CJC 1000 | INTRODUCTION TO CORRECTIONS

Miami Dade College School of Justice

Contains Material From

Corrections
in the 21st Century
sixth edition

Frank Schmalleger, PhD
Distinguished Professor Emeritus
University of North Carolina at Pembroke

John Ortiz Smykla, PhD
Distinguished University Professor
University of West Florida

McGraw Hill **Learning Solutions**

Boston   Burr Ridge, IL   Dubuque, IA   New York   San Francisco   St. Louis
Bangkok   Bogotá   Caracas   Lisbon   London   Madrid
Mexico City   Milan   New Delhi   Seoul   Singapore   Sydney   Taipei   Toronto

The McGraw·Hill Companies

Introduction to Corrections
Miami Dade College School of Justice
CJC 1000

This book is a McGraw-Hill Learning Solutions textbook and contains select material from *Corrections in the 21st Century,* Sixth Edition by Frank Schmalleger and John Ortiz Smykla. Copyright © 2013, 2011, 2009, 2007 by The McGraw-Hill Companies, Inc. Reprinted with permission of the publisher. Many custom published texts are modified versions or adaptations of our best-selling textbooks. Some adaptations are printed in black and white to keep prices at a minimum, while others are in color.

1 2 3 4 5 6 7 8 9 0 DIG DIG 14 13 12

ISBN-13: 978-0-07-768536-2
ISBN-10: 0-07-768536-9

Learning Solutions Consultant: Kimberly Wollschlager
Production Editor: Larry Jackson
Printer/Binder: Digital Impressions
Cover Images © 2012 JupiterImages Corporation

dedication }

For my granddaughters, Ava and Malia
—*Frank Schmalleger*

For my wife, Evelyn, and my granddaughter, Harper Grace
—*John Smykla*

About the Authors

Frank Schmalleger, PhD, is Distinguished Professor Emeritus at the University of North Carolina at Pembroke.

Dr. Schmalleger holds a bachelor's degree from the University of Notre Dame and both a master's and a doctorate in sociology from Ohio State University with a special emphasis in criminology. From 1976 to 1994, he taught criminal justice courses at the University of North Carolina at Pembroke, serving for many years as a tenured full professor. For the last 16 of those years, he chaired the Department of Sociology, Social Work, and Criminal Justice. As an adjunct professor with Webster University in St. Louis, Missouri, Dr. Schmalleger helped develop a graduate program in security management and loss prevention that is currently offered on U.S. military bases around the world. He taught courses in that curriculum for more than a decade, focusing primarily on computer and information security. Dr. Schmalleger also has taught in the New School for Social Research online graduate program, helping build the world's first electronic classrooms for criminal justice distance learning.

Dr. Schmalleger is the author of numerous articles and many books, including *Criminal Justice Today* (Prentice Hall, 2011), *Criminal Justice: A Brief Introduction* (Prentice Hall, 2013), *Criminology Today* (Prentice Hall, 2013), and *Criminal Law Today* (Prentice Hall, 2011). He is founding editor of the journal *Criminal Justice Studies* (formerly *The Justice Professional*) and has served as imprint advisor for Greenwood Publishing Group's criminal justice reference series.

Dr. Schmalleger is also the creator of a number of award-winning Web sites (including the former cybrary.info and crimenews.info). He is a member of the Academy of Criminal Justice Sciences, the American Society of Criminology, and the Society of Police Futurists International (where he is a founding member). Schmalleger's author website on Amazon.com can be viewed at http://www.amazon.com/Frank-Schmalleger/e/B001IGFLVI.

John Ortiz Smykla, PhD, is Distinguished University Professor at the University of West Florida. Previously, he was professor of criminal justice at the University of Alabama, where he served as chair of the criminal justice department for 10 years, and at the University of South Alabama, where he served as department chair of political science and criminal justice for 3 years.

Dr. Smykla teaches courses in corrections and research methods. He teaches online, face-to-face, and using a blended format at the University of West Florida. He has taught two-way interactive corrections courses across several campuses of the University of Alabama system and has supervised more than 70 master's and doctoral students. Dr. Smykla earned the interdisciplinary social science PhD in criminal justice, sociology, and anthropology from Michigan State University. He holds bachelor's and master's degrees in sociology from California State University at Northridge.

Dr. Smykla has authored or edited five corrections books. His coauthored data set *Executions in the United States, 1608–2003: The Espy File*, funded by a grant from the National Science Foundation, is one of the most frequently requested criminal justice data files from the University of Michigan's Inter-University Consortium for Political and Social Research.

Dr. Smykla has published more than 40 research articles on corrections issues, including "The Human Impact of Capital Punishment," "Effects of a Prison Facility on the Regional Economy," "Jail Type and Inmate Behavior," "Juvenile Drug Courts," "Drunk and Alone in a K-Mart Parking Lot: The Pedagogy of Simulations and Contemporary Attitudes Toward Drinking and Driving," and most recently "Correctional Privatization and the Myth of Inherent Efficiency." He is currently engaged in a five-year study of federal reentry court for the U.S. District Court, Northern District of Florida. Dr. Smykla has delivered more than 50 conference papers in the United States and abroad. In 1986, he was a Senior Fulbright Scholar in Argentina and Uruguay.

Dr. Smykla is a member of the Academy of Criminal Justice Sciences and the Southern Criminal Justice Association. In 1996, the Southern Criminal Justice Association named him Educator of the Year. In 1997, he served as program chair for the annual meeting of the Academy of Criminal Justice Sciences. In 2000, he served as president of the Southern Criminal Justice Association. In 2010, the University of West Florida named him a Distinguished University Professor.

Brief Contents

Expanded Contents

PART 5   ISSUES IN CORRECTIONS   427

Boxed Features

CAREER PROFILES

COMMISSION ON SAFETY AND ABUSE IN AMERICA'S PRISONS

ETHICS AND PROFESSIONALISM

PREFACE

Corrections, when seen as the control and punishment of convicted offenders, has been an important part of organized society from the earliest days of civilization. It has not always had a proud past, however. In pre-modern times, atrocious physical punishment, exile, and unspeakable torture were the tools used all too often by those called upon to enforce society's correctional philosophies—especially the strongly felt need for vengeance.

Important changes in correctional practice began around the time of the American Revolution when the purposes of criminal punishments were closely examined by influential reformers. More recently, corrections has become an important field of study in which scientific techniques are valued and reasoned debate is encouraged.

The best, however, is yet to come. Only within the past 30 years have conscientious corrections practitioners begun to embrace the notion of professionalism—wherein ethics, a sense of high purpose, a personal long-term career commitment, a respect for the fundamental humanity of those supervised, and widely agreed-upon principles and standards guide the daily work of correctional personnel. Corrections professionalism, although not yet as well known as police professionalism, has garnered support from policymakers and is winning respect among the public. It serves as this textbook's organizing principle.

Corrections in the 21st Century:

- provides an in-depth look at the past, present, and future of corrections;
- identifies the many *subcomponents* of modern-day corrections;
- highlights the *process* of modern-day corrections;
- focuses on the *issues* facing the correctional enterprise today;
- provides an appreciation for contemporary real-world correctional *practice;*
- examines the opportunities represented by new and developing corrections *technologies;* and
- points students in the direction of the still-emerging ideal of corrections *professionalism.*

It is our belief that a new age of corrections is upon us. It is an age in which the lofty goals of corrections professionalism will take their place alongside the more traditional components of a still-developing field. It is our hope that this textbook will play at least some small part in helping bring about a new and better correctional enterprise—one that is reasonable and equitable to all involved in the justice process.

THE SIXTH EDITION

The Sixth Edition of *Corrections in the 21st Century* contains a number of notable and exciting elements. Among these are feature articles provided by *Corrections Connection Network News (CCNN)* exclusively for this textbook, and *Reflections on the Future* essays written specifically for the Online Learning Center by well-known corrections practitioners and scholars.

The following changes have been made across the entire text to better focus reader attention on the key learning materials in each chapter:

- Correlation of end-of-chapter review questions to the objectives listed at the start of each chapter.
- Enhancement of the photo program to better grab student interest and draw readers into the text.
- Integration of additional evidence-based information throughout the book and frequent citation of the literature relating to such practices.
- A new focus on careers in corrections underscoring the book's professionalism theme with a career icon adjacent to specifically selected text to help students recognize information on careers in corrections, as well as direction in each chapter to the Appendix: Careers in Corrections located on the Online Learning Center.
- A number of new stories focusing on current events now open the chapters.
- Incorporation of reviews of the most recent data and literature throughout.

Significant chapter-specific content changes include the following:

Chapter 1

- An entirely new chapter opening vignette and associated photo.
- New line art depicting the growth in state and federal prison populations.
- Revision of two American Correctional Association correctional policy boxes.
- Extensive updating of the section on evidence-based corrections.

Chapter 2

- Inclusion of information on Arab TV personality Rosanna Yami whom a Saudi court sentenced to receive 60 lashes for her role in a Lebanese TV program that interviewed a Saudi man who boasted of his sex life.
- Inclusion of historical information on early Canon law.

Chapter 3

- The chapter opening story has been replaced with a new one.
- The story of Nushawn Williams has been updated.
- The federal Fair Sentencing Act (FSA) of 2010 is now discussed.

Chapter 4

- New research by the National Association of Pretrial Services Agencies' Diversion Committee on participants' completion rates.
- New discussion on the position of the federal judiciary against disclosure of the probation officer's sentencing recommendation.
- New discussion of diversion programs for veterans returning from wars in Afghanistan and Iraq.
- Latest data on the characteristics of adults on probation.
- Added coverage on community supervision technology.
- Updated research on Hawaii's Opportunity Probation with Enforcement (HOPE) program.

Chapter 5

- New research from the National Council on Crime and Delinquency on how much states

would save if only 80 percent of the nation's incarcerated nonserious, nonsexual offender population were given intermediate sanctions.
- Increased coverage on how states are using intermediate sanctions.
- Expanded coverage on the new types of drug courts: veterans treatment court, DWI court, family drug court, reentry court, juvenile drug court, reentry drug court, tribal healing to wellness court, and the Back to TRAC clinical justice model.
- A new Ethics and Professionalism insert on the International Community Corrections Association Code of Ethics.
- New coverage on how the fiscal crisis is influencing governors' and legislators' interest in intermediate sanctions.
- Current evaluation research on intermediate sanctions.

Chapter 6

- New research from the Justice Policy Institute that discusses the unintended negative consequences of building newer and bigger jails.
- Latest data on the characteristics of jail inmates, staff, and facilities.
- Still the only corrections book to discuss fourth-generation and pay-to-stay jails.
- Discussion of the most recent data on the decline in the jail suicide rate.
- Updated U.S. Department of Justice research on the prevalence of sexual victimization in the nation's jails.
- New material on how jails are generating new revenue by allowing inmates' relatives to use Aramark's "iCare" Web site to order meatball subs, pizza, cheeseburgers, and other foods for the inmate.
- Coverage of new research on successful jail reentry programs in Georgia and Ohio.
- New research on jail industry programs making headlines in California, Colorado, Louisiana, Massachusetts, Maine and Pennsylvania.
- Updated information on how some states are increasing state oversight of county jails.
- New correspondence from the American Correctional Association on the number of ACA-accredited jails and ACA's new "core" jail standards for small- and medium-size sized facilities.

Chapter 7

- New coverage of how cuts in corrections budgets are affecting personnel, salaries, benefits, overtime, programs, facilities, and services and how states are turning to evidence-based practices, the federal Second Chance Act, drug courts, veterans courts, reentry courts, technology, and assistance from professional associations and advocacy groups for guidance on the effective use of the funds they have.
- Latest data on characteristics of adults under jurisdiction of state and federal prisons.
- Discussion of how the movement in EBC and the economic downturn has caused a decline in state prison populations for the first time in four decades.
- Coverage of the federal court order mandating that California reduce its prison population by almost one-fourth over the next two to three years.
- Updated data on the cost of state and federal incarceration.
- New discussion of states' use of Justice Reinvestment.
- The section "Does Incarceration Work?" is updated with the latest evidence-based literature.

Chapter 8

- In response to the economic crisis, the chapter now contains updated material on how states are handling parolees' technical violations.
- More comprehensive analysis of federal attention on reentry beginning with the Clinton Administrations emphasis on reentry court, President Bush's 2004 State of the Union Address and passage of the Second Chance Act, and President Obama's request for $100 million more for reentry programs and establishment of the first-ever interagency Cabinet-level Reentry Council as well as state and local government initiatives.
- New research on reentry problems for African American women.
- New coverage of California's "non-revocable parole."
- Latest data on characteristics of adults on parole are included.
- Updated and expanded coverage on the question, "Can parolees vote?"
- New section on the question, "Is parole a right or privilege?"

Chapter 9

- Start of chapter learning objectives have been restructured along with end of chapter summary points and discussion questions.
- Correctional officer personality types have been further elaborated.
- A "Gender and Staffing" heading has replaced that of "Female Officers."
- Professionalism is better defined and corrections professionalism is discussed in detail.
- Mission and Vision statements from the Maryland Department of Public Safety and Correctional Services are now included.
- New Commission on Safety and Abuse in America's Prisons.
- New section on officer corruption has been added.
- The anti-terrorism material has been restructured.

Chapter 10

- Start of chapter learning objectives have been restructured along with end of chapter summary points and discussion questions.
- The chapter opening story has been replaced.
- The prison argot list has been updated and expanded.
- The information on sexual victimization within prison has been updated and expanded.
- New photo of inmates in the Malachi Dads program at Louisiana State Penitentiary at Angola.

Chapter 11

- A new introductory story opens the chapter.
- Some dated material has been removed, shortening the chapter slightly.
- Updated information on the impact of California's three strikes law on inmate populations in the state.
- Revised end of chapter decision making scenarios.

Chapter 12

- Updated coverage on how states are addressing the health care needs of special needs inmates.
- Latest data on the prevalence of HIV in prison.
- Updated states' testing policies for HIV/AIDS and TB.

- New coverage on what some states are doing to encourage HIV-infected inmates to continue treatment after leaving prison.
- Latest data on the characteristics of older inmates.

Chapter 13

- Updated statistics on the problem of prison crowding.
- New material on how states are reducing corrections spending.
- Updated coverage and statistics on the incidents and effects of sexual victimization in state and federal prisons, jails, ICE and U.S. military facilities, and correctional institutions in Indian territory.
- Updated statistics on percentage of STGs in prison and jail.
- New literature from the Colorado DOC arguing that the conditions of supermax confinement do not exacerbate the symptoms of mental illness nor create mental illness where none previously existed.
- New correspondence from the American Correctional Association on the number of ACA-accredited adult correctional institutions and adult local detention facilities.
- Updated and expanded coverage on privatization of community supervision.
- Expanded coverage on the problems of inmate cellphone use in prison and new federal legislation making inmate possession of a cellphone or wireless device a felony.
- Expanded coverage of how technology is being used for offender and officer recognition and tracking, and detection for prison security.

Chapter 14

- The start of chapter objectives have been substantially modified along with the end of chapter discussion questions and summary section.
- Information about the federal Adam Walsh Child Protection and Safety Act of 2006 was added.
- The timeline on crime victims' rights has been abbreviated.
- The American Correctional Association correctional policy box has been updated.
- The federally-run Dru Sjodin National Sex Offender Public Website is now highlighted.
- The Vision 21 initiative of the federal Office for Victims of Crime is now discussed.

Chapter 15

- Latest statistics on the number of people whose innocence was established after they were sent to death row, and the trends in capital punishment.
- Latest data on states that abolished capital punishment.
- New coverage of Illinois becoming the 16th state to abolish capital punishment.
- New material on the cost of the death penalty.
- Updated exhibit and text on the number of people executed since 1977 and prisoners under sentence of death.
- New material on "geography" as a factor in deciding the death penalty.
- New coverage on the shortage of sodium thiopental used in executions and how three states (Ohio, Oklahoma, and Washington) have responded.
- New coverage on the ban by the American Board of Anesthesiologists revoking the certification of any member who participates in an execution.
- Updated coverage and exhibit on compensating the exonerated.
- New coverage of former U.S. Supreme Court Justice John Paul Stevens and former supporter of capital punishment now arguing that capital punishment is hopelessly flawed, unconstitutional, shot with racism, skewed toward conviction, infected with politics, tinged with hysteria, and unreliable.

Chapter 16

- Start of chapter learning objectives have been restructured, along with the end of chapter summary section and discussion questions.
- The U.S. Supreme Court case of *Graham* v. *Florida* (2010) has been added.
- A new section on bullying has been added.
- The youth gang discussion has been modified and updated.
- The section on juvenile justice reform has been substantially modified.

ORGANIZATION

The Sixth Edition of *Corrections in the 21st Century* includes 16 chapters whose organization reflects aspects of the correctional process. Chapters are grouped into five parts, each of which is described in detail in the following paragraphs.

Part One, "Introduction to Corrections," provides an understanding of corrections by explaining the goals underlying the correctional enterprise and by describing the how and why of criminal punishments. Part One identifies professionalism as the key to managing correctional personnel, facilities, and populations successfully. Standard-setting organizations such as the American Correctional Association, the American Jail Association, the American Probation and Parole Association, and the National Commission on Correctional Health Care are identified, and the importance of professional ethics for correctional occupations and correctional administrators is emphasized.

Part Two, "Community Corrections," explains what happens to most convicted offenders, including diversion (the suspension of formal criminal proceedings before conviction in exchange for the defendant's participation in treatment), probation, and intermediate sanctions.

Part Three, "Institutional Corrections," provides a detailed description of jails, prisons, and parole. The reentry challenges facing inmates released from prisons are explained. Education, vocational preparation, and drug treatment programs that are intended to prevent reoffending also are explored.

Part Four, "The Prison World," provides an overview of life inside prison from the points of view of both inmates and staff. Part Four also describes the responsibilities and challenges surrounding the staff role. Chapter 12 focuses attention on special correctional populations, including inmates who are elderly, who have HIV/AIDS, and who are mentally and physically challenged. We have chosen to integrate our coverage of women in corrections—including information about the important NIC report titled "Gender Responsive Strategies: Research, Practice, and Guiding Principles for Women Offenders"—throughout the body of the text rather than isolating it in Chapter 12.

Part Five, "Issues in Corrections," explores some of the most controversial topics in contemporary corrections. Prison crowding, capital punishment, the conditional rights of prisoners, and juvenile corrections all can be found in this section of the text. Victims' rights and the role that correctional authorities can play in protecting and advancing those rights also are explored.

PEDAGOGICAL AIDS

Working together, the authors and editor have developed a learning system designed to help students excel in the corrections course. In addition to the many changes already mentioned, we have included a wealth of new photographs to make the book even more inviting and relevant.

To this same end, our real-world chapter-opening vignettes give the material a fresh flavor intended to motivate students to read on; our photo captions, which raise thought-provoking questions, actively engage students in the learning process. Carefully updated tables and figures highlight and amplify the text coverage. And chapter outlines, objectives, and reviews, plus marginal definitions and an end-of-book glossary, all help students master the material.

The Schmalleger/Smykla learning system goes well beyond these essential tools, however. As mentioned, *Corrections in the 21st Century* offers a unique emphasis on corrections professionalism, an emphasis that has prompted us to create a number of innovative learning tools that focus on the real world of corrections:

- A concentration on *Evidence-Based Corrections*—What actually works in correctional settings? that is, what correctional programs are effective in reducing recidivism and in preventing future crimes? Evidence-based corrections is an exciting new development in the corrections field, and a number of agencies, institutions, and organizations now emphasize the use of scientific evidence. Evidence-based policy, which builds on evidence-based corrections, is an approach that helps people make well-informed decisions about policies and programs by putting the best available evidence from research at the heart of policy development and implementation.

- *Career Profiles*—enlightening minibiographies of corrections professionals, such as a parole officer, a victims' advocate, a corrections officer, a youth counselor, and a substance abuse manager.

- *Offender Speaks* and *Staff Speaks*—intriguing interviews with offenders and practitioners that provide a balance of perspectives and further expand on the text's real-world emphasis.

- *Commission on Safety and Abuse in America's Prisons*—a series of boxes throughout the text highlighting the findings of this important national commission that was formed to examine conditions in American prisons following the abuse scandals at the military-run Abu Ghraib prison in Iraq. Each box in the series focuses on a subset of the commission's findings, such as correctional leadership, security, oversight and accountability, and measuring correctional effectiveness.

- *Ethics and Professionalism*—boxes that highlight ethical codes and critical concerns from America's premier corrections-related professional associations. Included are features from the American Correctional Association, the American Jail Association, the American Probation and Parole Association, International Association of Community Corrections, the International Association of Correctional Training Personnel, and others. Included in each Ethics and Professionalism box are author-created Ethical Dilemmas, which present students with ethical questions from the corrections field and guide them to an insightful resolution. Ethical Dilemmas are supplemented with Web-based resources maintained by the authors and specifically selected to help students navigate particular ethics-related issues.

- *Talking About Corrections*—Web-based on-demand audio features in which corrections professionals discuss important issues relating to today's correctional enterprise.

In addition to the features we have developed to further our goal of creating a uniquely practical, professionally oriented text, we also have included end-of-chapter review material to help students master the concepts and principles developed in the chapter:

- *Chapter Summary*—a valuable learning tool organized into sections that mirror the chapter-opening objectives exactly; the summary restates all of the chapter's most critical points.
- *Key Terms*—a comprehensive list of the terms defined in the margins of the chapter, complete with page references to make it easy for students to go back and review further.
- *Questions for Review*—objective study questions (exactly mirroring the chapter-opening objectives and summary) that allow students to test their knowledge and prepare for exams.
- *Thinking Critically About Corrections*—broad-based questions that challenge students to think critically about chapter concepts and issues.
- *On-the-Job Decision Making*—unique experiential exercises that enable students to apply what they have learned in the chapter to the daily work of correctional personnel.

SUPPLEMENTS

Visit our Online Learning Center Web site at www.mhhe.com/schmalleger6e for robust student and instructor resources.

For Students

Student resources include "Reflections on the Future" contributed essays with self-assessment quizzes, "Live Links" and "Corrections Connections Network News" feature articles, a "Careers in Corrections" guide, corrections-related Internet links, chapter-specific multiple-choice self-quizzes, and exercises.

For Instructors

The password-protected instructor portion of the Web site includes the instructor's manual, a comprehensive computerized test bank, PowerPoint lecture slides, and a variety of additional instructor resources.

Other dynamic instructor resources include:

 McGraw-Hill Higher Education and Blackboard have teamed up.

Blackboard, the Web-based course-management system, has partnered with McGraw-Hill to better allow students and faculty to use online materials and activities to complement face-to-face teaching. Blackboard features exciting social learning and teaching tools that foster more logical, visually impactful and active learning opportunities for students. You'll transform your closed-door classrooms into communities where students remain connected to their educational experience 24 hours a day.

This partnership allows you and your students access to McGraw-Hill's Create™ right from within your Blackboard course—all with one single sign-on. McGraw-Hill and Blackboard can now offer you easy access to industry leading technology and content, whether your campus hosts it, or we do. Be sure to ask your local McGraw-Hill representative for details.

Craft your teaching resources to match the way you teach! With McGraw-Hill Create™, www.mcgrawhillcreate.com, you can easily rearrange chapters, combine material from other content sources, and quickly upload content you have written such as your course syllabus or teaching notes. Find the content you need in Create by searching through thousands of leading McGraw-Hill textbooks. Arrange your book to fit your teaching style. Create even allows you to personalize your book's appearance by selecting the cover and adding your name, school, and course information. Order a Create book and you'll receive a complimentary print review copy in three to five business days or a complimentary electronic review copy (eComp) via e-mail in minutes. Go to www.mcgrawhillcreate.com today and register to experience how McGraw-Hill Create™ empowers you to teach your students your way.

With the CourseSmart eTextbook version of this title, students can save up to 50 percent off the cost of a print book, reduce their impact on the environment, and access powerful Web tools for learning. Faculty can also review and compare the full text online without having to wait for a print desk copy. CourseSmart is an online eTextbook, which means users need to be connected to the Internet in order to access it. Students can also print sections of the book for maximum portability. For further details, contact your sales representative or go to www.coursesmart.com.

 Tegrity Campus is a service that makes class time available all the time by automatically capturing every lecture in a searchable format for students to review when they study and complete assignments. With a simple one-click start and stop process, you capture all computer screens and corresponding audio. Students can replay any part of any class with easy-to-use browser-based viewing on a PC or Mac.

To learn more about Tegrity watch a 2-minute Flash demo at http://tegritycampus.mhhe.com.

McGraw-Hill's online courses provide interactive digital content and activities aligned to learning objectives that work with most learning management systems as a true cartridge. Designed to be used in conjunction with a textbook, McGraw-Hill's online course tools combine visual, auditory, and interactive elements to encourage all types of learners to connect and retain knowledge. Course content includes animation, graphics, streaming video, and interactive activities to enliven the content and motivate the learner. Specifically for the area of criminal justice, the McGraw-Hill online course content tools were developed around content areas that have been established by the Academy of Criminal Justice Sciences Minimum Standards of Criminal Justice Education. Preview the *Corrections* course content and more at www.OnlineLearning.com.

Course Management Systems—whether you use WebCT, Blackboard, e-College, or another course management system, McGraw-Hill will provide you with a *Corrections* cartridge that enables you either to conduct your course entirely online or to supplement your lectures with online material. And if your school does not yet have one of these course management systems, we can provide you with PageOut, an easy-to-use tool that allows you to create your own course Web page and access all material on the *Corrections* Online Learning Center.

Please contact your local McGraw-Hill representative for more information on any of the above supplements.

IN APPRECIATION

Writing a textbook requires a great deal of help and support. We would like to acknowledge and thank the many individuals on whom we relied. Special thanks go to William W. Sondervan, Director of Criminal Justice, Investigative Forensics and Legal Studies at the University of Maryland, and Ania Dobrzanska, Program Coordinator with the Moss Group in Washington, DC, for contributing the reading "Professionalism in Corrections" to the Online Learning Center; to Dennis Stevens formerly of Sacred Heart University, Fairfield, Connecticut for his research on special features; to Jody Klein-Saffran at the Federal Bureau of Prisons and Gary Bayens at Washburn University for their contributions to our chapters on parole and juvenile corrections, respectively; to Erika Overall and Major William Hayes of the Kent Division of the King County (Washington) Jail, Regional Justice Center for the photograph and schematic of the fourth-generation jail; to the criminal justice and legal studies faculty and staff and the dean of the College of Professional Studies at the University of West Florida for their encouragement and for the resources they made available; to Laura Joyce for her help in Web development; and to the many students who suggested ideas for chapter opening stories. We also gratefully acknowledge the contributions of the following individuals who helped in the development of this textbook.

Steve Abrams
California Department of Corrections
    and Rehabilitation
Santa Rosa, California

Stanley E. Adelman
University of Arkansas School of Law
Little Rock, Arkansas
University of Tulsa College of Law
Tulsa, Oklahoma

John Augustine
Triton College
River Grove, Illinois

Tom Austin
Shippensburg University
Shippensburg, Pennsylvania

Ken Barnes
Arizona Western College
Yuma, Arizona

Jeri Barnett
Virginia Western Community College
Roanoke, Virginia

Rose Johnson Bigler
Curry College
Milton, Massachusetts

Kathy J. Black-Dennis
University of Louisville
Louisville, Kentucky

Robert Bohm
University of Central Florida
Orlando, Florida

David A. Bowers Jr.
University of South Alabama
Mobile, Alabama

Greg Brown
Westwood College of Technology
Denver, Colorado

David E. Carter
Southern Oregon University
Ashland, Oregon

Vicky Dorworth
Montgomery College
Rockville, Maryland

Carrie L. Dunson
Central Missouri State University
Warrensburg, Missouri

Michael Earll
Western Technical College
La Crosse, Wisconsin

Hilary Estes
Southern Illinois University, Carbondale
Carbondale, Illinois

Robert Figlestahler
Eastern Kentucky University
Richmond, Kentucky

Lynn Fortney
EBSCO Subscription Services
Birmingham, Alabama

Don Drennon Gala
Federal Bureau of Prisons
Atlanta, Georgia

Donna Hale
Shippensburg University
Shippensburg, Pennsylvania

Homer C. Hawkins
Michigan State University
East Lansing, Michigan

Nancy L. Hogan
Ferris State University
Big Rapids, Michigan

Ronald G. Iacovetta
Wichita State University
Wichita, Kansas

Connie Ireland
California State University, Long Beach
Long Beach, California

James L. Jengeleski
Shippensburg University
Shippensburg, Pennyslvania

Brad Johnson
Atlanta, Georgia

Kathrine Johnson
University of West Florida
Ft. Walton Beach, Florida

John Calvin Jones
North Carolina A&T State University
Greensboro, North Carolina

Kay King
Johnson County Community College
Overland Park, Kansas

Mike Klemp-North
Ferris State University
Big Rapids, Michigan

Julius Koefoed
Kirkwood Community College
Cedar Rapids, Iowa

Michael Kwan
Salt Lake Community College
Taylorsville, Utah

Walter B. Lewis
St. Louis Community College at Meramec
Kirkwood, Missouri

Shelley Listwan
Kent State University
Kent, Ohio

Jess Maghan
Forum for Comparative Correction
Chester, Connecticut

Preston S. Marks
Keiser University

Alvin Mitchell
Delgado Community College
New Orleans, Louisiana

Etta Morgan
Pennsylvania State University
Capital College, Pennsylvania

Kathleen Nicolaides
University of North Carolina, Charlotte
Charlotte, North Carolina

Sarah Nordin
Solano Community College
Suisun City, California

Michael F. Perna
Broome Community College
Binghamton, New York

Scott Plutchak
University of Alabama at Birmingham
Birmingham, Alabama

Bobby B. Polk
Metropolitan Community College
Omaha, Nebraska

Wayne D. Posner
East Los Angeles College
Monterey Park, California

Barbara R. Russo
Wayne Community College
Goldsboro, North Carolina

John Sloan
University of Alabama at Birmingham
Birmingham, Alabama

Larry E. Spencer
Alabama State University
Montgomery, Alabama

Anthony C. Trevelino
Camden County College
Blackwood, New Jersey

Sheryl Van Horne
Radford University
Radford, Virginia

Shela R. Van Ness
University of Tennessee at Chattanooga
Chattanooga, Tennessee

Gennaro F. Vito
University of Louisville
Louisville, Kentucky

Brenda Vos
University of North Florida
Jacksonville, Florida

Kiesha Warren-Gordon
Ball State University
Muncie, Indiana

Anthony White
Illinois Central College
East Peoria, Illinois

Ed Whittle
Florida Metropolitan University at Tampa College
Tampa, Florida

Beth Wiersma
University of Nebraska at Kearney
Kearney, Nebraska

Robert R. Wiggins
Cedarville College
Cedarville, Ohio

Jeffrey Zack
Fayetteville Technical Community College
Fayetteville, North Carolina

Kristen M. Zgoba
Rutgers University
Piscataway, New Jersey

Dawn Zobel
Federal Bureau of Prisons
Alderson, West Virginia

We greatly acknowledge the assistance and support of the many dedicated professionals who provided original written contributions for the Web-available *Reflections on the Future* boxes that support this edition. They include:

Thomas J. Cowper, Police Futurists International

Richard S. Frase, University of Minnesota

Tara Gray, New Mexico State University

Edward A. Harrison, National Commission on Correctional Health Care

Herbert J. Hoelter, National Center on Institutions and Alternatives

Illinois Governor's Commission on Capital Punishment

Leslie W. Kennedy, Rutgers University

Ken Kerle, American Jail Association

Richard Kiekbusch, University of Texas–Permian Basin

James W. Marquart, University of Texas–Dallas

William L. Tafoya, University of New Haven

Morris L. Thigpen Sr., National Institute of Corrections, U.S. Department of Justice

Jeremy Travis, John Jay College of Criminal Justice

Mark Umbreit, University of Minnesota

Kathy Waters, Arizona Supreme Court

Alan C. Youngs, Lakewood, Colorado, Police Department (retired)

Finally, we want to acknowledge the special debt that we owe to the McGraw-Hill team, including sponsoring editor Bill Minick for keeping the project on track; marketing manager Leslie Oberhuber for seeing value in this textbook; developmental editor Kate Scheinman for her attention to the many day-to-day details that a project like this entails; project manager Lisa Bruflodt; permissions editor Sheri Gilbert; buyer Nicole Baumgartner; design coordinator Margarite Reynolds; photo researcher LouAnn Wilson; copy editor JaNoel Lowe; and indexer Coughlin Indexing. The professional vision, guidance, and support of these dedicated professionals helped bring this project to fruition. A hearty "thank you" to all.

Frank Schmalleger
John Smykla

Introduction to Corrections

Part One develops an understanding of corrections

by examining the purposes of correctional punishments and by exploring how offenders have been punished throughout history.

Today, crime rates are falling but the number of people under correctional supervision (on probation or parole or in jail or prison) is close to a peak. Get-tough-on-crime attitudes, the War on Drugs, and the reduction in the use of discretionary parole board release explain this peak.

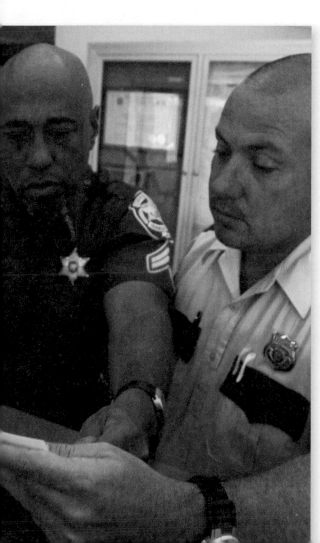

Professionalism is the key to effectively managing the growth in the correctional population. Standard-setting organizations such as the American Correctional Association, the American Jail Association, the American Probation and Parole Association, and the National Commission on Correctional Health Care offer detailed sets of written principles for correctional occupations and correctional administrators.

Nevertheless, professional credentialing in corrections is new. The seed was planted during the Enlightenment when reformers such as Cesare Beccaria and the Philadelphia Quakers shifted the focus of punishment away from the body and toward the soul and human spirit. Correcting the soul and human spirit required understanding the causes of crime and new reforms. To that end, the National Prison Association (now known as the American Correctional Association) met in Cincinnati, Ohio, in 1870 to advance correctional theory and practice. The assembly elected then Ohio

governor and future U.S. president Rutherford B. Hayes as the first president of the association. Today, the ACA remains the leader in advancing professionalism in corrections through education, training, and skills development.

The professional nature of corrections is also seen in the way sanctions are developed. From a time when theory and practice advocated indeterminate sentences to the legislatively mandated determinate sentences of today, correctional decision makers have had to use their knowledge of human behavior, philosophy, and law to construct sanctions that are fair and just. The correctional goals of retribution, just deserts, deterrence, incapacitation, rehabilitation, and restoration have produced the sanctions of probation, intermediate sanctions, jail, prison, and capital punishment.

What are the consequences of punishment? Choosing the best sanction means understanding the political, social, economic, human, and moral consequences of crime control. For that reason, corrections is a field in which complex decision making requires the skills of professional staff and administrators.

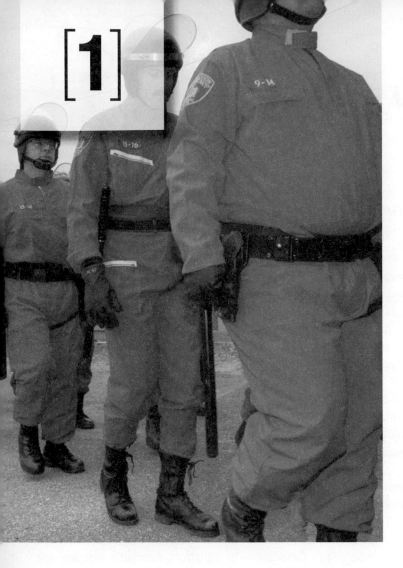

CORRECTIONS

An Overview

CHAPTER OBJECTIVES

After completing this chapter you should be able to do the following:

1 Describe the corrections explosion and explain why correctional populations continue to rise, even though the rate of serious crime in the United States has experienced a significant decline.

2 Describe how crime is measured in the United States, and list the kinds of crimes that cause people to enter correctional programs and institutions.

3 List and describe the various components of the criminal justice system, including the major components of the corrections subsystem.

4 Explain the importance of professionalism in the corrections field, and describe the characteristics of a true professional.

5 Define *evidence-based corrections,* and explain the important role that it plays in corrections professionalism today.

6 Understand what is meant by *social diversity,* and explain why issues of race, gender, and ethnicity are important in corrections today.

The use of evidence-based practices in corrections and public policy is now considered the gold standard for policy and program development.

—Richard Tewksbury and Jill Levenson, "When Evidence Is Ignored: Residential Restrictions for Sex Offenders," *Corrections Today*, December 2007, p. 34

In 2011, federal auditors reported that inmates in state prisons and jails had stolen at least $39 million from the IRS by filing false or fraudulent income tax returns.[1] A second audit found that 29 inmates received $50,000 in federal tax payments for electric vehicles they falsely claimed they had purchased.

Although prisoner tax scams are not new, the number of such cases has grown rapidly in recent years. Inmates typically use stolen social security numbers when filing and have refunds sent to friends and relatives who are not behind bars. Those collaborators then deposit a large portion of the refunds they receive into inmates' accounts.

On a related note, prisoners' use of outlawed cell phones to make calls from inside of correctional institutions has grown exponentially as the number of phones in general circulation has expanded. Recently, for example, California correctional officers seized nearly 6,000 banned cell phones from the state's prisoners, while officials with Maryland's Department of Public Safety and Correctional Services confiscated over 3,600 cell phones in the past three years.[2] In Mississippi, nearly 2,000 contraband phones were confiscated during the first half of 2010 alone. The issue of contraband cell phone use inside of prisons is discussed in a number of places throughout this book.

A corrections officer examines almost 2,000 cell phones that have been confiscated from prisoners at California State Prison Solano over the last few years. How does this photo illustrate at least some of the problems facing correctional personnel today?

Illicit cell phone usage, fraudulent tax return filing, and similar other outlawed[3] activities that occur behind prison bars illustrate the close connection that inmates retain to the outside society, and raise the question, "Do prisons really make us safe?"[4] What about other corrections programs, such as probation, parole, jails, alternative sentencing programs, and institutions for juvenile offenders? If they make our society a safer place in which to live, then the recent and rapid growth in correctional populations—discussed in the next section of this chapter—is understandable (although it may be economically difficult to maintain). If they don't contribute much to safety and security, however, then we must look elsewhere to understand why such rapid growth has occurred.

THE CORRECTIONS EXPLOSION

One amazing fact stands out from all the contemporary information about corrections: While serious **crime** in the United States consistently declined throughout much of the 1990s, and while such declines continued into the early years of the 21st century, the number of people under correctional

crime
A violation of a criminal law.

3

EXHIBIT 1–1   The Growth of Imprisonment in the United States

State prison populations 1925–2010

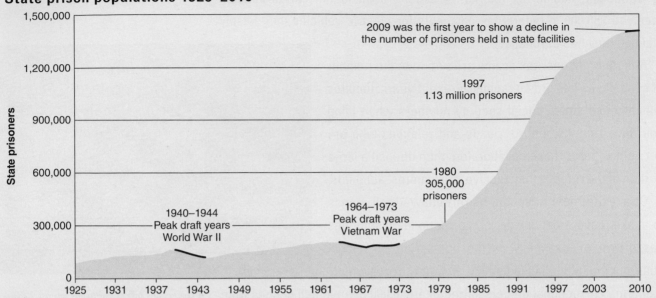

Source: Bureau of Justice Statistics, *Crime and Justice Atlas 2000* (Washington, DC: Bureau of Justice Statistics, 2001), pp. 42–43; and Heather C. West, William J. Sabol, and Sarah J. Greenman, *Prisoners in 2009* (Washington, DC: Bureau of Justice Statistics, 2010); and other years.

Federal prison populations 1925–2010

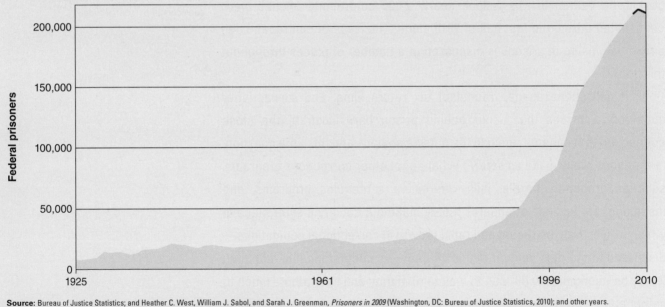

Source: Bureau of Justice Statistics; and Heather C. West, William J. Sabol, and Sarah J. Greenman, *Prisoners in 2009* (Washington, DC: Bureau of Justice Statistics, 2010); and other years.

prison

A state or federal confinement facility that has custodial authority over adults sentenced to confinement.

supervision in this country—not just the number of convicted offenders sent to **prison**—has continued to climb. Crime rates are approximately 20 percent lower today than they were in 1980. They are near their lowest level in 25 years. But the number of people on probation is up almost 300 percent since 1980, the nation's prison population has increased by more than 400 percent, and the number of persons on parole has more than doubled. Exhibit 1–1 illustrates trends in federal and state prison populations.

EXHIBIT 1–2	Number of Prisoners by Offense, 2009		
Type of Offense	**All**	**Male**	**Female**
Violent offenses	715,400	681,700	33,700
Property offenses	251,800	224,300	27,500
Drug offenses	251,400	225,900	25,500
Public-order offenses	125,900	119,000	6,900

Source: Adapted from Heather C. West, William J. Sabol, and Sarah J. Greenman, *Prisoners in 2009* (Washington, DC: Bureau of Justice Statistics, 2010), p. 30.

The question is, Why? Why the steady increase in correctional populations in the face of declining crime rates? The answer to this question, like the answers to most societal enigmas, is far from simple. Pursuit of the answer is important, however. As Franklin Zimring, director of the Earl Warren Legal Institute at the University of California at Berkeley, points out, "The change in the number of inmates tells us . . . about our feelings about crime and criminals."[5]

The answer has a number of dimensions. First, it is important to recognize that get-tough-on-crime laws, such as the three-strikes (and two-strikes) laws that were enacted in many states in the mid-1990s, have fueled rapid increases in prison populations. The conservative attitudes that gave birth to those laws are still with us. Noted criminal justice scholar John P. Conrad summarizes today's mood this way: "There is an unprecedented consensus on the necessity for strengthening criminal justice. This consensus can be summed up in one sentence. Criminals must be locked up and kept off the streets."[6] Conrad goes on to explain: "The vast expansion of corrections today has not come about without good cause. For the citizen on the streets, there is only one reasonable response to the violence he or she fears. Lock them up, and hang the expense."[7]

A second reason correctional populations have rapidly increased can be found in the nation's War on Drugs. The War on Drugs has led to the arrest and conviction of many offenders, resulting in larger correctional populations in nearly every jurisdiction (especially within the federal correctional system). In Exhibit 1–2, compare the total number of individuals incarcerated for drug offenses with, for example, the total incarcerated for property offenses. Drug arrests continue to increase. Although they account for a large portion of the nation's correctional population, they do not figure into the FBI's calculations of the nation's rate of serious crimes. Hence, the War on Drugs goes a long way toward explaining the growth in correctional populations even while the rate of "serious crime" in the United States appears to be declining.

Third, parole authorities, fearing civil liability and public outcry, have become increasingly reluctant to release inmates. This has contributed to a further expansion of prison populations.

Fourth, as some observers have noted, the corrections boom has created its own growth dynamic.[8] As ever increasing numbers of people are placed on probation, the likelihood of probation violations increases. Prison sentences for more violators result in larger prison populations. When inmates are released from prison, they swell the numbers of those on parole, leading to a larger number of parole violations, which in turn fuels further prison growth. Statistics show that the number of criminals being sent to prison for at least the second time has increased steadily, accounting for approximately 35 percent of the total number of admissions.[9]

EXHIBIT 1-3 Rate of Imprisonment in the United States, 1850-2009

Sources: Margaret Werner Cahalan, *Historical Corrections Statistics in the United States, 1850–1984* (Washington, DC: U.S. Department of Justice, 1986); and Heather C. West, William J. Sabol, and Sarah J. Greenman, *Prisoners in 2009* (Washington, DC: Bureau of Justice Statistics, 2010), p. 1.

Historical Roots of the Corrections Explosion

Seen historically, the growth of correctional populations may be more the continuation of a long-term trend than the result of recent social conditions. A look at the data shows that correctional populations have continued to increase through widely divergent political eras and economic conditions. Census reports show an almost relentless increase in the rate of imprisonment over the past 150 years. In 1850, for example, only 29 people were imprisoned in this country for every 100,000 persons in the population.[10] By 1890, the rate had risen to 131 per 100,000. The rate grew slowly until 1980, when the rate of imprisonment in the United States stood at 153 per 100,000. At that point, a major shift toward imprisonment began. While crime rates rose sharply in the middle to late 1980s, the rate of imprisonment rose far more dramatically. Today, the rate of imprisonment in this country is over 500 per 100,000 persons, although the rate may have peaked.[11] Exhibit 1–3 illustrates changes in the rate of imprisonment over the past 155 years. Probation statistics—first available in 1935—show an even more amazing rate of growth. Although only 59,530 offenders were placed on probation throughout the United States in 1935, more than 4.2 million people are on probation today.[12]

Correctional Employment

Growing correctional populations and increasing budgets have led to a dramatically expanding correctional workforce and enhanced employment opportunities within the field. According to historical reports, persons employed in the corrections field totaled approximately 27,000 in 1950.[13] By 1975, the number had risen to about 75,000. The most current statistics available show that the number of uniformed correctional officers in adult prisons alone has increased to more than 215,000.[14] When juvenile detention facility personnel, probation and parole officers, correctional

U.S. correctional populations have grown dramatically over the past 25 years, as this image of inmates living in a modified gymnasium at the Mule Creek State Prison in Ione, California, illustrates. What factors led to a substantial increase in the use of imprisonment in this country beginning in the 1980s?

EXHIBIT 1–4	Careers in Corrections	
Academic teacher	Field administrator	Psychologist
Activity therapy administrator	Fugitive apprehension officer	Recreation coordinator
Business manager	Human services counselor	Social worker
Case manager	Job placement officer	Statistician
Chaplain	Mental health clinician	Substance abuse counselor
Chemical dependency manager	Parole caseworker	Unit leader
Children's services counselor	Parole officer	Victim advocate
Classification officer	Presentence investigator	Vocational instructor
Clinical social worker	Probation officer	Warden/superintendent
Correctional officer	Program officer	Youth services coordinator
Dietary officer	Program specialist	Youth supervisor
Drug court coordinator	Programmer/analyst	

Note: Consult the Appendix: Careers in Corrections at www.mhhe.com/schmalleger6e for the steps involved in career planning, developing employability and job readiness, and finding the right job.

administrators, jailers, and other corrections professionals are added, the total number of persons employed in corrections today stands at more than 748,000.[15] Exhibit 1–4 shows some of the employment possibilities in corrections.

New prisons mean jobs and can contribute greatly to the health of local economies. Some economically disadvantaged towns—from Tupper Lake, in the Adirondack Mountains of upstate New York, to Edgefield, South Carolina—are cashing in on the prison boom, having successfully competed to become sites for new prisons. The competition for new prison facilities is reminiscent of the efforts states made some years ago to attract new automobile factories and other industries.

CRIME AND CORRECTIONS

The crimes that bring people into the American correctional system include felonies, misdemeanors, and minor law violations that are sometimes called *infractions*.

Felonies are serious crimes. Murder, rape, aggravated assault, robbery, burglary, and arson are felonies in all jurisdictions within the United States, although the names for these crimes may differ from state to state. A general way to think about felonies is to remember that a **felony** is a serious crime whose commission can result in confinement in a state or federal correctional institution for more than a year.

In some states a felony conviction can result in the loss of certain civil privileges. A few states make conviction of a felony and the resulting incarceration grounds for uncontested divorce. Others prohibit convicted felony offenders from running for public office or owning a firearm, and some exclude them from professions such as medicine, law, and police work.

Huge differences in the treatment of specific crimes exist among states. Some crimes classified as felonies in one part of the country may be misdemeanors in another. In still other states, they may not even be crimes at all! Such is the case with some drug law violations and with social order offenses such as homosexual acts, prostitution, and gambling.

Misdemeanors, which compose the second major crime category, are relatively minor violations of the criminal law. They include crimes such as petty theft (the theft of items of little worth), simple assault (in which the victim suffers no serious injury and in which none was intended), breaking and entering, the possession of burglary tools, disorderly conduct, disturbing the peace, filing a false crime report, and writing bad checks (although

felony

A serious criminal offense; specifically, one punishable by death or by incarceration in a prison facility for more than a year.

misdemeanor

A relatively minor violation of the criminal law, such as petty theft or simple assault, punishable by confinement for one year or less.

the amount for which the check is written may determine the classification of this offense). In general, misdemeanors can be thought of as any crime punishable by a year or less in confinement.

Within felony and misdemeanor categories, most states distinguish among degrees, or levels of seriousness. Texas law, for example, establishes five felony classes and three classes of misdemeanor—intended to guide judges in assessing the seriousness of particular criminal acts. The Texas penal code then specifies categories into which given offenses fall.

A third category of crime is the **infraction**. The term, which is not used in all jurisdictions, refers to minor violations of the law that are less serious than misdemeanors. Infractions may include such violations of the law as jaywalking, spitting on the sidewalk, littering, and certain traffic violations, including the failure to wear a seat belt. People committing infractions are typically ticketed—that is, given citations—and released, usually upon a promise to appear later in court. Court appearances may be waived upon payment of a fine, which is often mailed in.

Measuring Crime

Two important sources of information on crime for correctional professionals are the FBI's Uniform Crime Reporting Program (UCR) and the Bureau of Justice Statistics' National Crime Victimization Survey (NCVS). Corrections professionals closely analyze these data to forecast the numbers and types of **correctional clients** to expect in the future. The forecasts can be used to project the need for different types of detention and rehabilitation services and facilities.

The Crime Funnel

Not all crimes are reported, and not everyone who commits a reported crime is arrested, so relatively few offenders enter the criminal justice system. Of those who do, some are not prosecuted (perhaps because the evidence against them is insufficient), others plead guilty to lesser crimes, and others are found not guilty. Some who are convicted are diverted from further processing by the system or may be fined or ordered to counseling. Hence, the proportion of criminal offenders who eventually enter the correctional system is small, as Exhibit 1–5 shows.[16]

CORRECTIONS AND THE CRIMINAL JUSTICE SYSTEM

Corrections is generally considered the final stage in the criminal justice process. Some aspects of corrections, however, come into play early in the process. Keep in mind that although the term **criminal justice** can be used to refer to the justice *process*, it can also be used to describe our *system* of justice. Criminal justice agencies, taken as a whole, are said to compose the **criminal justice system**.

The components of the criminal justice system are (1) police, (2) courts, and (3) corrections. Each component, because it contains a variety of organizations and agencies, can be termed a *subsystem*. The subsystem of corrections, for example, includes prisons, agencies of probation and parole, jails, and a variety of alternative programs.

The *process* of criminal justice involves the activities of the agencies that make up the criminal justice system. The process of criminal justice begins when a crime is discovered or reported.

infraction
A minor violation of state statute or local ordinance punishable by a fine or other penalty, but not incarceration, or by a specified, usually very short term of incarceration.

correctional clients
Prison inmates, probationers, parolees, offenders assigned to alternative sentencing programs, and those held in jails.

criminal justice
The process of achieving justice through the application of the criminal law and through the workings of the criminal justice system. Also, the study of the field of criminal justice.

criminal justice system
The collection of all the agencies that perform criminal justice functions, whether these are operations or administration or technical support. The basic divisions of the criminal justice system are police, courts, and corrections.

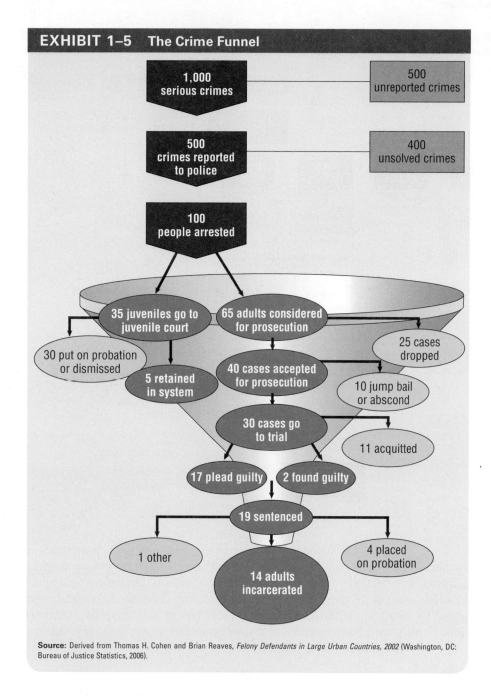

EXHIBIT 1–5 **The Crime Funnel**

Source: Derived from Thomas H. Cohen and Brian Reaves, *Felony Defendants in Large Urban Countries, 2002* (Washington, DC: Bureau of Justice Statistics, 2006).

Court decisions based on the due process guarantees of the U.S. Constitution require that specific steps be taken in the justice process. Although the exact nature of those steps varies among jurisdictions, the description that follows portrays the most common sequence of events in response to serious criminal behavior. Exhibit 1–6, which diagrams the American criminal justice system, indicates the relationship among the stages in the criminal justice processing of adult offenders.

Entering the Correctional System

The criminal justice system does not respond to all crime because most crimes are not discovered or reported to the police.[17] Law enforcement agencies learn about crimes from the reports of citizens, through discovery by a police officer in the field, or through investigative and intelligence work. Once a law enforcement agency knows of a crime, the agency must

EXHIBIT 1–6   The Adult Criminal Justice System

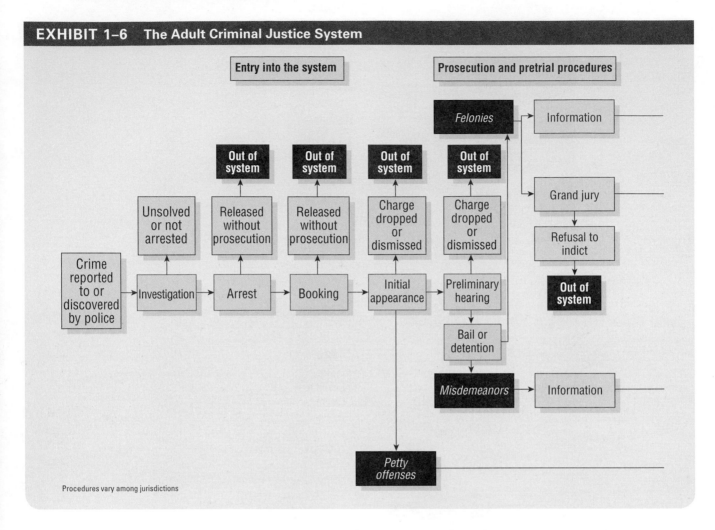

Procedures vary among jurisdictions

identify and arrest a suspect before the case can proceed. Sometimes a suspect is found at the scene; other times, however, identifying a suspect requires an extensive investigation. Often no one is identified or apprehended—the crime goes unsolved. If an offender is arrested, booked, and jailed to await an initial court appearance, the intake, custody, confinement, and supervision aspects of corrections first come into play at this stage of the criminal justice process.

Prosecution and Pretrial Procedure

After an arrest, law enforcement agencies present information about the case and about the accused to the prosecutor, who decides whether to file formal charges with the court. If no charges are filed, the accused must be released. The prosecutor can also drop charges after filing them. Such a choice is called *nolle prosequi;* and when it happens, a case is said to be "nolled" or "nollied."

A suspect charged with a crime must be taken before a judge or magistrate without unnecessary delay. At the initial appearance, the judge or magistrate informs the accused of the charges and decides whether there is probable cause to detain him or her. Often, defense counsel is also assigned then. If the offense charged is not very serious, the determination of guilt and the assessment of a penalty may also occur at this stage.

In some jurisdictions, a pretrial-release decision is made at the initial appearance, but this decision may occur at other hearings or at another

EXHIBIT 1–6 *(continued)*

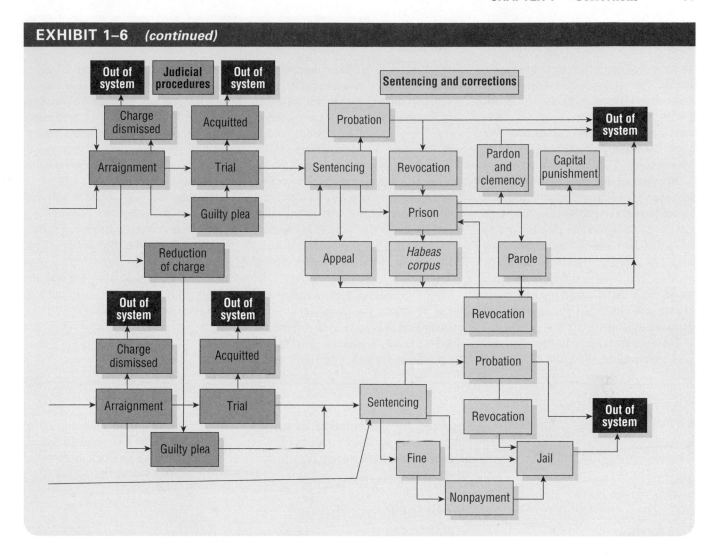

time during the process. Pretrial release on bail was traditionally intended to ensure appearance at trial. However, many jurisdictions today permit pretrial detention of defendants accused of serious offenses and deemed dangerous, to prevent them from committing crimes in the pretrial period. The court may decide to release the accused on his or her own recognizance, into the custody of a third party, on the promise of satisfying certain conditions, or after the posting of a financial bond. Conditions of release may be reviewed at any later time while charges are still pending.

In many jurisdictions, the initial appearance may be followed by a preliminary hearing. The main function of this hearing is to determine whether there is probable cause to believe that the accused committed a crime within the jurisdiction of the court. If the judge or magistrate does not find probable cause, the case is dismissed. However, if the judge finds probable cause for such a belief, or if the accused waives the right to a preliminary hearing, the case may be bound over to a grand jury.

A grand jury hears evidence against the accused, presented by the prosecutor, and decides if there is sufficient evidence to cause the accused to be brought to trial. If the grand jury finds sufficient evidence, it submits an indictment to the court.

Not all jurisdictions use grand juries. Some require, instead, that the prosecutor submit an information (a formal written accusation) to the court. In most jurisdictions, misdemeanor cases and some felony cases

Very few of us do not think about beating the system. After all, the system deprives us of the freedom we cherish. It stands for all that we resent: lack of choice, restricted movement, denial of access to loved ones. We resent the walls, bars, uniforms, being told what to do, what programs we must take.

Moralists argue that we get exactly what we deserve, and many citizens believe that we are treated too well. Few of us can argue that we didn't know what we were getting into when we made the bad choices that landed us in prison. None of us arrived by accident, and if we are honest with ourselves, we'll acknowledge a whole series of destructive behaviors that preceded our committal to a "monastery of the damned."

In view of status and our chances of success upon release, the future doesn't look particularly bright. It's damn depressing to have to accept our collective reality. Hope is found in beating the system, the smart way. The smart way is not the path many of us have continually taken: defiance, conflict with "the man." AA members are familiar with the slogan "I can only change myself, not others." It is always easier to project blame for our inadequacies onto others. But until we come to terms with our individual reality, separate the crime from the man, decide that the "I am" is capable of much more than the label implies—we're doomed to failure.

The administration uses education statistics to create the illusion of massive programming. It is up to us to demand the delivery. Enroll in courses. Develop the thirst to learn. Ask for help from peer tutors.

An education is the ultimate form of restorative justice. The entire population benefits when just one con becomes literate. Educated cons have reason to lift their heads in self-assurance. We are better able to articulate our needs, better able to negotiate collectively, better able to see a future for ourselves.

Whether "the man" wants to acknowledge it or not, educated prisoners get respect from everybody inside and outside the prison. Adult education and training at every level—whether basic literacy, high school, college or university—are vital. The positive skills we learn in prison can't be taken away from us at the gate.

Joseph E. McCormick
A prisoner

---

proceed by the issuance of an information. Some jurisdictions require indictments in felony cases. However, the accused may choose to waive a grand jury indictment and, instead, accept service of an information for the crime.

Judicial Procedures

adjudication

The process by which a court arrives at a final decision in a case.

arraignment

An appearance in court prior to trial in a criminal proceeding.

nolo contendere

A plea of "no contest." A no-contest plea may be used by a defendant who does not wish to contest conviction. Because the plea does not admit guilt, however, it cannot provide the basis for later civil suits.

Adjudication is the process by which a court arrives at a decision in a case. The adjudication process involves a number of steps. The first is **arraignment.** Once an indictment or information is filed with the trial court, the accused is scheduled for arraignment. If the accused has been detained without bail, corrections personnel take him or her to the arraignment. At the arraignment, the accused is informed of the charges, advised of the rights of criminal defendants, and asked to enter a plea to the charges.

If the accused pleads guilty or pleads *nolo contendere* (accepts a penalty without admitting guilt), the judge may accept or reject the plea. If the plea is accepted, no trial is held and the offender is sentenced at this proceeding or at a later date. The plea may be rejected if, for example, the judge believes that the accused has been coerced. If this occurs, the case may proceed to trial. Sometimes, as the result of negotiations between the prosecutor and the defendant, the defendant enters a guilty plea in expectation of reduced charges or a light sentence. *Nolo contendere* pleas are often entered by those who fear a later civil action and who therefore do not want to admit guilt.

If the accused pleads not guilty or not guilty by reason of insanity, a date is set for trial. A person accused of a serious crime is guaranteed a trial by jury. However, the accused may ask for a bench trial, in which the judge, rather than a jury, serves as the finder of fact. In both instances, the prosecution and defense present evidence by questioning witnesses, and the judge decides issues of law. The trial results in acquittal or conviction of the original charges or of lesser included offenses. A defendant may be convicted at trial only if the government's evidence proves beyond a reasonable doubt that the defendant is guilty, or if the defendant knowingly and voluntarily pleads guilty to the charges.

Sentencing and Sanctions

After a guilty verdict or guilty plea, sentence is imposed. In most cases, the judge decides on the sentence, but in some states, the sentence is decided by the jury, particularly for capital offenses, such as murder.

To arrive at an appropriate sentence, a court may hold a sentencing hearing to consider evidence of aggravating or mitigating circumstances. In assessing the circumstances surrounding a criminal act, courts often rely on presentence investigations by probation agencies or other designated authorities. Courts may also consider victim impact statements.

The sentencing choices available to judges and juries frequently include one or more of the following:

- the death penalty;
- incarceration in a prison, a jail, or another confinement facility;
- community service;
- probation, in which the convicted person is not confined but is subject to certain conditions and restrictions;
- fines, primarily as penalties for minor offenses; and
- restitution, which requires the offender to provide financial compensation to the victim.

In many states, *mandatory minimum* sentencing laws require that persons convicted of certain offenses serve a minimum prison term, which the judge must impose and which may not be reduced by a parole board or by "good-time" deductions.

After the trial, a defendant may request appellate review of the conviction to see if there was some serious error that affected the defendant's right to a fair trial. In some states, the defendant may also appeal the sentence.

At least one appeal of a conviction is a matter of right. Any further appeal (to a state supreme court or in the case of federal court convictions, to the U.S. Supreme Court) is *discretionary*, which means that the higher court may or may not choose to hear the further appeal. After losing all their available *direct* appeals (also known as *exhaustion of state remedies*), state prisoners may also seek to have their convictions reviewed *collaterally* in the federal courts via a writ of *habeas corpus*. In states that have the death penalty, appeals of death sentences are usually automatic, and extensive federal *habeas corpus* review often takes place before the sentence of death is actually carried out.

The Correctional Subsystem

After conviction and sentencing, most offenders enter the correctional subsystem. Before we proceed with our discussion, it is best to define the term *corrections*. As with most words, a variety of definitions can be found.

In 1967, for example, the President's Commission on Law Enforcement and Administration of Justice wrote that *corrections* means "America's prisons, jails, juvenile training schools, and probation and parole machinery." It is "that part of the criminal justice system," said the commission, "that the public sees least of and knows least about."[18]

Steven Hayes, (left), was sentenced to death by a Connecticut jury in 2011 for his role in a home invasion that culminated in the rape and murder of a mother and her two daughters. His partner in crime, Joshua Komisarjevsky, (right), pled guilty to homicide and received a life sentence. Who decides what happens to defendants after they enter the correctional system?

Years later, in 1975, the National Advisory Commission on Criminal Justice Standards and Goals said in its lengthy volume on corrections, "*Corrections* is defined here as the community's official reactions to the convicted offender, whether adult or juvenile."[19] The commission noted that "this is a broad definition and it suffers . . . from several shortcomings."

We can distinguish between institutional corrections and noninstitutional corrections. A report by the Bureau of Justice Statistics (BJS) says that **institutional corrections** "involves the confinement and rehabilitation of adults and juveniles convicted of offenses against the law and the confinement of persons suspected of a crime awaiting trial and adjudication."[20] BJS goes on to say that

institutional corrections

That aspect of the correctional enterprise that "involves the incarceration and rehabilitation of adults and juveniles convicted of offenses against the law, and the confinement of persons suspected of a crime awaiting trial and adjudication."

> correctional institutions are prisons, reformatories, jails, houses of correction, penitentiaries, correctional farms, workhouses, reception centers, diagnostic centers, industrial schools, training schools, detention centers, and a variety of other types of institutions for the confinement and correction of convicted adults or juveniles who are adjudicated delinquent or in need of supervision. [The term] also includes facilities for the detention of adults and juveniles accused of a crime and awaiting trial or hearing.

According to BJS, **noninstitutional corrections**, which is sometimes called *community corrections*, includes "pardon, probation, and parole activities, correctional administration not directly connectable to institutions, and miscellaneous [activities] not directly related to institutional care."

As all these definitions show, in its broadest sense, the term *corrections* encompasses each of the following components, as well as the process of interaction among them:

noninstitutional corrections (also *community corrections*)

That aspect of the correctional enterprise that includes "pardon, probation, and parole activities, correctional administration not directly connectable to institutions, and miscellaneous [activities] not directly related to institutional care."

- the *purpose* and *goals* of the correctional enterprise;
- jails, prisons, correctional institutions, and other *facilities*;
- probation, parole, and alternative and diversionary *programs*;
- federal, state, local, and international correctional offices and *agencies*;
- counseling, educational, health care, nutrition, and many other *services*;
- correctional *clients*;
- corrections *volunteers*;

EXHIBIT 1–7   **American Correctional Association**

Public Correctional Policy on Role of Corrections Policy

The overall role of corrections is to enhance public safety and social order. Adult and juvenile correctional systems should:

- implement court-ordered sanctions and provide supervision of those accused of unlawful behavior prior to and after adjudication in a safe and humane manner;
- offer the widest range of correctional programs that are based on exemplary practices, supported by research and promote pro-social behavior;
- provide gender- and culturally-responsive programs and services for preadjudicated and adjudicated offenders that will enhance successful reentry to the community and that are administered within the least restrictive environment consistent with public, staff and offender safety;
- address the needs of victims of crime;
- routinely review correctional programs and reentry services to ensure that they are addressing the needs of offenders, victims, and the community; and
- collaborate with other professions to improve and strengthen correctional services and to support the reduction of crime and recidivism.

Source: Copyright © American Correctional Association.

- corrections *professionals;*
- fiscal appropriations and *funding;*
- various aspects of criminal and civil *law;*
- formal and informal *procedures;*
- effective and responsible *management;*
- community *expectations* regarding correctional practices; and
- the machinery of *capital punishment.*

When we use the word *corrections,* we include all of these elements. Fourteen elements, however, make for an unwieldy definition. Hence, for purposes of discussion, we will say that **corrections** refers to all the various aspects of the pretrial and postconviction management of individuals accused or convicted of crimes. Central to this perspective is the recognition that corrections—although it involves a variety of programs, services, facilities, and personnel—is essentially a management activity. Rather than stress the role of institutions or agencies, this definition emphasizes the human dimension of correctional activity—especially the efforts of the corrections professionals who undertake the day-to-day tasks. Like any other managed activity, corrections has goals and purposes. Exhibit 1–7 details the role of corrections as identified by the American Correctional Association (ACA).

corrections

All the various aspects of the pretrial and postconviction management of individuals accused or convicted of crimes.

The Societal Goals of Corrections The ACA statement about the purpose of corrections is addressed primarily to corrections professionals. It recognizes, however, that *the* fundamental purpose of corrections "is to enhance social order and public safety." In any society, social order and public safety depend on effective social control. Some forms of social control take the form of customs, norms, and what sociologists refer to as *mores* ('mȯr-ˌāz). **Mores** are behavioral standards that embody a group's values. Violation of these standards is a serious wrong. They generally forbid such activities as murder, rape, and robbery. **Folkways,** in contrast, are time-honored ways of doing things. Although folkways carry the force of tradition, their violation is unlikely to threaten the survival of the group.

mores

Cultural restrictions on behavior that forbid serious violations—such as murder, rape, and robbery—of a group's values.

folkways

Time-honored ways of doing things. Although they carry the force of tradition, their violation is unlikely to threaten the survival of the social group.

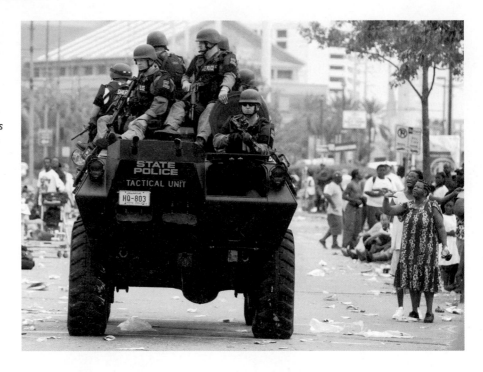

A Louisiana State Police SWAT team drives past flood victims waiting for rescue in New Orleans after powerful Hurricane Katrina made landfall in 2005 and flooded much of the city. The officers had been deployed to restore order in the stricken city after looters took advantage of the social disorder that followed in the hurricane's wake. What role does the criminal justice system play in the maintenance of social order?

criminal law (also *penal law*)

That portion of the law that defines crimes and specifies criminal punishments.

Societal expectations, whatever form they take, are sometimes enacted into law. The **criminal law**, also called *penal law*, is the body of rules and regulations that define public offenses, or wrongs committed against the state or society, and specify punishments for those offenses. Social control, social order, and public safety are the ultimate goals of criminal law.

The correctional subsystem is crucial in enforcing the dictates of the law because the rewards and punishments it carries out play a significant role in society's control of its members.

PROFESSIONALISM IN CORRECTIONS

Only a few decades ago, some writers bemoaned the fact that the field of corrections had not achieved professional status. Happily, much has changed over the past several years. By 1987, Bob Barrington, who was then the executive director of the International Association of Correctional Officers, was able to proclaim, in a discussion about prisons, that "correctional facilities . . . run smoothly and efficiently for one basic reason: the professional and forward-thinking attitudes and actions of the correctional officers employed."[21]

Some writers on American criminal justice have said that the hallmark of a true profession is "a shared set of principles and customs that transcend self-interest and speak to the essential nature of the particular calling or trade."[22] This definition recognizes the selfless and ethical nature of professional work. Hence, "professionals have a sense of commitment to their professions that is usually not present among those in occupational groups."[23] Work within a profession is viewed more as a "calling" than as a mere way of earning a living. "Professionals have a love for their work that is above that of employment merely to receive a paycheck."[24]

profession

An occupation granted high social status by virtue of the personal integrity of its members.

Although it is important to keep formal definitions in mind, for our purposes, we will define a **profession** as an occupation granted high social status by virtue of the personal integrity of its members. We can summarize

Offices of the American Correctional Association (ACA) in Alexandria, Virginia. The ACA is a leading proponent of professionalism in corrections. What does corrections professionalism entail?

the *attitude* of a true professional by noting that it is characterized by the following:

- a spirit of public service and interest in the public good;
- the fair application of reason and the use of intellect to solve problems;
- self-regulation through a set of internal guidelines by which professionals hold *themselves* accountable for their actions;
- continual self-appraisal and self-examination;
- an inner sense of professionalism (i.e., honor, self-discipline, commitment, personal integrity, and self-direction);
- adherence to the recognized ethical principles of one's profession (see the Ethics and Professionalism box in this chapter); and
- a commitment to lifelong learning and lifelong betterment within the profession.

Most professional occupations have developed practices that foster professionalism among their members.

Standards and Training

Historically, professional corrections organizations and their leaders have recognized the importance of training. It was not until the late 1970s, however, that the American Correctional Association (ACA) Commission on Accreditation established the first training standards. The commission did the following:

- specified standards for given positions within corrections;
- identified essential training topics;
- set specific numbers of hours for preservice (120) and annual in-service training (40); and
- specified basic administrative policy support requirements for training programs.[25]

Ethics and Professionalism

American Correctional Association Code of Ethics

1. Members shall respect and protect the civil and legal rights of all individuals.

2. Members shall treat every professional situation with concern for the welfare of the individuals involved and with no intent to gain personally.

3. Members shall maintain relationships with colleagues to promote mutual respect within the profession and improve the quality of service.

4. Members shall make public criticism of their colleagues or their agencies only when warranted, verifiable, and constructive.

5. Members shall respect the importance of all disciplines within the criminal justice system and work to improve cooperation with each segment.

6. Members shall honor the public's right to information and share information with the public to the extent permitted by law subject to individuals' right to privacy.

7. Members shall respect and protect the right of the public to be safeguarded from criminal activity.

8. Members shall refrain from using their positions to secure personal privileges or advantages.

9. Members shall refrain from allowing personal interest to impair objectivity in the performance of duty while acting in an official capacity.

10. Members shall refrain from entering into any formal or informal activity or agreement that presents a conflict of interest or is inconsistent with the conscientious performance of duties.

11. Members shall refrain from accepting any gifts, services, or favors that are or appear to be improper or imply an obligation inconsistent with the free and objective exercise of professional duties.

12. Members shall clearly differentiate between personal views/statements and views/statements/positions made on behalf of the agency or Association.

13. Members shall report to appropriate authorities any corrupt or unethical behaviors for which there is sufficient evidence to justify review.

14. Members shall refrain from discriminating against any individual because of race, gender, creed, national origin, religious affiliation, age, disability, or any other type of prohibited discrimination.

15. Members shall preserve the integrity of private information; they shall refrain from seeking information on individuals beyond that which is necessary to implement responsibilities and perform their duties; members shall refrain from revealing nonpublic information unless expressly authorized to do so.

16. Members shall make all appointments, promotions, and dismissals in accordance with established civil service rules, applicable contract agreements, and individual merit, rather than furtherance of personal interests.

17. Members shall respect, promote, and contribute to a workplace that is safe, healthy, and free of harassment in any form.

Adopted by the Board of Governors and Delegate Assembly in August 1994.

Source: Copyright © American Correctional Association.

Ethical Dilemma 1–1: In light of tight state budgets and overcrowded prisons, should governors use their authority to provide early release to some inmates? If so, under what circumstances? For more information, go to Ethical Dilemma 1–1 at www.justicestudies.com/ethics06.

Ethical Dilemma 1–2: You are the warden of the only medium security prison in your state. Your nephew is sentenced to serve 10 years in your institution. Using the ACA Code of Ethics as a guide, determine what ethical issues you will face. For more information, go to Ethical Dilemma 1–2 at www.justicestudies.com/ethics06.

Ethical Dilemma 1–3: One of your fellow correctional officers accepts candy and snacks from one of the inmates. She doesn't ask for the snacks, nor does she do any favors for the inmate. Should you report this activity? Will you report it? Using the ACA Code of Ethics, determine the ethical issues, if any, involved in this behavior. For more information, go to Ethical Dilemma 1–3 at www.justicestudies.com/ethics06.

Ethical Dilemmas for every chapter are available online.

Following ACA's lead, virtually every state now requires at least 120 hours of preservice training for correctional officers working in institutional settings; many states require more. Probation and parole officers are required to undergo similar training in most jurisdictions, and correctional officers working in jails are similarly trained.

Agencies such as the Palm Beach (Florida) County Sheriff's Office understand that 40 hours of training every four years is not sufficient to maintain the proficiency of skills or the continuous development of staff. The Palm Beach County Sheriff's Office requires all certified correctional officers to participate in a minimum of 40 hours in-service training annually. This program is designed to develop not only technical skills but also the overall well-being of the officer.

In most training situations there is not the need, time, or resources to transfer detailed knowledge of theoretical concepts. Required outcomes must apply a practical balance between understanding the reason an action is done in a particular way and having the ability to apply procedures correctly.

It is important to define performance indicators and targets against these objectives, which are acceptable and practical expected levels of achievement. Knowledge assessment techniques need to be integrated into training to enable assessment of whether adequate competencies have been achieved by each officer.

The Palm Beach County Sheriff's Office mandates the attendance and curriculum for 24 of the 40 hours. This 24-hour block attended by all officers consists of firearms, defensive tactics, first aid/CPR and blood-borne pathogens, and CJSTC (Criminal Justice Standards & Training Commission)–mandated courses. The remaining 16 hours are chosen by the individual officer from a training catalog compiled each year by the Bureau of Training. The available classes for selection by the officer range from yoga, nutrition, and retirement planning to advanced handgun and pressure point controlling techniques.

The presented materials in these in-service classes are not intended to be a comprehensive course in technical development and skills. Rather the lessons are meant to be a supplement that will give the officers an enhanced perspective on how to develop their skills and themselves. Not only do the lessons give the officers helpful tips and concepts, but they also are meant to provide them with insight on good methods to use.

There is no such thing as a common knowledge of an unstated objective. Objectives need to be defined to ensure accountability. When determining the objectives of training, training managers should also define the indicators by which they can judge whether training programs are successful. This will make evaluation of training considerably more relevant.

Captain Alan Fuhrman
Palm Beach County Sheriff's Office
Planning & Research Unit
West Palm Beach, Florida

Through training, new members of a profession learn the core values and ideals, the basic knowledge, and the accepted practices central to the profession. Setting training standards ensures that the education is uniform. Standards also mandate the teaching of specialized knowledge. Standards supplement training by doing the following:

- setting minimum requirements for entry into the profession;
- detailing expectations for those involved in the everyday life of correctional work; and
- establishing basic requirements for facilities, programs, and practices.

From the point of view of corrections professionals, training is a matter of personal responsibility. A lifelong commitment to a career ensures that those who think of themselves as professionals will seek the training needed to enhance their job performance.

Basic Skills and Knowledge

In 1990, the Professional Education Council of the American Correctional Association developed a model entry test for correctional officers. The test was intended to increase professionalism in the field and to provide a standard criminal justice curriculum.[26]

The council suggested that the test could act "as a quality control measure for such education, much as does the bar exam for attorneys." The standard entry test was designed to "reveal the applicant's understanding of the structure, purpose, and method of the police, prosecution, courts, institutions, probation, parole, community service, and extramural

Melanie Estes

Day Youth Counselor • United Methodist Family Services • Richmond, Virginia

Melanie Estes has been with the agency for only a few years and is currently one of two senior counselors. She completed a four-year degree in criminal justice in 1997 and is planning to attend graduate school in social work at Virginia Commonwealth University.

As a youth counselor, Estes assists in developing, implementing, evaluating, and modifying individual and group treatment plans. She ensures that daily routine and expectations are followed in the residential home. It is also her responsibility to plan, oversee, and evaluate daily and weekly schedules of agency program activities. She is the liaison between the agency and the residents' social workers, probation officers, parents, and any others who may be involved in the youths' treatment. She keeps all parties informed of residents' progress.

As a staff member, Estes's foremost duty is to act as a change agent for clients in the program. She believes that it is important that staffers learn that their interactions and interventions with one another are as crucial to the habilitative process as their interactions and interventions with youth. As a team member, she is asked to evaluate her coworkers' performance and to provide support, feedback, and training for other team members. Once a month, she is the chairperson and recorder for the weekly team meeting.

> *"Working with troubled juveniles is challenging and rewarding, especially with abandoned and abused children. I'm not kidding anyone when I say that it is hard to maintain a healthy balance between friend and caretaker. But one of the greatest experiences I ever had is to help at-risk youth."*

Talking about CORRECTIONS

WORKING IN TODAY'S PRISONS AND JAILS

Visit *Live Talk* at **Corrections .com** (www.mhhe.com/ schmalleger6e) and listen to the program "Working in Today's Prisons and Jails," which relates to ideas discussed in this chapter.

---

corrections professional

A dedicated person of high moral character and personal integrity who is employed in the field of corrections and takes professionalism to heart.

---

programs." It was also designed to "test for knowledge of various kinds of corrections programs, the role of punitive sanctions and incapacitation, and perspective on past experience and current trends."

More recently, Mark S. Fleisher of Illinois State University identified four core traits essential to effective work in corrections.[27] The traits are as follows:

- **Accountability:** "Correctional work demands precision, timeliness, accountability and strong ethics." Students may drift into patterns of irresponsibility during their college years. Once they become correctional officers, however, they need to take their work seriously.
- **Strong Writing Skills:** Because correctional officers must complete a huge amount of paperwork, they need to be able to write well. They should also be familiar with the "vocabulary of corrections."
- **Effective Presentational Skills:** "A correctional career requires strong verbal skills and an ability to organize presentations." Effective verbal skills help officers interact with their peers, inmates, and superiors.
- **A Logical Mind and the Ability to Solve Problems:** Such skills are essential to success in corrections because problems arise daily. Being able to solve them is a sign of an effective officer.

In sum, we can say that a **corrections professional** is a dedicated person of high moral character and personal integrity who is employed in the field of corrections and takes professionalism to heart. He or she understands the importance of standards, training, and education and the need to be proficient in the skills required for success in the correctional enterprise. The corrections professional recognizes that professionalism leads to the betterment of society, to enhanced social order, and to a higher quality of life for all.

Standard-Setting Organizations

A number of standard-setting **professional associations** in the field of corrections have developed models of professionalism. Among them are the American Correctional Association (ACA), the American Probation and Parole Association (APPA), and the American Jail Association (AJA).

Standard-setting organizations like these offer detailed sets of written principles for correctional occupations and corrections administration. The ACA, the APPA, and the AJA, for example, all have developed standards to guide training and to clarify what is expected of those working in corrections. Moreover, many professional associations have developed codes of ethics, outlining what is moral and proper conduct. Some of these codes will appear in later chapters.

Correctional associations also offer training, hold meetings and seminars, create and maintain job banks, and produce literature relevant to corrections. They sometimes lobby legislative bodies in an attempt to influence the development of new laws that affect corrections.

Future chapters will present ACA policies. The ACA policies are important because they guide the development of training and because they influence the work environment of many agencies and institutions.

In 1999, the ACA, through its national Commission on Correctional Certification, established a program for certifying correctional staff, from line officers to executive leaders. **Certification** is part of a process called *credentialing* that focuses specifically on the individual. Its counterpart is accreditation, a formal process that highlights the quality of a facility in an effort to ensure that it meets health, safety, and other correctional standards. Accreditation is discussed in more detail in Chapter 13. ACA certification began officially in January 2000 when the first Certified Corrections Executive (CCE) application was accepted by the ACA. The first CCE examination was administered in August 2000.[28]

There are four categories of ACA Certified Corrections Professional (CCP), extending from those who work at the highest organization levels to personnel employed at the line level, working directly with offenders. Those categories are: (1) Certified Corrections Executive (CCE), (2) Certified Corrections Manager (CCM), (3) Certified Corrections Supervisor (CCS), and (4) Certified Corrections Officer (CCO). Applicants for certification must pass a 200-item multiple-choice examination, document their corrections experience, show compliance with the ACA's Code of Ethics, and meet minimum requirements for formal education. Educational requirements increase with each certification level. While a high school diploma or equivalent is required of those seeking CCO certification, CCS and CCM certification seekers are required to hold two-year college degrees (or its equivalent), while those applying for certification at the CCE level must hold a four-year college degree (or equivalent). According to the ACA, the organization's certification program creates the *opportunity* for a lifetime of progressive professional achievement. Anyone successfully completing the certification process is designated as a Certified Corrections Professional (CCP).[29] Recertification happens at three-year intervals and requires a specified number of continuing education contact hours.

professional associations
Organized groups of like-minded individuals who work to enhance the professional status of members of their occupational group.

certification
A credentialing process, usually involving testing and career development assessment, through which the skills, knowledge, and abilities of correctional personnel can be formally recognized.

Education is an important component of any successful profession. Shown here are three educational institutions offering undergraduate programs in criminal justice—two with a corrections emphasis. What role does the American Correctional Association see for higher education in advancing the corrections profession?

The purpose of the ACA Professional Certification Program is "to uphold standards for competent practice." Moreover, certification provides an opportunity "for staff to be recognized as qualified correctional practitioners."

Like the ACA, the AJA, through its five-member Jail Manager Certification Commission (JMCC), offers a program for the certification of jail administrators, managers, and supervisory personnel. The first Certified Jail Managers (CJMs) were recognized in 1997.[30]

Education

Education is another component, besides basic job skills and job-specific training, of true professionalism. Training, by itself, can never make one a true professional, because complex decision-making skills are essential for success in any occupation involving intense interpersonal interaction—and

---

EXHIBIT 1–8   American Correctional Association

Public Correctional Policy on Higher Education

The field of corrections, in cooperation with higher education, should contribute to the improvement of the professional practice of corrections. Academic programs concerned with criminal justice, juvenile justice and corrections should:

- provide a pool of qualified candidates for correctional service, and assist in the delineation of dimensions of work responsibilities that may emerge as a result of changing social, economic, political and technological trends;
- promote understanding, both for correctional practitioners and for the public at large, of the complex social, ethical, political and economic factors that influence all areas of corrections;
- Challenge assumptions about crime and corrections, and stimulate change when change is needed;
- partner with criminal justice, juvenile justice and corrections organizations to promote and support ethical standards in research, planning and evaluation in all areas;
- engage in public service related to corrections, including informational programs, volunteer programs and opportunities for training, such as internships and practicums to enhance the relationship between the academic community and correctional practitioners;
- encourage colleges and universities to provide opportunities for research and the publication of research findings;
- Support, through program and faculty development, the evolution of corrections as a distinct professional discipline;
- Implement programs in corrections at the associate degree level that can serve as a minimum requirement for full professional status as a correctional employee; and
- partner with correctional agencies to promote and facilitate learning initiatives for employees.

Source: Copyright © American Correctional Association.

---

they can be acquired only through general education. Education builds critical-thinking skills, it allows the application of theory and ethical principles to a multitude of situations that are constantly in flux, and it provides insights into on-the-job difficulties.

Correctional education that goes beyond skills training is available primarily from two- and four-year colleges that offer corrections curricula and programs of study (see Exhibit 1–8). Courses in corrections are also typically found in undergraduate and graduate programs in criminal justice. The day will come when at least a two-year degree will be required for entry into the corrections profession.

EVIDENCE-BASED CORRECTIONS

Corrections professionalism today includes recognition of the importance of scientific studies of corrections, referred to as **evidence-based corrections.** Evidence-based corrections is focused on determining what works in correctional settings; that is, what correctional programs are effective in reducing recidivism and in preventing future crimes. In any discussion of evidence-based corrections (also known as *evidence-based penology*), it is important to remember that the word *evidence* refers to scientific evidence, not to criminal evidence. Corrections professionals who adhere to an evidence-based philosophy acknowledge the problem-solving potential

evidence-based corrections (also *evidence-based penology*)

The application of social scientific techniques to the study of everyday corrections procedures for the purpose of increasing effectiveness and enhancing the efficient use of available resources.

EVIDENCE-BASED CORRECTIONS

of social science research methods, read correctional publications and journals, and keep abreast of the latest findings in their field.

The beginning of the evidence-based movement in corrections can be traced to the 1997 publication of a lengthy report to the U.S. Congress, entitled *Preventing Crime: What Works, What Doesn't, What's Promising*.[31] The report, known as a *meta-analysis* because it assessed more than 500 previously completed studies of various crime prevention programs, looked at the effectiveness of correctional programs in seven different settings: families, police, community, place security, labor markets, schools, and the criminal justice system.

Researchers discovered that a number of the evaluated programs could be declared successful. Successful efforts became known as *what works* programs; defined as those that are reasonably certain to reduce recidivism. Other programs were found likely to fail to reduce recidivism, and were listed in the category of *what does not work*. Finally, some programs, which fell into a middle ground, were termed *promising*.

In 2008, the National Institute of Corrections (NIC) awarded a grant to address evidence-based decision making in local criminal justice agencies to the Center for Effective Public Policy, in partnership with other groups. The goal of the ongoing initiative is to build a systemwide framework that will result in a useful evidence-based decision-making model. The model is intended to help criminal justice policymakers by providing them the information, processes, and tools needed to achieve measurable reductions in pretrial misconduct and in postconviction reoffending.

The principal product of the initial phase of the NIC initiative was the 2010 publication of *A Framework for Evidence-Based Decision Making in Local Criminal Justice Systems*.[32] As the initiative continues to unfold, the NIC and its collaborators are seeking to create and fund pilot projects to demonstrate the value of approaches that are supported by research, and that produce positive and measurable outcomes. The NIC is an agency within the federal Bureau of Prisons that provides assistance to federal, state, and local corrections agencies. It has offices in Washington, D.C., and Aurora, Colorado.

Also in 2010, under the direction of Assistant U.S. attorney general Laurie O. Robinson, the Office of Justice Programs (OJP), an arm of the U.S. Department of Justice, announced an agencywide Evidence Integration Initiative, called E2I. Like the NIC partnership, E2I is an ongoing effort to integrate science and research into OJP's programs. The initiative also seeks to generate quality evidence in the form of research and statistical evaluations. Most importantly, according to Robinson, "We are working to move evidence into practice by funding evidence-based programs."[33]

Evidence-based corrections is an exciting new development in the corrections field, and many other agencies, institutions, and organizations are beginning to emphasize the use of scientific evidence. Among them is the Center for Evidence-Based Corrections at the University of California, Irvine. The center stresses the use of scientific studies in corrections as useful in the creation of evidence-based policy. Evidence-based policy, says the center, "is an approach that helps people make well-informed decisions about policies and programs by putting the best available evidence from research at the heart of policy development and implementation."[34] This approach, says the center, "stands in contrast to opinion-based policy, which relies heavily on either the selective use of evidence . . . or on the untested views of individuals or groups, often inspired by ideological views and speculative conjecture."

Another notable proponent of evidence-based corrections is the Philadelphia-based Pew Center on the States. In 2009, the center released a report subtitled "The Long Reach of American Corrections," in which it

Assistant U.S. attorney general Laurie O. Robinson speaking to the National Association of Drug Court Professionals (NADCP) in 2011. Robinson recently announced creation of the Evidence Integration Initiative (called E2I) within the federal Office of Justice Programs. What is evidence-based corrections?

noted that while states may take different paths toward creating an effective correctional system, they should ensure that the options they consider "are rooted in today's robust body of research," and "should always develop and implement policies based on the best available science."[35] According to Pew, the implementation of evidence-based practices can result in decreases in crime of up to 30 percent while non-evidence-based programs "tend to see no decrease and even a slight increase in crime."

Evidence-based corrections helps to inform this book, and is discussed in a number of the chapters that follow.

SOCIAL DIVERSITY IN CORRECTIONS

The corrections profession faces a number of social issues that are of special concern to Americans today. Contemporary issues include questions about the purposes and appropriateness of punishment in general and the acceptability of capital punishment in particular; the usefulness of alternative or nontraditional sanctions; the privatization of correctional facilities; and the rights and overall treatment of prisoners. At the forefront of today's issues are those involving concerns about gender, race, ethnicity, and other forms of social diversity.

While a number of these issues are discussed in later chapters, this brief section provides definitions of some of the terms that will be discussed and suggests some structure for what is to follow.

Some terms, such as *race,* are not easy to define. Historical definitions of race have highlighted some supposed biological traits, such as skin color, hair type, or shape of the skull and face. Eighteenth-century European physical anthropologists distinguished between white, black, and Asian (or "yellow") races. The notion of race, however, is now generally recognized as a social construct and is not seen as an objective biological fact. Moreover, racial distinctions have blurred throughout American society, which has long been characterized as a melting pot. Nonetheless, when asked, the majority of Americans today still identify themselves as members of a particular racial group.

To say that race is a social construct means that racial distinctions are culturally defined. It does *not* mean, however, that such distinctions are without consequences. On the contrary, great social significance is often attached to biological or other indicators of race, and race plays a crucial role in social relations. *Racism,* which is also socially constructed, can be the result. **Racism** has been defined as social practices that explicitly or implicitly attribute merits or allocate value to members of racially categorized groups solely because of their race.[36] In the field of corrections, as in other social endeavors, it is racism (rather than race itself) that is the real issue because it can lead to forms of racial discrimination, including inequities in hiring and promotion for those working in corrections, and to unfairness in the handling of inmates or other correctional clients because of their race.

racism
Social practices that explicitly or implicitly attribute merits or allocate value to individuals solely because of their race.

Considerable overlap exists between the concept of race and that of *ethnicity.* In contemporary usage, both terms imply the notion of lineage, or biological and regional as well as cultural background and inheritance. Of the two, however, ethnicity is most closely associated with cultural heritage. Members of an ethnic group generally share a common racial, national, religious, linguistic, and cultural origin. Hence, from an ethnic perspective, a person might identify himself or herself as Hungarian, even though he or she has never lived in Hungary, does not speak Hungarian, and knows little of the history of the Hungarian nation. Ethnic differences can lead to serious consequences, as prison gangs built around ethnicity demonstrate.

At first blush, the term *gender* seems more straightforward than race or ethnicity because it relates to differences between the sexes. In fact,

Kathleen Dennehy (left), former Massachusetts commissioner of corrections, and Dora Schriro (right), director of the commissioner of corrections for New York City. In recent years, the number of women working in corrections has increased significantly. Do you think that gender bias exists within the correctional career field today?

many critical issues that concern correctional administrators today reflect a rapid increase in the number of women entering correctional service.

For many years, corrections was a male-dominated profession. Although the correctional process has always involved some women, historically most women in the profession have attended to the needs of the small number of females held in confinement. It wasn't until the 1970s that women began to enter the corrections professions in significant numbers. Many went to work in facilities that housed males, where they soon found themselves confronting *gender bias* from an entrenched macho culture.

Today, women working in correctional facilities largely have been accepted, as evidenced by the fact their proportion is more than double the proportion of female law enforcement officers: Twenty-six percent of sworn correctional officers in the United States are women, while only 13 percent of police officers are female. As Exhibit 1–9 shows, however,

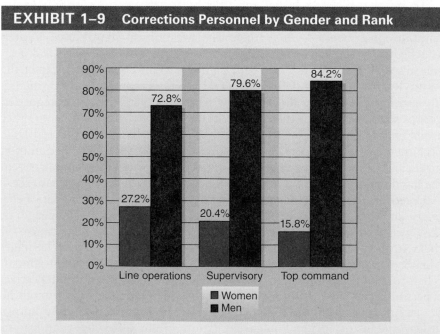

EXHIBIT 1–9   Corrections Personnel by Gender and Rank

Source: From "Equality Denied: The Status of Women in Policing, 2001," p. 9. Copyright © National Center for Women and Policing. www.womenandpolicing.org.

COMMISSION ON SAFETY AND ABUSE IN AMERICA'S PRISONS: FIGHTING PRISON ABUSE

" What happens inside jails and prisons does not stay inside jails and prisons. It comes home with prisoners after they are released and with corrections officers at the end of each day's shift. . . . We must create safe and productive conditions of confinement not only because it is the right thing to do, but because it influences the safety, health, and prosperity of us all. "

—Commission on Safety and Abuse in America's Prisons

In 2004, the world was shocked to see photos of mistreated prisoners at the American-run Baghdad Central Detention Facility in Iraq—a lockup formerly known as Abu Ghraib prison. The photos showed shackled and naked prisoners being threatened with dogs, piled on top of one another, and being taunted by their captors. At least one inmate died after being abused, and the Pentagon launched an investigation into alleged atrocities at the facility. Eventually a small number of soldiers were court-martialed, reduced in rank, or pleaded guilty to charges of abusing detainees.

The Abu Ghraib scandal highlighted the important role of good correctional practice and inspired top American corrections representatives to issue a statement saying that the "ill treatment and torture of incarcerated individuals whether by military personnel, intelligence personnel, or civilian corrections staff is condemned by corrections professionals."[1] The statement was signed by the presidents of the American Correctional Association, the Association of State Correctional Administrators, the International Association of Correctional Officers, and the executive directors of the American Jail Association, the American Probation and Parole Association, the National Sheriffs' Association, the North American Association of Wardens and Superintendents, and others.

The Abu Ghraib scandal led to the creation of the Commission on Safety and Abuse in America's Prisons. The commission, organized by the New York–based Vera Institute of Justice, and sponsored by private foundations and major law firms, was formed to examine conditions in U.S. correctional facilities. After a year of fact-finding public hearings throughout the country, the commission (also known as the *Vera Commission*) issued a comprehensive report in 2006. Excerpts from the commission's report are presented in boxes throughout this text.

Source: Excerpts from *Confronting Confinement: A Report of the Commission on Safety and Abuse in America's Prisons* by John J. Gibbons and Nicholas de B. Katzenbach, June 2006. Copyright © 2006, Vera Institute of Justice.
1. See "The State of Corrections," *Criminal Justice Washington Letter*, May 28, 2004.
Note: The full 126-page report, *Confronting Confinement: A Report of the Commission on Safety and Abuse in America's Prisons,* can be accessed on the Internet at www.prisoncommission.org.

The infamous Abu Ghraib prison near Baghdad, Iraq. Photos of prisoner abuse by American military personnel at the facility in 2004 highlighted the need for proper training and high correctional standards. How can better training improve standards?

women working in corrections tend to be concentrated in the lower ranks and are underrepresented in supervisory positions. According to the National Center for Women in Policing, women of color hold 12.9 percent of corrections positions, 9.7 percent of top command positions, and 9.1 percent of supervisory positions.[37]

Race, ethnicity, and gender are all aspects of social diversity—although diversity in society extends to many other areas as well, such as economics, religion, education, intellectual ability, and politics. Keep in mind, as you read through this textbook, that in the field of corrections diversity issues can be described from four perspectives: (1) as they impact individual correctional clients, (2) as they determine correctional populations and trends, (3) as they affect the lives and interests of those working in the field of corrections, and (4) as they change the structure and functioning of correctional institutions, facilities, and programs.

REVIEW AND APPLICATIONS

SUMMARY

1 Although crime rates are at their lowest level in more than 20 years, correctional populations have been increasing because of get-tough-on-crime-attitudes, the nation's War on Drugs, and the increasing reluctance of parole authorities, fearing civil liability and public outcry, to release inmates. Moreover, growth in correctional populations and in spending on prisons and jails has led to a dramatically expanding correctional workforce, and to enhanced employment opportunities within the field.

2 Two important sources of crime statistics are the FBI's Uniform Crime Reporting Program and the National Crime Victimization Survey, published by the Bureau of Justice Statistics. The crimes that bring people into the American correctional system include felonies, which are relatively serious criminal offenses; misdemeanors, which are less serious crimes; and infractions, which are minor law violations.

3 Criminal justice agencies are said to make up the criminal justice system. The main components of the criminal justice system are police, courts, and corrections. Each can be considered a subsystem of the criminal justice system. The major components of the corrections subsystem are jails, probation, parole, and prisons. Jails and prisons are examples of institutional corrections, while probation and parole are forms of noninstitutional corrections.

4 Professionalism in corrections is important because it can win the respect and admiration of others outside of the field. Moreover, professionals are regarded as trusted participants in any field of endeavor. This chapter also discussed seven aspects of a professional attitude.

5 Evidence-based corrections is the application of social scientific techniques to the study of everyday corrections procedures for the purpose of increasing effectiveness and enhancing the efficient use of available resources. When discussing evidence-based corrections, it is important to remember that the word *evidence* refers to scientific, not criminal, evidence.

6 Social diversity encompasses differences of race, gender, and ethnicity and is important in corrections today because it impacts individual correctional clients, influences correctional populations and trends, affects the lives and interests of those working in the field of corrections, and may help determine the structure and functioning of correctional institutions, facilities, and programs.

KEY TERMS

QUESTIONS FOR REVIEW

1 Why have correctional populations in the United States dramatically increased over the past few decades? How does the rise in correctional populations compare with changes in crime rates over time?

2 What are the kinds of crimes that cause offenders to enter correctional institutions? To enter other kinds of correctional programs?

3 What are the major components of the criminal justice system? What aspects of the corrections subsystem can you identify?

4 Explain the importance of professionalism in corrections and list the seven characteristics of a professional attitude.

5 What is evidence-based corrections? What role does it play in corrections professionalism today?

6 What is meant by the term *social diversity,* and why is the issue of social diversity important in corrections today?

THINKING CRITICALLY ABOUT CORRECTIONS

Vision

Dianne Carter, former president of the National Academy of Corrections, once said, "Too often in corrections, only worker skills are targeted for training, and the organization misses a significant opportunity to communicate its vision and mission."[38] Do you agree or disagree with this statement? Why?

Professionalism

Harold Williamson, a writer in the corrections field, has noted, "Higher levels of professionalization require greater amounts of training and usually involve increased specialization when compared to lesser professionalized activity. Higher levels of professionalization also involve the learning of more abstract knowledge and information."[39] Do you agree? Why or why not?

ON-THE-JOB DECISION MAKING

Training

Today is the first day of your job as a correctional officer. A severe statewide shortage of officers required you to begin work immediately before training, which you are scheduled

to attend in three months. When you arrive at the facility, you are ushered into a meeting with the warden. He welcomes you and gives you a brief pep talk. He asks if you have any concerns. You tell him, "Well, I feel a little uneasy. I haven't gone through the academy yet." "Don't worry," he says, "all our new recruits get on-the-job experience before a slot in the academy opens up. You'll do fine!" He shakes your hand and leads you to the door. After you leave the warden's office, you are given a set of keys and a can of mace. The shift supervisor, a sergeant, gives you a brief tour of the prison. Then he tells you that as you learn your job, you will spend most of your time with another officer, though pairing up will not always be possible.

The officer you are assigned to accompany is Harold Gates. At first, you follow Officer Gates across the compound, getting more familiar with the layout of the facility. Then you spend an uneventful afternoon working with Officer Gates in the yard. At 4:30, Officer Gates instructs you to make sure that all inmates have left the classroom building in preparation for a "count." As you enter the building, you encounter a group of six inmates heading toward the door. Before you can move to the side, one of the inmates walks within an inch of you and stares at you. The others crowd in behind him. You can't move. You are pinned to the door by the men. The man directly in front of you is huge—over 6 feet tall and about 280 pounds. His legs look like tree trunks, and his arms are held away from his body by their sheer bulk. You're staring at a chest that could easily pass as a brick wall. With a snarl he growls, "What do you want?"

1. How do you respond? Would you feel more confident responding to a situation like this if you had had some training?

2. If you tell the inmates that it's time for a count and to move along, what will you do next? Will you ask anyone for guidance in similar future situations or just chalk up the encounter to a learning experience? To whom might you talk about it?

3. Suppose you are a manager or supervisor at this facility. How would you handle the training of new recruits?

Leadership

You are a correctional officer at the McClellan Correctional Facility. You and your coworkers have been following, with high interest, the events at Brownley, another correctional facility located approximately 35 miles away. Prisoner rioting at Brownley during the past four days has left 4 correctional officers and 19 prisoners seriously hurt. It now appears, though, that while tensions remain high, the riot has been contained and the prisoners at Brownley are settling back down. The uneasy truce, however, mandates resolution of the issues that led to the riot in the first place.

The main issue leading to the riot was the prisoners' claims of mistreatment at the hands of certain members of the Brownley correctional staff. State correctional administrators have determined that an essential first step in preventing future riots is replacement of certain members of the correctional staff at Brownley. You are called to your supervisor's office, where she informs you that you are being reassigned temporarily to Brownley, with a possibility that the reassignment may become permanent.

This news does not make you happy. The logistical impact alone is irritating, because it will mean a significant commute each day. More important, though, is that you will be leaving a cohesive team of skilled and dedicated correctional officers with whom you have developed a close bond. You trust each other, and you trust your leaders. There's no telling what you will encounter at Brownley.

Your worst fears are realized when you report for your first shift and your new sergeant takes you aside. "We can't let them win on this," he says. "You know the drill. Stay on 'em hard, and don't cut 'em any slack. We need to let them know from the get-go that things haven't changed—we're still in charge, whether they like it or not, and we ain't gonna take any guff from the likes of them!"

It is immediately apparent to you that your sergeant has a strong "us-against-them" perspective. Your experience tells you that such an attitude at the leadership level likely induces similar, often stronger attitudes at the correctional officer level, and your common sense tells you that this is probably the root of the problem at Brownley.

1. How do you respond to your new sergeant?

2. If you elect to keep this information to yourself, how will you establish yourself with the Brownley inmates as a CO who does not subscribe to the other CO's practices without appearing weak or exploitable?

3. If you elect to bring this information to the attention of someone higher up in the supervisory chain, how will you deal with potential adverse reactions from your new coworkers?

For additional information, please see: www.mhhe.com/schmalleger6e

PUNISHMENTS

A Brief History

[2]

CHAPTER OBJECTIVES

After completing this chapter you should be able to do the following:

1 Describe the types of punishment prevalent in ancient times.

2 List and describe the major criminal punishments used throughout history.

3 Explain the role of torture in the justice systems of times past.

4 Explain the ideas that led to the use of incarceration as a criminal punishment and as an alternative to earlier punishments.

5 Explain the role of correctional reformers in changing the nature of criminal punishment.

> *No man shall be forced by Torture to confesse any Crime against himselfe nor any other unlesse it be in some Capitall case, where he is first fullie convicted by cleare and suffitient evidence to be guilty. After which if the cause be of that nature, That it is very apparent there be other conspiratours, or confederates with him, Then he may be tortured, yet not with such Tortures as be Barbarous and inhumane.*
>
> —Massachusetts Body of Liberties of 1641, Section 45

corporal punishments
Physical punishments, or those involving the body.

THE STOCKS.

An offender in the stocks in Colonial times. Early punishments were often both physical and public. What purposes did such punishments serve?

Before the advent of prisons in the Western world, **corporal punishments** were often imposed for serious crimes. Some, although not regularly administered, were especially gruesome. In 1757, Robert-François Damiens was sentenced to be quartered publicly in Paris for attempting to kill King Louis XV. As the executioners took their places, it was announced that

the flesh will be torn from his breasts, arms, thighs and calves with red-hot pincers, his right hand, holding the knife with which he committed said [crime], burnt with sulphur, and, on those places where the flesh will be torn away, poured molten lead, boiling oil, burning resin, wax and sulphur melted together and then his body drawn and quartered by four horses and his limbs and body consumed by fire, reduced to ashes and his ashes thrown to the winds.[1]

As it turned out, Damiens was a very muscular man. He remained conscious throughout the tortures, although a report tells us that he "uttered horrible cries." When it came time for him to be quartered, the four horses were unable to pull him apart—even after repeated attempts. Finally, six horses were used, and when they were still unable to disjoint the prisoner, his muscles had to be "cut through with knives."

Gruesome as this story may be, it illustrates the relative newness of our present system of corrections, which depends largely on the use of fines, probation, imprisonment, and parole. This chapter traces the historical and cultural roots of our present system.

PUNISHMENTS IN ANCIENT TIMES

Before the large-scale building of prisons began in 17th-century Europe, a variety of practices, based on the law and justice concepts of certain cultural groups, various practices were used to punish wrongdoers and maintain civil order. We will briefly highlight some of these practices and the traditions that have influenced modern correctional practices.

Ancient Greece

In the cultural history of punishments, the Greek city-states provide the earliest evidence that public punishment is part of the Western tradition—and that its roots are in ideas of law and justice. Of all the city-states, the practices of Athens are the best documented. This documentation, which ranges from the writings of orators and philosophers to plays and poetry, tells us that many early crimes were punished by execution, banishment, or exile. Greek poets described stoning the condemned to death, throwing them from high cliffs, binding them to stakes (similar to crucifixion), and cursing them ritually. In many cases, the bodies of executed criminals were regarded as dishonored and were prevented from being buried. Their bodies were left to scavengers and the elements, serving as a warning to anyone contemplating similar crimes.

Other punishments in ancient Athens included "confiscation of property, fines, and the destruction of the condemned offenders' houses."[2] Public denunciation, shaming (*atimia*), imprisonment, and public display of the offender were also used. Criminal punishments in ancient Greece sometimes included civil penalties, such as loss of the ability to transfer property, to vote, and to marry.

Ancient Israel

The chief record of ancient Hebrew history is the Bible. It describes the law and civilization of the ancient Hebrews, including their criminal law and penology. Punishments used by the Hebrews mentioned in the Old Testament included banishment, beating, beheading, blinding, branding and burning, casting down from a high place, crushing, confiscation of property, crucifixion, cursing, cutting asunder, drowning, exile, exposure to wild beasts, fining, flaying, hanging, imprisonment, mutilation, plucking of the hair, sawing asunder, scourging with thorns, slavery, slaying by spear or sword, use of the stocks, stoning, strangulation, stripes, and suffocation.[3] Michel Foucault, the French historian, says that the purpose of physical punishments was primarily revenge. "It was as if the punishment was thought to equal, if not to exceed, in savagery the crime itself," he writes.[4]

A stoning in pre-Christian times. How do ancient punishments and the philosophies that influenced them contribute to today's understanding of the role of criminal punishment in society?

Early Rome

The Twelve Tables, the first written laws of Rome, were issued in 451 B.C. Conviction of some offenses required payment of compensation, but the most frequent penalty was death. Among the forms of capital punishment were burning (for arson), throwing from a cliff (for perjury), clubbing to death (for writing insulting songs about a citizen), hanging (for stealing others' crops), and decapitation. Not mentioned in the Twelve Tables were several other forms of capital punishment in vogue in ancient Rome. For killing a close relative, the offender was subjected to the *culleus*, which consisted of confining the offender in a sack with an ape, a dog, and a serpent, and throwing the sack into the sea. Vestal virgins who had violated their vows of chastity were buried alive. As an alternative to execution, offenders might choose exile. Offenders who went into exile lost their citizenship, freedom, and immovable property. If they returned to Rome, they could be killed by any citizen.[5]

PHYSICAL PUNISHMENTS

In Western societies, the practice of corporal punishment carried over into the Christian era. Physical punishments were imposed for a wide variety of offenses during the Middle Ages. Physical punishments were also used in the American colonies: "The whole baggage of corporal punishments, as they existed in England, were brought to this country, and flourished, especially in New England where the precepts of Calvinism adorned them with pious sanctions."[6] The Puritans, for example, sometimes burned witches and unruly slaves; made wide use of the stocks, the pillory, and the ducking stool; branded criminal offenders; and forced women convicted of adultery to wear "scarlet letters."

The purpose of punishment is for people to learn from what they have done wrong. For example, when you were a child and you got caught sneaking a cigarette from your father's pack, the punishment was a spanking and getting sent to your room until told to come out. Well, most kids learn from this. Then you have the hard-headed ones such as myself who did not learn. I had to do this over and over and over again. Repeat the punishment until I got it right. I beat my head against the wall too many times and it ended up hurting too much.

If there were no punishment, it would be one place I would not want to live. There would be total chaos throughout the world. Back to the wild, wild west days. I also believe that the punishment should fit the crime. Myself, I've spent 10 years 3 months in prison which I deserved to do. I did wrong, and this is my example of how the punishment should fit the crime. I was convicted of 11 armed robberies which I said I did over 10 years. I've met people in prison who did one armed robbery and they have been in since the early 1970s. I do not feel that is right.

Gary James Campbell
Palm Beach Detention Center, Florida

Michael Fay, the American teenager who was caned in Singapore in 1994. Corporal punishments like caning, which involves whipping with a bamboo rod, are still used in more than two dozen countries as criminal sanctions. Fay, who was 18 years old when caned, had spray-painted some parked cars. Can corporal punishment be an effective criminal deterrent?

As justice historian Pieter Spierenburg notes, many physical punishments during the Middle Ages and in "early modern Europe" were *theatrical punishments*.[7] That is, they were corporal punishments carried out in public. Spierenburg divides punishments that were both physical and public into five degrees of severity: (1) whipping or flogging; (2) burning of the skin; (3) mutilation, or "more serious encroachments on bodily integrity"; (4) a merciful instant death; and (5) a torturous and prolonged death.[8]

Flogging

Flogging (or whipping) has been the most common physical punishment through the ages.[9] The code established by Moses, for example, authorized flogging, and Roman law specified flogging as a punishment for certain forms of theft. Flogging was common in England during the Middle Ages as punishment for a wide variety of crimes. In England, women were flogged in private, but men were whipped publicly.[10]

The construction of flogging whips varied greatly, from simple leather straps or willow branches to heavy, complicated instruments designed to inflict a maximum of pain. A traditional form of whip was the cat-o'-nine-tails, consisting of nine knotted cords fastened to a wooden handle.

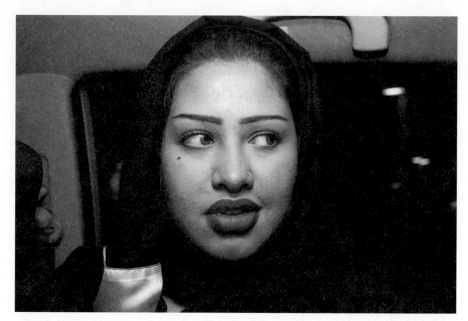

Arab TV personality, Rosanna Yami. In 2009, Yami, who lives in Saudi Arabia, was sentenced by a Saudi court to receive 60 lashes for her role in a Lebanese TV program that interviewed a Saudi man who boasted of his sex life. The man was sent to prison, and Yami was later pardoned by the Saudi king. Why are physical punishments, like flogging, still used in some parts of the world?

The "cat" got its name from the marks it left on the body, which were like the scratches of a cat. One especially cruel form of the whip, the Russian knout, was made of leather strips fitted with fishhooks. When a prisoner was whipped, the hooks would dig into the body, ripping away a proverbial "pound of flesh" with each stroke. A thorough whipping with the knout could result in death from blood loss.

Flogging was also widely used in the American colonies to enforce discipline, punish offenders, and make an example of "ne'er-do-wells" (shiftless and irresponsible individuals). As a mechanism for enforcing compliance with prison rules, flogging survived into the 20th century. As late as 1959, Harry Elmer Barnes and Negley K. Teeters were able to write, "Floggings have been prison practice down to our own times, and deaths have occurred due to over-severe whippings in southern prison camps and chain-gangs. Tying prisoners up by their hands and allowing them to hang suspended with their toes barely touching the floor or ground has been a common method of enforcing discipline."[11]

Branding

Branding, a type of mutilation, was practiced by Roman society. Criminals were branded with a mark or letter signifying their crimes. Brands, which were often placed on the forehead or another part of the face, served to warn others of an offender's criminal history.

The last documented incident of facial branding of English criminals occurred in 1699.[12] After that year, offenders were branded on the hand because it was feared that more obvious marks would reduce employment possibilities. Branding was abolished in England during the last half of the 18th century.

The French branded criminals on the shoulder with the royal emblem. They later switched to burning onto the shoulder a letter signifying the crime of which the offender had been convicted.

Branding was also practiced in the early American colonies. The East Jersey Codes of 1668 and 1675, for example, ordered that burglars be branded on the hand with the letter *T* (for *thief*). After a second offense, the letter *R* (for *rogue*) was burned into the forehead. Maryland branded blasphemers with the letter *B* on the forehead. Women offenders were not branded but were forced to wear letters on their clothing.

Mutilation

Mutilation was another type of corporal punishment used in ancient and medieval societies. Archaeological evidence shows that the pharaohs of ancient Egypt and their representatives often ordered mutilation.[13] In ancient Rome offenders were mutilated according to the law of retaliation, or *lex talionis*. *Lex talionis*, as a punishment philosophy, resembles the biblical principle of "an eye for an eye and a tooth for a tooth."

Medieval justice frequently insisted that punishment fit the crime. Hence, "thieves and counterfeiters had their hands cut off, liars and perjurers had their tongues torn out, spies had their eyes gouged out, sex criminals had their genitals removed, and so forth."[14] Blasphemers sometimes had their tongues pierced or cut out and their upper lips cut away.[15]

Mutilation had a deterrent effect; the permanently scarred and disfigured offenders served as warnings to others of what would happen to criminals. Sometimes, mutilation served merely as a prelude to execution. The right hand of a murderer, for example, was sometimes cut off before he was hanged.[16]

Instant Death

According to Spierenburg, beheading, hanging, and garroting (strangulation by a tightened iron collar) were the most common means of merciful or instant death.[17] Instant death was frequently reserved for members of the nobility who had received capital sentences (usually from the king) or for previously honorable men and women who ran afoul of the law. Decapitation, especially when done by the sword, was regarded as the

A 1786 German woodcut depicts a public execution by burning. What purpose did such public dispensing of justice serve?

most honorable form of capital punishment—since a sword was a symbol that was both noble and aristocratic. Hanging, says Spierenburg, "was the standard nonhonorable form of the death penalty." For women, however, hanging was considered indecent. Garroting tended to replace hanging as a capital punishment for women.

Lingering Death

The worst fate a criminal offender—especially one convicted of heinous crimes—might meet in medieval Europe was a slow or lingering death, often preceded by torture. Some offenders were burned alive, while others were "broken on the wheel." Breaking on the wheel was a procedure that broke all of the major bones in the body. A person who had been broken on the wheel and was still alive was often killed by an executioner's blow to the heart.

Offenders who were to be hanged sometimes had their arms and legs broken first; others were whipped or burned. Burning alive, a practice used in France until the 18th century, was undoubtedly one of the period's cruelest forms of capital punishment.

The Role of Torture

A variety of other corporal punishments were employed, some of which involved torture. Pain was central to retaliatory punishments, and it was used to extract confessions and get information. "Torture," said one source, "is the twisting (torsion) from its subjects of guilty secrets."[18] The use of torture in medieval England was based on a theory that knowledge of one's own guilt, or of the guilt of others, was an offense in itself. Moreover, the theory went, such knowledge was a kind of property that rightly belonged to the state. Hence, forcing an offender to relinquish such "property," by any means necessary, was a right of the government.

Tortures of all kinds were also used during the Middle Ages in an effort to gain confessions from heretics. Heresy was considered a crime against the church and against God. At the time, there was no separation between church and state in many Western societies, and church courts were free to impose punishment as they saw fit. Believers were sure that the heretic's soul was condemned to eternal damnation and that confession would lead to salvation. As a result, torture flourished as a technique for saving souls. Some saw the suffering induced by corporal punishments as spiritually cleansing. Others compared it to the suffering of Jesus on the cross. They argued that physical pain and suffering might free the soul from the clutches of evil.

A common medieval torture was the rack—a machine that slowly stretched a prisoner until his or her joints separated. In another method of torture, red-hot pincers called *hooks* were used to pull the flesh away. Thumbscrews were used as their name implies. In *cording*, an offender's thumbs were tied tightly together behind the back by a rope that passed through a support in the ceiling. Weights were then tied to the ankles, and the person was hoisted into the air by his or her thumbs. Stones were used to crush confessions out of offenders: First a convict was covered with boards, and then suffered as one stone after another was placed on top of them.

Exile and Transportation

In a number of early societies, exile, or banishment, sometimes took the place of corporal and capital punishment. The ancient Greeks permitted offenders to leave the Greek state and travel to Rome, where they might gain citizenship. Early Roman law also established the punishment of exile. Exile was regarded as akin to a death sentence, because the banished person could no longer depend on his or her former community for support and protection. He or she could generally be killed with impunity if attempting to reenter the area.

Exile was practiced in some European communities into the 1800s. One historical study, for example, revealed that, between 1650 and 1750, 97 percent of the noncapital sentences handed down in Amsterdam included banishment.[19] Sentences of banishment drove petty offenders out of a municipality and kept known offenders out of town. But banished criminals resurfaced quickly in neighboring towns, and many communities in Europe confronted a floating population of criminals—especially petty thieves.

Though it was rarely practical to banish offenders from an entire province or nation, England practiced for more than 200 years a form of criminal exile known as *transportation*. An English law authorizing the transportation of convicts to newly discovered lands was passed in 1597. The law was intended primarily to provide galley slaves for a burgeoning English merchant fleet. Soon, however, public support grew for the transportation system as a way of ridding England of felons. As a result, large numbers of convicts were sent to America and other English colonies. One writer estimates that, by the beginning of the American Revolution, 50,000 prisoners had been sent to the New World. Most of them "were sold as indentured servants in the southern colonies, where their market value was greater than in New England."[20]

After the American Revolution, convicted felons began piling up in English jails with no place to go. Legislation was soon passed authorizing prisoners to be housed aboard floating prison ships called *hulks*. Many of these vessels were abandoned merchant ships or broken-down warships. Hulks were anchored in rivers and harbors throughout England. They were unsanitary, rat infested, and unventilated, and the keepers flogged the inmates to force them to work. Disease ran rampant in the hulks, sometimes wiping out all the prisoners on a ship, as well as the crew and nearby citizens. This "temporary" solution lasted about 80 years.

The system of hulks eventually proved impractical, and England soon began shifting its convict population to Australia, which Captain Cook had come upon in 1770. Convict transportation to Australia began in earnest in 1787,[21] with English convicts being transported to New South Wales, Norfolk Island, and Van Diemen's Land— now known as Tasmania (see Exhibit 2–1). The journey was long and demanding, and conditions on prison ships were often ghastly. Many convicts did not survive the trip. Those who did were put to work at heavy labor when they reached their destinations, helping develop the growing region.

Devil's Island, the infamous French prison where many political prisoners were held. What role did transportation play in the criminal punishments of times past?

Soon convicts who had served their sentences began to receive land grants. In 1791, the governor of New South Wales initiated a program to give released convicts up to 30 acres of land each, along with enough tools, seeds, and rations to last 18 months.

English transportation of criminals began to wane in 1853, when Parliament abolished transportation for prisoners with sentences of fewer than 14 years. Opposition to transportation was especially strong among the free settlers who had begun to populate Australia and nearby regions.

EXHIBIT 2–1 Van Diemen's Land

Van Diemen's Land, an island off the southern coast of Australia that is known today as Tasmania, served as a destination in the English system of convict transportation during the early 1800s. The paragraphs that follow, which were written in 1832, give some historical insight into the practice.

Van Diemen's Land was discovered so long ago as the year 1642, by the Dutch navigator Tasman, who gave it the name which it still bears, in honour of his employer Anthony Van Diemen, the then governor of the Dutch possessions in India. It was not, however, till the year 1804 that the country was taken possession of by England. In the early part of that year Colonel David Collins, having been appointed Governor of the projected settlement, arrived on the island with about four hundred prisoners in charge and a force of fifty marines under his command. He was accompanied also by several gentlemen, commissioned to fill the various situations on the new government. They fixed their headquarters on the site of the present capital, to which they gave the name of Hobart Town, after Lord Hobart, the then Secretary for the Colonies. The Colony . . . being thus founded, continued to take root, although at times suffering very great hardships. . . . No sheep or cattle were imported till three years after the settlement of the island. For some time after this, indeed, the colony was looked upon merely as a place of punishment for persons convicted of crimes in New South Wales, numbers of whom accordingly continued to be sent to it every year. Governor Collins died in 1810; and in 1813 Lieutenant-Colonel Davey arrived as his successor.

From about this time the colony began to be considered in a new light. The population consisted no longer merely of the convicts and the garrison; but, besides many persons who, having been originally crown prisoners, had obtained their freedom by servitude or indolence, embraced a considerable number of settlers who had arrived in successive small parties from the neighbouring colony of New South Wales. Hitherto the only places with which Van Diemen's Land was allowed to hold any communication had been New South Wales and England: That restriction was now done away with, and the two colonies were placed, in respect to foreign commerce, on precisely the same footing. . . .

In 1817 Colonel Davey was succeeded in the government by Colonel Sorell. The first object which engaged the attention of the new governor was the suppression of an evil under which the colony had for some years been suffering, the ravages of the bush-rangers, as they were called, or prisoners who had made their escape and roamed at large in the woods. The capture and execution of the principal leaders of these marauders in a short time put an end, for the present, to their destructive inroads.

About 1821 may be said to have begun the emigration from England, which has since proceeded almost with uninterrupted steadiness. . . . In December 1825, Van Diemen's Land was declared entirely independent of New South Wales; and an executive and legislative Council were appointed as advisers to the Governor, the members of both being named by the Crown. In 1827 the island was divided into eight police districts, each of which was placed under the charge of a stipendiary magistrate.

Source: The Society for the Diffusion of Useful Knowledge, *The Penny Magazine*, vol. 1, no. 1, March 31, 1832.

In 1867, the practice of transportation officially ended, although England continued to send inmates from India to its penal colony in the Andaman Islands until World War II.

France also experimented with transportation. Beginning in 1791, French authorities sent prisoners in large numbers to Madagascar, New Caledonia, the Marquesas Islands, and French Guiana. Devil's Island, in the Caribbean Sea, off the coast of French Guiana, continued to function as a prison until 1951. The island was named for the horrors associated with imprisonment there. It was the site of an infamous penal colony that was used mostly for political prisoners. The island was also made famous by the Dreyfus Affair, which began in 1894 when French Captain Alfred Dreyfus (1859–1935)

In the late 18th century, the English government began turning broken-down war vessels and abandoned transport ships into hulks to house prisoners. What event caused the prison overcrowding that made these hulks necessary?

was convicted of treason by a court-martial, sentenced to life imprisonment, and sent to the island. Thirty-six years later, Dreyfus was exonerated after it was demonstrated that the original charges against him were the result of anti-Semitism in the French military and had no factual basis.

The only Western nation to practice transportation into the 1990s was Russia, which sent prisoners to Siberia as late as 1990. Siberia is a cold and formerly desolate region in what is now central and eastern Russia. It stretches from the Ural Mountains to the Pacific Ocean. The extensive area was annexed by Russia in stages during the 16th and 17th centuries. It was used as a place of exile for political prisoners beginning in the early 17th century. In 1741, the Russian Count Biron was found guilty of treason, but his sentence of death by quartering was changed to exile to Siberia.[22] Hard labor in Siberia became a common sentence for criminal offenders in Czarist Russia, and it is estimated that hundreds of thousands of vagrants, felons, political prisoners, and even voluntary exiles were sent to Siberia under the Czars to force settlement of the region and to develop its natural resources. During Joseph Stalin's rule (1928–1953), Siberian prison camps forced tens of millions of victims into a vast labor system. The brutal conditions in these camps resulted in millions of deaths and have been graphically described in the works of Aleksandr Solzhenitsyn.[23] After Stalin's death, the camp population greatly decreased, although some still hold a few criminal offenders. The major industrial cities of today's prosperous Russian Arctic, including Kolyma, Norilsk, and Vorkuta, began as camps constructed by prisoners.

Found guilty of the offense of impiety in Athens in 399 B.C., Socrates chose poison over imprisonment. What was the goal of most early penalties for crimes?

Public Humiliation

Many corporal punishments were carried out in public, primarily to deter other potential lawbreakers. Some other forms of punishment depended on public ridicule for their effect. These included the stocks and the pillory.

Stocks held a prisoner in a sitting position, with feet and hands locked in a frame. A prisoner in the pillory was made to stand with his or her head and hands locked in place. Both devices exposed the prisoner to public scorn. While confined in place, prisoners were frequently pelted with eggs and rotten fruit. Sometimes they were whipped or branded. Those confined to the pillory occasionally had their ears nailed to the wood, and they had to rip them free when released. England abolished the pillory in 1834; according to at least one source, the pillory was still in use in Delaware in 1905.[24]

Confinement

Confinement by chaining or jailing has been a punishment since ancient times. In China, Confucius wrote about prisons being built around 2000 B.C., and the Old Testament describes imprisonment in Babylon and during Egypt's Middle Kingdom (2040–1640 B.C.).[25] At times, confinement served functions other than punishment for crimes. In early Greece, for example, prisons were used to punish convicted offenders, to enforce the payment of debts, to hold those awaiting other punishments, and to detain foreigners who might otherwise flee before their cases could be heard.[26] Until the 1600s and the development of prisons as primary places of punishment, prisons were used to detain people before trial; to hold prisoners awaiting other punishments, such as death or corporal punishment; to force payment of debts and fines; and to hold and punish slaves.

Early European prisons were rarely called *prisons*. They went by such names as *dungeon, tower,* and *gaol* (from which we get the modern term *jail*). Some places used as prisons had been built for other purposes. The Tower of London, for example, was originally a fortified palace that had been used as an arsenal. The French Bastille began as a fortified city gate leading into Paris. Judicial proceedings were not necessary before imprisonment in such places, nor was a formal sentence. As a result, anyone thrown into a dungeon at the behest of authorities was likely to stay there until granted clemency or until death.

INCARCERATION AS PUNISHMENT

Church-run prisons were in place by the 6th century, and they were relatively commonplace by the 9th century. Early Canon (or church) law, forbade the drawing of blood as punishment and stressed contrition—principles that were served well by the solitude of imprisonment. Church prisons, which were not under the control of secular society, were built around the extensive system of church-run monasteries that existed throughout Europe during the middle ages.[27]

According to Pieter Spierenburg, a Dutch justice historian, a form of secular punishment that emerged around the year 1500 was *penal bondage,* which included all forms of incarceration.[28] Spierenburg explained, "Courts came to use it almost as frequently as physical sanctions. Instead of being flogged or hanged, some offenders were incarcerated in workhouses or forced to perform labor in some other setting." According to Spierenburg, the word *bondage* means "any punishment that puts severe restrictions on the condemned person's freedom of action and movement, including but not limited to imprisonment."

Among the forms of penal bondage imposed on criminals, vagrants, debtors, social misfits, and others were forced labor on public works projects and forced conscription into military campaigns. Later, houses of correction also subjected inmates to strict routines.

One early form of incarceration developed in France. For at least 200 years, prisoners were regularly assigned to French warships as galley slaves. After the naval importance of galleys had declined, French naval officials continued to have custody of convicted offenders. By the mid-1700s, they had begun to put convicts to work in the shipyards of Toulon, Brest, and Rochefort. At night these prisoners were sheltered in arsenals, where they slept chained to their beds. As Spierenburg notes, "the arsenals were in fact labor camps where convicts had to remain within an enclosed space, so the penalty was more akin to imprisonment than to public works."

The public works penalty, sometimes called *penal servitude,* became especially popular in Germany and Switzerland in the 1600s and 1700s. According to Spierenburg, "convicts dug ore in mines, repaired ramparts, built roads or houses, or went from door to door collecting human waste."[29]

The House of Correction (1550–1700)

Midway between corporal punishments and modern imprisonment stands the workhouse or the house of correction. The development of workhouses was originally a humanitarian move intended to manage the unsettling social conditions of the late 16th and early 17th centuries in England. The feudal system had offered mutual protection for land-owning nobles and for serfs, who were tied to the land. By 1550, that system was breaking down in Europe. Hordes of former serfs roamed the countryside, unable to earn a living. Many flocked to the cities, where they hoped to find work in newly developing industries. The change from an agrarian economy to an industrial one displaced many persons, resulted in growing poverty, and increased the numbers of beggars and vagrants.

Vagrancy became a crime, and soon anyone unable to prove some means of support was imprisoned in a workhouse. The first workhouse in England was called Bridewell because it was located in Bridewell Palace, which was given to London by King Edward III and opened as a prison in 1556.[30] Soon, the word **bridewell** entered the language as a term for a workhouse. English Parliament ordered workhouses to be created throughout England. Parliament intended that those housed in workhouses be taught habits of industry and frugality and that they learn a trade.

At first, prisoners in workhouses were paid for the work they did. Work included spinning, weaving, clothmaking, the milling of grains, and baking. Soon, however, as the numbers of prisoners grew, the workhouse system deteriorated. As workhouses spread through Europe, they became catchall institutions that held the idle, the unemployed, the poor, debtors, insane persons, and even unruly individuals whose families could not cope with them. According to one writer, imprisonment in a workhouse could serve "as a tool of private discipline. . . . The family drew up a petition explaining why the individual should be imprisoned, and the authorities decided whether or not to consent. Usually, private offenders were confined because of conduct considered immoral."[31]

Hence, workhouses served as informal repositories for people the community regarded as "inconvenient," irresponsible, or deviant—even if their behavior did not violate the criminal law. In the midst of this large population of misfits and unwanted persons could be found a core group of criminal offenders. In 1706 the British Parliament passed legislation "permitting judges to sentence felons to the house of correction for up to two years."[32]

By the end of the 17th century, houses of correction had become mere holding cells with little reformative purpose. Nonetheless, because workhouses relied primarily on incarceration rather than corporal punishments, they provided a model for prison reformers bent on more humanitarian correctional practices.

The Emergence of the Prison

Two main elements fueled the development of prisons as we know them today. The first element was a philosophical shift away from punishment of the body toward punishment of the soul or human spirit. By the late 1700s in Europe and America, a powerful movement was under way to replace traditional corporal punishments with deprivation of personal liberty as the main thrust of criminal sentencing. Michel Foucault explains the shift this way:

The punishment-body relation [was no longer] the same as it was in the torture during public executions. The body now serves as an instrument or

bridewell

A workhouse. The word came from the name of the first workhouse in England.

Bridewells were penal institutions for social outcasts—ranging from vagrants to petty criminals—who were forced to work under strict discipline. What social conditions prompted governments to establish such houses of correction?

intermediary: If one intervenes upon it to imprison it or to make it work, it is in order to deprive the individual of a liberty that is regarded both as a right and as property. The body, according to this penalty, is caught up in a system of constraints and privations, obligations and prohibitions. Physical pain, the pain of the body itself, is no longer the constituent element of the penalty.[33]

The transition from corporal punishments to denial of liberties found its clearest expression in the work of the Philadelphia Society for Alleviating the Miseries of Public Prisons. The society, established by the Pennsylvania Quakers in 1787, had as its purpose the renovation of existing prisons and jails and the establishment of the prison as the basic form of criminal punishment. Thanks largely to the widely publicized works of the society, Pennsylvania became in April 1794 the first state to abolish permanently the death penalty for all crimes except first-degree murder, and it adopted a system of fines and imprisonment in place of corporal punishments.[34] The new Pennsylvania criminal code was important because it "marked the first permanent American break with contemporary juristic savagery, was the forerunner of the reform codes of other American states, and was the essential basis of Pennsylvania criminal jurisprudence until the next systematic revision in 1860."[35]

The second element fueling the development of modern prisons was the passage of laws preventing the imprisonment of anyone except criminals. Civil commitments to prison ended, and a huge class of social misfits were removed from prisons and dealt with elsewhere. Primary among this group were debtors, who historically had been cast into jails as a result of civil rulings against them. John Howard's study of English jails found 2,437 debtors among the 4,084 prisoners he encountered.[36] Many others were vagrants who had committed no "intentional" crime.

According to Pieter Spierenburg, the Dutch were the first Europeans to segregate serious criminals from vagrants and minor delinquents, and Dutch courts were the first European courts to begin substituting imprisonment for corporal punishments.[37] The workhouse in Amsterdam, which opened in 1654, "represented the first criminal prison in Europe," says Spierenburg. By the start of the 1700s, Dutch "courts frequently imposed sentences of imprisonment. During the third quarter of the 17th century, the Amsterdam court did so in one-fifth of its criminal cases; a century later, it did so in three-fifths. By the 1670s, the court of Groningen-City imposed imprisonment in two-fifths of criminal cases." Even so, the imprisonment of debtors persisted in Holland for another 100 years, and Dutch prisons of the period held both criminal and civil "convicts."

These ideas—that "doing time" was often the most appropriate punishment for criminal activity and that incarceration should be imposed only on criminal offenders—soon combined with a burgeoning emphasis on reformation as the primary goal of criminal sentencing. Reformation, argued many prison advocates of the time, could best be achieved by enforced solitude.

In 1776, the British philanthropist Jonas Hanway published a book titled *Solitude in Imprisonment*. Hanway's work appears to have had a significant influence on prison advocates. He argued that the interruption of transportation provided a much-needed opportunity to reexamine prevailing policies for dealing with prisoners. Hanway suggested that reformation should be the primary goal of criminal sentencing and said that it was plainly not being met by sentencing practices then in existence. Solitary confinement, said Hanway, would force the prisoner to face his

Talking about CORRECTIONS

SECURITY TECHNOLOGIES IN CORRECTIONS

Visit *Live Talk* at **Corrections.com** (**www.justicestudies.com/talking06**) and listen to the program "Security Technologies in Corrections," which relates to ideas discussed in this chapter.

I am a psychologist for the New Hampshire Department of Corrections working in a mental health unit at a correctional institution. My job is to lead a treatment program for offenders with moderate to severe Axis 1 (illness-type) mental disorders. Correctional counselors, nurses, or other mental health employees refer inmates to my supervisor, the Chief of Mental Health. If he thinks the inmate may have a serious illness-type mental disorder, he gives the case to me. Then either I or one of my team members carefully read the inmate's offender record and medical chart, do a thorough interview, and, with the client's written permission, write for information from mental health professionals who have worked with the client. Usually, the psychiatrist on the team will see the inmate also. If we think the person does have a disorder appropriate for us to treat, we develop a treatment plan and schedule the individual for a treatment team meeting, attended by a nurse, the correctional counselor, the psychiatrist, my team members, and myself. We talk with the client about goals and interventions. These may include nonaddictive psychotropic medications, psychotherapy (individual and group), case management, and monitoring. When it's appropriate, we refer clients to other programs at the prison—for example, the sexual offender program or the substance abuse program. As the clients approach release, we do our best to set them up with mental health and other resources in the community, so that they will remain in good mental health and so that a worsening of their mental disorder does not contribute to their reoffending.

Laura Magzis
Psychologist
Mental Health Unit
New Hampshire State Prison for Men

or her conscience—leading to reformation: "The walls of his prison will preach peace to his soul, and he will confess the goodness of his Maker, and the wisdom of the laws of his country."[38]

THE REFORMERS

Prisons, as institutions in which convicted offenders spend time as punishment for crimes, are relatively modern. They came about largely as a result of growing intellectualism in Europe and America and as a reaction to the barbarities of corporal punishment.

The period of Western social thought that began in the 17th century and lasted until the dawn of the 19th century is known as the Age of Enlightenment. One author explains, "The phrase was frequently employed by writers of the period itself, convinced that they were emerging from centuries of darkness and ignorance into a new age enlightened by reason, science, and a respect for humanity."[39] The Enlightenment, also known as the *Age of Reason*, was more than a set of fixed ideas. Enlightenment thought implied an attitude, a method of knowing based on observation, experience, and reason.

One of the earliest representatives of the Enlightenment was the French social philosopher and jurist Charles de Montesquieu (1689–1755) whose masterwork, *The Spirit of Laws*, was published in 1748. Montesquieu wrote that governmental powers should be separated and balanced in order to guarantee individual rights and freedom. He strongly believed in the rights of individuals. His ideas influenced leaders of both the American Revolution and the French Revolution.[40]

Another celebrated philosopher of the Enlightenment was the French writer Voltaire, who satirized both the government and the religious establishment of France. Voltaire twice served time in the Bastille and chose exile in England over prison for additional offenses. He deeply admired the English atmosphere of political and religious freedom.

A number of important thinkers influenced the justice systems of Western nations and the directions the correctional enterprise would take over the next 200 years. We will now turn our attention to those individuals.

William Penn

William Penn (1644–1718), regarded as the founder of Pennsylvania, was the son of Sir William Penn, a distinguished English admiral. During his youth, Penn traveled widely throughout Europe, served in the Royal Navy, and studied law. In 1667, he converted to the Quaker faith and by the next year found himself confined in the Tower of London as punishment for promoting the faith. While imprisoned, he wrote a paper titled "No Cross, No Crown." After release, he was again imprisoned on a number of occasions, causing him to seek refuge in America. In 1682, Penn obtained a charter creating the Commonwealth of Pennsylvania, and naming him governor. Gathering together hundreds of Quakers, Penn set sail for the New World. The colony he founded promoted religious tolerance, and it was soon attracting persecuted minorities from England, Germany, Holland, and Scandinavia.

Penn's influence on the criminal law of this country and on the coming age of imprisonment was most visible in the "Great Act" of 1682. Through that single piece of legislation, the Pennsylvania Quakers reduced capital offenses to the one crime of premeditated murder and abolished all corporal punishments as they had existed under English code.

John Howard

John Howard (1726–1790) was born to a deeply religious English family. On a trip to Portugal as a young man, Howard was taken prisoner by pirates when the British merchant ship on which he was traveling was captured by a French privateer.[41] He and his fellow passengers were kept below deck in subhuman conditions. When they arrived in France, he was imprisoned in a French dungeon, but he was later released in exchange for a French naval officer.

In 1773, Howard was appointed high sheriff of Bedfordshire. He was shocked at the abysmal conditions that existed in English jails of the time, and he set out on a quest for prison reform. He began arguing for the abolishment of spiked collars and chains, which prisoners were made to wear, and he argued against the common practice of paying jailers for release. Within a few years, Howard had visited almost every county in England, Wales, and Scotland, traveling no fewer than 7,000 miles in 1779 alone. He also inspected prisons in a number of other countries, including France, Belgium, Holland, Italy, Germany, Spain, Portugal, Denmark, Sweden, and Russia.

Although most prisons Howard visited were like those in England, he found one—the Maison de Force in Ghent, Belgium—that embodied the highest standards of its day.

Howard's greatest legacy was his 1777 book, *The State of the Prisons in England and Wales*,[42] in which he described the abysmal state of English prisons. *The State of the Prisons* also contained descriptions of clean and well-run institutions, prisons in which the sexes were separated, and jails in which inmates were kept busy at productive work.

Howard's book promoted the notion that the fundamental business of corrections should be to reform rather than to punish, and he argued that every citizen must accept responsibility for the criminal justice system of the society in which he or she lives. *The State of the Prisons* appealed to policymakers looking for alternatives to existing systems, and it fueled the efforts of prison reformers in both Europe and America. Many of the principles described in Howard's book later became the foundation for the English Penitentiary Act of 1779, which established a decisive shift toward the use of imprisonment rather than transportation and capital punishment.

A plaque in Warrington, NW of London honoring John Howard, the great English prison reformer. Howard proposed the idea that the fundamental business of corrections should be to reform rather than to punish. How does his work influence corrections today?

As Randall McGowen, corrections historian at the University of Oregon, explains, "Howard's contribution was to make the prison the center of focus, shifting all other forms of punishment to the margins. He fostered a vital change of perspective at the very time that judges were sentencing greater numbers of felons to confinement. Howard's book created the impression that the prison was the natural and inevitable shape of punishment."[43]

Howard died of the plague in Russia in 1790. At the time, he was in the midst of his sixth tour of European prisons and was about to leave on a trip to study prisons in Turkey and Asia. On his tomb are engraved these words:

whosoever Thou Art
Thou Standest at the
Grave of Thy friend

Cesare Beccaria

Cesare Beccaria (1738–1794), an Italian jurist and criminologist, was one of the first to argue against capital punishment and inhumane treatment of prisoners. What writing by Beccaria influenced the criminal justice systems of Western Europe?

Cesare Beccaria (1738–1794) was born in Italy, the eldest son of an aristocratic family. By the time he reached his mid-20s, Beccaria had formed, with his close friends Pietro and Alessandro Verri, an intellectual circle called the Academy of Fists.[44] The academy took as its purpose the reform of the criminal justice system. Through the Verri brothers, Beccaria became acquainted with the work of French and British political writers such as Montesquieu, Thomas Hobbes (1588–1679), Denis Diderot (1713–1784), Claude-Adrien Helvetius (1715–1771), and David Hume (1711–1776).

In 1764 Beccaria published an essay titled *On Crimes and Punishments*. Although the work was brief, it was, perhaps, the most exciting essay on law of the 18th century. In the essay, Beccaria outlined a utilitarian approach to punishment, suggesting that some punishments can never be justified because they are more evil than any "good" they might produce. The use of torture to obtain confessions falls into that category, said Beccaria. Beccaria also protested punishment of the insane, a common practice of the times, saying it could do no good because insane people cannot accurately assess the consequences of their actions. Beccaria said that *ex post facto* laws, or laws passed after the fact, imposed punishment unfairly, because a person could not calculate the risk of acting before a law against a specific action was passed. He also argued against the use of secret accusations, the discretionary power of judges, the inconsistency and inequality of sentencing, the use of personal connections to obtain sentencing reductions, and the imposition of capital punishment for minor offenses.

Beccaria proposed that punishment could be justified only if it was imposed to defend the social contract—the tacit allegiance that individuals owe their society, and the obligations of government to individuals. It is the social contract, said Beccaria, that gives society the right to punish its members.

Beccaria also argued that punishment should be swift because swift punishment offers the greatest deterrence. When punishment quickly follows a crime, said Beccaria, the ideas of crime and punishment are more closely associated in a person's mind. He also suggested that the link between crime and punishment would be stronger if the punishment somehow related to the crime.

Finally, said Beccaria, punishments should not be unnecessarily severe. The severity of punishment, he argued, should be proportional

Zaira Tena

Correctional Officer • New Mexico Women's Correctional Facility • Grants, New Mexico

Zaira Tena is employed by Corrections Corporation of America (CCA) as a correctional officer at the New Mexico Women's Correctional Facility in Grants, New Mexico. This is Tena's first job in corrections. She was attracted to CCA and a career in corrections because of the benefits that CCA offered her.

Tena attended Laramie County Community College in Laramie, Wyoming, before joining CCA. The company provided additional training in interpersonal communication, special-needs inmates, crisis intervention, infectious diseases, suicide prevention, first aid, CPR, and firearms, giving her the skills she needs to ensure the health, welfare, and safety of prison employees and inmates. Because Tena especially enjoys recreation, she also coordinates the institution's recreation activities.

Tena's enthusiasm for her own career and professional development shows in her advice to people thinking about a career in corrections. Wisely, she is taking her own advice. She plans to stay in corrections and hopes one day soon to become assistant shift commander at the Grants women's facility.

> *"I like my job. I like working with people. What I learned and what I'd tell someone is, be very professional, firm, fair, and consistent at all times, and be able to work under a lot of pressure."*

to the degree of social damage caused by the crime. Treason, Beccaria said, is the worst crime because it most harms the social contract. Below treason, Beccaria listed crimes in order of declining severity, including violence against a person or his property, public disruption, and crimes against property. Crimes against property, he said, should be punished by fines.

When his essay was translated into French and English, Beccaria became famous throughout much of Europe. Philosophers of the time hailed his ideas, and several European rulers vowed to follow his lead in the reform of their justice systems.

Jeremy Bentham

Philosopher and jurist Jeremy Bentham (1748–1832) was born in London. As a young child, he was considered a prodigy, having been found, at the age of 2, sitting at his father's desk reading a multivolume history of England.[45] He began to study Latin at the age of 3. When Bentham was 12, his father, a wealthy attorney, sent him to Queen's College, Oxford, hoping that he would enter the field of law.

After hearing lectures by the leading legal scholar of the day, Sir William Blackstone (1723–1780), young Bentham became disillusioned with the law. Instead of practicing law, he decided to criticize it, and he spent the rest of his life analyzing the legal practices of the day, writing about them, and suggesting improvements.

Bentham advocated **utilitarianism,** the principle that the highest objective of public policy is the greatest happiness for the largest number of people. Utilitarianism provided the starting point for Bentham's social analysis, in which he tried to measure the usefulness of existing institutions, practices, and beliefs against a common standard. Bentham believed that human behavior is determined largely by the amount of pleasure or pain associated with a given activity. Hence, he suggested, the purpose of law should be to make socially undesirable activities painful enough to keep people from engaging in them. In this way, said Bentham, "good" can be achieved.

utilitarianism
The principle that the highest objective of public policy is the greatest happiness for the largest number of people.

hedonistic calculus

The idea that people are motivated by pleasure and pain and that the proper amount of punishment can deter crime.

Bentham's idea, that people are motivated by pleasure and pain and that the proper amount of punishment can deter crime, became known as **hedonistic calculus.** Bentham's hedonistic calculus made four assumptions:

1. People by nature choose pleasure and avoid pain.
2. Each individual, either consciously or intuitively, calculates the degree of pleasure or pain to be derived from a given course of action.
3. Lawmakers can determine the degree of punishment necessary to deter criminal behavior.
4. Such punishment can be effectively and rationally built into a system of criminal sentencing.

Bentham is also known as the inventor of the *panopticon* (from a Greek word meaning "all-seeing")—a type of prison he proposed building in England as early as 1787. The panopticon was intended to put utilitarian ideas to work in the field of penology.

Key to the panopticon was its unique architecture, which consisted of a circular, tiered design with a glass roof and with a window on the outside wall of each cell.[46] The design made it easy for prison staff, in a tower in the center of the structure, to observe each cell (and its occupants). Within the wheel-like structure, walls separated the cells to prevent any communication between prisoners. Speaking tubes linked cells with the observation platform so that officers could listen to inmates.

The panopticon, also called an *inspection house,* was intended to be a progressive and humanitarian penitentiary. Bentham thought of it as a social experiment. The design was touted as being consistent with the ideals of utilitarianism because only a few officers would be subject to the risks and unpleasantness of the inspection role, while many prisoners would benefit from this enlightened means of institutional management.

Jeremy Bentham (1748–1832), an English philosopher and social reformer. He spent his life trying to reform the law. His innovative plan for a prison, called the panopticon, consisted of a huge structure covered by a glass roof. A central tower allowed guards to see into the cells, which were arranged in a circle. Although the British government did not use Bentham's plan, several U.S. prisons did, including one in Joliet, Illinois, known as Stateville Correctional Center. What is the name given to Bentham's principle that the highest object of public policy is the greatest happiness for the greatest number of people?

After years of personally promoting the concept, Bentham saw his idea for an innovative penitentiary die. The panopticon was never built in England, and in 1820, government officials formally disavowed it. The concept may have fallen victim to the growing emphasis on transportation, which delayed all prison construction in England. Another significant factor in the demise of the panopticon ideal, however, was Bentham's insistence that panopticons be built near cities to deter crime among the general population. Although a number of sites were chosen for construction, nearby residents always protested plans to build any sort of prison in their neighborhoods. Despite Bentham's failure ever to construct a facility completely true to his panopticon plan, he will always be remembered for his idea that order and reform could be achieved in a prison through architectural design.

Sir Samuel Romilly

Sir Samuel Romilly (1757–1818) was an English legal reformer who worked ceaselessly to lessen the severity of existing criminal law in his home country. Romilly, once described as "the flower of the English reform movement,"[47] attacked laws that authorized capital punishment for a host of minor felonies and misdemeanors.

Romilly's dedication to his cause drew the admiration from a number of reformers. M. Dumont, once described as "the leading orator of the French Revolution," said of Romilly, "[He is] always tranquil and orderly yet has an incessant activity. He never loses a minute; he applies all his mind to what he is about. Like the hand of three watches, he never stops."[48] Another contemporary said of Romilly that "in the House of Commons he looked like Apollo surrounded by crowds of satyrs and goats. . . . This man it was who led the fight to get the gentleness of the English character expressed in its laws."[49]

Romilly entered Parliament in 1806, and in 1810 proposed a reexamination of the Penitentiary Act of 1779. As a result, the government appointed the Holford Committee to examine issues associated with penal reform. Until his early death in 1818, Romilly fought to reduce the number of English capital crimes. He succeeded in getting passed a bill abolishing the death penalty in cases of "private stealing from the person," and he won the abolition of the death penalty in cases of soldiers and sailors found absent without leave. At the time of his death, 200 offenses were still punishable by sentence of death. The movement he began, however, continued to flower. By 1840, the number of capital crimes in England had been reduced to 14, and by 1861 the number fell to 4 (treason, murder, piracy, and setting fire to arsenals).

Romilly's work and the results it produced led others to recognize the need for alternatives to capital punishment as a means of dealing with the large majority of offenders.

Sir Robert Peel

Sir Robert Peel (1788–1850) was a British parliamentary leader bent on seeing the ideas of Romilly, Bentham, and others incorporated into English law. Peel is best known in the history of criminal justice for establishing a police force that influenced the development of policing throughout much of the rest of the world. His force, the London Metropolitan Police, became known as the Met.

Prior to Peel's time, agents of law enforcement often meted out "justice" as they saw fit, sometimes apprehending the offender and punishing him

Sir Robert Peel, founder of the London Metropolitan Police. Punishment, said Peel, should not be imposed by the police, but by specialists in penology. In what other ways did Peel influence the field of corrections?

or her on the spot. Peel and other legal reformers of the day worked to identify the fundamental function of the police as the investigation of crime and the apprehension of criminals. Peel insisted that the police should be responsible for investigation and arrest only, while the trial, defense, and conviction phase of the justice process should reside entirely in the hands of another body, the judiciary.[50] Punishment, he said, should not be imposed by the police, but by specialists in the field of penology. In Peel's words, it is necessary for the police "to recognize always the need for strict adherence to police executive functions and to refrain from even seeming to usurp the powers of the judiciary or avenging individuals or the state and of authoritatively judging guilt and punishing the guilty."

In effect, while working to formalize police administration, Peel pointed out the need for other specialists in the administration of justice such as attorneys, magistrates, and correctional personnel. Peel was also primarily responsible for legislation, Peel's Gaol Act of 1823, aimed at reforming British jails. The Gaol Act required that men and women be segregated while in jail and mandated the supervision of female prisoners by female correctional personnel.[51]

Elizabeth Fry

Elizabeth Fry (1780–1845), a strict Quaker committed to religious and philanthropic work, campaigned during the early 1800s to "expose the plight of women in prison and to promote better conditions for them."[52] While most Enlightenment era thinkers had been influenced by a belief in utilitarian principles, Fry's reformist activities grew out of her religious faith.

Fry had been strongly influenced by a delegation of American Quakers who visited London's notorious Newgate prison in 1813. Their report said that they had been horrified to find "blaspheming, fighting, dram-drinking, half-naked women" occupying part of the facility. A few months later, Fry visited the jail herself and found that women were being held in what she described as "filthy" conditions. From then on Fry campaigned for reform of the conditions under which women were confined, arguing that women should be treated "tenderly" and "with gentleness and sympathy so that they would submit cheerfully to the rules and cooperate willingly in their own reform."[53]

Fry formed the Ladies Association for the Reformation of Female Prisoners in Newgate and, later, the British Ladies Society for the Reformation of Female Prisoners. Fry's influence was also felt in the United States where concerned women banded together under the banner of prison reform in order to draw attention to the welfare of women prisoners.

Fry and her followers, including American feminist leader Dorothea Dix, believed that women are more likely than men to change and that appeals "to the heart" would be more effective with women offenders than with men. In her 1825 publication, *Observations on the Siting, Superintendence, and Government of Female Prisoners*, Fry provided concrete ideas on how women's prisons should be run. "Especially important for women," she argued, "were cleanliness, plain decent clothing, and warm, orderly surroundings."[54]

Mary Belle Harris

Another American woman reformer who was influenced by Fry was Mary Belle Harris (1874–1957). Harris, who was born in Pennsylvania, eventually became the first warden of the Federal Institution for Women in Alderson, West Virginia, when it opened in 1927. She had turned to a career in corrections only after already having been a teacher, social worker, and archeologist.

Harris came to Alderson after serving as superintendent of the Women's Workhouse on Blackwell Island (New York), as superintendent of the State Reformatory for Women at Clinton, New Jersey, and as assistant director of the section on Reformatories and Detention Homes for the U.S. War Department.

Known as a vocal advocate of correctional reforms and as an avid supporter of the reformation ideal, Harris believed that reformation, not punishment should be the primary focus of most correctional programs and institutions. Harris also believed that the criminality of women was largely the result of their social roles and specifically their economic dependency upon men. As a result, She advocated training programs that would permit women prisoners to become financially independent upon release. At Alderson, Harris oversaw the development of programs designed to break the cycle of dependency. Her work became widely known and served as a model for women's prisons throughout the nation.

Mary Belle Harris (1874–1957), the first warden of the Federal Institution for Women at Alderson, West Virginia. What historical role have women played in the development of the field of corrections?

Before retiring in 1941, Harris wrote a number of books describing her experiences in corrections. Among them are *I Knew Them in Prison* (1936) and *The Pathway of Mattie Howard to and from Prison: The Story of the Regeneration of an Ex-Convict and Gangster Woman* (1937).

Sanford Bates

Sanford Bates (1884–1972) was the first director of the Federal Bureau of Prisons (BOP), a position he held from 1930 until 1937. Before becoming the bureau's director, Bates served in the Massachusetts state legislature, was commissioner of Penal Institutions in Boston from 1917 to 1919, and held the position of commissioner of the Massachusetts Department of Corrections. Bates became superintendent of Prisons, U.S. Department of Justice, in 1929. While in that post, he prepared the legislation that established the Federal Bureau of Prisons in 1930.

During his tenure as director of the BOP, Bates authored a number of books including *Prisons and Beyond*.[55] In *Prisons,* Bates wrote that "the perplexing problem confronting the prison administrator of today is how to devise a prison so as to preserve its role of a punitive agency and still reform the individuals who have been sent there." Although the BOP began operations during the Great Depression, Bates believed in rehabilitation and in the value of inmate labor, thinking that work provided both a sense of purpose and a tool for reformation. Consequently, he began Federal Prison Industries (FPI), and served as its chair from 1934 until his death in 1972. Bates created FPI programs involving work on prison farms, public lands, military bases, and highway construction, thereby largely avoiding the ire of labor unions that were seeking jobs for their members. Under Bates's leadership, the U.S. federal prison system became one of the most progressive and adequately financed correctional systems in the world.

Sanford Bates (1884–1972), first director of the Federal Bureau of Prisons. Why did Bates believe in the value of inmate labor?

Bates believed that prisoner rehabilitation offered the best hope of protecting society from crime.[56] He also became president of the American Correctional Association and, after retiring as director of the BOP, served as executive director of the Boys Clubs of America, parole commissioner for

New York State, and New Jersey state commissioner of Institutions and Industries. Today, the Sanford Bates Library, a collection of over 5,000 personal papers, books, and monographs, is housed at Sam Houston State University's George J. Beto Criminal Justice Center.

George J. Beto

Like Bates, George J. Beto (1916–1991), director of the Texas Department of Corrections from 1962 until 1972, believed in the goal of rehabilitation—promoting it as a goal to be achieved in prisons everywhere. Under Beto's leadership, the Texas prison system became known for its order and stability.

Beto began his career as a Lutheran minister but became interested in reformation after serving on the Texas Prison Board, a volunteer organization that oversaw the entire state prison system. As a board member, Beto initiated one of the earliest General Education Development (GED) testing programs for prisoners in the nation.[57] He also served for a time on the Illinois Parole Board, frequently visiting the Stateville Prison in Joliet, Illinois.

Beto drew special attention to the importance of preparing inmates for release back into society. On October 11, 1970, as he delivered the presidential address at the Centennial Congress of Correction of the American Correctional Association in Cincinnati, Beto told attendees:

> The future will bring an expanded use of pre-release programs. It is sheer folly to keep a man in prison two or three or four or five years and, at the termination of his sentence or upon parole, release him with a few dollars, a cheap suit, and the perfunctory ministrations of the dismissing officer. To an even greater degree, the future will witness programs which devote themselves to easing the inmate's transition from the most unnatural society known to man—prison society—to the free world. . . . We must blur the line between the institution and the community.[58]

During his tenure as director of the Texas Department of Corrections, Beto earned the nickname "Walking George" for his habit of showing up unannounced at prisons at any hour of the day or night and conducting

George J. Beto (1916–1991), director of the Texas Department of Corrections from 1962 to 1972. What did Beto mean when he said, "We must blur the line between the institution and the community"?

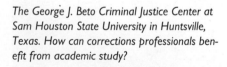

The George J. Beto Criminal Justice Center at Sam Houston State University in Huntsville, Texas. How can corrections professionals benefit from academic study?

on-the-spot inspections. He's best known, however, for having developed a program of prisoner management called the Texas control model. The control model was built on the belief that inmates were in prison because of a lack of self-control, necessitating the need for strong external controls. The control model depended upon strict rule enforcement, and prisoners were punished for even minor infractions of prison regulations. Beto was convinced that discipline, order, and control were necessary in order to provide a safe environment for inmates to better themselves.[59] Before he left the position of director, Beto convinced the state legislature to enact a law requiring state agencies to buy prison-made goods, thereby greatly expanding opportunities for inmate labor in Texas.

Other correctional reformers, including John Augustus, Alexander Maconochie, Sir Walter Crofton, and Zebulon Brockway, are discussed later in this text.

REVIEW AND APPLICATIONS

SUMMARY

1 Corporal, or physical, punishments were the most common response to crime for centuries before criminals began to be incarcerated.

2 Criminal punishments of the past generally consisted of flogging, branding, mutilation, exile, transportation, and public humiliation.

3 Torture of all kinds was used during the Middle Ages in an effort to gain confessions. Torture was justified by the belief that guilty knowledge was properly the property of the king or the state, and that exceptional means could be used to recover it.

4 Many reformers based their ideas on Enlightenment principles, including the use of reason and deductive logic to solve problems. They laid the groundwork for the use of imprisonment as an alternative to traditional punishments.

5 Beginning in the mid-1700s, a number of correctional reformers fought the use of corporal punishments and sought to introduce more humane forms of punishment. Among those reformers were Cesare Beccaria, Jeremy Bentham, and John Howard.

KEY TERMS

corporal punishments, p. 32   utilitarianism, p. 47   hedonistic calculus, p. 48
bridewell, p. 42

QUESTIONS FOR REVIEW

1 What are corporal punishments? What has been the purpose of corporal punishments throughout history? List and describe at least four corporal punishments used in the past for criminal offenders.

2 Describe the major criminal punishments used throughout history. Which ancient civilization

provided the earliest evidence that physical punishment is part of Western society tradition?

3 What role did torture play in the application of corporal punishments? How was the use of torture justified?

4 What cultural developments contributed to the creation of prisons as an alternative to corporal punishments?

5 Which important thinkers discussed in this chapter adapted principles born of the Enlightenment and applied them to the field of law and corrections? Describe the contributions each made to the field.

THINKING CRITICALLY ABOUT CORRECTIONS

Corporal Punishment

In 1994 Michael Fay, an American teenager convicted of spray-painting parked cars, was flogged in Singapore. The flogging (called *caning* because it was done with a bamboo rod) sparked an international outcry from opponents of corporal punishment. In this country, however, it also led to a rebirth of interest in physical punishments—especially for teenagers and vandals.

The last official flogging of a criminal offender in the United States took place in Delaware on June 16, 1952, when a burglar was tied to a whipping post in the state's central prison and was given 20 lashes. Since then, no sentencing authority in this country has imposed whipping as a criminal punishment, and most jurisdictions have removed all corporal punishments from their statutes. Moreover, corporal punishment, other than capital punishment, is now forbidden in U.S. prisons under the Eighth Amendment. Amnesty International, however, reports that whipping is still in use in parts of the world for certain kinds of prisoners.

After the Fay flogging, lawmakers in eight states introduced legislation to institute whipping or paddling as a criminal sanction. Mississippi legislators proposed paddling graffitists and petty thieves, Tennessee lawmakers considered punishing vandals and burglars by public caning on courthouse steps, the New Mexico Senate Judiciary Committee examined the feasibility of caning graffiti vandals, and Louisiana looked into the possibility of ordering parents (or a correctional officer if the parents refused) to spank their children in judicial chambers. So far, none of the proposals has become law.

1. Would a return to corporal punishments, in the form of whipping or paddling, be justified for some offenders? Why or why not?
2. Might paddling be appropriate for some juvenile offenders? Why or why not?
3. Do you think that any state legislatures will eventually pass legislation permitting the paddling or whipping of criminal offenders? Why or why not?

Capital Punishment

Proponents frequently cite deterrence as a benefit of the death penalty. Some studies refute this contention. When confronted with such studies, proponents sometimes respond that execution "will definitely deter the executed offender." They also argue that death is the only thing that the offender really "deserves."

1. How would you respond to the proponents' first argument?
2. How would you respond to the proponents' second argument?

ON-THE-JOB DECISION MAKING

Counseling

You are a parole officer for the state corrections system. You are so burdened with paperwork that you rarely get out of the office to see any of your 200 clients—even though you are supposed to make regular home visits.

While you are shuffling papers one day, one of your clients, Bob Boynton, knocks at your door. It is time for him to make his monthly report. You tell him to have a seat, and you ask him the usual questions: "Have you been in trouble with the law since I saw you last?" "Are you still working?" "Are you paying your bills on time?"

Before you finish the interview, Boynton says, "You know, I'm never going to get anywhere this way. I need a better education. The time I spent in prison was wasted. They didn't teach me anything. I need to learn a skill so that I can make more money. If I can't earn better money I won't be able to pay my bills—and I'm afraid that I'll be tempted to get into the drug business again. I don't want to do that!"

You tell Boynton that there are a number of training schools in the area that can teach him a skill. Some of the computer classes offered at the local community college, you've heard, can lead to jobs paying decent wages. Boynton says, "I don't have a high school diploma. I can't get into the college. I'll never learn computers. I'm just too old. Besides, I need to work with my hands."

You go through the list of schools and training centers in the area, but Boynton raises an objection to each one. You sense that Boynton is trying to transfer responsibility for his success or failure to you. What should you do to get him to take responsibility for himself, yet provide support and guidance for his efforts?

Dispute Resolution

As a newly assigned assistant warden, you are responsible for discipline within your correctional facility. During your initial meeting with the warden, he said that your predecessor had a well-earned reputation among the inmate population as one who unfailingly sided with the correctional staff in all disputes between staff and inmates, no matter how egregious the staff member's behavior. Warden Cowen specifically asked you to establish yourself as a fair and impartial arbiter to reduce inmate concerns of injustice in dispute resolution.

An incident on your second day on the job presents you with a dilemma that even Solomon might be at a loss to resolve. Correctional Officer Tim Dashe is a six-year veteran with absolutely no record of abusive behavior toward inmates. In fact, during your transitional briefing into this job, your predecessor cited Dashe as one of the stalwarts on your staff, particularly praising his professionalism, maturity, good judgment, and reliability.

Inmate Deon Kussick has been incarcerated for 13 years without a single blemish on his record. Quiet, mature, and intelligent, Kussick is considered one of the "go-to" inmates when the administration needs cooperation from the prisoners to resolve a problem.

Inexplicably, Dashe and Kussick got into a fight this morning. A real knock-down drag-out, the fight is now the buzz of conversation among both the prisoner population and the correctional staff. Not surprisingly, tension is rising between the prisoners and the staff as both elements back "their" man and claim that the other man was responsible for the fight.

While it is clear that something is amiss, both Dashe and Kussick are closemouthed about the reason or reasons behind the fight. Their vague explanations are of the "It was just one of those things" variety. Obviously, though, there is a significant point of contention between the two men that, unless resolved, might lead to another confrontation. You can't resolve it, however, if you can't figure out what it is.

For you, the situation is particularly delicate, and the stakes are high. The correctional staff is waiting to see if you will back their fellow officer, the inmates are watching to see if you will be impartial in your handling of the incident, and the warden is evaluating your ability to handle a crisis. What you do will establish your reputation for loyalty (among the staff) and fairness (among the inmates) and serve as an indicator (to the warden) of your reliability and judgment.

One of the old-timers among the inmates sidled up a few minutes ago and, with a casualness that belied his intense interest, asked this simple question: "Watcha gonna do, chief?"

1. What are you going to do?

2. Why?

For additional information, please see: www.mhhe.com/schmalleger6e

[3]

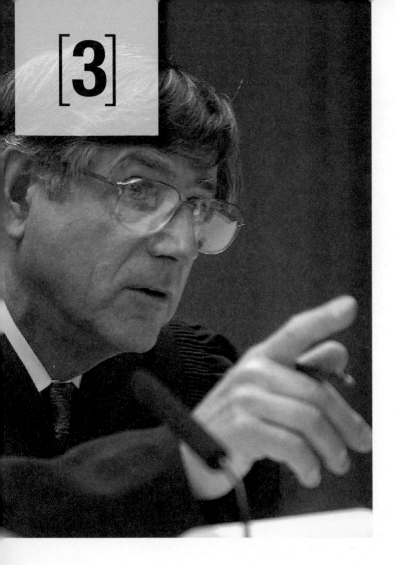

SENTENCING

To Punish or to Reform?

CHAPTER OBJECTIVES

After completing this chapter you should be able to do the following:

1 Describe sentencing philosophy and identify the central purpose of criminal punishment.

2 Name the seven goals of criminal sentencing.

3 List and explain the sentencing options in general use today.

4 Explain what a model of criminal sentencing is and identify models in use today.

5 Describe three-strikes laws and their impact on the correctional system.

6 Identify and explain some major issues related to fair sentencing.

> *We will not punish a man because he hath offended, but that he may offend no more; nor does punishment ever look to the past, but to the future; for it is not the result of a passion, but that the same thing be guarded against in time to come.*
>
> —Seneca, the younger, Roman Philosopher, 3 B.C.–A.D. 65

In 2011, the Washington, D.C.-based Sentencing Project released its annual report on the state of sentencing in the United States. Among the policy recommendations included in the report was one to "enact sentencing reform measures to control prison growth."[1] The Sentencing Project, which is a national nonprofit organization engaged in research and advocacy of criminal justice policy, noted that in today's difficult economy, "Many states are looking closely at ways to reduce correctional costs as they seek to address limited resources."

In fact, the Sentencing Project found that in 2010, at least 23 state legislatures and the District of Columbia adopted 35 different sentencing-related policies intended to reduce prison populations while eliminating barriers for released prisoners attempting to reenter society.

Vermont lawmakers, for example, codified into statute their plan to reduce that state's incarceration rate to 300 (per 100,000 residents) or fewer. The Vermont legislation established a coalition of stakeholders within the state's criminal justice system, and directed them to work cooperatively to reduce the incarceration rate to a number as close to the target rate as possible. To assist in reducing the rate of imprisonment, Vermont lawmakers established a new sentencing option of home confinement that criminal court judges could impose for sentences of 180 days or less.

In another example, Illinois lawmakers in 2010 raised the financial threshold for the crime of felony theft from $300 to $500 and for felony retail theft from $150 to $300. As a direct result of the legislation, fewer property crime offenders are now being sentenced to prison in Illinois.

Sentencing is a court's imposition of a penalty on a convicted offender. A **sentence** is the penalty imposed.

This chapter concerns the nature, history, purpose, and philosophy of criminal sentencing. One of the most crucial issues surrounding sentencing is whether to punish or to reform. The punish-or-reform debate has a long history and continues to concern many people today. We turn now to an examination of the history of sentencing philosophy.

sentencing
The imposition of a criminal sanction by a sentencing authority, such as a judge.

sentence
The penalty a court imposes on a person convicted of a crime.

SENTENCING: PHILOSOPHY AND GOALS

Philosophy of Criminal Sentencing

Western society has a long tradition of punishing criminal offenders. Historically, offenders were banished, exiled, killed, or tortured. Corporal, or physical, punishments became common during the Middle Ages, replacing executions as the preferred penalty. Physical punishments such as flogging and mutilation, though severe in themselves, deterred rampant use of the death penalty. Eventually, as we shall see in later chapters, imprisonment and a variety of other sentencing alternatives replaced corporal punishments as criminal sanctions.

Contemporary sentencing of offenders is still intimately associated with historical notions of punishment. Crimes are frequently seen as *deserving* of punishment. We often hear it said that the criminal must "pay a debt to society" or that "criminals deserve to be punished." John Conrad puts it another way: "The punishment of the criminal is the collective reaction of the community to the wrong that has been done."[2] Conrad goes on to say, "It is the offender's lot to be punished."

Philosophers have long debated *why* a wrongful act should be punished. Many social scientists suggest that criminal punishment maintains and defends the **social order.** By threatening potential law violators and by making the lives of violators uncomfortable, they say, punishments reduce the likelihood of future or continued criminal behavior.

Still, one might ask, instead of punishing offenders, why not offer them psychological treatment or educate them so that they are less prone to future law violation? The answer to this question is far from clear. Although criminal sentencing today has a variety of goals, and educational and treatment programs are more common now in corrections, punishment still takes center stage in society's view. Some writers, such as Conrad, have suggested that society will always *need* to punish criminals because punishment is a natural response to those who break social taboos.[3] Others disagree, arguing that an enlightened society will choose instead to reform lawbreakers through humanitarian means.

The Goals of Sentencing

In 2010, New York state officials refused to let Nushawn Williams out of Erie County's Wende Correctional Facility under the state's civil confinement statute. The law, aimed primarily at predatory sex offenders, permits judges to order certain inmates held after the expiration of their sentences if releasing them would represent a danger to the public. Williams was 22 years old in 1999 when he was sentenced to 4 to 12 years in prison for statutory rape and two counts of reckless endangerment. Williams, a convicted drug dealer from Chautauqua County, New York, had been accused of infecting as many as 103 teenage girls and young women with the AIDS virus in a series of drugs-for-sex encounters.[4] At trial, prosecutors were able to show that Williams had sex with the women while knowing he was HIV-positive. Williams, who kept a journal of his many "conquests," was originally charged with one count of reckless endangerment for each sexual encounter and with first-degree assault for each partner who subsequently became infected. The statutory rape conviction stemmed from his having had sex with a 13-year-old girl who later tested positive for the

social order

The smooth functioning of social institutions, the existence of positive and productive relations among individual members of society, and the orderly functioning of society as a whole.

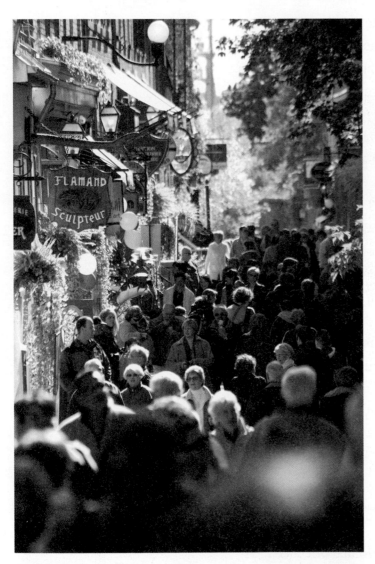

A crowded city street. Many social scientists say that criminal punishments help maintain social order. What would a society without order be like?

EXHIBIT 3–1	Goals of Criminal Sentencing
Goal	**Rationale**
Revenge	Punishment is equated with vengeance and involves an emotional response to criminal victimization.
Retribution	Punishment involves a "settling of scores" for both society and the victim.
	Victims are entitled to "get even."
Just deserts	Offenders are morally blameworthy and deserving of punishment.
	Punishment restores the moral balance disrupted by crime.
Deterrence	Punishment will prevent future wrongdoing by the offender and by others.
	Punishment must outweigh the benefits gained by wrongdoing.
Incapacitation	Some wrongdoers cannot be changed and need to be segregated from society.
	Society has the responsibility to protect law-abiding citizens from those whose behavior cannot be controlled.
Rehabilitation or Reformation	Society needs to help offenders learn how to behave appropriately.
	Without learning acceptable behavior patterns, offenders will not be able to behave appropriately.
Restoration	Crime is primarily an offense against human relationships and secondarily a violation of a law.
	All those who suffered because of a crime should be restored to their previous sense of well-being.

AIDS virus. During trial, prosecutor James Subjack told jurors, "It takes an individual with no regard for human life to do something like this."[5]

The Williams case demonstrates a crucial component of contemporary sentencing philosophy: that people must be held accountable for their actions and for the harm they cause. From this perspective, the purpose of the criminal justice system is to identify persons who have acted in intentionally harmful ways and (where a law is in place) to hold them accountable for their actions by imposing sanctions. Seen this way, our justice system is primarily an instrument of retribution.

Sentencing, however, also has a variety of other purposes. As shown in Exhibit 3–1, the goals of sentencing are (1) revenge, (2) retribution, (3) just deserts (or the fact of deserving punishment), (4) deterrence, (5) incapacitation, (6) rehabilitation or reformation, and (7) restoration.

Revenge   One of the earliest goals of criminal sentencing was revenge. **Revenge** can be described as both an emotion and as an act in response to victimization. Victims sometimes feel as though an injury or insult requires punishment in return. When they act on that feeling, they have taken revenge.

While we think of vengeance as a primitive need, it can still play an important role in contemporary societies and even in modern justice systems. The "tit-for-tat" exchange of terrorist attacks for military incursions

revenge

Punishment as vengeance; an emotional response to real or imagined injury or insult.

between the Palestinians and Israelis that is taking place as this book goes to press is one example of a highly charged emotional situation in which calls for revenge seem to play an important—and sometimes guiding—role. Similarly, had the terrorists who perpetrated the 9/11 attacks been captured (instead of dying in the suicide attacks), there can be little doubt that many Americans would have sought revenge on the perpetrators through our justice system—as was done with Zacarias Moussaoui, the "twelfth highjacker," who was in jail at the time of the 9/11 attacks.

retribution

A sentencing goal that involves retaliation against a criminal perpetrator.

Retribution   Retribution involves the payment of a debt to both the victim and society and, thus, atonement for a person's offense. Historically, retribution was couched in terms of "getting even," and it has sometimes been explained as "an eye for an eye, and a tooth for a tooth." *Retribution* literally means "paying back" the offender for what he or she has done. Retribution is predicated on the notion that victims are *entitled* to reprisal.

Because social order suffers when a crime occurs, society is also a victim. Hence, retribution, in a very fundamental way, expresses society's disapproval of criminal behavior and demands the payment of a debt to society. It is not always easy to determine just how much punishment is enough to ensure the debt is paid.

just deserts

Punishment deserved. A just deserts perspective on criminal sentencing holds that criminal offenders are morally blameworthy and are therefore *deserving* of punishment.

Just Deserts   Retribution is supported by many sentencing schemes today—although the concept is now often couched in terms of **just deserts** even though there is a difference between retribution and just deserts. The concept of just deserts de-emphasizes the emotional component of revenge by claiming that criminal acts are *deserving* of punishment, that offenders are *morally blameworthy,* and that they must be punished. In this way, just deserts restores the moral balance to a society wronged by crime.

Andrew von Hirsch, who identified the rationales underlying criminal punishment, says that when someone "infringes the rights of others . . . he deserves blame [and that is why] the sanctioning authority is entitled to choose a response that expresses moral disapproval: namely, punishment."[6] Hence, from a just deserts point of view, justice *requires* that punishments be imposed on criminal law violators.

Of all the purposes of punishment that are discussed here, only retribution and just deserts are past oriented. That is, they examine what has already occurred (the crime) in an effort to determine the appropriate sentencing response.

deterrence

The discouragement or prevention of crimes through the fear of punishment.

Deterrence   A third goal of criminal sentencing is **deterrence.** Deterrence is the discouragement or prevention of crimes similar to the one for which an offender is being sentenced. Unlike retribution and just deserts, deterrence is future oriented in that it seeks to prevent crimes from occurring. Two forms of deterrence can be identified: specific and general.

specific deterrence

The deterrence of the individual being punished from additional crimes.

Specific deterrence is the deterrence of the individual being punished from committing additional crimes. Long ago, specific deterrence was achieved through corporal punishments that maimed offenders in ways that precluded their ability to commit similar crimes in the future. Spies had their eyes gouged out and their tongues removed, rapists were castrated, thieves had their fingers or hands cut off, and so on. Even today, in some countries that follow a strict Islamic code, the hands of habitual thieves are cut off as a form of corporal punishment.

general deterrence

The use of the example of individual punishment to dissuade others from committing crimes.

General deterrence occurs when the punishment of an individual serves as an example to others who might be thinking of committing a crime—thereby dissuading them from their planned course of action. The **pleasure-pain principle,** which is central to modern discussions of general deterrence, holds that actions are motivated primarily by the desire to experience pleasure and avoid pain. According to this principle, the threat of loss to anyone convicted of a crime should outweigh the potential pleasure to be gained by committing the crime.

For punishment to be effective as a deterrent, it must be relatively certain, swiftly applied, and sufficiently severe. *Certainty, swiftness,* and *severity* of punishment are not always easy to achieve. The crime funnel, described in Chapter 1, demonstrates that most offenses do not end in arrest, and most arrests do not end in incarceration. Although it may not be easy for all offenders to get away with crime, the likelihood that any individual offender will be arrested, successfully prosecuted, and then punished is far smaller than deterrence advocates would like it to be. When an arrest does occur, an offender is typically released on bail, and, because of an overcrowded court system, the trial, if any, may not happen until a year or so later. Moreover, although the severity of punishments has increased in recent years, modern punishments are rarely as severe as those of earlier centuries. Arguments over just how much punishment is enough to deter further violations of the criminal law rarely lead to any clear conclusion.

Incapacitation Many believe that the huge increase in the number of correctional clients has helped lower the crime rate by incapacitating more criminals. Many of these criminals are behind bars, and others are on supervised regimens of probation and parole. **Incapacitation** restrains offenders from committing additional crimes by isolating them from free society. A recent report by the National Center for Policy Analysis, for example, observed that a "major reason for [the] reduction in crime is that crime has become more costly to the perpetrators. The likelihood of going to prison for committing any type of major crime has increased substantially."[7]

The report claims that "the best overall measure of the potential cost to a criminal of committing crimes is *expected punishment*." Expected punishment, says the report, "is the number of days in prison a criminal can expect to serve for committing a crime." The center calculated expected punishment by multiplying the median sentence imposed for each crime by the probabilities of being apprehended, prosecuted, convicted, and sentenced. Crime rates are declining, says the report, because expected prison stays are significantly longer today for every category of serious crime than two decades ago.

A number of studies have claimed to show that incapacitating offenders through incarceration is cost-effective. Such studies conclude that imprisoning certain types of offenders (especially career or habitual offenders) results in savings by eliminating the social costs of the crimes offenders would be likely to commit if they were not imprisoned. Those social costs include monetary loss, medical costs of physical injury, and time lost from work.

One of the most frequently cited studies attempting to quantify the net costs of incarceration was done by Edwin Zedlewski.[8] Zedlewski used a RAND Corporation survey of inmates in three states (Michigan, Texas, and California) to estimate the number of crimes each inmate would commit if not imprisoned. In the survey, the average respondent reported committing anywhere from 187 to 287 crimes annually just before being incarcerated. To calculate the cost associated with each crime, Zedlewski divided the total criminal justice expenditures in the United States by the total number of crimes committed in the United States. From this he concluded that the average crime "costs" $2,300. Multiplying $2,300 by the

pleasure-pain principle
The idea that actions are motivated primarily by a desire to experience pleasure and avoid pain.

incapacitation
The use of imprisonment or other means to reduce an offender's capability to commit future offenses.

Well, here I am, about two and one-half years into my life sentence. The worst part so far for me has been the loneliness. I'm close to 3,000 miles away from my family. I really don't have anyone right now. I think my family is still digesting the fact that I'm in prison. I don't hear from them very often.

With all the time I have alone in my cell, my brain works overtime. I think about all the people I've hurt, whether physically, emotionally, or financially. I think about my crime every day of my life. I took a human life. What makes a man do that? I don't really know. All I can remember is the anger I felt and the hurt feelings. I can remember my heart hurting so bad that I couldn't function normally anymore. I cried all the time and I couldn't eat or sleep. At first it was all jealousy and then it was anger and pain. I guess it all came to a head that night. I had never felt that much rage before in my life. When it was over, I was holding a lifeless body in my arms. I couldn't speak or move. All I could feel was my soul leaving my body. It was an emptiness that I hope I never feel again. It was like I too had died that night.

I remember the day I was sentenced like it was yesterday. I knew ahead of time what I was getting, but it didn't make it any easier. The tears, the stares, the looks, and the glares were all directed in court from people who were once my friends. I was sentenced to life so I couldn't hurt anyone else ever again (or at least I thought so). I called home that afternoon to let my family know that it was all over and that I was going down for life. My father told me that my mom had tried to kill herself by putting a .38 in her mouth. By a miracle of God, my dad had called home at that very moment and talked her out of it. She was so depressed about me, plus she was addicted to painkillers because she had so many back operations. I wanted so much to comfort her, but I couldn't. I didn't know how.

I remember the time I saw my father cry. It was a day I'll never forget. It was a day or two after I was arrested and a week before I was extradited to Arizona when he came to visit me in the county jail in Pennsylvania. I was so nervous. We hadn't talked in years. He didn't like me much at all because I had disappointed him so many times over the years. I couldn't blame him. I was a failure in his eyes as well as mine. I walked down the hallway to where my father was sitting. I sat down in a chair and looked at him through the glass that separated us. He looked so broken and so sad. We picked up the phones and started to talk. The tears just started to run down his face. I had a lump in my throat so that I couldn't swallow. My heart was bleeding inside and the pain was unbearable to see a rock of a man crumble before me because of what I had done. I wanted to end my life right there. My father didn't deserve what I was putting him through. He tried so hard to be a good father. He was strict but fair. I know it wasn't easy for him. I was his stepson. All through my childhood, he never treated me like less than his own son. As I looked into my father's eyes, I wished that he could hug me and I could cry too.

I guess I should thank God for letting me live for 31 years. I tried to destroy myself so many times with drugs, alcohol, and suicide attempts. In a way, prison has saved my life. I would have died at a young age from drugs or alcohol, or maybe the suicide attempts would have worked sooner or later. I'm just thankful I was able to overcome the demons in my life. I'm a better person now. I'm responsible, caring, and able to be kind. I guess that's all part of growing up, and that's what I've done the past few years. I still have a long way to go, but it's a start.

George Killian, #82256
ASPC-Eyman Complex, Meadows Unit Florence, Arizona

---

correctional econometrics
The study of the cost-effectiveness of various correctional programs and related reductions in the incidence of crime.

187 crimes estimated to be committed annually by a felon, Zedlewski calculated that society saves $430,100 per year for each felon who is incarcerated. Figuring that incarceration costs society about $25,000 per prisoner per year, he concluded that prisons produce a cost–benefit return to society of 17 to 1 ($17 saved for every $1 spent)—leading him to strongly support increased incarceration.

Three years after Zedlewski's work, well-known criminologist John DiIulio performed a cost–benefit analysis using a survey of Wisconsin prisoners. The study, called "Crime and Punishment in Wisconsin," led to the conclusion that prisons saved taxpayers in Wisconsin approximately $2 for every dollar they cost.[9]

Studies such as those by Zedlewski and DiIulio are part of the growing field of correctional econometrics. **Correctional econometrics** is the study of the cost-effectiveness of various correctional programs and related reductions in the incidence of crime. Recent studies have identified a decreasing return associated with the expanded use of incarceration. In 2006, for example, the Washington State Institute for Public Policy conducted an econometric study of how state incarceration rates affect county crime rates in Washington. Institute researchers concluded that "a 10 percent increase (or decrease) in the incarceration rate leads to a statistically significant 3.3 percent decrease (or increase) in crime rates."[10] The study noted, however, that diminishing returns "begin to erode the crime reduction effects as incarceration rates are increased." Other research found that "the effect of prison growth on crime diminishes as the scale of imprisonment increases."[11] In fact, this second study stated that "when the incarceration rate reaches a certain point (the inflection point), a further increase in prison population actually produces an increase in crime."

Rehabilitation or Reformation   The goal of **rehabilitation or reformation** is to change criminal lifestyles into law-abiding ones. Rehabilitation has been accomplished when an offender's criminal patterns of thought and behavior have been replaced by allegiance to society's values. Rehabilitation focuses on medical and psychological treatments and on social skills training, all designed to "correct" the problems that led the individual to crime.

A subgoal of rehabilitation is **reintegration** of the offender with the community. Reintegrating the offender with the community means making the offender a productive member of society—one who contributes to the general well-being of the whole.

Rehabilitation, which became the focus of American corrections beginning in the late 1800s, led to implementation of indeterminate sentencing practices (soon to be discussed), probation, parole, and a separate system of juvenile justice. During the 1970s, however, rehabilitation came under harsh criticism. As American society experienced disruptions brought about by economic change, the decline of traditional institutions, and fallout from the war in Vietnam, conservatives blamed the rehabilitative ideal for being too liberal, and liberals condemned it for providing an unfair basis for coercive action against disenfranchised social groups.[12] About the same time, an influential and widely read study by Robert Martinson, which evaluated rehabilitation programs nationwide, reported that few, if any, produced real changes in offender attitudes.[13] Dubbed the "nothing works doctrine," Martinson's critique of rehabilitation as a correctional goal led some states to abandon rehabilitation altogether or to de-emphasize

rehabilitation (also *reformation*)
The changing of criminal lifestyles into law-abiding ones by "correcting" the behavior of offenders through treatment, education, and training.

reintegration
The process of making the offender a productive member of the community.

As a goal of sentencing, incapacitation restrains offenders from committing more crimes by isolating them from society. Does this threat of social isolation encourage law-abiding behavior?

it in favor of the goals of retribution and incapacitation. In other states, attempts at rehabilitation continued but were often muted.

Today, some governments and private organizations are reembracing rehabilitation, emphasizing treatment and education. According to Francis T. Cullen and Paul Gendreau, it is time to give the rehabilitative ideal a second chance. They call for *reaffirming rehabilitation*. "Many [rehabilitative] programs fail to work," say Cullen and Gendreau, "because they either are ill-conceived (not based on sound criminological theory) and/or have no therapeutic integrity (are not implemented as designed)." "We would not be surprised," they write, "if young children turned out to be illiterate if their teachers were untrained, had no standardized curriculum, and met the children once a week for half an hour."[14] Until recently, contend Cullen and Gendreau, many correctional treatment programs were in such a state.

Other writers hold that continued efforts at rehabilitation are mandatory for any civilized society. "In order to neutralize the desocializing potential of prisons," says Edgardo Rotman, "a civilized society is forced into rehabilitative undertakings. These become an essential ingredient of its correctional system taken as a whole. A correctional system" with no "interest in treatment," says Rotman, "means . . . de-humanization and regression."[15]

Rehabilitation typically implies the notion of treatment, in the belief that offenders who receive appropriate counseling, psychological treatment, psychiatric intervention, or drug therapy will be less prone to repeat criminality. California's Proposition 36, officially known as the Substance Abuse Crime Prevention Act of 2000 (SACPA), is indicative of the return to rehabilitation now occurring. Passed by the state's voters in 2000, it became effective on July 1 of that year. The law's purpose, stated in Section 3(c), is to "enhance public safety by reducing drug-related crime and preserving jails and prison cells for serious and violent offenders, and to improve public health by reducing drug abuse and drug dependence through proven and effective drug treatment strategies." It seeks to accomplish that goal by mandating probation for any person convicted of a nonviolent drug possession offense, and it requires participation in, and completion of, proven and effective community-based treatment programs as a condition of probation.

According to a recent study of the social and financial consequences of Proposition 36 by researchers at UCLA, the initiative had cost California more than $600 million in its first two years.[16] Nonetheless, a net savings resulted from diverting thousands of nonviolent drug offenders from prisons, saving the state $2.50 for every $1 spent on diversion. Researchers found a significant problem, however, in the fact that drug-related rearrest rates for offenders diverted from prison to treatment under the initiative was 48 percent higher than for those who remained in the criminal justice system.[17] According to the researchers, Proposition 36 placed unmanageable burdens on residential drug treatment programs, resulting in relatively ineffective outpatient treatment for many clients who, prior to passage of the Proposition, would have been enrolled in inpatient programs instead.

restoration

The process of returning to their previous condition all those involved in or affected by crime—including victims, offenders, and society.

restorative justice

A systematic response to wrongdoing that emphasizes healing the wounds of victims, offenders, and communities caused or revealed by crime.

Restoration In recent years, a new goal of criminal sentencing, known as **restoration**, has developed. **Restorative justice** is based on the belief that criminal sentencing should involve restoration and justice for all involved in or affected by crime.

Advocates of restorative justice (or, as some agencies refer to it, *community justice* or *reparative justice*) believe that crime is committed not just against the state but also against victims and the community. Restorative

Erich Parsons
Deputy Sheriff • Palm Beach County, Florida

Erich Parsons is deputy sheriff with the Palm Beach County Sheriff's Department in West Palm Beach, Florida. A 44-year-old Army veteran and grandfather of five, he attended Johnson Bible College in Knoxville, Tennessee, where he received a bachelor of arts degree, and has been an ordained minister since 1986. He has been with the department since 2000, working the midnight to 8 A.M. shift.

Deputy Parsons had no educational background in law enforcement. While working in his family's business in the late 1990s (as a glazier in the family glass factory), he tore his rotator cuff, and he says that during his stay in the hospital he became interested in the job.

"Part of my desire to move on to something of this caliber was the need for significance. I felt that even though I was comfortable where I was and who I was, I like challenges. I'm a kid from the streets—grew up fast. So my penchant was to reach youth, and the training I took in theology was youth ministry–specific. I felt that my greater outreach perhaps would be those individuals in the county level as opposed to the state level, that the street kids needed more than just the church setting."

On a typical day, Deputy Parsons will handle unresolved issues from the previous shift; handle new arrests, fingerprints, and photographs; "and try to maintain order as we're doing all that," he says.

"I love my job," he says. "My satisfaction is to know that I've done my job the best I was able to do, with what was available to me."

> *"Even though I see the charges as they come in on the rough arrests, I try not to judge them. I know sometimes they're in bad situations. I try to maintain the dignity of an individual. Usually they reciprocate, and say, 'Thank you for treating me human.'"*

justice is especially concerned with repairing the harm to the victim and the community. Harm is repaired through negotiation, mediation, and empowerment rather than through retribution, deterrence, and punishment. A restorative justice perspective allows judges and juries to consider **victim-impact statements** in their sentencing decisions. These are descriptions of the harm and suffering that a crime has caused victims and their survivors. Also among the efforts being introduced on behalf of victims and their survivors are victim assistance and victim compensation programs.

Advocates of restorative justice believe not only that the victim should be restored by the justice process but also that the offender and society should participate in the restoration process. To this end, efforts at restoration emphasize the successful reintegration of offenders into the community as well as victims' rights and needs. Another aspect of involving offenders in restoration is having them actively address the harm they have caused. The system strives to accomplish this by holding them directly accountable and by helping them become productive, law-abiding members of their community.[18] Restorative justice programs try to personalize crime by showing offenders the consequences of their behavior.

Restorative justice is based on the premise that because crime occurs in the context of the community, the community should be involved in addressing it. Particular restorative justice or community justice programs might use any of the following: (1) victim–offender mediation, (2) victim–offender reconciliation, (3) victim-impact panels, (4) restorative justice panels, (5) community reparative boards, (6) community-based courts, (7) family group conferences, (8) circle sentencing, (9) court diversion programs, and (10) peer mediation.

Restorative justice seeks to restore the health of the community, repair the harm done, meet victims' needs, and require the offender to contribute

victim-impact statement

A description of the harm and suffering that a crime has caused victims and survivors.

EXHIBIT 3–2 Restorative Justice Principles

The following principles were developed by the Restorative Justice Consortium in order to provide a working basis for particular settings involved in the practice of restorative justice, including adult criminal justice, youthful offenders, schools, the workplace, prisons, and communities.

1. Principles relating to the interests of all participants
   a. Voluntary participation based on informed choice
   b. Avoidance of discrimination, irrespective of the nature of the case
   c. Access to relevant agencies for help and advice
   d. Ongoing access to various established methods of dispute resolution
   e. Processes that do not compromise the rights under the law of the participants
   f. Commitment not to use information in a way that may prejudice the interests of any participant in subsequent proceedings
   g. Protection of personal safety
   h. Protection of and support for vulnerable participants
   i. Respect for civil rights and the dignity of persons
2. Principles relating to those who have sustained harm or loss
   a. Respect for their personal experiences, needs, and feelings
   b. Acknowledgment of their harm or loss
   c. Recognition of their claim for amends
   d. Opportunity to communicate with the person who caused the harm or loss, if that person is willing
   e. Entitlement of victim to be the primary beneficiary of reparation
3. Principles relating to those who caused the harm or loss to others
   a. The opportunity to offer reparation, including before any formal requirement
   b. Reparation appropriate to the harm done and within the person's capacity to fulfill it
   c. Respect for the dignity of the person making amends
4. Principles relating to the interests of local community and society
   a. The promotion of community safety and social harmony by learning from restorative processes and the taking of measures that are conducive to the reduction of crime or harm
   b. The promotion of social harmony through respect for cultural diversity and civil rights, social responsibility, and the rule of law
   c. Opportunity for all to learn mediation and other methods of nonviolent resolution of conflict
5. Principles relating to agencies working alongside the judicial system
   a. Settlement outside the judicial system, except when this is unworkable due to the level of harm done, the risk of further harm, issues of public policy, or disagreement about the critical facts
   b. Avoidance of unfair discrimination by ensuring that rights under the law are not compromised
   c. Provision of a wide and flexible range of opportunities to enable those who have caused loss or harm to make amends
6. Principles relating to the judicial system
   a. A primary goal of repairing harm
   b. Restorative requirements that are fair, appropriate, and workable
   c. Opportunities for community reparation or reparation to others who have suffered harm or loss when a restorative requirement is appropriate but victims decline to participate
   d. Enforcement of community reparation when a restorative requirement is appropriate but those who have caused harm or loss decline to participate
   e. Valuing of voluntary offers to repair harm or loss by those who have caused it
   f. Privileged status of content of restorative meetings, subject to public interest qualifications
7. Principles relating to restorative justice agencies
   a. Commitment to needs-based practice
   b. Safeguarding of legal human rights
   c. The participation of restorative justice practitioners who are seen to be neutral
   d. The participation of restorative justice practitioners who act impartially
   e. Maintenance of neutrality and impartiality by restorative justice practitioners who play no other role in the case
   f. Commitment of restorative justice agencies to keep confidential the content of restorative meetings, subject to the requirements of the law
   g. Participant commitment to confidentiality about the contents of restorative meetings
   h. Facilitation of the engagement of weaker parties in negotiation
   i. Upholding of respectful behavior in restorative processes
   j. Upholding of equality of respect for all participants in restorative processes, separating this from the harm done
   k. Engagement with good practice guidelines within the restorative justice movement
   l. Commitment by the agency to the use of constructive conflict resolution in general and of internal grievance and disciplinary procedures in specific
   m. Commitment to the accreditation of training, services, and practitioners
   n. Commitment to continually improved practice

Source: Restorative Justice Principles. Copyright © Restorative Justice Consortium.

to those repairs. Thus, the criminal act is condemned, offenders are held accountable, offenders and victims are involved as participants, and repentant offenders are encouraged to earn their way back into the good graces of society. Restorative justice principles, developed by the Restorative Justice Consortium, are shown in Exhibit 3–2.

EXHIBIT 3–3   **American Correctional Association**

Public Correctional Policy on Sentencing

The American Correctional Association actively promotes the development of sentencing policies that should:

- be based on the principle of proportionality. The sentence imposed should be commensurate with the seriousness of the crime and the harm done;
- be impartial with regard to race, ethnicity, and economic status as to the discretion exercised in sentencing;
- include a broad range of options for custody, supervision, and rehabilitation of offenders;
- be purpose-driven. Policies must be based on clearly articulated purposes. They should be grounded in knowledge of the relative effectiveness of the various sanctions imposed in attempts to achieve these purposes;
- encourage the evaluation of sentencing policy on an ongoing basis. The various sanctions should be monitored to determine their relative effectiveness based on the purpose(s) they are intended to have. Likewise, monitoring should take place to ensure that the sanctions are not applied based on race, ethnicity, or economic status;
- recognize that the criminal sentence must be based on multiple criteria, including the harm done to the victim, past criminal history, the need to protect the public, and the opportunity to provide programs for offenders as a means of reducing the risk for future crime;

- provide the framework to guide and control discretion according to established criteria and within appropriate limits and allow for recognition of individual needs;
- have as a major purpose restorative justice—righting the harm done to the victim and the community. The restorative focus should be both process and substantively oriented. The victim or his or her representative should be included in the "justice" process. The sentencing procedure should address the needs of the victim, including his or her need to be heard and, as much as possible, to be and feel restored to whole again;
- promote the use of community-based programs whenever consistent with public safety; and
- be linked to the resources needed to implement the policy. The consequential cost of various sanctions should be assessed. Sentencing policy should not be enacted without the benefit of a fiscal-impact analysis. Resource allocations should be linked to sentencing policy so as to ensure adequate funding of all sanctions, including total confinement and the broad range of intermediate sanction and community-based programs needed to implement those policies.

Source: Copyright © American Correctional Association.

Not only is restorative justice having an impact on U.S. sentencing practices (Exhibit 3–3), but also it is becoming influential internationally. A United Nations report on the international acceptance of restorative justice principles in 35 member countries, for example, found that the concept has received considerable international attention by both practitioners and policymakers who view it as an alternative approach to more common criminal justice practices. According to the report, restorative justice is seen as offering promising concepts and options if taken as a supplement to established criminal justice practices. In general, says the report, restorative justice principles are seen as a complement to established justice systems and practices but not as a replacement for existing systems.[19]

SENTENCING OPTIONS AND TYPES OF SENTENCES

Options

Legislatures establish the types of sentences that can be imposed. The U.S. Congress and the 50 state legislatures decide what is against the law and define crimes and their punishments in the jurisdictions in which they have control. Sentencing options in wide use today include the following:

- fines and other monetary sanctions;
- probation;
- alternative or intermediate sanctions such as day fines, community service, electronic monitoring, and day reporting centers;

EXHIBIT 3–4   Adults on Probation, in Jail, in Prison, or on Parole in the United States

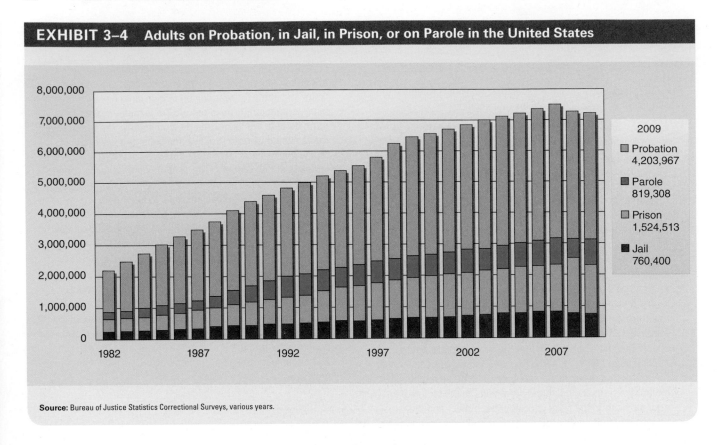

Source: Bureau of Justice Statistics Correctional Surveys, various years.

- incarceration; and
- death penalty.

As punishment for unlawful behavior, fines have a long history. By the 5th century B.C., Greece, for example, had developed an extensive system of fines for a wide variety of offenses.[20] Under our modern system of justice, fines are usually imposed as punishment for misdemeanors and infractions. When imposed on felony offenders, fines are frequently combined with another punishment, such as probation or incarceration.

Fines are only one type of monetary sanction used today. Others include the court-ordered payment of the costs of trial, victim restitution, various fees, forfeitures, donations, and confiscations. **Restitution** consists of payments made by a criminal offender to his or her victim as compensation for the harm caused by the offense. While fines are usually paid to the government, restitution may be paid directly to the victim (or paid to the court, which turns it over to the victim). Some innovative courts have ordered offenders to donate specified amounts to specified charities in lieu of a fine.[21] Restitution is an example of a restorative justice sentencing option.

With a sentence of probation, the convicted offender continues to live in the community but must comply with court-imposed restrictions on his or her activity and freedom of movement. Alternative sanctions or intermediate sentencing options (which are discussed in detail in Chapters 4 and 5) usually combine probation with some other punishment, such as community service or house arrest with electronic monitoring. A sentence of incarceration, or total confinement away from the community, is used when the community needs to be protected from further criminal activity by an offender. The death penalty, or capital punishment, is the ultimate sentence. Exhibit 3–4 displays recent trends in four correctional options.

restitution

Payments made by a criminal offender to his or her victim (or to the court, which then turns them over to the victim) as compensation for the harm caused by the offense.

Types of Sentences

A sentence is generally imposed by a judge. Sentencing responsibility can also be exercised by a jury or a group of judges, or it may be mandated by statute. **Mandatory sentences** are those that are required by law under certain circumstances—such as conviction of a specified crime or of a series of offenses of a specified type. Mandatory sentences may add prison time to sentences for offenders who carried weapons during the commission of their crimes, who used or possessed illegal drugs, or who perpetrated crimes against elderly victims. Such sentences allow judges no leeway in sentencing.

Even when there is no mandatory sentence, judges cannot impose just any sentence. They are still limited by statutory provisions. They also are guided by prevailing sentencing goals. A judge usually considers a **presentence report (PSR)**. This report, prepared by the probation department attached to a court, is a social and personal history as well as an evaluation of the offender. Finally, judges' sentencing decisions are influenced by their own personal convictions and characteristics.

Once the sentence is chosen, the judge must decide how it will be served, especially if more than one sentence is being imposed. Sentences can be consecutive or concurrent. **Consecutive sentences** are served one after the other. When a person is convicted of multiple offenses, a judge might impose, for example, a sentence of 10 years for one offense and 20 years for another. If the sentences are to run consecutively, the offender will begin serving the second sentence only after the first one expires. **Concurrent sentences** are served together. If the sentences in the example are to run concurrently, the 10-year sentence will expire when the offender has served one-half of the 20-year sentence. The offender will then need to serve the remainder of the 20-year sentence before being released. When multiple sentences are imposed, most are ordered to be served concurrently.

mandatory sentences

Those that are required by law under certain circumstances—such as conviction of a specified crime or of a series of offenses of a specified type.

presentence report (PSR)

A report prepared by the probation department of a court that provides a social and personal history as well as an evaluation of a defendant as an aid to the court in determining a sentence.

consecutive sentences

Sentences served one after the other.

concurrent sentences

Sentences served together.

SENTENCING MODELS

A **model of criminal sentencing** is a strategy or system for imposing criminal sanctions. Sentencing models vary widely (see Exhibit 3–5). Over the past 100 years, a shift has occurred from what might be called a *judicial model of sentencing* to an *administrative model*. Judges generally have far less discretion in sentencing decisions today than they previously had. The majority of sentences imposed in American courts today follow legislative and administrative guidelines.

Sentencing in 19th-century America involved mostly fines, probation, and "flat" prison sentences. **Flat sentences** specify a given amount of time to be served in custody and allow little or no variation from the time specified. A typical flat sentence might be stated as "five years in prison." Flat sentences generally mean that an offender has to complete the sentence imposed and cannot earn an early release.

model of criminal sentencing

A strategy or system for imposing criminal sanctions.

flat sentences

Those that specify a given amount of time to be served in custody and allow little or no variation from the time specified.

Indeterminate Sentencing

By the close of the 19th century, sentencing reform in the United States began replacing the flat sentence with indeterminate sentences.[22] At the time, the criminal justice system was coping with a rapidly expanding and increasingly diverse prison population, increased efficiency of police and courts, and other factors. Overcrowded prisons and the warehousing of inmates resulted.[23]

EXHIBIT 3–5 Sentencing Models

Determinate Sentencing

Sentencing to a fixed term of incarceration that may be reduced by good time. Usually, explicit standards specify the amount of punishment and a set release date, with no review by a parole board or other administrative agency. Postincarceration supervision may be part of the sentence.

Indeterminate Sentencing

Sentencing in which an administrative agency, generally a parole board, has the authority to release an incarcerated offender and to determine whether an offender's parole will be revoked for violation of the conditions of release. In one form of indeterminate sentencing, the judge specifies only the maximum sentence length (a fixed term); the associated minimum is automatically implied but is not within the judge's discretion. In the more traditional form of indeterminate sentencing, the judge specifies maximum and minimum durations within limits set by statute. The judge has discretion over the minimum and maximum sentences.

Presumptive Guidelines Sentencing

Sentencing that meets all the following conditions: (1) the appropriate sentence for an offender in a specific case is presumed to fall within a range authorized by guidelines adopted by a legislatively created sentencing body, usually a sentencing commission; (2) judges are expected to sentence within the range or provide written justification for departure; and (3) the guidelines provide for review of the departure, usually by appeal to a higher court. Presumptive guidelines may employ determinate or indeterminate sentencing structures.

Voluntary/Advisory Guidelines Sentencing

Recommended sentencing policies that are not required by law. They serve as a guide and are based on past sentencing practices. The legislature has not mandated their use. Voluntary/advisory guidelines may use determinate or indeterminate sentencing structures.

Mandatory Minimum Sentencing

A minimum sentence that is specified by statute for all offenders convicted of a particular crime or a particular crime with special circumstances (e.g., robbery with a firearm or selling drugs to a minor within 1,000 feet of a school). Mandatory minimums can be used in both determinate and indeterminate sentencing structures. Within an indeterminate sentencing structure, the mandatory minimum requires the inmate to serve a fixed amount of time in prison before being eligible for release with the approval of a parole board. Under a determinate sentence, the offender is required to serve a fixed amount of time in prison before being eligible for release.

indeterminate sentence

A sentence in which a judge specifies a maximum length and a minimum length, and an administrative agency, generally a parole board, determines the actual time of release.

In an **indeterminate sentence**, the judge specifies a maximum length and a minimum length, within limits set by statute, and a parole board determines the actual time of release. The parole board's determination depends on its judgment of whether the prisoner has been reformed, has been cured, or has simply served enough time. An example of an indeterminate sentence is "5 to 10 years in prison." A second form of indeterminate sentencing requires the judge to specify only the maximum sentence length, with the associated minimum set by statute. Some states, for example, require an offender to serve as little as one-quarter of the sentence before becoming eligible for parole.

With an indeterminate sentence, discretion is distributed, not only among the prosecutor, defense counsel, and judge, but also to prison officials and the parole board, which have considerable influence over an offender's length of stay. Prison officials have discretion over the amount of **good time** an inmate earns, which can affect parole eligibility, the discharge date, or both. The parole board decides the actual release date for most inmates. The result is a system of sentencing in which few people understand or can predict who will be imprisoned and for how long.

Under indeterminate sentencing, punishments are made to fit the criminal rather than the crime. Proponents of indeterminate sentences assume that crime is a product of individual deviation from the norm and that rehabilitation can be achieved within a prison system designed to punish, not treat, inmates. They also assume that prison personnel have the knowledge to impose treatment or to predict recidivism accurately enough to justify their discretion regarding when an inmate should be released. The use of indeterminate sentences has prompted numerous accusations of disparity in sentencing as well as protests from inmate groups, penologists, and other critics of the penal system. These protests have spurred a movement for sentencing reform.

good time
The number of days or months prison authorities deduct from a sentence for good behavior and for other reasons.

Determinate Sentencing

A **determinate sentence** (also known as a *fixed sentence*) specifies a fixed period of incarceration, which can be reduced for good time served. The term is generally used to refer to the sentencing reforms of the late 1970s. Determinate sentences are generally based on the incapacitation and deterrence goals of sentencing. The theory behind determinate sentencing is that criminals will be off the streets for longer periods of time. The other advantage, supporters say, is that prisoners know when they will be released. In most determinate sentencing models, parole is limited or is replaced by the use of good-time credits. With good time, inmates are able to reduce their sentences by earning credits. The amount of the reduction depends on the number of credits earned. Good-time credits can be earned by demonstrating good behavior and not being "written up" for violating prison rules. They can also be earned by participating in educational programs, community service projects, or medical experiments. The procedure for earning credits and the number that can be earned vary from state to state. Prison administrators generally favor determinate sentencing and good-time credits because they aid in controlling prison populations.

determinate sentence (also *fixed sentence*)
A sentence of a fixed term of incarceration, which can be reduced by good time.

Guideline Sentencing

As we have seen, the sentences that judges impose are regulated by law. As part of the movement to eliminate sentencing disparities, some states, as well as the federal government, have enacted sentencing guidelines for judges to follow. The guidelines fall into two categories.

Voluntary/Advisory Sentencing Guidelines Among the earliest guided sentencing innovations in the United States was the experiment with voluntary guidelines, also called *advisory guidelines*. These are recommended sentencing policies that are not required by law. Usually, they are based on past sentencing practices and serve as a guide to judges. Voluntary or advisory guidelines have had disappointing results because they are often not enforced and are sometimes ignored. More importantly, the guidelines are voluntary; judges can simply ignore them. A review of all the major studies conducted on voluntary and advisory guidelines reveals low compliance by judges and, hence, little reduction in disparity.[24]

sentencing commission

A group assigned to create a schedule of sentences that reflect the gravity of the offenses committed and the prior record of the criminal offender.

Presumptive Sentencing Guidelines By the early 1980s, states had begun to experiment with the use of presumptive sentencing guidelines. These models differ from determinate sentences and voluntary or advisory guidelines in three respects. First, the guidelines are developed, not by the legislature, but by a **sentencing commission** that often represents diverse interests, including private citizens as well as all segments of the criminal justice system. Second, the guidelines are explicit and highly structured, relying on a quantitative scoring instrument. Third, the guidelines are not voluntary or advisory. Judges must adhere to the sentencing system or provide a written rationale for departure.

The forces stimulating presumptive sentencing guidelines were the same as those that had driven the moves to determinate sentencing and voluntary or advisory guidelines: issues of fairness and prison crowding. These concerns provided the impetus for states to adopt guidelines, replace indeterminate sentencing with determinate sentencing, and abolish or reduce discretionary parole release. The first four states to adopt presumptive sentencing guidelines were Minnesota (1980), Washington (1981), Pennsylvania (1982), and Florida (1983).

The state of Washington's Sentencing Reform Act (SRA) of 1981 (as amended), for example, is based on a determinate sentencing model. The law mandated creation of a Sentencing Guidelines Commission, which developed a set of sentencing guidelines "to ensure that offenders who commit similar crimes and have similar criminal histories receive equivalent sentences."[25] The state's presumptive sentencing schedules, which apply to all felonies committed in the state after June 30, 1984, are structured "so that offenses involving greater harm to a victim and to society result in greater punishment." According to the Sentencing Guidelines Commission, "The guidelines apply equally to offenders in all parts of the state, without discrimination as to any element that does not relate to the crime or to a defendant's previous criminal record."

As is typically the case in presumptive sentencing states, Washington's guidelines specify a standard sentence range based on the seriousness of an offense combined with an offender's criminal history "score." In Washington State, a defendant's criminal history includes his or her prior adult felony convictions in any state or federal court or in another country and dispositions in juvenile court. Misdemeanors are not counted except when related to current convictions of felony traffic offenses (e.g., driving under the influence of alcohol or drugs may figure into a defendant's criminal history when felony convictions for crimes such as vehicular assault occur). Judges use forms provided by the state's sentencing commission in calculating an offender's score for sentencing purposes. Crimes representative of each "seriousness level" are shown in Exhibit 3–6.

As in other presumptive sentencing states, in Washington judges may sentence offenders outside the standard ranges found in the state's sentencing grid. Sentences that fall outside established guidelines, however, are not permitted if based solely on determinations of fact made by the sentencing judge—a limitation imposed by the U.S. Supreme Court in the 2004 case of *Blakely* v. *Washington*. In 2005, Washington's sentencing law was changed to require that aggravating circumstances that might lead to sentencing enhancements be proved to a jury.

EXHIBIT 3–6 State of Washington: Representative Crimes by Level of Seriousness

Level of Seriousness	Representative Offense	Level of Seriousness	Representative Offense
XVI	Aggravated Murder in the First Degree[a]	V	Third Degree Child Molestation
XV	First Degree Murder		First Degree Custodial Sexual Misconduct
	Homicide by Abuse		Domestic Violence Court Order Violation
	First Degree Malicious Explosion		First Degree Extortion
XIV	Second Degree Murder		Persistent Prison Misbehavior
XIII	Second Degree Malicious Explosion		Possession of a Stolen Firearm
	First Degree Malicious Placement of an Explosive		Stalking
XII	First Degree Assault	IV	Second Degree Arson
	First Degree Rape		Second Degree Assault
XI	First Degree Manslaughter		Bribing a Witness
	Second Degree Rape		Counterfeiting
X	First Degree Child Molestation		Knowingly Trafficking in Stolen Property
	Indecent Liberties (with Forcible Compulsion)		Threats to Bomb
	First Degree Kidnapping	III	Third Degree Assault
	Leading Organized Crime		Second Degree Burglary
IX	Controlled Substance Homicide		Communication with a Minor for Immoral Purposes
	Inciting Criminal Profiteering		Criminal Gang Intimidation
	First Degree Robbery/Sexual Exploitation		Harassment
	Vehicular Homicide, by Being Under the Influence of Intoxicating Liquor or Any Drug		Intimidating a Public Servant
			Maintaining a Dwelling or Place for Controlled Substances
VIII	First Degree Arson		Manufacture, Deliver, or Possess with Intent to Deliver Marijuana
	Deliver or Possess with Intent to Deliver Methamphetamine		Patronizing a Juvenile Prostitute
	Hit and Run—Death		Possession of Incendiary Device
	Second Degree Manslaughter		Possession of Machine Gun or Short Barreled Shotgun or Rifle
	First Degree Promoting Prostitution		Tampering with a Witness
	Vehicular Homicide, by the Operation of Any Vehicle in a Reckless Manner	II	First Degree Computer Trespass
VII	First Degree Burglary		Create, Deliver, or Possess a Counterfeit Controlled Substance
	Drive-by Shooting		Health Care False Claims
	Indecent Liberties (without Forcible Compulsion)		Theft of Rental, Leased, or Lease-Purchased Property (Valued at $1,500 or More)
	Involving a Minor in Drug Dealing		Unlicensed Practice of a Profession or Business
	Use of a Machine Gun in Commission of a Felony	I	Attempting to Elude a Pursuing Police Vehicle
VI	First Degree Incest		False Verification for Welfare
	Intimidating a Judge		Forged Prescription
	Intimidating a Juror/Witness		Taking a Motor Vehicle Without Permission
	Theft of a Firearm		Unlawful Use of Food Stamps

[a]Aggravated murder in the first degree is first-degree murder under certain circumstances. Among them are (a) the victim was a law enforcement officer or firefighter performing his or her official duties; (b) the defendant was serving a term of imprisonment in a state institution at the time of the homicide; (c) the defendant solicited another person to commit the crime for pay, and so on. To learn the statutory elements of each of the offenses listed here, view Title 9 of the Revised Code of Washington (the state's criminal law) online at www.mrsc.org/rcw.htm. Visit the state of Washington Sentencing Guidelines Commission at www.sgc.wa.gov, where you can read the state's online adult sentencing guidelines manual. The manual contains a comprehensive list of all felonies defined by state law along with their location in the sentencing grid.

Federal Sentencing Guidelines In the early 1980s, the U.S. Congress focused its attention on disparity in sentencing.[26] Congress concluded that the sentencing discretion of federal trial judges needed boundaries. The resulting legislation, termed the Sentencing Reform Act (SRA) of 1984,[27] created the United States Sentencing Commission. The nine-member commission, first organized in October 1985, is a permanent body charged with formulating and amending national sentencing guidelines. The commission's guidelines apply to all federal criminal offenses committed on or after November 1, 1987.

Federal sentencing guidelines take into account a defendant's criminal history, the nature of the criminal conduct, and the particular circumstances surrounding the offense. Congress required that all federal trial judges follow the guidelines in their sentencing decisions. Deviations from the guidelines were permitted only when a judge provided a written justification setting forth specific reasons as to why a sentence outside of the range specified by the guidelines was appropriate.

Federal sentencing guidelines have been subject to change, and the commission may submit guideline amendments to Congress each year between the beginning of the regular congressional session and May 1. Suggested amendments automatically take effect 180 days after submission unless Congress rejects them.

Early challenges to the constitutionality of federal sentencing guidelines were resolved by the 1989 case of *Mistretta* v. *United States,* in which the U.S. Supreme Court upheld the 1984 SRA and ruled that Congress had acted properly in delegating authority to the U.S. Sentencing Commission in the creation of sentencing guidelines.

In addition to creating the U.S. Sentencing Commission, the SRA abolished parole for federal offenders sentenced under the guidelines. As a consequence, sentences imposed on convicted federal offenders today are essentially the sentences that will be served. Under federal law, however, inmates may earn up to 54 days of credit (time off their sentences) each year for good behavior.

The Legal Environment and Sentencing Guidelines A number of U.S. Supreme Court cases focused on the authority that judges retain in deciding to depart from sentencing guidelines and on the application of **sentencing enhancements.** In 1994, in the case of *Nichols* v. *United States,* the Court held that "an uncounseled misdemeanor conviction," because no prison term was imposed, is valid when used to enhance punishment at a subsequent conviction. (An "uncounseled conviction" is one in which the defendant was not represented by an attorney.)

In the 2002 case of *United States* v. *Cotton,* the Court found that sentences imposed by a federal judge were not improper even though the judge based those sentences on a quantity of drugs that he had estimated and that had not been alleged in the original indictment brought against the defendants. The *Cotton* defendants had been charged with conspiracy to distribute and to possess with intent to distribute a "detectable amount" of cocaine and cocaine base in the city of Baltimore. Under federal law, the penalty for such offenses is "not more than 20 years."[28] After the jury returned a finding of guilt, the judge made an independent finding of drug quantity (more than 500 grams of cocaine base) and then imposed enhanced penalties (up to life) as allowed under federal law. The judge's finding, the Court concluded, was based on "overwhelming and uncontroverted evidence" that the defendants "were involved in a vast drug conspiracy."

sentencing enhancements

Legislatively approved provisions that mandate longer prison terms for specific criminal offenses committed under certain circumstances (such as a murder committed because of the victim's race or a drug sale near a school) or because of an offender's past criminal record.

In the far-reaching case of *Apprendi* v. *New Jersey* (2000), however, the Supreme Court limited the fact-finding authority of state judges in sentencing decisions. The case involved Charles Apprendi, a New Jersey defendant who had pleaded guilty to unlawfully possessing a firearm—an offense that carried a prison term of 5 to 10 years under state law. Prior to imposing sentence, however, the judge found that Apprendi had fired a number of shots into the home of an African-American family living in his neighborhood. The judge further determined that Apprendi had done so to frighten the family and to convince them to move. Statements made by Apprendi, said the judge, classified the shooting as a hate crime. The judge then applied a sentencing enhancement provision under New Jersey's hate crimes statute and sentenced Apprendi to 12 years in prison—2 years beyond the 10-year maximum authorized by statute for the weapons offense to which he had confessed. Significantly, the sentence was imposed without the benefit of a jury-based fact-finding process and with the judge alone making the determination that a hate crime had taken place. In overturning the state court's finding, the Supreme Court reasoned that Apprendi's due process guarantees were violated when the judge—not a jury—made a factual determination that did not require proof beyond a reasonable doubt. In the words of the Court, "Under the Due Process Clause of the Fifth Amendment and the notice and jury trial guarantees of the Sixth Amendment, any fact (other than prior conviction) that increases the maximum penalty for a crime must be charged in an indictment, submitted to a jury, and proven beyond a reasonable doubt."

Blakely v. *Washington* (2004) built on the Court's holding in *Apprendi.* In *Blakely,* the Court ruled that no criminal sentence in *state* courts can be enhanced beyond the allowable maximum guideline for an offense unless the facts used to determine the enhanced sentence are found by a jury or the defendant waives the right to a jury or admits the facts in a guilty plea.

In 2007, in the case of *Cunningham* v. *California,* the U.S. Supreme Court found that California's determinate sentencing law (DSL) violated a defendant's right to trial by jury because it placed sentence-elevating fact finding within the province of judges. In that case, a judge following the requirements of the DSL had sentenced John Cunningham to a term of 16 years in prison based on a posttrial sentencing hearing in which he identified six aggravating factors and only one mitigating factor. Cunningham had earlier been found guilty of the continuous sexual abuse of a child younger than 14.

In 2005, in the combined cases of *United States* v. *Booker* and *United States* v. *Fanfan,* the U.S. Supreme Court turned its attention to the constitutionality of *federal* sentencing practices that used what it called "extra-verdict determinations of fact" in the application of sentencing enhancements. The combined cases raised two issues: (1) whether fact finding done by judges under federal sentencing guidelines violates the Sixth Amendment right to trial by jury and (2) if so, whether the guidelines are themselves unconstitutional. Consistent with its findings in *Blakely,* the Court found that, on the first question, defendant Freddie Booker's drug trafficking sentence had been improperly enhanced under federal sentencing guidelines on the basis of facts found solely by a judge. Under a mandatory guidelines system, the Court said, a sentence cannot be increased based on facts found by a judge that were neither admitted by the defendant nor found by a jury. Consequently, Booker's sentence was ruled unconstitutional and invalidated. On the second question, the

Ralph Howard Blakely in Grant County (Washington) Superior Court on March 22, 2005. Blakely, made famous for his role in the 2004 U.S. Supreme Court case of Blakely v. Washington, *was sentenced to 35 years in prison for plotting to have his ex-wife and daughter murdered. What did the Court rule in* Blakely v. Washington?

Court did not strike down the federal guidelines, as some thought might happen. Instead, it held that the guidelines could be taken into consideration by federal judges during sentencing but that they should no longer be regarded as mandatory. In effect, the combined decision in *Booker* and *Fanfan* made the federal sentencing guidelines merely advisory and gave federal judges wide latitude in imposing punishments. The result is that today federal judges must take the guidelines into account when sentencing, but they are no longer required to impose a sentence within the range prescribed by the guidelines.

The Court continues to clarify its decisions in the sentencing arena. In 2007, for example, in the case of *Rita* v. *United States*, the Court held that federal appeals courts hearing challenges from defendants about prison time may presume that federal criminal sentences are reasonable if they fall within U.S. sentencing guidelines.[29] Significantly, the justices wrote, that "even if the presumption increases the likelihood that the judge, not the jury, will find 'sentencing facts,' it does not violate the Sixth Amendment." Congress has been reconsidering federal sentencing law in light of *Booker*. In the meantime, some expect the federal courts to be flooded with inmates appealing their sentences.

The Federal Fair Sentencing Act

In 2010, President Barack Obama signed the federal Fair Sentencing Act (FSA) into law. The act reduced a previous disparity in the amounts of powder cocaine and crack cocaine specified by the federal sentencing guidelines and eliminated what had been a mandatory minimum sentence under federal law for simple possession of crack cocaine. As a result of the FSA, a first conviction for simple possession of any amount of crack cocaine, like simple possession of powder cocaine, is subject to a penalty range of zero to one year of imprisonment regardless of quantity.

Prior to enactment of the FSA, federal sentencing guidelines drew a strong distinction between crack and regular (or powdered) cocaine and typically led to much stiffer sentences for anyone convicted of crack possession. Because many crack users come from the African American community, the disparity in previous law resulted in a disproportionate

President Barack Obama signs the Fair Sentencing Act into law on August 3, 2010. What is the purpose of the law?

number of blacks being incarcerated for extended periods. Before passage of the FSA, blacks received longer sentences than whites, not because they received differential treatment by judges but because they comprised the large majority of those convicted of trafficking in crack cocaine.

The FSA's provisions do not apply to people who were sentenced for a federal crack offense prior to August 3, 2010. Consequently, on December 17, 2010, another bill was introduced in the U.S. House of Representatives to make the FSA's changes to federal crack cocaine sentencing laws retroactive—that is, to apply them to people who had already been sentenced for crack offenses. The new bill is called the Fair Sentencing Clarification Act (FSCA). Under FSCA, which has not yet become law, a motion for a crack sentence reduction would have to be made by the sentencing court, the Bureau of Prisons, or the defendant in order to obtain a sentence reduction for those already serving prison time.

The research arm of the U.S. Sentencing Commission estimates that 12,835 offenders in federal prisons would be eligible to receive a reduced sentence under the FSCA, should it become law.[30]

Even if the FSCA never becomes law, however, the U.S. Sentencing Commission has recognized that "in the sound discretion of the court, a reduction in the term of imprisonment may be appropriate for previously sentenced, qualified defendants."[31] The Commission also noted that "a reduced guideline range is sufficient to achieve the purposes of sentencing," but that "such a discretionary reduction does not otherwise affect the lawfulness of a previously imposed sentence, does not authorize a reduction in any other component of the sentence, and does not entitle a defendant to a reduced term of imprisonment as a matter of right."[32]

Mandatory Minimum Sentencing

Mandatory minimum sentencing refers to the imposition of sentences required by statute for those convicted of a particular crime or a particular crime with special circumstances, such as robbery with a firearm or selling drugs to a minor within 1,000 feet of a school, or for those with a particular type of criminal history. By 1994, all 50 states had enacted one or more mandatory minimum sentencing laws,[33] and Congress had enacted numerous mandatory sentencing laws for federal offenders. Mandatory minimum sentencing rationales dominated the 1980s and early 1990s.

By the start of the 21st century, many states had adopted sentence enhancements, usually mandating longer prison terms for violent offenders with records of serious crimes. Mandatory sentence enhancements aim to deter known and potentially violent offenders and to incapacitate persistent criminals through long-term incarceration.[34] Such sentence enhancements have come to be known as *three-strikes laws* (and, in some jurisdictions, *two-strikes laws*).

Three-strikes laws vary in breadth. Some stipulate that both the prior convictions and the current offense must be violent felonies; others require only that the prior felonies be violent. Some three-strikes laws count only prior adult convictions; others permit consideration of juvenile adjudications for violent crimes. Under California's three-strikes law, an offender who is convicted of a qualifying felony and has two prior qualifying felony convictions must serve a minimum of 25 years. The law also doubles prison terms for offenders convicted of a second violent felony.[35]

Rationales Mandatory sentences have two goals—deterrence and incapacitation. The primary purposes of modest mandatory prison terms

mandatory minimum sentencing
The imposition of sentences required by statute for those convicted of a particular crime or a particular crime with special circumstances, such as robbery with a firearm or selling drugs to a minor within 1,000 feet of a school, or for those with a particular type of criminal history.

Many of today's mandatory sentencing laws were passed in reaction to public outcries against especially violent or well-publicized criminal acts. Does mandatory sentencing fulfill the goals of deterrence and incapacitation?

(e.g., three years for armed robbery) are specific deterrence for already-punished offenders, and general deterrence for prospective offenders. If the law increases the imprisonment rate, it also serves the goal of incapacitation, leaving fewer offenders free to victimize the population at large. The intent of three-strikes (and even two-strikes) laws is to incapacitate selected violent offenders with very long terms—25 years or even life.

Mandatory sentencing laws have become highly politicized. By passing mandatory sentencing laws, legislators can convey that they deem certain crimes especially grave and that people who commit these crimes deserve, and can expect, harsh sanctions. Such laws typically are a rapid and visible response to public outcries following heinous or well-publicized crimes.

Impact Mandatory sentencing has had significant consequences that deserve close attention. Among them are its impact on crime and the operations of the criminal justice system. The possibility that the consequences will be different for different groups of people also bears examination.

Crime Evaluations of mandatory minimum sentencing have focused on two types of crimes—those committed with handguns and those related to drugs (the offenses most commonly subject to mandatory minimum penalties in state and federal courts). An evaluation of the Massachusetts law that imposed mandatory jail terms for possession of an unlicensed handgun concluded that the law was an effective deterrent of gun crime, at least in the short term.[36]

However, studies of similar laws in Michigan[37] and Florida[38] found no evidence that crimes committed with firearms had been prevented. An evaluation of mandatory sentence enhancements for gun use in six large cities (Detroit, Jacksonville, Tampa, Miami, Philadelphia, and Pittsburgh) indicated that the laws deterred homicide but not other violent crimes.[39] An assessment of New York's Rockefeller drug laws was unable to support their claimed efficacy in deterring drug crime in New York City.[40]

The Criminal Justice System Today's busy criminal courts rely on a high rate of guilty pleas to speed case processing and thus avoid logjams. Officials can offer inducements to defendants to enter these pleas.

At least in the short term, mandatory sentencing laws may disrupt established plea-bargaining patterns by preventing a prosecutor from offering a short prison term (less than the new minimum) in exchange for a guilty plea. However, unless policymakers enact the same mandatory sentences for several related crimes, prosecutors can usually shift strategies and bargain on charges rather than on sentences.

Most state-level two- and three-strikes laws leave judges no discretion to deviate from the sentences dictated by legislatures. Another central feature of such laws is the extraordinary length of the prison terms they require. Offenders serving life sentences in California and North Carolina under such legislation, for example, become eligible for parole only after serving 25 years, those in New Mexico after 30 years, and those in Colorado after 40 years. Three-strikes laws in some states mandate life without the possibility of parole. Two- and three-strikes laws came about in response to public concerns about crime and the growing belief that many serious offenders were being released from prison too soon.[41] Proponents view such legislation as the best way to deal with the persistent, serious violent offender—the proverbial three-time loser.

Two- and three-strikes laws are a form of **habitual offender statute.** Although habitual offender laws have been on the books in a number of jurisdictions since at least the 1940s, the older laws were often geared to specific types of prior offenses, such as crimes of violence, sex offenses, or crimes perpetrated with guns. Moreover, most early habitual offender laws allowed enhanced sentences but did not make them mandatory as do two- and three-strikes legislation.[42]

habitual offender statute
A law that (1) allows a person's criminal history to be considered at sentencing or (2) makes it possible for a person convicted of a given offense and previously convicted of another specified offense to receive a more severe penalty than that for the current offense alone.

THREE-STRIKES MODELS— WASHINGTON AND CALIFORNIA

During the last decade of the 20th century, 26 states and the federal government enacted new habitual offender laws that fell into the three-strikes category.[43] Washington State was the first of those to do so.[44] California soon followed with a considerably broader version of the three-strikes law. As those laws were being implemented, people debated the impact they would have on the criminal justice systems of those states. Proponents predicted the laws would curb crime and protect society by warehousing the worst offenders for a long time. Opponents argued that defendants facing lengthy mandatory sentences would be more likely to demand trials, slowing the processing of cases, and that more offenders would serve long terms of incarceration, causing prison populations already at crisis levels in many states to rise.[45]

Although they were enacted within months of each other amid the same "three-strikes-and-you're-out" rallying cry, and they count many of the same offenses as strikes, the Washington and California laws differ in three important ways. First, in Washington, all three strikes must be for felonies specifically listed in the legislation. Under the California law, only the first two convictions must be from the state's list of "strikeable" crimes (which include most violent offenses and many drug offenses); *any* subsequent felony can count as the third strike. Second, the California law contains a two-strikes provision, by which a person convicted of any felony after one prior conviction for a strikeable offense is to be sentenced to twice the term he or she would otherwise receive. There is no two-strikes provision in the Washington law. Third, the sanctions for a third strike differ. The Washington statute requires a life term in prison without the possibility of parole for a person convicted for the third time of any of the

I am a director and regional administrator for the state prison system, and I supervise nursing students in a locked ward with criminally insane clients. In addition, I'm a researcher for the National Commission on Correctional Health Care. The commission surveys prisons, jails, juvenile facilities, and immigration facilities all over the United States. I have directed teams in 29 states, in facilities ranging from 38 to 1,000 beds. Part of my job in prison is to consult with and transport clients to other countries, which have in the past included Spain, Portugal, Canada, Panama, and Venezuela.

I love this field and encourage students who want a challenge and a career that is interesting to give corrections, especially work with the criminally insane, a look. Every day and every interaction with our clients is different. No two days are alike, and no two situations are similar.

Dr. Roger Childers
Supervisor
Psychiatric Unit for the Criminally Insane
Bryce Hospital
Tuscaloosa, Alabama

"most serious offenses" listed in the law. In California a "third-striker" has at least the possibility of being released after 25 years.[46]

California's law came under attack for the seeming ease with which offenders who commit relatively minor crimes can be sentenced to prison for a long time. The law, however, found a powerful ally in the Supreme Court. In 2001, for example, the Ninth U.S. Circuit Court of Appeals ruled in *Andrade* v. *Attorney General of the State of California*[47] that two consecutive 25-years-to-life sentences imposed on a California man, Leandro Andrade, who was twice caught shoplifting videotapes from a Kmart, constituted cruel and unusual punishment under the Eighth Amendment to the U.S. Constitution.

On March 5, 2003, however, the U.S. Supreme Court overturned the lower court's finding and ruled that Andrade's two consecutive 25-years-to-life sentences did not violate the Eighth Amendment's proscription against cruel or unusual punishment.[48] In effect, the Court held that it is *not* cruel and unusual punishment to impose a possible life term for a conviction of a non-violent felony committed by a defendant with a history of serious or violent convictions.

In another 2003 case, *Ewing* v. *California*,[49] the U.S. Supreme Court upheld the conviction and sentence of Gary Ewing under California's three-strikes law. Ewing, who had a lengthy record of prior convictions, had received a 25-years-to-life sentence following his conviction for felony grand theft of three golf clubs. In writing for the Court, Justice Sandra Day O'Connor said that states should be able to decide when repeat offenders "must be isolated from society . . . to protect the public safety," even when nonserious crimes trigger the lengthy sentence.

In 2004, Californians voted down Proposition 66—a ballot initiative that would have changed the state's three-strikes law so that only specified serious or violent crimes could be counted as third strikes. Passage of the proposition would also have meant that only previous convictions for violent or serious felonies, brought and tried separately, would have qualified for second- and third-strike sentence increases.

California's three-strikes law remains firmly in place. In its current form, it punishes anyone who commits a third felony, regardless of its severity, with a mandatory sentence of 25-years-to-life if the first two felonies were violent or serious.

Impact on Local Courts and Jails

When three-strikes laws were first passed in Washington and California, some analysts projected a much greater impact on local criminal justice systems in California, because the California law had a much broader scope.[50]

They predicted that California courts would be overwhelmed as defendants facing enhanced penalties demanded jury trials. The added time to process cases through trials and the reluctance of courts to grant pretrial release to defendants facing long prison terms, they said, would cause jail populations to explode as the number of jail admissions and the length of jail stays grew.

Early evidence from California supported these predictions. A review of 12,600 two- and three-strikes cases from Los Angeles, for example, showed that two-strikes cases took 16 percent longer to process and three-strikes cases 41 percent longer than nonstrike cases.[51] In addition, strikes cases were three times as likely to go to trial as nonstrike felonies and four times as likely as the same types of cases before the law took effect. This effect led to a 25 percent increase in jury trials as well as an 11-percentage-point rise in the proportion of the jail population awaiting trial, from 59 percent before the law was enacted to 70 percent.

According to more recent data, however, at least some California counties have learned how to handle the changes brought about by the law. A recent survey of eight California counties with populations of more than 1 million identified several that were successfully disposing of two- and three-strikes cases early in the process.[52] In addition, data from the Los Angeles County Sheriff's Department suggest that the pace of strikes cases coming into that system may be slowing.[53]

Impact on State Prison Systems

The impact of the Washington and California laws on state corrections departments has not been as severe as projected. Planners in Washington had expected that 40 to 75 persons would be sentenced under three-strikes provisions each year. The actual numbers, however, have been much lower. During the first three years the law was in effect, only 85 offenders—not the 120 to 225 projected—were admitted to the state prison system under the three-strikes law.[54]

A similar overestimate of the impact the California law would have on prisons there was made. As of April 2009, 25 percent of the inmate population in the state of California was incarcerated under the state's three-strikes law. According to a 2010 report by the California State Auditor, the cost of housing striker inmates "for the additional years they were sentenced to under the three strikes law represents a substantial liability to the State."[55] The auditor estimated that the additional years imposed by the three-strikes law amount to $19.2 billion in additional costs over the duration of the incarceration of the state's current striker inmates. Even though the sheer number of cases affected by the law is significantly higher than that for any other state, the numbers are not as high as originally projected. Still, according to some experts, three-strikes laws may be having a real, but subtle, impact on the California prison system. Such laws, they say, funnel increasingly older persons into correctional institutions and ensure that they will remain there for a very long time.[56] The result is an inmate population that is getting older. The aging of America's inmate population, which has begun to concern policymakers across the country, is discussed in more detail in Chapter 12.

The Current Applicability of Three-Strikes Laws and Habitual Offender Statutes   According to the Washington, D.C.-based Sentencing Project, only a handful of states have convicted more than a hundred individuals using two- and three-strikes statutes—even though more than half of all states have such laws on the books. The Sentencing Project says that only Georgia, South Carolina, Nevada, Washington, and Florida are actually using three-strikes legislation "to any significant extent."[57]

Talking about CORRECTIONS

SENTENCING TRENDS

Visit *Live Talk* at **Corrections** .com (**www.justicestudies** .com/talking06) and listen to the program "Sentencing Trends," which relates to ideas discussed in this chapter.

There is also evidence of a movement away from mandatory minimum sentences in a number of jurisdictions where such sentences have been blamed for prison crowding and budgetary problems. In Louisiana, for example, where prison populations increased from 25,260 to 38,000 in the six years following the state's 1995 implementation of mandatory sentences, the legislature eliminated mandatory prison time for crimes such as residential burglary, Medicaid fraud, prostitution, theft of a firearm, and possession of small amounts of controlled substances. "This [was] an attempt to bring under control a system that was bankrupting the state and was not reducing crime," said state senator Donald R. Cravins.[58]

In similar legislative action, other states, including Connecticut, Indiana, and North Dakota, have eliminated some laws that required certain offenders to serve long prison terms without the possibility of parole. Likewise, in 2001, Mississippi passed a law establishing parole eligibility for nonviolent first-time offenders who have served only 25 percent of their sentences—reducing the figure from what had been a required 85 percent under previous law.[59]

The economic problems that have caused some states to use habitual offender statutes less frequently or to release repeat offenders early are present in almost all regions of the country. Some states, however, have moved to release nonviolent and relatively minor drug offenders in order to address budgetary shortfalls in their correctional systems but have refused to shorten the sentences of habitual felons.

ISSUES IN SENTENCING

Many sentencing reforms have been an attempt to reduce disparity in sentencing and make the process fairer. The term **fair sentencing**, or *fairness in sentencing*, has become popular in recent years. Although fair sentencing today often refers to fairness for *victims*, many suggest that any truly fair sentencing scheme must incorporate fairness for both victims and offenders. These are the issues related to fairness in sentencing:

- proportionality;
- equity;
- social debt; and
- truth in sentencing.

fair sentencing

Sentencing practices that incorporate fairness for both victims and offenders. *Fairness* is said to be achieved by implementing principles of proportionality, equity, social debt, and truth in sentencing.

Proportionality

Proportionality is the sentencing principle that the severity of punishment should match the seriousness of the crime for which the sentence is imposed. To most people today, the death penalty would seem grossly disproportional to the offense of larceny—even if the offender had a history of such violations. However, this was not always the case. Larceny *was* punishable by death in medieval England. On the other hand, probation would seem disproportional to the crime of murder—although it is occasionally imposed in homicide cases.

proportionality

The sentencing principle that the severity of punishment should match the seriousness of the crime for which the sentence is imposed.

Equity

Equity is the sentencing principle that similar crimes and similar criminals should be treated alike. The alternative to equity is *disparity,* in which similar crimes are associated with different punishments in different jurisdictions or in which offenders with similar criminal histories receive

equity

The sentencing principle that similar crimes and similar criminals should be treated alike.

widely differing sentences. Disparity can also result from judicial discretion when judges hold widely different sentencing philosophies. In a jurisdiction with wide leeway for judges to determine sentences, one judge might treat offenders very harshly while another may be lenient. Under such circumstances, now largely eliminated by sentencing reform, one burglar, for example, might receive a sentence of 30 years in prison upon conviction, but his partner in crime is merely put on probation simply because he appears before a more lenient judge.

Recently, racial and ethnic disparities have become the focus of concern in the sentencing practices of a number of states.[60] In 2008, for example, Connecticut and Iowa both passed legislation requiring minority impact statements to be included in any legislation that changes the current criminal penalty structure.[61] The statements are intended to assess the potential impact of criminal justice-related legislation on racial and ethnic minorities prior to passage. Also in 1988, the Illinois general assembly enacted Senate Bill 2476, which created the Commission to Study Disproportionate Justice Impact. The Committee is charged with studying the degree to which the criminal sentencing structure in Illinois disproportionately affects communities of color.

Wayne Ford, an Iowa state representative, authored that state's Minority Impact Statement Bill and told reporters, "I believe that we need to be tough on crime, but we must also make sure that our laws are fair and equitable."[62] Ford initiated the legislation after the release of a 2007 report by the Washington, D.C.–based Sentencing Project entitled *Uneven Justice: State Rates of Incarceration by Race and Ethnicity*. The report revealed that Iowa imprisons blacks at a rate 13 times that of whites—more than double the national average.

Social Debt

Social debt is the sentencing principle that the severity of punishment should take into account the offender's prior criminal behavior. As we have seen, a number of laws designed to recognize social debt have recently been passed. Among them are three-strikes and two-strikes laws. Although there is considerable variation in such laws among states, the primary characteristic of these laws is that they "call for enhanced penalties for offenders with one or more prior felony convictions."[63] They require a repeat offender to serve several years in prison in addition to the penalty imposed for the current offense.

social debt
The sentencing principle that the severity of punishment should take into account the offender's prior criminal behavior.

Truth in Sentencing

Until the sentencing reforms of the 1970s, the laws of many states enabled convicted offenders to be released from prison long before they had served their full sentences. Inmates frequently had *good time* deducted from their sentences or time off for good behavior. *Gain time* could be earned for going to school, learning a trade, or doing volunteer work. Moreover, many states mandated routine parole eligibility after inmates had served one-quarter or even one-fifth of their sentences.

Recent truth-in-sentencing laws have changed such practices by requiring offenders to complete sentences very close to the ones they are given. **Truth in sentencing** requires an offender to serve a substantial portion of the sentence and reduces the discrepancy between the sentence imposed and actual time spent in prison (see Exhibit 3–7). The Violent Crime Control and Law Enforcement Act of 1994 includes a truth-in-sentencing

truth in sentencing
The sentencing principle that requires an offender to serve a substantial portion of the sentence and reduces the discrepancy between the sentence imposed and actual time spent in prison.

EXHIBIT 3–7   Average Prison Time Served Compared with Court Sentence in Florida, 1998–2009

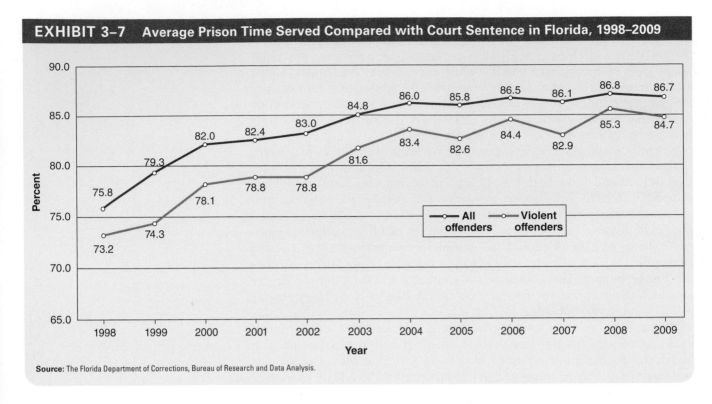

Source: The Florida Department of Corrections, Bureau of Research and Data Analysis.

provision. To qualify for federal aid under the act, a state must amend its laws so that an imprisoned offender serves at least 85 percent of his or her sentence before being released. Parole eligibility and good-time credits are generally restricted or eliminated in truth-in-sentencing laws.

By 1998, 27 states and the District of Columbia had met the 85 percent federal truth-in-sentencing requirement. Another 13 states had adopted truth-in-sentencing laws requiring certain offenders to serve a specified portion of their sentences.[64] Three states—Idaho, Nevada, and New Hampshire—require inmates to serve 100 percent of the minimum sentence they receive before they become eligible for release.

Broader Issues

Today's two main sentencing initiatives—guideline-based determinate sentencing and restorative justice—represent different attempts to achieve sentencing fairness. The two, however, appear to be inherently at odds with one another. That is because determinate sentencing requires a top-down approach in which an authoritative decision-making body imposes strict limits on the sentencing process, whereas restorative justice emphasizes community involvement at the grassroots level. "All this," say some experts, "suggests that, at its philosophical core, restorative justice appears to be incompatible with sentencing guidelines."[65]

One way of addressing the differences between these two approaches would be to seek greater community involvement in the development of sentencing guidelines. In fact, many states have encouraged local participation in the guideline-development process. Similarly, some guideline states encourage the use of local sentencing options such as community-based sanctions (which are discussed in more detail in Chapters 4 and 5). For example, North Carolina, a guideline state, assigns county officials the responsibility for developing and recommending local community sentencing options for certain categories of offenders.

Still, community sentencing may be appropriate only for relatively minor offenders, and traditional grid-based guidelines offer little leeway for sentencing offenders convicted of serious crimes. Some authors have suggested creation of a hybrid system of "restorative sentencing guidelines" to resolve the problem. Under the system, a new restorative sentencing option would be created and made applicable to less serious offenders. For such offenders, the traditional guideline grid, based on severity of offense and prior record, would not apply.

REVIEW AND APPLICATIONS

SUMMARY

1 The philosophy underlying criminal sentencing is that people must be held accountable for their actions and the harm they cause. Western society has a long tradition of sentencing criminal offenders to some form of punishment. Many social scientists suggest that the central purpose of criminal punishment is to maintain social order.

2 The goals of criminal sentencing today are (1) revenge, (2) retribution, (3) just deserts, (4) deterrence, (5) incapacitation, (6) rehabilitation or reformation, and (7) restoration.

3 Sentencing options in use today include fines and other monetary sanctions, probation, alternative or intermediate sentences, incarceration, and capital punishment.

4 A model of criminal sentencing is a strategy or system for imposing criminal sanctions. Sentencing models vary widely among the jurisdictions in the United States. These models include indeterminate sentences, determinate sentences, voluntary or advisory sentencing guidelines, presumptive sentencing guidelines, and mandatory minimum sentencing.

5 Recent laws have increased penalties for criminal offenses, particularly violent crimes, and for repeat offenders. Many such laws are three-strikes laws. The rationale for such laws is simple: Offenders convicted repeatedly of serious offenses should be removed from society for long periods of time. Many three-strikes laws mandate a life sentence for the third violent felony conviction. Analysts of three-strikes laws predicted that courts would be overwhelmed as more defendants, facing enhanced penalties, demanded jury trials. The added time to process cases and the reluctance to grant pretrial release to defendants facing long prison terms, said analysts, would cause jail populations to explode as the number of admissions and the length of jail stays grew. The actual effects of the laws have been similar to the effects predicted but to a lesser extent.

6 *Fair sentencing* often refers to fairness for *victims*. Fair-sentencing advocates, however, suggest that any truly fair sentencing scheme must incorporate fairness for both victims and offenders. Issues related to fairness in sentencing are proportionality, equity, social debt, and truth in sentencing.

KEY TERMS

sentencing, p. 57
sentence, p. 57
social order, p. 58
revenge, p. 59
retribution, p. 60
just deserts, p. 60

deterrence, p. 60
specific deterrence, p. 60
general deterrence, p. 60
pleasure-pain principle, p. 61
incapacitation, p. 61
correctional econometrics, p. 62

rehabilitation, p. 63
reintegration, p. 63
restoration, p. 64
restorative justice, p. 64
victim-impact statement, p. 65
restitution, p. 68

QUESTIONS FOR REVIEW

1 Define *sentencing,* describe sentencing philosophy, and name the central purpose of criminal punishment.

2 What are the seven goals of criminal sentencing?

3 What are the major sentencing options in wide use in the United States today?

4 What is a sentencing *model*? How have American models of criminal sentencing changed over the past 100 years?

5 What are three-strikes (and two-strikes) laws? What consequences might three-strikes (and two-strikes) laws have for the criminal justice system and for the corrections subsystem?

6 What is fair sentencing? What are some of the major issues relating to fair sentencing today?

THINKING CRITICALLY ABOUT CORRECTIONS

Rehabilitation

Edgardo Rotman says, in *Beyond Punishment,* "Rehabilitation . . . can be defined tentatively and broadly as a right to an opportunity to return to (or remain in) society with an improved chance of being a useful citizen and staying out of prison."[66] Do you agree that offenders have a right to rehabilitation? Why or why not?

Mandatory Sentencing

Mandatory sentencing laws for drug possession offenses were initially hailed as the best method for toughening the government's response to the growing drug problem. Critics now complain that, in practice, mandatory sentencing rules lead to excessive punishments for many low-level offenders and to unwarranted leniency for the high-volume dealers who were the original targets of the new laws.

Furthermore, critics contend that plea bargaining is the culprit. Faced with lengthy prison terms, many arrested big-time dealers readily provide the names of numerous "little fish" in the drug distribution chain to prosecutors who are too quick to abandon prosecution of a single high-volume dealer in favor of procuring numerous convictions of low-level dealers.

Should mandatory sentencing laws be amended to prohibit plea bargaining in cases in which the accused is charged with trafficking in quantities exceeding an established volume?

In view of the dramatic impact mandatory sentencing has had on prison population growth, should the sentences of current inmates be reviewed with an eye toward reducing, appropriately, the sentences of the previously mentioned little fish?

ON-THE-JOB DECISION MAKING

Recidivism

You have spent the past six years as a counselor at a minimum-security state correctional facility. Your effectiveness has earned you a strong reputation throughout the Department of Corrections as a specialist in prerelease counseling, a program designed to prepare inmates for their return to society upon parole or completion of their sentence.

Lately, a series of highly publicized violent crimes has been committed by former inmates of the state's super-maximum-security facility. All were released recently upon completion of their sentences, and all had moved almost directly from their cell back to the criminal lifestyle that originally landed them in prison.

Hard-line correctional officers insist that because those incarcerated in the "supermax" are the worst of the worst, they cannot be trusted to behave during prerelease counseling. The safety risks such inmates represent, they say, make leaving them in their cells until the law requires they be set free the only sensible course of action. What happens after that, in the hard-liners' opinions, is both the decision and responsibility of the former inmate.

Reformers insist that immediate recidivism is the likely outcome of releasing inmates directly from a harsh, totally controlled lockdown environment. They call for significant transitional counseling as essential for helping inmates adjust to free society and also for defusing their angry urge to make society pay for the harsh life from which they are being released.

Both the governor and the commissioner of corrections face daily media demands to explain what the administration is going to do about this problem. In particular, the governor is under the gun because his opponent in the upcoming and hotly contested gubernatorial race has seized on this as an issue that demonstrates "this governor's inability, or unwillingness, to take the tough steps necessary to protect the good citizens of our state."

You have been asked to speak at a meeting to develop potential courses of action to address this problem. The meeting will be chaired by the corrections commissioner, and various wardens, assistant wardens, and senior correctional specialists from throughout the state will attend. It is likely but not yet confirmed that the governor will also attend.

1. What issues will you address?
2. How might you resolve the conflict between the need to protect counselors and staff from the often violent behavior of supermax inmates and the need to provide this critical prerelease counseling to these troubled inmates?
3. How would you respond to hard-line corrections officers who contend that what happens after release is not their problem?

For additional information, please see: www.mhhe.com/schmalleger6e

Institutional Corrections

Part Three examines jail, prison, and parole.

These three correctional components account for 3.2 million offenders daily.

How much have jail inmates, facilities, and staff changed since the country's first jail officially opened in Philadelphia in 1773? As you will learn, many of today's jails are large and some are quickly adapting high technology to their purposes. Even though only 6 percent of the nation's 3,365 locally operated jails are "mega" jails (having 1,000 or more cells), they hold

50 percent of the jail population. And why is it that with only 94 percent of all jail capacity occupied nationwide, jail staff perceive that jails are overcrowded? Staffing has not kept up with the increase in the jail population. Are privatization and accreditation solutions? You will decide.

Prisons also first developed in Pennsylvania. In 1790, a wing of the Walnut Street Jail was devoted to long-term incarceration and served as a model for the world's first prison, the Eastern State Penitentiary, in 1829. The architecture of jails and prisons changed over the years from linear to podular. Prisoner supervision approaches also changed, from indirect to direct. Regardless of all

the changes, overcrowding remains a problem.

Each day, almost 2,000 people will leave prison. How prepared are they to reenter society? Did they receive the educational and vocational preparation and drug treatment they need to minimize their likelihood of reoffending? Unfortunately, probably not. Prisons simply do not have the resources to rehabilitate all inmates under their care. The federal Second Chance Act, passed by Congress in 2008, now hopes to help offenders make successful transitions from prison or jail back to the community by providing employment assistance, substance abuse treatment, housing, family programming, mentoring, victim support, and other services to reduce reoffending and violations of probation and parole.

[6] JAILS

Way Stations Along the Justice Highway

> *Informed people know that jails today have become the biggest mental hospitals in the United States with the largest three being Los Angeles County Jail system, number one, New York City Department of Corrections, number two, and Cook County Department of Corrections, Chicago, number three. Many of these inmates with mental health problems also have an addiction to alcohol/drugs, what people today refer to as co-occurring disorders.*
>
> —Ken Kerle, former managing editor of *American Jails*

When it comes to downsizing, former Detroit Mayor Kwame Kilpatrick didn't think he'd be going from his swanky 4,000-square foot mansion at 9240 Dwight Street in the Berry Subdivision Historic District to a bare-bones 150-square-foot cell at the Wayne County Jail at 570 Clinton Street.[1] But on Tuesday, October 28, 2008, Kilpatrick was sentenced to serve two concurrent four-month jail sentences at the Wayne County Jail for his part in a sex-and-text-message scandal. Judge David Groner also ordered Kilpatrick to pay the city of Detroit $1 million over a five-year probationary period. Kilpatrick cannot run for elected office during his probation. He also loses his license to practice law and forfeits his mayor's pension.

Kilpatrick pleaded guilty to obstruction of justice, admitting he lied during a civil trial to conceal an extramarital affair with his chief of staff, Christine Beatty, and he pleaded no contest, acknowledging that he shoved and cursed police officers who were at his sister's home trying to serve a subpoena to one of his friends.

In court he said, "I lied under oath in the case of Gary Brown and Harold Nelthrope [two former Detroit police officers who in 2003 filed a civil lawsuit claiming they were fired for investigating reports of misconduct by two of Kilpatrick's former bodyguards] (. . .) I did so with an intent to mislead the court and jury and to impede and obstruct the fair administration of justice." He went on to say that he lied under oath twice more. It was during those court proceedings in 2003 that one of the officers revealed Kilpatrick's affair with Christine Beatty.

Kilpatrick had to give up his diamond-studded earrings, custom-tailored flashy suits, monogrammed shirt cuffs, spa treatments, and Las Vegas hotels and restaurants. In jail he wore a hand-me-down green jumpsuit, ate boxed lunches of what some call "mystery meat," and lived in cell 14J-4 with stained walls, slight water pressure, and three small, barred windows—definitely not the walls of bowed, arched, and leaded glass that he enjoyed at the mayor's mansion that opened onto a spectacular view of the mansion's grounds and the Detroit River. His new accommodations cost the Wayne County taxpayers $115 a night, a far cry from what Kilpatrick was used to spending in hotels in Las Vegas.

Kilpatrick served 99 days at the Wayne County Jail after receiving good time. But his freedom did not last long. On May 25, 2010, Kilpatrick was sentenced to 18 months to 5 years in prison for hiding assets from the court in order to avoid making payments on his $1 million court-ordered restitution. On June 23, 2010, federal prosecutors also indicted Kilpatrick on 19 additional counts of mail and wire fraud, filing false tax returns, and income tax invasion. If found guilty on the new charges, Kilpatrick faces an additional 28 years in prison.

In 2002, at age 31, Kwame Kilpatrick was the youngest person ever elected mayor of Detroit, the country's 11th largest city. However, in 2008, Kilpatrick resigned his office as part of a plea agreement to two felonies for obstruction of justice and was sentenced to serve two concurrent four-month jail sentences at the Wayne County Jail followed by five years on probation. During his probationary period, he has to pay the city of Detroit $1 million and he cannot run for elected office. He also lost his license to practice law and forfeited his mayor's pension. For Kilpatrick and the other 837,833 women and men in jail today, what is the purpose of jail?

Kilpatrick's story isn't much different from the thousands of men and women who enter our nation's jails each day, many with substance addictions. Most are not as educated or politically and economically fortunate, but the offense similarities are surprising. As you'll read in this chapter, jails are often disparaged in corrections, but in many places, that image is changing. Today's jails have opportunities that were unheard of just a decade ago. Citizen advocates, community linkages, judicial oversight, and jail professionalism are changing the ways jails are operating. These windows of opportunity can leverage jails to successfully perform their functions.

PURPOSE OF JAILS

jails

Locally operated correctional facilities that confine people before or after conviction.

total admission

The total number of people admitted to jail each year.

average daily population (ADP)

Sum of the number of inmates in a jail or prison each day for a year, divided by the total number of days in the year.

Except for six states that run combined jail/prison systems (Alaska, Connecticut, Delaware, Hawaii, Rhode Island, and Vermont), **jails** are locally operated correctional facilities that confine people before or after conviction. Jails are different from prisons (the subject of Chapter 7) in a number of ways that you will learn about as you read. The fundamental difference between jail and prison is the nature of their populations.[2]

Total admission is the total number of persons admitted to jail each year, which falls between 10 million and 13 million. That translates into about 34,000 people released from jails each day, and about 238,000 released each week.

The **average daily population (ADP)**, on the other hand, is the sum of the number of inmates in a jail or prison each day for a year divided by the total number of days in the year. Jail ADP at midyear 2009 was 767,992. Prison total admission is currently estimated at 730,860 a year, and prison ADP on January 1, 2010, was 1,613,740 adults (see Chapter 7). The *daily* population of jails is lower than that of prisons, but the *annual* total of people incarcerated in jails is higher. Put another way, it takes almost two years for the nation's state and federal prison population to turn over once; the jail population turns over almost 17 times each year. The jail population is, thus, dynamic, and the prison population is static. The changing nature of jail populations raises significant issues and problems that form the core of this chapter.

On June 30, 2009, local jail authorities held or supervised 848,826 offenders, an increase of 2.4 percent from midyear 2008.[3] Jail authorities supervised approximately 8.3 percent of these offenders (70,213) in alternative programs outside jail facilities (see Exhibit 6–7). A total of 767,620 were housed in local jails.

Inmates sentenced to jail usually have a sentence of 1 year or less. Seventy percent are released within 3 days; however, an estimated 20 percent will spend at least 1 month, 12 percent at least 2 months, and 4 percent will spend more than 6 months.[4]

At midyear 2009, the majority of the nation's jail population (62 percent—an all-time high for the third year in a row) was pretrial detainees.

Jails also incarcerate persons in a wide variety of other categories. Jails are used to do the following:

- Receive persons awaiting court action on their current charge.
- Readmit probation and parole violators and bail-bond absconders.

- Detain juveniles until custody is transferred to juvenile authorities.
- Hold persons with mental illness until they are moved to appropriate health facilities.
- Hold individuals for the military.
- Provide protective custody.
- Confine persons found in contempt.
- Hold witnesses for the courts.
- Hold inmates about to be released after completing a prison sentence.
- Transfer inmates to federal, state, or other authorities.
- House inmates for federal, state, or other authorities because of crowding of their facilities.
- Operate some community-based programs as alternatives to incarceration.
- Hold inmates sentenced to short terms (generally under one year) of incarceration.

Almost 40 percent of the nation's jails like the one pictured are small (less than 50 cells), holding only 3 percent of the jail population. Most small jails were built in the early part of the 20th century. What management style does this jail suggest?

For all their important roles and responsibilities, jails have been a disgrace to every generation.[5] Many of the nation's 3,365 locally operated jails are old, overcrowded, poorly funded, scantily staffed by underpaid and poorly trained employees, and given low priority in local budgets. Yet a strong groundswell of support is rising for the nation's jails. Tomorrow's jail professionals have tremendous opportunities to continue that momentum. Progress is being made because of new emphases on jail education, staff selection and training, professional associations, standards, technology, accountability, and laws, among other things. Groups such as the American Jail Association (AJA) are advancing jail professionalism through training, information exchange, technical assistance, publications, and conferences. Members of the AJA include sheriffs, jail administrators, judges, attorneys, educators, correctional staff, jail inspection officials, health care providers, and clergy. The AJA mission statement is shown in Exhibit 6–1. This chapter will explore the problems of jails of the past and present and discuss direction for the 21st century.

JAILS IN HISTORY

It is believed that King Henry II of England ordered the first jail built, in 1166. The purpose of that jail was to detain offenders until they could be brought before a court, tried, and sentenced. From that beginning, jails spread throughout Europe but changed in scope and size over time.

With the development of workhouses and poorhouses in the 15th and 16th centuries in England, sheriffs took on the added responsibility of supervising vagrants, the poor, and the mentally ill. These institutions, despite their distinct names, were indistinguishable from jails. Their squalid, unhealthy conditions and the sheriffs' practice of demanding money from persons under their charge caught the attention of 18th-century Enlightenment reformers. One such reformer was the English sheriff John Howard. In 1779, England's Parliament passed the four jail reforms that Howard proposed: secure and sanitary structures, jail inspections, elimination of

I've been on the job 21 years, and it's been wonderful—it's been an excellent career. I would tell anybody to step into it. It's so rewarding—it can be so stressful, but there are so many rewards. I'm a hands-on person; I enjoy working with people. We don't always see people coming into jail pretty—you see them at their lowest—and if you can help that person to move up, I guess that's where the reward comes in.

Prior to this, I worked at the state hospital, so I worked with the mentally challenged and the handicapped. Then I had my second child and went into day care, and I baby-sat the sheriff's grandson. I always told him, "If there's ever an opening, keep me in mind," so I went for an interview and got a position.

I have never been afraid of my position; I've never been afraid of working with individuals. I've had a wonderful captain—he always trained in the adage "Treat them as you'd like to be treated if you were behind bars." I've always used that as my outlook with the individuals that I come into contact with here. You never know; you could be falsely charged with something—it could be you behind bars.

People in the community do not know what it is like to be locked up. And in a sense, I'm locked up for eight hours a day, or if I have to stay longer. When we work the floor, we're basically prisoners too. We don't realize what it's like for somebody to be away from their family—sure, they've messed up. But if we can give them a TV or send them to a GED class or a religious class, that is taking their minds off of thoughts of suicide, thoughts of "I'm worthless." I've been through I don't know how many attempted suicides, and it's not a pretty sight. You have to step into a prisoner's eyes and see where they're at but not step down to their level.

Some people say that we're just glorified babysitters, but if you feel that way, you're in the wrong position. We're not here to find these people guilty—we're here to meet their needs while they're incarcerated.

Right now I'm in charge of the transport area—I deal a lot with probation and courts and see to it that people are transported to where they need to be. So I've got to keep the rapport good and open with probation and the court. That's one area that I really work hard at. But my work ethic is maybe different than some—because when I'm here, I'll do whatever I can to help anybody out. I love my job, and you don't hear too many people say that after so many years. You can always find something good in a person.

Terrie Butterfield
Sergeant
Kandiyohi County Jail
Willmar, Minnesota

EXHIBIT 6–1   American Jail Association

Mission Statement

To band together all those concerned with or interested in the custody and care of persons awaiting trial, serving sentences, or otherwise locally confined; to improve the conditions and systems under which such persons are detained.

To advance professionalism through training, information exchange, technical assistance, publications, and conferences.

To provide leadership in the development of professional standards, pertinent legislation, management practices, programs, and services.

To present and advance the interests, needs, concerns, and proficiency of the profession as deemed appropriate by the membership and their representatives.

Copyright © American Jail Association.

---

fees, and an emphasis on reforming prisoners. To this day, the John Howard Association and *Howard Journal* carry Howard's ideas forward.

First Jail in the United States

The first jail in the United States was the Walnut Street Jail in Philadelphia, built in 1773. The jail housed offenders without regard to sex, age, or offense. Following the jail's opening, conditions quickly deteriorated. According to some, the jail became a "promiscuous scene of unrestricted

The Walnut Street Jail, started in Philadelphia in 1773, originally housed offenders without regard to sex, age, or offense. Following its redesignation as a penitentiary in 1790, it housed only convicted felons. Which religious group's principles influenced correctional institutions in Pennsylvania?

intercourse, universal riot, and debauchery."[6] The Philadelphia Quakers had wanted the Walnut Street Jail to be a place where inmates reformed themselves through reflection and remorse.

In 1790 the Philadelphia Society for Alleviating the Miseries of Public Prisons and the General Assembly of Pennsylvania designated a wing of the Walnut Street Jail a penitentiary. Implementing Quaker beliefs, the penitentiary emphasized prisoner reform through reflection and penitence and rehabilitation through good conduct. Sixteen solitary cells were added to the facility and workshops were built. Alcohol and prostitution were prohibited; prisoners were segregated by sex, age, and offense; diets were monitored; guardians were appointed to care for minors; and religious, health care, and educational services were provided. Debtors were housed separately from the general inmate population and had no such privileges. Their prison conditions were pitiful, and many debtors starved.[7]

In 1798 a fire destroyed the workshops at Walnut Street. The destruction brought about disillusionment and idleness. Rising costs crippled the jail's budget. Disciplinary problems rose with overcrowding, and escape and violence increased. The number of inmates who were destitute vagrants or debtors soared as did the incidence of disease. There were political conflicts between the religious Quakers and the non-Quaker prison board members. Prisoners rioted on March 27, 1820, and on October 5, 1835, the Walnut Street Jail closed. State prisoners were transferred to the new Eastern State Penitentiary in Philadelphia, the first institution of its kind in the world (see Chapter 7). County inmates and those awaiting trial were transferred to a new county jail.

By the close of the 19th century, most cities across the United States had jails to hold persons awaiting trial and to punish convicted felons. The sheriff became the person in charge of the jail. As crime increased and urban centers expanded, jails grew in importance, as did the sheriffs' control over jails.

United States Jails in the 20th Century

On any given day, America's jails serve a variety of functions. They detain people awaiting arraignment or trial, 62 percent at midyear 2009. They confine offenders serving short sentences for less serious offenses. Jails also serve as surrogate mental hospitals, a topic we return to later in this chapter and in Chapter 12. They frequently detain people with drug or alcohol dependency. They are the first stop on the social services highway for the homeless, street people, and some with extremely poor physical health, especially those with HIV, AIDS, and tuberculosis (TB). We expand on the characteristics of today's jail population later in this chapter.

Some historians refer to America's jails as the "poorhouse of the twentieth century," the dumping grounds for society's problems.[8] Jails in 20th-century America evolved into institutions of social control not only for people who committed criminal acts but also for those who made up the underclass in American society.

rabble management

Control of people whose noncriminal behavior is offensive to their communities.

John Irwin, former California prison inmate turned college professor, called the purpose of jails **rabble management;** that is, the control of persons whose noncriminal behavior is offensive to their communities.[9] They are not the offenders we are afraid of. They are the ones we are mad at, and for them there are other alternatives such as the intermediate sanctions discussed in the previous chapter.

The central purpose of the 20th-century jail was to detain the most disconnected and disreputable persons who were arrested more because they were offensive than because they had committed crimes. They were individuals of whom all were aware yet whom society ignored: public nuisances, derelicts, junkies, drunks, vagrants, the mentally ill, and street people. One study in Las Vegas, Nevada, found that most jail inmates were incarcerated not because of their threat to society, but for their inability to post bail and pay fines, essentially making the jail a poorhouse.[10]

Therefore, the purpose of America's 20th-century jails must be understood in relation to the composition of the jail population. Jails not only confined people before and after conviction but also held those who did not fit into the mainstream of American society. Moreover, because jails housed society's outcasts, there was no incentive to improve jail conditions. Today, good business practices are driving the design and operation of well-run facilities.

Architecture and Inmate Management

In an attempt to better manage and control inmate behavior, jails have progressed through four phases of architectural design. Each design is based on a particular philosophy of inmate management and control.

first-generation jail

Jail with multiple-occupancy cells or dormitories that line corridors arranged like spokes. Inmate supervision is intermittent; staff must patrol the corridors to observe inmates in their cells.

First-Generation Jails First-generation jails were built in a linear design that dates back to the 18th century, when prison and jail design was shifting from single-cell and religious emphasis to congregate housing and secular administration (more on the history of correctional architecture is presented in Chapter 7).

In a typical **first-generation jail,** inmates live in multiple-occupancy cells or dormitories. The cells line corridors that are arranged like spokes. Inmate supervision is sporadic or intermittent; staff must patrol the corridors to observe inmates in their cells. Contact between jailers and inmates is minimal unless there is an incident to which jailers must react (see Exhibit 6–2).

The design of such linear jails reflects the assumption that inmates are violent and destructive and will assault staff, destroy jail property, and try to escape. The facility is designed to prevent these behaviors. Heavy metal bars separate staff from inmates. Reinforced metal beds, sinks, and toilets

EXHIBIT 6–2 First-Generation Jail—Intermittent Surveillance

Cells line corridors in first-generation jails. Unable to observe all inmate housing areas from one location, prison and jail staff must patrol inmates' living areas to provide surveillance. What are the consequences of first-generation jails?

are bolted to the ground or wall. Reinforced concrete and razor wire surround the facility.

The biggest problem with first-generation jails is the inability of an officer to see what is going on in more than one or two cells at a time. That limitation gave rise to the second-generation jails of the 1960s.

Second-Generation Jails Second-generation jails emerged in the 1960s to replace old, run-down linear jails and provide officers the opportunity to observe as much of the housing area as possible from a single vantage point.

Second-generation jails adopted a different philosophical approach to construction and inmate management. In a **second-generation jail**, staff remain in a secure control booth overlooking inmate housing areas, called *pods* (see Exhibit 6–3). Although visual surveillance increases in such jails, surveillance is remote, and verbal interaction with inmates is even less frequent than in first-generation jails. Property destruction is minimized because steel and cement continue to define the living areas. Outside, fences and razor wire continue to discourage escapes as well as unauthorized entry. Second-generation jails have been termed *podular remote-supervision facilities.*

Although staff can observe activity in common areas, or *dayrooms,* they are unable to respond quickly to problems or even to interact effectively with inmates because of the intervening security control booth. In both the first- and second-generation jails, the biggest problem is that staff and inmates are separated. As David Parrish, former detention commander for the Hillsborough County Sheriff's Department (Tampa, Florida) put it, "Staff managed the hallways and control rooms, generally about 10 percent of the facility, while inmates ran the housing areas, roughly 90 percent."[11]

Third-Generation Jails **Third-generation jails,** also known as *direct-supervision jails,* emerged in 1974 when the Federal Bureau of Prisons opened three Metropolitan Correctional Centers (MCCs) in New York, Chicago, and San Diego. These three federal facilities were the first

second-generation jail

Jail where staff remain in a secure control booth surrounded by inmate housing areas called *pods* and surveillance is remote.

third-generation jail (also *direct-supervision jail*)

A jail where inmates are housed in small groups, or pods, staffed 24 hours a day by specially trained officers. Officers interact with inmates to help change behavior. Bars and metal doors are absent, reducing noise and dehumanization.

EXHIBIT 6–3 **Second-Generation Jail—Remote Surveillance**

Inmate living areas are divided into pods, or modules, in which cells are clustered around dayrooms that are under remote observation by staff in a secure control room. What are the consequences of second-generation jails?

jails planned and designed to be operated under the principles of unit management, which later became known as *direct supervision* (see Exhibit 6–4 for a list of the nine principles of direct supervision). The housing unit design of such jails is podular. Inmates' cells are arranged around a common area, or dayroom. There is no secure control booth for the supervising officer, and there are no physical barriers between the officer and the inmates. Direct supervision places a single deputy directly in a "housing pod" with between 32 and 64 inmates. The officer may have a desk or table for paperwork, but it is in the open dayroom area.

In a third-generation jail, the inmate management style is direct supervision. An officer is stationed in the pod with the inmates, much like a teacher in a classroom. The officer moves about the pod and interacts with the inmates to manage their behavior. Advocates of direct supervision tell us that when correctional officers are in constant and direct contact with inmates, they get to know them and can recognize and respond to trouble before it escalates into violence.

The pod contains sleeping areas, dayroom space, all necessary personal hygiene fixtures, and sufficient tables and seats to accommodate

EXHIBIT 6–4 **Nine Principles of Direct Supervision**

1. *Effective control:* The unit officer is the secure perimeter.
2. *Effective supervision:* Continuous supervision is maintained by the unit officers.
3. *Competent staff:* Correctional standards guide recruitment.
4. *Staff and inmate safety:* Performance-based data are collected.
5. *Manageable and cost-effective operations:* There are more architectural choices, commercial-grade furnishings, and equipment options.
6. *Effective communication:* Direct communication exists between inmates and officers, officers and supervisors.
7. *Classification and orientation:* Know with whom you are dealing; intense supervision is maintained for the first 12 to 72 hours.
8. *Justice and fairness:* Unit officers exercise primary informal discipline.
9. *Ownership of operations:* Inmate policy decisions are guided by a team approach.

EXHIBIT 6–5   Third-Generation Jail—Direct Supervision

Cells are grouped in housing units, or pods. Each pod has a central dayroom. Prison staff are stationed inside the housing unit to encourage direct interaction between inmates and staff. What are the consequences of direct-supervision jails?

unit capacity. Officers are not separated from inmates by a physical barrier. Officers provide frequent, nonscheduled observation of and personal interaction with inmates (see Exhibit 6–5). Due to the close contact, officers are expected to detect signs of tension between inmates and defuse the situation by either talking with inmates or by restricting privileges. They do this by using their communication skills training to maintain a nonviolent environment. Furnishings are used to reduce inmate stress caused by crowding, excessive noise, lack of privacy, and isolation from the outside world. Bars and metal doors are absent, reducing noise and the dehumanization common in first- and second-generation jails.

Direct-supervision jails facilitate staff movement, interaction with inmates, and control and leadership over pods. By supervising inmate activities directly, the staff can help change inmate behavior patterns rather than simply react to them. Staff control inmate behavior through the enforcement of boundaries of acceptable behavior and the administration of consequences for violating the boundaries. Observing unacceptable behavior and administering consequences is less likely to occur in first- and second-generation jails where staff supervision is sporadic and remote.

Some researchers tell us that pods and direct supervision provide a safer and more positive environment for inmates and staff than do first- and second-generation jails.[12] But other researchers have found few differences between the perceptions of officers in new generation versus traditional facilities.[13] In one study, new generation officers were no more satisfied with their jobs, did not feel more connected to their coworkers, did not believe communication was improved, did not feel any greater sense of personal involvement in their work, and were just as likely to see their jobs as monotonous and routine as officers working in the more traditional facility. Possible reasons for the lack of difference include the short history of direct supervision, little supporting data, and the belief among sheriffs and jail administrators that direct-supervision facilities are not as "safe" or "strong" as remote-supervision facilities because of distance and physical separation from inmates.[14] Simply put, many agencies are not comfortable removing the "barriers" between "us and them."

The first direct-supervision county jail in the United States was the Martinez Detention Facility in Contra Costa, California. It opened in

Talking about CORRECTIONS

DIRECT SUPERVISION: CHANGING THE FACE OF JAIL DESIGN

Visit *Live Talk* at **Corrections .com (www.justicestudies .com/talking06)** and listen to the program, "Direct Supervision: Changing the Face of Jail Design," which relates to ideas discussed in this chapter.

January 1981. Today, an estimated 349 of the 3,365 local jails use direct supervision, but as one researcher has asked, "Are they really direct-supervision jails?"[15] After receiving surveys from half of the direct-supervision jails, Christine Tartaro, professor of criminal justice at the Richard Stockton College of New Jersey, found that while many jails are being called direct supervision, few of them truly are. Only 40 percent said their facilities operate under a unit management structure, and few offered any inmate services other than recreation on the pod. The majority operated under traditional centralized management and a few used elements of both. Tartaro also found that half of the direct-supervision jails offered correctional officers no more than two days of communication skills training even though the training requirements for learning to communicate with a diverse group of inmates are difficult and need more than one or two days of instruction. The majority of Professor Tartaro's sample (70 percent) also identified their jail's furnishings and fixtures as vandalism resistant and half bolted their furniture to the floor, conveying the message that inmates are expected to misbehave. (The first MCCs outfitted inmate living areas with normalized commercial fixtures, furnishings, and finishes.) Furthermore, because of jail crowding, the majority of the inmates in direct-supervision facilities are no longer housed in single cells. Tartaro believes that jails that are only partially implementing the direct-supervision model are not secure or well-run facilities. This may explain why there are few differences between the perceptions of officers in new generation versus traditional facilities. This risks giving a bad reputation to those that are truly operating under the nine principles of direct supervision as escapes, riots, violence, or no change in the officers' perceptions of their work environments occurs in the partially implemented third-generation jails. This leads us to the newest development in architectural design and philosophy of inmate management, fourth-generation jails.

Fourth-Generation Jails Over the past few decades, architects and correctional planners have worked together to improve direct-supervision jails in two important ways, thereby introducing the next phase of jail development, **fourth-generation jails.** First, they introduced the concept of "borrowed light." Directing natural light into the dayroom where staff work and inmates spend most of their day makes them more alert and interactive with one another, and improves attitudes. In most jails, even third-generation jails, staff and inmates are isolated inside, unable to tell night from day, or experience the positive effects of daylight. In fourth-generation jails, sunlight bathes the dayroom. Light passes into the sleeping cells through the large windows in the cell doors. On sunny days, lighting can be turned down, thereby saving electricity.

The second improvement is programmatic. Third-generation jails isolate the officer with the inmates. (Recall from Professor Tartaro's research that the majority of third-generation jails do not offer any inmate services on the housing unit other than passive recreation—for example, watching TV, reading, and playing cards and board games.) The fourth-generation jail brings program services, staff, volunteers, visitors, and even vending machines to the housing unit, thereby reducing the feeling of isolation in the unit. Proponents of fourth-generation jails argue that this improvement adds significantly to the correction officer's ability to carry out the nine principles of direct supervision (see Exhibit 6–4). The only known fourth-generation jail in operation to date is the King County Regional Justice Center in Kent, Washington (see Exhibit 6–6).[16]

fourth-generation jail

Jail that incorporates natural light into the dayroom where staff work and inmates spend most of their day, and brings program services, staff, volunteers, and visitors to the housing unit.

EXHIBIT 6–6 Fourth-Generation Jail—Direct Supervision, Natural Light, and Pod-Based Programming

Natural light illuminates the podular design where staff work and inmates spend most of their day under the principles of direct supervision. Program services and visitation also take place on the pod. What are the consequences of fourth-generation jails?

CHARACTERISTICS OF JAIL INMATES, FACILITIES, AND STAFF

Who is in jail? Why are they there? How many jails are there? How many people work in jails? What do we know about the operation and administration of jail facilities? To these and related questions we now turn our attention.

Jail Inmates

With the exception of a change in conviction status (number of jail inmates unconvicted and convicted) and the sheer number of inmates under jail supervision, the characteristics of jail inmates have changed slightly over the past decade. Since 2000, 9 out of 10 jail inmates have been male; 4 out of 10 have been white; 4 out of 10 have been black; and 1 percent or less have been juveniles.

In June 2009, local jail authorities held or supervised 837,833 offenders. This was the first decline in the nation's local jail population since the federal government began its annual survey of jails in 1982 when the jail population was 223,551. Growth in the U.S. jail population has been slowing since 2005.

During the 12 months ending June 30, 2009, the nation's jail population dropped by nearly 18,000 inmates from a year earlier. Most of the decline occurred in large jails (those with inmate populations of 1,000 or more). Reasons for the decline are many including the third straight year of declining crime rates and the economic downturn that has taken a heavy toll on city and county budgets.

In 2009, 8.3 percent of these offenders (70,213) were supervised outside jail facilities (see Exhibit 6–7). A total of 767,620 were housed in local jails. Jails also held more than 24,200 immigrants (asylum-seekers, people suspected of being in the United States illegally, and legal immigrants convicted of crimes) for the U.S. Immigration and Customs Enforcement, nearly double the number held in 2000.

One not-so-promising statistic is the steady percentage increase in the number of jail inmates who are pretrial detainees (62 percent in 2009,

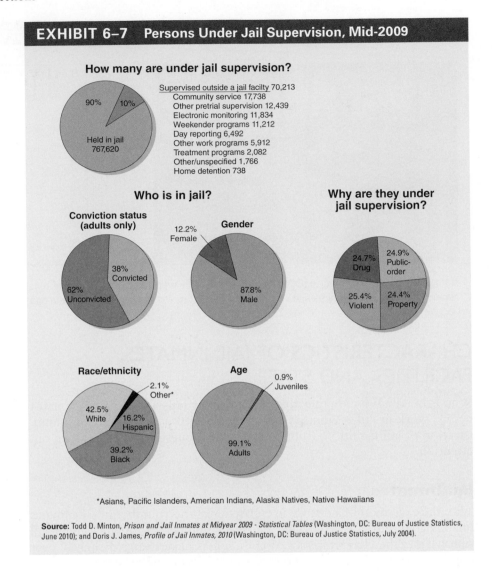

EXHIBIT 6–7   Persons Under Jail Supervision, Mid-2009

How many are under jail supervision?

90%   10%

Held in jail
767,620

Supervised outside a jail facilty 70,213
Community service 17,738
Other pretrial supervision 12,439
Electronic monitoring 11,834
Weekender programs 11,212
Day reporting 6,492
Other work programs 5,912
Treatment programs 2,082
Other/unspecified 1,766
Home detention 738

Who is in jail?

Why are they under jail supervision?

Conviction status (adults only)

38% Convicted
62% Unconvicted

Gender

12.2% Female
87.8% Male

24.7% Drug
24.9% Public-order
25.4% Violent
24.4% Property

Race/ethnicity

42.5% White
2.1% Other*
16.2% Hispanic
39.2% Black

Age

0.9% Juveniles
99.1% Adults

*Asians, Pacific Islanders, American Indians, Alaska Natives, Native Hawaiians

Source: Todd D. Minton, *Prison and Jail Inmates at Midyear 2009 - Statistical Tables* (Washington, DC: Bureau of Justice Statistics, June 2010); and Doris J. James, *Profile of Jail Inmates, 2010* (Washington, DC: Bureau of Justice Statistics, July 2004).

up from 56 percent in 2000), leading one of the country's most respected voices in jail issues, Dr. Ken Kerle, to write that "this is another unhappy sign that inmate processing is slowing down."[17] If more jail inmates are not being tried, convicted, or sentenced, jail resources become overburdened, crowding results, and the conditions of confinement worsen.

The Bureau of Justice Statistics and others have compiled a profile of inmates in local jails. Note that at the time of arrest:

- 80 percent earned less than $2,000 a month before they were locked up.
- 75 percent who had mental health problems also had co-occurring substance abuse or dependency issues;
- 68 percent had not seen a health care provider since incarceration;
- 64 percent suffered from some form of mental illness;
- 55 percent of females had been sexually or physically abused;
- 50 percent grew up in homes without both parents;
- 46 percent were not taking their medication at the time of arrest;
- 44 percent had less than a high school education;
- 40 percent had a criminal history;

- 39 percent had a chronic medical condition;
- 33 percent were on probation;
- 33 percent were unemployed at the time of arrest;
- 25 to 87 percent had traumatic brain injury;
- 25 percent had dental problems;
- 14 percent were homeless at the time of arrest;
- 13 percent of males had been sexually or physically abused;
- 12 percent were on parole;
- 5 percent of women were pregnant at the time of arrest; and
- 1.3 percent were HIV positive.

Despite this gloomy picture, jails are in a unique position to help persons leaving jail and resuming life in the community. Today more and more policymakers are recognizing that because jail inmates usually have shorter lengths of stay than state or federal inmates, and the community location of most jail facilities means less time away from family, friends, treatment providers, faith institutions, and other social supports. They also realize that jails have opportunities to develop strategies to reduce the criminalization of persons with mental illness and combat this list of problems with interventions and reentry programs prior to release. This chapter, along with Chapters 7, 8, and 12, discusses some of those opportunities.

Another way to look at the nation's jail population is to consider the rate of incarceration. Jail populations give us a count of the total number held in jail (e.g., 837,833 offenders held or supervised in mid-2009). Because of differences in total population, however, such counts do not allow for accurate comparison of jurisdictions. Rates of jail incarceration, expressed as the number of jail inmates per 100,000 residents age 18 and older, provide for a more meaningful and useful analysis of trends in incarceration. With rate data, we can compare changes over time. Exhibit 6–8 shows changes in the jail incarceration rate from 2000 through 2009. Note that the incarceration rate increased from 226 jail inmates per 100,000 adults in 2000 to 259 jail inmates per 100,000 adults in 2007, and then declined somewhat in 2008 and 2009.

Gender and Jail Populations There has been an upsurge in the number of women incarcerated in the United States, explained, in part, by guideline sentencing, under which gender is not considered an appropriate consideration. Though females have historically been treated more leniently than men at sentencing, guideline sentencing has tended to limit or end this practice.

The number of women in jail has more than quintupled over the past 25 years, from 19,000 in 1985 to a peak of 100,520 in 2007. Since then the number has declined to 99,600 in 2008 and 93,700 in 2009. The absolute number of women in jail is much smaller than the absolute number of men. However, their impact on jail operations is significant, raising concerns about the adequacy of jail facilities and the services provided.

The typical female jail inmate is poor, is a high school dropout with low skills, has held mainly low-wage jobs, is young (25 to 29), is unmarried with one to three children, and belongs to a racial minority.

Almost one-half of women and one-third of men in jail are first-time offenders (49 versus 37 percent).[18] Almost half of the women and men in jail were under the influences of alcohol or drugs at the time of the offense. Forty-six percent had members of their immediate families sentenced to prison.

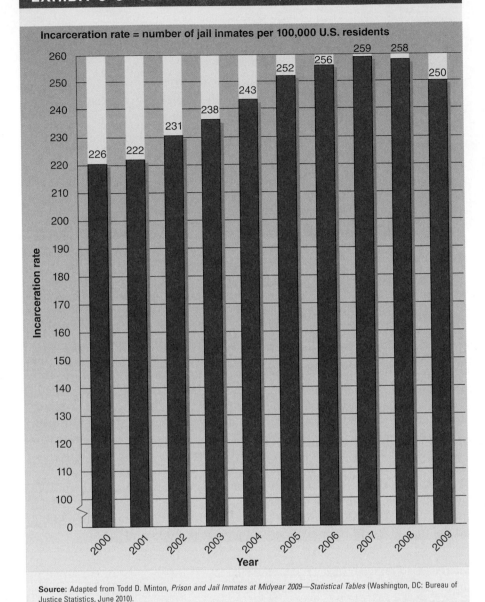

EXHIBIT 6–8   Jail Incarceration Rate, 2000–2007

Incarceration rate = number of jail inmates per 100,000 U.S. residents

Source: Adapted from Todd D. Minton, *Prison and Jail Inmates at Midyear 2009—Statistical Tables* (Washington, DC: Bureau of Justice Statistics, June 2010).

Two of every 10 grew up in a home where one or both parents abused drugs, alcohol, or both. And more than one-half of the women (55 percent) and 13 percent of the men had been physically or sexually abused before age 18. Women in jail need targeted interventions that address these issues.

This profile also raises troubling concerns about the children of jailed mothers. Two-thirds of women in jail are mothers with children under age 18 who were living with them prior to detention. When mothers go to jail, children become silent victims. The children may already have been victims if their mothers used drugs during pregnancy. Young children, not yet capable of understanding why their mother is gone, where she has gone, and if or when she will return, may develop depression and feelings of abandonment. Even children who are fortunate enough to be placed with emotionally supportive caregivers must cope with seeing their mother only through a glass barrier and hearing her voice only over the phone. Studies have shown that children of incarcerated mothers have more behavioral problems at home and in school and are four times as likely to become juvenile delinquents as children from similar socioeconomic backgrounds with parents at home. Maintaining bonding with children and family is the most difficult female inmate experience.[19] Recognizing that children should not be made to suffer for the poor choices of their parents and recognizing that support for family maintenance is a societal value, some jails are establishing visitation and parenting programs that accommodate this need. Through such programs, jail administrators have the opportunity to become leaders in preserving families and reducing crime.

Some scholars believe that many women in jail do not pose a threat to public safety but are jailed because they do not have the financial resources to make bail. Seventeen percent are charged with violent offenses.[20] Most are charged with property offenses (32 percent), drug offenses (29 percent), and public-order offenses (21 percent). This suggests some differences are needed in women's facility bed space and program space from men's facility space (for example, there may need to be less high-security bed space and more substance abuse programming space).

The increase in the number of women in jail has required that local officials identify and try to meet the needs of female inmates, yet severe limitations in resources often impede the provision of programs and services for women in jail. Jails are not prepared to house and treat rapidly rising female populations. They have difficulty providing appropriate housing, bed space, programs, jobs, mental health care, and other services. Women in jail have high needs for education, job training, health care, mental health care, alcohol and drug abuse counseling, and parenting skills development. Properly classifying women according to their risks and needs is beyond the scope of most jails in the United States.[21] The National Institute of Justice surveyed 54 jails and found that the same classification instrument was used for both male and female inmates in 50 jails. The survey found no effort to gauge women inmates' different needs, circumstances, and risk profiles.[22]

Recently the state of Maryland proposed building a new 800-bed jail for women in Baltimore costing taxpayers over $181 million for construction alone plus the additional annual operating costs of approximately $32 million. The Justice Policy Institute, a nonprofit research and public policy organization in Washington, DC, published a brief document in January 2011 that advocated against the new jail. The Institute argued that evidence from other jurisdictions that built new jails shows that:

1. The addition of a new jail frequently eliminates pressure to reduce the number of people held in jail.

2. Women who now are released either on bail or on their own recognizance may be detained in these facilities in the future because more and better space is available.

3. Other systems such as law enforcement may see additional beds as an invitation to arrest more women for minor offenses, even when crime is down.

4. Net-widening can result and be detrimental to the individual woman and her community.[23]

The Institute argued that Maryland should redirect the money toward proven cost-effective public safety strategies, such as education, job training, housing for the city's vulnerable homeless population, and treatment for people who are either involved in—or at risk of becoming involved in—the justice system.

Ignoring problems relating to women in jail increases a jail's exposure to litigation and liability. The National Institute of Corrections argues against doing nothing: "The 'get tough on inmates' mood, combined with decreasing levels of accountability for maintaining some level of minimum standards, raises the specter of decreased funding for jails, corresponding cutbacks in staff and training, and the rebirth of the sorts of very brutal, barbaric, and often dangerous conditions that led to the initial wave of court intervention in the early 1970s."[24]

Women are normally housed in a "women's unit," often an afterthought built inside facilities designed for men or simply a replica of the men's facility design. Such design fails to take into account the different needs of women. For example, the traditional jail bunks and fixed-seating arrangements in the jail's dayroom or at dining room tables may present safety and comfort issues for women who are pregnant in jail. In addition, jailed women seldom have access to programs and services provided to male inmates. Special programming designed specifically for their unique needs as women and mothers is not offered.[25]

Another deficiency affecting women in jail is jail staffing. Either there are no female correctional officers or there are too few to ensure around-the-clock supervision of women in jail. The result too often is that women inmates are exploited and abused by male staff. In 1975, a North Carolina jury found Joan Little, then 20 years old, not guilty of the murder of 62-year-old Clarence Alligood, a correctional officer in the Beaufort County Jail. Alligood had entered Little's cell and sexually attacked her. She argued that she killed him in self-defense with the ice pick he had brought into her cell. Ken Kerle, managing editor of *American Jails,* argues that the best defense for a jail against female inmates' allegations of sexual harassment by male staff is to have a female officer present at all times.[26]

Recently the National Institute of Corrections released a report to help jail and prison administrators more effectively manage the women in their care.[27] According to the researchers, women offenders behave the way they do because of four factors. Understanding these factors in combination with each other will help jail administrators consider how to adjust policies and procedures and how to assess and improve services to women in their care. They are:

1. **Pathways perspective.** Women in jail often have histories of sexual and/or physical abuse and substance abuse and are clients of mental health services. These women typically are unskilled, earn low incomes, have sporadic work histories, and are single parents. Thus, understanding how women enter the criminal justice system helps jails improve their responses.

2. **Relational theory and female development.** Relational theory describes the different ways women and men develop. An important difference suggested by the research is that women develop a sense of self and self-worth when their actions arise out of, and lead back into, connections with others even if this means establishing dysfunctional relationships. Many women offenders are drawn into criminal activity because of their relationships with others. Knowing this explains why jail staff often perceive that communicating with female offenders is more difficult and time-consuming than communicating with male inmates.

3. **Trauma theory.** Trauma is the injury done by violence and abuse and it is largely unrecognized by the women offenders themselves.

Mental health services that understand past trauma and its effect on current behavior are needed to respond to trauma.

4. **Addiction theory.** When substance abuse treatment programs for women are combined with additional pathway factors (mental illness, trauma, abuse), jail-based treatment is successful.

Ethnicity and Jail Populations Whites comprise nearly 70 percent of the U.S. population but only 43 percent of the jail population. In the general population, Hispanics make up almost 16 percent, and blacks make up 12.7 percent, but in jail, their populations are 16 percent and 39 percent, respectively.

In December 2009, the Bureau of Justice Statistics published its eighth report on jails in Indian country in the United States.[28] (*Indian country* is a statutory term that includes all lands within an Indian reservation; dependent Indian communities; and Indian trust allotments, or lands held in trust for tribes or their members.) The bureau reported that 82 Indian country facilities held 1,882 adults and 253 juveniles. Five of the 10 largest jails in Indian country are in Arizona. In 2008, together these 5 jails held 25 percent of the total inmate population.

In 2004, the Department of the Interior inspector general delivered a report to Congress detailing the present conditions of Indian jails in the United States.[29] The inspector general wrote, "It became abundantly clear that some facilities we visited were egregiously unsafe, unsanitary, and a hazard to both inmates and staff alike. BIA's detention program is riddled with problems and, in our opinion, is a national disgrace with many facilities having conditions comparable to those found in third-world countries . . . our assessment found evidence of a continuing crisis of inaction, indifference, and mismanagement throughout the BIA detention program. . . . Our anxiety over the detention program remains heightened, however, not only because of what we found during our site visits but, more importantly, because of what we fear remains undiscovered at the sites we did not visit."[30]

To correct these deficiencies, the inspector general offered 25 recommendations that called for strong leadership, attention from senior management, regular compliance checks, alternatives to detention for intoxicated inmates, on-site medical assistance, improved employee recruiting and training, increased staffing, and regular meetings to encourage best practices.

Explanations for the overrepresentation of minorities in jail abound, not the least of which is how the U.S. Census Bureau defines *race*. The decennial census measures race and ethnicity differently than did the previous census. First, the census item on *race* (on which people identify themselves as white, black, or of other races and ethnicities) and the item on Hispanic identity are separate. This means that one can be both black and Hispanic. Second, for the first time in 2000, census respondents could check more than one race, an attempt by the Census Bureau to identify multiracial people. One result is that blacks and Hispanics are not two distinct groups. In 2000, about 1.7 million blacks were also estimated to be Hispanic. How does one determine which group is larger? Should blacks be deducted from the Hispanic population or the other way around? Does one grouping take precedence over the other?

Another explanation for minority overrepresentation in jail has to do with the function of jails as pretrial detention centers. The jail population is heavily influenced by bail decisions. A number of researchers have found that judges impose higher bail—or are more likely to deny bail

Minorities comprise approximately 28 percent of the U.S. population but they make up over 55 percent of the jail population. What are the explanations for the overrepresentation of minorities in jail?

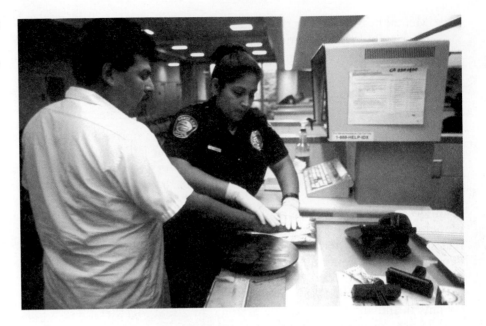

altogether—if the defendant is a racial minority.[31] Still another reason is the impact of the war on drugs and on law enforcement strategies of racial profiling. Other researchers have argued that the war on drugs has had a particularly detrimental effect on black males.[32] Across the past two decades, more black males than white males have been detained for drug offenses. Researchers at the University of Nebraska argue that police are *reactive* in responding to crimes against persons and property but are *proactive* in dealing with drug offenses. "There is evidence," they write, "to suggest that they [police] target minority communities—where drug dealing is more visible and where it is thus easier to make an arrest—and tend to give less attention to drug activities in other neighborhoods."[33]

Mental Illness and Jail Populations How jails became the institution of choice to manage increasing numbers of people with mental illness and what can be done about it is discussed in more depth in Chapter 12. Here we point out that incarceration—especially jail—has become the nation's default mental health treatment provider and the problems associated with that approach.

At midyear 2007, almost two-thirds (64 percent) of all jail inmates had a mental health problem compared to about 11 percent of the general adult population.[34] When researchers investigated the prevalence of "serious" mental illnesses defined as major depressive disorders, bipolar disorders, schizophrenia, and delusional disorders using structured clinical interviews with 20,000 adults entering five jails, they found that almost 15 percent of the men and 31 percent of the women had a serious mental illness.[35] As we will show in Chapter 12, persons living with mental illness are swept into the criminal justice system because of the failures of the public mental health system and the lack of adequate treatment in most poor communities. Today there may be as many as eight times more people with mental illness in the nation's jails (over 478,000) than there are in mental health hospitals (60,000).[36] The Los Angeles County Jail is the largest psychiatric inpatient facility in the United States with more than 3,400 prisoners suffering with mental health problems.[37] New York's Rikers Island is second with 3,000, and Chicago's Cook County Jail is third with over 1,500. In six states, jails actually function as quasi-mental health centers. State statutes in Alaska, Kentucky, Mississippi, Montana, New Mexico, and Wyoming authorize jails to hold individuals awaiting transfer to a mental health facility.[38]

Despite the large number of jail inmates with mental illness, these individuals are not often fit subjects for retribution or punishment. James Gondles, executive director of the American Correctional Association, said, "The notion that the prospect of incarceration will deter an individual with a mental illness from committing a crime does not apply to a population that cannot fully comprehend the consequences of its actions, especially in cases where crime is a direct result of illness."[39] Other experts tell us that the criminal justice system is ill-equipped to meet the special needs of persons with mental illness who are incarcerated or on supervised release in the community."[40]

Until recently, community and institutional punishment of persons with mental illness received little public policy attention. However, the U.S. Department of Health and Human Services' SAMSHA, the Mentally Ill Offender Treatment and Crime Reduction Act of 2003, and a Congressional report titled *Incarceration of Youth Who Are Waiting for Community Mental Health Services in the United States*[41] indicate that policymakers at all levels of government are taking notice of the burden that incarceration of persons with mental illness in jail and prison places on an already overcrowded criminal justice system and the tragic consequences that imprisonment of such individuals can have on families and communities.

Sixty-four percent of jail inmates have mental health problems compared to about 11 percent of the general population. Why are these individuals not fit subjects for retribution or punishment?

Over the years, the nation's sheriffs have also said that jails are not equipped to meet the complex needs of persons living with mental illness and asked county and general hospitals to accept them as patients. The sheriffs spelled out six objections as part of a resolution as to why jails should not be used in this manner:

1. The mentally ill person has usually committed no crime.
2. County jails are overcrowded.
3. Small county sheriffs' officers are not specially trained for the proper handling and care of a mental patient.
4. Many jails do not have proper or adequate detention rooms for the mentally ill.
5. Detention in the county jail is unfair to the patient as well as to the corrections officers.
6. Psychiatrists agree that a patient originally detained in a jail is much more difficult to treat and readjust, and incarceration can contribute to the further decompensation of many people with mental illness.[42]

SAMSHA, the Act of 2003, the Congressional report, and the nation's sheriffs promote the diversion of individuals with mental illness from the nation's jails, collaboration between the justice system and the mental health communities, and treatment and training. Since 2004, 13 states have passed legislation creating or expanding mental health courts to provide alternative sentencing for nonviolent offenders with mental health problems.[43] We complete our discussion of the incarceration of persons who are mentally ill in Chapter 12.

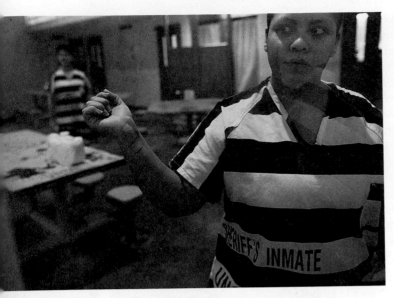

Suicide, homicide, and sexual victimization are challenging problems for jail administrators. Describe the problem and what jail leadership can do about it.

Suicide, Homicide, Sexual Victimization, and Jail Populations

The problems of suicide, homicide, and sexual victimization are challenging ones for jail administrators. In 2003, Congress passed and President Bush signed the Prison Rape Elimination Act that requires the U.S. Department of Justice to report on the incidence of rape and other forms of sexual victimization in correctional facilities. As we describe below, some states are taking bold steps to reduce the incidence of suicide, homicide, and sexual victimization in our nation's jails.

The good news is that the jail suicide rate is declining. Twenty-five years ago, there were 47 suicides per 100,00 jail inmates. In 2000, the rate declined to 49. Today it stands at 36 per 100,000 jail inmates.[44] Reasons for the decrease include better suicide prevention programming, better training of jail staff, more in-depth inquiry of suicide risk factors during the intake process, search practices that remove dangerous items from the prisoners, increased inspection of cells, and a closer working relationship with health care personnel in delivering and maintaining adequate health care services to inmates. Still, suicide is the single leading cause of unnatural deaths in local jails, accounting for 29 percent of all jail deaths between 2000 and 2007. (Heart disease is the leading cause among illness deaths in local jails, accounting for 22 percent of all deaths in local jails.)

Kentucky successfully reduced its jail suicides from 17 to 4 per year by cross-training jail personnel and mental health providers, developing new screening instruments for arresting and booking officers, establishing a telephonic service that allows jail staff to call a licensed mental health professional for risk management consultation 24 hours a day, and establishing a statewide data collection and analysis system.[45] However, the sad news is the jail suicide rate is still over three times what it is for the general U.S. population (11 per 100,000).

The situation for small jails is even worse. The suicide rate for jails with 50 or fewer beds was 169 per 100,000; in the largest jails (those with an ADP of 1,000 or more inmates), the suicide rate was 27 per 100,000 inmates.[46] The reasons are that smaller jails tend to be older and poorly staffed, are less able to provide sight and sound separation for inmates of different ages or genders, are less likely to use volunteers to deliver religious or rehabilitative programs, typically pay lower wages, find it difficult to comply with standards for physical or mental health care, use fewer classification, and offer less inmate supervision.

The majority of jail inmate suicides typically occur within the first week of incarceration with nearly a quarter occurring within the first two days of admission (time of day is not a factor), are mostly violent offenders (violent offenders who commit suicide outnumber nonviolent offenders by a margin of 3-to-1), and are typically committed by hanging. The majority of inmates who commit suicide have a high school education, are unmarried, white, male, and between the ages of 25 and 44. Over one-third have a history of serious mental illness of the type described earlier.

The consequences of inmate suicide are lost lives, the devastation to families, the short- and long-term psychological effects on other inmates and correctional staff, expensive investigations and litigation, and medical care costs.

Homicide in jail is another concern of jail administrators, and here the news is not good. In 2000, 17 jail inmates were murdered. In 2006, the number increased to 36 and decreased to 20 in 2007. The literature on jail homicides offers very few insights other than revealing that kidnapping offenders are the most likely victims of jail homicides, followed by violent offenders, property offenders, and then public-order offenders. Drug offenders have the lowest homicide victimization rate. The majority of jail homicide victims are male, mostly between the ages of 18 and 54, and evenly split between white and black.

A section of the Prison Rape Elimination Act also requires the U.S. Department of Justice to provide a list of local jails according to the prevalence of sexual victimization. The Justice Department defines **sexual victimization** as all types of sexual activity, for example, oral, anal, or vaginal penetration; handjobs; touching of the inmate's buttocks, thighs, penis, breasts, or vagina in a sexual way; abusive sexual contacts (unwanted contacts with another inmate or any contacts with staff that involved touching of the inmate's buttocks, thigh, penis, breasts, or vagina, in a sexual way); and both willing and unwilling sexual contact. The Justice Department reported that 3.1 percent, approximately 24,000 of all jail inmates nationwide, experienced one or more incidents of sexual victimization in 2008–2009.[47] Most jail inmates reported that the incident involved jail staff. Some said the incident involved another inmate, and some said both other inmates and staff had victimized them. The majority (6,900) who reported that the incident involved jail staff said the sex or sexual contact was unwilling as a result of physical force, pressure, or offers of special favors or privileges. An equally large number of jail inmates (8,400) said they willingly had sex or sexual contact with staff. The Justice Department is clear to note, however, "Regardless of whether an inmate reported being willing or unwilling, any sexual contact between jail inmates and staff is illegal."[48]

Because the Justice Department study is based on a sample of jail inmates but not a complete enumeration of all jail inmates nationwide, an *exact* ranking of jails by sexual victimization rates is not possible. With this limitation in mind, however, the jails with the highest rates of inmate-on-inmate sexual victimization are Orleans Parish (South White Street Jail), Louisiana (7.5 percent), Madison County Detention Facility, Alabama (5.5 percent), and Miami–Dade County Pretrial Detention Center, Florida (5.1 percent). Jails with the highest rates of staff sexual misconduct are Caroline County Jail, Maryland (10 percent), Eastern Shore Regional Jail, Virginia (9.9 percent), and Clallam County Correctional Facility, Washington (6.1 percent).

Other findings from the Justice Department study are:

- Female inmates in jail were more than twice as likely as male inmates to report experiencing inmate-on-inmate sexual victimization.

- Sexual activity with jail staff was reported by 2.1 percent of male jail inmates and 1.5 percent of female jail inmates.

- Rates of inmate-on-inmate sexual victimization in jail were significantly higher among inmates who were white or multiracial, had a college degree, a sexual orientation other than heterosexual, and experienced sexual victimization before coming to jail.

- Rates of reported staff sexual misconduct were lower among white inmates, lower among inmates ages 25 or older, higher among inmates with a college degree, and higher among inmates who had experienced sexual victimization before coming to jail.

sexual victimization

All types of sexual activity, for example, oral, anal, or vaginal penetration; handjobs; touching of the inmate's buttocks, thighs, penis, breasts, or vagina in a sexual way; abusive sexual contacts.

- Nineteen percent of jail inmates who reported inmate-on-inmate sexual victimization said they were victimized within the first 24 hours after admission compared to 4 percent of female inmates in jail.
- More than 40 percent of inmates who reported inmate-on-inmate victimization said the incident occurred between 6 pm and midnight.
- Among male victims of staff sexual misconduct, 64 percent of those in jails reported sexual activity with female staff. An additional 18 percent of jail inmates reported sexual activity with both female and male staff.
- Among inmates who reported staff sexual misconduct, 30 percent of male victims in jail and 4 percent of female victims in jail said they were victimized by staff within the first 24 hours.

Stopping sexual victimizations in local jails will not be easy. It will require jail leadership taking a zero tolerance approach, better staff and inmate training, creating an environment where all inmate victims feel free to report the incident without reprisal, tough sanctions against staff and inmate offenders, and possibly facility remodeling to eliminate blind spots.

Juveniles and Jail Populations Over the past 25 years, there has been a dramatic reversal in the theory and practice of punishing juveniles, as Chapter 16 will explain. In the mid-1970s, juvenile offenders were deemed to have special needs, so Congress passed the Juvenile Justice and Delinquency Prevention Act of 1974. The act contains four core requirements that participating states must address to receive federal juvenile justice grants:

1. Status offenders may not be held in secure confinement.
2. Juveniles generally may not be held in jails and lockups in which adults are confined.
3. When juveniles are temporarily detained in the same facilities as adults, they must have no "sight or sound" contact with adult inmates.
4. States are required to demonstrate efforts to reduce the disproportionate number of minority youth who come into contact with the juvenile justice system.

By 1996, however, in the face of pressure to increase punishment for juvenile offenders, new legislation allowed cities and states to detain juvenile offenders for up to 12 hours in an adult jail before a court appearance and made it easier to house juveniles in separate wings of adult jails. That shift in philosophy and policy has increased the percentage of juveniles held as adults in adult jails. At midyear 1995, 76 percent of the 7,800 juveniles confined in the nation's jails were held as adults. Today, it is 81 percent (5,847 held as adults and 1,373 held as juveniles). Under current law, juveniles can be held in adult jails once they have been declared "adult" for the purpose of prosecution.

The incarceration of juveniles in adult jails is criticized for a number of reasons. Holding juveniles in adult jails places young people at greater risk of being physically, sexually, and mentally abused by adult offenders. Juvenile girls are especially vulnerable to sexual assault. Juveniles in adult jail are almost eight times more likely to commit suicide than are juveniles in juvenile detention centers. One explanation is that juveniles are held in isolated parts of adult jails where they receive less staff support and supervision. Another is that jail staff are not trained to recognize depression in juveniles.

As late as midyear 2008, the U.S. Congress discussed bills that would bar most juveniles charged as adults from being detained in adult jails unless a court finds, after a hearing, that it is in the interest of justice to do so. However, to date the Congress has not acted on any of the proposals.

Jail Facilities

Occupancy   The capacity to house jail inmates has kept pace with the jail population. For more than 10 years the nation's jail rated capacity has averaged only 94 percent. Rated **capacity,** which is the maximum number of beds or inmates allocated to each jail facility by a state or local rating official, has remained below 100 percent since 1995. (The other ways to measure capacity are discussed in Chapter 7.)

Public Versus Private   Of the nation's 3,365 jails, 47 are privately operating under contract to local governments.[49] Texas leads the nation in private jail operations with approximately one-fifth of its inmates (3,469) and facilities (eight). Tennessee has the second-largest number of inmates (2,278) in privately operated jails, followed by Florida (1,931). Across the country, another 15 percent of jails are under federal court order or consent decree (most often for crowding or other confinement conditions). Another 11 percent have been ordered to limit populations.

Size, Location, and Budget   At midyear 2009, almost 40 percent of the nation's jails had an average daily population of fewer than 50 inmates and held less than 3 percent of the jail population. In contrast, 6 percent of the nation's jails, referred to as *megajails,* had average daily populations of 1,000 or more inmates.[50] Megajails held 50 percent of the nation's jail population by midyear 2009.[51] Typically these large facilities are located in major metropolitan and urban areas. Jail operating budgets are highest in New York (almost $1.1 billion) and lowest in North Dakota ($3.5 million).[52] The average annual cost to incarcerate one jail inmate is approximately $24,000.[53]

Today a number of local jails charge inmates housing fees and medical co-pay fees. It is not known how common this is across the United States, but several states have adopted the practice. For example, more than half of the 95 jails currently operating in the state of Kansas charge a housing fee ranging from $10 to $70 a day. According to the researchers, the overriding reasons jails assess housing fees are the economic recession, jail crowding, and the need to cover operating costs (e.g., medical, food, utilities, staff, and transportation).[54] However, out of concern for gender-responsive services for females, some are asking what impact medical co-pays will have on female offenders who statistically enter correctional facilities with more medical problems than do males and who will have to pay extra for something that is a result of being female.[55]

Almost 80 jails in the United States are also generating new revenue by allowing well-behaved inmates a chance to receive meatball subs, cheeseburgers, and pizza and wings complete with celery, blue cheese, and a Pepsi ordered by their relatives on Aramark's "iCare" Web site. (Aramark is one of the nation's largest businesses providing food to educational institutions, restaurants, hospitals, and other businesses.) Aramark tailors its menus to each jail's rules. Prices generally run from $7 to $14

rated capacity

The maximum number of beds or inmates allocated to each jail facility by a state or local rating official.

Nicole Brockett, a 22-year-old bartender in Los Angeles, served 21 days for DUI at the Santa Ana City Jail, one of a dozen pay-to-stay jails in California, instead of incarceration at the nearby county jail. Brockett paid $82 per day for living conditions that the jail says are "a world away from cement and steel bars." What are the advantages and disadvantages of pay-to-stay jail?

for a hot meal and $20 to $100 for a junk-food box. Jails receive revenue on every dollar. For example, the Bexar County Jail in San Antonio, Texas, makes 45 cents on every dollar in sales and projected its revenue would hit $500,000 in 2010. Will programs like this create envy, violence, and extortion among inmates? Will overindulgence in junk food lead to health problems and potentially raise taxpayer costs for inmate health care? It's too early to tell what impact Aramark's "iCare" food service for jails will have. Jail staff including Captain Richard Fisher of the Rock Island County Jail, Illinois, say "Jails are always run better when your inmates are happy." But others cringe. Sheriff Joe Arpaio of Maricopa County, Arizona, who serves his jail inmates only "nutraloaf," a brick-hard concoction made from blending together dry milk, vegetables and bread dough, says pepperoni pizza is not his idea of jail food. "Instead of calling it a jail, let's call it the Hilton," he said.[56]

pay-to-stay jail (also *self-pay jails*)

An alternative to serving time in a county jail. Offenders convicted of minor offenses are offered privileges for a fee from $75 to $127 per day.

Pay-to-Stay Jail   In addition to charging inmates housing, food, and medical co-pay fees as a way to offset jail operations, some jurisdictions have added **pay-to-stay jails**, also referred to as *self-pay jails*. The concept of pay-to-stay is surging after actors such as Keifer Sutherland, star of "24," and Gary Collins, star of countless TV shows, served their sentences for DUI at the Glendale, California, city jail in 2008. The Beverly Hills Police Department, California, opened its pay-to-stay jail in late 2009.

Pay-to-stay jails are an alternative to serving time in a county jail and offer privileges to offenders (sometimes called *clients*) convicted of minor offenses such as DUI and non-drug-related offenses who pay $75 to $127 per day. Estimates are that there are approximately 13 pay-to-stay jails in California.[57] Exhibit 6–9 compares six pay-to-stay jails in southern California in terms of cost per day, number of beds available, amenities, what inmates are allowed to bring in, and eligibility criteria. For example, persons convicted of DUI and sentenced to 21 days in the Santa Ana City Jail will pay over $1,700 for the extra privileges. Recently, an assistant sheriff of Orange County (California) was convicted of perjury and misuse of public funds. He served his sentence of 243 days at the Fullerton City Jail and paid $18,000 for a private cell, bathroom, and shower stall; use of his cell phone; and food brought by his visitors and even pizza delivery.

EXHIBIT 6–9   Comparison of Six Pay-to-Stay Jails

	Price per Day	Beds in the Program	What Inmate Gets	What Inmate Can Bring	Who Cannot Come
Santa Ana	$82	30	Work furlough, daily visitation	Nothing	Anyone who has assaulted someone in law enforcement; people who need protective custody
Seal Beach	$70 plus $100 application fee[1]	30	Work furlough, (if approved), up to 2-hour approved daily visitation	Books, games, iPods	Violent offenders
Montebello	$75 plus $100 application fee	10	Work furlough, up to 2-hour daily visitation	Books, games, iPods	Violent offenders
Pasadena	$127 plus $58 one-time administrative fee	20	Work furlough daily visitation	A Bible or book, watch (no jewelry), and up to $20 in cash	Anyone with a history of violent behavior or drug background arrest or with serious medical problems requiring multiple medications
Fullerton	First two consecutive days, $100, $75 thereafter	2	Visitors twice weekly	Cell phone, reading materials, official court papers, pillow and blanket, small food deliveries	Drug or alcohol addicts in withdrawal, epileptics with a history of seizures, those who are mentally deranged, those with suicidal tendencies or history of attempts, those with contagious diseases
Beverly Hills	$110 plus $24 application fee	2 (but can accommodate more)	Outgoing collect calls and weekend and holiday visitation	Clean clothes, a pair of regular shoes, a pair of shower shoes, glasses or contact lenses, one key, photo identification, a non-expensive watch, a maximum of $50 in cash, travel-size toothbrush, toothpaste, and deodorant, contact lens solution, appropriate reading material, a pillowcase, pillow, his or her own food in the form of commercially prepackaged and sealed frozen meals. No cell phone, blackberry, laptop, or other electronic or telecommunication device	Anyone with a history of violence, sex or drug abuse, or arson or has a situation or condition that may endanger the health, safety, or welfare of the other pay-to-stay inmates or the jail staff

1. $15 a day extra for GPS bracelets if required.

Source: Jennifer Steinhauer, "For $82 a Day, Booking a Cell in a 5-Star Jail," *The New York Times*, April 29, 2007, www.nytimes.com (accessed April 30, 2007). Updated by authors.

Offenders normally petition the court at their sentencing proceedings to serve their sentence at a pay-to-stay jail. If the court agrees and the city accepts the offender's application, the offender is housed separately from other inmates but may have minimal contact with the general inmate population during meal service. Most pay-to-stay jail inmates are required to work several hours a day outside their cells in food preparation, laundry, facility sanitation, vehicle washing, and so on, even if they work elsewhere in the community or attend school. The accommodations are usually cleaner and safer.

Supporters of the self-pay model argue that pay-to-stay jails benefit everyone: Paying inmates generate cash for the community (the Pasadena, California, city jail collected $234,000 from pay-to-stay clients at the rate of $127 a night in 2008, and the Burbank, California, city jail collected

$109,000 at the rate of $85 a night[58]); taxpayers pay less to house offenders in city rather than county jails; offenders can serve their time in a smaller, nonviolent facility; and paying inmates are generally easier to deal with.

On the other hand, critics charge that pay-to-stay jails create inherent injustices, offering cleaner, safer alternatives to those who can afford it. The concept of offering a cleaner, safer jail is valid, they say, but the criterion of inmates paying for it is not. To date, there is no research to support the claims of self-pay jails or whether offenders who pay for their own jail stay are less likely to recidivate.

Jail Staff

Twenty years ago, staffing was cited as the number-one concern in a survey of 2,452 jails.[59] Dr. Ken Kerle, the former managing editor of *American Jails*, says this is still a major problem.[60] Today, an estimated 297,600 people work in the nation's jails.[61] Women comprise one-third of all jail employees (one-fourth of all corrections officers). Sixty-six percent of all jail corrections officers are white, 24 percent are black, 8 percent are Hispanic, and 2 percent are of other races. Minority employees are underrepresented relative to their proportion among inmates. Consult the Appendix: Careers in Corrections at the Online Learning Center Web site for the steps involved in career planning, developing employability and job readiness, and finding the right job.

In spite of the fact that there are more jail beds than inmates, as noted earlier, jail staff perceive that jails are overcrowded because there are not enough staff on shift to handle the workload properly. Jail staff think of a jail as overcrowded if, due to staff shortages, inmate counts, bed checks, and cell searches are not performed and inmate programs such as visitation and outdoor recreation are postponed.[62] Because most jails are locally funded, local politics determine how much staff a county government allocates to operate the county jail. How much is the county willing to spend on the jail compared to other county agencies such as roads, police, and fire?

Most jails spend 75 to 90 percent of their budgets on salaries. One jail post operating 24 hours a day, seven days a week requires five officers when sick time, vacation, and other leaves are factored in. This partially explains why county officials are reluctant to increase staffing to correspond with an increase in inmate population. Yet understaffing poses a threat to inmate and staff security and safety. Too often inadequate staffing leads to inmate lockdowns to prevent escape and ease the handling of prisoners. Furthermore, without appropriate staff supervision, little can be done to protect inmates from one another in multiple-occupancy cells.

Other problems of jail staff include substandard pay compared to that of other employees in the criminal justice system, low job prestige, high turnover, and inadequate systems for recruitment, selection, and training. The National Sheriff's Association (NSA) believes that too often "warm bodies are taken off the street, put into uniform, given a set of keys, and told to go to work."[63] Concerning salaries, the NSA wrote, "Jail officer careers will never achieve the status they deserve so long as counties continue to pay jail officers less money than the officers assigned to law enforcement. . . . No person wants to make a career where the reward is lousy wages. You can't attract the people who have the potential to be the best officers by paying them wages in the poverty range."[64]

Lupe Valdez is sheriff of Dallas County, Texas. She is the only female sheriff in Texas, the only Hispanic female sheriff in the United States, and she is openly gay. Her department has an operating budget of $132 million, employs 2,250 personnel, and operates the seventh largest jail in the United States. At midyear 2009, the ADP of the Dallas County Jail was 6,039. Its rated capacity is 8,097. Why are staffing issues a major concern of most jails today?

Although the Palm Beach County Florida Sheriff's Department starts certified jail corrections officers at $47,220, not all jails can do this. Nevertheless, most jails can help officers find satisfaction in their work by setting clearly defined goals, identifying the officer's job obligations and performance expectations, and providing jail officers adequate organizational resources to perform their jobs. Attracting and retaining jail employees depends on engaging in effective recruitment, providing meaningful preservice and inservice training and career development, and developing responsive management and leadership.

JAIL ISSUES

In May and June 2007, 45 sheriffs and jail administrators from across the United States met to discuss the most important issues facing jails today and make recommendations to the Justice Department.[65] The jail managers cited inmate mental health as their top concern and recommended that the government give jails more support in that area.

All 45 jail managers agreed that inmates are arriving in jail with more serious and costly mental health problems that they (the jail managers) are responsible for treating. They said they need other agencies and resources in the community to help share the burden of the treatment. Jails may be able to do a relatively good job of stabilizing a mentally ill person while he or she is in jail, but jails are incapable of dealing with long-term needs, so once released, the inmates get into trouble again and come back to jail. Earlier in this chapter, we detailed the issue of mental illness and jail populations.

We conclude this chapter by elaborating on other concerns of jail managers: privatization, reentry, accreditation, workforce development, and evidence-based practices.

Privatization

Privatization is defined as a contract process that shifts public functions, responsibilities, and capital assets, in whole or in part, from the public sector to the private sector. We expand on the issue of *correctional* privatization in Chapter 13. Our focus here is on *jail* privatization.

Jails can be privatized in one of three ways: through private management, private sector development, or private services provision. In private management, private firms have total responsibility for the operation of a facility. This is the most common application of the term *privatization* and the most controversial aspect of the private sector's involvement in corrections.

In private sector development, the private sector develops, designs, and finances or arranges for the financing of jails. This often involves owning the jail and leasing it back to the jurisdiction through a lease/purchase contract, which serves as an alternative to a public bond issue or tax increase.

In private services provision, jails contract with private vendors to run services such as health and dental care, alcohol and drug treatment, mental health services, food service, training, and programming. This is the most familiar privatization model and the least controversial.

The debate between proponents and opponents of jail privatization surfaced early and continues today. Pressures for privatization come from escalating costs and crowded jails as well as from general dissatisfaction with county government. Jail privatization is sometimes seen as a practical option when a jurisdiction needs to update facilities quickly in

privatization

A contract process that shifts public functions, responsibilities, and capital assets, in whole or in part, from the public sector to the private sector.

Jose M. Ortiz-Cruz

Correctional Officer • Florida Department of Corrections
• Hendry Correctional Institution • Immokalee, Florida

Jose Ortiz-Cruz has been a correctional officer with the Florida Department of Corrections for 1½ years. He works at the Hendry Correctional Institution, a mixed-security men's facility with a rated capacity of 1,229 inmates.

Officer Ortiz-Cruz's work assignment is twofold. He is responsible for the security, transport, care, custody, and control of all prison inmates. He is also a member of the Crisis Negotiation Team. He received specialized training to handle all inmate hostage situations, suicides, and cell extractions.

Officer Ortiz-Cruz was born in Puerto Rico. He is fluent in Spanish and communicates with the prison's Spanish-speaking prisoner population. The best part of his job is the pride he takes in his work. The hardest part, he says, is having to tell grown men what to do.

Officer Ortiz-Cruz is currently working on his undergraduate degree at Edison State College in Naples, Florida. In 2009 he was promoted to sergeant. In five years he would like to be a lieutenant with the Florida DOC.

His advice to persons interested in working in a state prison? "Respect is something that is earned, not given. They are inmates. That is their punishment for the crime they committed. It is not our job to make their lives more miserable. Stay professional at all times, be on time, be reliable, and have a positive attitude at your institution. Be firm, fair and consistent and you will have a great career in corrections."

> *"Be firm, fair and consistent and you will have a great career in corrections."*

response to a court order for additional capacity. Advocates of privatization claim that private operators can operate facilities more efficiently and cost-effectively.

Opponents of jail privatization dispute cost comparisons or dismiss them altogether. Some insist that the fundamental point is that it is the responsibility of local governments to operate jails, not to delegate power and liability. Opponents believe that the administration of justice is a basic function of government and a symbol of state authority and should not be delegated. From this perspective, jails are, as John J. DiIulio Jr., University of Pennsylvania professor of politics, religion, and civil society, put it, "a public trust to be administered on behalf of the community and in the name of civility and justice."[66]

Opponents also fear that if we privatize jails, we risk enabling private corporations to use their political influence to continue programs not in the public interest. For example, would private contractors keep jail occupancy rates high to maintain profit? Might private contractors accept only the best inmates, leaving the most troublesome for public facilities to handle?

Turning a jail over to a private corporation also raises questions about accountability. Who is responsible for monitoring the performance of the private contractor? Who will see that local laws and regulations are followed? As jail incarceration rates continue to rise, the debate over privatizing jails and the competition for new contracts will continue.

Professional associations have addressed jail privatization through policy statements that range from cautious (American Correctional Association) to negative (American Jail Association and the National Sheriff's Association). The American Federation of State, County and Municipal Employees has been opposed from the beginning, and the

American Bar Association has urged a moratorium until more information is available.

Jail Reentry (Begins at Entry)

Another solution to jail crowding is jail **reentry**, the process of transition that offenders make from prison or jail to the community. (We return to a discussion of reentry in Chapter 8.) It seems only natural to add jail reentry to the list of strategies so that fewer people, once released, return to jail.

reentry

The transition offenders make from prison or jail to the community.

Most jails limit their reentry efforts to basic adult and secondary education (55 percent), faith-based and drug-related counseling (70 percent), fee-for-service health care (39 percent), and mental health screening at intake and psychotropic medication (78 percent).[67] Less effort is put into vocational education (6 percent), job seeking (15 percent), or life skills (21 percent). As evidence suggests, improving inmate job skills, helping inmates find jobs upon release, and increasing inmate wage potential all have a significant impact on recidivism.[68] We find success stories in small rural jails and in large urban jails. Researchers studied the jail reentry transition program in Auglaize County, Ohio, a small rural county in western Ohio with a population of 46,000. The program provides a comprehensive approach to addressing inmate problems that range from medical and mental health issues to drug and alcohol addiction. A team composed of jail management; security, mental health, and chemical dependency counselors; and staff from the Ohio Department of Job and Family Services perform an assessment immediately at intake and design an Reentry Accountability Plan that focuses on services such as employment placement, drug and alcohol treatment, mental health counseling, and educational support. Case managers serve as advocates and mentors and help offenders with wraparound services after release. Researchers carefully matched 72 program participants with 72 nonparticipants and one year after release, 82 percent of program participants had not committed another crime versus only 12 percent of the nonparticipantrs.[69]

A different jail reentry approach is underway in Atlanta, Georgia. There judges require housing and treatment options to be in place before persons with mental illness are released from the Fulton County Jail. Jail staff, together with the public defender's office and the local Social Security office, helps jail inmates apply for Social Security's Supplemental Security Income (SSI) to address the difficulties of people who are homeless and suffer from mental illness.[70] SSI is accompanied by federal Medicaid benefits. It provides a monthly payment that can be used to provide for basic needs and to access many subsidized housing programs. We know, for example, that housing is critical for jail inmates with mental illness. The Bureau of Justice Statistics reports that inmates with mental illness are more than twice as likely to be homeless in the 12 months prior to arrest than inmates without mental illness.[71] Thus, housing is key to successful reentry, and for people with mental illness leaving jail, SSI is key to accessing housing. Exhibit 6–10 shows what some of the jails across the United States are doing in jail reentry.

Educational, Vocational, and Inmate Work Programs Many jail inmates have poor reading skills. National studies show that more than 40 percent of all jail inmates have less than a ninth-grade education.[72] They also have substance abuse problems and few job skills. They frequently cannot find jobs after they are released or can find only low-paid or temporary work. As a result, in part, they often return to a life of crime.

The last time I was in jail was in the spring of 2001. I was in for a Driving After Revocation offense. I was on probation for Controlled Substance at the time.

I have known for six years that I am HIV-positive. When I went to jail, I was on several medications which were preventing the acceleration of the virus. The only thing different for me as an inmate was that I needed medication every day, several times a day. The jail staff contacted my physicians regarding my medication, dosages, etc.

I did not have any problems getting my medications as prescribed. The jail nurse dispensed them. But they gave them out with the rounds of others. So they did not single me out or draw attention to me.

The jail staff followed confidentiality policies. I did not have any problems with anyone else, except specific staff members, knowing about my condition. I didn't have any specific dietary needs, so that wasn't an issue. I felt the same when I left the jail as when I entered.

Anonymous

EXHIBIT 6–10 Jail Reentry

To date, reentry policies and programs have primarily targeted people released from state and federal prisons. However, jail reentry has at least as much of an impact on public safety, if not more. Although the nation's jail capacity is lower than its prison capacity—there are approximately 691,000 jail beds, compared to 1.4 million prison beds—admissions and releases from jails far exceed those from prisons. According to the Bureau of Justice Statistics 2004 Survey of Large Jails, 20 percent of jail inmates serve at least one month, and only 4 percent serve more than six months. As a result, the jail population is continuously turning over, resulting in approximately 12 million admissions and releases per year.

The short sentences served in jail and the proximity of jails to inmates' home communities have important implications—both positive and negative—for the role of local jails in addressing the challenges of prisoner reentry, highlighted as follows:

- **Mental illness.** Sixteen percent of both jail inmates and state prisoners report a mental condition or overnight stay in a mental hospital. However, only 41 percent of jail inmates with mental illness receive mental health services compared to 61 percent of state prisoners with mental illness.
- **Substance abuse and dependence.** More than two-thirds (68 percent) of jail inmates are dependent on or abuse drugs or alcohol, but only 18 percent receive treatment or participate in other substance abuse programs after entering jail. Sixty-nine percent of jail inmates are regular drug users, and 29 percent of convicted jail inmates report drug use at the time of their offense.
- **Limited employability.** Fifty-seven percent of jail inmates were working full-time the month prior to their arrest. Thirty percent of all jail inmates reported personal earnings totaling less than $300 per month.
- **Extensive criminal histories.** Three-fourths of jail inmates have served a prior probation or incarceration sentence, and nearly a quarter (24 percent) have served three or more prior sentences to incarceration. More than half of all jail inmates have a current criminal justice status at the time of arrest.

Source: Adapted from Nancy G. La Vigne, Amy L. Solomon, Karen A. Beckman, and Kelly Dedel, *Prisoner Reentry and Community Policing: Strategies for Enhancing Public Safety* (Washington, DC: U.S. Department of Justice, Office of Community Oriented Policing Services, March 2006).

Too many jails simply warehouse inmates and care little about education or job skills. It costs taxpayers money to provide educational services to jail inmates—the same people who already have financially and psychologically burdened society through their crimes. Education does not guarantee that an offender will remain free of crime upon release. However, consider the alternative: More than 40 percent of defendants on pretrial release have one or more prior convictions. The cost of

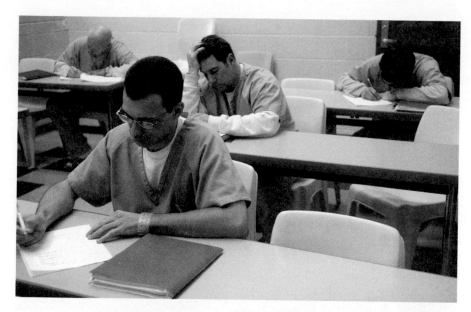

Jail inmates at the Onondaga County Justice Center (Syracuse, New York) take a test at their small-engine repair class. The class is divided between work, tests, and hands-on engine work. What do you believe will happen if educational and vocational programs are not available for jail inmates?

keeping one inmate in jail for one year ranges from $20,000 to $40,000. Studies also show that inmates who earn their GEDs while incarcerated are far less likely to return to crime. Educational and vocational programs help offenders help themselves, they boost self-esteem, and they encourage legitimate occupations upon release. Overall, it costs less to educate offenders and teach them job skills than to do nothing to change their attitudes, abilities, and outlooks. Ignoring an offender's educational and vocational deficiencies leaves the offender with fewer marketable skills or qualifications when released, increasing the chance of a return to crime.

On an average day, nearly 20 percent of all jail inmates work at least six hours a day. Some jails go further, creating opportunities for inmates to learn work habits and skills that are in demand in the community, earn wages that apply to their fines, court costs, and family obligations, provide quality goods to consumers, and reduce inmate idleness. Jail industries making headlines include:[73]

- **Lafayette Parish, Louisiana.** Inmates manufacture and deliver can liners for trash and garbage use to government or nonprofit agencies in the state of Louisiana. In 2009, total sales reached over $200,000.

- **Two Bridges Regional Jail, Maine.** Inmates in one of the newest jail industries programs in the country design and fabricate wood items.

- **Franklin County Jail, Pennsylvania.** Inmates produce the newsletter for the Council for the Arts and wash, dry, and deliver uniforms for the Chambersburg Cardinals, a minor league football team.

- **Los Angeles Sheriff's Department Jail Enterprise Unit, California.** Inmates produce lunch and trash bags for the sheriff's food service unit, saving the sheriff's office over $100,000 annually instead of purchasing the bags. The Unit is expanding to market the bags to other government agencies within Los Angeles County.

- **Arapahoe County, Colorado.** Inmates are involved in a wide array of recycling initiatives. In 2007, the program earned almost $300,000, and about one-fourth of the revenues were paid to inmates as wages.

A faith-based organization encourages jail inmates to form a circle and ask their victims for forgiveness. Major life events such as incarceration are linked to a greater tendency to turn to spirituality or religion. What do you think is the role of jail ministry?

- **Hampden County Jail, Massachusetts.** Inmates enroll in a Culinary Arts Program at Springfield Technical Community College and operate the Olde Armory Grille. They gain experience in food preparation and delivery.

Elsewhere across the country, jail inmates are involved in animal grooming, auto repair, body work and detailing, events setup and breakdown, computer data entry, digital imaging, furniture assembly and repair, graphics, laundry, silk-screening, telephone marketing, and welding.

Jail Ministry

Very little is written about the use and effects of jail ministry and faith-based programming in jail. Too often the topic is looked at skeptically by outsiders who believe that inmates pretend to "find God" as a convenient way to obtain release or forgiveness. However, getting into trouble and then turning to religion is supported by the "coping" literature, which links major life events to a greater tendency to turn to spirituality or religion. What we will explore here, however, is not the research supporting the veracity of inmates' claims of conversion but instead the partnership between government and faith-based organizations to meet the nation's corrections needs. We will also consider the experiences of those who minister to jail inmates.

Religious belief can make a difference in people's lives and can assist in tackling social problems. Much crime is the result of people making the wrong moral choices. Churches and religious organizations can provide the moral and spiritual aspects to correctional programs. There are not enough correctional officers, probation or parole officers, or police to prevent every ex-offender from committing another crime, so help from other partners is needed. Pat Nolan, vice president of Prison Fellowship Ministries writes, "The way society will be able to reduce crime is if during their time of incarceration, offenders have been transformed and internalized a moral code that allows them to exercise self-restraint and be good citizens after they are released. . . . It will be helpful to look upon local churches as partners to help teach inmates these important lessons during their incarceration and to act as mentors as they re-enter their communities."[74]

Recently, researchers conducted a study to investigate the impact of religious programs on two matched groups of adult male prisoners in New York.[75] They found that inmates most actively involved in Bible studies (meaning they attended 10 or more classes over the course of one year) were less likely than inmates who attended fewer classes (or none) to commit institutional infractions or, if they did, the infractions were not as serious as the infractions of those who attended fewer classes (or none); and inmates most actively involved in Bible studies were less likely than inmates who attended fewer classes (or none) to be arrested during a one-year follow-up. Subsequent research found that differences in rearrest peaked at two and three years after release. The average time to rearrest for the inmates who were most actively involved in Bible studies was 3.8 years versus 2.3 years for inmates who attended fewer classes (or none). However, differences between the two groups diminished after that and were not statistically significant in years four through eight. Over time, the effects of Bible study attendance are diminished in importance. Risk for arrest in years four through eight was explained by other factors such as prior record, race, and age.

Those who minister to jail inmates tell us there are at least five benefits of jail chaplaincy. First, most jail chaplains believe that the cycle of crime can be broken only one life at a time. Jail inmates must experience an inner conversion before they change their behavior. Jail chaplains can assist in that conversion. Second, jail chaplains can help jail staff with their emotional and family problems. An on-site chaplain can help staff deal with problems daily as they develop. Third, jail chaplains are in a unique position to mediate and moderate tensions and conflicts between inmates and staff before they get serious. Pleading for nonviolence is a chaplain's strong tool. Inmates usually see a jail chaplain as neutral. The chaplain has the unique opportunity to speak his or her mind and be seen as someone who cares enough to confront and comfort. Fourth, the public perceives ministering to the disadvantaged as legitimate, and so such ministry helps the community remember those they would just as soon forget (recall the concept of inmates as "rabble," discussed earlier in this chapter). In the role as community liaisons, chaplains help raise the awareness about and sensitivity to jail issues and interests. The ability of chaplains to involve the public as jail volunteers is an added benefit. And fifth, jail chaplains can help inmates confront the truth about themselves and reverse the "everything is relative" attitude that offenders develop to justify their crimes.

In the following excerpt, a chaplain shares some thoughts about his two years on the job:[76]

> A chaplain occupies a unique place in an inmate's thinking. She or he is not seen as "one of them"; we are not associated so much with the institution or judicial system. That gives us unique opportunities to speak openly and be viewed not as someone who has a sinister hidden agenda, but as someone who cares enough to confront.

Jail Standards, Inspection, and Accreditation

Dr. Ken Kerle, former managing editor of *American Jails* and probably the most known advocate today for improving our nation's jails, wrote recently, ". . . jail inspection is about as popular in many places as a skunk in the living room and many county officials, including sheriffs, would just as soon avoid it altogether. It is no accident that 12 states today have no jail inspections and 8 states with inspection standards have no enforcement agency to compel compliance."[77] Florida is one example. According to the *Orlando Sentinel,* "When it comes to grading Central Florida's jails, no bell curve exists. Every facility generates near-perfect grades and glowing reviews."[78] Florida's Model Jail Standards inspection is a voluntary, peer-accreditation system of part-time inspectors, people usually employed as corrections managers, law enforcement officers, or fire inspectors somewhere else in Florida. Many Florida jails are also inspected through another peer-based system administered by the Florida Corrections Accreditation Commission, but accreditation is optional. Such oversight raises questions about the state's ability to oversee its jails. Members from the Florida Corrections Accreditation Commission and inspectors measuring the Florida Model Jail Standards recently each gave the Osceola County Jail nothing but praise just before two inmates escaped, another incident in which an inmate was accidentally released, and failure to note that razor wire had been incorrectly installed—issues that led to the disciplining of 30 officers, demotions of two captains, resignation of the jail director, and firing of the county manager. "If almost every jail is reaccredited by meeting 100 percent of the standards reviewed and if every facility meets an overwhelming majority of the Florida Model Jail Standards, then are these detention facilities truly being tested?" asked the *Orlando Sentinel*.

On the other hand, other populous states such as Illinois, New York, Pennsylvania, Ohio, and Texas mandate state oversight of county jails. Texas, for example, has the Commission on Jail Standards, an independent state agency with the authority to develop standards, conduct inspections, and fine or close down jails if they fail to comply. New York state statute allows the Commission of Corrections' jail investigators to visit any of the state's prisons or county jails at any time and may view any records they deem necessary to complete their duties. The Commission has a $3 million budget and a full-time nine-member board appointed by the governor. They may close any correctional facility if it is unsafe, unsanitary, or inadequate. Any person who does not obey its orders is guilty of a misdemeanor. The American Bar Association agrees with independent oversight and authority to act. It recommends that all federal, state, tribal, and territorial governments create independent bodies with broad authority and access to corrections facilities.[79]

Jail standards now govern inmate health care; the use of force; protection of inmates from violence; provision of services including food, clothing, shelter, protection from fires, and exercise; searches of all types; access to mail and reading materials, practice of one's faith; and inmate discipline. The task for jail managers is to translate jail standards into understandable and objective guidelines. For example, a court ruling that lighting in an inmate's cell may not be so low as to present an unreasonable risk of serious harm to inmates may leave a jail manager guessing as to how much light to have in the jail. However, a standard stating that lighting in inmate cells must be "at least 20 foot-candles at desk level" turns the vague statement into a measurable objective.

Today, jail compliance with standards set forth by the American Correctional Association (ACA) has become the best defense to ensure that jails are operating properly and highlight where improvements are needed. Two ACA publications, *Standards for Adult Local Detention Facilities* and *Standards for Small Jail Facilities,* cover the standards for the services, programs, and operations they consider essential to good jail management. Jails that comply with 100 percent of the mandatory standards and 90 percent of the nonmandatory ones are awarded accreditation.

Jail accreditation is a process through which correctional facilities and agencies can measure themselves against nationally adopted standards and through which they can receive formal recognition and accredited status. We will expand on the issue of correctional accreditation in Chapter 13.

jail accreditation
Process through which correctional facilities and agencies can measure themselves against nationally adopted standards and through which they can receive formal recognition and accredited status.

Ethics and Professionalism

Code of Ethics for Jail Officers

As an officer employed in a detention/correctional capacity, I swear (or affirm) to be a good citizen and a credit to my community, state, and nation at all times. I will abstain from questionable behavior which might bring disrepute to the agency for which I work, my family, my community, and my associates. My lifestyle will be above and beyond reproach, and I will constantly strive to set an example of a professional who performs his/her duties according to the laws of our country, state, and community and the policies, procedures, written and verbal orders, and regulations of the agency for which I work.

On the job I promise to

KEEP the institution secure so as to safeguard my community and the lives of the staff, inmates, and visitors on the premises.

WORK with each individual firmly and fairly without regard to rank, status, or condition.

MAINTAIN a positive demeanor when confronted with stressful situations of scorn, ridicule, danger, and/or chaos.

REPORT either in writing or by word of mouth to the proper authorities those things which should be reported and keep silent about matters which are to remain confidential according to the laws and rules of the agency and government.

MANAGE and supervise the inmates in an evenhanded and courteous manner.

REFRAIN at all times from becoming personally involved in the lives of the inmates and their families.

TREAT all visitors to the jail with politeness and respect and do my utmost to ensure that they observe the jail regulations.

TAKE advantage of all education and training opportunities designed to assist me to become a more competent officer.

COMMUNICATE with people in or outside of the jail, whether by phone, written word, or word of mouth, in such a way so as not to reflect in a negative manner upon my agency.

CONTRIBUTE to a jail environment which will keep the inmate involved in activities designed to improve his/her attitude and character.

SUPPORT all activities of a professional nature through membership and participation that will continue to elevate the status of those who operate our nation's jails. Do my best through word and deed to present an image to the public at large of a jail professional, committed to progress for an improved and enlightened criminal justice system.

Adopted by the American Jail Association Board of Directors on November 10, 1991, Revised May 19, 1993.

Source: Copyright © American Jail Association.

Ethical Dilemma 6–1: Female offenders have an average of 2.5 children. Increasing numbers of incarcerated, pregnant, and/or parenting women being sentenced to jail have resulted in many more children being separated from their mothers. Should jail administrators concern themselves with providing services for families of jail inmates? For more information go to Ethical Dilemma 6–1 at www.justicestudies.com/ethics06.

Ethical Dilemma 6–2: Sometimes administrators must make hard decisions when faced with budget cuts. As a jail administrator, you must cut one position, either a correctional officer or a teacher. Which position will you cut? Why? For more information go to Ethical Dilemma 6–2 at www.justicestudies.com/ethics06.

Ethical Dilemmas for every chapter are available online.

Although jails were slow to respond to the standards movement, their response has picked up in recent years. As of February 25, 2011, 131 adult local detention facilities were ACA accredited. ACA acts on agency requests for accreditation at its annual Winter Conference and Summer Congress of Correction.[80]

There are several reasons jails have been slow to adopt national standards or seek national accreditation. First, accreditation is expensive and time-consuming. Many jails do not have the resources to commit to it. This is especially true of small jails that are already overburdened. Second, jails hold relatively few long-term inmates. Few inmates are in a jail long enough to file a successful legal action regarding poor conditions in the jail. Knowing this, some jail administrators may not be willing to undergo the expense and burden of seeking accreditation. Third, some states have their own standards that jails must meet.

There are, however, at least five reasons for jails to have national accreditation:

1. Accreditation by the ACA indicates that a jail adheres to strict standards to protect the health and safety of staff and inmates.
2. Being accredited may help a jail defend itself against lawsuits over conditions of incarceration.
3. In preparing for the accreditation review, the sheriff's office may evaluate all operations, procedures, and policies, leading to better management practices.
4. With accreditation come professional recognition and status, greater appreciation by the community, and a sense of pride in the achievement and in the hard work that went into it. As Edward Sturdivant, accreditation manager for the Clarke/Frederick/Winchester Regional Jail, Winchester, Virginia, put it, "Accreditation shows that we as a profession are willing to police ourselves and that we are dedicated to getting the job done right the first time. It also holds us to a higher standard so that society does not have to do it for us."[81]
5. And recently, ACA in conjunction with the American Jail Association, National Sheriff's Association, National Institute of Corrections, and the Federal Bureau of Prisons developed a set of core jail standards to establish minimum practices for small- and medium-size facilities. This new option makes certification easier now for small- and medium-size jails.

Workforce Development

Jail staff assume enormous responsibility, and we expect them to conduct themselves as professionals. Before 1970, training and education for jail officers were virtually nonexistent for several reasons. Jail officers often aspired to be law enforcement officers, or they were using jail work as their last stop on the road to retirement. Many people also believed that education and training for jail staff were unnecessary because the work was unsophisticated and could be learned on the job.

Since 1970, however, the image of jail staff has changed. Thanks to organizations such as the American Jail Association and the American Correctional Association; national, state, and local commissions on jail issues; and studies by practitioners, consultants, and academic researchers, jail work is now recognized not only as difficult but also as a career path that is different from law enforcement and requires different attitudes and skills. Jail staff perform work that is vital, complex, and potentially hazardous, even under the best of circumstances.

Many communities today have been affected by recent immigration trends, and sometimes those new trends set up cultural barriers between jail staff and inmates. The 45 sheriffs and jail administrators who met in May and June 2007 to make recommendations on jail issues to the Justice Department noted that jails deal with the most diverse populations in society, from race and religion to age, education, ethnicity, sexual orientation, disabilities, language, and intellectual competence. Yet two-thirds of jail staff are white males, as we pointed out earlier, and many staff are not prepared to deal effectively with the challenges involved in managing such a diverse population.

To conduct themselves as professionals, jail staff must have strong communication skills, knowledge of the psychology of behavior, multi-cultural sophistication, ethnic and racial tolerance, human management expertise, endurance, and fitness. Even more important, they must, for their own mental well-being, be able to understand and tolerate the stress of a potentially explosive environment. The American Jail Association's Code of Ethics for Jail Officers is shown in the Ethics and Professionalism box.

In 1978, the ACA pioneered correctional accreditation. In 1999, it embarked on another milestone in the process of bringing professionalism into corrections by developing a national Commission on Correctional Certification (CCC) and an online Corrections Academy.

Just as accreditation provides an opportunity for facilities to be recognized, certification is an opportunity for jail staff to be recognized as qualified correctional practitioners. The ACA certification process requires applicants to meet the educational requirements of the category within which they seek certification (for example, the category of correctional executive requires a college degree; correctional managers and supervisors require an associate degree; correctional officers require a high school diploma). Next applicants must pass a national examination developed by the National Institute of Corrections for the job tasks and related competencies associated with the job category. Finally, applications enter into "candidacy status," a two-year period during which they must pass a certification examination. Those who pass the certification exam become Certified Corrections Professionals for three years. Maintaining that status involves becoming recertified and obtaining a specified number of continuing education credits. Through the efforts of the ACA's Commission on Correctional Certification, jail personnel are on the road to upgrading their public image and professional stature and achieving the status of other professions that rely on universal compliance with a self-imposed credentialing process.

Evidence-Based Practices

The final priority identified by the group of sheriffs and jail administrators in 2007 relates to evidence-based practices. The body of jail-related research is very small compared to what is known about prisons, yet the sheriffs and jail administrators agreed that if more was known about what works in jails, they would be able to improve everything from efficiency and cost-effectiveness to public safety, agency accountability, and proactive planning.

A year later, researchers reported on what evidence-based practices are used in the nation's jails to treat substance abuse. Of 13 key evidence-based practices recommended by the National Institute on Drug Abuse, the researchers found that jail administrators reported implementing an average of only 1.6 (see Exhibit 6–11).[82] Only four best practices are used in more than half of all jails: (1) comprehensive treatment methods to address offenders' multiple needs; (2) engagement with community agencies to provide services for drug-involved offenders; (3) use of positive incentives to encourage inmate behavior; and (4) use of standardized substance abuse assessment tools to understand the extent and impact of drug usage.

In spite of the fact, however, that half of the jails use these four evidence-based practices, the jails have not conducted the rigorous evaluations that are necessary to show the impact the practices have on reduced criminal activity.

EVIDENCE-BASED CORRECTIONS

EXHIBIT 6–11   Percentage of Jails That Use Evidence-Based Practices to Treat Substance Abuse

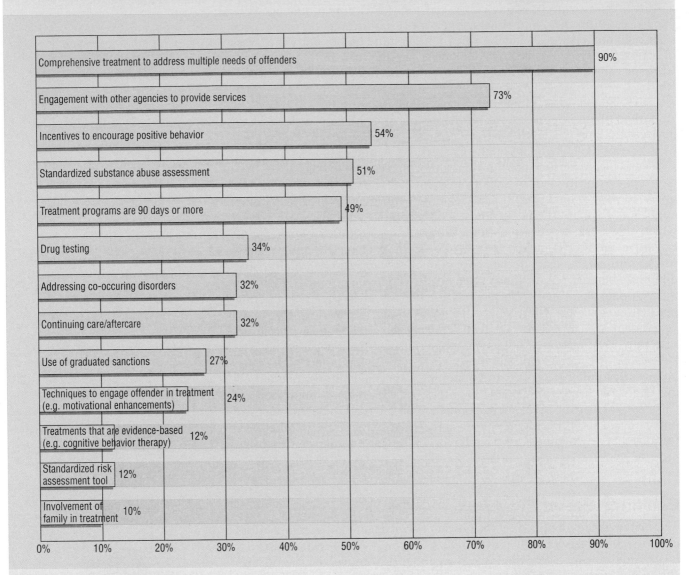

Source: Adapted from Peter D. Friedman, Faye S. Taxman, and Craig E. Henderson, "Evidence-Based Treatment Practices for Drug-Involved Adults in the Criminal Justice System," *Journal of Substance Abuse Treatment,* vol. 32, no.3 (2007), pp. 267–277.

REVIEW AND APPLICATIONS

SUMMARY

1 There are 3,365 locally operated jails in the United States. Besides incarcerating people who have sentences of a year or less, jails serve a number of purposes. They hold people awaiting trial, probation and parole violators, adults and juveniles awaiting transfer, and prison inmates about to be released. Sometimes they operate community-based programs. The jail population is different from the prison population in terms of total admissions and average daily population.

2 The *daily* population of jails is lower than that of prisons, but the *annual* total of people incarcerated in jails is higher.

3 Jails emerged in Europe in the 12th century to detain offenders for trial. In the 15th and 16th centuries, the poor and unemployed were detained alongside criminals. The first jail in America was the Walnut Street Jail. Quakers designed it according to their principles of religious reflection and penance. It fell short of reaching its goals and closed in 1835.

4 American jails have progressed through four phases of architecture and inmate management: first-generation jails (linear design and sporadic supervision), second-generation jails (pod design and remote supervision), third-generation jails (pod design and direct supervision), and fourth-generation jails ("borrowed light" and less isolation).

5 By mid-2009, jails held or supervised 837,833 offenders. An estimated 38 percent of jail inmates are convicted offenders. Women represent 12.2 percent of the jail population; nonwhites, 57.5 percent; and juveniles, 0.9 percent. Almost two-thirds of all jail inmates have a mental health problem, and there are more people with mental illness in jail than there are in mental health hospitals. Jail suicides are down, jail homicides are up, and 3.1 percent of all jail inmates experienced one or more incidents of sexual victimization involving another inmate or staff. By mid-2009, 94 percent of jail capacity was occupied. Forty-seven jails are privatized. The most (eight) are in Texas. Almost 300,000 people work in jails. The increase in the jail population is outpacing the growth in jail staff. The problems of jail staff include low pay and prestige, high turnover, and inadequate systems for recruitment, selection, and training.

6 Advocates of privatization claim they can build and operate jails more efficiently than can government. Opponents argue they cannot, or they dismiss the cost issues altogether. For them, operating a jail is a basic function of government and a symbol of state authority and should not be delegated.

7 Jail vocational and educational programs are important avenues for managing inmates, reducing recidivism, and successful reentry. They keep inmates occupied, boost self-esteem, and help inmates find jobs after release.

8 Jails are partnering with faith-based organizations to meet the needs of jail inmates. Jail chaplaincy can influence jail inmates in five ways. First, chaplains can help inmates with the inner conversion needed to break the cycle of crime. Second, a jail chaplain can help staff deal with day-to-day problems. Third, a jail chaplain can mediate and moderate tensions and conflicts between inmates and staff. Fourth, jail chaplaincy can involve the public as jail volunteers and remind people that inmates exist. And fifth, chaplains can help inmates confront the truth about themselves.

9 Jail standards, inspection, and accreditation are important for five reasons. First, inspection and accreditation indicate that a jail adheres to strict standards. Second, accreditation may help a jail defend itself against lawsuits over conditions of incarceration. Third, through inspection and accreditation, the sheriff's office may evaluate all jail operations, procedures, and policies, leading to better management practices. Fourth, accreditation generates professional recognition and status, greater appreciation by the community, and a sense of pride. And fifth, the ACA in conjunction with the American Jail Association, National Sheriff's Association, National Institute of Corrections, and the Federal Bureau of Prisons now has a set of core jail standards to establish minimum practices for small- and medium-size facilities. This new option makes certification easier for small- and medium-size jails.

10 It is important for jail staff to conduct themselves as professionals because jail work is difficult and carries enormous responsibility. It requires a special attitude, communication skills, knowledge of the psychology of behavior, multicultural sophistication, endurance, and fitness. Together, college education and jail training prepare jail staff to work as professionals. In 1999, the American Correctional Association established the Commission on Correctional Certification (CCC). The purpose of the CCC is to recognize jail staff as qualified correctional practitioners using a self-imposed credentialing process.

11 The National Institute on Drug Abuse recommends 13 key evidence-based practices to treat substance abuse. Jails implement an average of only 1.6. Four evidence-based practices are used in more than one-half of all jails. However, jails have not conducted scientific evaluations to show the impact the practices have on reduced criminal activity.

KEY TERMS

jails, p. 174
total admission, p. 174
average daily population (ADP), p. 174
rabble management, p. 178
first-generation jail, p. 178

second-generation jail, p. 179
third-generation jail, p. 179
direct-supervision jail, p. 179
fourth-generation jail, p. 182
sexual victimization, p. 193
rated capacity, p. 195

pay-to-stay jail, p. 196
self-pay jails, p. 196
privatization, p. 199
reentry, p. 201
accreditation, p. 206

QUESTIONS FOR REVIEW

1 Jails serve a number of purposes. Which do you believe is the most important and why?

2 Describe how jail populations are different from prison populations.

3 Summarize the history of jails.

4 Explain how first-, second-, third-, and fourth-generation jails are different.

5 What can you infer from the characteristics of jail inmates, facilities, and staff?

6 What ideas can you add to the arguments for and against jail privatization?

7 How do jail vocational and educational programs affect inmate behavior, recidivism, and reentry?

8 What criteria would you use to assess the impact that faith-based organizations and jail chaplains have on jail inmates and staff?

9 What ideas can you add to the arguments for and against jail standards, inspection, and accreditation?

10 What might happen if jail staff did not conduct themselves as professionals?

11 Explain how jails could do more to implement evidence-based practices to treat substance abuse and demonstrate their impact on reduced criminal activity.

THINKING CRITICALLY ABOUT CORRECTIONS

Mentally Ill Inmates

Explain why mentally ill jail inmates are not yet subjects for incarceration as some suggest, and why jails are ill-equipped to meet their needs.

Evidence-Based Practices

Why are evidence-based practices necessary for jails?

ON-THE-JOB DECISION MAKING

Promoting Direct Supervision

You are the administrator of a new county jail with the architecture and philosophy of direct supervision. The new jail replaced a jail built in 1912. Some of the senior staff have begun complaining to you about direct supervision. They say they don't like to interact with inmates. They talk about "the good old days" when inmates were "on the other side" of the reinforced glass and steel bars. There's even been a letter to the editor in the local newspaper complaining that the new jail doesn't "look like a jail."

1. What could you tell the senior staff about direct-supervision philosophy that might ease their concerns?

2. What strategies might you use to educate the public about the benefits of direct supervision?

Jail Standards, Inspection, and Accreditation

Imagine that you have just been elected as the first college-educated sheriff of a large county with a megajail (more than 1,000 beds). Your state has jail standards but inspection is done by a jail committee from another county and there is no enforcement agency to compel compliance. At the annual state sheriffs' meeting, you give a talk on the issues you see with neighboring counties inspecting each other's jails and the lack of enforcement to compel compliance. What will you say?

For additional information, please see: www.mhhe.com/schmalleger6e

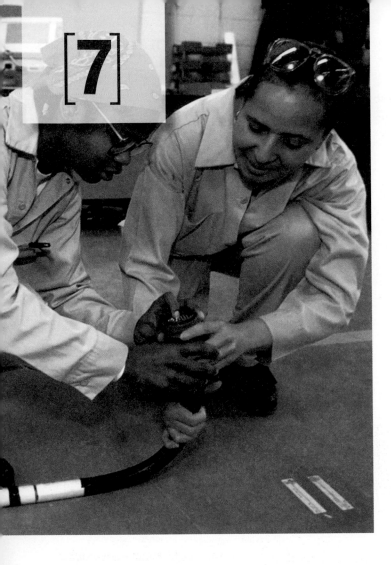

[7]

PRISONS TODAY

Change Stations or Warehouses?

CHAPTER OBJECTIVES

After completing this chapter you should be able to do the following:

1 Explain the differences between the Pennsylvania and Auburn prison systems.

2 Outline the nine eras of prison development.

3 Describe the characteristics of today's prisoners and discuss reasons for the incarceration of women and minority prisoners.

4 Explain prisoner classification and its purposes.

5 Discuss the arguments for and against faith-based correctional institutions.

6 Explain what the evidence-based literature says about prison industries.

7 Report on the availability of education and health care programs for prisoners.

8 Compare state and federal prison organization and administration.

9 Discuss the question "Does incarceration work?"

> "It is not that we do not know how to create meaningful changes to our prison and mental health systems, it is that we do not have the will to do so. It is far easier to put people who are dangerously ill behind walls and fences; in that way, we will never have to acknowledge their suffering.
>
> —Elaine Lord, former superintendent of the Bedford Hills Correctional Facility, New York State's maximum security facility for women"

A 13-year-old boy is not your average criminal, but Kody Scott was not your average 13-year-old boy. Born in Los Angeles in 1963, Kody grew up with his mother and five brothers and sisters. It was a childhood full of hardship, violence, and instability. Tired of being bullied in elementary school, Kody chose never to be a victim again. He joined the Eight Tray Gangster Crips and earned the nickname "Monster" when he beat and stomped a robbery victim into a coma. Witnesses told the police that the person was a "monster," and the name stuck.[1]

Kody spent the next 13 years with the Crips living up to his nickname, becoming progressively more violent and vicious. He dropped out of school after the sixth grade and became a hero to the Crips. But eventually, in detention, he began to question his way of life. At the California Youth Training School, he met Muhammad Abdullah who led the Muslim worship services and led Kody to understand that what he was doing was self-destructive when the real enemy was the American social system that kept minorities from advancing. For almost a decade, Kody was in and out of prison for armed robbery, assault, illegal possession of a weapon, and parole violation. As an adult, Kody turned to Islam, left the Crips, joined the New Afrikan Independence movement, and changed his name to Sanyika Shakur.

In 1993, Shakur published his autobiography, *Monster: The Autobiography of a L.A. Gang Member.* It describes how he was drawn into gang life, his experiences as a gangster both on the streets and in prison, and his eventual transformation into Islam. The book sold over 100,000 copies.

In March 2007, however, Scott was once again arrested by the Los Angeles Police Department for parole violations and allegedly breaking into the home of an acquaintance and beating him in order to steal his car. He pleaded no contest and was sentenced to six years in state prison. He is one of almost 172,000 inmates under the jurisdiction of the California Department of Corrections and Rehabilitation.[2] He is incarcerated under the name Kody Scott, inmate D07829 at the Pelican Bay State Prison, 700 miles north of Los Angeles. In 2008, he also published his first book of fiction, *T.H.U.G. L.I.F.E.,* about an L.A. gang member and his attempts to free himself.

Later in this chapter we will learn more about state and federal prison systems. We begin the chapter with a look at the history of American prisons.

His legal name is Kody Scott, inmate D07829, incarcerated since 2007 at the Pelican State Bay Prison, 700 miles north of Los Angeles, for parole violations and breaking into the home of an acquaintance and beating him in order to steal his car. His friends and family call him Sanyika Shakur, a name he gave himself when he turned to Islam and the New Afrikan Independence movement. Scott's criminal career began when he was 13 years old. He beat and stomped a robbery victim into a coma. Witnesses told police that the person was a "monster," and the name stuck. In 1993, Scott published his autobiography, Monster: The Autobiography of a L.A. Gang Member. *The book describes how he was drawn into gang life and his eventual transformation into Islam. The book sold over 100,000 copies. In 2008, he published his first book of fiction* T.H.U.G. L.I.F.E. *about an L.A. gang member and his attempts to free himself. How could Scott use his writing skills in prison? What about on his release to stay crime free?*

Then we will discuss the composition of the prison population, programs for prisoners, and the way America's prisons are organized and administered. We conclude with the question "Does incarceration work?"

HISTORY OF PRISONS IN AMERICA

Prisons are relatively modern social institutions, and their development is distinctly American. Until the mid-18th century, fines, banishment from the community, corporal punishment, and execution were the primary forms of punishing offenders. By the latter part of the century, incarceration was championed as a more humane form of punishment. It reflected and fueled a shift from the assumption that offenders were inherently criminal to a belief that they were simply not properly trained to resist temptation and corruption. The two prison systems that emerged in the United States—the Pennsylvania system and the Auburn system—were copied throughout the world.

The Pennsylvania and Auburn prison systems developed in the United States at the turn of the 19th century. Pennsylvania Quakers advocated a method of punishment more humane than the public corporal punishment used at the time. The Quakers shifted the emphasis from punishing the body to reforming the mind and soul. Together with an elite group of 18th-century Philadelphians, they ushered in the first **penitentiary**, a place for reform of offenders through repentance and rehabilitation. They believed prisoners needed to be isolated from each other in silence to repent, to accept God's guidance, and to avoid having a harmful influence on each other. Known as the **Pennsylvania system** or the *separate system*, this method was first used at the Walnut Street Jail, which the Quakers reorganized in 1790 as the country's first penitentiary. The Eastern State Penitentiary, constructed in 1829, was also based on these principles. The prison was designed for solitary confinement and labor, with instruction in labor, morals, and religion. To make the isolation less severe and to help inmates prepare for employment after release, prison officials permitted inmates to work by themselves in their cells at various occupations, such as shoemaking, weaving, tailoring, and polishing marble. For the first time in American history, rehabilitation and deterrence emerged as goals of corrections.

The solitary confinement of the Pennsylvania system was expensive, and it reportedly drove prisoners insane and further hardened criminal tendencies. Reformers responded with what has been termed the **Auburn system**: regimentation, military-style drill, silence unless conversation was required in workshops, congregate working and eating, separation of prisoners into small individual cells at night, harsh discipline, shaved heads, black-and-white striped uniforms, and industrial workshops that contracted with private businesses to help pay for the institution. Prison factories in the 19th century produced shoes, barrels, carpets, engines, boilers, harnesses, clothing, and furniture—goods that could not be produced under the "solitary" system of Pennsylvania or not in quantities sufficient to make a profit. This merchandise was sold on the open market to American consumers or exported to Canada and Latin America, and the proceeds helped support prison operations. The first prison to use this system opened in Auburn, New York, in 1819. The Auburn system, congregate by day and separate by night, eventually gave way to congregate cells at night and removal of the restrictions against talking.

penitentiary

The earliest form of large-scale incarceration. It punished criminals by isolating them so that they could reflect on their misdeeds, repent, and reform.

Pennsylvania system (also *separate system*)

The first historical phase of prison discipline, involving solitary confinement in silence instead of corporal punishment; conceived by the American Quakers in 1790 and implemented at the Walnut Street Jail.

Auburn system

The second historical phase of prison discipline, implemented at New York's Auburn prison in 1815. It followed the Pennsylvania system and allowed inmates to work silently together during the day, but they were isolated at night. Eventually sleeping cells became congregate and restrictions against talking were removed.

Prison reform in the United States caught the attention of prison officials around the world. The Pennsylvania system of isolation and silence became popular in Europe. In the United States, the two competing philosophies of prison life clashed, and the debate over which system was superior raged on for decades. Supporters of the Pennsylvania system argued that it made it easier to control prisoners and prevented prisoners from learning bad habits from each other. Supporters of the Auburn system claimed that prisoners' spirits needed to be broken before true reform could begin and that their system of harsh discipline and congregate but silent labor accomplished that. Auburn supporters also argued that their prison system was cheaper to build and that the use of contract labor would keep down costs.

A system that was congregate by day (and eventually by night as well) seemed more compatible with the political and economic tone of the time. The Pennsylvania system represented a traditional approach to production: handcrafted labor in solitary cells. In contrast, the Auburn system reflected the emerging developments of the Industrial Revolution: power machinery, factory production, and division of labor. The attractiveness of the Auburn system's perceived economic benefits as well as a belief in the rehabilitative value of hard work settled the debate. Thus, the congregate system became the preferred model of incarceration in the United States. In 1913, Eastern State Penitentiary, the epitome of the Pennsylvania system, converted to the Auburn system, ending the great debate. Congregate prisons have been the mode ever since. Today, however, new voices are calling for a return to long-term solitary confinement in supermax prisons (one of several topics discussed in Chapter 13).

Stages of Development

Prisons in America have progressed through nine stages of development (see Exhibit 7–1). Many of these changes were influenced by cultural movements in society. As you review the historical stages, think about how the goals of imprisonment changed in each era as society changed.

The Eastern State Penitentiary, completed in 1829, was designed on the Quakers' principle of solitary confinement in silence with instruction in labor, morals, and religion. What name was given to this separate system of prisoner management?

EXHIBIT 7–1   Stages of Prison History in the United States

Stage	Penitentiary Era	Mass Prison Era	Reformatory Era	Industrial Era
Years	1790–1825	1825–1876	1876–1890	1890–1935
Goal	Rehabilitation and deterrence	Incapacitation and deterrence	Rehabilitation	Incapacitation
Characteristics	Separate and silent Congregate and silent	Congregate labor and living spaces without silence Contract prison labor	Indeterminate sentencing Parole	Public accounts industries Contract labor State-use labor Convict lease Public works labor
Examples of Institutions	Walnut Street Penitentiary, Philadelphia, PA Eastern State Penitentiary, Cherry Hill, PA Auburn Prison, Auburn, NY	Sing Sing Prison, Ossining, NY San Quentin State Prison, San Quentin, CA	Elmira, NY Indiana Reformatory for Women and Girls, Indianapolis, IN	Most major prisons
Related Events	1819 Congregate, silent system implemented in Auburn Penitentiary, New York. 1829 Eastern State Penitentiary opens under the Pennsylvania prison model.	1841 John Augustus begins the practice of probation in Massachusetts. 1871 *Ruffin* v. *Commonwealth* establishes that convicted felons not only forfeit liberty but also are slaves of the state; this provides the legal justification for courts to maintain a "hands-off doctrine." 1913 Eastern State Penitentiary converts to the Auburn prison model.	1876 The first women's prison, the Indiana Reformatory for Women and Girls, opens. 1876 Zebulon Brockway appointed warden at Elmira Reformatory and initiates first parole system in the United States. 1878 First probation law is passed in Massachusetts.	1899 First juvenile court established in Cook County (Chicago), Illinois. 1914–1918 World War I begins and ends. 1929 Hawes-Cooper Act passed to regulate interstate sale of prison-made goods. 1929 Great Depression begins. 1930 Federal Bureau of Prisons is established.

EXHIBIT 7–1 Stages of Prison History in the United States *(continued)*

Punitive Era	Treatment Era	Community-Based Era	Warehousing Era	Just Deserts Era
1935–1945	1945–1967	1967–1980	1980–1995	1985–Present
Retribution	Rehabilitation	Reintegration	Incapacitation	Retribution
Strict punishment and custody	Medical model Emerging prisoner unrest	Intermediate sanction: halfway houses, work release centers, group homes, fines, restitution, community service	Sentencing guidelines End of discretionary parole release Serious crowding More prison riots	Just deserts Determinate sentencing Truth in sentencing Three-strikes law Serious crowding
U.S. Penitentiary, Alcatraz, CA	Patuxent Institution, Jessup, MD	Major prison riots (Attica, NY; Santa Fe, NM)	Most major prisons	Spreading through the United States
1934 Alcatraz ("Hellcatraz") opens. 1939 Great Depression ends. 1939–1945 World War II begins and ends. 1942–1945 Japanese and Japanese American relocation centers open and close.	1950 Federal Youth Corrections Act passed to create treatment for offenders under the age of 22 in the federal system. 1964 *Cooper* v. *Pate* formally recognizing the constitutional rights of prisoners. 1967 *In re Gault,* U.S. Supreme Court rules that juvenile offenders are entitled to state-provided counsel and due process guarantees. 1967 President Johnson's Commission on Law Enforcement and Administration of Justice recommends changing the criminal justice system.	1970 Massachusetts becomes first state to close down all of its juvenile reform schools. 1974 Robert Martinson's "What Works" is published and is used by politicians as reason to pull resources from prisons. 1976 Maine is first state to abolish discretionary parole board release. 1979 Prison Industry Enhancement (PIE) certification program repeals limitations on interstate commerce in prison-made goods.	1980s President Reagan declares "war on drugs." 1984 Federal Sentencing Reform Act imposes mandatory sentences for specific crimes. 1993 Three-strikes-and-you're-out laws spread across the United States. 1994 Congress passes the Violent Crime Control and Law Enforcement Act, which increases financial incentives for states to put more violent criminals in prison.	1994 Federal Bureau of Prisons opens its supermax prison. 1995 Eight states reinstate chain gangs. 1999 Number of people incarcerated in the United States exceeds 2 million for the first time. 2004 Abuse of prisoners at Abu Ghraib prison in Baghdad, Iraq, by U.S. military personnel becomes public. 2007 Evidence-based research and economic recession shape correctional practice.

EVIDENCE-BASED CORRECTIONS

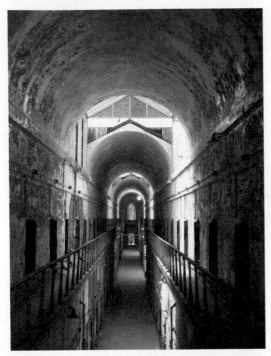

Interior view of a cellblock at Eastern State Penitentiary. Linear design and sporadic inmate supervision characterized Eastern State. What problems emerged at Eastern State that caused the demise of the Pennsylvania system?

public accounts system

The earliest form of prison industry, in which the warden was responsible for purchasing materials and equipment and for overseeing the manufacture, marketing, and sale of prison-made items.

contract system

A system of prison industry in which the prison advertised for bids for the employment of prisoners, whose labor was sold to the highest bidder.

Remember too that old ways did not disappear when new ways emerged. Rather, new thinking challenged the thinking of previous eras and facilitated the development of new correctional policy, including the shift toward professionalism in corrections. Most often, new ideas simply developed alongside existing ones.

Penitentiary Era (1790–1825) The first era in prison history was the penitentiary era. In 1790, the renovated Walnut Street Jail opened with a penitentiary wing that emphasized the Quakers' religious belief in prisoner reform through reflection, penitance, and rehabilitation through good conduct. From that beginning, two competing prison systems merged, the Pennsylvania system of separate and silent confinement and the Auburn system of harsh discipline and congregate but silent labor. The era witnessed the demise of the Pennsylvania system and the building of 30 state prisons on the Auburn pattern of congregate by day and separate by night. This pattern eventually changed to congregate both day and night.

Mass Prison Era (1825–1876) The second era was the mass prison era. During that period, the idea of prison as a place for punishment flourished across the United States. As a result, 35 more Auburn-system prisons were built, including Sing Sing in New York State in 1825, San Quentin in California in 1852, and Joliet in Illinois in 1858. Most were built by prisoners who quarried the stones on-site.

Reformatory Era (1876–1890) The third era was the reformatory era. Influenced by progressive beliefs that education and science were vehicles for controlling crime, the first reformatory for young men opened at Elmira, New York, in 1876. The reformatory, whose prisoners had indeterminate sentences (a sentence for which a judge specifies a maximum length and a minimum length and for which an administrative agency, generally a parole board, determines the actual time of release), used a grading system that led to early release on parole and offered academic education, vocational training, individual rehabilitation, and military instruction and discipline. During this era, 20 reformatories opened for men, as well as the first prison for women, Mount Pleasant in Ossining, New York, and the first reformatory for women, the Indiana Reformatory for Women and Girls in Indianapolis. Massachusetts passed the first probation law in 1878, extending progressive belief into community supervision as well.

Industrial Era (1890–1935) Fourth was the industrial era. During this time, inmates worked in prison industries. The first prisons had used the **public accounts system** for work. The warden at the Walnut Street Jail determined the product, purchased materials and equipment, and oversaw the manufacture, marketing, and sale of prison-made items. At Auburn, prison industries expanded to include copper, weaving, tailor, blacksmith, and shoemaking shops. However, as more states adopted the Auburn model, the **contract system** replaced the public accounts system. Under the contract system, the prison advertised for bids for the employment of prisoners, whose labor was sold to the highest bidder. The desire to increase profits for the prison and the private contractor often led to exploitation of the prisoners under this system.

During the industrial era, prisons progressed from the public accounts and contract systems of the Pennsylvania and Auburn prisons to *convict lease, state use,* and *public works* systems. Which system was used in a state depended on the region the state was in and the period in which the transition was made.

The **convict lease system** was prevalent in the post–Civil War South and functioned as a replacement for the institution of slavery. Many southern prisons had been destroyed during the war. Southern states found it easier to relinquish supervision of their prisoners to a lessee. The lessee either employed prisoners as slave labor for private businesses within a state institution or transported them to work elsewhere in the state. Railway, lumber, and coal mining companies leased the highest numbers of inmates. Lessees housed, fed, clothed, and disciplined inmates. The convict lease system generated income for the prison and reduced overhead because the contractors were responsible for feeding and sheltering the convicts they leased. Left to the mercy of the contractors, however, leased convicts were subjected to terrible abuses of nearly unimaginable brutality.

From attempts to deal with this problem emerged the state use system. Under the **state use system,** prisoners manufactured products for use by state governments and their agencies, departments, and institutions. By putting inmates to work manufacturing products for sale exclusively to government agencies, prisons were better able to keep inmates occupied while reducing direct competition with the private sector and avoiding the exploitative character of inmate leasing. As the western states developed, a **public works system** emerged. This system used inmates to build public buildings, roads, and parks.

In time, national labor organizations saw prison industries as unfair competition and lobbied Congress to regulate prison industry. In 1929, the Hawes-Cooper Act banned the interstate shipment of prison-made goods. The Ashurst-Sumners Act of 1935 prohibited carriers from accepting prison-made goods for transportation. Ashurst-Sumners also mandated the labeling of prison-made goods. In 1940, Congress passed the Sumners-Ashurst Act, forbidding the interstate transportation of prison-made goods for private use, regardless of whether a state banned importation of prison goods (products manufactured for the federal government or other state governments were exempt). Thus, much of the private market was closed to goods made by inmates. Today, it is a violation of federal law for state prisons to sell their products in interstate commerce unless they are certified by a federal program known as Prison Industry Enhancement (PIE). Under provisions of the PIE program, inmates must be paid the same wages as free workers engaged in similar work. They must also be allowed to keep 20 percent of what they earn. The rest of their wages can be withheld to pay income taxes, child support obligations, room and board charges, and restitution to victims and to victim assistance funds. We return to a discussion of PIE later in this chapter.

It was also during the industrial era that the federal Bureau of Prisons (BOP) was established in 1930. We return to a discussion of the BOP later in this chapter.

The Industrial Revolution ushered in the era of the industrial prison. The era had good intentions. What were they and what happened?

convict lease system

A system of prison industry in which a prison temporarily relinquished supervision of its prisoners to a lessee. The lessee either employed the prisoners within the institution or transported them to work elsewhere in the state.

state use system

A system of prison industry that employs prisoners to manufacture products consumed by state governments and their agencies, departments, and institutions.

public works system

A system of prison industry in which prisoners were employed in the construction of public buildings, roads, and parks.

Punitive Era (1935–1945) The closing of prison industries ushered in the punitive era, with its emphasis on strict punishment and custody. The holding of prisoners in the Big House, in complete idleness, monotony, and frustration, characterized this era. The "escape proof" federal prison on the island of Alcatraz in San Francisco Bay opened on the eve of this era. It became the prototype of the latter-day supermax prisons that we will discuss in Chapter 13. It was retrofitted with the latest security hardware then available and staffed with an elite corps of officers. It opened in 1934 to receive the toughest prisoners in the federal BOP.

Treatment Era (1945–1967) The sixth era, treatment, emerged in response to prison riots across the United States. After World War II, the prison population exploded. Overcrowding, idleness, poor food, and other deprivations led prisoners to take matters into their own hands. Prison riots erupted in California, Colorado, Georgia, Illinois, Louisiana, Massachusetts, Michigan, Minnesota, New Jersey, New Mexico, Ohio, Oregon, Pennsylvania, Utah, and Washington. The riots aroused public support for prisoner rehabilitation.

medical model

A philosophy of prisoner reform in which criminal behavior is regarded as a disease to be treated with appropriate therapy.

Reform through classification, therapy, and increased use of the indeterminate sentence was the focus of the **medical model,** in which criminal behavior was regarded as a disease to be treated. If the diagnosis showed poor socialization and inadequate work skills as the factors that caused a person to turn to crime, the prescription could involve a combination of social skills counseling and vocational training. Maryland's Patuxent Institution with legions of mental health experts promised to predict dangerousness accurately and to release only those prisoners who were no longer a threat to the community. However, Patuxent failed to keep that promise. Scholars and advocacy groups also began finding fault with the medical model. They argued that it did not have as favorable an effect on recidivism as supporters argued it would have. They also argued that the medical model encouraged inmates to give the false impression that they were rehabilitated and suitable for early release. Above all was the view that the medical model was a form of coercion and that genuine changes in human behavior could not be coerced. In addition, the social and political unrest of the 1960s had found its way into the nation's prisons. A race riot broke out at San Quentin in 1967, and protests, riots, and killings occurred in other prisons. Corrections experts believed that a new approach was needed—one in which offenders were supervised in the community rather than imprisoned in fortresslike institutions.

Community-Based Era (1967–1980) Community-based corrections mostly developed after the 1960s although some community-based programs had begun a century earlier. New York City Quakers opened the Isaac T. Hopper Home in 1845 as a shelter for released inmates; Zebulon Brockway opened the Detroit House of Corrections in 1861 as a shelter for released women; the Philadelphia House of Industry opened in 1889; and Maude Ballington Booth opened Hope Hall, a refuge for ex-inmates in New York, in the 1890s. After that, the community-based concept lay dormant until the 1950s when church groups founded more halfway houses (St. Leonard's House in Chicago and Crenshaw House in Los Angeles) and then until 1967 when President Lyndon Johnson's crime commission came to the conclusion that the community was a source of offenders' problems. The commission recommended that offenders be rehabilitated by using community resources. More halfway houses, community corrections centers, intensive supervision probation programs, work release centers, and the like quickly spread across the United States. By the end of the 20th century, halfway houses—which were practically unknown a century earlier—were an indispensable part of corrections.

Observers soon discovered that the community-based approach did not lower the crime rate, reduce the prison population, or make the community safer. With the goals of community corrections unmet, the community-based era gave way, and President Nixon ushered in the country's attitude of "get tough on crime."

Warehousing Era (1980–1995) During the warehousing era, indeterminate sentencing was replaced by determinate sentencing in all states. Discretionary parole board release was abolished in a number of states and the federal government, and the pendulum swung from rehabilitation to incapacitation. President Reagan declared "war on drugs," federal sentencing reform mandated sentences for specific crimes, and three-strikes-and-you're-out and truth-in-sentencing laws swept across the United States. Within 15 years, the number of people under correctional supervision jumped from 1.8 million to almost 6 million. Prisons were operating over capacity, and controlling prisoners in such an environment was difficult. For staff and inmates alike, the nation's prisons were dangerous places to be. Extreme crowding resulted in violent outbreaks, which further hardened the attitudes of correctional policymakers and caused them to crack down even more.

Just Deserts Era (1985–present) Along with the get-tough policies of the warehousing era emerged a distinct but parallel vision of corrections. The just deserts philosophy focuses on punishment and provides a philosophy that supports the practice of warehousing. Chain gangs, striped uniforms, and boot camps have been resuscitated, parole has been cut back to 19th-century levels, and corrections has become as much of a political football as at any time in its history. Under the philosophy of just deserts, offenders are punished because they deserve it, the sanction used depending on the seriousness of the offense. Just deserts is not concerned with inmate rehabilitation, treatment, or reform. It separates treatment from punishment. Prisons today provide opportunities for inmates to improve themselves, but participation is not mandatory, nor is it a condition of release as it was for most of the 20th century. Change is facilitated, not coerced. Determinate sentencing, capital punishment, truth in sentencing, and three-strikes laws have grown in popularity. As we move into the 21st century, supermax and "no-frills" prisons are becoming the trend.

WHO IS IN PRISON TODAY?

On January 1, 2010, 1,613,740 adults were under the jurisdiction of state and federal prison authorities—208,118 held in federal prisons and 1,405,622 held in state prisons.[3] For the first time in nearly four decades, state prison populations declined largely because of the movement in evidence-based corrections that started over a decade ago and more recently because of the economic downturn that made policymakers and taxpayers more aware of the financial price of incarceration. For example, a number of populous states experienced significant reductions in their prison populations across the first decade of the 21st century: New York revised its harsh drug laws, and its prison population declined 16 percent.

EXHIBIT 7–2	**Prison Statistics Among the States and the Federal Government, January 1, 2010**				
Number of Prisoners Under Jurisdiction		**Incarceration Rate per 100,000 Population of Sentenced Prisoners**		**Number of Female Prisoners Under Jurisdiction**	
5 Highest					
Federal	208,118	Louisiana	881	Federal	11,780
California	171,275	Mississippi	702	Texas	11,620
Texas	171,249	Texas	648	California	10,735
Florida	103,915	Oklahoma	657	Florida	7,283
New York	58,687	Georgia	526	Ohio	3,989
5 Lowest					
North Dakota	1,486	Federal	61	Vermont	98
Wyoming	2,075	Maine	150	Maine	135
Maine	2,206	Minnesota	189	New Hampshire	167
Vermont	2,220	New Hampshire	206	North Dakota	174
New Hampshire	2,731	North Dakota	228	Wyoming	214

Source: Adapted from Heather C. West, William J. Sabol, and Sarah J. Greenman, *Prisoners in 2009* (Washington, DC: U.S. Department of Justice, Bureau of Justice Statistics, December 2010).

Maryland improved its use of evidence-based practices and saw almost a 6 percent reduction. Michigan invested more in offender reentry (Chapter 8) and achieved a 5 percent reduction. And New Jersey reduced the number of low-risk people on parole returning to prison because of technical violations, and its prison population fell by almost 15 percent. Overall prison populations fell in 24 states from 2008 to 2009. The remaining 26 state departments of corrections reported increases in their prison populations.

Some say the reduction was long overdue because crime rates have declined for the past 15 years.[4] Why, then, did it take so long? Marc Mauer, executive director of the public safety performance project of the Pew Center on the States, said the lag was partly the result of longer sentences and partly because of tough standards in many states for revoking parole.[5] Today 1 in every 143 U.S. persons is under the jurisdiction of a state or federal prison. If we include all correctional populations (probation, parole, jail, and prison), 1 in every 32 adults is under correctional control. Twenty-five years ago it was 1 in every 77. This explosion in the correctional population presents enormous challenges for public safety and public spending as this and other chapters explain.

The imprisonment rate—the number of sentenced prisoners per 100,000 U.S. residents—declined slightly for the second straight year, falling to 502 per 100,000 from 506 per 100,000 in 2007. Imprisonment rates decreased in 28 states, increased in 18, and did not change in 4. The rate of imprisonment ranged from 150 people per 100,000 in Maine (the lowest) to 881 people per 100,000 in Louisiana (the highest). The federal system led the country with the most inmates (208,118); North Dakota had the fewest (1,486; see Exhibit 7–2).

When prison and jail incarceration rates are combined, the United States imprisons 756 people per 100,000 population, up from 684 in 2000, and 601 in 1995. That's more than any other country in the world. Russia is second with 629 prisoners per 100,000 followed by Rwanda (604), St. Kitts and Nevis (588), Cuba (531), U.S. Virgin Islands (512), British Virgin

Islands (488), Palau (478), Belarus (468), Belize (455), Bahamas (422), Georgia (415), American Samoa (410), Grenada (408), and Anguilla (401).[6] Almost three-fifths of countries (59 percent) have rates below 150 per 100,000. With less than 5 percent of the world's population, the United States has almost a quarter of the world's prisoners.

States with almost identical populations and crime rates have widely different rates of incarceration. For example, in 2009, Wisconsin had a population of 5.6 million residents, a crime rate of 2,685 offenses per 100,000 population, and an incarceration rate of 369 per 100,000.[7] Minnesota had 5.2 million residents, a crime rate of 2,884 offenses per 100,000 population, and an incarceration rate of only 189 per 100,000 population. With similar population and crime rates, Wisconsin's incarceration rate was almost twice as much as Minnesota's. What causes these disparities among states and their prison use? An interesting answer to this question was provided by Bowers and Waltman. Their investigation of felony sentencing in the United States found that the preferences of the public weigh heavily on the sentencing of violent offenders. More recently, world leaders of the prison administrations of the 45 member countries of the Council of Europe concluded that levels of imprisonment are usually influenced more by political decisions than by levels of crime or rates of detection of crime. They also concluded that jurisdictions can choose to have high or low rates of imprisonment, and this choice is reflected in the sentencing patterns adopted by legislatures.[8] Today as states grapple with the economic downturn, we can see how political decisions about what constitutes dangerousness or seriousness impact prison populations. A decade ago nonviolent offenders and parole violators would have been incarcerated. Today's economic problems find legislators and policymakers reducing prison time for nonviolent offenders and establishing programs like California's nonrevocable parole (which we discuss in Chapter 8).

State and Federal Inmates Held in Privately Operated Facilities

The issue of correctional privatization, including the pros and cons of building and operating private prisons, is discussed in depth in Chapter 13. The focus here is on the current use of privately operated correctional facilities.

On January 1, 2010, 32 states and the federal system held 129,336 prisoners in 107 privately operated prisons, up from 77,854 inmates in 101 private prisons in 2000.[9] The federal system (35,087), Texas (19,207), Florida (9,812), Arizona (8,971), Oklahoma (5,989), Mississippi, (5,286), Georgia (5,129), Tennessee (5,108), and Colorado (4,957) reported the largest number of inmates in private facilities on January 1, 2010. By region (excluding federal), 62 percent (58,737) of the private prisoner correctional population is in the South and 28 percent (26,194) is in the West. Before leaving office in January 2011, California governor Arnold Schwarzenegger signed contracts with Corrections Corporation of America and GEO Group, Inc., two of the largest private prison groups in the United States, to ship almost 6,000 California prisoners to Michigan and Minnesota, bringing the total number of California inmates housed in private prisons to almost 15,500 at an annual cost of $365 million to California taxpayers. (California is under federal court order to reduce the number of inmates in its overcrowded prisons by as much as one-third, or as many as 55,000, over the next three years. California's prison capacity is about 80,000. It currently holds twice that number. A decision in the case is expected in the spring or summer of 2011.)

COMMISSION ON SAFETY AND ABUSE IN AMERICA'S PRISONS: PREVENTING CRIME

"If you put poor, underprivileged young men together in a large institution without anything meaningful to do all day, there will be violence. If that institution is overcrowded, there will be more violence. If that institution is badly managed . . . [including] poor mental health care, there will be more violence. And if there is inadequate supervision of the staff, if there is ineffective discipline, if there is a code of silence, if there are inadequate investigations, there will be even more violence.

—Donald Specter, Director of the Prison Law Office in California,
summarizing the driving factors of violence in his testimony to the Commission.

The ability of a correctional facility to protect prisoners and staff from physical harm is a fundamental measure of the success or failure of that institution. Corrections administrators do not want to run violent facilities. When individuals under their care are seriously hurt, administrators are likely to experience those breaches in safety as personal and professional failures. Emotions run high because lives, careers, and reputations are at stake and because assessing levels of violence in America's prisons and jails is a very difficult thing to do.

Jack Beck, an attorney and director of the Prison Visiting Project at the Correctional Association of New York, told the commission that the lowest levels of tension and violence seem to exist in facilities where staff clearly follow policies, where there is meaningful communication between prisoners and staff, and where prisoners feel respected. All of these qualities flow from good leadership.

Witness after witness told the commission that violence in prisons and jails is not inevitable. Donald Specter, director of the Prison Law Office in California, told the commission, "Prisons don't have to be as dangerous and as violent as they are. The culture of our prisons virtually dictates the level of violence that you will have in them. And if you change that culture, you will reduce the violence."

The following six recommendations focus on preventing violence in America's prisons and jails:

Reduce Crowding
States and localities must commit to eliminating the crowded conditions that exist in many of the country's prisons and jails and work with corrections administrators to set and meet reasonable limits on the number of prisoners that facilities can safely house.

Promote Productivity and Rehabilitation
Invest in programs that are proven to reduce violence and to change behavior over the long term.

Use Objective Classification and Direct Supervision
Incorporate violence prevention in every facility's fundamental classification and supervision procedures.

Use Force, Nonlethal Weaponry, and Restraints Only as a Last Resort
Dramatically reduce the use of nonlethal weapons, restraints, and physical force by using nonforceful responses whenever possible, restricting the use of weaponry to qualified staff, and eliminating the use of restraints except when necessary to prevent serious injury to self or others.

Employ Surveillance Technology
Make good use of recording surveillance cameras to monitor the correctional environment.

Support Community and Family Bonds
Reexamine where prisons are located and where prisoners are assigned, encourage visitation, and implement home call reform.

Source: Excerpts from *Confronting Confinement: A Report of the Commission on Safety and Abuse in America's Prisons* by John J. Gibbons and Nicholas de B. Katzenbach, June 2006. Copyright © 2006, Vera Institute of Justice. Note: The full 126-page report, *Confronting Confinement: A Report of the Commission on Safety and Abuse in America's Prisons,* can be accessed on the Internet at www.prisoncommission.org.

State and Federal Inmates Held in Local Jails
On January 1, 2010, 35 states and the federal system housed 5.4 percent (86,653) of their prisoner populations in local jails. For many jurisdictions, housing state and federal inmates contributes to the problem of jail crowding. By region, most state and federal inmates are housed in jails

EXHIBIT 7–3 Persons Under the Jurisdiction of State or Federal Prisons, January 1, 2010

How many persons are under the jurisdiction of state and federal correctional authorities?

13% Federal prisoners
87% State prisoners

1,405,622 State prisoners
208,118 Federal prisoners
1,613,740 Total

Who is in prison?

Gender
7.0% Women
93.0% Men

Race/ethnicity*
37% White
22% Hispanic
41% Black

*Hispanics may be of any race

Age
5% 55 or older
16% 18–24
15% 45–54
34% 25–34
30% 35–44

Why are they in prison?

State prisoners
52% Violent offenses[a]
18% Drug offenses
9% Public order offense[c]
18% Property offenses[b]

a. Violent offenses include murder, rape, assault, and robbery.
b. Property offenses include burglary, larceny/theft, motor vehicle theft, and fraud and other property.
c. Public order offenses include weapons, drunk driving, vice, morals and decency offenses, liquor law violations, and other public order offenses.

Federal prisoners
51% Drug offenses
6% Property offenses
8% Violent offenses
35% Public order offenses

Source: Heather C. West, William J. Sabol, and Sarah J. Greenman, *Prisoners in 2009* (Washington, DC: U.S. Department of Justice, Bureau of Justice Statistics, December 2010).

in the South (84 percent), followed by the West (6 percent), Midwest (4 percent), and Northeast (3 percent).

Gender

Women represent the fastest-growing population in correctional facilities. Over the past decade, the number of women prisoners under state or federal jurisdiction has increased from 68,468 (in 1995) to 113,462 (in 2010), an increase of 66 percent. On January 1, 2010, women prisoners constituted 7.0 percent of the U.S. prison population (see Exhibit 7–3).

On January 1, 2010, 113,462 adult women were under state or federal prison jurisdiction, 30 percent of them in California, Texas, and federal prisons. Women represent the fastest-growing correctional population. Why are women in prison, and what will it take to reduce women's incarceration?

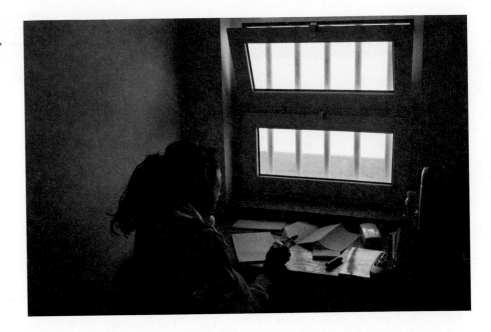

The rate of incarceration for women was 67 per 100,000 female residents, compared with 949 men per 100,000 male residents. On January 1, 2010, California, Texas, and the federal system held 30 percent of all female inmates. See Exhibit 7–2 for the jurisdictions with the highest and lowest female prison populations.

Beth Richie, a professor of criminal justice and women's studies at the University of Illinois at Chicago, and Elaine Lord, former superintendent of the Bedford Hills Correctional Facility (New York's maximum-security prison for women), who quit her job after 20 years because she stopped believing in the confinement of mentally ill women, describe the racial/ethnic profile of women in prison as one of the most vivid examples of racial disparity in the United States and prison as the worst environment possible for mothers and women with mental illness.[10]

The majority of women in prison are women of color. Two-thirds are black, Hispanic, or of other nonwhite ethnic groups. They are also young and poor. Only one-third graduated from high school or earned a GED. Two-thirds have a history of physical or sexual abuse, and 3.5 percent are HIV positive. Three-fourths suffer from major depression and manic psychotic disorders. Sadly, the corrections literature suggests that, despite the fact that some women do quite well putting their lives back together when they are released from prison, most are likely to return to the same disenfranchised neighborhoods and difficult situations without having received any services to address their underlying problems. If it is true, as the corrections literature suggests, that prior arrest history predicts postprison recidivism, then the outlook for women prisoners is bleak: 65 percent of women in prison have a history of prior convictions. One-half have three or more convictions.

Scholars debate the reasons for the increase in women's incarceration over men's. Some suggest that as women moved into jobs from which they were formerly excluded, they gained the opportunities and skills to commit criminal acts for which incarceration was appropriate punishment. Others disagree, saying that poverty of young, female, single heads of households has contributed to the increase in women's crime and incarceration, particularly for property and drug offenses. One scholar put it this way: "The war on drugs has translated into a war on women."[11]

The number of state, federal, and private confinement correctional facilities in the United States is 1,292. Minorities make up almost two-thirds of the prison population. Why is that so?

Others think the criminal justice system is becoming more "gender blind" due to the emergence of "get-tough" attitudes and sentencing policies. Instead of seeing women offenders as weaker and giving them differential, if not preferential, treatment, judges and juries now sentence women more harshly whether they are first-time drug offenders or they have committed crimes against persons or property. The combined effects of harsh drug laws, changing patterns of drug use, and mandatory sentencing policies have lead to a significant increase in women's incarceration. Almost one-third of women in state prisons and over one-half of women in federal prisons are serving time for nonviolent, drug-related offenses. Quite likely, the reason for the increase in women's incarceration is a product of all these theories. To reduce women's incarceration is to understand and implement programs about women's development, trauma, and addiction discussed in Chapter 6.

Race

The primary observation to be made about the prison population in the United States is that minorities are strikingly overrepresented. Although minorities comprise only 20 percent of the U.S. population, they make up 63 percent of all incarcerated offenders. Conversely, whites are underrepresented: over 80 percent of the general population but only 37 percent of the prison population.

Research conducted by The Sentencing Project on state rates of incarceration show us that:[12]

- Blacks are incarcerated at nearly six times the rate of whites.
- Hispanics are incarcerated at nearly double the rate of whites.
- States exhibit substantial variation in the ratio of black to white incarceration, ranging from a high of 13.6:1 in Iowa to a low of 1.9:1 in Hawaii.
- States with the highest black to white ratio are disproportionately in the Northeast and Midwest, including Iowa, Vermont, New Jersey, Connecticut, and Wisconsin.
- States with the highest Hispanic to white ratio are also disproportionately in the Northeast and Midwest, including Massachusetts, Pennsylvania, New York, New Hampshire, and New Jersey.

The lifetime likelihood of a black male spending time in prison at some point in his life is 32 percent, a Hispanic male has a 17 percent chance, and a white male has a 6 percent chance.[13]

As is the case with so many other criminological controversies, there is a debate over the relationship between race and crime. Official prison data suggest that the reason more minorities are disproportionately in prison, and for longer terms, is differential crime offending. Almost 60 percent of the persons in prison for violent offenses on January 1, 2010, were minority, and 65 percent were in prison for drug offenses. Recently, two Washington State Supreme Court Justices stunned audiences when they said they didn't believe that anyone was in prison because of age, race, disability, and other factors. One of the Justices referred to those who represent the poor as "poverty pimps" and used the words "you people" when stating that African Americans commit crimes in their own communities. Shirley Bondon, manager of Washington State's Administrative Office of Courts who oversees programs to remove barriers in the legal system, said she couldn't believe a Justice of the Supreme Court would make comments like that in her presence. Brandon said she took the comments personally as though the Justices were saying that she and all African Americans had a predisposition for criminality. "I was offended," she added.[14]

Others argue that the higher arrest rates, convictions, and sentences to prison of blacks are a function of racial profiling and racism in the criminal justice system. After reviewing 32 state-level studies of the decision to incarcerate and length of sentence imposed, Cassia Spohn, professor of criminology and criminal justice at Arizona State University, concluded there is ample evidence among these studies that, controlling for other relevant factors, blacks and Hispanics are more likely to be incarcerated than whites and, in some jurisdictions, receive longer sentences. And others have found gross racial disparities when arrest and incarceration for drug dependence and abuse are examined at the city and county levels.[15] While government statistics indicate that African Americans and whites use and sell drugs at similar rates, African Americans are admitted to prison for drug offenses at 10 times the rate of whites in the 198 largest counties in the United States. The rate of admission to prison for drug offenses is 25 per 100,000 for whites and 262 per 100,000 for African Americans, suggesting there are differences in the way counties construct policies concerning drug offenses. What are those practices that arrest and incarcerate more African American drug offenders? One factor is that 51 percent of African Americans live in metropolitan areas, compared with 21 percent of whites. Generally speaking, drug use is higher in urban areas, there are more law enforcement resources in urban areas, and there are more drug arrests in urban areas. Law enforcement practices are also a factor. Drug transactions in low-income, minority areas are more likely to be in public and between strangers, making it easier for police to make arrests whereas drug dealing by whites is more likely to occur in clubs, bars, and private homes. Prosecutorial discretion in deciding which cases to bring to trial and which pleas to accept and the ability of African Americans to afford private attorneys are other reasons.

Still others argue that although discriminatory practices exist, it is improbable that criminal justice bias alone could account for the disproportionate arrest rates of blacks. They suggest the social problems of unemployment, economic deprivation, social disorganization, and social isolation of the nation's inner cities as additional causes. The inner city, the residence of most of the nation's poor, experiences by far the highest violence rates. Middle-class communities have more resources to deal with offenders, especially drug offenders, and get them into treatment. In low-income communities, those resources are not available, so a drug problem is more likely to develop into a criminal justice problem.

These levels of racial disparity are causing some states to implement racial impact statements. Just as policymakers routinely require analysis of the fiscal or environmental impact of proposed new laws, some have proposed that legislators do the same before implementing new sentencing laws. In 2008, Iowa and Connecticut (two states with some of the highest black-to-white ratios of incarceration) took the lead among the states and enacted racial impact statements. The analysis of crime and sentencing data will project relative racial composition of new prison sentences.

Age

The nation's population is aging, and this is reflected in the prison population. Middle-aged and older inmates make up a growing portion of the prison population. In 2000, 56 percent of the nation's prisoners were between 18 and 34 years old, 40 percent were between 35 and 54, and 4 percent were over 55. In 2010, for the third straight year, the representation of 18- to 34-year-olds had decreased to 50 percent, the presence of 35- to 54-year-olds had increased to 45 percent, and the presence of inmates 55 and older had increased to 5 percent (see Exhibit 7–3). In Chapter 12, we'll discuss the issues surrounding older prisoners in more detail.

Most Serious Offense

Another characteristic to compare is the most serious offense of which a prisoner was convicted. On January 1, 2010, 52 percent of state prisoners were held for violent offenses, up from 46 percent in 1995. The percentage of state prisoners held for property offenses dropped from 23 percent in 1995 to 18 percent in 2008, and the percentage held for drug offenses dropped from 22 to 18 percent across the same time period. Still, the number of inmates doing time for drug violations in state and federal prison is triple what it was a decade ago. Convictions for public order offenses stayed the same at 9 percent.

Among federal inmates, persons sentenced for drug offenses constituted the largest group (51 percent) on January 1, 2010, similar to what it was in 1995. Immigration, weapon, and other public order offenders made up approximately 35 percent of the federal prison population at the beginning of 2010, up from 18 percent in 1995. The percentage of violent offenders in federal prison in 2010 was 8 percent, similar to what it was in 1995. And property offenders constituted 6 percent in 2010, paralleling what it was in 1995 (see Exhibit 7–3).

PROGRAMS FOR PRISONERS

Among the most important elements of an inmate's institutional experience, whether in federal or state prison, are the programs and services available. Today there is evidence-based research supporting the success rates against recidivism for correctional programs and services in education (academic and vocational), drug and alcohol, mental health, anger management, faith-based interventions, job readiness, and other programs.

EVIDENCE-BASED CORRECTIONS

Some programs and services such as recreation and personal wellness do not directly indicate a reduction in recidivism, but, as you will read later in this chapter, experts tell us that personal wellness and recreation are vehicles to promote health and prevent disease, a goal for all of us.

But what does success mean? According to one of the best reviews of the current evidence of the effectiveness of adult correctional programming by Aos and his colleagues at the Washington State Institute for Public Policy, it means reducing recidivism by 5 to 15 percent.[16] Chapter 12 discusses special prison populations and programs for inmates who are drug offenders and mentally ill.

Classification

Researchers with the Pennsylvania Department of Corrections use the following analogy to make the point that criminal justice agencies often attempt to determine what is wrong with offenders by relying on subjective assessments of offenders' likelihood of reoffending:

> Imagine that a couple goes to the grocery store, fills a cart with their desired items, walks to the checkout lane, and the clerk simply eyeballs their selections and says, "looks like about $200 worth to me." They probably would not be too happy with this approach. Of course, if they felt it was an underestimate, they might be willing to let it go, but most people would expect a more systematic means of tallying the bill. Indeed, the widespread use of bar-coded scanners is yet the latest attempt to take human error out of the cashier process.[17]

classification

The process of subdividing the inmate population into meaningful categories to match offender needs with correctional resources.

The analogy demonstrates the importance of classification, the principal management tool for allocating scarce prison resources efficiently and minimizing the potential for escape or violence. Prisoner **classification** is the process of subdividing the inmate population into meaningful categories to match offender needs with correctional resources. As prisons become more crowded, classification decisions play a significant role. Because classification lies at the heart of inmate programming, we emphasize it here.

Classification is based on the premise that there are wide differences among prisoners. Its purpose is to assign inmates to appropriate prison housing and to help staff understand, treat, predict, and manage prisoner behavior. Prior to the 19th century, when most prisons were privately operated (a topic we return to in Chapter 13), a detainee's financial condition determined his or her classification. For example, until the early 19th century, the keeper at Newgate Prison (England) was allowed to collect fees for reception, discharge, supervision, and accommodation (single vs. multiple occupancy cells).[18] It wasn't until 1832 that Newgate offenders were separated by age and offense severity.

One hundred years ago, the Elmira Reformatory in Elmira, New York, classified offenders as "specimens" and labeled them either "Mathematical Dullards," "Those Deficient in Self-Control," or "Stupid."[19] Today, the classifications are more sophisticated. The belief is that "somewhere between the extremes of 'all offenders are alike' and 'each offender is unique' lies a system (or systems) of categorization along pertinent dimensions that will prove to be of value in reaching correctional goals."[20]

The American Correctional Association believes that classification is one of the most important features of an effective correctional treatment system. ACA's policy statement on classification is presented in Exhibit 7–4. What does ACA recommend a correctional agency do to balance the public's need for protection, the needs of offenders, and the efficient and effective operation of the correctional system?

| EXHIBIT 7–4 | American Correctional Association |

Public Correctional Policy on Classification

Introduction

Proper classification of offenders promotes public, staff, and offender safety. It is a continuing process basic to identifying and matching offender needs to correctional resources. Classification also serves as a tool for identifying gaps in correctional services. This continuing process involves all phases of correctional management.

Policy Statement

Classification should balance the public's need for protection, the needs of offenders, and the efficient and effective operation of the correctional system. In developing and administering its classification system, a correctional agency should:

A. develop written classification policies that establish criteria specifying different levels of security, supervision, and program involvement; establish procedures for documenting and reviewing all classification decisions and actions; describe the appeal process to be used by individuals subject to classification; and specify the time frames for monitoring and reclassifying cases;

B. develop the appropriate range of resources and services to meet the identified risk and program needs of the population served;

C. base classification decisions on rational assessment of objective and valid information, including background material (criminal history, nature of offense, age, gender, social history, educational needs, medical/mental health needs, etc.), as well as information regarding the individual's current situation, adjustment, and program achievement;

D. train all personnel in the classification process and require specialized training for those directly involved in classification functions;

E. use the classification process to assign individuals to different levels of control on the basis of valid criteria regarding risk (to self and others) and individual needs, matching these characteristics with appropriate security, level of supervision, and program services;

F. involve the offender directly in the classification process;

G. assign appropriately trained staff to monitor individual classification plans for progress made and reclassification needs;

H. objectively validate the classification process and instruments, assess on a planned basis the degree to which results meet written goals, and, as needed, refine the process and instruments; and

I. provide for regular dissemination of classification information to all levels of correctional staff and ensure that all staff understand the nature and purpose of proper classification of offenders.

Source: Copyright © American Correctional Association.

Types of Classification There are two types of prisoner classification: external and internal. **External classification** determines an inmate's security level (maximum, close, medium, minimum, or community) for *interinstitutional* placement. For example, maximum-security inmates are placed in a maximum-security facility. External classification answers the question "Where should I put this inmate?"

Internal classification is *intrainstitutional* placement. Once an inmate arrives at the institution, she or he undergoes a classification review. Classification staff review an inmate's behavior, personality, and educational, chemical dependency, medical, and mental health needs. Staff then assign inmates to housing units or cellblocks, work, and programming based on their risk, needs, and time to serve. The Pennsylvania Department of Corrections develops a unique correctional plan for each prisoner

external classification
Interinstitutional placement of an inmate that determines an inmate's security level.

internal classification
Intrainstitutional placement that determines, through review of an inmate's background, assignment to housing units or cellblocks, work, and programming based on the inmate's risk, needs, and time to serve.

EXHIBIT 7–5   Pennsylvania's Prisoner Intake Process

The Intake Process

The PA DOC intake process is designed to be completed in two weeks, as shown in the following table. However, it can take up to four to six weeks to establish medical, mental health, initial custody, and programming requirements for the prisoners.

Identifying the Prisoner

During day 1, the prisoner's identification is verified and he/she is strip searched, photographed, and fingerprinted; court documents are reviewed; and the prisoner's property is inventoried. Each prisoner bathes and receives baseline drug tests for illicit substances and medical and mental health screens. Additionally, the prisoner is interviewed by custody staff to identify potential security threat group membership and by a counselor to determine the need for separating the prisoner from other prisoners or staff members. Each prisoner also is issued a prisoner handbook in English, Spanish, or Braille. At the end of the first day, the prisoner has been identified, assigned to a cell, and has received institutional clothing and toiletries.

On day 2, a counselor provides formal orientation during which basic institutional rules and procedures are explained.

During the next 7 business days, the prisoner receives a full medical examination and takes a series of academic achievement, psychological, and substance abuse tests. As indicated by the results from the written tests, the psychologist and drug and alcohol treatment specialist conducts clinical interviews with the prisoner. In addition, the medical staff interview the prisoner about his/her medical history. DNA samples are collected from prisoners convicted of murder, stalking, and/or a sex-related offense. By the end of the 10th day at the intake center, prisoners have medical, mental health, education, and substance abuse ratings that indicate their level of need for services and/or treatment. These ratings are forwarded to classification staff for custody, facility, work, and programming assignments.

Classification

Classification staff use PACT [Pennsylvania Assessment and Classification Tool]—a fully automated classification system that synthesizes data collected throughout the intake process to establish a prisoner's custody level and to recommend housing, work detail, treatment, and programming assignments—to classify and assess the needs of prisoners. They also develop electronically a classification summary that is used by staff at the long-term facility to plan with the prisoner his/her institutional program and work assignments. The facility placement recommendation considers the prisoner's custody level, separation and regionalization issues, program needs, and bed space availability. Because PACT and the classification summary are automated, the counselor simply reviews the preliminary custody assessment, annotates any applicable administrative or discretionary overrides, recommends a preliminary custody level, and generates a form for recording the custody assessment and facility placement recommendations and decisions.

Initial Classification

Classification staff use PACT to determine the prisoner's custody level and facility placement. The initial custody level is based on seven discrete items: severity of current offense, severity of criminal history, escape history, institutional adjustment, number of prior institutional commitments, time to expected release, and stability factors (e.g., current age, marital status, and employment at arrest). A facility placement recommendation also is made during the initial classification process. It addresses custody, program, medical, and mental health needs; case management/case planning; and other specific prisoner or institution needs (e.g., electrician, maintenance technician, plumber).

Administrative overrides—based on the prisoner's legal status, current offense, and sentence—can change classification recommendations. Discretionary overrides by the case manager are permitted based on the prisoner's security threat group affiliation; escape history; nature of current offense; and behavior, mental health, medical, dental, and program needs. Information about cases for which discretionary overrides are recommended is forwarded electronically to the appropriate staff for approval. Multiple levels of review by classification supervisory staff and the central office are required for all overrides.

Reclassification

The reclassification process parallels the initial classification process. Regularly scheduled custody reassessments are conducted as part of the prisoner's annual review. Reassessments are also conducted following major misconduct reports and select minor violations, significant changes in the prisoner's program needs, time credits, escape time, sentence continuations, detainers, prerelease applications, unusual incident reports, transfer requests, and as needed to ensure the safety and security of the facility.

Reclassification is based on the severity of current offense, severity of criminal history, escape history, history of institutional violence, number and severity of misconduct reports during the previous 18 months, current age, program participation, work performance, and housing performance. As with the initial classification, these items are tallied on the PACT to create the total score. Again, mandatory and discretionary override factors are considered and reviewed.

EXHIBIT 7–5 Pennsylvania's Prisoner Intake Process *(continued)*

Overview of Pennsylvania's Prisoner Intake Process

Tasks	Conducted	Who Is Tested?	Personnel Responsible for Task	Instrument(s) and/or Process(es) Used
Day 1				
Identification	Yes; mandatory	All prisoners	Records staff	Court orders, AFIS, and LiveScan
Medical screen within 24 hours	Yes; mandatory	All prisoners	Health care staff	Medical screen
Mental health screen	Yes; mandatory	All prisoners	Intake office and mental health staff	Mental health screen
Drug testing	Yes; mandatory	All prisoners	Health care	Urine test
Prisoner separation	Yes; mandatory	All prisoners	Security staff and counselors	Interview and court documents
Gang membership	Yes; mandatory	All prisoners		Tattoos, criminal and institutional records, and interview
Days 2–10				
Academic achievement	Yes; mandatory	All prisoners	Education staff	TABE and WRAT
IQ tests	Yes; mandatory	All prisoners	Psychology staff	Beta III and WAIS
Vocational aptitude	No; not required			
Substance abuse	Yes; mandatory	All prisoners	Drug treatment staff	TCUDDS
Psychological	Yes; mandatory	All prisoners	Psychology staff	PAI, GBA, and clinical interview
Physical exam	Yes; mandatory	All prisoners	Health care staff	Physical exam, blood work, and interview
DNA testing	Yes; not required	Prisoners convicted of murder, stalking, and/or a sex-related crime	Lab technicians	Blood work
Days 11–15				
Criminal history	Yes; mandatory	All prisoners	Records staff	NCIC, presentence investigation, DOC MIS, and court orders
Social history	Yes; mandatory	All prisoners	Classification staff	Interview and presentence investigation
Institutional adjustment	Yes; mandatory	All prisoners	Classification staff	Jail documents and DOC MIS
Custody level	Yes; mandatory	All prisoners	Classification staff	PACT
Internal classification	Yes; mandatory	All prisoners	Classification staff	Custody and needs assessments
Security level/facility	Yes; mandatory	All prisoners	Classification staff	PACT
Prisoner separation	Yes; mandatory	All prisoners	Classification and security staff	Self-reports and court documents
Victim notification	Yes; not required	Only prisoners with a victim	District attorney's office	Offense type

Source: Adapted from Patricia L. Hardyman, James Austin, and Johnette Peyton, *Prisoner Intake Systems: Assessing Needs and Classifying Prisoners* (Washington, DC: U.S. Department of Justice, National Institute of Corrections, February, 2004).

PRIDE Enterprises is an internationally recognized general manufacturing and services company. A private, not-for-profit corporation founded in 1981, PRIDE Enterprises has experience and expertise in working in a secure prison environment providing on-the-job training, job placement, and support for ex-offenders to help them successfully transition back into society after a period of incarceration. PRIDE operates 38 diverse industries in 22 correctional institutions throughout Florida. It has received national and international attention as a model for public/private partnerships, especially regarding the privatization of government functions.

PRIDE consists of 200 employees and 2,000 inmate workers, and its products and services yield annual sales of over $60 million. The state has not provided any funds to the corporation, and since its inception PRIDE has contributed over $121 million to the State of Florida in cash, inmate wages, investment in state property, victim restitution, and job training, placement, and support services.

PRIDE's customer base is divided between state government (55%), nonstate government (22%), and private sector (23%).

Current production ranges from simple assembly to full-scale manufacturing in digital technology, custom design and production, industrial manufacturing, construction and assembly, retrofitting and refurbishing, and distribution and fulfillment.

Now in its 23rd year, PRIDE is encouraged by the current national focus on the potential of inmate workers to become an asset to America's economy.

Pamela J. Davis
President and CEO
PRIDE Enterprises of Florida
www.peol.com

that identifies problem areas and treatment needs to be addressed by the prisoner during incarceration (see Exhibit 7–5). In approximately two-thirds of the states, the processes of internal and external classification are done at the same time.[21] Classification staff recommend both an inmate's security level and housing assignments and programming. The remaining states defer internal classification to the facility to which the prisoner is transferred.

A survey by the National Council on Crime and Delinquency (NCCD) found that only nine states had a formal internal classification system that used structured scoring instruments, staff specialists who were formally trained to use them, and a reclassification process to update previously classified prisoners.[22] NCCD found that some kind of internal classification process exists in all prison systems to assign newly arrived inmates to housing units, work assignments, and programs, but these processes are usually informal and rely on subjective criteria. Most (86 percent) state correctional agencies use the same classification assessment criteria for both males and females.[23] However, a few states—including Idaho, Massachusetts, New York, and Ohio—have developed gender-specific classification instruments that acknowledge that the nature and extent of women's criminal behavior and the ways in which they respond to supervision and incarceration make a difference.

Three of the best-known systems of internal classification are the Adult Internal Management System (AIMS), the Prisoner (or Client) Management Classification (PMC) system, and behavior-based systems (BBSs). AIMS is used by several facilities in the federal BOP and a number of state departments of corrections including Missouri, Ohio, South Dakota, and Washington. Its purpose is to reduce institutional predatory behavior by identifying inmates who are likely to be incompatible in terms of housing and inmates who are most likely to pose a risk to the safe and secure operation of a facility. AIMS uses personality checklists that are designed to determine an inmate's ability to be housed successfully with other inmates.

PMC uses a semistructured attitudinal interview to assist staff in identifying potential predators and victims and those inmates who require

My Incarceration

No one other than one who has been incarcerated can really identify with what this is like. Even those who are charged with the responsibility of keeping us on this side of the fence cannot really feel what we feel.

Because good social norms of society are missing elements in the prison setting, how can one expect antisocial behaviors to change? Incarceration forces a man to redefine what is normal. So naturally you will find us gravitating to that which we can best relate to. This can be on a peer level, a racial level, a spiritual level, or a level where we use gambling, sex, drugs, alcohol, food, television, and so on, as a way of coping. Some of us consciously use these devices to escape from reality or replace some missing aspect of our being. Others lack the cognitive ability to understand these dynamics and fall prey to the prison mentality. Thus you have a large number of offenders who, once they get out of the system, find themselves not equipped or in some cases less equipped to be productive members of society. My awareness of the so-called prison mentality can be attributed only to my relationship with my lord and savior Jesus Christ.

My Offense and Punishment

My crime is capital murder. I was sentenced to Life Without the Possibility of Parole. In other words, I was given a living death sentence. It would've been real easy for me to adapt to the prison culture and mentality if the opportunity for positive endeavors had not become available. To be honest, for a short time I did take part in the prison gambling industry. In my mind, this was the lesser of the many evils associated with prison life. I was only lying to myself. There are so many variables to the gambling industry in prison. In some cases it could mean your life.

What the Faith-Based Restorative Justice Dorm Has Meant to Me

This brings me to October of '98, when the DOC was ordered by the prison commissioner to open up honor dorms at all its facilities. That month I made the decision to apply for the honor dorm. At the time, I wanted only to be a part of something positive. I also made a promise to my mother, shortly after coming to prison, that I would not do anything to make her cry again, as long as I could help it. So to begin with the honor dorm gave me the opportunity and the environment to keep the promise I made to my mother.

The Impact on My Life

The restorative justice community, where the definition of respect, problem solving, and normal behavior more closely emulate that in society, has been a good foundation for me to begin the work of earning my way back into society. It may be hard for those who have never been incarcerated to understand the culture and mentality of the prison environment. If one could put aside the media's portrayal of prison life, they could see that there are good things happening behind these walls. One of the most effective programs that I've had an opportunity to be a part of is the *Faith-Based Restorative Justice Honor Dorm*. The "faith-based" aspect of the dorm promotes and encourages spirituality both structured and nonstructured, which allows even the nonbeliever to have the opportunity of exposure to God's word and believers to practice their faith communally or individually. The dorm's guiding philosophy, *restorative justice,* allows an offender to begin the work of understanding how his crime has affected the person or persons and his community that were directly harmed by his crime. For me personally, this area of focus in the dorm has helped me become an advocate for victims' rights. Coming from an offender's point of view this may seem strange, but to me, it is only a natural outcome of restorative justice. I truly am sorry for the pain I've caused those who were affected by my crime. Believe me when I say that this approach does make a difference to offenders' accountability, responsibility, and ownership of crime. I know because it has made a difference in my life. Our restorative justice community provides the physical environment that allows men to begin the work of living a life reflective of how one wants to be perceived by society. Through its class curriculums, our restorative justice community gives men the tools that are needed to be productive members in their current community and future communities outside these walls when released.

Prospects for the Future

I have seen how this restorative justice subcommunity has influenced the general population over the past five years. I envision a future where the prison mentality will be a reflection of the Faith-Based Restorative Justice community philosophy. I envision a future where positive behavior is promoted as opposed to deviant behaviors. I envision a spiritually based restorative healing mission, in an environment conducive for these concepts to be practiced, which eventually spreads throughout the entire prison.

Tony Joyce

---

special programs or supervision. The attitudinal items tap the inmate's attitude regarding the current offense; criminal history; family relationships; relationships with staff, inmates, and peers; and plans after release. In addition, other items assess the inmate's social status and demeanor during the interview.

BBSs assess inmates according to behavioral measures as reflected by disciplinary records and work performance in contrast to personality and

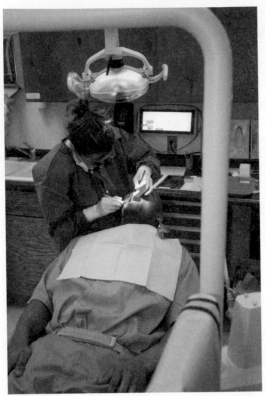

Classification of incoming inmates is based on many factors, including medical, dental, and mental health care needs; custody needs; institutional risk; work skills; and educational needs. Classification serves the custody goals of a prison but tends to label prisoners. Is such labeling appropriate?

attitude scales. Florida, Illinois, New Jersey, and Oregon use BBSs. Inmates are scored according to their level of aggression, which is determined by the severity and frequency of institutional misconduct and gang-related activities. Staff who use a BBS conduct a historical assessment of the inmate to achieve an understanding of an inmate's potential behavior. Staff review a host of factors such as type of disciplinary incidents, days spent in segregation, time remaining to serve, external custody level, and needs assessment. The factors are scored and placed into grids that identify the inmate's housing type, potential cellmates, and treatment and program needs.

Advantages of Classification Good internal classification systems offer a number of advantages. First, separating inmates by risk level and program needs puts extremely aggressive inmates in high security while those who require less or are at risk of being victimized are kept in low security. Within those levels of security, prisoners' needs may also be considered. Does the facility offer drug and alcohol treatment? Sex offender treatment? Anger management training? GED preparation? Such classification offers prisoners a chance for counseling, education, or vocational training, and it may keep aggressive inmates from assaulting passive inmates.

Second, a good classification system minimizes misclassification, thus promoting a safe environment for inmates and staff. When prisons are over capacity, as they are today, staff feel pressure to classify inmates quickly, which often results in misclassification. A good classification system will include safeguards against misclassification. For example, when there is not enough space in maximum-security facilities, a good system will direct staff to house only the lowest-risk high-security inmates in medium-security facilities.

Third, a good classification system more accurately places inmates and more effectively deploys staff. Without good classification, the tendency is to place inmates in more secure, more expensive prisons than necessary. Good classification controls the inmate population, assigns inmates to appropriate security levels, and better deploys staff.

Fourth, a good classification system enhances prison security by reducing tension in prison. Misclassification can jeopardize a prison's security and increase violence and escapes. A review of the major developments and trends in prisoner classification over a recent 20-year period found significant improvement in classification technology (e.g., computer software to help collect, store, and manage the data) and more sophisticated assessment of risk and of medical, mental health treatment, and education needs.[24]

Orientation to the Institution

While the process of internal classification is being conducted, state and federal prison systems provide inmates an orientation to the institution. For several weeks, as shown in Pennsylvania's prisoner intake process (Exhibit 7–5), inmates participate in an admission and orientation program. It provides an introduction to all aspects of the institution and includes screening by staff from the case management, medical, and mental health units. Inmates receive copies of the institution's rules and regulations, including the inmate discipline policy, and they are introduced to the programs, services, policies, and procedures of the facility.

Increasingly, prison systems such as the Louisiana State Penitentiary at Angola use inmates to orient new arrivals to prison life. According to some researchers, North Carolina conducts one of the most detailed orientations, which includes videos about the facility, prisoner responsibilities, and diseases as well as questionnaires about drug use, potential visitors, and family background.[25]

Unit Management and Faith-Based Honor Dorms and Prisons

Unit management is based on the idea that cooperation is most likely in small groups that have lengthy interactions.[26] A unit is a self-contained living area for 50 to 200 inmates that is managed semiautonomously within the larger institution. Third- and fourth-generation jails discussed in Chapter 6 are unit management systems.

In the federal system and in a number of states, prisons use a **unit management system.** The purpose of dividing prisons into functional units, each with its own permanently assigned staff and a unit manager who serves as a "mini warden," was largely to improve program delivery. Many units—drug treatment units, in particular—were established to focus on specific program needs. The unit team—typically composed of the unit manager, one or more case managers, two or more correctional counselors, and a unit secretary—is directly responsible for the inmates living in that unit. Unit staff receive input from other employees involved in an inmate's progress (such as work supervisors, teachers, and psychologists) and meet with the inmate on a regular basis to develop, review, and discuss the work assignments and programs the inmate should be involved in as well as any other needs or concerns.

Traditional correctional institutions make decisions through a centralized and hierarchical management structure whereas unit management strives to decentralize decision making. When decisions are made at the unit level, they are made with better information and by staff who know the inmates better. Unit management gives inmates direct daily contact with the staff who make most of the decisions about their daily lives. It results in improved inmate access to staff and greater staff access to inmates, providing staff with an awareness of significant inmate concerns and potential problems. Unit management also means that not all units will be managed in the same way. Having different management methods is a strength because different inmates require different management approaches.

The success of unit management is affected by internal classification. Inmates who are assigned to a given institution are then assigned to a specific unit based on their risks and needs. After the processes of internal classification and initial orientation, each inmate meets with the unit team to formulate a program plan, which may include drug treatment, education, and vocational training as well as institution maintenance jobs or other work assignments. The unit team reviews the inmate's progress and makes changes in the program plan as needed. Unit management emphasizes candid, open communication between staff and inmates. Direct and frequent communication helps staff know inmates, understand their needs, and respond appropriately to those needs.

The principles of classification and unit management have produced another type of prison housing—*faith-based*—in which inmates volunteer to be housed in facilities that provide special activities and classes, religious and secular, aimed at character development and personal growth.[27] Today, nearly half of state and federal prison systems are operating or developing at least one residential faith-based program,[28] and recently

unit management system

A method of controlling prisoners in self-contained living areas and making inmates and staff (unit manager, correctional counselor, and unit secretary) accessible to each other.

Trinity Broadcasting Network (TBN) introduced four faith-based television channels that it offers free of charge to prisons and jails. TBN says its faith-based programming provides positive, life-affirming television programs to address the needs of offenders through faith-based assistance. TBN is now available in Florida, Mississippi, Ohio, South Carolina, South Dakota, and Texas.[29]

Supporters of faith-based initiatives argue that such programs *may* reduce recidivism and improve other postrelease outcomes; are generally free or low cost because they are provided by volunteer groups (Mears cites the case in Oregon where faith volunteers contributed the equivalent of 121 full-time staff positions valued at roughly $4.5 million[30]); may improve in-prison behavior (such as more compliance with rules, participation in treatment, and physical and mental health among inmates); and lessen the dehumanization of incarceration and are unlikely to harm anyone.

On the other hand, opponents argue that faith-based prisons programs may not be effective; may actually cost taxpayers; promote a religious orientation and hence may be unconstitutional as reported in a recent legal challenge to a taxpayer-supported prison program in Iowa run by Charles Colson's Prison Fellowship; may actually lessen offender accountability for their crimes; and may coerce some inmates into certain kinds of religious activity.

In spite of its growth, however, only a few studies have examined the effectiveness of faith-based prisons. The few studies that have, Mears and O'Connor say, suffer from measurement problems, research design issues, and data collection and interpretation.[31] Both researchers concluded that it will be difficult to know the potential that faith-based services, lives, and interventions have to offer corrections until research improves.

Recently researchers from the Urban Institute in Washington, DC evaluated two of the three faith-based prisons run by the Florida Department of Corrections: Lawtey, a men's facility in Raiford, about 40 miles from Jacksonville; and Hillsborough, a women's facility in Riverview, about 23 miles from Tampa.[32] The researchers found that one year after release there was no difference in the reincarceration rate between the women and men released from the faith-based prisons and a matched sample released from other Florida prisons. Due to the small sample sizes, however, the researchers called for further research.

Others tell us that faith-based programming in prison should not be contingent on the issue of program effectiveness for several reasons. "First, regardless of social science findings, prisoners have a right to express their religious views. . . . Second . . . the real outcome or purpose of religion in prison is not only to reduce anti-social behavior/criminal behavior or relapse into criminal activity, but also to counteract the tendency of prisons to dehumanize people and help prisoners prevent a further decline in their humanity. . . . Finally . . . [researchers] question whether we can accurately tap into the deeper religious dimensions of that person's motivations and thereby assess whether a particular individual has changed."[33]

On the legal front, in 2007, the Eighth Circuit of the U.S. Court of Appeals affirmed the ruling of federal judge Robert Pratt of the U.S. District Court for the Southern District of Iowa who found that a taxpayer-supported prison program in Iowa run by Charles Colson's Prison Fellowship was unconstitutional because it was so intertwined with the state and funded in part by taxpayers. The appellate court concluded that taxpayers' aid "advanced religion." However the Court did not order the program to reimburse the state of Iowa the $1.53 million that Judge Pratt had ordered. The court ruled that state officials acted in good faith in contracting for the program.

On June 25, 2007, the U.S. Supreme Court ruled in *Hein* v. *Freedom From Religion Foundation, Inc.* that taxpayers cannot challenge a White House initiative that promotes federal grants to religious charities. The Court said executive initiatives like faith-based programming, paid for with discretionary funds, is different from specific programs funded by the legislature. This important ruling means that presidents have a lot of power to spend discretionary money in favor of religion without any review by the courts.

Examples of faith-based housing units within a prison can be seen in the Offender Speaks boxes in this chapter and in Chapter 12. They were written by inmates living in a faith-based honors dorm at Alabama's Holman Correctional Facility, a maximum-security prison of 1,000 inmates, including over 200 on death row. Approximately 200 inmates live in the prison's faith-based honors dorm. The dorm uses the principles of restorative justice discussed in Chapter 3 and encourages and promotes both structured and unstructured opportunities for inmate spirituality as a foundation on which to build successful reentry initiatives.

Daily Routine

A typical prison day begins with breakfast at 6:30 A.M. For inmates with prison jobs, work begins about 7:30 A.M. By this time, inmates are expected to have cleaned their personal living areas and made their beds. After work and the evening meal, inmates may participate in organized or individual recreation, watch television, or engage in personal hobbies. In most prisons, inmates must remain in their quarters after the 10 P.M. count. The weekend and holiday routines are somewhat more relaxed depending on the level of prison security.

Prisons regularly count inmates to ensure that all are where they are supposed to be. How often inmates are counted varies considerably. In some prisons, formal inmate counts are taken five times a day, including a morning count at 6, an afternoon count at 4, and three counts between 10 p.m. and morning. Informal counts may be conducted in program areas at various times during the day to ensure that inmates are in the proper place. Emergency counts may be held at any time. On weekends and holidays, when routines are more relaxed, counts are still made.

After serving his four-month federal prison sentence in 2005, Baltimore Ravens running back Jamal Lewis described his daily prison routine to reporters: "I wasn't used to getting up early (4:30 A.M.) and having guards watching you every minute. And having to stand there three times a day and be counted. But you make the best of it."[34] Lewis held a job in the prison tool room, handing out equipment to work details. He told reporters that his worst problem in prison was the lack of privacy and that the thing he missed most during his incarceration was his freedom. "It's not about Jamal Lewis; it's not about the football player. You know you're just another number in the prison cell."

Work Assignments

Work is a very important part of institutional management and offender programs. Meaningful work programs are the most powerful tool prison administrators have in managing crowding and idleness, which can lead to disorder and violence. And now the news on prisoner work assignments is even better. The evidence-based reviews introduced in Chapter 1 and mentioned throughout the text show that the average prison industry program reduces the recidivism rate of participants by almost 6 percent.

Some prison industries achieve better results, some worse. On average, however, researchers find that the typical prison industry can be expected to reduce recidivism by 6 percent.[35]

Prison work is generally of one of three types: operational assignments within the institution, community projects, or prison industry.

Operational Assignments In operational assignments within the institution, inmates perform tasks necessary to the functioning of the facility or larger corrections system. Institutional maintenance assignments including farm and other agricultural activities are the largest single option for inmate work. Forty-five states, the District of Columbia, and the BOP pay inmates a wage for services rendered to the institution. The average wage range for institutional maintenance work is $0.99 to $3.98 per day. Inmates working in institutional maintenance perform the following types of work: laundry, heating and air conditioning repair, building maintenance and custodial service, landscaping and grounds maintenance, and food preparation and service.

Community Projects Many correctional institutions allow inmates to gain work experience through community projects. Through them offenders contribute their labor to benefit the community while developing job skills in a practical, nonprison setting. Community work usually takes the form of construction, landscaping, horticulture, and agriculture activities. Construction/repair of public property and parks development and maintenance are by far the most common types of community work activities. Examples of other community projects include building houses for low-income persons, painting municipal swimming pools, providing snow removal services, providing backup firefighting services, and delivering antidrug programs in schools. In South Carolina, inmates who meet the criteria for community work build playground equipment, pick up trash on state highways, maintain and clean up state parks, aid flood victims, clean up debris after storm damage, and provide skilled labor for Habitat for Humanity. Inmate work organizations also raise money for the Special Olympics and other charities.

Inmates at the Snake River Correctional Institution, Ontario, Oregon, make calls arranging business meetings for the consulting firm Perry Johnson. What are the benefits of prison industry for inmates, their families, and victims while in prison and after release, the institution, the business community, and taxpayers?

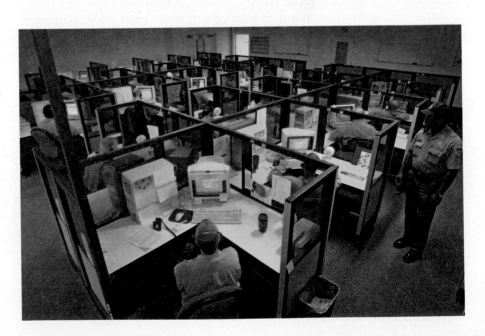

State Prison Industries and the Prison Industry Enhancement Certification Program (PIECP) PIECP allows inmates to work for a private employer in a "free-world" occupation and earn the prevailing wage. Created by Congress in 1979, PIECP encourages states and local correctional agencies to form partnerships with private companies to give inmates real work opportunities.

How much does the electorate support PIECP? Eighty-two percent of U.S. voters said that job training is very important for a person to reintegrate successfully into society after incarceration.[36] Their faith in prison industry programs is supported by the what-works literature introduced in Chapter 1. Of the 30 rigorous evaluations of prison industries examined by the Washington State Institute for Public Policy, an agency created by the state legislature to conduct research on policy issues, the studies showed an average 6 percent reduction in recidivism due to prison industry.

The PIE certification program has two primary objectives: First, to generate products and services that enable prisoners to make a contribution to society, help offset the cost of their incarceration, compensate crime victims, and provide inmate family support. And second, to provide a means of reducing prison idleness, increasing inmate job skills, and improving the prospects for successful inmate transition to the community upon release.

Currently, PIE certification programs operate in 37 states and 4 counties in the United States. These programs manage over 175 business partnerships with private industry.[37] By the end of 2005, 6,555 offenders were employed in the program. PIECP generated more than $33 million for victims' programs, $21 million for inmate family support, $97.5 million for correctional institution room and board costs, $46.6 million in state and federal taxes, and $14 million in mandatory inmate savings.

In addition to PIE certification programs, there are hundreds of innovative prison industry programs across the United States. Inmates in Maine, Mississippi, Nevada, Ohio, and Virginia train guide dogs to aid visually impaired persons, hearing dogs to assist those who are deaf and hearing impaired, and service dogs to assist individuals suffering from various physical needs. Other Nevada inmates learn building construction while still others learn to employ resistance-free training methods to tame and train wild horses in order to improve their adoptability. Women inmates at the Belfair Mission Creek Corrections Center in Washington are taken to the rivers and canals around Hood Canal and are paid $1 an hour to spray pesticides in order to save salmon habitats. The women can become licensed at handling and spraying pesticides. At the Louisiana State Penitentiary in Angola, a maximum-security prison, inmates built Prison View, a nine-hole golf course that is on prison property and open to the public. Although inmates cannot play, they learned landscape design, horticulture, and groundskeeping. Inmates in Nebraska and 34 other states volunteer for a one-year-long rigorous Braille translation program certified by the Library of Congress. They earn between 38 cents and $1.08 an hour with at least half making 54 cents or less. However, over the past few years, even prison work budgets have been cut because of the nation's economic downturn. In 2009, 23 states cut funding for prison industries. In North Carolina, prison industry sales decreased 10 percent in 2009 from the previous fiscal year due to statewide budget cuts.

One of the best-known prison industry programs operates at the Eastern Oregon Correctional Institution in Pendleton, Oregon, the famous mill town known for Pendleton fabrics. There prisoners make a line of T-shirts, jackets, and jeans known as Prison Blues®. Oregon Corrections Enterprises owns the business. It operates a 47,000-square-foot factory on the prison grounds, a type of industrial park with bars. All 50 inmates working in the factory are paid prevailing industry wages, which range from a base of $7.80 to $9.58 per hour. They can also earn bonus incentives for quality and productivity.

What Impact Does PIECP Have? In June 2006, researchers at the University of Baltimore asked whether PIECP inmates return to prison less frequently or enter more successful employment than inmates in traditional prison industries and those who did not work at all.[38] The researchers found that PIECP inmates became tax-paying citizens more quickly and remained in that status longer than inmates who worked in traditional prison industries or not at all. Furthermore, 82 percent of PIECP inmates were not arrested in their first year following release, compared to 77 percent of inmates who worked in traditional prison industry jobs, and 76 percent of those who were not employed at all while in prison.

Although the results of the PIECP study are positive, they are not conclusive because participants in the three groups were not randomly assigned to groups. Prisoners volunteered to participate in the PIECP and traditional prison industries. Therefore, inmates who worked either in PIECP or traditional prison industries were "self-selected" and may have had different motivations and backgrounds than other inmates, which may have led to better outcomes.

Federal Prison Industries and UNICOR In the federal system, legislation authorizing the establishment of paid inmate work programs was introduced into Congress in 1934. However, the American Federation of Labor (AFL) voiced its opposition, arguing that federal prison industries have an unfair competitive advantage over the public sector because they pay their inmates less than a private company worker would be paid for carrying out similar assignments. President Franklin Roosevelt took a personal interest in the matter and called AFL president William Green and BOP director Sanford Bates to the Oval Office. Together, the three men were able to draw out Green's objections to the proposed legislation and his suggestions for improvement, and ultimately the AFL withdrew its opposition. On June 23, 1934, President Roosevelt signed the law that authorized the establishment of **Federal Prison Industries (FPI)**, and on December 11, 1934, he issued Executive Order 6917, which formally created FPI. FPI is a federal work program in which inmates are paid. Better known by its trade name, **UNICOR**, FPI is a self-supporting corporation owned by the federal government and overseen by a governing board appointed by the president.

Since 1934, FPI has operated factories and employed inmates in America's federal prisons. When the United States entered World War II in December 1941, FPI manufactured bomb fins and casings, TNT cases, parachutes, cargo nets, and wooden pallets for the military. It also handled the military's laundry and built, remodeled, and repaired military patrol boats, tugboats, and barges. FPI also contributed in another way to the war effort. It trained inmates to move directly into jobs in defense

Many state correctional systems channel prison labor into industrial and commercial programs. One such program is the Prison Blues® brand of jeans, T-shirts, work shirts, and yard coats manufactured by Oregon Corrections Enterprises, a division of the Oregon Department of Corrections. What benefits to inmates do such work programs provide?

Federal Prison Industries (FPI)

A federal, paid inmate work program and self-supporting corporation.

industries after release from prison. During the 1990–1991 Persian Gulf War, FPI provided Kevlar helmets, camouflage battle uniforms, lighting systems, sandbags, blankets, cables for the Patriot missile system, and night-vision eyewear for military use during Operation Desert Shield and Operation Desert Storm. Today FPI in Tennessee sews the military vests worn by U.S. soldiers and Marines fighting in Afghanistan and Iraq. Other products manufactured by UNICOR are electronic cable assemblies, executive and modular furniture (FPI ranks ninth in such manufacture in the United States), metal pallet racks, stainless-steel food service equipment, mattresses, towels, utility bags, brooms, thermoplastics, military helmets, and government forms. UNICOR also provides services such as data entry, sign making, and printing.

The mission of FPI is to employ and provide job skills training to the greatest practical number of inmates confined within the federal Bureau of Prisons; contribute to the safety and security of federal correctional facilities by keeping inmates constructively occupied; produce market-priced quality goods for sale to the federal government; operate in a self-sustaining manner; and minimize FPI's impact on private business and labor. FPI operates about 100 factories in seven business areas: clothing and textiles, electronics, fleet management and vehicular components, industrial products, office furniture, recycling activities, and service. Virtually all of FPI's electronic sales and the vast majority of FPI's clothing and textile sales are in support of the Department of Defense's war effort in Iraq.

Making war supplies notwithstanding, FPI is not immune to the nation's economic pinch. Slightly more than 7,000 federal prisoners were cut from FPI work rolls in 2009 and 2010 as several factories closed. In 2010, only 16,115 of the nation's 208,118 federal inmates were employed in FPI jobs, down from 23,152 in 2008. Federal corrections officials are concerned that workforce cuts could spark inmate unrest in overcrowded institutions where industry jobs have kept prisoners occupied and out of recreation yards and housing units.[39]

What Impact Does UNICOR Have? There is very little independent research on whether UNICOR reduces criminal activity. Over 10 years ago, the federal BOP released a study that compared the postrelease activities of a group of inmates who had participated in UNICOR programs with those of another group of inmates who had not. The study found that inmates employed by UNICOR were 24 percent more likely, upon release, to become employed and remain crime free for as long as 12 years after release than those who were not involved in UNICOR programs. Another study showed that inmates employed in federal prison industries had survival times (measured by the number of days before recommitment) that were 20 percent longer than those of the comparison group.[40] However, independent evaluations have neither confirmed nor denied the BOP's findings. Without independent evaluations, we do not know whether, and how much, UNICOR reduces criminal activity.

Today UNICOR is being questioned by Congress. Critics argue that because federal agencies are required to purchase products and services from UNICOR if those goods can be delivered in a timely manner and the prices are considered competitive, UNICOR does not have to compete to receive federal contracts. Critics note that UNICOR regularly ranks in the upper third among the top 100 federal contractors behind corporate giants like Exxon Mobil, and 72nd among top Department of Defense contractors ahead of Motorola and Tyco. Critics argue that the result is an unfair competitive advantage and the loss of jobs in the private sector.

UNICOR

The trade name of Federal Prison Industries. UNICOR provides such products as U.S. military uniforms, electronic cable assemblies, and modular furniture.

Talking about CORRECTIONS

SENTENCING TRENDS

Visit *Live Talk* at **Corrections .com** (**www.justicestudies .com/talking06**) and listen to the program "Correctional Education," which relates to ideas discussed in this chapter.

Support for abolishing UNICOR's preferential status has been gaining momentum in Congress since 2000, and several pieces of federal legislation have chipped away at UNICOR's preferential status.

Education and Recreation Programs

The majority of prisoners cannot read or write well enough to function in society. In fact, the illiteracy rate among prisoners is two and one-half times that of the U.S. adult population.[41]

According to a report by the Bureau of Justice Statistics, an estimated 40 percent of state prison inmates, 27 percent of federal inmates, 47 percent of inmates in local jails, and 31 percent of those serving probation sentences had not completed high school or its equivalent (GED) while about 18 percent of the general population failed to attain high school graduation.[42] In Philadelphia alone, almost one-third of inmates read at a second- or third-grade level and have fifth-grade math skills.[43] A survey of inmate education programs conducted by the American Correctional Association found that of the more than 1 million persons incarcerated, only 283,000 were participating in educational programs.[44] This may be due in part to the higher rate of learning disabilities found among inmates.[45] An estimated 30 to 50 percent of inmates have a learning disability compared with 5 to 15 percent of the general adult population.

However, can prison education programs rehabilitate prisoners so that they eventually contribute constructively to society upon reentry? The Correctional Education Association (CEA) believes they can. CEA is a nonprofit professional association serving educators and administrators around the world committed to educating prisoners. CEA conducted one of the nation's largest investigations on the impact of correctional education on rearrest, reconviction, reincarceration, and on employment outcomes. CEA's *Three-State Recidivism Study* compared 1,373 correctional education participants and 1,797 nonparticipants in three states—Maryland, Minnesota, and Ohio—for three years after release from prison.[46] Key findings are:

1. For rearrest, correctional education participants had statistically significant lower rates of rearrest (48 percent) when compared to the comparison group of nonparticipants (57 percent).

2. For reconviction, correctional education participants had statistically significant lower rates of reconviction (27 percent) when compared to the control group of nonparticipants (35 percent).

3. For reincarceration, correctional education participants had statistically significant lower rates of reincarceration (21 percent) when compared to the control group of nonparticipants (31 percent).

4. For each of the three years wage earnings were reported, data showed that correctional education participants had higher earnings than nonparticipants.

Overall, CEA's results reveal a statistically significant correlation between participation in education and a lower rate of recidivism in each state. The evidence-based corrections research conducted by the Washington State Institute for Public Policy and Dr. Doris MacKenzie, criminologist at the University of Maryland, confirm that corrections-based educational programs are effective in reducing recidivism.[47] Once correctional education participants are released, they are about 10 to 20 percent less likely to reoffend than the average released prisoner. And for every reincarceration prevented by

EVIDENCE-BASED CORRECTIONS

Maura Gardiner hands out a quiz to students in the geography class she teaches for inmates at the Carl Robinson Correctional Institution in Enfield, Connecticut. Gardiner is director of business and industry services at Enfield's Asnuntuck Community College, which runs the program offering college courses at the prison. What is the illiteracy rate among prisoners compared to that of the general population? Why are there so few prisoners enrolled in education classes?

education, states save about $20,000. According to Laurie Robinson, assistant attorney general at the Office of Justice Programs, U.S. Department of Justice, "While literacy alone will never be a vaccine against criminality, it is one of many skills needed to function—and function well—as a responsible and law-abiding adult in our society."[48]

Education is also an opportunity for prisoners to earn good time credits (also called *earned time*), first introduced in Chapter 3. In at least 21 states, inmates can earn time off their sentences by participating in or completing educational courses. In Nevada, for example, an inmate can earn 10 days per month for participation in an education program, and an additional 60, 90, or 120 days for obtaining a certificate, diploma, or degree, respectively.

So if corrections-based educational programs are effective in reducing recidivism, why are only 283,000 inmates enrolled? There are a number of reasons. First, correctional educators face substantial hurdles in delivering effective instruction. Inmates do not enter prison or jail to attend classes. They often do not see the importance of gaining an education, and many have a history of educational failure. They do not enroll in programs or participate in classes with the same enthusiasm as the non-institutionalized population. Even negative peer pressure can discourage inmates from joining programs. Correctional educators face the challenge of motivating inmates to involve themselves in educational programming because they know that programming inside correctional facilities greatly influences what happens once inmates are released. Emphasizing the relevance of education to inmates, helping inmates experience success in learning, and developing an institutional culture that endorses the importance of education are vital components as correctional facilities work to achieve rehabilitation through education. Second, educational programming has not been a high priority in correctional budgeting, particularly because the beginning of the warehousing era. The bulk of correctional spending has been on security. Third, educational programming cannot be delivered given the present state of overcrowding. As of January 1, 2010, 19 states and the federal system were operating their prisons at more than 100 percent of capacity.[49] California's prisons

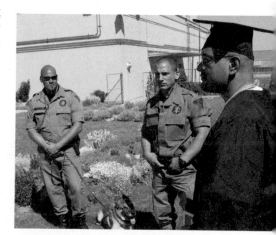

On May 21, 2009, Eduardo Barba, who is serving 30 years for two second-degree felonies at the Utah State Prison, received his Associate of Arts degree in architectural technology from Utah State University. Barba was one of three students chosen to speak during the ceremony. Why is prisoner education important?

were operating at close to 200 percent. And fourth, many states, such as California, Florida, Illinois, Iowa, and Kentucky are slashing correctional education budgets because of the current budget crisis.[50] What we know, though, is that states have a responsibility to ensure public safety and cannot abandon this duty in times of budgetary crisis. Prison education programs prevent more crimes than increasing incarceration rates and lengthening sentences—and cost far less. They even save states money on correctional budgets by reducing the number of offenders who return to prison in the future.

Recreation is another important prison program, and here the courts have made numerous rulings that guarantee prisoners some minimal amount of time in recreational activities. However, the specifics about the nature and extent of recreation programming in prison and inmates' participation in such programs are not known. What is known is that recreation and organized sports can make doing time more bearable and, as a result, make the jobs of correctional officers easier. Recreation programs can also be used as an incentive for good behavior, and by reducing tension, they can cut the number of prison assaults. Physical and mental health experts tell us that recreation programs can be a vehicle for teaching ways to promote health and prevent disease. Inmates who play hard are more likely to stay fit, possibly reducing health costs. Nutrition experts know that eating healthful food, participating in a regular exercise program, and stopping smoking are central to maintaining good health in prison. They also reduce the cost of prison health care.

Physical and Mental Health Care

Good health care plays an important role in the day-to-day operations of a correctional facility. Investments in prisoner health care mean fewer correctional disturbances, disciplinary actions, and inmate injuries and less negative publicity for the institution. For the nation's one-half million correctional employees and thousands of daily visitors to prisons and jails, good health care also reduces their risk of becoming infected from inmates with communicable diseases.

The public health suffers when good health care is not provided as it did in 1989 in New York City when 80 percent of tuberculosis cases were traced to people released from jail and prison. In Los Angeles, a meningitis outbreak in the county jail spread to surrounding neighborhoods. Thus, our policies toward prisoners have a direct impact on the public health of everyone.

Providing inmates adequate health care is of concern to the courts and professional associations. In 1976, the U.S. Supreme Court established a constitutional standard in the Texas case of *Estelle* v. *Gamble*. Gamble claimed that prison officials had inflicted undue suffering when they failed to provide adequate health care for an injury that he sustained while working on a prison assignment. Even though the case was found in favor of the Texas Department of Criminal Justice, the Court ruled that "deliberate indifference to serious medical needs" constitutes cruel and unusual punishment, which is prohibited by the Eighth Amendment of the U.S. Constitution. Over time, the Court redefined the decision and established that inmates have the right to seek medical care, professional medical judgment, care that is ordered, informed consent; refusal of treatment; and medical confidentiality. However, the Court also made clear that such a right did not mean that prisoners have unqualified access to health care. Lower courts have held that the Constitution does not require the medical care provided prisoners to be perfect, the best obtainable, or even very good.[51] According to an excellent review of legal health care standards and the legal remedies available to prisoners, the courts support the **principle of least eligibility:** that prison conditions—including the delivery of health care—must be a step below those of the working class and people on welfare. As a result, prisoners are denied access to medical specialists, second opinions, prompt delivery of medical services, technologically advanced diagnostic techniques, the latest medications, and up-to-date medical procedures.

California, with the nation's largest correctional health care system, spent 20 percent ($974.5 million) of the state's corrections budget on inmate health care in 2004. Despite that amount of money and after 25 years of litigation, on Friday, July 1, 2005, senior U.S. district judge Thelton Henderson announced the most sweeping federal takeover of a prison health care system in the nation's history.[52] In San Francisco, Henderson said that he was taking control of California's troubled prison health care system, saying he was driven to act by "stunning testimony" that medical malpractice or negligence had been causing, on average, one death each week. Henderson said he would appoint a receiver, accountable only to him, to run the almost $1 billion-a-year medical system plagued by inadequate staffing, red tape, and personnel procedures that protect dangerous doctors and nurses. Henderson ordered immediate short-term fixes, mostly in costs for physicians, nurses, pharmacists, and top-level managers, and the installation of a new, computerized record-tracking system costing the state an extra $100 million a year. Four years later, a three-judge panel of the Ninth Circuit Court of Appeals upheld Henderson's decision and ordered California to reduce its prison population by almost one-fourth over the next two to three years. Even though former California governor Arnold Schwarzenegger said, "I don't blame the courts for stepping in to try to solve the health care crisis that we have, because the fact of the matter is, for decades the state of California hasn't really taken it seriously. It hasn't really done something about it." California appealed to the U.S. Supreme Court.[53] The Court's decision is expected sometime in the spring or summer 2011.

The problems of inmate health care are not confined to California, however. Nationally, an estimated 800,000 prisoners suffer from a chronic medical condition that requires medical attention but that most inmates are not receiving: diabetes, hypertension, a prior heart attack, or a previously diagnosed cancer.[54] Almost two-thirds of the states charge inmates a medical copay that averages $3 except for inmates who have a chronic disease, an emergency situation, or a work-related injury for which a staff member ordered medical help or for inmates who are indigent. In 2005, state prisons earned over $4.2 million in medical copayments from inmates.[55]

One new area of inmate health care that is sparking controversy is the shackling of pregnant women during labor and delivery. In October 2010, the Rebecca Project for Human Rights and the National Women's Law Center published a report card that graded federal and state policies on prenatal care, shackling during labor and delivery, and alternative sentencing programs.[56] On prenatal care, 38 states received failing grades for their failure to institute adequate prenatal care despite the fact that many women in prison have high-risk pregnancies. Thirty-six states received failing grades for their use of restraints on the belly and arms of incarcerated women during labor and delivery, thereby restricting the

principle of least eligibility

The requirement that prison conditions—including the delivery of health care—must be a step below those of the working class and people on welfare.

mother's movements and the doctor's access to the patient and increasing the risk of a compromised birth. Seventeen states received a failing grade for their lack of adequate access to family-based programs for nonviolent women who are parenting. And 38 states received a failing grade for not offering prison nurseries to new mothers who are incarcerated.

On the federal level, the researchers were not able to assign a letter grade because they did not have access to data. But they reviewed the policies of the federal Bureau of Prisons (BOP) and the Immigration and Customs Enforcement (ICE) agency of the Department of Homeland Security. (ICE detains women, both pregnant and parenting, who violated civil immigration laws pending deportation.) The researchers reported (1) that the BOP's prenatal care policy is comprehensive in addressing the unique needs of incarcerated pregnant women, but information on the actual care provided is sparse, and reports indicate that access to prenatal care is inconsistent, (2) the BOP prohibits the shackling of pregnant women during labor and delivery but there is no information regarding the implementation of the policy, (3) the BOP has a program called Mothers and Infants Nurturing Together (MINT), which provides alternative community-based sentencing for women who have recently given birth and have less than five years left on their prison terms, but the program serves only a small portion of mothers in federal prison, and access is restricted to mothers with newborns, and (4) the BOP does not operate any prison nurseries.

The researchers found that ICE (1) is in the process of revising its policies regarding the confinement of pregnant women detained for immigration violations, (2) has no prohibition on shackling pregnant detainees, (3) has alternatives to detention yet immigration attorneys report inconsistent implementation as well as government resistance to having pregnant women detainees released into the community, and (4) has poor conditions for families with children in detention.

National health care organizations—such as the American Medical Association and the National Commission on Correctional Health Care—insist on alleviating the pain and suffering of all people, regardless of their status. They believe that no distinction should be made between inmates and free citizens. We will return to the health care issues in Chapter 12.

PRISON ORGANIZATION AND ADMINISTRATION

All 50 states and the BOP operate prisons. In addition, four local jurisdictions in the United States operate prison systems: Cook County (Chicago), Illinois; Philadelphia; New York City; and Washington, DC. It is estimated that there are 1,292 state, federal, and private confinement facilities: 102 federal and 1,190 state.[57] (Private confinement facilities operate under contract to state or federal correctional authorities and are included in those counts).

Jurisdictions use a variety of capacity measures to reflect both the space available to house inmates and the ability to staff and operate an institution. Some use rated capacity (first introduced in Chapter 6), which is the number of beds or inmates a state official assigns to an institution. Some use **operational capacity**, the number of inmates that a facility's staff, existing programs, and services can accommodate. Others use **design capacity**, the number of inmates that planners or architects intend for the facility. For instance, an architect might design a prison for 1,100 inmates.

operational capacity
The number of inmates that a facility's staff, existing programs, and services can accommodate.

design capacity
The number of inmates that planners or architects intend for the facility.

Administrators might add more staff, programs, and services to be able to confine 1,300 in the same space. The design capacity was 1,100, but the operational and rated capacities are 1,300. The institution is operating 18 percent above design capacity.

On January 1, 2010, the federal prison system was operating at 36 percent over capacity. Overall, state prisons were operating between 1 percent and 40 percent over capacity. We return to the issue of prison capacity and overcrowding in Chapter 13.

State Prison Systems

Organization The administration of state prisons is a function of the executive branch of government. The governor appoints the director of corrections, who in turn appoints the wardens of the state prisons. A change in governors often means a change in state prison leadership and administration.

The organization of most state prison systems involves a central authority, based in the state capital. Local communities, private contractors, or the state itself may provide prison services (from treatment and education to maintenance and repair). This method of organizational structure and delivery of services across wide geographic areas is often criticized for its fragmentation; duplication of structure, effort, and services; lack of coordination; and ambiguous goals. Still, for legal control and for maintaining an equitable distribution of resources, a centralized model has been maintained while in other areas of corrections (e.g., community corrections and probation), services are often decentralized.

As we explained about the organization and administration of probation in Chapter 4, there is no correct way to organize corrections. Any arrangement that helps corrections reach its goals is appropriate. The organizational styles found across the United States developed over time and are the result of political interaction and accommodation among government agencies and interest groups.

Size and Costs State departments of corrections vary in size. In 2010, one of the smallest was South Dakota's, with over 900 employees working in juvenile and adult institutions and community services and an annual operating budget of $108 million. The largest was California's, with almost 66,000 employees and an annual operating budget of $9.8 billion.[58] An estimated 455,000 people work in adult correctional facilities: 66 percent are correctional officers; 12 percent are clerical, maintenance, and food service workers; 10 percent are professional/technical staff; 3 percent are educators; 2 percent are administrator; and 7 percent are other.[59] Male employees outnumber female employees by a ratio of 2 to 1. Nineteen percent of all correctional facility staff are black, and 7 percent are Hispanic. In the summer of 2010, a survey conducted by the American Correctional Association reported on correctional officer wages while in training, entry level after training, and after the first year of employment. The highest wages for training are $45,166 in Massachusetts, $40,000 in New Jersey, and $36,600 in California. For entry level after training, highest wages are $45,288 in California, $45,166 in Massachusetts, and $40,000 in New Jersey. After one year of employment, highest wages are $60,660 in California, $53,674 in New Jersey, and $48,653 in Massachusetts.[60]

Twenty years ago, the United States spent about $7 billion on corrections. Today that number is more than $52 billion. Corrections is the

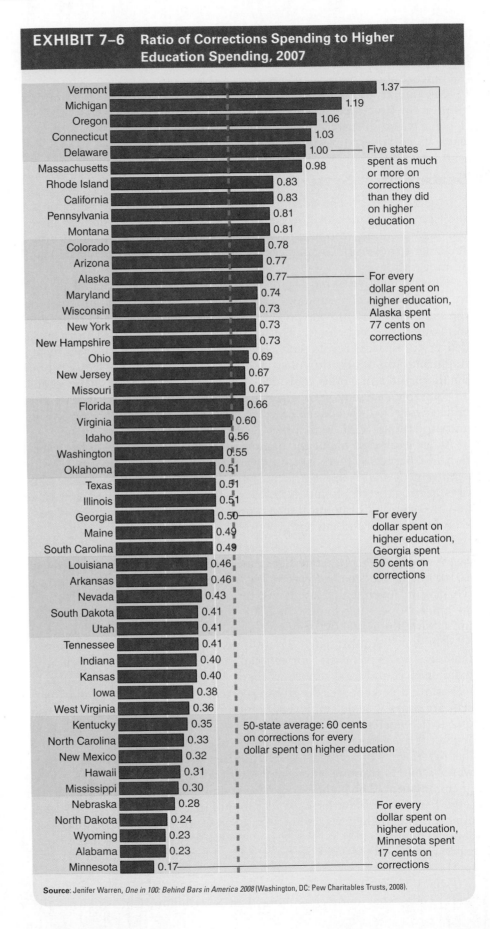

EXHIBIT 7–6　Ratio of Corrections Spending to Higher Education Spending, 2007

State	Ratio
Vermont	1.37
Michigan	1.19
Oregon	1.06
Connecticut	1.03
Delaware	1.00
Massachusetts	0.98
Rhode Island	0.83
California	0.83
Pennsylvania	0.81
Montana	0.81
Colorado	0.78
Arizona	0.77
Alaska	0.77
Maryland	0.74
Wisconsin	0.73
New York	0.73
New Hampshire	0.73
Ohio	0.69
New Jersey	0.67
Missouri	0.67
Florida	0.66
Virginia	0.60
Idaho	0.56
Washington	0.55
Oklahoma	0.51
Texas	0.51
Illinois	0.51
Georgia	0.50
Maine	0.49
South Carolina	0.49
Louisiana	0.46
Arkansas	0.46
Nevada	0.43
South Dakota	0.41
Utah	0.41
Tennessee	0.41
Indiana	0.40
Kansas	0.40
Iowa	0.38
West Virginia	0.36
Kentucky	0.35
North Carolina	0.33
New Mexico	0.32
Hawaii	0.31
Mississippi	0.30
Nebraska	0.28
North Dakota	0.24
Wyoming	0.23
Alabama	0.23
Minnesota	0.17

Five states spent as much or more on corrections than they did on higher education

For every dollar spent on higher education, Alaska spent 77 cents on corrections

For every dollar spent on higher education, Georgia spent 50 cents on corrections

50-state average: 60 cents on corrections for every dollar spent on higher education

For every dollar spent on higher education, Minnesota spent 17 cents on corrections

Source: Jenifer Warren, *One in 100: Behind Bars in America 2008* (Washington, DC: Pew Charitables Trusts, 2008).

EXHIBIT 7–7	States with the Highest and Lowest Reported Average Annual Operating Costs per Inmate		
Highest		**Lowest**	
Rhode Island	$44,860	Louisiana	$13,009
Massachusetts	43,026	Alabama	13,019
New York	42,202	South Carolina	13,170
Alaska	42,082	Mississippi	13,428
Maine	35,012	South Dakota	14,157

Source: Pew Charitable Trusts, *Public Safety, Public Spending: Forecasting America's Prison Population 2007–2011* (Washington, DC: Pew Charitable Trusts, 2007).

fourth-largest category of states' spending following education, Medicaid, and transportation. The vast majority of funds that go to state corrections systems—9 of every 10 dollars—goes to prisons.[61] Some ask if the money spent on state corrections encroaches on funds for higher education because the money has to come from somewhere. Is there discussion about this kind of trade-off? Jennifer Gonnerman, a reporter for the *Village Voice,* writes, "When parents get a tuition bill for their kids' college education, I always think they should get a little note that says tuition went up $200 last year because we decided to build two new prisons. Then we can all decide whether we think that's a good use of our money or not."[62] Others have said, "Every additional dollar spent on prisons, of course is one dollar less that can go to preparing for the next Hurricane Katrina, educating young people, providing health care to the elderly, or repairing roads and bridges."[63] Exhibit 7–6 shows the ratio of corrections to higher education spending in 2007. Vermont, Michigan, Oregon, Connecticut, and Delaware spend as much money or more on corrections as they do on higher education.

States spend, on average, approximately $28,648 a year to incarcerate one offender.[64] Others believe the cost is even higher, $40,000.[65] And depending on the prison security level, the capital costs of building one prison cell can be as much as $100,000.[66] States with the highest and lowest reported average annual operating costs per inmate are shown in Exhibit 7–7.

Reasons for the variation between states in the cost of operating prisons include differences in the cost of living, employees' salaries and benefits, climate, and inmate-to-staff ratios. High inmate-to-staff ratios are most common in states reporting low average costs per inmate; low inmate-to-staff ratios predominate in states with high average annual costs per inmate. For example, New York, one of the states with the highest reported average annual operating cost per inmate ($42,202), has an inmate-to-staff ratio of 2.0:1. Alabama, on the other hand, has one of the lowest reported average annual costs per inmate ($13,019) and an inmate-to-staff ratio of 7.1:1.

However significant reductions in corrections budgets, a move that would have been unheard of during the tough-on-crime days of the 1980s and 1990s is forcing every correctional agency to make deep cuts to balance the states' general fund budgets.[67] For example, in fiscal year 2010, the corrections budget in Connecticut was reduced by approximately 5 percent, 12 percent in Kansas, 3 percent in Michigan, and 7 percent in Washington. Over two-thirds of the states and the federal BOP cut personnel, salaries, benefits, and overtime. Almost one-half downsized programs. Forty-four states either closed facilities, reduced their number of beds, or proposed selling prison facilities. And one-fourth reduced food services.

Corrections professionals, legislatures, and governors in these and other states have seized the opportunity to rethink prison growth, change the face of corrections without sacrificing public safety, and actually turn the fiscal crisis into "the mother of invention." State policymakers turned to evidence-based corrections for guidance about making more effective use of the funds they have. They turned to the federal Second Chance Act (discussed in Chapter 8) for funding to assist with successful reentry of prisoners returning home. States channeled money into drug courts and veterans courts (discussed in Chapter 5) and reentry courts (discussed in Chapter 8) that keep offenders in the community and have been shown to maintain or enhance public safety at less expense than imprisonment. States also reduced prison sentences for good behavior and other forms of early release. They invested in technology, for example, the use of videoconferencing to avoid physically transporting inmates for court appearances. And they turned to professional associations, such as the American Correctional Association, the American Jail Association, and the American Probation and Parole Association, and independent centers such as the Vera Institute of Justice in New York City that provide technical assistance to help leaders in government improve criminal justice policy.

New York, the fourth largest state prison system, reduced its prison population by 20 percent from 1999 to 2009 by increasing its use of diversion for prison-bound cases to treatment and other alternatives to incarceration, scaling back its harsh Rockefeller drug laws, and increasing the use of release programs and incentives to shorten time served in prison for people convicted of drug violations and other nonviolent crimes. Michigan, which has the 8th largest state prison system, reduced its prison population by 12 percent from 2006 to 2009 by scaling back mandatory drug sentences, increasing parole grants, reducing technical violations, and enhancing its use of community corrections. New Jersey, with the 19th largest state prison system, reduced its prison population by 19 percent from 1999 to 2009 by increasing parole grants, reducing parole revocations, and scaling back drug sentencing guidelines. And Kansas, which has the 34th largest state prison system, reduced its prison population by 5 percent from 2003 to 2009 by scaling back drug sentencing guidelines, improving community supervision, reducing technical revocations, and investing a portion of the savings from reduced spending on prisons into infrastructures and civic institutions such as abuse treatment, housing, education, and jobs located in high-risk neighborhoods, a practice known as **justice reinvestment**.

These experiences demonstrate that controlling prison growth is not an intractable problem and corrections can develop policy responses that reverse the prison buildup of the past 25 years while promoting public safety and doing more with less. Researchers with the Sentencing Project concluded their investigation of the impact of the fiscal crisis on corrections by writing, "The renewed interest in evidence-based programming, along with the harsh realities of the fiscal crisis, offers an opportunity to take a broad look at the use of incarceration and the prospects for reducing its scale in ways that better promote public safety."[68]

justice reinvestment
The practice of reducing spending on prisons and investing a portion of the savings into infrastructure and civic institutions located in high-risk neighborhoods.

Security Level Prisons are classified by the level of security they provide. A **maximum- or close/high-security prison** is designed, organized, and staffed to confine the most violent and dangerous offenders for long periods. It imposes strict controls on the movement of inmates and their visitors, and custody and security are constant concerns. The prison has a highly secure perimeter with watchtowers and high walls. Inmates live in single- or multiple-occupancy barred cells. The staff-to-inmate ratio is high, routines are highly regimented, and prisoner counts are frequent. Programs, amenities, and privileges are few. There are 372 maximum- and close/high-security correctional facilities in the United States confining 36 percent of the prisoner population.[69]

Inmates in a **medium-security prison** are considered less dangerous than those in maximum-security prisons and may serve short or long sentences. Medium-security prisons impose fewer controls on inmates' and visitors' freedom of movement than do maximum-security facilities. Outwardly, medium-security prisons often resemble maximum-security institutions, and they, too, have barred cells. The staff-to-inmate ratio is generally lower than in a maximum-security facility. Medium-security prisons place more emphasis on treatment and work programs than do maximum-security prisons, and the level of amenities and privileges is slightly higher. Forty-two percent of the prisoner population is serving time in 480 medium-security correctional facilities.[70]

A **minimum-security prison** confines the least dangerous offenders for both short and long periods. It allows as much freedom of movement and as many privileges and amenities as are consistent with the goals of the facility while still following procedures to avoid escape, violence, and disturbance. The staff-to-inmate ratio is low, and inmates live in dormitory housing or private rooms. Some leave the institution for programming in the community. There are 969 minimum-security correctional institutions in the United States confining 22 percent of the prisoner population.[71] They are sometimes referred to as **open institutions** because they have no fences or walls surrounding them.

maximum- or close/high-security prison

A prison designed, organized, and staffed to confine the most dangerous offenders for long periods. It has a highly secure perimeter, barred cells, and a high staff-to-inmate ratio. It imposes strict controls on the movement of inmates and visitors, and it offers few programs, amenities, or privileges.

medium-security prison

A prison that confines offenders considered less dangerous than those in maximum security, for both short and long periods. It places fewer controls on inmates' and visitors' freedom of movement than does a maximum-security facility. It, too, has barred cells and a fortified perimeter. The staff-to-inmate ratio is generally lower than that in a maximum-security facility, and the level of amenities and privileges is slightly higher.

minimum-security prison

A prison that confines the least dangerous offenders for both short and long periods. It allows as much freedom of movement and as many privileges and amenities as are consistent with the goals of the facility. It may have dormitory housing, and the staff-to-inmate ratio is relatively low.

open institution

A minimum-security facility that has no fences or walls surrounding it.

Maximum-security prisons confine the most violent and dangerous offenders for long periods. They are surrounded by high walls and gun towers. What percent of the prisoner population is confined in maximum-security prisons?

Medium-security prisons incarcerate less dangerous inmates than maximum-security prisons. They impose fewer controls on inmates' freedom of movement and place more emphasis on treatment and work programs. What percent of the prisoner population is confined in medium-security prisons?

Federal Bureau of Prisons

The BOP is an entirely separate system from state and local prison systems. Before the 1890s, the federal government did not operate its own prisons. Instead, the Department of Justice paid state prisons and county jails to house people convicted of committing federal crimes. The public outcry over the convict lease system, however, motivated the passage of a federal law prohibiting the leasing of federal offenders. Many state prisons and county jails subsequently became reluctant to house federal offenders because it was not economically advantageous to incarcerate inmates they could not lease. Moreover, the expansion of federal law enforcement activities and the enactment of new federal laws in the late 19th century

Minimum-security prisons confine the least dangerous offenders. They are sometimes referred to as open institutions because they have no fences or walls surrounding them. What percent of the prisoner population is confined in minimum-security prisons?

Michelle Galaviz

Classification Officer • Florida Department of Corrections • Lake City Work Release Center • Lake City, Florida

Michelle Galaviz is a classification officer at the Lake City Work Release Center with the Florida Department of Corrections. She started her career with the Florida DOC in September 2007 shortly after earning her bachelor's degree in criminal justice from the University of West Florida. Prior to her employment with the Florida DOC, she worked as a correctional officer in a county jail in Georgia. Michelle plans to go to graduate school and earn a master's degree in administration with a specialization in criminal justice. Her goal is to better understand and apply the principles of administration to the criminal justice system and grow professionally with the Florida DOC.

Michelle points to two areas where her classes at the University of West Florida are helping her as a classification officer. Classes in judicial process and the American criminal justice system help her understand Florida's sentencing structure and answer questions that inmates and their families have about the inmate's sentence. The communication skills she learned in Human Behavior & Social Environment, Moral Issues in Criminal Justice, and Social Problems and Sociology help her communicate what is happening to inmates and their families. Michelle says, "When you get to use what you learned, it makes all that studying worthwhile!"

Being a classification officer requires focusing on details, being self-motivated and self-disciplined, and showing lots of patience. Michelle says this is a job where you wear a coat of many colors. "In one coat color you are the classifier, making sure that the inmates are classified properly and do not have any conflicts within the facility or with a facility they may be transferring to. You are responsible for completing any appointments, ranging from progress reviews to release appointments. In the next coat color you become a counselor. In your appointments with inmates you discuss the issues they are having. This may be anything from family problems to problems with other inmates. In this coat, you are also responsible for answering any questions or issues that the family may have. Then put on another coat, it is time to become a clerk/typist. In this coat you are responsible for keeping all inmate files, hard- and computer-copy, up-to-date and accurate. This means that you have to do some filing and some typing."

Michelle's advice to persons interested in working as a corrections counselor is this: "The most important thing to remember when doing this job is that you are dealing with real people and their lives and that is not something that you want to mess up; so pay attention to what you are doing, check yourself, double check and don't rush. Pay attention to details, be self-motivated and self-disciplined, and show lots of patience. It is not an easy job and there is not a lot of praise involved; this is one of those jobs you have to have a passion for!"

> *"The most important thing to remember when doing this job is that you are dealing with real people and their lives and that is not something that you want to mess up; so pay attention to what you are doing, check yourself, double check and don't rush. Pay attention to details, be self-motivated and self-disciplined, and show lots of patience. It's not an easy job and there's not a lot of praise involved; this is one of those jobs that you have to have a passion for!"*

led to an increase in the prosecution of federal lawbreakers and to overcrowding in the prisons where they were held. With a growing population of federal prisoners and the growing reluctance of nonfederal prisons to house them, the federal government had no choice but to build prisons of its own. Congress authorized the establishment of three federal prisons in 1891: U.S. penitentiaries at Atlanta (Georgia), Leavenworth (Kansas), and McNeil Island (Washington).

Bureau of Prisons In 1930, the BOP was established to provide more progressive and humane care for 13,000 federal inmates, to

EXHIBIT 7–8 Federal Bureau of Prisons' Mission Statement

It is the mission of the Federal Bureau of Prisons to protect society by confining offenders in the controlled environments of prison and community-based facilities that are safe, humane, and appropriately secure and that provide work and other self-improvement opportunities to assist offenders in becoming law-abiding citizens.

Source: Federal Bureau of Prisons, July 1998.

professionalize the prison service, and to ensure consistent and centralized administration of the 11 federal prisons in operation at that time. Between 1940 and 1980, the BOP held steady with approximately 25 institutions and some 25,000 inmates. Most of the BOP's growth in institutions and inmates occurred in the 1980s as a result of federal law enforcement efforts and new legislation that altered sentencing in the federal criminal justice system. From 1980 to 1989, the federal inmate population doubled, from 25,000 to more than 58,000. During the 1990s, the population doubled again as efforts to combat illegal drugs and illegal immigration contributed to increasing conviction rates. Today the federal prison population stands at 208,118 (36 percent—almost 75,000 prisoners—over capacity). More than a quarter are noncitizens imprisoned for immigration crimes (crimes committed by illegal immigrants) because some countries such as Cuba and Vietnam refuse to take back their convicted citizens, leaving the BOP to hold the foreigners indefinitely. Following President Obama's State of the Union Address on January 25, 2011, the BOP, in discussion with the White House Office of Management and Budget, proposed increasing the amount of time deducted from federal prison terms for good behavior, which would immediately qualify some 4,000 federal inmates for release and another 4,000 over the next 10 years as one strategy to reduce BOP spending.[72]

Exhibit 7–8 shows the mission statement of the BOP. The central office in Washington, DC, 6 regional offices, 2 staff training centers, 116 confinement institutions, and 22 community corrections offices that oversee residential reentry centers and home confinement programs carry out this mission. The BOP also houses the National Institute of Corrections (NIC), which advises and assists state and local correctional agencies throughout the country, primarily through technical assistance, training, and information services. The attorney general appoints the director of the BOP. Harley G. Lappin was sworn in as the seventh director of the BOP on April 4, 2003. He retired May 7, 2011. Thomas Kane is acting director until the attorney general appoints a permanent director.

The BOP employs more than 37,500 people nationwide. Almost 28 percent of the BOP workforce is female and one-third is minority. Thirty percent of BOP personnel have completed some college. Another 30 percent have a bachelor's degree or further education.

The BOP budget for 2011 is $6.1 billion, the same as for 2010 unless Congress and the president provide a new funding amount through an appropriations bill.[73] The largest portion, $2.7 billion, was for institution security and administration, including the costs of facility maintenance, motor pool operations, and other administrative functions for all BOP facilities. The second highest cost was $2.2 billion for inmate care and programs. This included the costs of all food, medical supplies, clothing, welfare services, transportation, staff salaries, academic courses, social and occupational education courses, religious programs, psychological services, and drug abuse treatment. The starting salary of a federal correctional officer is approximately $30,000. Starting federal salaries are slightly higher in areas where prevailing local pay levels are higher. Other employment opportunities with the BOP include accountant, attorney, chaplain, clinical psychologist, contract specialist, correctional treatment specialist, dental hygienist, dentist, drug treatment specialist, employee services specialist, health system administrator, information technology specialist, legal instruments examiner, medical records technician, physician, recreation specialist, registered nurse, nurse practitioner, pharmacist, physical therapist, physician assistant, safety specialist, secretary, teacher, and training instructor. Consult the Appendix: Careers in Corrections at the Online Learning Center Web site for the steps involved in career planning, developing employability and job readiness, and finding the right job. The average annual cost to incarcerate a federal prisoner was $28,284 in 2010.

Institutions and Security Level On January 1, 2010, 208,118 inmates were under the jurisdiction of the federal prison system (24,031 federal prisoners were held in privately operated facilities). The BOP operates 116 confinement institutions of several different security levels to confine appropriately a broad range of federal offenders. The classification of facilities by security level is based on such factors as the presence of gun towers, security barriers, or detection devices; the types of housing within the institution; internal security features; and the staff-to-inmate ratio. Each facility is placed in one of five groups—minimum security, low security, medium security, high security, and administration:

- **Minimum-security institutions,** also known as *federal prison camps (FPCs),* have dormitory housing, a relatively low staff-to-inmate ratio, and limited or no perimeter fencing. These institutions are work and program oriented. Many are adjacent to larger institutions or on military bases where inmates help serve the labor needs of the institution, military base, or other federal entities such as the National Park Service and U.S. Forest Service. Approximately 17 percent of BOP inmates are in minimum-security facilities.
- **Low-security federal correctional institutions (FCIs)** have double-fenced perimeters, mostly dormitory housing, and strong work and program components. The staff-to-inmate ratio in these institutions is higher than in minimum-security facilities. Approximately 38 percent of BOP inmates are in low-security facilities.
- **Medium-security FCIs** have fortified perimeters (often double fences with electronic detection systems), cell housing, and a wide variety of work and treatment programs. They have an even higher staff-to-inmate ratio than do low-security FCIs, providing even more internal controls. Approximately 29 percent of BOP inmates are in medium-security facilities.
- **High-security institutions,** known as *U.S. penitentiaries (USPs),* have highly secure perimeters (featuring walls or reinforced fences), multiple- and single-occupancy cell housing, close staff supervision, and strict movement controls. Approximately 11 percent of BOP inmates are in high-security facilities.

- **Administrative institutions** have special missions, such as detention of noncitizens or pretrial offenders, treatment of inmates with serious or chronic medical problems, or containment of extremely dangerous or escape-prone inmates. Approximately 5 percent of BOP inmates are in administrative facilities. Exhibit 7–9 shows the locations of all BOP facilities.

DOES INCARCERATION WORK?

In June 2002, the Bureau of Justice Statistics reported on the recidivism of 272,111 prisoners discharged from 15 states and tracked for three years after their release in 1994.[74] Overall, 68 percent were rearrested within three years and 25 percent were resentenced to prison for a new crime. More than two-thirds of the recidivism occurs within the first year after incarceration. Recidivism statistics released by the BOP aren't any better. On March 18, 2010, BOP director Harley Lappin told the House of Representatives Subcommittee on Commerce, Justice, Science, and Related Agencies that 40 percent of inmates return to federal prison. This means that of the 60,00 federal inmates released in 2009, 24,000 will be reincarcerated. Lappin admitted that the BOP leaves a lot to be desired, saying, "I don't think we're doing a good enough job."[75]

After reading statistics like these, you might wonder whether incarceration works. The answer depends on whom you ask and how he or she interprets the question. What does "work" mean? Does it refer to the prevention of rearrest, reconviction, or reincarceration? Should a new offense be related to previous ones? What if a new offense occurs 5 or 10 years after release from prison? Should the prison experience deter potential *and* actual offenders? Should it lower the crime rate? If so, by how much, how fast, and at what cost? What about criminological theories that link crime to forces outside the individual and over which the offender has little or no control such as his or her biological or psychological makeup, social structures, and even the more radical explanations that link crime to economic development, race, class, and gender? Politicians and researchers see the question differently. Governors and directors of corrections see the question straightforwardly: Were it not for prison, there would be more crime. Removing convicted offenders from the community ensures public safety, and the cost of incarceration is the price tag for ensuring that safety.

Researchers feel the effectiveness question can be answered only with randomly designed experiments in which identically matched offenders are randomly assigned to prison or to other punishments. Even if such experiments were possible, there are differences between prisoners and people not sent to prison, and these differences will influence future offending.

The common expectation is that crime rates will decline as the number of persons incarcerated increases and that crime will increase if incarceration rates fall. If you look at the relationship between the crime index and the prison population over the past 10 years, you might reach the conclusion that as the nation's prison population grew, crime fell and, therefore, the experiment in locking up more people lowered the nation's volume of crime. For example, David Muhlhausen, a policy analyst at the Heritage Foundation, argues that increasing incarceration decreases crime. "Considering that there are still about 12 million crimes a year," Muhlhausen concludes, then "maybe we're not incarcerating enough

EXHIBIT 7–9   Institutions of the Federal Bureau of Prisons

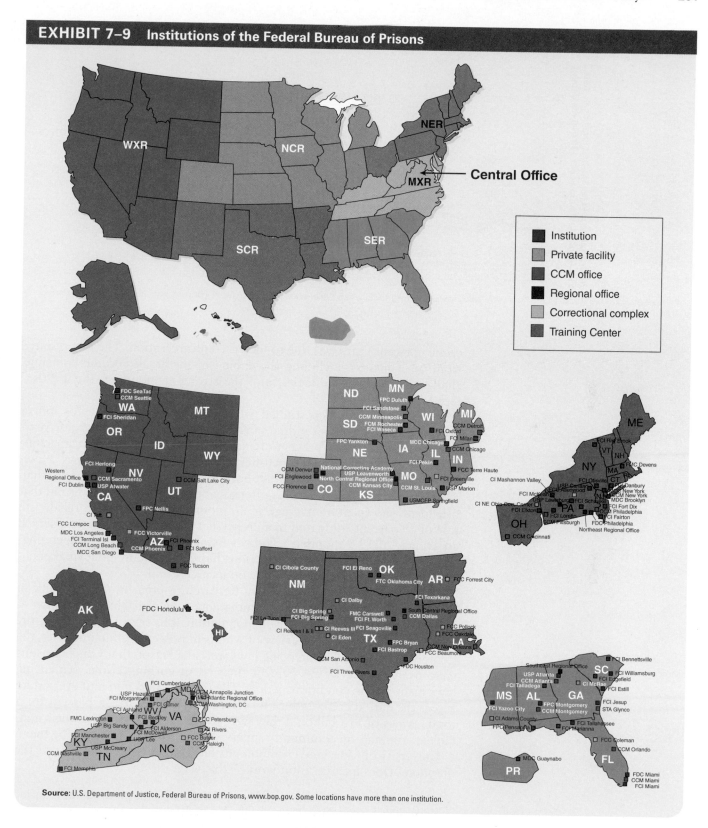

Source: U.S. Department of Justice, Federal Bureau of Prisons, www.bop.gov. Some locations have more than one institution.

people."[76] Unfortunately, if you look at the past quarter century of prison buildup, you find that as the prison population increased, crime increased, decreased, increased, and decreased. There is simply no strong or consistent relationship between incarceration rate and crime rate.[77] Bruce Western of Harvard University estimated that only 10 percent of the decline in

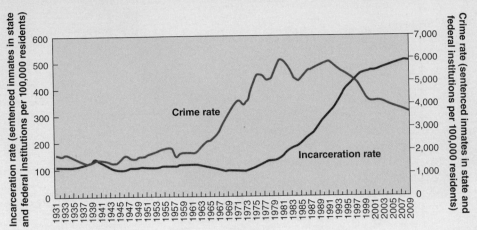

EXHIBIT 7–10   National Crime and Imprisonment Trends, 1931–2009

Source: Adapted from Pew Charitable Trusts, *Public Safety, Public Spending: Forecasting America's Prison Population 2007–2011* (Philadelphia: Pew Charitable Trusts, 2007) and updated by the authors.

crime in recent years was due to increased incarceration. The rest resulted from other factors, including the ebbing of the crack cocaine epidemic, changes in policing strategies, and the strong economy of the 1990s.[78] (See Exhibit 7–10.)

Researchers have also studied whether locking up people for longer periods of time enhances public safety. Putting people in prison for years or even decades should prevent offenders from reoffending by incapacitating them or deterring would-be offenders from committing crimes. However, a review of 50 studies dating back to 1958 and involving more than 336,000 offenders with various offenses and criminal histories found that offenders who spent an average of 30 months in prison had a recidivism rate of 29 percent compared to a 26 percent rate among those who served an average of 12.9 months.[79] Today's fiscal crisis and a growing emphasis on using evidence-based corrections has caused many policymakers to question our logic and our reliance on incarceration.

The Center for Economic Policy Research, a bipartisan think tank in Washington, DC was recently commissioned by the Ohio legislature to help that state reduce its prison population (the seventh largest in the nation). After a thorough review of who is in prison in Ohio and why, the Center said the state's sentencing laws were the reason that Ohio's prisons were overcrowded by 26 percent. Instead of curbing crime, sentencing laws made prison conditions worse. The Center said Ohio and every state across the nation could reduce its corrections budget by 25 percent for a total savings of $15 billion if they were to place just one-half of their nonviolent criminals on community supervision instead of incarcerating them.

University of Maryland criminologist Dr. Doris MacKenzie answers the question "Does incarceration work?" this way:

> In summary, there is evidence that incapacitation has the potential for reducing crime in the community. The difficulty lies in determining the amount of crime prevented and how much should be considered a large reduction in crime. Questions also revolve around the costs of such policies in terms of money and impact on future generations in inner cities.[80]

Questions such as whether one can determine the amount of crime prevented through incarceration; whether that reduction is large enough; whether the amount spent on that reduction is worth it; and whether the impact of incarceration on families and communities left behind is acceptable, speak to the importance of justice reinvestment to project the consequences of incarceration. Until then, there is no indication that we have come any closer in reaching consensus on the question of whether incarceration works.

REVIEW AND APPLICATIONS

SUMMARY

1 The Pennsylvania and Auburn prison systems emerged in the United States at the turn of the 19th century. The Pennsylvania system isolated prisoners from each other to avoid harmful influences and to give prisoners reflection time so they might repent. The Auburn system allowed inmates to work together during the day under strict silence. At night, however, prisoners were isolated in small sleeping cells. With time, sleeping cells became congregate and restrictions against talking were removed.

2 There have been nine eras in U.S. prison history:
- Penitentiary era (1790–1825)
- Mass prison era (1825–1876)
- Reformatory era (1876–1890)
- Industrial era (1890–1935)
- Punitive era (1935–1945)
- Treatment era (1945–1967)
- Community-based era (1967–1980)
- Warehousing era (1980–1995)
- Just deserts era (1985–present)

3 On January 1, 2010, 1,405,622 people were under the jurisdiction of state correctional authorities, and 208,118 people were under the jurisdiction of the federal prison system. Of these state and federal inmates, 7 percent were female, 37 percent were white, 41 percent were black, and 22 percent were Hispanic. Reasons for the increase in women prisoners include women's presence in the U.S. labor market, which has brought about increased opportunities for crime; the increased poverty of young, female, single heads of households, which means that more women are turning to crime to support themselves and their families; changes in the criminal justice system, which no longer affords women differential treatment; and the combined effects of harsh drug laws, changing patterns of drug use, and mandatory sentencing policies. Reasons for the increase in minority prisoners include an increase in serious criminal activity that results in incarceration; racial profiling and racism by the criminal justice system; and the prevalence of social conditions that exist in the nation's inner cities, which is where most minorities in the United States regardless of race live, and the fact that large urban areas have the highest violence rates.

4 Classification is the principal management tool for allocating scarce prison resources efficiently and minimizing the potential for escape or violence. The purpose is to assign inmates to appropriate prison housing and to help staff understand, treat, predict, and manage prisoner behavior. There are two types of classification, external and internal. External classification determines an inmate's security level (maximum, close, medium, minimum, or community). Internal classification determines an inmate's assignment to housing units or cellblocks, work, and programming based on the inmate's risk, needs, and time to serve.

5 Today, nearly half of state and federal prison systems are operating or developing at least one residential faith-based program. Supporters of faith-based initiatives argue that such programs may reduce recidivism and improve other postrelease outcomes; are generally free or low cost because they are provided by volunteer groups; may improve in-prison behavior; lessen the dehumanization of incarceration; and are unlikely to harm anyone. Opponents argue that faith-based programs may not be effective; may actually cost taxpayers; promote a religious orientation and hence could be unconstitutional; may lessen offender accountability for their crimes; and may coerce some inmates into certain kinds of religious activity.

6 The evidence-based literature on prison industries shows that the average prison industry program reduces the recidivism rate of participants by almost 6 percent.

7 The illiteracy rate among prisoners is two and one-half times that of the U.S. adult population. Only 283,000 inmates participate in educational programs. Evidence-based literature shows that corrections-based educational programs are effective in reducing crime. Specifics about the nature and extent of recreation programming in prison and inmates' participation in them is not known, but recreation and organized sports can make doing time easier, be used as an incentive, reduce tension, promote health, prevent disease, and reduce prison health care costs. In 1976, the U.S. Supreme Court ruled in *Estelle* v. *Gamble* that inmates have a constitutional right to reasonable, adequate health care for serious medical needs. However, the Court also made clear that such a right did not mean that prisoners have unqualified access to health care.

8 All 50 states, the Federal Bureau of Prisons (BOP), and four local jurisdictions operate correctional institutions. State prison administration, a function of the executive branch of government, is most often organized around a central authority operating from the state capital. There are three levels of state prison security: maximum, for the most dangerous offenders serving long sentences; medium, for less dangerous offenders serving long or short sentences; and minimum, for the least dangerous offenders. Most state are either medium or minimum security. The BOP operates 116 federal confinement correctional facilities. The BOP operates minimum-security prisons known as *federal prison camps,* low- and medium-security facilities known as *federal correctional institutions,* high-security institutions known as *U.S. penitentiaries,* and administrative institutions with special missions, such as detention of illegal immigrants, treatment of people with chronic medical problems, and containment of extremely dangerous or escape-prone inmates. The majority of federal prisoners are confined in low- and medium-security facilities.

9 Whether incarceration works depends on whom you ask and how he or she interprets the question. Politicians and researchers see the question differently. Governors and directors of corrections see the question straightforwardly: Were it not for prison, there would be more crime. Researchers feel the question can be answered only with randomly designed experiments. There is no indication that we have come any closer to reaching consensus on the question of whether incarceration works.

KEY TERMS

penitentiary, p. 216
Pennsylvania system, p. 216
separate system, p. 216
Auburn system, p. 216
public accounts system, p. 220
contract system, p. 220
convict lease system, p. 221
state use system, p. 221
public works system, p. 221

medical model, p. 222
classification, p. 232
external classification, p. 233
internal classification, p. 233
unit management system, p. 239
Federal Prison Industries (FPI), p. 244
UNICOR, p. 244
principle of least eligibility, p. 249

operational capacity, p. 250
design capacity, p. 250
justice reinvestment, p. 254
maximum- or close/high-security prison, p. 255
medium-security prison, p. 255
minimum-security prison, p. 256
open institution, p. 257

QUESTIONS FOR REVIEW

1 Explain the differences between the Pennsylvania and Auburn prison systems.

2 Summarize the eras of prison development.

3 What can you infer from the characteristics of today's prisoners and the reasons for the incarceration of women and minority inmates?

4 Are there criteria you would add to prisoner classification schemes?

5 Summarize the literature and the issues on the program effectiveness of faith-based institutions.

6 Discuss the impact of the evidence-based literature on prison industries.

7 What ideas can you add to the reasons for including education, recreation, and health care programs for prisoners?

8 Evaluate the strengths and limitations of the various ways prisons are organized and administered.

9 What ideas can you add to the question "Does incarceration work?"

THINKING CRITICALLY ABOUT CORRECTIONS

Internal Classification

Review the three internal classification systems discussed in this chapter (Adult Internal Management system, Prisoner Management Classification system, and behavior-based systems). AIMS and PMC use personality and attitude measures (what inmates say they'll do—sometimes called a *casework model*) to assign inmates to housing units or cellblocks, work, and programming. BBS employs a behavioral model (how the inmate has behaved in the past) to determine internal classification. Write a list of three advantages and disadvantages of each approach (casework model of personality and attitude versus behavioral). Which method do you think is better to determine internal classification, and why?

Does Incarceration Work?

This chapter concludes with the statement, "Thus, there is no indication that we have come any closer in reaching consensus on the question of whether incarceration works." After more than 200 years of prison history, what is it about the question "Does incarceration work?" that makes it so difficult to reach consensus? Do you think there's a model muddle in corrections, meaning that adult prisons set more goals than their resources can accomplish? Do you see areas where the goals of adult prisons conflict with one another and thus make it difficult to answer the question "Does incarceration work?" If you had the ability to remove the confusion, what goal(s) would you set for adult prisons and which measures of effectiveness would you employ?

ON-THE-JOB DECISION MAKING

High-Tech Recruiting

Imagine that you are the recruiting manager for your state's department of corrections. You know that recruiting for corrections has never been easy, but you are very tech savvy and excited to unveil your department's new and cutting-edge recruitment strategy. Forget the pen and paper—you now have keyboards and Web sites, search engines and aggregators, tweets, friending, and fan pages. How will you update your department's image? What kind of "branding" will you use that focuses on your state's unique opportunities? What will your "splash" page look like? What digital, online, print, out-of-home (posters, postcards, radio, TV), and internal (employee referral program, new hire surveys, climate surveys, and exit interview) strategies will you use? How can you use Google's Adwords? What about banner ads and where? What about aggregators such as Indeed.com and SimplyHired.com? What about a fan page on Facebook? What about a careers page on Twitter and to tweet about upcoming testing dates, new job openings, and other important events? And what about a channel on YouTube? What will you expect to get out of this, and how will you know you have achieved it?

Advancing Prison Education Programming

As the newly appointed director of prison education programming, you remember two things from your undergraduate corrections course: first, few inmates participate in prison education programs; second, while literacy alone will not prevent crime, it is one of the many skills needed to function well as a responsible and law-abiding adult in our society.

Your warden would like to create a model prison education program and asks you (1) what can be done with little or no budget increase to encourage more inmates to participate in prison education and (2) how will you know whether your strategies have been effective? What will you tell the warden?

For additional information, please see: www.mhhe.com/schmalleger6e

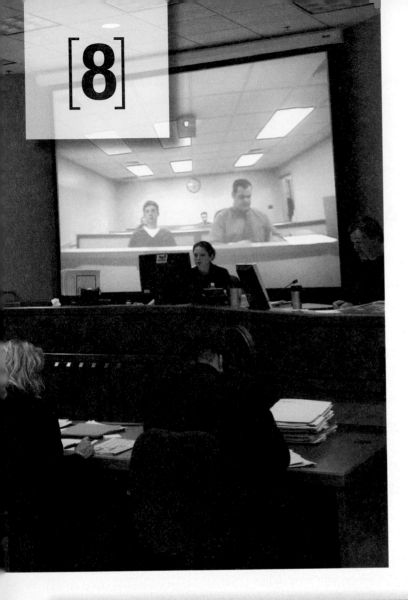

PAROLE

Early Release and Reentry

CHAPTER OBJECTIVES

After completing this chapter you should be able to do the following:

1 Present a brief history of American parole development.

2 Understand the function of parole in the criminal justice system.

3 Define *parole* and explain the parole decision-making process.

4 Describe the characteristics of the parole population.

5 Explain the circumstances under which parole may be revoked.

6 Summarize current issues in parole.

> *We must create a pathway for people coming out of prison to get the jobs, skills, and education they need to leave a life of crime. That means supporting effective training and mentoring programs to help people transition into jobs. That means reevaluating the laws against hiring people with a criminal record so that we don't foreclose legal and effective ways out of poverty and crime. That also means giving former prisoners parenting skills so they can give their children the sense of hope and opportunity that so many of them were denied.*
>
> —President Barack Obama

Every president of the United States except William Harrison and James Garfield has exercised his right under Article II, Section 2, Clause 1 of the United States Constitution to grant **clemency** in the form of reprieves and pardons.[1] A **reprieve** (also referred to as *commutation*) reduces the severity of a punishment, but the person remains "guilty." A **pardon** removes both punishment and guilt, which is why pardons are more likely to be controversial.

President Franklin D. Roosevelt granted the most acts of clemency—3,687. Besides Harrison and Garfield, the fewest were granted by Presidents George Herbert Walker Bush (77), Zachary Taylor (38), John Adams (21), and George Washington (16).

Since the middle of the 20th century, President Eisenhower granted 1,157 acts of clemency, President Kennedy 575, President Johnson 1,187, President Nixon 926, President Ford 409, President Carter 566, President Reagan 406, President George Herbert Walker Bush 77, President Bill Clinton 456, and President George W. Bush 189. With less than one month in office, President Barack Obama had already received 30 petitions for pardon and 44 for commutation.

Among the most controversial pardons in U.S. history are George Washington's pardon of leaders of the Whiskey Rebellion, James Madison's pardon of Latiffe's pirates after the War of 1812, Andrew Johnson's pardon of Confederate soldiers after the Civil War, Harry Truman's pardon of those who violated World War II Selective Service laws, Jimmy Carter's pardon of Vietnam War draft dodgers, Gerald Ford's pardon of former President Richard Nixon one month after Nixon resigned over Watergate and Ford assumed the presidency, Bill Clinton's pardon of fugitive financier Marc Rich, and George Herbert Walker Bush's pardon of six Reagan administration officials involved in the Iran-Contra scandal.

Persons seeking presidential clemency submit a formal petition to the pardon attorney in the Department of Justice. The petition is 23 pages long. Most offenders, however, do not petition for presidential clemency. The most they hope for is **parole,** the conditional release of a prisoner prior to completion of the imposed sentence, under the supervision of a parole officer.

clemency

Kindness, mercy, forgiveness, or leniency, usually relating to criminal acts.

reprieve

An executive act that reduces the severity of punishment (e.g., from death to life imprisonment) but the person remains guilty.

pardon

An executive act that removes both punishment and guilt.

Every president of the United States except William Harrison and James Garfield has exercised his right under Article II, Section 2, Clause 1 of the United States Constitution to grant clemency in the form of reprieves and pardons. With less than one month in office, President Barack Obama had already received 30 petitions for pardon and 44 for commutation. However, most offenders do not petition for presidential clemency. The most they hope for is parole. What are the differences between clemency, commutations, pardons, and parole?

parole
The conditional release of a prisoner, prior to completion of the imposed sentence, under the supervision of a parole officer.

Parole has been used for early release from prison for more than a century, but never before have so many individuals been released from prison. Almost 2,000 persons are released from prison every day, some with only $5 to $100 in gate money. (*Gate money* refers to the predetermined amount of money, bus ticket, or clothing given to eligible inmates upon discharge from prison. Both the amount of money provided and the source of the monies vary from jurisdiction to jurisdiction.) As you will learn in this chapter, nationally, about two-thirds of them will be rearrested within three years—30 percent within the first six months—and one-half will return to prison within that same period.

While it was once politically taboo to speak of providing resources for prisoners, these startling statistics have brought many lawmakers throughout the United States, both liberal and conservative, to the same conclusion: The nation's correctional system is correcting very little. That reality has sparked a movement to improve prisoner "reentry," a buzzword that's on the lips of politicians from coast to coast.

PAROLE AS PART OF THE CRIMINAL JUSTICE SYSTEM

Parole is usually granted by authorities in the correctional system—responsibility for offenders passes from the judicial system to the correctional system upon imprisonment. Release on parole may be mandatory or discretionary. **Discretionary release** is at the paroling authority's discretion within boundaries established by the sentence and by law. **Mandatory release** is early release after a specific period of time as specified by law. In those states that permit discretionary release, state laws give correctional officials the authority to change, within certain limits, the *length* of a sentence. Correctional officials may also change the *conditions* under which convicted offenders are supervised—they may release offenders from prison to supervision in the community or to an outside facility. The American Probation and Parole Association (APPA), the nation's largest association of probation and parole professionals, supports discretionary parole (see Exhibit 8–1).

discretionary release
Early release based on the paroling authority's assessment of eligibility.

mandatory release
Early release after a time period specified by law.

Historical Overview

The parole concept has its roots in an 18th-century English penal practice—indentured servitude. Judges transferred custody of physically fit condemned felons to independent contractors, paying those contractors a fee to transport the prisoners to the American colonies and sell their services for the duration of their sentences to the highest bidder. This practice was similar to today's parole in that the indentured servant had to comply with certain conditions to remain in supervised "freedom." This practice was discontinued with the beginning of the American Revolutionary War in 1775 because English offenders were joining colonial forces against England.

EXHIBIT 8–1   American Probation and Parole Association

Policy Statement on Discretionary Parole

Definition

Parole can refer to both a guidelines process and a discretionary decision. Both of these methods of parole have merit. This position statement addresses only discretionary parole. Discretionary parole is a decision to release an offender from incarceration whose sentence has not expired, on condition of sustained lawful behavior that is subject to supervision and monitoring in the community by parole personnel who ensure compliance with the terms of release.

APPA Position

The American Probation and Parole Association supports discretionary parole as an integral and important part of a criminal justice system that is committed to public safety, victim and community restoration and the reintegration of offenders as law-abiding and productive citizens.

Discretionary parole decisions are based on a number of factors that weigh the need for punishment, successful community reintegration and victim and community restoration. These factors include the nature of the crime; the offender's criminal history, behavior in prison, social background and risk posed to the community; and information from crime victims and affected communities. Discretionary parole decisions enhance public safety by working to keep dangerous offenders incarcerated and that other offenders carefully selected for release receive the necessary structure and assistance to become law-abiding citizens in the community in which they reside.

Discussion

Parole is rooted in the fundamental belief that offenders can be motivated to make positive changes in their lives. Offenders are more likely to cooperate with correctional authorities if release is conditioned on good behavior, and after release the likelihood of their becoming law abiding is increased when offered assistance. The result is enhanced public safety.

Discretion is inherent at every level of the criminal justice system. Police exercise discretion when determining whom to arrest and charge. The court system uses discretion to decide whom to indict, whom to release pre-trial, whether to go to trial, and what criminal penalties to recommend. Judges use their discretion to determine the appropriate level of punishment given the circumstances of the crime and the offender's criminal history. They may sentence one offender to probation and another to prison for the same offense.

Parole boards closely examine and consider each offender's entire record, recognizing that correctional authorities can better manage inmates who have an incentive to follow institutional rules. The possibility of parole also provides inmates with an incentive to participate in programs that build competency skills. Parole boards know that the great majority of offenders sent to prison will eventually be released.

Parole boards are in a unique position to listen to and address the needs and concerns of crime victims and communities. Parole board control over offenders and communication with victims provides the framework for victim assistance and community restoration from the damage of crime.

During periods when there are an inadequate number of correctional beds, parole boards apply a rational process, targeting for release those inmates who pose the least risk to community safety. Parole boards are the only component of the criminal justice system that can weigh all of the factors and release only those offenders who can be best managed under community supervision, thus providing a powerful enhancement to public safety.

The core services offered by parole—investigations, victim advocacy, release planning, community supervision, immediate response to violations, and treatment services—provide optimum public protection. Parole is a powerful partner to both the courts and to victims. Parole boards ensure that the victim's voice is both heard and heeded, creating a natural and valuable ally for victims and victim advocacy groups.

The American Probation and Parole Association is committed to promoting discretionary parole as an integral and important part of the criminal justice system, designed to enhance the protection of victims and promotion of community safety.

Source: American Probation and Parole Association.

From 1775 through 1856, English offenders were sent to Australia as punishment. Those who committed more felonies in Australia were transported to England's most punitive prison on Norfolk Island, 1,000 miles off the east coast of Australia. In 1840, British Navy Captain Alexander Maconochie was appointed superintendent of the penal colony. Maconochie favored indeterminate sentences rather than fixed sentences. He recommended and in part implemented a marks system to measure the prisoner's progress toward release from prison, and he urged a system of graduated release and aftercare of prisoners to resettle them in the community. He developed a "ticket of leave" system, which moved inmates through stages: imprisonment, conditional release, and complete restoration of liberty.

Inmates moved from one stage to the next by earning "marks" for improved conduct, frugality, and good work habits. Although Maconochie had control over island tickets of leave, he could not control a graduated return to society in England. Maconochie's ideas did not blend well with the official English position on punishment, which was rooted in deterrence and relied on the infliction of suffering. He was removed in 1844 and the penal colony at Norfolk Island lapsed into a period of extraordinary brutality before it closed in 1856. Maconochie is referred to as the founder of parole.

In 1854, Sir Walter Crofton, director of the Irish prison system, implemented a system that was based on Maconochie's ticket of leave system. Crofton's version required that upon conditional release, a former inmate do the following:

1. Report immediately to the constabulary on arrival and once a week thereafter.
2. Abstain from any violation of the law.
3. Refrain from habitually associating with notoriously bad characters.
4. Refrain from leading an idle and dissolute life without means of obtaining an honest living.
5. Produce the ticket of leave when asked to do so by a magistrate or police officer.
6. Not change locality without reporting to the constabulary.[2]

The former inmate who did not comply with the conditions of release was reimprisoned. Crofton's system of conditional release is considered the forerunner of modern American parole.

Use of the term *parole* for early release from prison began with a letter from Dr. S. G. Howe of Boston to the Prison Association of New York in 1846. Howe wrote, "I believe there are many [prisoners] who might be so trained as to be left upon their parole (a promise made with or confirmed by a pledge of one's honor) during the last period of their imprisonment with safety."[3]

Early American Parole Development The first legislation authorizing parole in the United States was enacted in Massachusetts in 1837, and the Elmira Reformatory in New York, which opened in 1876, was the first U.S. correctional institution to implement an extensive parole program. Zebulon Brockway, the institution's first superintendent, implemented a system of upward classification. The first grade was Brockway's personal interview with the new inmate. The second grade was the prison regime that Brockway established for the prisoner: a mix of labor (in the iron foundry or factories, on the farm, or on the maintenance crew), formal schooling, mandatory religious service, and military drill. An inmate in the second grade who earned three marks each for labor, education, and behavior each month for six months was promoted to the third grade. Six months after achieving the third-grade promotion, the inmate was granted a parole hearing before Brockway and five other Elmira staff members. Paroled inmates made their own living and work arrangements. Elmira employees and community volunteers provided parole supervision. Failure to comply with conditions of parole meant parole revocation and return to Elmira's second grade.[4]

By 1889, 12 states had implemented parole programs; by 1944, all 48 states had enacted parole legislation.

Captain Alexander Maconochie, who became superintendent of the British penal colony on Norfolk Island, Australia, in 1840, implemented a "ticket of leave" system to ease inmate transition from custody to freedom. Later, Sir Walter Crofton, director of the Irish prison system, implemented a system based on Maconochie's ideas. How did their systems influence current parole procedures?

Parole Development in the Early 20th Century The 1920s and early 1930s were a turbulent period in the United States. During Prohibition, organized crime increased, street gang warfare escalated, and the media provided obsessive coverage of criminals and their activities. Prison riots erupted in response to prisoner idleness and arbitrary rules and punishment. Prisons and the parole system failed to rehabilitate offenders.

The Wickersham Commission, a commission on law enforcement and observance appointed by President Herbert Hoover, issued a report in 1931 that advocated uniformity in state parole practices by recommending that states establish centralized policymaking boards to write standards and guidelines for parole practices.[5] This report included a list of the "essential elements" of a good parole system:

1. indeterminate sentence law permitting the offender to be released (conditionally) at the time when he or she is most likely to make a successful transition back to society;
2. provision of quality release preparation—in the institution—for the offender who is reentering the community;
3. familiarity by the parole officer with the home and environmental conditions of the offender before he or she leaves the institution; and
4. sufficient staffing levels to ensure an adequate number of parole officers to supervise parolees.[6]

The Wickersham Commission reported that parole was logical because it was an inexpensive way to supervise offenders. Moreover, the commission reported, the parolee earns money whereas the prisoner cannot support himself or herself and cannot contribute financially to his or her family. By 1944, all of the states had passed parole legislation.[7]

Despite the fact that all states had enacted parole legislation by the mid-1940s, opposition to it was strong. The attitude that parole boards were turning hardened criminals loose on society sparked a series of angry attacks through national and state commissions, investigatory hearings, editorials and cartoons, press releases, and books.[8] Opponents claimed that parole had a dismal performance record, its goals were never realized, parole board members and parole officers were poorly trained, and parole hearings were little more than hastily conducted, almost unthinking interviews.

In spite of the gap between its goals and reality, parole fulfilled important functions for officials in the criminal justice system. Wardens supported parole because the possibility of earning parole served as an incentive for offenders, making it easier to keep peace. Wardens also used parole to control prison overcrowding by keeping the number of people being released on parole about equal to the number of new prisoner admissions. Legislators supported parole because it cost less than incarceration. District attorneys supported parole because they felt it helped with plea bargaining. Without parole, district attorneys argued, there was little motivation for defendants, particularly those facing long prison sentences, to plead guilty to lesser crimes. District attorneys also supported parole because parolees could be returned to prison without new trial proceedings.

Together, these groups made a claim to the public that parole actually extended state control over offenders because parolees were supervised. Eventually, the public accepted the claim that parole was tough on criminals and that abolishing parole would end state control over dangerous persons.

Parole Development in the Late 20th Century   Opposition to parole resurfaced in the 1960s and 1970s, this time as part of a larger political debate about crime, the purposes of sanctioning, and the appropriateness of the unlimited discretion afforded various sectors of the criminal justice system (paroling authorities in particular). During this period, the debate on correctional policy addressed both the assumptions of the rehabilitative ideal and the results of indeterminate sentencing and parole.

In the 1970s, research indicated that prison rehabilitation programs had few positive benefits. Parolees were not rehabilitated, as parole advocates had claimed.[9] This position was supported on all sides of the political spectrum, including by those who believed that prisons "coddled" dangerous criminals and by those who questioned the ethics of coercing offenders into submitting to unwanted treatment as a condition of release.[10] These research findings led to many of the sentencing reforms of the 1970s and 1980s and helped usher in the warehousing and just deserts eras discussed in Chapter 7. During a time when supporting parole represented a "soft" stance on crime and when crime rates and recidivism were up, the public did not want prisoners released on parole.

In 1987, the American Probation and Parole Association voiced its support of parole and objected to efforts to abolish it. Nevertheless, in that same year, six states abolished discretionary parole board release. By the year 2000, 16 states and the federal government had abolished it, and another four states had abolished discretionary parole release for certain violent offenses or other crimes against a person. The APPA position statement on parole is presented in Exhibit 8–2.

Reentry

At the beginning of this chapter, we introduced the subject of parole reentry. We expand on that here.

Reentry is the use of programs targeted at promoting the effective reintegration of offenders back to communities upon release from prison and jail.

Reentry has occurred since the Walnut Street Jail opened in 1773. However, the scale of offender reentry is larger today than ever before, and we face enormous challenges in managing the reentry of persons leaving prison and jail. Ninety-five percent of all prisoners will be released prior to the expiration of their sentences. In just 20 years, the number of inmates being released from prison has quadrupled. Almost 2,000 offenders leave state and federal prison every day and according to the largest recidivism study ever conducted in the United States, two of every three are rearrested within three years of their release—30 percent within the first six months—and half are returned to prison in that same period.[11]

Why is corrections not correcting? There are many reasons. Among them are the following:

- **Parole supervision:** Most parole officers manage large caseloads and typically meet with offenders for about 15 minutes once or twice a month. Why should we expect such a small amount of contact to make a large difference?

- **Shift in parole function:** Parole has shifted from a service orientation to a surveillance-oriented, control-based strategy centered on monitoring behavior, detecting violations, and enforcing rules. Surveillance technologies such as the Global Positioning System, remote-control monitoring, and drug testing make it easier to monitor behavior and detect violations. However, what academics and practitioners have been telling us for years—that surveillance alone does not change criminal behavior—is in fact a reality. To reduce a parolee's criminal activity, parole agencies and officers must employ evidence-based practices that focus on individual-level change and are shown to work such as academic and vocational education, cognitive-behavioral treatment, and drug courts.

- **Responses to technical violations:** Violators of probation and parole represent the fastest-growing category of admissions to jail and prison, one-third nationally, and 60 to 70 percent in some states such as California.[12] Legislators are beginning to realize that as the correctional populations swell, so do corrections budgets. American taxpayers spent almost $30 billion for corrections in 2001. Today it's more than $52 billion.

EVIDENCE-BASED CORRECTIONS

The current budget crisis has changed the way that several states now respond to probation and parole violators. Kansas allows probation and parole officers to decide whether those who violate early release conditions for nonviolent offenses should go back to prison. Tennessee accelerates prison releases for probation and parole violators who are sent back to prison and complete drug abuse and other counseling programs. Arizona lets probation and parole violators end their community supervision early by applying "good time" (time that is subtracted from a person's sentence for positive behavior, program completion, etc.) against their sentences, thereby reducing the chances they could be sent back to prison for condition violations. Other changes are taking place in Louisiana, Mississippi, Oklahoma, and Wyoming.

Politicians on both sides of the aisle now agree that there is simply not enough money to build our way out of the problem. Why not reallocate the money to evidence-based practices that are shown to reduce criminal activity in the hope of a more promising return? The growth in the correctional population must be managed, and policymakers must do a better job of ensuring that ex-offenders become productive, healthy members of families and communities after their release from jail and prison.

Talking about CORRECTIONS

HOUSING AND REENTRY

Visit *Live Talk* and watch the program "What Works to Keep Young Men from Returning to Jail?" which relates to ideas discussed in this chapter.

Offender Problems   Research shows that when people are released from jail and prison, their job prospects are dim, their chances of finding a place to live are bleak, and their health is poor. Fewer than half have a job lined up before leaving prison. Three-fourths still have a substance abuse problem. Over one-third have a physical or mental disability. Almost one in five has hepatitis C. More than half have dependent children who rely on these reentering adults for financial support. Only one-third participated in educational programs while incarcerated, and even fewer participated in vocational training.[13] (See Exhibit 8–3.) These former inmates will work fewer weeks each year and earn less money as well as have limited upward mobility than if they had never been incarcerated. Research also shows that returning prisoners are increasingly concentrated in communities that are often crime ridden and lack services and support systems.[14] For example, in Illinois, 51 percent of prisoners released from state correctional institutions in 2001 returned to Chicago, and 34 percent of them returned in just 6 of Chicago's 77 neighborhoods. And, no services were located in two of those six neighborhoods. Regrettably, parole violations and new crimes are often committed because offenders reentering the community lack the skills and support to adapt to community life. But as we will discuss later, now that we know that there are geographic concentrations of returning prisoners to a handful of neighborhoods in most large cities, we have an opportunity to place our reentry efforts in those areas.

Prisoner reentry problems are magnified for women leaving prison, especially minority women. Nearly two-thirds of the women confined in jails and state and federal prisons are black, Hispanic, or of other nonwhite ethnic groups. As reported in Chapter 6 and 7, women in prison have a high rate of prior sexual or physical abuse, high rates of positive-HIV status and other sexually transmitted diseases, and high alcohol, drug use, and addiction rates at the time of arrest. "In most of their communities," writes Beth Richie of the University of Illinois at Chicago, "there are few services and very limited resources available to assist women in the process of reentry."[15]

The situation is even more grim when we look at the reentry problems for African American women.[16] African American women leaving

EXHIBIT 8–3   Service Needs of State and Federal Prisoners

Area of Need	Prevalence (Percentage of All Prisoners)
Substance abuse	75
Physical or mental disability	83
No high school diploma	86
No diploma or GED	40
Earned less than $600/month prior to incarceration	50
Homeless before or after incarceration	10

Source: The Council of State Governments, *The Report of the Re-Entry Policy Council: Charting the Safe and Successful Return of Prisoners to the Community* (Lexington, KY: The Council of State Governments, 2005), p. 49.

prison have unique needs in the areas of family and health care that current reentry systems do not consider. African American children are more likely than white or Hispanic children to have a parent who is incarcerated. They are also more likely to be in foster care and remain there longer than white or Hispanic children. Due to their time in poverty, jail, and prison, African American women are more vulnerable to becoming HIV positive. AIDS is the number one killer of African American women between the ages of 25 and 34. Compounding the problem is a generation of African American men who are not present in the community to assist with childcare and provide an income for the home. Reentry services have not accounted for the additional challenges that African American women face but that white and Hispanic women do not. Although the challenges facing African American women leaving prison are daunting, in recent years the United States has witnessed a surge of policy interest and innovation in response to these realities that we point out shortly.

Reentry Programs to Help Ex-Offenders With so many problems and such high rearrest rates, it has become clear to many that simply placing an offender in prison does not deter future criminal behavior. The U.S. prison and parole systems have become a revolving door that cities and towns across the nation were not prepared to handle.

Researchers have found that on reentry, parolees need transportation and better money management skills. They need food, clothing, and a place to live. They need a birth certificate, a Social Security card, a photo ID, and financial assistance. Those with children need parenting classes and childcare, help with child support payments, and help resolving custody issues. They need health insurance, medical treatment, substance abuse treatment, mental health services, and help obtaining federal disability benefits. They need to work on their personal relationships, and many need and want a mentor or a spiritual or religious advisor. Many need anger management training. Most need a job and job training. People who are elderly, terminally ill, mentally ill, or physically or developmentally disabled may have significantly different needs with respect to housing, employment, family support, substance use, and criminal involvement. Women parolees on reentry have gender-specific needs with respect to childcare, protection from sexual harassment and abusive relationships, reproductive health problems, few job-related skills or experiences to support themselves or their children, and housing that is safe, secure, and affordable.[17]

EVIDENCE-BASED CORRECTIONS

Recently, the Legal Action Center (LAC) published the results of an exhaustive two-year study of legal obstacles that people with criminal records face when they attempt to reenter society and become productive, law-abiding citizens. LAC developed a report card to "grade" how states deal with seven roadblocks that criminals face upon reentry: employment, public assistance and food stamps, housing benefits, voting, access to criminal records, parenting, and driving. States were graded from 1 (being the best) to 10 (the worst). Scores ranged from 10 to 48. States with the lowest overall scores have the fewest barriers to reentry. State scores are shown in Exhibit 8–4.

In response to the roadblocks, we see policymakers at all levels of government showing unprecedented interest in the record number of people coming out of prisons and jails.

The surge of national policy interest and innovation in reentry began during the Clinton administration when Attorney General Janet Reno called for new approaches to inmate reentry including reentry courts (we discuss them later in this chapter). It continued under the George W. Bush administration with the Serious and Violent Offender Reentry Initiative (SVORI), which is legislation to fund reentry services such as life-skills training, dental and medical assistance, needs and risk assessments, treatment and release plans,

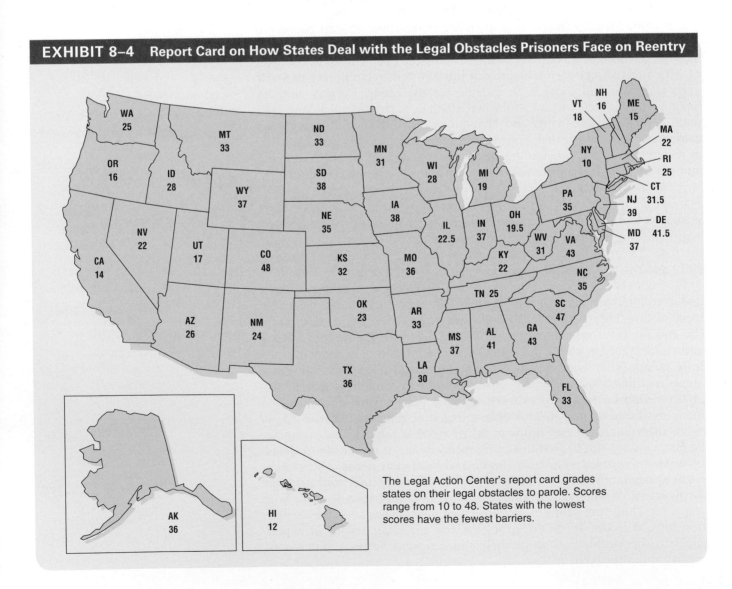

EXHIBIT 8–4   Report Card on How States Deal with the Legal Obstacles Prisoners Face on Reentry

The Legal Action Center's report card grades states on their legal obstacles to parole. Scores range from 10 to 48. States with the lowest scores have the fewest barriers.

and job placement at three key phases: just prior to release from prison, during the first few months after release, and for several years postrelease as participants assume more productive roles in the community. In his 2004 State of the Union address, President Bush voiced his administration's interest in reentry when he declared that "America is the land of second chance, and when the gates of the prison open, the path ahead should lead to a better life." President Bush followed up on his declaration when he signed into law the Second Chance Act (SCA) and Congress called for $330 million for prisoner reentry programs. Whereas SVORI targets helping serious and violent offenders, the SCA provides grants to local and state governments as well as nonprofit and faith-based organizations to improve and expand reentry programs for persons on parole; create new programs for substance abuse treatment, individual and family-based counseling, education, housing, mentoring, reentry courts, training parolees for technology-based jobs; and create pilot programs to move some elderly federal prisoners from prison to home confinement. President Obama signaled his support for a national reentry strategy with a request for $100 million more for reentry programs and in January 2011, Attorney General Eric Holder convened the first-ever interagency Cabinet-level Reentry Council with representatives from 16 federal departments and offices. The mission of the council is to make communities safer by reducing recidivism and victimization; to assist those returning from prison and jail in becoming productive, tax-paying citizens; and to save taxpayer dollars by lowering the direct and collateral costs of incarceration.

State and local governments have been equally busy in addressing reentry issues. Elected officials in Baltimore, Boston, and Chicago have passed "ban the box laws" that require employers to ask the "have-you-ever-been-convicted" question. Other states have created reentry councils to coordinate health, housing, welfare, employment, education, and other social service agencies to improve prospects for men and women leaving prison. And local governments are creating innovative programs such as Chicago's Offender Notification Forums that require some types of offenders to attend a forum hosted by representatives from state and local law enforcement agencies, the community, and service providers. The content of the forum is designed to stress to offenders the consequences should they choose to pick up a gun as well as the choices they must make to ensure that they do not reoffend. After the start of the program, there was a 37 percent decrease in monthly homicide rates in the target neighborhood compared with the previous three years.[18] The American Correctional Association's policy statement favoring reentry is shown in Exhibit 8–5.

EVIDENCE-BASED CORRECTIONS

Eligibility for Reentry An inmate's eligibility for parole is determined by the sentence received from the court as set by law. The **parole eligibility date** is the earliest date on which an inmate might be released. State statutes usually dictate parole eligibility dates and specify what portion of a sentence an offender must serve before being considered for release.

An offender's parole eligibility date is also affected by good time credit first discussed in Chapter 3. At least 31 states and the federal government provide some type of good time incentives. Many states such as California, Michigan, and Washington have either already increased time off for good behavior from one-third to as much as one-half of sentence time or are considering doing so in order to reduce overcrowding and the corrections budget.[19]

parole eligibility date
The earliest date on which an inmate might be paroled.

> ## EXHIBIT 8–5   American Correctional Association
>
> ### Public Correctional Policy on Reentry of Offenders
>
> **Introduction:**
>
> Successful reentry of offenders in the community is in the best interest of society. Reentry programs enhance public safety, help prepare offenders for transition to responsible citizenship, can help reduce future criminal behavior, remove the barriers that make it difficult for offenders to reenter their communities, and develop necessary community support.
>
> **Policy Statement:**
>
> The American Correctional Association fully supports evidence-based practices and reentry programs, and encourages the elimination of any local, state and federal laws and policies that place barriers on the offender's successful reentry. Therefore, public and private agencies at the federal, state and local levels should:
>
> A. Advocate for the review and revision of existing laws and regulations that inhibit the successful reentry of offenders;
> B. Initiate individualized transitional planning during intake to a facility.
> C. Provide recidivism-risk and reentry-needs assessments and associated services and programs during incarceration;
> D. Provide an expedited process to obtain appropriate legal identification prior to or upon release;
> E. Assist the offender in accessing appropriate housing upon release;
> F. Provide sufficient staff trained to supervise and motivate offenders released to the community;
> G. Encourage institution and community supervision staff to integrate work efforts to assure a comprehensive continuum of supervision and services;
> H. Develop community partnerships and support networks for providing to provide a seamless and timely connection between pre- and post-release programs and services;
> I. Provide information and assistance to address health care needs following release such as obtaining Medicaid, medical and substance abuse treatment, and other health and psychological services. Provide a sufficient supply of prescription medication upon release;
> J. Provide information and assistance to offenders to gain employment upon release, such as pre-employment readiness training, job identification and retention skills training, and job placement services;
> K. Ensure that offenders who have served in the U.S. military are provided with information regarding the benefits and services to which they may be entitled, and are referred at discharge, to the Department of Veterans' Affairs or local veteran service organizations; and
> L. Provide services to facilitate successful family and community reunification.
>
> Source: Copyright © American Correctional Association.

paroling authority

A person or correctional agency (often called a *parole board* or *parole commission*) that has the authority to grant parole, revoke parole, and discharge from parole.

Granting Parole—The Paroling Authority Every jurisdiction in the United States has a paroling authority. In most states, a **paroling authority** is a correctional agency (often called a *parole board* or *parole commission*) that has statutory authority to grant parole, set conditions of parole, supervise parolees, revoke parole, and discharge from parole. For jurisdictions with determinate sentencing and no discretion for the timing of release, the paroling authority still may determine conditions of release.

Parole boards vary in size from 3 members (Alabama, Hawaii, Montana, North Dakota, Washington, and West Virginia) to 10 or more (Michigan, 10; Connecticut, 11; Ohio, 11; Illinois, 12; Texas, 18; and New York, 19). Of the 52 jurisdictions—the 50 states, the District of Columbia, and the federal government—only 34 have full-time salaried parole board members. Minnesota's paroling authority is its Commissioner of Corrections.[20]

I work in a city of 80,000, which currently has no supervision for parolees who have been serving sentences of two years or more in a federal facility. Currently, there are 30 to 40 such individuals in unsupervised conditions. There are also many more who are assigned to halfway houses in nearby communities, making life unnecessarily difficult on some of these individuals.

We are trying to bring a 12-bed facility into the community. We are facing strenuous resistance, including death threats—ironic, isn't it?—of both the NIMBY (not in my back yard) and the NOPE (not on planet earth) variety. Some of the resistance, I'm sure, is based on fear that we are bringing criminals into the community. One obvious answer is that many of these individuals came from the community in the first place.

One really hard question to answer is whether the local property values will be negatively affected. That's a realistic concern for everyone. Yet the most recent material that I have been able to find is from the early 1980s. It suggests that there is no clear effect on property values and that most people on a street are unaware that such accommodations are there, once they have been there a while. Of course, if these former offenders are released into the community without any preparation or socialization, they won't have a chance, let alone a halfway chance, of following the rules and becoming a positive contributor to the community that denies them.

Linda Deutschmann
Halfway House Worker
Brookhaven, Kansas

Research has indicated that parole board decision making relies primarily on two factors, criminal history and institutional behavior.[21] A national survey of parole board members said that the most important factors in the decision to grant or deny parole were the nature of the inmate's offense and the inmate's prior criminal record, attitude toward the victim, institutional adjustment (as measured by the inmate's participation in prison programs), and insight into the causes of past criminal conduct.[22] Least important are the inmate's physical health and age, prison conditions, and the public awareness of the case. Studies of parole in Colorado found that, in order to process the large volume of cases, parole boards find it necessary to develop a routine and to look for a few factors that will decide their cases for them:

> The parole board first considers the inmate's current and prior offenses and incarcerations. Parole board members also determine if the inmate's time served is commensurate with what they perceive as adequate punishment. If it is not, the inmate's institutional behavior, progress in treatment, family circumstances, and parole plan will not outweigh the perceived need for punishment.[23]

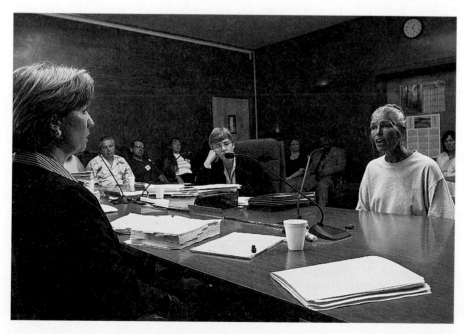

A parole board meets to consider a release candidate. While discretionary release by parole boards was at one time very common, it has been eliminated in many jurisdictions. Does parole provide offenders with an effective opportunity to reintegrate into society?

Not all parole authorities use the same release criteria. Observations of federal parole hearings, for example, suggest that an inmate's institutional behavior and program participation are given little importance in release decisions.[24] "Noncompliance with required treatment programs or poor institutional behavior may be reasons to deny parole, but completion of treatment programs and good institutional behavior are not sufficient reasons to grant parole."[25]

salient factor score (SFS)
Scale, developed from a risk-screening instrument, used to predict parole outcome.

In the 1970s, the United States Parole Commission developed the **salient factor score (SFS)**, a risk assessment instrument to estimate an inmate's likelihood of recidivating following his or her release from prison. The SFS has been revised several times since the pilot project in 1972.

Today, the SFS is a series of six static factors based on an objective scale through empirically validated research. Static factors are ones that do not change over time and are known to be related to recidivism, such as age at first conviction, prior incarcerations, number and severity of previous arrests or convictions, and supervision failures. The primary benefits of using the SFS are that the items are objective, easily scored, few in number, and unable to be manipulated by offenders.

The salient factor score used by the U.S. Parole Commission today is shown in Exhibit 8–6. Each of the six items' responses is weighted. The total score (a range from 0 to 10) is then calculated. The higher the total score, the lower the likelihood of recidivism. The total score is then placed into one of four risk categories (Poor, 0–3; Fair, 4–5; Good, 6–7; and Very Good, 8–10). Where the SFS intersects with the offense characteristics shown in the first vertical column (category one represents the least serious offenses; category eight represents the most severe) gives the range (in months) of incarceration judges may order at sentencing.

Today, risk assessment instruments have become an integral part of the parole process. Parole boards in jurisdictions across the United States use various types of risk assessments as shown in Exhibit 8–7.

Granting Parole—The Hearing In general, parole hearings are attended by victims, the applicant, the institutional representative, and hearing examiners or parole board members. A two-year study of 5,000 parole hearings in Colorado found that the parole board heard too many cases to allow for individualized treatment.[26] The time for a typical parole hearing was 10 to 15 minutes. Unusual cases take longer.

In today's high-tech environment, a number of states such as West Virginia are experimenting with video conferencing equipment that links that state's seven regional jails and three prisons. Instead of requiring the five parole board members to travel around the state to conduct parole hearings at each institution, the new system is expected to save on travel costs and also permit crime victims to testify without having to be in the same room as the offender. Parole boards in other states such as Michigan now use more "data-driven" or evidence-based release policies to identify people who pose lower risks to public safety.

The final decision to grant or deny parole is based on both eligibility guidelines and the interview. If parole is granted, a contract that defines the release plan is executed and the inmate is given a release date. The inmate who is conditionally released to community supervision is called a **parolee**.

parolee
A person who is conditionally released from prison to community supervision.

The trend among parole authorities is to grant or deny parole on the basis of risk to the community. If parole is denied, the common reasons are "not enough time served," "poor disciplinary record," "need to see movement to lower security and success there," and "lack of satisfactory

EXHIBIT 8–6   United States Parole Commission Salient Factor Score

Item A. Prior Convictions/Adjudications (*Adult or Juvenile*)............................ ☐

    None = 3; One = 2; Two or three = 1; Four or more = 0

Item B. Prior Commitment(s) of More than 30 Days (*Adult/Juvenile*) .... ☐

    None = 2; One or two = 1; Three or more = 0

Item C. Age at Current Offense/Prior Commitments...................................... ☐

26 years or older	Three or fewer prior commitments = 3
	Four prior commitments = 2
	Five or more commitments = 1
22–25 years	Three or fewer prior commitments = 2
	Four prior commitments = 1
	Five or more commitments = 0
20–21 years	Three or fewer prior commitments = 1
	Four prior commitments = 0
19 years or younger	Any number of prior commitments = 0

Item D. Recent Commitment Free Period (three years) .... ☐

No prior commitment of more than 30 days (adult or juvenile) or released to the community from last such commitment at least 3 years prior to the commencement of the current offense = 1; Otherwise = 0

Item E. Probation/Parole/Confinement/Escape Status Violator This Time ....☐

Neither on probation, parole, confinement, or escape status at the time of the current offense; nor committed as a probation, parole, confinement, or escape status violator this time = 1; Otherwise = 0

Item F. Older Offenders.. ☐

If the offender was 41 years of age or older at the commencement of the current offense (and the total score from Items A–E above is 9 or less) = 1; Otherwise = 0

Total Score... ☐

parole program" (proposed home, work, or treatment in the community). In that case, the inmate remains in prison, and a date is set for the next review. The waiting period between hearings depends on the jurisdiction and the inmate's offense.

For example, on Tuesday, September 7, 2010, the New York State Parole Board denied parole for the sixth time to Mark David Chapman, the man who shot and killed John Lennon in 1980. The panel of three board members concluded in written comments that Chapman's "discretionary release remains inappropriate at this time and incompatible

EXHIBIT 8–6   United States Parole Commission Salient Factor Score (continued)

Offense Characteristics	Offender Chracterisistics: Parole Prognosis			
Severity of Offense Behavior	Very Good Risk (10–8)	Good Risk (7–6)	Fair Risk (5–4)	Poor Risk 3–0)
Category One	≤4 months	≤8 months	8–12 months	12–16 months
Category Two	≤6 months	≤10 months	12–16 months	16–22 months
Category Three	≤10 months	12–16 months	18–24 months	24–32 months
Category Four	12–18 months	20–26 months	26–34 months	34–44 months
Category Five	24–36 months	36-48 months	48–60 months	60–72 months
Category Six	40–52 months	52–64 months	64–78 months	78–100 months
Category Seven	52–80 months	64–92 months	78–110 months	100–148 months
Category Eight*	100+ months	120+ months	150+ months	180+ months

*Note: For category eight, no upper limits are specified due to the extreme variability of the cases within this category. For decisions exceeding the lower limit of the applicable guideline category by more than 48 months, the commission will specify the pertinent case factors upon which it relied.

with the welfare of the community."[27] The New York State Division of Parole received 75 letters arguing against Chapman's release, including one from Lennon's 77-year-old widow, Yoko Ono, who said she believed Chapman posed a risk to her, Lennon's two sons, the public, and even to himself. Chapman was sentenced to 20 years to life in 1980. According to New York law, Chapman is entitled to a parole hearing every two years.

EXHIBIT 8–7	Risk Assessment Instruments Used by Other Jurisdictions Across the United States	

Jurisdiction	Use a Risk Instrument?	Description of Instrument
Alabama	Yes	A 12-item instrument that consists of 11 static factors and 1 dynamic factor.
Alaska	No	
Arizona	No	
Arkansas	Yes	A 14-item instrument that examines 4 categories of predictors; all items are static.
California	No	
Colorado	Yes	An 8-item instrument that consists of 1 dynamic factor and 7 static factors.
Connecticut	Yes	A 5-item instrument consisting of static factors.
Delaware	No	
Florida	No Response	
Georgia	Yes	There are 10 risk factors examined, 6 static factors and 4 dynamic factors.
Hawaii	No	
Idaho	No Response	
Illinois	No	
Indiana	No Response	
Iowa	No Response	
Kansas	No Response	
Kentucky	Yes	A 9-item instrument that consists of 5 static items and 4 dynamic items.
Louisiana	No	
Maine	No Response	
Maryland	Yes	A 9-item risk instrument that has 5 static risk factors and 4 dynamic risk factors.
Massachusetts	No	
Michigan	Yes	This instrument consists of 34 items with a combination of static and dynamic factors.
Minnesota	Yes	
Mississippi	No	
Missouri	No Response	
Montana	Yes	A 7-item instrument that consists of 6 static factors and 1 dynamic factor.
Nebraska	Yes	A 9-item instrument that consists of 8 static factors and 1 dynamic factor.
Nevada	No	
New Hampshire	No	
New Jersey	Yes	A 54-item instrument that contains both static and dynamic factors.
New Mexico	No	
New York	Yes	A 17-item instrument that consists of static factors.
North Carolina	No	

EXHIBIT 8–7	Risk Assessment Instruments Used by Other Jurisdictions Across the United States (continued)

Jurisdiction	Use a Risk Instrument?	Description of Instrument
North Dakota	No Response	
Ohio	Yes	A 6-item instrument that consists of static factors.
Oklahoma	No Response	
Oregon	No	
Pennsylvania	Yes	A 54-item instrument that contains both static and dynamic factors.
Rhode Island	No Response	
South Carolina	Yes	A 10-item instrument that consists of 7 static factors and 3 dynamic factors.
South Dakota	Yes	The instrument contains 6-items on static factors for the risk assessment and 3 items for the needs assessment.
Tennessee	Yes	A 10-item instrument consisting of static risk factors.
Texas	Yes	An instrument consisting of static factors; used for sex offender risk assessment.
Utah	Yes	A 7-item instrument that consists of static risk factors.
Vermont	Yes	A 13-item instrument that consists of 7 static risk factors and 6 dynamic risk factors.
Virginia	No	
Washington	Yes	A 54-item instrument that contains both static and dynamic factors.
West Virginia	Yes	A 10-item instrument that contains 5 static factors and 5 dynamic factors.
Wisconsin	No	
Wyoming	No	
U.S. Parole Commission	Yes	A 6-item instrument that consists of static factors.

Source: Shamir Ratansi and Stephen M. Cox, *State of Connecticut Assessment and Validation of Connecticut's Salient Factor Score* (New Britain, CT: Connecticut Statistical Analysis Center, Central Connecticut State University, Department of Criminology and Criminal Justice, October 2007).

Conditions of Parole Paroling authorities set specific conditions for parole on a case-by-case basis (see Exhibit 8–8). Parolees must comply with these conditions, averaging three years, which may include restitution, substance abuse aftercare, remote-electronic monitoring, and/or house arrest, among others.

Parolees are technically in state custody; they have merely been granted the privilege of living in the community instead of prison. Parole officers, who work closely with the parolee and the paroling authority, carry out the supervision of parolees. They can initiate parole revocation hearings and return parolees to prison if they threaten community safety or

Kenneth Wong

State Parole Agent • California Department of Corrections and Rehabilitation

Kenneth Wong is a state parole agent with the California Department of Corrections and Rehabilitation. Before joining the San Francisco parole office in 1990, Wong worked three and one-half years as a correctional officer at the California State Prison at San Quentin and one and one-half years as an auto mechanic. Wong completed the automotive program of the College of Alameda and later enrolled in courses in human behavior at the University of California at Hayward.

As a parole officer, Wong works closely with police and social service agencies. He conducts antinarcotic testing, refers parole violators to the State Board of Prison Terms, and helps parolees make a smooth transition from prison to the community. His paramount concern is community protection.

Wong's advice to people interested in corrections is simple: "If you like working with people who've been in prison and if you have the patience to listen to their problems and make positive referrals and provide advice, then you should apply. The job is challenging, and there is always something new."

In 1996, the California Probation, Parole, and Correctional Association recognized Ken Wong as Parole Agent of the Year. The association said Wong's job performance was exemplary and that he made a significant contribution to the field of corrections.

Wong plans to spend his career with the California Department of Corrections and Rehabilitation. He would like to pursue management positions, beginning with parole unit supervisor.

> *"I like being a parole agent because the job allows me to help people who got caught up in the criminal justice system and assist them with a smooth transition from prison back into society by providing a range of services. The most exciting thing about my job is I get to help parolees perform acceptably in the community and remove those who cannot."*

otherwise violate the conditions of release. Depending on the severity of the crime and the risk presented by the offender, parole supervision can incorporate several types of contact with and "examination" of the parolee, including drug testing, setting of a curfew, remote-location monitoring, and employment verification.

The conditions under which parolees must live are very similar in form and structure to those for probationers. Sometimes the rules are established by law, but more often they are established by the paroling authority. The paroling authority can require any of the following forms of release: standard parole supervision, parole with enhanced treatment and programming conditions, halfway house placement, intensive supervision, parole with remote-electronic monitoring or voice and location tracking, or release with follow-up drug testing and payment of supervision fees and restitution.

Types of Parole Release on parole may be mandatory or discretionary. Discretionary parole decisions are made by a paroling authority such as a parole board or parole commission after its members review a case to determine whether they believe the prisoner is ready to be returned to the community. The criteria used to reach the decision vary from state to state, as discussed earlier. Discretionary parole decisions occur in jurisdictions using indeterminate sentencing.

EXHIBIT 8–8 **Sample State Conditions of Parole**

State of Alaska

Standard Conditions of Parole

The following standard conditions of parole apply to all prisoners released on mandatory or discretionary parole, in accordance with AS 33.16.150(a).

1. REPORT UPON RELEASE: I will report in person no later than the next working day after my release to the parole officer located at the PAROLE OFFICE and receive further reporting instructions. I will reside at _____.

2. MAINTAIN EMPLOYMENT/TRAINING/TREATMENT: I will make a diligent effort to maintain steady employment and support my legal dependents. I will not voluntarily change or terminate employment without receiving permission from my parole officer to do so. If discharged or if employment is terminated (temporarily or permanently) for any reason, I will notify my parole officer the next working day. If I am involved in an education, training, or treatment program, I will continue active participation in the program unless I receive permission from my parole officer to quit. If I am released, removed, or terminated from the program for any reason, I will notify my parole officer the next working day.

3. REPORT MONTHLY: I will report to my parole officer at least monthly in the manner prescribed by my parole officer. I will follow any other reporting instructions established by my parole officer.

4. OBEY LAWS/ORDERS: I will obey all state, federal, and local laws, ordinances, orders, and court orders.

5. PERMISSION BEFORE CHANGING RESIDENCE: I will obtain permission from my parole officer before changing my residence. Remaining away from my approved residence for 24 hours or more constitutes a change in residence for the purpose of this condition.

6. TRAVEL PERMIT BEFORE TRAVEL OUTSIDE ALASKA: I will obtain the prior written permission of my parole officer in the form of an interstate travel agreement before leaving the state of Alaska. Failure to abide by the conditions of the travel agreement is a violation of my order of parole.

7. NO FIREARMS/WEAPONS: I will not own, possess, have in my custody, handle, purchase, or transport any firearm, ammunition, or explosives. I may not carry any deadly weapon on my person except a pocket knife with a 3" or shorter blade. Carrying any other weapon on my person such as a hunting knife, axe, club, etc. is a violation of my order of parole. I will contact the Alaska Board of Parole if I have any questions about the use of firearms, ammunition, or weapons.

8. NO DRUGS: I will not use, possess, handle, purchase, give, or administer any narcotic, hallucinogenic, (including marijuana/THC), stimulant, depressant, amphetamine, barbiturate, or prescription drug not specifically prescribed by a licensed medical person.

9. REPORT POLICE CONTACT: I will report to my parole officer, no later than the next working day, any contact with a law enforcement officer.

10. DO NOT WORK AS AN INFORMANT: I will not enter into any agreement or other arrangement with any law enforcement agency which will place me in the position of violating any law or any condition of my parole. I understand the Department of Corrections and Parole Board policy prohibits me from working as an informant.

11. NO CONTACT WITH PRISONERS OR FELONS: I may not telephone, correspond with, or visit any person confined in a prison, penitentiary, correctional institution or camp, jail, halfway house, work release center, community residential center, restitution center, juvenile correctional center, etc. Contact with a felon during the course of employment or during corrections-related treatment is not prohibited if approved by my parole officer. Any other knowing contact with a felon is prohibited unless approved by my parole officer. I will notify my parole officer the next working day if I have contact with a prisoner or felon.

12. CANNOT LEAVE AREA: I will receive permission from my parole officer before leaving the area of the state to which my case is assigned. My parole officer will advise me in writing of limits of the area to which I have been assigned.

13. OBEY ALL ORDERS/SPECIAL CONDITIONS: I will obey any special instructions, rules, or order given to me by the Alaska Board of Parole or by my parole officer. I will follow any special conditions imposed by the Alaska Board of Parole or my parole officer.

Source: State of Alaska Board of Parole, *Parole Handbook, Appendix II: Conditions of Parole,* June 1998.

Mandatory parole release is set by law and occurs in jurisdictions using determinate sentencing. It requires the correctional authority to grant parole after the inmate serves a specific period of time as required by law. Exhibit 8–9 compares discretionary and mandatory parole release.

EXHIBIT 8–9	Comparing Discretionary Release and Mandatory Release	
	Discretionary Release	**Mandatory Release**
Release date	Decided by parole board	Determined by law
Criteria	Based on parole board guidelines	None[1]
Postrelease supervision	Yes	Maybe

1. Corrections authorities may have discretion to grant or deny good-time credits in mandatory release cases.

Source: Adapted from Jeremy Travis and Sarah Lawrence, *Beyond the Prison Gates: The State of Parole in America* (Washington, DC: Urban Institute, 2002). Copyright © 2002 The Urban Institute.

Historically, most states have used discretionary parole release. But over the past few decades, the balance between the two methods of parole release has shifted. In 1977, 69 percent of parolees received discretionary parole board release. States began moving away from discretionary prison release policies in the 1980s in favor of determinate sentences and mandatory prison release. (We will return to a discussion of this trend later in this chapter.) Consistent with the adoption of truth in sentencing and other mandatory release statutes, mandatory prison release is increasing, while discretionary parole release is decreasing. Exhibit 8–10 shows how much the share of prison releases by type changed from 1977 to 2010.

Mandatory release is the most common method of release from prison today. Some argue that abandonment of discretionary release in favor of mandatory release has detrimental effects. Proponents of discretionary parole board release argue that parole boards serve a salutary function by requiring inmates to focus their efforts on successful reentry from prison to the community. Without the prospect of discretionary release, inmates have fewer incentives for engaging in good behavior or participating in

EXHIBIT 8–10   Percentage of All Prison Releases, 1977 and 2010

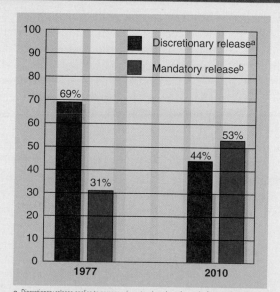

a. Discretionary release applies to persons who entered parole as the result of a parole board decision.
b. Mandatory release applies to persons who entered parole because of determinate sentencing statutes, good time provisions, or emergency release.

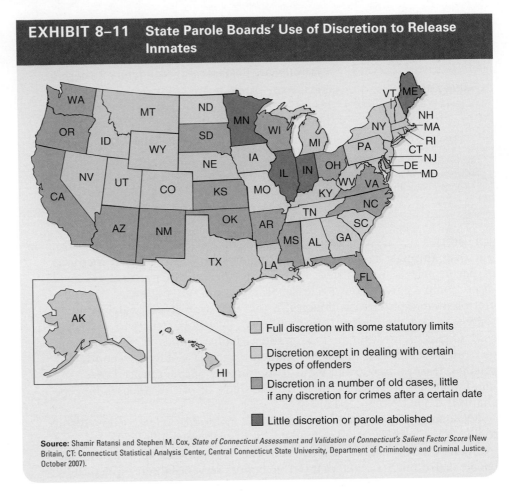

EXHIBIT 8–11   State Parole Boards' Use of Discretion to Release Inmates

☐ Full discretion with some statutory limits

☐ Discretion except in dealing with certain types of offenders

▨ Discretion in a number of old cases, little if any discretion for crimes after a certain date

▉ Little discretion or parole abolished

Source: Shamir Ratansi and Stephen M. Cox, *State of Connecticut Assessment and Validation of Connecticut's Salient Factor Score* (New Britain, CT: Connecticut Statistical Analysis Center, Central Connecticut State University, Department of Criminology and Criminal Justice, October 2007).

rehabilitative programs, and prison administrators have fewer mechanisms for relieving institutional crowding.

Exhibit 8–11 shows the amount of discretion that state parole boards have to release inmates. Parole boards in 24 states have nearly full discretion within statutory limits. In six states, parole boards have discretion except in cases involving certain violent offenses. Sixteen states have either abolished parole boards or the parole boards have discretion only in a small number of cases that occurred before a certain date but no discretion or limited discretion with cases after a specific date. And four states have either completely abolished parole or have very limited discretion. Later in the chapter we return to a discussion of the "abolish parole" movement.

In January 2010, the California legislature introduced a new type of release from prison called **nonrevocable parole (NRP)**.[28] NRP is a type of unsupervised parole that, unlike regular parole, cannot be revoked for technical violations. Persons allowed NRP are no longer under the jurisdiction of the California Department of Corrections and Rehabilitation, and they do not report to a parole officer. Persons are discharged from NRP after one year. Only offenders convicted of non-violent, nonsexual, low-level crimes who have been assessed and determined not to be a serious risk to the public are eligible for NRP. In addition, the offenders must have demonstrated acceptable behavior in prison and must have made progress with any substance abuse issues.

nonrevocable parole (NRP)

A type of unsupervised parole that cannot be revoked for technical violations; the person does not report to a parole officer.

In the first year of operation, some 6,500 prisoners received NRP at an estimated cost savings of $100 million. They will be returned to prison only if they are arrested for a new offense, convicted, and sentenced to a term of incarceration in the same manner as any other criminal defendant.

Proponents of NRP argue that it removes low-level offenders from parole supervision, reduces the average parole officer caseload from 70 parolees to 45, allows the state to focus parole supervision on the most serious and violent parolees, allows law enforcement to continue to conduct warrantless searches on these parolees, reduces the number of parolees returned to custody for parole violations, and reduces the need for bed space in county jails and state prisons. Critics note that they recognize the need to reduce crowding and cut costs but not at the expense of public safety. It is too early to tell what impact NRP will have, but if it costs less than regular parole and does not contribute to an increase in serious and violent crime, chances are other states will consider adopting it.

CHARACTERISTICS OF PAROLEES

The tremendous increase in the prison population discussed in Chapter 7 has given many people a sense of safety and security. However, the majority of the population is also unconcerned—or unaware—that at least 95 percent of those who enter prisons eventually return to the community, and most do so in about two and one-half years. Some have put it this way: More prisoners in results in more prisoners out!

Almost 2,000 prisoners each day leave prison. About one in five leaves prison with no postrelease supervision because of changes in sentencing legislation that allow some prisoners to "max out" (serve their full sentences) and leave prison with no postcustody supervision as discussed previously. On January 1, 2010, 819,308 American adults were on parole, down 5,526 from one year earlier and the second year in a row that the nation's parole population declined.[29] Eighty-eight percent of those adults were state parolees; the rest were federal. In midyear 2006, the Bureau of Justice Statistics estimated that 14,000 full-time parole officers were supervising the nation's parole population, each with a caseload of about 38 active parolees.[30] (Some agencies supervise both parolees and probationers.) Men and women made up nearly equal percentages of full-time employees. Consult the Appendix Careers in Corrections at the Online Learning Center Web site for the steps involved in career planning, developing employability and job readiness, and finding the right job.

The basic demographics of parolees have not changed much over the past 20 years. The typical adult parolee is a white, non-Hispanic male on mandatory parole and under active parole supervision for more than one year. The median age is 34, with an 11th-grade education. Women make up 12 percent of the parole population (see Exhibit 8–12). The region with the highest number of parolees is the South, followed by the West, Northeast, and Midwest.

Not all who are sent to prison are released on parole. Those who are the most serious offenders (those who have life sentences or who face the death penalty) or who have disciplinary problems while incarcerated generally are not paroled. Instead, they live out their lives in prison or are released when they have served their entire sentences.

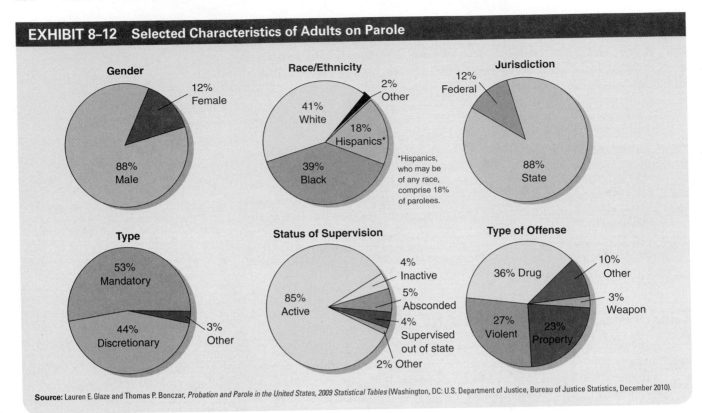

EXHIBIT 8–12   Selected Characteristics of Adults on Parole

Source: Lauren E. Glaze and Thomas P. Bonczar, *Probation and Parole in the United States, 2009 Statistical Tables* (Washington, DC: U.S. Department of Justice, Bureau of Justice Statistics, December 2010).

Trends in the Parole Population

The estimated number of adults under community supervision and incarceration from 1995 through 2010 is shown in Exhibit 8–13. Notwithstanding the slight decrease in the number of persons on parole over the past two years, the nation's parole population increased 88,161 over the past decade, resulting from states' increased use of parole as a way to reduce prison crowding and spending. According to one criminologist, "The numbers of returning offenders dwarf anything known before, the needs of released inmates are greater, and corrections has retained few rehabilitation programs."[31] Many parolees have long histories of criminal or gang involvement and few marketable skills. Most employers are also reluctant to hire ex-offenders. A survey in five major cities revealed that two of three employers would not knowingly hire an ex-offender (regardless of the offense), and one of three companies said they had checked the criminal records of their most recent hires.[32] Furthermore, there are increased employment restrictions on parolees convicted of felonies who want to practice a profession that requires licensing (for example, law, real estate, medicine, nursing, physical therapy, teaching, dentistry, engineering, pharmacy, and barbering). Thirty-three states (and the District of Columbia) impose some kind of legal restriction on public employment after a felony conviction.[33]

Countering employer reluctance means having more recent proof that the ex-offender is motivated to change and has used the period of incarceration productively to prepare for success in the community. Why should we even care about employment for persons who have been convicted? The short answer is that the benefits of increased employment go far beyond those with prior convictions and their immediate families. Communities are stronger when the individuals who live there are gainfully employed. Taxpayers benefit: Reduced recidivism means lower costs

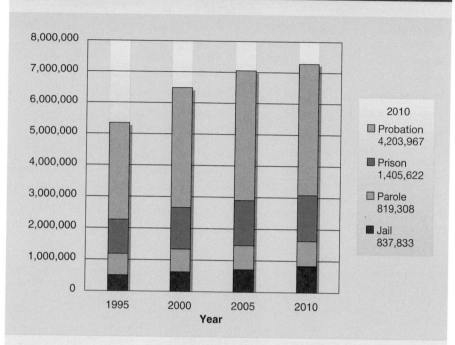

EXHIBIT 8–13   Trends in the Correctional Population, 1995, 2000, 2005, and 2010

2010
- Probation 4,203,967
- Prison 1,405,622
- Parole 819,308
- Jail 837,833

Source: Bureau of Justice Statistics publications: *Jail Inmates at Midyear 2009, Statistical Tables; Prisoners in 1995; Prisoners in 2007; Probation and Parole in the United States, 1998; Probation and Parole in the United States, 2000; Probation and Parole in the United States, 2005;* and *Probation and Parole in the United States, 2009.*.

to the criminal justice system and fewer victims. For employers, more people competing for jobs means better-quality employees. What we find in many communities across the United States today is that increasing employment opportunities for persons released from prison is not just the "right" thing to do—it is also the "smart" thing to do.

Hoping to prevent parolees from being shut out of the workforce, we mentioned earlier that some major cities are eliminating questions from their job applications that ask whether prospective employees have ever been convicted of a crime.[34] Baltimore, Chicago, Los Angeles; Memphis; Minneapolis; New Haven and Norwich, Connecticut; and San Francisco and Oakland, California, have dropped or are considering dropping the criminal history question from job applications except for sensitive positions such as with police and schools and involving large amounts of money. And it's not only in the employment arena that parolees have problems. An estimated 5.3 million people in the United States have lost their voting rights as the result of a felony conviction. Although some believe that disenfranchisement of felons is an acceptable penalty for crime, others argue that denying large segments of the population the right to vote is likely to cause further alienation and make people less willing to participate in legitimate free-world activities. We return to the issue of parolees' voting later in this chapter.

Exhibit 8–14 defines parole populations among the states on January 1, 2010. California had the largest number of adults on parole, followed by Texas and Pennsylvania. Pennsylvania also had the highest rate of parole supervision, which means it used parole more than any other state; Maine used parole the least.

| EXHIBIT 8–14 | Selected Parole Populations Among the States, January 1, 2010 | | | | |

Ten States with the Largest Parole Populations	Number Supervised	Ten States with the Highest Rates of Supervision	People Supervised per 100,000 Adult U.S. Residents	Ten States with the Lowest Rates of Supervision	People Supervised per 100,000 Adult U.S. Residents
California	106,035	Arkansas	967	Maine	3
Texas	104,943	Pennsylvania	761	Florida	30
Pennsylvania	75,112	Louisiana	758	South Carolina	46
New York	49,950	Oregon	754	North Carolina	50
Illinois	33,162	Texas	581	Nebraska	61
Louisiana	25,863	South Dakota	446	Massachusetts	65
Michigan	24,374	Wisconsin	443	North Dakota	71
Georgia	24,029	Missouri	430	Rhode Island	71
Oregon	22,394	California	383	Delaware	76
Arkansas	21,166	Kentucky	378	Virginia	76

Source: Adapted from Lauren E. Glaze and Thomas P. Bonczar, *Probation and Parole in the United States, 2009* (Washington, DC: U.S. Department of Justice, Bureau of Justice Statistics, December, 2010).

Does Parole Work?

Parole rates, like probation rates, should be viewed in context. Parole starts with a population of 100 failures (i.e., convicted felons). How realistic is it then to expect parole, after conviction and the debilitating aspects of prison, to magically succeed with criminals where the home, the school, the police, and the courts have all arguably failed?

Still the most common way to answer the question "Does parole work?" is to ask what percentage of people placed on parole supervision complete their parole term successfully. There are at least four ways to view success.

The first way to view success may include those who do not return to prison. A second view may include those who are not rearrested while under parole supervision. A third may include those who do not commit any technical violations. The fourth takes a broader view and focuses on issues such as stable employment, adequate housing, and healthy family and personal relationships. Data on the first three ways of defining parole success are available and are discussed in the following text. Data on the fourth view are not routinely collected and are beyond the scope of this chapter but they are important and should be considered.

Parole Success The U.S. Department of Justice's Bureau of Justice Statistics defines parole as successful if the parolee completes a term of community supervision without returning to prison or jail or absconding. Using this definition, 51 percent of people discharged from parole in 2009 (that is, people leaving active parole supervision in the community) were successful. The percentage of persons discharged from parole who were deemed successful has been relatively stable for the past 20 years. Fifty percent of adults leaving parole in 1990 were successful. In 2000, the rate dipped to 43 percent.

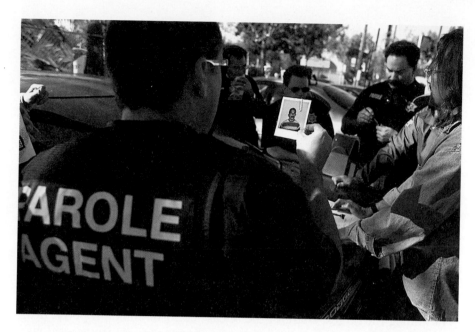

A parole officer questions one of his parolees about a suspected new offense violation. One reason for revoking parole is the parolee's arrest for a criminal offense. What are other reasons for which parole may be revoked?

Researchers in Tennessee found that first-time releases to state parole do better than rereleases.[35] In every year during the 1990s, first-time releases to state parole were more successful than rereleases. In 1990, 56 percent of first-time releases were successful compared with 15 percent of rereleases. In 1999, of those exiting parole, 63 percent of first-time releases were successful, compared to 21 percent of rereleases.

The researchers also found that success on parole depends on the method of release—whether it is discretionary or mandatory. In every year between 1990 and 1999, state prisoners released by a parole board had higher success rates than those released through mandatory release. Between 1990 and 1999, the percent of successful discretionary parole board releases varied between 50 and 56 percent while the percent of successful mandatory releases ranged between 24 and 33 percent.

When the researchers combined method of release and status of parolee (first time vs. rerelease), first-time mandatory parole releases had a higher success rate (79 percent) than did first-time discretionary parole board releases (61 percent). However, when researchers looked at the success of parolees rereleased from state prison, they found just the opposite: Discretionary parole board releases in 1999 who had been rereleased from prison were more successful (37 percent) than were mandatory parolees (17 percent).

The research results can be an important tool for allocating resources. Knowing that method of release and status of parolee (first-time vs. rerelease) are related to success on parole may suggest different sets of parole conditions depending upon method of release and status of parolee, allowing for a better distribution of fiscal and human resources.

Parole Failures Rates of relapse and recidivism are high, especially in the vulnerable period immediately following release. In fact, two-thirds of all parolees are rearrested within three years, 30 percent within the first six months of release.

The number of parole violators returned to prison continues to increase. Of the nearly 552,611 adults who exited parole in 2009, 185,550 (34 percent) were returned to prison either with a new sentence

(26 percent) or revocation (71 percent) or to receive treatment (less than 1 percent), up from 27,177 in 1980 and 160,000 in 1995. The numbers are so high that parole failures account for a growing proportion of all new prison admissions.

Shouldn't parole supervision produce lower recidivism? The obvious answer is yes. However, if you look only at broad national statistics on the impact of parole supervision, the data are not encouraging. For example, researchers at the Urban Institute discovered that parole supervision has little effect on the rearrest rates of released prisoners.[36] (Mandatory parolees—who represent the largest share of released prisoners—are no better off in terms of rearrest than prisoners released without supervision [inmates released at the expiration of their sentence].) Those screened by parole boards are less likely to be rearrested, but the difference is relatively small. Furthermore, this small difference may be due to factors other than supervision given that parole boards may base their decision on such factors as attitude, motivation, and preparedness for release.

The public safety impact of supervision is minimal and often nonexistent among the largest share of the release cohort—male property, drug, and violent offenders. Supervision does not appear to improve recidivism outcomes for violent offenders or property offenders released to mandatory parole. Supervision is associated with lower rearrest rates only among discretionary parolees who had been incarcerated for a property offense. In fact, for male drug offenders, mandatory release to supervision predicts higher rearrest rates than for unconditional releasees or discretionary parolees. These higher rates may reflect the fact that mandatory parolees are a higher-risk population than discretionary parolees and face heightened surveillance (such as drug testing) compared with unconditional releasees. In short, while postprison supervision may have modest effects on recidivism in some cases, it does not appear to improve rearrest rates for the largest subsets of released prisoners. The answer is to look beyond the broad sweep of national statistics and examine what impact parole supervision has on women, those with few prior arrests, public order offenders, and technical violators. When those questions are asked, we find rearrest rates as much as 16 percentage points lower than rates observed with unconditional release. In addition, persons with combinations of these characteristics (e.g., females with few prior arrests who were incarcerated for a public order offense) who were released to supervision were predicted to have even lower rearrest rates.

Once again, research results can be an important tool for allocating resources.

Why are they returning? Parole may be revoked for two reasons. A *technical violation* occurs when any of the technical conditions of parole (e.g., find and keep a job, live at home, sign no contracts, pay restitution and fees, perform community service, attend drug and alcohol abuse counseling) are violated. The second type of violation is a *new offense violation*. This involves arrest for the commission of a new crime. A new offense violation might involve a technical violation. For example, an arrest for selling drugs and a positive test for drug use would be a violation for a new offense and a technical violation.

For about the past decade, Department of Justice statistics show that approximately one-third of adults who exited parole were returned to incarceration. Of the parole violators returned to prison, one-fourth were returned for a new conviction and almost three-fourths for a technical violation. For example, California releases approximately 120,000 parolees every year, and every year about 75,000 of them return to prison for violating their parole on technical terms, such as missing an appointment with a parole officer or moving without permission. The Justice Department adds that a significant number of these are attributable to incomplete and/or inadequate release planning, imposition of unrealistic rules, and ineffective case management.[37] Other scholars tell us that violations are sometimes a function of clients' symptoms or their difficulties in following directions. For example, parolees with serious mental illness might violate the technical conditions of supervision because of cognitive impairment, delusions, confusion, or side effects of psychotropic medications. The Justice Policy Institute estimates that if states reduced by half the number of people sent back to prison for technical violations, they could save about $1.1 billion in incarceration costs.[38] Statistics such as these help us understand why California divided its parole population into two categories: those who pose little or no risk outside prison and for whom nonrevocable parole is appropriate, and those who need regular, or even enhanced, supervision.

When a violation occurs, a revocation hearing date is set. (Revocation hearings are discussed in Chapter 4.) The purpose of a revocation hearing is to determine whether the violation warrants the parolee's removal from the community. During a revocation hearing the parolee has certain rights of due process because he or she could lose conditional freedom; but the parolee is not entitled to a full adversary hearing, as would be the case in a new criminal proceeding. If the parolee violates the conditions of parole, a revocation hearing could return the offender to prison to serve the remainder of the original sentence plus any new sentence that might be given because of new violations.[39]

Researchers recently examined over 114,000 cases of parole violation in California and found that the parole board exercises a significant amount of discretion in deciding which parole violators are returned to prison and which are permitted to remain in the community.[40] They found that one's race, ethnicity, and gender affect the likelihood that parole violators were reimprisoned. Men and parolees of color were more likely than women and white parolees to be returned to prison. The authors assert that the findings are evidence of conscious or unconscious bias by parole boards, although they caution that other characteristics that were not measured in the study such as employability, addiction, or family stability may also influence the decision to reimprison. If the board hears fewer cases of parole violation in the future as one might expect as a result of the newly implemented nonrevocable parole, it will be interesting to learn whether and, if so, how the discretion changes.

What, however, lies at the heart of parole success and failure? We hear and read a lot about the importance of providing parolees opportunities for work, reuniting families, and providing housing. These are important needs for reentering ex-prisoners as this chapter has explained. However, Dr. Bonita Veysey, Rutgers University professor of criminal justice, tells us that individual-level change is required before opportunities for work, reuniting families, and providing housing make a difference. We know from the evidence-based literature discussed in this book that a person must first change her or his cognitive reasoning; the way she or he perceives; reflects, thinks about life reasons; and solves problems before moving toward a different way of life. Giordano and colleagues refer to this change as cognitive transformation.[41] Quite possibly the reason that parole has failed to reduce criminal activity and returns so many ex-offenders to prison is that parole programs focus on providing offenders opportunities for jobs and housing and reuniting families but do not

EVIDENCE-BASED CORRECTIONS

American Probation and Parole Association Code of Ethics

- I will render professional service to the justice system and the community at large in effecting the social adjustment of the offender.
- I will uphold the law with dignity, displaying an awareness of my responsibility to offenders while recognizing the right of the public to be safeguarded from criminal activity.
- I will strive to be objective in the performance of my duties, recognizing the inalienable right of all persons, appreciating the inherent worth of the individual, and respecting those confidences which can be reposed in me.
- I will conduct my personal life with decorum, neither accepting nor granting favors in connection with my office.
- I will cooperate with my co-workers and related agencies and will continually strive to improve my professional competence through the seeking and sharing of knowledge and understanding.
- I will distinguish clearly, in public, between my statements and actions as an individual and as a representative of my profession.
- I will encourage policy, procedures, and personnel practices, which will enable others to conduct themselves in accordance with the values, goals, and objectives of the American Probation and Parole Association.
- I recognize my office as a symbol of public faith and I accept it as a public trust to be held as long as I am true to the ethics of the American Probation and Parole Association.
- I will constantly strive to achieve these objectives and ideals, dedicating myself to my chosen profession.

Source: American Probation and Parole Association 2009.

Ethical Dilemma 8–1: Offenders often leave prison without job skills, money, or personal coping skills. Should they be released on parole? Is parole working? What can agencies do to assist parolees? For more information, go to Ethical Dilemma 8–1 at www.justicestudies.com/ethics06.

Ethical Dilemma 8–2: A woman with young children is a repeat offender who has again violated her parole. Should she remain in the community, or should she return to prison? What are the issues? Should a parolee's gender make a difference in treatment? For more information, go to Ethical Dilemma 8–2 at www.justicestudies.com/ethics06.

Ethical Dilemmas for every chapter are available online.

---

emphasize individual-level change. Again, to quote Dr. Veysey, "Telling someone to stop being criminal may work for a period of time, but that person needs a replacement identity, and this identity may be chosen only by the individual who is in the process of change."

For parole and other correctional interventions to work and reduce criminal activity, two things are needed: a cognitive transformation within the individual and a supportive environment in which change is likely to occur. The evidence-based literature tells us, for example, that vocation and academic education and drug treatment change individuals, and these changes result in a person's ability to find and keep employment and to improve social functioning and relationships with others. Making these changes will not be easy. For if it were, we would not have the statistic that two of every three parolees are rearrested within three years of their release and one-half are returned to prison in that same period.

ISSUES IN PAROLE

Over the past few decades, the face of parole has changed. This chapter concludes with a discussion of several important issues in parole, including voting rights, reentry courts, successful reintegration programs involving victims, the abolition of discretionary parole board release, prisoner reentry and community policing, and community-focused parole. Also, we look to the U.S. Supreme Court for the answer to the question, "Is parole a right or a privilege?"

Can Parolees Vote?

Among the many issues being debated by legislators and correctional policymakers in planning for successful reentry is felon disenfranchisement, meaning depriving persons who have been convicted of felonies of the right to vote. Currently, an estimated 5.3 million people in the United States have lost their voting rights as the result of a felony conviction. The U.S. Constitution, Article 1, Section 2, gives the matter of voting rights to the states. Only two states—Maine and Vermont—do not deny persons the right to vote based on a criminal conviction; even prisoners may vote by absentee ballot.

Over the past decade, 23 states have amended felony disenfranchisement policies in an effort to reduce their restrictiveness and expand voter eligibility.[42] For example,

- Nine states either repealed or amended lifetime disenfranchisement laws.
- Three states expanded voting rights to persons under community supervision (probation and parole).
- Eight states eased the restoration process for persons seeking to have their right to vote restored after completing sentence.
- Three states improved data and information sharing.

In addition to disenfranchisement by law, there is confusion among election officials about their state's felony disenfranchisement policies.[43] For example, almost one-fourth of Ohio's boards of elections misinformed callers posing as people with felony convictions, telling them that they could not vote while under community supervision, although Ohio state law denies voting rights to felons only while they are incarcerated. During the research, 13 of Ohio's 88 boards of elections said they did not know the state's law on whether people on probation or parole could vote.

We present the arguments for and against felon disenfranchisement next. As you read them, remember that they have not been scientifically proved. They sound rational on the surface, but social science research has yet to validate them.

Only Maine and Vermont do not place any restrictions on the right to vote for people with felony convictions. Missy Shea of the Vermont Secretary of State's office helps at Marble Valley Regional Correctional Facility in Rutland with the voter registration process. An estimated 5.3 million people in the United States have lost their voting rights as a result of a felony conviction. What are the arguments for and against felon disenfranchisement?

There are at least four arguments in support of felon disenfranchisement. First, inmates should be denied the right to vote as a matter of principle because they committed a felony. Second, states have the right to deny felons the right to vote as added punishment, just as they have the right to restrict felons from certain occupations. Third, denying felons the right to vote sends a message about respect for the law and acts as a deterrent to crime. And fourth, felons should be denied the right to vote because they cannot be trusted to make politically informed decisions.

On the other hand, there are five arguments against felon disenfranchisement. First, voting is not a privilege but a right guaranteed by the Constitution, and states don't have the right to take it away. Second, felon disenfranchisement laws are unfair to minorities who are treated unfairly by the criminal justice system—one of every eight adult black males is ineligible to vote. Third, felon disenfranchisement laws are not an effective form of punishment because most ex-felons did not vote before incarceration. Fourth, removal of an inmate's right to vote is inconsistent with reentry. Offenders should be encouraged to accept more responsibility for their future roles in the community, not less. John Timoney, former Miami police chief and president of the Police Executive Research Forum, put it this way: "I do not think we should give criminals an excuse for not reforming themselves because they are bitter about having had one of their most important rights—the right to vote—taken away. I think it is better to remove any obstacles that stand in the way of offenders resuming a healthy, full, productive life . . . my sense is, once you've cleared the four walls of the jail, your right to vote should be restored."[44] And fifth, once we open the door by declaring that a certain group of people does not deserve the basic right to vote, then which group of people might be the next we attempt to restrict?

Reentry Courts

It is incumbent on criminal justice policymakers who are interested in greater public safety and more efficient use of public tax dollars to consider how we might better handle the challenges of the almost 2,000 offenders who leave prison each day. Because of the potential threats that parolees pose to victims, families, children, and communities, investing in effective parole programs may be one of the best investments we make.

One of the latest innovations in helping offenders released from prison make a successful adjustment to the community is the reentry court. A **reentry court** manages the return to the community of individuals released from prison, using the authority of the court to apply graduated sanctions and positive reinforcement and to marshal resources to support the prisoner's reintegration. The U.S. attorney general has proposed that reentry courts operate like drug courts or other problem-solving courts (domestic violence court, community court, family court, gun court, and DWI court).[45] In drug court, for example, a judge is limited to managing a caseload of drug-involved offenders. The judge requires an offender to make regular court appearances and participate in drug treatment and testing. If the drug offender violates the conditions of release, the judge administers a predetermined range of graduated sanctions that do not automatically require return to prison (except for new crimes or egregious violations). Frequent appearances before the court, offers of assistance, and the knowledge of a predetermined range of sanctions for violations of the conditions of release assist the offender in getting back on track.

The U.S. Department of Justice proposes that a reentry court have six core elements:

• **Assessment and planning:** Correctional administrators and the reentry judge meet with inmates who are near release to explain the

Los Angeles County Superior Court Judge Michael Tynan congratulates Melanie Hightower for graduating from the Second Chance Women's Reentry Court. Reentry courts manage the return to the community of individuals released from prison. What are the core elements of reentry court that facilitate an individual's successful return?

reentry court

A court that manages the return to the community of individuals released from prison.

reentry process, assess inmates' needs, and begin building links to a range of social services, family counseling, health and mental health services, housing, job training, and work opportunities that support reintegration.

- **Active judicial oversight:** The reentry court sees all prisoners released into the community with a high degree of frequency, maybe once or twice a month. Also involved are the parole officer and others responsible for assessing the parolee's progress. In court, offender progress is praised, and offender setbacks are discussed.

- **Case management of support services:** The reentry court acts as a service broker and advocates on behalf of parolees for "wraparound services" such as substance abuse treatment, job training, employment, faith instruction, family member support, housing, and community services.

- **Accountability to the community:** Reentry courts appoint broad-based community advisory boards to develop and maintain accountability to the community. Advisory boards also help courts negotiate the sometimes difficult task of brokering services for parolees and advocate on their behalf.

- **Graduated sanctions:** Reentry courts establish a predetermined range of graduated sanctions for violations of the conditions of release that do not automatically require return to prison.

- **Rewarding success:** Reentry courts incorporate positive judicial reinforcement actions after goals are achieved. Examples include negotiating early release from parole or conducting graduation ceremonies similar to those used in drug courts.

Models of four reentry courts are shown in Exhibit 8–15.

According to the U.S. Department of Justice, "The successful completion of parole should be seen as an important life event for an offender, and the court can help acknowledge that accomplishment. Courts provide powerful public forums for encouraging positive behavior and for acknowledging the individual effort in achieving reentry goals."[46] The U.S. Department of Justice is promoting the idea and asking communities to experiment with it, depending upon statutory framework, caseload considerations, administrative flexibility, and levels of collaboration among the judiciary, corrections officers, parole officers, police, business community, religious institutions, community organizations, and the like. Whichever form a reentry court takes, developing new ways that communities can manage and support offenders after release from prison with assistance in securing employment, housing, substance abuse treatment, family counseling, and other services is essential to our ability to reduce crime and keep communities safe.

The largest reentry court in operation today is in Richland County, Ohio. The court accepted its first parolees in 2000. Reentry court supervision lasts a minimum of one year. During this time, parolees appear in court each month to discuss their progress. They receive an average of 12 monthly intensive supervision contacts, undergo random drug and alcohol testing, and are required to participate in remote-location monitoring. The idea involves constant attention coupled with swift and consistent consequences. Jeffrey Spelman studied the Richland County reentry court and found that the felony rearrest rate for graduates of the year-long program was 4 percent within one year of their release into the community.[47] The contrast between the 4 percent rearrest rate in Richland

EXHIBIT 8–15 Models of Reentry Court

The Fort Wayne, Indiana, Reentry Program

One judge-centered reentry court model is operating in Ft. Wayne, Indiana, which borrows heavily from the drug court experience: that is, an ongoing, central role for a judge, a "contract" drawn up between court and offender, discretion on the judge's part to impose graduated sanctions for various levels of failure to meet the conditions imposed, and the promise of the end of supervision as an occasion for ceremonial recognition. In Ft. Wayne, the reentry court judge has been vested with authority by the Indiana Parole Commission to act on the Commission's behalf in supervising released adult offenders. A transition team comprised of treatment providers, corrections staff, law enforcement, employment trainers, and family counselors, is assigned to the offender to assist with the development, monitoring, and enforcement of the reentry plan that is implemented upon release from the institution. This plan is based on assessments (e.g., risk, educational, vocational, mental health, and substance abuse) and developed with the offender and his or her support system. This plan becomes the guide by which the offender's reentry into the community is managed. Many of the offenders have been connected with a network of mentors who help guide their transition back into the community.

With the reentry plan completed and upon the offender's release from commitment, the offender appears before the reentry court judge for formalization or ordering of the reentry plan, depending on the offender, the support system, and the agencies of government representing the community. Typically, an offender will have to remain drug free, make restitution to his or her victim and reparation to the community, participate in programs that had begun in commitment (work, education, emotions management, parenting classes, etc.), refrain from committing crime, and comply with any other terms and conditions of the reentry plan. The offender is also required to appear before the reentry court judge on a regular basis to determine if the plan remains appropriate and effective and if the offender is in compliance.

The Ohio Reentry Court Program

The Richland County Common Pleas Court in partnership with the Ohio Department of Rehabilitation and Correction developed a comprehensive reentry program that addresses all offenders sent from prison and returned to Richland County, Ohio. The Richland County reentry court program began in January 2000, following its selection by the U.S. Department of Justice's call for a concept paper on establishing a reentry court to enhance accountability of offenders being released from prison with judicial oversight, stronger supervision, and an emphasis on addressing issues which make reentering society difficult. The reentry court was fully operational and became a part of the judicial process January 1, 2001. Through early assessment and planning, the reentry court addresses the basic issues that lead most offenders to crime and which most often resurface when they return. By establishing reentry release plans at sentencing, offenders are presented with those areas that they must address before release back into the community. The probation and parole supervision system must also address the reentry needs of the offender prior to release, and during supervision to make prosocial reintegration more successful. Already the benefits of this collaborative process have begun to surface, not only with the increased success of offenders returning to the community but

also with the closer collaborations between the criminal justice, law enforcement, social service, and treatment communities to assist them.

The Iowa Reentry Program

The Iowa reentry court project is a pilot initiative and is a collaboration between the Iowa Department of Corrections, the Iowa Parole Board, and the city of Cedar Rapids and targets offenders who have mental health disorders or who have been dually diagnosed with mental health and substance abuse problems. This program in Cedar Rapids is operational. Another program is being implemented in Des Moines and focuses on the 22 percent of offenders who refuse treatment and parole as well as paroled offenders who are not typically assigned to a parole officer. The Iowa reentry court makes use of an administrative law judge (ALJ) under the jurisdiction of the parole board, and relies on a Community Accountability Board that works with the ALJ. Composed of local service providers, probation and parole officers, victims, and other interested citizens, the accountability board identifies community service and support opportunities and develops accountability mechanisms for the successful reentry of released inmates.

A Reentry Coordinator in the Department of Corrections Offender Services Office works with institutional counseling staff who are preparing offenders for participation in the reentry process. Staff are now working to identify special needs of at-risk inmates through assessment and diagnosis in the prison setting and will begin pre-release treatment and planning to connect them with community resources. Upon release from confinement, parolees will meet with the Community Accountability Board and ALJ at least monthly.

The West Virginia Reentry Program

The Division of Juvenile Services has implemented a juvenile reentry court initiative targeting adjudicated youth (male and female) who have been committed to the West Virginia Industrial Home for Youth and the Davis Center and who will be returning to Grant, Mineral, or Tucker counties. The Industrial Home for Youth is the state's most secure committed facility and the Davis Center is a medium-secure facility. These counties are located in the panhandle region in a fairly remote part of the state. This initiative is modeled after the OJJDP-supported Intensive Community-Based Aftercare Program (IAP) currently being replicated by juvenile justice systems throughout the country. In addition to intensive case management provided to youth while in confinement and upon return to the community, collaborative partnerships have been formed with the Circuit Court and Juvenile Probation, local law enforcement, faith communities, and local school systems.

Youth are oriented into the program at the time of commitment to the Industrial Home for Youth. Youth returning to Grant, Mineral, and Tucker Counties are assessed for eligibility. Upon return to the community, youth attend monthly court hearings before the Juvenile Court judge. An aftercare case manager is immediately assigned to the case. Along with the juvenile probation officer, the aftercare case manager will provide intensive supervision and surveillance with frequent contacts in the school, at home, and at work if applicable. Advisory boards in each of the counties have been established to allow community members to provide valuable input to the restorative justice process

Source: "Serious and Violent Offender Reentry Initiative Appendices," U.S. Department of Labor Employment and Training Administration, (accessed September 5, 2007).

County's reentry court and BJS data from a 15-state recidivism study that found a one-year rearrest rate of 44 percent suggests that reentry court is capable of making a difference in the lives of individuals even if they are terminated from the program. However, only time and further research will test the accuracy of these early results.

Reintegration Involving Victims

Successful reintegration programs also involve victims.[48] Victims and victim organizations can assist in the reintegration of parolees by providing parole board members and parole officers with relevant information, offering their experience and expertise, and encouraging offender accountability.

Each year, about 30 million people in America become victims of crime. Most states give victims the right to (1) be notified about parole proceedings, (2) be heard on matters relating to the offender's parole, (3) be present at parole proceedings, and (4) receive restitution as a condition of parole. These rights are designed to ensure that the views of victims are taken into account before decisions about parole are made and to help victims prepare themselves for the offender's release. Victim input can highlight the need for strict supervision or special conditions such as restitution orders, order of protection, or mandated treatment in order to discourage reoffending and encourage reintegration.

Programs involving victims operate in a number of ways. Some encourage victims to volunteer relevant information to parole officers. For example, in stalking cases, victims can tell parole officers whether offenders are in areas where they are not supposed to be. Other programs encourage victim–offender communication. In these programs, victims educate offenders about the impact of the crime and generate remorse in the hope that they can change offender behavior in the future. Whether the program features one-on-one conversation or a victim talking to an audience of imprisoned or paroled offenders, the aim is to convey to offenders the consequences of their actions in terms of the victims' pain and suffering. We return to a discussion of how corrections agencies participate in meeting victims' needs in Chapter 14.

The U.S. District Court for the Northern District of Florida graduated its first seven reentry court participants on March 30, 2011. The Robert A. Dennis, Jr. Reentry Court was established in 2010 by U.S. District Court Chief Judge Casey Rodgers. The program accepts offenders on federal supervised release who have a minimum of 36 months of supervision remaining, agree to abstain from alcohol and drug use, participate in a drug and alcohol evaluation, and engage in a variety of treatment modalities to address issues of substance abuse. Participants stay in the program for at least one year. Those who finish the program earn up to one year early termination from the original term of supervision. How can reentry court benefit the offender and the community?

Abolition of Discretionary Parole Board Release

Earlier in this chapter we discussed that there was strong opposition to parole in the 1930s and that opponents wanted to abolish it. They argued that parole boards were turning hardened criminals loose on society, parole had a dismal performance record, its goals were never realized, parole board members and parole officers were poorly trained, and parole hearings were little more than hastily conducted, almost unthinking interviews. In spite of the gap between goals and this 1930s reality, parole fulfilled important functions for wardens, legislators, and district attorneys.

The movement to abolish discretionary parole boards resurfaced in the 1970s when the concept of "just deserts"—the idea that offenders deserve punishment for what they do to society—was being discussed.[49] However, states did not do away with parole altogether; they restructured it. As the data in Exhibit 8–16 show, by the end of 2000, 16 states

I was on parole for 30 months after doing 16 years straight on a very lengthy sentence. When I got out, I paroled to a place where I had never been before—everything was new to me and the only person I knew in my whole town was my wife. Starting over again was great, I made new friends, got a good job, joined the church, and integrated back into society just like I was supposed to.

Then it happened. I began to fall apart for a very simple reason—I stopped doing what my parole officer told me to do and started doing what I wanted to do. Subsequently, I was violated and returned to prison to do more time on my sentence, and that is where I sit at this writing.

There are good people and bad people in the world, and parole officers are the same. I was lucky and got a good one. From day one she told me that whether or not I succeeded was entirely up to me. She laid out a simple plan for me to follow, which I did for a while. Even when I started breaking the rules, instead of punishing me she put me in places that offered help for the issues I had. Finally, I left her no choice but to violate me, and she did just that.

Parole is a good idea because the inmate will have some of the awesome powers of the state at his disposal to help with the reintegration process. Done alone, the process can be terrifying. If the inmate does not

define and address his own situation while he is in prison, the chance of that person making it on parole is slim to none. On the other hand, if the inmate has truly applied himself and has identified and addressed the "thing" that makes him able to break the law, parole is an excellent idea.

For myself, I know this: If I would have done what I needed to do while doing 16 years in prison, I would not be sitting here now praying for the chance to be free again and live a normal life.

Anonymous

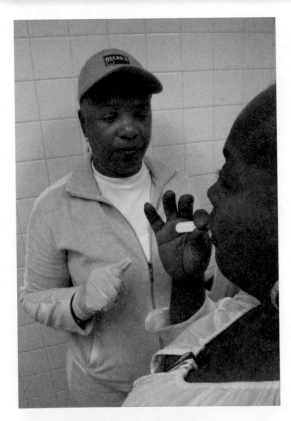

A parolee blows into a disposable plastic mouthpiece. The parole officer then attaches the mouthpiece to a portable handheld breath-testing machine that digitally registers the parolee's blood-alcohol level. Other portable alcohol technology tests urine, skin, and hair. What are the advantages of such technology in supervising parolees?

and the federal government had abolished discretionary release from prison by a parole board for all offenders. Another four states had abolished discretionary parole release for certain violent offenses or other crimes against a person. In these states, postrelease supervision still exists and is referred to as "mandatory supervised release," "controlled release," or "community control." Parole boards still have discretion over inmates who were sentenced for crimes committed prior to the effective date of the law that eliminated parole board release and the responsibility to place offenders under either conditional or supervised release, the authority to return an offender to prison for violating the conditions of parole or supervised release, and the power to grant parole for medical reasons.

Why did some states abolish discretionary release from prison by a parole board? There are at least four reasons.

First, scholars concluded that indeterminate sentencing and discretionary parole did not achieve offender rehabilitation, which was unfair because it was based solely on parole board judgment without explicit standards of fairness and equity in sentencing. Studies showed that wide disparities resulted when the characteristics of the crime and the offender were taken into account, and decisions were influenced by the offender's race, socioeconomic status, and place of conviction. Recall that earlier in this chapter we discussed a recent study in California in which researchers found that one's race, ethnicity, and gender affected the parole board's decision to return some parole violators to prison and let others remain in the community. Men and parolees of color were more likely than women and white parolees to be returned to prison. Second, eliminating discretionary parole appeared to be tough on crime. Third, parole boards' lack of openness in the decision-making process, in which boards made their parole decisions on a case-by-case basis without benefit of a written set of policies and procedures, prompted criticism. Today only 30 states make their parole board votes public. The rest are kept secret.[50] Fourth, state politicians were able to convince the public that parole was the cause of the rising crime problem and that abolition was the solution.

Prisoner Reentry and Community Policing

Reentry isn't just for corrections anymore for two reasons. First, the fourfold increase in the number of persons being released each year from state and federal prisons over the past two decades into crime-ridden neighborhoods that lack services and support systems is more than community corrections officers can handle. There has not been a fourfold increase in the number of community supervision officers as Chapter 4 pointed out, and for that reason probation and parole agencies are experimenting with privatization in community corrections (see Chapter 13).

Second, in spite of all the efforts being made at prisoner reform, offenders are still leaving prison unprepared for successful reentry as this chapter has pointed out. Not enough prisoners are receiving education or vocational training. Not enough prisoners are receiving alcohol and drug treatment. Not enough prisoners are receiving life skills. These challenges not only impact prisoners but also threaten public safety. Prisoners who are not prepared to lead productive, law-abiding lives will reoffend. (We found earlier in this chapter that more than two-thirds are rearrested for a new crime within three years—30 percent within the first six months—and 51 percent are returned to prison during that same period either for a new crime or for a technical violation of the conditions of their release.) Communities that provide prisoners the services and environment to transition successfully into the community will also protect themselves from further harm.

One way some communities are responding to the problems of prisoner reentry is to involve community policing with reentry initiatives. The argument for involving community policing in reentry is this: Because the majority of ex-offenders are rearrested within three years, making contact with former prisoners is part of the everyday business of law enforcement. In fact, researchers at the Urban Institute say that "arrest frequencies for returning prisoners are 30 to 45 times higher than for the general population. Police agencies stand to benefit from their involvement in reentry because successful efforts to reduce reoffending among released prisoners can, by definition, prevent future crimes and help improve community relations with police."[51] In places where we find corrections and law enforcement officers as partners in reentry, the chief executives of these agencies can ensure that collaborative efforts are publicly framed in terms of safety issues, effectively combatting any allegations that reentry is "soft on crime." They can attest that when police and corrections do not collaborate, officers on the street encounter the same men and women. Law enforcement agencies are also able to send an important message to people leaving prison. They inform ex-offenders that through collaboration with corrections they are willing to help

EXHIBIT 8–16	States That Have Abolished Discretionary Release, 2000
For All Offenders	**For Certain Violent Offenders**
Arizona	Alaska
California[1]	Louisiana
Delaware	New York
Florida[2]	Tennessee
Illinois	
Indiana	
Kansas[3]	
Maine	
Minnesota	
Mississippi	
North Carolina	
Ohio[4]	
Oregon	
Virginia	
Washington	
Wisconsin	

1. In 1976 the Uniform Determinate Sentencing Act abolished discretionary parole for all offenses except some violent crimes with a long sentence or a sentence to life.
2. In 1995 parole eligibility was abolished for offenses with a life sentence and a 25-year mandatory term.
3. It excludes a few offenses, primarily first-degree murder and intentional second-degree murder.
4. It excludes murder and aggravated murder.

Source: Adapted from Timothy A. Hughes, Doris James Wilson, and Allen J. Beck, *Trends in State Parole, 1999–2000* (Washington, DC: U.S. Department of Justice, Bureau of Justice Statistics, October 2001).

them find the supports and services they need while holding ex-prisoners accountable for their actions.[52]

The community policing approach is to analyze and understand the reasons behind repeat offending and create partnerships with local businesses, residents, government agencies, and other stakeholders to solve underlying crime problems and prevent future offending.

Joint supervision of parolees by teams of police and parole officers is the most common way that police currently contribute to prisoner reentry efforts. Team supervision usually takes the form of police accompaniment on parole home visits, parole ride-alongs on police patrols, and parole involvement in policing activities, such as attending community meetings and staffing neighborhood substations. The team approach sends the message that community corrections is not soft on crime. It also contributes additional eyes and ears to enhance surveillance and assistance to community supervision. Exhibit 8–17 illustrates the example of community police practice in offender reentry in the Ogden (Utah) City Police Department.

Another way police are helping with reentry is more personal. Grand Rapids, Michigan, police lieutenant Ralph Mason met James Churchill in prison when Churchill was nearing the end of a 10-year prison term for armed robbery. Mason called Churchill two months after he was released from prison and told him about a job at a friend's industrial plumbing company, which was also willing to provide training. Nine months later when *USAToday* published the story "Unlikely Mentors Give Felons Help," Churchill was still employed at the plumbing company and earning $21 per hour.[53] One of Churchill's former bosses said he is one of the company's hardest workers, well liked by all 40 employees, and added, "I trust him completely." Churchill lives with his grandmother, building a relationship with his 11-year-old daughter, and saving for a car. "Everything is coming in small steps," he says. "I figure the harder I work, the more things will come. I just have to take it slow."

Community-Focused Parole

Earlier we said that communities that provide prisoners the services and environment to transition successfully into the community will also protect themselves from further harm. Community policing and prisoner reentry is one strategy.

Another is community-focused parole, a process of engaging the community so the community engages parole.[54] The process requires at least three changes to current parole practice.

The first is to capture a mission statement that the public understands. Some parole agencies are adopting public safety in addition to offender reform as a definition of their services. By raising their profile in the community as agencies that deliver public safety and highlighting that in their mission statement, parole agencies could decentralize parole officers into local neighborhoods (perhaps utilizing neighborhood police substations) and form collaborative partnerships with police and others similar to what community police do with local businesses, residents, government agencies, and other stakeholders to solve underlying crime problems and prevent future offending.

A second change is visibility. Unless the work of parole is made visible to the community, it will not result in the service being valued or supported. For many citizens, the issue of prisoners and their return to

| EXHIBIT 8-17 | Prisoner Reentry and Community Policing |

Ogden (Utah) City Police Department

Project T.E.A.M.

Team Enforcement and Monitoring (Project T.E.A.M.) was formed in response to crimes committed by the high number of individuals returning to a small area within Ogden City, Utah. Assessments of reentry patterns revealed that nearly 12 percent of the population in one eight-block neighborhood were under either probation or parole supervision. This high concentration of ex-offenders resulted in unmanageable caseloads for Weber County community supervision officers and restricted the amount of one-on-one contacts with clients. The goal of the Project T.E.A.M. collaborative is to improve the capacity of criminal justice agents to monitor and support reentry transitions by linking participants to social service organizations. To do so, the project has granted the police authority to act as community supervision agents. Although this authorization is contingent upon the individual signing a waiver, the incentive to participate is attractive to many releasees because it is often offered as an alternative to returning to prison for technical violations. The primary role for police includes strengthening the deterrence message communicated during the face-to-face introductory notification sessions, during which the consequences of noncompliance, especially for weapons offenses, are explained. In addition, police support supervision activities by conducting random curfew checks and home visits. This program benefits parole agents who typically have 60 to 80 offenders on their caseload, giving them extra support from the police to supervise higher risk parolees. For police, face-to-face meetings foster positive interactions with former prisoners and provide police with important context to individual circumstances of reentry.

Key Program Elements

- **Encouraging Compliance.** Individuals returning to Weber County on parole attend a meeting with police officers on the day of their release during which they are informed of the consequences of not abiding by the law. They are specifically informed that they may be federally prosecuted if they possess or use a firearm. If a parolee commits a technical violation, he or she is offered the option of joining the program instead of returning to prison. Participation in T.E.A.M. is contingent on the individual signing a contract that permits police officers to act in the capacity of parole officers and may include a curfew requirement or alcohol restrictions among other stipulations.
- **Increasing Surveillance.** The police have the same powers that the parole officer has over the parolee, including the right to make unannounced visits and search without a warrant or consent if they believe the individual is participating in criminal activity. Twice a month a police officer joins a parole officer in conducting visits to every high-risk parolee in the county.
- **Connecting to Services.** The program offers participants opportunities to receive education and employment support, including access to general equivalency diploma classes, computer courses, and career centers. Participants are linked with relevant social service organizations in the community during notification sessions.

Note: Partners include the Ogden City Police Department, all law enforcement agencies within Weber County, the Utah Department of Corrections, the Weber County Adult Probation and Parole Office, Ogden City's Enterprise Community, Safe Haven, and the Utah Department of Workforce Services.

Source: Adapted from Nancy G. La Vigne, Amy L. Solomon, Karen A. Beckman, and Kelly Dedel, *Prisoner Reentry and Community Policing: Strategies for Enhancing Public Safety* (Washington, DC: U.S. Department of Justice, Office of Community Oriented Policing Services, March 2006).

society is met with fear. However, scientifically conducted public opinion polls show that the public supports offender job training, treatment, and education. Media relations can help create a positive image and increase visibility regarding the work of parole. Other examples are participating in local events and using a highly visible offender community service work program that involves nonprofit organizations.

The third change—building partnerships—is central to any community-oriented initiative. Strategies that raise an agency's profile and elicit support are critical to the development of a community-focused parole service. Appearances on local news shows, articles in local newspapers, meetings with neighborhood associations, and sponsoring of local events such as Relay for Life are ways that parole agencies show they care about the community and can educate it about strategies in place to support and supervise returning prisoners.

The literature on community-oriented policing has found that proactive crime prevention strategies can yield long-term crime reduction benefits. It stands to reason then that community-focused parole can also have a positive impact on community safety.

Is Parole a Right or a Privilege?

Since the establishment of parole in the 18th century, students, researchers, inmates, corrections officials, lawyers, and judges have debated the issue of whether parole is a right or a privilege. Most recently, a federal appeals court judge in California reversed the decision of the California parole board and state courts for denying parole to Damon Cooke, who had been convicted of the attempted murder of a friend in Berkeley in 1991. Cooke was sentenced to an indeterminate term of seven years to life in prison with the possibility of parole.

Under California law, the parole board is required to set a release date unless a lengthy period of incarceration is necessary to protect the public. The level of proof required to make that decision is, according to California law, whether "some evidence" supports the conclusion that the inmate is unsuitable for parole because he or she currently is dangerous.

In November 2002, the California parole board determined that Cooke was not yet suitable for parole, basing its decision on the "especially cruel and callous manner" of his crime, his failure to participate in rehabilitative programs, his failure to develop marketable skills, and three incidents of misconduct while in prison.

At the parole hearing, the board admitted that Cooke had received a favorable psychological report, but it dismissed the report as not credible because it included several inconsistent and erroneous statements. The board denied Cooke's parole, saying he "would pose an unreasonable risk to society if released from prison." Cooke filed a petition with the State Superior Court, California court of appeals, and the California Supreme Court. All three were denied.

In 2004, Cooke filed a petition with the federal district court challenging the parole board's decision. The district court also denied his petition. However, in 2010, the 9th Circuit Court of Appeals reversed the district court's decision noting that there was no evidence that Cooke would pose a threat to public safety if released.

The California attorney general's office appealed to the U.S. Supreme Court. Without hearing arguments in the case, on January 24, 2011, the Justices unanimously reversed the opinion of the 9th Circuit.[55] The Justices said, "There is no right under the federal Constitution to be conditionally released before the expiration of a valid sentence, and the states are under no duty to offer parole to their prisoners."[56] "That should have been the beginning and the end"[57] of the matter in the federal courts, they said. The Justices went on to say that the only issue that should have been of federal interest was procedural, namely, what is the process for decision making, not whether the state court decided the case correctly.[58] The Court noted that under its 1979 decision of *Greenholtz* v. *Inmates of the Nebraska Penal and Correctional Complex*, Cooke received adequate due process when he was allowed an opportunity to be heard, to speak at his parole hearing, and to contest the evidence against him. He was afforded access to his records in advance, and he was provided a statement of the reasons for denial of parole. Thus, there had been no denial of due process.

Absent a future challenge on different grounds or heard by different Justices, the issue of whether parole is a right or a privilege seems to be settled for now. Parole is a privilege. The Court has made it clear that no prisoner has a liberty interest in being released before his or her sentence expires because the trial and appeals processes have ensured that the state has lawfully deprived the person of his or her interest in being free from confinement.

REVIEW AND APPLICATIONS

SUMMARY

1 Early English judges spared the lives of condemned felons by exiling them first to the American Colonies and then to Australia as indentured servants. Captain Alexander Maconochie, superintendent of the British penal colony on Norfolk Island, devised a "ticket of leave" system that moved inmates through stages. Sir Walter Crofton used some of Maconochie's ideas for his early release system in Ireland. In the United States, Zebulon Brockway implemented a system of upward classification.

2 Paroling authorities play powerful roles in the criminal justice system. They determine the length of incarceration for many offenders and can revoke parole. The paroling authority's policies have a direct impact on an institution's population. Paroling authorities use state laws and information from courts and other criminal justice agencies to make release decisions.

3 *Parole* is the conditional release of a prison inmate prior to sentence expiration with supervision in the community. The parole process of release begins in the courtroom when the judge sentences an offender to either a determinate or an indeterminate sentence. After serving a certain portion of his or her sentence, an offender is eligible for parole release. That aspect varies from state to state. If an inmate maintains good conduct for a certain amount of time preceding the parole hearing and is granted parole, he or she must live in accordance with specified rules and regulations in the community. If a parolee either violates the technical conditions of parole or commits a new crime, he or she may have parole revoked.

4 On January 1, 2010, 819,308 American adults were on parole, down 5,526 from one year earlier and the second year in a row that the nation's parole population declined. Eighty-eight percent are state parolees. The typical adult parolee is a white, non-Hispanic male, on mandatory parole and under active parole supervision for more than one year. His median age is 34, and he has an 11th-grade education. Women make up 12 percent of the parole population. The region with the highest number of parolees is the South, followed by the West, Northeast, and Midwest.

5 Parole may be revoked for a technical violation (failure to comply with one of the conditions of parole) or for a new offense violation (commission of a crime). Two-thirds of all parolees are rearrested within three years, typically within the first six months of release. Of the nearly 552,611 adults who exited parole in 2009, 185,550 (34 percent) were returned to prison either with a new sentence (26 percent), revocation (71 percent), or to receive treatment (less than 1 percent), up from 27,177 in 1980 and 160,000 in 1995.

6 This chapter discussed seven current issues in parole: inmate voting, reentry court, reintegration involving victims, abolition of parole, community policing and reentry, community-focused parole, and whether parole is a privilege or right. Only Maine and Vermont do not place any restrictions on the right to vote for people with felony convictions. Reentry court requires the parolee make regular court appearances for progress assessment. Reintegration involving victims encourages victims to educate offenders about the impact of the crime and generate remorse in the hope that they can change offender behavior in the future. Today, 16 states and the federal government have abolished discretionary release from prison by a parole board for all offenders. Another four states have abolished discretionary parole release for certain violent offenses or other crimes against a person. In community policing and reentry we find joint supervision of parolees by teams of police and parole officers. The goal of community-focused parole is to engage the community so the community engages parole. And finally, the U.S. Supreme Court made it clear that parole is a privilege, not a right.

KEY TERMS

clemency, p. 267

reprieve, p. 267

pardon, p. 267

parole, p. 268

discretionary release, p. 268

mandatory release, p. 268

parole eligibility date, p. 277

paroling authority, p. 278

salient factor score (SFS), p. 280

parolee, p. 280

nonrevocable parole (NRP), p. 288

reentry court, p. 298

QUESTIONS FOR REVIEW

1 Explain the history of parole development in the United States.

2 Outline how parole functions in the criminal justice system.

3 Describe parole and the parole decision-making process.

4 What can you infer from the characteristics of the parole population?

5 What do you think about the circumstances under which parole may be revoked?

6 Critique the current issues in parole.

THINKING CRITICALLY ABOUT CORRECTIONS

Reentry and Cognitive Transformation

When this chapter discussed parole success and failure, it quoted Dr. Bonita Veysey, who says that individual-level change is required before opportunities for work, reuniting families, and providing housing make a difference in a parolee's life. Others refer to this change as cognitive transformation. How can parole agencies help offenders achieve cognitive transformation and successful reentry?

Abolish Parole?

Sixteen states and the federal government have abolished discretionary parole board release from prison in favor of mandatory release. Another four states abolished it for certain violent offenses or other crimes against a person. Proponents of discretionary prison release argue that abandonment of discretionary release has a detrimental effect. They believe that parole boards serve a salutary function by requiring inmates to focus their efforts on successful reentry from prison to the community. They argue that without the prospect of discretionary prison release, inmates have fewer incentives for cognitive transformation and opportunities for work, reuniting with families, and housing. Critically examine the issues of this debate.

ON-THE-JOB DECISION MAKING

Nonrevocable Parole

To help your state reduce prison crowding and the money it spends on prisons, your parole agency decides it is going to study California's nonrevocable parole law and urge your state legislature to adopt something similar. Go to the California Department of Corrections and Rehabilitation Web site http://www.cdcr.ca.gov/. Click first Parole and then Non-Revocable Parole tabs. Study the eligibility criteria. Are there criteria you believe should be added to the list or possibly deleted? Defend your position to a legislative subcommittee on criminal justice.

Mentors and Offender Reentry

As chief parole officer in your area, write a two-page proposal recommending the involvement of mentors in offender reentry. Include what you believe are the advantages of mentoring for offender reentry and strategies for recruiting, training, and matching mentors with parolees.

For additional information, please see: www.mhhe.com/schmalleger6e

The Prison World

Part Four explores life inside prison

for inmates and staff, the legal challenges surrounding their roles and responsibilities, and the special needs of inmates who are elderly, infected with HIV or AIDS, or mentally or physically challenged.

Custodial staff are most directly involved in the daily work of managing the inmate population. The extent to which correctional officers share beliefs, values, and behaviors is largely a function of the correctional officer subculture and each individual's personality.

Prisoners, too, develop a subculture that helps them adjust to the self-doubt, reduced self-esteem, and deprivations they experience as a result of confinement. Inmate subculture is also based on the life experiences that prisoners bring with them when they enter confinement. One question that we try to answer concerns why men's prisoner subculture encourages isolation while women's prisoner subculture encourages relationships.

For a century, prisoners were considered civilly dead, and prisons operated entirely without court intervention. However, in 1970, the U.S. Supreme Court declared that, if states were going to operate prisons, they would have to do so according to the dictates of the Constitution. Since then, prisoners have reclaimed many of their conditional rights under the U.S. Constitution. But today, changes in state and federal statutes have slowed the pace of prisoners' rights cases, and the U.S. Supreme Court seems to have become less sympathetic to prisoners' civil rights claims.

Inmates with special needs—those who are elderly, suffer from HIV, AIDS, or other chronic diseases, or are mentally or physically challenged—present significant problems for correctional managers. Special needs inmates may be more prone to violence and disruption. They frequently require close monitoring to reduce the risk of suicide, and they may tax scarce medical resources and become targets of abuse by other inmates.

The preprison drug use and sexual activity of many prisoners has brought HIV, AIDS, and tuberculosis into jails and prisons. Managing these problems requires training in early detection, treatment, classification, staff education, and adequate funding. These problems are compounded by the fact that many prisoners have co-occurring physical and mental health problems.

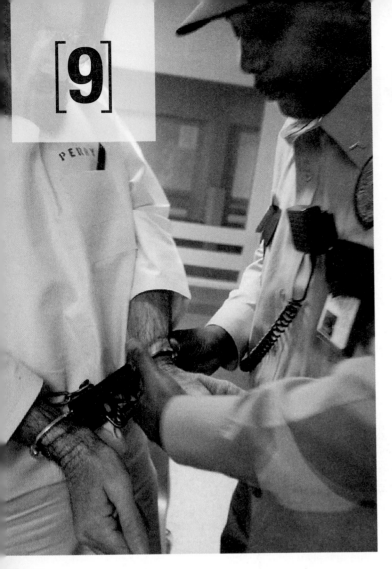

[9]

THE STAFF WORLD

Managing the Prison Population

CHAPTER OBJECTIVES

After completing this chapter you should be able to do the following:

1 List the staff roles within the organizational hierarchy of correctional institutions.

2 Identify the types of power available to correctional officers and list and describe the most common correctional officer personality types.

3 List and describe the seven correctional officer job assignments.

4 Identify five significant correctional staff issues.

5 Detail the nature of workplace corruption among correctional personnel and explain its causes.

6 Explain the impact that terrorism is having on prisons and on the operation of correctional institutions today.

> *Corrections is not a business where only one sex, race, religion, or type of person can succeed. It takes men and women of all races, religions, and color to create a dynamic and effective workforce to manage diverse inmates and solve the problems we face.*
>
> —Dora Schriro, former Missouri director of corrections

Recently, American Correctional Association (ACA) executive director James A. Gondles Jr. issued a special media statement titled "*Guard* Must Go."[1] Gondles was objecting to the use of the word *guard* by the media to describe correctional officers. "The role of correctional officers," said Gondles, "is to ensure that offenders complete their sentences in a way that sufficiently addresses the wide range of problems they often bring with them, while maintaining corrections' paramount duty—public safety."

Gondles pointed to the fact that the ACA had taken action to eliminate the word *guard* from its publications, advertisements, and announcements more than 20 years earlier and that doing so had now become official policy. Rejecting the term *guard,* Gondles said, was necessary "because it implies that the job is inherently passive and demands nothing more than watching locked-up inmates. Nothing could be further from the truth."

In contrast, said Gondles, the term *correctional officer* "embodies the diverse skills officers employ each day—communication skills, cultural awareness, first aid, suicide prevention, emergency response preparedness, program and service delivery, and the proper use of force."

James A. Gondles Jr., American Correctional Association executive director. Why does Director Gondles reject use of the word guard in describing today's correctional officers?

THE STAFF HIERARCHY

Practically speaking, a prison of any size has a number of different staff roles—each with its own unique set of tasks. **Roles** are the normal patterns of behavior expected of those holding particular social positions. **Staff roles** are the patterns of behavior expected of correctional staff members in particular jobs. Eventually, many people internalize the expectations others have of them, and such expectations can play an important part in their self-perceptions.

Ideally, today's correctional staff members have four main goals:

1. to provide for the security of the community by incarcerating those who break the law;
2. to promote the smooth and effective functioning of the institution;
3. to ensure that incarceration is secure but humane; and
4. to give inmates the opportunity to develop a positive lifestyle while incarcerated and to gain the personal and employment skills they need for a positive lifestyle after release.[2]

Prison staff are organized into a hierarchy, or multilevel categorization, according to responsibilities. An institution's hierarchy generally has a warden or superintendent at the top and correctional officers at a lower level. A typical correctional staff hierarchy includes the following:

- administrative staff (wardens, superintendents, assistant superintendents, and others charged with operating the institution and its programs and with setting policy);

roles

The normal patterns of behavior expected of those holding particular social positions.

staff roles

The patterns of behavior expected of correctional staff members in particular jobs.

- clerical personnel (record keepers and administrative assistants);
- program staff (psychologists, psychiatrists, medical doctors, nurses, medical aides, teachers, counselors, caseworkers, and ministers—many of whom contract with the institution to provide services);
- custodial staff (majors, captains, lieutenants, sergeants, and correctional officers charged primarily with maintaining order and security);
- service and maintenance staff (kitchen supervisors, physical plant personnel, and many outside contractors); and
- volunteers (prison ministry, speakers, and other volunteers in corrections).

custodial staff

Those staff members most directly involved in managing the inmate population.

program staff

Those staff members concerned with encouraging prisoners to participate in educational, vocational, and treatment programs.

Organizational charts graphically represent the staff structure and the chain of command within an institution. An organizational chart for a typical medium-to-large correctional institution is shown in Exhibit 9–1. **Custodial staff** are most directly involved in managing the inmate population through daily contact with inmates. Their role is to control prisoners within the institution. **Program staff,** on the other hand, are concerned with encouraging prisoners to participate in educational, vocational, and treatment programs. Custodial staff, who make up over 60 percent of

EXHIBIT 9–1   Organizational Chart of a Typical Midsize or Large Correctional Institution

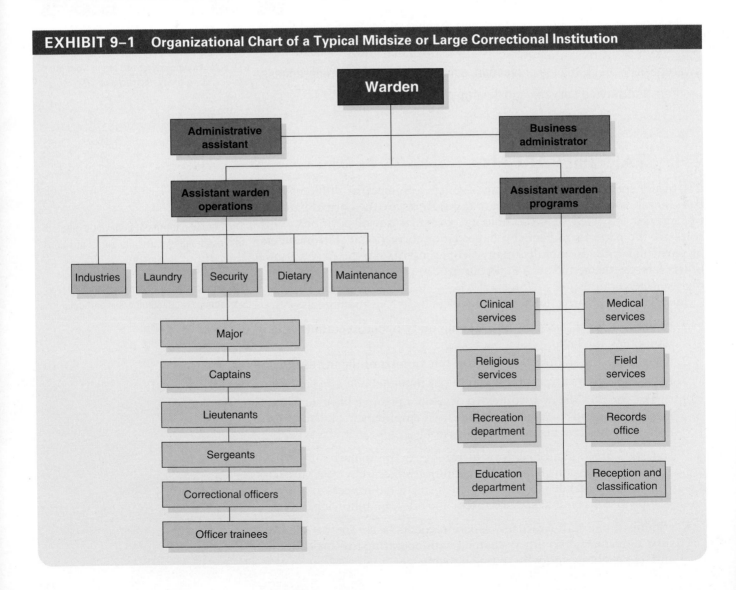

prison personnel, are generally organized in a military-style hierarchy, from assistant or deputy warden down to correctional officer. Program staff generally operate through a separate organizational structure and have little in common with custodial staff.

To a great extent, prison management involves managing relationships—among employees, between employees and inmates, and among inmates. Prisons are unique in that most of the people in them (the inmates) are forced to live there according to the terms of their sentence; they really do not want to be there. Such a situation presents tremendous challenges. The people on the front lines dealing around the clock with such challenges are the correctional officers.

THE CORRECTIONAL OFFICER— THE CRUCIAL PROFESSIONAL

Although security is still the major concern, correctional officers today are expected to perform a variety of other tasks. As one commentator has said,

> Correctional officers have more responsibilities [now] than in the past and their duty is no longer to merely watch over the prisoners. They now have to play several roles in keeping prisoners in line. They have to be "psychiatrists" when prisoners come to them with their problems, and they have to be "arbitrators and protectors" when inmates have complaints or problems with each other, while still watching out for their own safety. In these situations, the wrong decision could offend someone and start a riot. This makes correctional officers "prisoners" of the daily emotional and physical moods of the inmates.[3]

Don Josi and Dale Sechrest explain it this way: "Correctional officers today must find a balance between their security role and their responsibility to use relationships with inmates to change their behavior constructively. They routinely assume numerous essential yet sometimes contradictory roles (e.g., counselor, diplomat, caretaker, disciplinarian, supervisor, crisis manager), often under stressful and dangerous conditions."[4]

Josi and Sechrest then go on to say, "These divergent and often incompatible goals can prove problematic; role conflict, role diffusion, and role ambiguity may be difficult if not impossible to avoid."[5]

Bases of Power

Correctional officers rely on a variety of strategies to manage inmate behavior. After surveying correctional officers in five prisons, John Hepburn identified five types of officers' power, according to the bases on which they rest: legitimate power, coercive power, reward power, expert power, and referent power.

Legitimate Power Correctional officers have power by virtue of their positions within the organization. That is, they have formal authority to command. As Hepburn says, "The prison guard has the right to exercise control over prisoners by virtue of the structural relationship between the position of the guard and the position of the prisoner."[6]

Coercive Power Inmates' beliefs that a correctional officer can and will punish disobedience give the officer coercive power. Many correctional officers use coercive power as a primary method of control.

Securing an inmate in preparation for a trip back to his cell. Correctional officers need to elicit inmates' cooperation to effectively carry out their custodial duties. What are some techniques officers might use?

gain time

Time taken off an inmate's sentence for participating in certain positive activities such as going to school, learning a trade, and working in prison.

Reward Power Correctional officers dispense both formal and informal rewards to induce cooperation among inmates. Formal rewards include assignment of desirable jobs, housing, and other inmate privileges. Correctional officers are also in a position to influence parole decisions and to assign good-time credit and **gain time** to inmates. Informal rewards correctional officers use include granting special favors and overlooking minor infractions of rules.

Expert Power Expert power results from inmates' perceptions that certain correctional officers have valuable skills. For example, inmates seeking treatment may value treatment-oriented officers. Inmates who need help with ongoing interpersonal conflicts may value officers who have conflict-resolution skills. Such officers may be able to exert influence on inmates who want their help.

Referent Power Referent power flows from "persuasive diplomacy." Officers who win the respect and admiration of prisoners—officers who are fair and not abusive—may achieve a kind of natural leadership position over inmates.

Some years before Hepburn's study, Gresham Sykes wrote that correctional officers' power can be corrupted through inappropriate relationships with inmates.[7] Friendships with prisoners, as well as indebtedness to them, can corrupt. According to Sykes, staff members who get too close to inmates and establish friendships are likely to find their "friends" asking for special favors. Similarly, officers who accept help from inmates may one day find that it is "payback time." In difficult or dangerous situations, help may be difficult to decline. In such cases, staff members must be careful not to let any perceived indebtedness to inmates influence their future behavior.

The Staff Subculture

Prison life is characterized by duality. An enormous gap separates those who work in prisons from those who live in them. This gap has a number of dimensions. One is that staff members officially control the institution

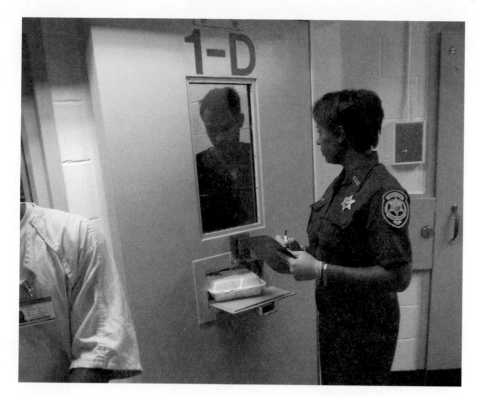

A correctional officer talks with an inmate. Effective communication is one way of overcoming the differences in beliefs, values, and behaviors between inmates and prison staff. What barriers to communication might such differences create?

and enforce the rules by which inmates live. Other formal and informal differences exist, including differences in background, values, and culture. Primarily, however, the relationship between correctional officers and inmates can be described as one of structured conflict.[8]

Structured conflict is a term that highlights the tensions between prison staff members and inmates that arise out of the correctional setting. In one sense, the prison is one large society in which the worlds of inmates and staff bump up against one another. In another sense, however, the two groups keep their distance from each other—a distance imposed by both formal and informal rules. Conflict arises because staff members have control over the lives of inmates, and inmates often have little say over important aspects of their own lives. The conflict is structured because it occurs within the confines of an organized institution and because, to some extent, it follows the rules—formal and informal—that govern institutional life.

Both worlds—inmate and staff—have their own cultures. Those cultures are generally called *subcultures* to indicate that both are contained within and surrounded by a larger culture. One writer has defined **subculture** as the beliefs, values, behavior, and material objects shared by a particular group of people within a larger society.[9] That is the definition we will use. The subcultures of inmates and correctional officers exist simultaneously in any prison institution. The beliefs, values, and behavior that make up the **staff subculture** differ greatly from those of the inmate subculture. Additionally, staff members possess material objects of control, such as keys, vehicles, weapons, and security systems.

Kauffman has identified a distinct correctional officer subculture within prisons.[10] Those beliefs, values, and behaviors set correctional officers apart from other prison staff and from inmates. Their beliefs and values form an "officer code," which includes the following:

- Always go to the aid of an officer in distress.
- Do not "lug" (bring in for inmate use) drugs or other contraband.

structured conflict

The tensions between prison staff members and inmates that arise out of the correctional setting.

subculture

The beliefs, values, behavior, and material objects shared by a particular group of people within a larger society.

staff subculture

The beliefs, values, and behavior of staff. They differ greatly from those of the inmate subculture.

- Do not rat on other officers.
- Never make a fellow officer look bad in front of inmates.
- Always support an officer in a dispute with an inmate.
- Always support officer sanctions against inmates.
- Do not be a "white hat" or a "goody two-shoes."
- Maintain officer solidarity in dealings with all outside groups.
- Show positive concern for fellow officers.

Gender and Ethnicity of Correctional Officers

The American Correctional Association (ACA) says that most correctional personnel at state and local levels are white males.[11] Two-thirds of female custodial and administrative staff members are white (see Exhibit 9–2). Thirty-two percent of corrections personnel are members of minority groups. Of these, most are black.

Ideally, the ethnic breakdown of correctional staff should closely approximate the ethnic breakdown of the population of the United States. According to the U.S. Census Bureau,[12] out of a 2000 population of about 282 million people, 34.7 million (12.3 percent) were black, 35.3 million (12.5 percent) were Hispanic, and 13.1 million (4.7 percent) were members of other minority groups. Exhibit 9–3 compares ethnic groups as a proportion of prison personnel and as a proportion of the U.S. population.

From Exhibit 9–3, it is easy to see that blacks are overrepresented among correctional personnel. Although only 12 percent of the U.S. population, they account for 21 percent of the correctional workforce. Hispanics are

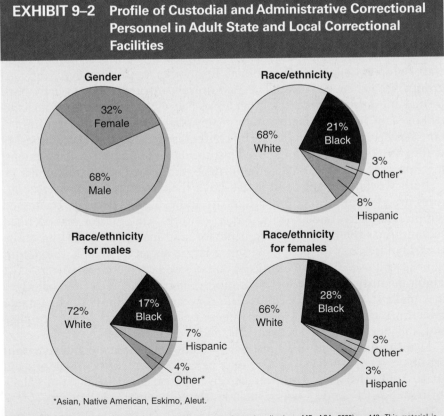

EXHIBIT 9–2   Profile of Custodial and Administrative Correctional Personnel in Adult State and Local Correctional Facilities

*Asian, Native American, Eskimo, Aleut.

Source: American Correctional Association, *Vital Statistics in Corrections* (Lanham, MD: ACA, 2000), p. 143. This material is copyrighted. The reproduction, distribution, or inclusion in other publications of this material is prohibited without prior written permission from the American Correctional Association, Alexandria, VA.

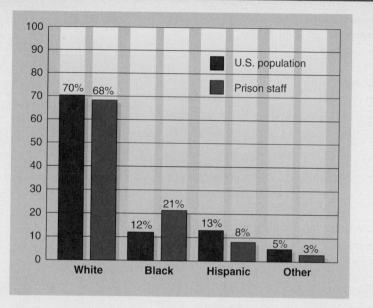

EXHIBIT 9–3   Ethnic Groups as a Proportion of the U.S. Population and as a Proportion of Prison Staff

Sources: American Correctional Association, *Vital Statistics in Corrections* (Lanham, MD: ACA, 2000). Population statistics derived from U.S. Bureau of the Census, *National Population Estimates of the United States: July 1, 2001* (Washington, DC: U.S. Government Printing Office, 2001), retrieved June 20, 2003, from http://eire.census.gov/popest/data/national/tables/asro/US-EST2001-ASRO-04.pht.

underrepresented (accounting for 13 percent of the country's population and just 8 percent of the correctional workforce), as are other minorities (5 percent of the population, 3 percent of correctional staff). Whites, on the other hand, are slightly underrepresented.

Twenty-seven percent of federal Bureau of Prison employees (8,097) are female.[13] About 20 percent of correctional staff members in federal institutions are black. In juvenile facilities, females make up slightly more than 42 percent of the correctional workforce.

The American Correctional Association also says that approximately 13 percent of all correctional staff positions are supervisory (i.e., above the level of sergeant). Females hold 16 percent of all supervisory positions but fewer positions at the level of warden or superintendent.[14] Consult the Appendix: Careers in Corrections at the Online Learning Center Web site for the steps involved in career planning, developing employability and job readiness, and finding a job in corrections.

Correctional Officer Personalities

The staff subculture contributes to the development of **correctional officer personalities.** Those personalities reflect the personal characteristics of the officers as well as their modes of adaptation to their jobs and institutional conditions, the requirements of staff subculture, and institutional expectations.[15] We will next explore the common personality types that have been identified.[16]

The Dictator The dictator likes to give orders and seems to enjoy the feeling of power that comes from ordering inmates around. Correctional officers with dictator personalities are often strongly disliked by prisoners and may face special difficulties if taken hostage during a prison uprising.

correctional officer personalities

The distinctive personal characteristics of correctional officers, including behavioral, emotional, and social traits.

First Lieutenant Gary F. Cornelius

Programs Director • Fairfax County Adult Detention Center • Fairfax County Office of the Sheriff • Fairfax, Virginia

First Lieutenant Gary Cornelius is programs director with the Fairfax County Adult Detention Center in Fairfax, Virginia. He has held this position since October 1995 but has been with the sheriff's department since 1978.

He earned his bachelor of arts and social sciences with a focus in criminal justice from Edinboro State College in Pennsylvania in 1974. He later completed specialized police courses at the Northern Virginia Criminal Justice Academy Basic Police School as well as the U.S. Secret Service. He is a former officer of the Uniformed Division of the Secret Service.

Lieutenant Cornelius is also the author of five books, including *The Twenty Minute Trainer, The Correctional Officer: A Practical Guide,* and *The Art of the Con: Avoiding Offender Manipulation.* "Writing gives me a chance to share what I have learned and to learn new concepts through research," he says.

His duties include the development and oversight of inmate programs, ranging from recreation to rehabilitation and substance abuse. He oversees inmate education, manages volunteers and college interns, and supervises other staff members in charge of inmate recreation.

Cornelius says he enjoys watching his efforts—and the efforts of his teammates—result in positive changes. "Probably the best thing about my job is working with good people who care about both jail security and making programs work for the betterment of inmates," he says. "The most difficult aspect is convincing staff of the need for programs, rehabilitative efforts, and volunteers. And trying to get through the old-fashioned 'jailhouse mentality.'"

What are the skills that serve him best in his day-to-day affairs? "Tolerance for others' points of view, patience, not giving up, and diplomatic people skills when dealing with both civilians and sworn staff," he says.

> *"Having staff work together on an idea and watching operations improve is one of the best parts of this job."*

Some dictator officers cross the line by personally degrading inmates under their charge through the use of profanity or racist language or by displays of religious and ethnic intolerance. Certain aspects of the dictator personality may lead to illicit and illegal activities by forcing inmates to provide sexual and other favors.

The Friend The correctional officer who tries to befriend inmates is often a quiet, retiring, but kind individual who believes that close friendships with inmates will make it easier to control the inmates and the work environment. Inmates, however, usually try to capitalize on friendships by asking for special treatment, contraband, and the like.

The Merchant Merchant-personality correctional officers (also called *rogue officers* or *rotten apples*) set themselves up as commodity providers to the inmate population. If an inmate needs something not easily obtained in prison, the merchant will usually procure it—at a cost. Often such behavior is a violation of institutional rules, and it can lead to serious violations of the law as the merchant correctional officer smuggles contraband into the institution for the "right price." We will discuss correctional officer corruption in more detail later in this chapter.

The Turnkey Turnkey officers do little beyond the basic requirements of their position. A turnkey usually interacts little with other officers and does the minimum necessary to get through the workday. Unmotivated and bored, the turnkey may be seeking other employment. Some turnkey officers have become disillusioned with their jobs. Others are close to retirement.

The Climber The correctional officer who is a climber is set on advancement. He or she may want to be warden or superintendent one day and is probably seeking rapid promotion. Climbers are often diligent officers who perform their jobs well and respect the corrections profession. Climbers who look down on other officers, however, or attempt to look good by making coworkers look bad, can cause many problems within the institution.

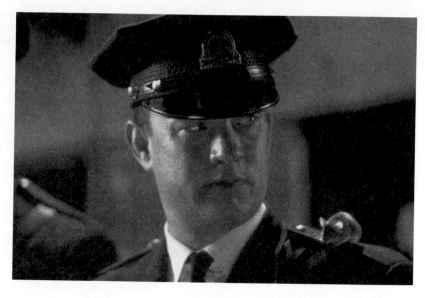

Tom Hanks as a correctional officer in The Green Mile. *This chapter describes a variety of correctional officer personality types. Which do you think is the most common? The least?*

The Reformer The reformer constantly finds problems with the way the institution is run or with existing policies and rules. He or she always seems to know better than anyone else and frequently complains about working conditions or supervisors.

The Do-Gooder The do-gooder is another type of reformer—one with a personal agenda. A devoutly religious do-gooder may try to convert other correctional officers and inmates to his or her faith. Other do-gooders actively seek to counsel inmates, using personal techniques and philosophies that are not integrated into the prison's official treatment program.

Although the personalities described here may be exaggerated, their variety suggests that correctional officer personalities result from many influences, including the following:

- general life experiences;
- biological propensities;
- upbringing;
- staff subculture;
- working conditions; and
- institutional expectations and rules.

CORRECTIONAL OFFICER JOB ASSIGNMENTS

Seven different correctional officer roles or job assignments have been identified.[17] They are classified by their location within the institution, the duties required, and the nature of the contact with inmates. The seven types are as follows:

1. **Block officers** are responsible for supervising inmates in housing areas. Housing areas include dormitories, cell blocks, modular living units, and even tents in some overcrowded prisons. Safety and security are the primary concerns of block officers. Conducting counts, ensuring the orderly movement of prisoners, inspecting personal property, overseeing inmate activity, and searching prisoners are all part of the block officer's job. Block officers also lock and

block officers

Those responsible for supervising inmates in housing areas.

Ms. Eagle, a teacher in the Delaware Prison Life Skills Program, invited family members twice to come to the prison. On one occasion, she had the family members and students break into small groups—I wasn't in the same group with my mom—to discuss what various family members should do when someone comes home very late at night. Then each group reported its solutions to the whole class. In my group, a mom actually had a son who was going through this problem. The groups help each family to see how other families would solve the problem, and they also help everyone to see that everyone has the same problems.

An inmate in the Delaware Prison Life Skills Program

---

unlock cells and handle problems that arise within the living area. Block officers are greatly outnumbered by the inmates they supervise. Hence, if disturbances occur, block officers usually withdraw quickly to defensible positions within the institution.

work detail supervisors

Those who oversee the work of individual inmates and inmate work crews.

2. **Work detail supervisors** oversee the work of individual inmates and inmate work crews assigned to jobs within the institution or outside it. Jobs assigned to inmates may include laundry, kitchen, and farm duties, as well as yard work and building maintenance. Work detail supervisors must also keep track of supplies and tools and maintain inventories of materials. Prison buildings are sometimes constructed almost exclusively with the use of inmate labor—creating the need for large inmate work details. On such large projects, supervising officers usually work in conjunction with outside contractors.

industrial shop and school officers

Those who ensure efficient use of training and educational resources within the prison.

3. **Industrial shop and school officers** work to ensure efficient use of training and educational resources within the prison. Such resources include workshops, schools, classroom facilities, and associated equipment and tools. These officers oversee inmates who are learning trades, such as welding, woodworking, or automobile mechanics or who are attending academic classes. Ensuring that students are present and on time for classes to begin, protecting the school and vocational instructors, and securing the tools and facilities used in instruction are all part of the job of these officers. The officers work with civilian instructors, teachers, and counselors.

yard officers

Those who supervise inmates in the prison yard.

4. **Yard officers** supervise inmates in the prison yard. They also take charge of inmates who are (1) moving from place to place, (2) eating, or (3) involved in recreational activities. Like other officers, yard officers are primarily concerned with security and order maintenance.

administrative officers

Those who control keys and weapons and sometimes oversee visitation.

5. **Administrative officers** are assigned to staff activities within the institution's management center. They control keys and weapons. Some administrative officers oversee visitation. As a result, they have more contact with the public than other officers do. Many administrative officers have little, if any, contact with inmates.

perimeter security officers

Those assigned to security (or gun) towers, wall posts, and perimeter patrols. These officers are charged with preventing escapes and detecting and preventing intrusions.

6. **Perimeter security officers** (also called *wall post officers*) are assigned to security (or gun) towers, wall posts, and perimeter patrols. They are charged with preventing escapes and detecting and preventing intrusions (such as packages of drugs or weapons thrown over fences or walls from outside). Perimeter security can become a routine job because it involves little interaction with

other officers or inmates and because relatively few escape attempts occur. Newer institutions depend more heavily on technological innovations to maintain secure perimeters, requiring fewer officers for day-long perimeter observation.

7. **Relief officers** are experienced correctional officers who know and can perform almost any custody role in the institution. They are used to temporarily replace officers who are sick or on vacation or to meet staffing shortages.

relief officers

Experienced correctional officers who know and can perform almost any custody role within the institution, used to temporarily replace officers who are sick or on vacation or to meet staffing shortages.

CORRECTIONAL STAFF ISSUES

Gender and Staffing

On a pleasant Sunday morning a few years ago, a high-custody female inmate at the Chillicothe (Missouri) Correctional Center was sitting in a dormitory, drinking her morning coffee. Having a good time, surrounded by friends, the inmate began laughing. Soon, however, the laughter turned to choking. Unable to breathe, she turned blue. Correctional officer Lisa Albin rushed to her side and found her hanging onto her bed, unable to speak. Albin remained calm as she applied the Heimlich maneuver to the inmate. After three attempts, the trapped coffee cleared the inmate's windpipe and she began breathing again. After the incident, the inmate wrote a letter of thanks to the superintendent, saying, "If it had not been for Mrs. Albin I could have very well died in that room. She literally saved my life and I will be forever grateful to her and for the training she received."[18]

Literature and films almost invariably portray correctional officers as "tobacco-chewin', reflective sunglasses-wearin', chain-gang-runnin', good ol' boys."[19] Today's officer generally defies this stereotype, and women working in corrections have helped erode this otherwise persistent myth (Exhibit 9–4).

EXHIBIT 9–4 | **American Correctional Association**

Public Correctional Policy on Employment of Women in Corrections

The American Correctional Association affirms the value of women employees and supports equal employment opportunities for women in adult and juvenile correctional agencies. To encourage the employment of women in corrections, correctional agencies should:

- ensure that recruitment, selection, and promotional opportunities for women are open and fair;
- assign female employees duties and responsibilities that provide career development and promotional opportunities equivalent to those provided to other employees;
- provide all levels of staff with appropriate training on developing effective and cooperative working relationships between male and female correctional personnel;
- provide all levels of staff with appropriate education and training in cross-gender supervision; and
- conduct regular monitoring and evaluation of affirmative action practices and be proactive in achieving corrective actions.

Female correctional officers competently perform day-to-day custodial tasks. Are there any areas of a male prison that female correctional officers should be barred from supervising?

Like most women working in male-dominated professions, female correctional officers face special problems and barriers—many of which are rooted in sexism. Prisons are nontraditional workplaces for women. As a consequence, female correctional officers—especially those working in men's prisons—often find themselves in a confusing situation. As one author explains it, "On the one hand, to be female is to be different, an outsider. On the other hand, female guards have much in common with and are sympathetic to their male peers as a result of their shared job experience."[20]

According to studies, female correctional officers typically say that they perform their job with a less aggressive style than men.[21] This difference in style seems due mostly to differences in life experiences and to physical limitations associated with women's size and strength. Life experiences prepare most women for helping roles rather than aggressive ones. As a consequence, women are more likely to rely heavily on verbal skills and intuition. Female correctional officers use communication rather than threats or force to gain inmate cooperation. They tend to talk out problems. Studies have also found that female correctional officers rely more heavily than male correctional officers on established disciplinary rules when problems arise. Male staff members, on the other hand, are more likely to bully or threaten inmates to resolve problems.

According to research, 55 percent of female officers indicate that their primary reason for taking a job in corrections is an interest in human service work or in inmate rehabilitation.[22] In striking contrast, only 20 percent of male officers give this as their primary reason for working in corrections.

Perhaps as a result of such attitudes, gender makes a dramatic difference in the number of assaults on correctional officers. One national survey of maximum-security prisons in 48 states, the District of Columbia, and the Federal Bureau of Prisons showed that female officers were assaulted only about one-fourth as often as male officers.[23]

Although female correctional officers may take a different approach to their work, the skills they use complement those of male staff members. As one expert writes, "Women may humanize the workplace in small ways by establishing less aggressive relationships with inmates."[24]

Studies also show that male officers, by and large, believe that female officers competently perform day-to-day custodial tasks. Most male staff members are "pro-woman," meaning that they applaud the entry of women into the corrections profession.[25] Many male correctional officers do express concerns about women's ability to provide adequate backup in a crisis, however. It is important to note that the need to use force in prison is relatively rare and that officers generally do not respond to dangerous situations alone. Nonetheless, some female correctional officers report that in emergencies, some male officers adopt a protective, chivalrous attitude toward them. Women generally report that they resent such "special treatment" because it makes them feel more like a liability than an asset in an emergency.

Another issue concerning women in today's workplace is personal and sexual harassment. Studies show that few female correctional officers personally experience unwanted touching or other forms of sexual harassment. The forms of harassment women most commonly experience are physical (nonsexual) assaults, threats, unfounded graphic sexual rumors about them, and demeaning remarks from peers, inmates, and supervisors.[26]

A fair amount of harassment is tolerated in the correctional officer subculture. It is viewed as customary and is often accorded little significance. The response to any form of harassment, however, is determined by the officer experiencing it. He or she can tolerate it, resist it, or report it. Female correctional officers, however, express fear of being ostracized if they complain.

One writer has made the following recommendations for improving the acceptance of women as correctional officers:[27]

1. Require managers and guards to undergo training to sensitize them to the concerns of women working in prisons.
2. Establish a strong policy prohibiting sexual and personal harassment with significant consequences for harassers.
3. Screen male job candidates for their ability and willingness to develop relationships of mutual respect with female colleagues.

Stress

In all occupational categories, employers estimate that more than 25 percent of all reported sick time is due to stress.[28] Stress—tension in a person's body or mind resulting from physical, chemical, or emotional factors—appears to be more commonplace in prison work than in many other jobs. Nonetheless, it is often denied. As one early writer on correctional officers' stress observed, "Most officers . . . try to disguise the toll taken by the job and make the best of what is often a frustrating situation. Though not immune to the pressures of the workplace, these officers project a tough, steady image that precludes sharing frustrations with other coworkers or family members. Some of these officers may be particularly vulnerable to stress."[29]

Correctional officers frequently deny that they are under stress, fearing that admitting to feelings of stress might be interpreted unfavorably. One correctional lieutenant, an 11-year veteran, reported repeatedly observing new correctional employees succumbing to the effects of stress by becoming depressed or turning to alcohol for relief. Although she wanted to intervene, she said she "couldn't" because "no one in law enforcement is allowed to show any emotion or signs of weakness."[30]

In misguided attempts to deal with the effects of stress, many COs resort to self-medication or other tactics to deal with feelings that they may not readily admit, even to themselves. Unfortunately, such ineffective methods do not alleviate the pressure and may instead make it worse.

Stress among correctional officers has a number of sources. Feelings of powerlessness, meaninglessness, social isolation, and self-estrangement all contribute to stress. Some authors have identified job alienation as the major source of stress among COs.[31] Correctional officers rarely participate in setting the rules they work under and the policies they enforce; as a result, they may feel alienated from those policies and rules and from those who create them.

stress

Tension in a person's body or mind, resulting from physical, chemical, or emotional factors.

One of the most interesting aspects of my job as a corrections officer is the fact that it allows me to interact with people from different socioeconomic backgrounds. Some are at the top of their careers and others at the bottom, not sure who they are, or where they're going. The job has taught me respect for the law and has given me the opportunity to progress as an individual.

As a corrections officer I consider myself to be a professional. I don't think of myself as a guard but as someone who has been given the responsibility of rebuilding, retraining, and restoring. Being a corrections officer takes enthusiasm, dedication, and a desire to help people overcome difficult situations. We have good listening skills and the ability to interpret and respond to changes in inmates' behavior. As a corrections officer, I work to rehabilitate inmates who have behavior problems, and to manage them by talking calmly, rather than threatening them with violence or punishment.

I'm also a field-training officer (FTO) and I teach new officers how to do the job right; be fair but firm, show compassion but not weakness, be able to react and respond quickly, treat people with respect, give the inmates someone to look up to, and finally, conduct yourself in a manner that creates and maintains respect for you and your department.

Marquis L. Westry
Corrections Corporal
Mobile County Metro Jail
Mobile, Alabama

Other factors that create stress follow:

- work overload;
- family conflict;[32]
- lack of autonomy or control over one's life;
- threat of job loss;
- role conflict or role ambiguity;
- conflicts with coworkers;
- conflicts with supervisors;
- problematic organizational culture;
- difficult working environment;
- insufficient resources to reach one's goals;
- inadequate job training;
- overqualification for one's current position;
- supervisors' problematic attitudes; and
- changes in the work environment.

Symptoms of stress can be psychological, behavioral, or physical. Psychological symptoms of stress include anxiety, irritability, mood swings, sadness or depression, low self-esteem, emotional withdrawal, and hypersensitivity (to others and to what others say). Behavioral symptoms of stress include an inability to make decisions, increased interpersonal conflict, blocked creativity and judgment, poor memory, lowered productivity, and difficulty concentrating. The physical symptoms of stress include insomnia, headaches, backaches, gastrointestinal disturbances, fatigue, high blood pressure, and frequent illnesses.

Poorer job performance and exhaustion are the results of stress. When stress reaches an unbearable level, burnout can occur. Burnout, a severe reaction to stress, is "a state of physical and emotional depletion that results from the conditions of one's occupation."[33]

Studies have shown that a person's ability to tolerate stress depends on the frequency, severity, and types of stressors confronted.[34] Stress tolerance also depends on a number of personal aspects, including past experiences, personal values and attitudes, sense of control, personality, residual stress level, and general state of health.

Authorities suggest a number of techniques for avoiding or reducing job stress. Among them are the following:[35]

1. Communicate openly. Tell people how you feel.
2. Learn not to harbor resentment, not to gossip, and to complain less often.
3. Learn to feel confident in your skills, your values and beliefs, and yourself.
4. Develop a support system. Close friends, pets, social activities, and a happy extended family can all help alleviate stress.
5. Be a good and conscientious worker, but don't become a workaholic.
6. Learn to manage your time and do not procrastinate.
7. Make it a habit to get a good night's sleep.
8. Exercise regularly.
9. Watch your diet. Avoid excessive fat, sugars, salt, red meat, and caffeine.
10. Learn some relaxation exercises such as self-affirmation, mental imaging, deep breathing, stretching, massage, or yoga.
11. Try to have fun. Laughter can combat stress quite effectively.
12. Spend time cultivating self-understanding. Analyze your feelings and your problems—and recognize your accomplishments.
13. Set goals and make plans. Both bring order and direction to your life.

One especially effective strategy for coping with job stress is to develop clear and favorable role definitions. According to J. T. Dignam and colleagues, "Officers who have more opportunities for receiving assistance and goal clarification from supervisors and coworkers [are] less likely to experience role ambiguity than those for whom such support is not available or sought. Further, the risk of burnout or other deleterious consequences of occupational stress may be reduced for those who are 'insulated' by social support."[36]

Similarly, another group of researchers found that "support from colleagues or supervisors may be one of the most important factors ameliorating stress in the workplace."[37] The same researchers also found that when correctional officers felt "rewarding companionship" with fellow correctional officers, they reported fewer stressful events (even when objective measures showed an actual rise in such events). Most researchers agree that candidates need more extensive and thorough training to prepare them for the psychological and sociological consequences of becoming correctional officers.

> **Talking about CORRECTIONS**
>
> **OFFICER STRESS**
> Visit *Live Talk* at **Corrections .com** (**www.justicestudies .com/talking06**) and listen to the program "Officer Stress," which relates to ideas discussed in this chapter.

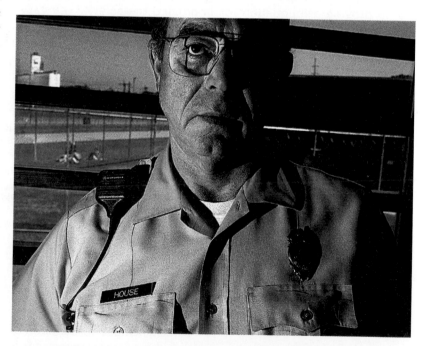

Stress is an unhappy outcome of the correctional officer's job. How does on-the-job stress arise in the correctional officer's role? How might it be reduced?

Staff Safety

Staff safety is a major stressor for individual correctional officers and a primary management concern for correctional administrators. Safety planning

COMMISSION ON SAFETY AND ABUSE IN AMERICA'S PRISONS: CORRECTIONAL LEADERSHIP

"What ultimately makes a correctional institution work has to do with the hearts and minds and spirits of those who people it, not with bricks and mortar, shatterproof glass, pre-fab cells or organizational charts.

—Sheriff Michael Ashe, Hampden County, Massachusetts

The public rarely thinks about people in prison and thinks even less often about the men and women who manage and work in these same facilities. When we do look closely, what we see is a poorly understood profession that shoulders tremendous responsibilities and faces incredible challenges, usually without adequate resources and support. Yet this labor force is responsible for operating jails and prisons that must safely and humanely accommodate an estimated 13.5 million people annually. When corrections professionals fail to meet the demands of the job, for whatever reason, they endanger prisoners and officers alike and, at the extreme, cripple entire facilities. The failures are felt beyond the facility walls when officers and prisoners return to their families and their communities.

The recommendations for reform outlined in this box are intended to acknowledge and build on the underlying strengths of the workforce and its leaders in two broad ways: by improving the institutional culture in correctional facilities and by supporting corrections professionals at every level. Progress in these areas would provide a foundation for improving the safety and effectiveness of America's prisons and jails.

The relationship between prisoners and corrections officers is at the very core of the culture of confinement. Too often, that relationship is uncaring and antagonistic, punctuated by moments of overt hostility, aggression, and physical violence.

Today there are statewide efforts in places as far apart as Oregon, Arizona, Massachusetts, and Maryland to change the fundamental culture of prisons. Corrections administrators in these states understand that an "us-versus-them" mentality ultimately jeopardizes the safety and health of prisoners and staff and over time harms the families and communities to which prisoners and staff belong. Their efforts at culture change should be supported, imitated, and improved upon so that no one has to live or work in a dehumanizing environment and so that our correctional facilities serve the public's interests. The culture of these institutions cannot change, however, unless efforts are made to build a highly qualified workforce and to cultivate and support great leaders.

The following three recommendations suggest ways to meet all of these goals:

Promote a Culture of Mutual Respect

Create a positive culture in jails and prisons grounded in an ethic of respectful behavior and interpersonal communication that benefits prisoners and staff.

Recruit and Retain a Qualified Corps of Officers

Enact changes at the state and local levels to advance the recruitment and retention of a high-quality, diverse workforce and otherwise further the professionalism of the workforce.

Support Today's Leaders and Cultivate the Next Generation

Governors and local executives must hire the most qualified leaders and support them politically and professionally, and corrections administrators must, in turn, use their positions to promote healthy and safe prisons and jails. Equally important, we must develop the skills and capacities of middle-level managers, who play a large role in running safe facilities and are poised to become the next generation of senior leaders.

Source: Excerpts from *Confronting Confinement: A Report of the Commission on Safety and Abuse in America's Prisons* by John J. Gibbons and Nicholas de B. Katzenbach, June 2006. Copyright © 2006, Vera Institute of Justice. Note: The full 126-page report, *Confronting Confinement: A Report of the Commission on Safety and Abuse in America's Prisons,* can be accessed on the Internet at www.prisoncommission.org.

must include consideration of the following elements (adapted, in part, from studies of staff safety needs in both juvenile[38] and adult[39] institutions):

- a functionally designed physical plant that limits inmate movement and incorporates technologically advanced security systems, perimeter barriers, and rooms, doors, and locks;

- a behavior management system that establishes clear guidelines for acceptable behavior, reward systems to reinforce expected behavior, and disciplinary systems to discourage unacceptable behavior;
- appropriate staff and inmate relationships (in particular, staff must be aware of, and prepared to respond to, the dangers posed by prison gangs);
- policies and procedures, published in a manual and distributed to staff and supervisors, that support consistent implementation of rules and regulations and prevent the risk of staff letdowns resulting from excessive routine;
- shift scheduling that ensures a mutually supportive balance of senior and junior staff because a sound mix of age and experience facilitates the achievement of inmate control while providing opportunities for on-the-job development of junior officers by senior officers;
- effective supervision at every level;
- comprehensive staff training that ensures all correctional officers and their supervisors know every rule, regulation, policy, and procedure that affects their particular job (if, as the saying goes, knowledge is power, such training is key to empowering the staff to maintain a controlled, safe environment); and
- development of, and training for, a sound action plan that addresses all contingencies.

In addition to advocating thorough planning as just outlined, Stewart and Brown[40] urge continuing research to identify what works, what doesn't work, and emerging trends in staff safety. In particular, they recommend development of a safety program tailored to the needs of correctional officers nationwide. It should be modeled, they suggest, on safety programs designed for police officers, probation officers, and other officers in law enforcement.

Job Satisfaction

High levels of stress reduce the satisfaction correctional officers get from their jobs. In a sad indictment of the corrections field, a 1996 study found that correctional officers were significantly different from most other groups of correctional employees. "They showed the lowest levels of organizational commitment, possessed the highest levels of skepticism about organizational change, were the least positive about careers in corrections and the rehabilitation of offenders, possessed the lowest levels of job satisfaction, were the least involved in their jobs, and were described as having the poorest work habits and overall job performance."[41] In a separate study, correctional supervisors and managers were found to have much higher levels of job satisfaction and professionalism.[42]

One reason for the difference in job satisfaction between supervisory personnel and those on the front lines of corrections work is that correctional officers often feel alienated from policymaking.[43] As one writer puts it, "when looking at the atmosphere and environment of a state or federal prison, it would seem obvious what correction personnel like least about working there: surveys of personnel who resign or quit show that their biggest problems are with supervisory personnel rather than inmates."[44]

Correctional officers' job satisfaction appears to be tied to the amount of influence they feel they have over administrative decisions and policies. Officers who feel they have some control over the institution and over their jobs seem much more satisfied than officers who believe they have no control. Hence, it appears that correctional officers' job satisfaction can be greatly enhanced by caring administrators who involve the officers in policymaking.

For some correctional officers, the perception that their profession suffers a generally poor public image[45] further reduces their job satisfaction. Compared to local and state police officers and agents of the various federal law enforcement organizations, correctional officers may be viewed as the "poor relations" of the law enforcement family. As one researcher wrote, "Most people do not know of a child who says, I want to be a correctional officer when I grow up."[46]

Media portrayals of correctional officers exacerbate the situation. Movies and television often depict COs as lowly qualified "guards" (considered a derogatory title; "guards work at Macy's and banks")[47] whose primary function seems to be abusing prisoners. Correctional officers "believe they are seen as brutes, only a shade better than the people behind bars."[48] Consequently, COs have a difficult time overcoming these images as they attempt to convey the significance and professional demands of their positions to civic leaders and the public.[49]

There is evidence, however, that job satisfaction among correctional officers is rising. The rise may be partly due to increasing awareness of what correctional officers find most important in the work environment. Recent studies have identified the most important determinants of job satisfaction among correctional officers as (1) working conditions, (2) the level of work-related stress, (3) the quality of working relationships with fellow officers, and (4) length of service.[50]

In one of the most significant studies to date, treatment-oriented correctional staff reported far higher levels of job satisfaction than did custody-oriented staff.[51] The study was of survey data collected from 428 Arizona correctional service officers (CSOs) and 118 correctional program officers (CPOs). Job satisfaction was significantly greater among the human-services-oriented CPOs than among the traditional-custody-oriented CSOs. The findings suggest that additional attention should be given to enhancing and enriching the duties of correctional officers, extending their control over and involvement in prisoners' activities, and redefining their roles more as service workers than as control agents.

Determinants of job satisfaction appear to differ for male and female correctional officers. One study found that the quality of working relationships with other officers, the amount of stress experienced at work, the length of service as a correctional officer, and educational level were all positively related to job satisfaction for males.[52] Women officers, on the other hand, appeared to place more emphasis on the quality of working relationships with all other correctional officers (not just the ones with whom they worked) and tended to be happier in prisons at lower security levels. Other studies have related higher job satisfaction among white female officers to the officers' positive evaluation of the quality of supervision. In other words, white female correctional officers tend to be happier in prisons that they believe are well run.[53]

Professionalism

A common difference between a professional and a nonprofessional is that a professional learns every aspect of the job whereas a nonprofessional avoids the learning process and often considers it a waste of time. Professionals seek to prevent mistakes at all costs, but if they occur, the professional does not let them slide; nonprofessionals tend to ignore or hide them. A professional tries to be great, whereas a nonprofessional just tries to get by at what he or she does.

Professionalism is commitment to a set of agreed-upon values aimed at improving the organization while maintaining the highest standards of

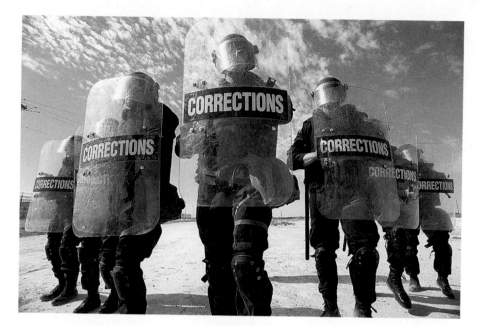

excellence and dissemination of knowledge.[54] In addition to having knowledge and skills, professionals must present humanistic qualities: selflessness, responsibility and accountability, leadership, excellence, integrity, honesty, empathy, and respect for coworkers and prisoners.

Professional correctional organizations that operate at the national level, such as the American Correctional Association (discussed in Chapter 1, and mentioned elsewhere in this chapter), have qualified and well-trained employees, well-run professional development departments, and well-developed standards of conduct. Such organizations provide the support needed for operating agencies and individual correctional facilities to achieve fairness in handling inmates and correctional personnel while documenting and addressing issues that may arise in inmate and employee conduct. These organizations also help to define common sets of values that establish the tone and climate for day-to-day operations in correctional facilities.

The vision provided by professional organizations helps build confidence that employees will be professional and will have integrity, respect, the ability to engage in teamwork, the motivation for continued learning, and commitment to the profession.

According to William Sondervan, former commissioner of the Maryland Division of Corrections and previous director of professional development for the American Correctional Association, professionalism in corrections is vitally important to the integrity, safety, and security of correctional agencies and institutions.[55] Corrections professionalism, says Sondervan, requires that any correctional organization establish or clarify the following three elements:

- **purpose**—the reason for an organization's existence;
- **mission**—what is done to support the organization's purpose; and
- **vision**—the planned future direction of the organization.

Together, says Sondervan, purpose, mission, and vision provide a roadmap for the development of professionalism within an organization.

Exhibit 9–5 depicts the formal mission, vision, and goals of the Maryland Department of Public Safety and Correctional Services, and Exhibit 9–6 lists the values and beliefs that support the department's mission and vision statements.

purpose

The reason for an organization's existence.

mission

That which is done to support an organization's purpose.

vision

The planned future direction of an organization.

EXHIBIT 9–5	Maryland Department of Public Safety and Correctional Services, Mission and Vision Statement

Mission

The Department of Public Safety and Correctional Services protects the public, its employees, and detainees and offenders under its supervision.

Vision

The Maryland Department of Public Safety and Correctional Services will be nationally recognized as a department that believes its own employees are its greatest strength, and values the development of their talents, skills, and leadership.

We will be known for dealing with tough issues like gang violence, by capitalizing on the strength of interagency collaboration.

We will be nationally known as the department that takes responsibility for the greatest of problems, and moves quickly and quietly to bring about successful change.

The Department of Public Safety and Correctional Services will be known as one of the national leaders in the development and use of technology through system interoperability.

Others will look to this department for its effective leadership and evidence-based practices.

We will be known for our belief in the value of the human being, and the way we protect those individuals, whether they are members of the public, our own employees, those we are obligated to keep safe and in custody, or victims of crime.

The Maryland Department of Public Safety and Correctional Services will be known as an organization that focuses on its mission and takes care of its people.

Source: Maryland Department of Public Safety and Correctional Services (DPSCS) available at http://www.dpscs.state.md.us/aboutdpscs/ (accessed July 24, 2011).

EXHIBIT 9–6	Maryland Division of Correction Values
Integrity	We are a principle-based organization. We recognize and respect the dignity of all individuals. We strive for and expect honesty, truth and respect in our service to customers and stakeholders.
Dedication	We are committed to fulfilling our mission by serving our customers and stakeholders with concern and sensitivity under challenging circumstances.
Teamwork and Communication	We value results-oriented teamwork as an essential tool to accomplish our mission. We encourage open, effective communication throughout the Division to efficiently integrate our internal and external partnerships.
Public Trust and Confidence	We value public trust and confidence. We strive to assure our citizens that we are good stewards of the public's resources entrusted to us. Through community outreach, we hope to inspire public confidence in the **P**rofessional **R**esults **I**n **D**aily **E**fforts **(PRIDE)** we take in our duties.
Professionalism	We value effective leadership and strive for impartiality and fairness in the workplace. We encourage personal and professional development. We recognize and reward dedication and commitment to competence and the highest standards of achievement.

Source: Maryland Department of Public Safety and Correctional Services (DPSCS); available at http://www.dpscs.state.md.us/aboutdpscs/ (accessed July 24, 2011).

International Association of Correctional Officers: The Correctional Officer's Creed

To speak sparingly . . . to act, not argue . . . to be in authority through personal presence . . . to correct without nagging . . . to speak with the calm voice of certainty . . . to see everything and to know what is significant and what not to notice . . . to be neither insensitive to distress nor so distracted by pity as to miss what must elsewhere be seen. . . .

To do neither that which is unkind nor self-indulgent in its misplaced charity . . . never to obey the impulse to tongue lash that silent insolence which in time past could receive the lash . . . to be both firm and fair . . . to know I cannot be fair simply by being firm, nor firm simply by being fair. . . .

To support the reputations of associates and confront them without anger should they stand short of professional conduct . . . to reach for knowledge of the continuing mysteries of human motivation . . . to think; always to think . . . to be dependable . . . to be dependable first to my charges and associates and thereafter to my duty as employee and citizen . . . to keep fit . . . to keep forever alert . . . to listen to what is meant as well as what is said with words and with silences.

To expect respect from my charges and my superiors yet never to abuse the one for abuses from the other . . . for eight hours each working day to be an example of the person I could be at all times . . . to acquiesce in no dishonest act . . . to cultivate patience under boredom and calm during confusion . . . to understand the why of every order I take or give. . . .

To hold freedom among the highest values though I deny it to those I guard . . . to deny it with dignity that in my example they find no reason to lose their dignity . . . to be prompt . . . to be honest with all who practice deceit that they not find in me excuse for themselves . . . to privately face down my fear that I not signal it . . . to privately cool my anger that I not displace it on others . . . to hold in confidence what I see and hear, which by telling could harm or humiliate to no good purpose . . . to keep my outside problems outside . . . to leave inside that which should stay inside . . . to do my duty.

Source: Copyright © 2000 Bob Barrington.

Ethical Dilemma 9–1: There are reports that find sexual misconduct is a problem in prisons for women. These reports state that male staff victimize women inmates. Should only female staff work in prisons for women? What are the issues? For more information go to Ethical Dilemma 9–1 at www.justicestudies.com/ethics06.

Ethical Dilemma 9–2: Stress among correctional staff is widespread, and your facility has a stress-reduction program. You are feeling very stressed, but you are afraid to take advantage of the program, thinking it may reflect poorly on you at promotion time. Do you participate in the program anyway? For more information go to Ethical Dilemma 9–2 at www.justicestudies.com/ethics06.

Ethical Dilemmas for every chapter are available online.

While the development of an appropriate mission statement is vital at the organizational level, the development of a sense of personal ethics is crucial to daily on-the-job success. In support of personal ethics, the International Association of Correctional Officers has published a Correctional Officer's Creed (see the Ethics and Professionalism box), which summarizes the duties and responsibilities of a correctional officer.

Officer Corruption

In 2009, 24 members of the violent Black Guerrilla Family prison gang were arrested in Maryland following a seven-month long investigation into the smuggling of contraband into Baltimore-area prisons.[56] Four of those arrested were state correctional officers. Using bribes, threats, and promised favors, leaders of the gang were able to coerce the officers into smuggling contraband to imprisoned associates and extorting money from other inmates. The favored prisoners feasted on salmon, shrimp, and other delicacies while smoking expensive cigars and drinking premium vodka. Using smuggled cell phones, they were able to arrange for attacks on witnesses and rival gang members living outside the prison. One of

> **Talking about CORRECTIONS**
>
> **DEDICATION TO THE FIELD**
>
> Visit *Live Talk* at **Corrections.com** (**www.justicestudies.com/talking06**) and listen to the program "Dedication to the Field," which relates to ideas discussed in this chapter.

the corrupt officers, a woman who played a central role in facilitating the gang's illegal activities, is reported to have provided sexual favors for inmates in return for money.

In another incident that apparently stemmed from correctional officer corruption, 76-year-old convicted mass murderer Charles Manson was caught with a mobile phone in his prison cell at California's Corcoran State Prison in February 2011. It was the second time in two years that officers had confiscated a phone from Manson during a cell search. Manson, who is serving a life sentence, was convicted in the 1969 murders of seven people, including pregnant actress Sharon Tate.

Legislative analysts for the state of California estimate that more than 10,000 cell phones made their way into California prisons in 2010.[57] According to those same analysts, prison employees are the main source of smuggled phones that end up in the hands of prisoners. A recent California state inspector general's report detailed the story of how a single corrections officer made $150,000 a year smuggling phones to inmates. Although his activities were eventually discovered and he was fired, he was not criminally prosecuted because it is not against the law in California to take cell phones into prisons—even though it is a violation of prison rules for inmates to possess them. To address the issue more fully in 2011, state senator Alex Padilla called on California Governor Jerry Brown to mandate the periodic searching of correctional officers reporting for work.

Other forms of correctional officer corruption and job malfeasance include the misuse of confidential information, drinking and abusing drugs while on duty, sleeping on duty, unnecessary roughness or brutality against inmates, racism, and filing false disciplinary reports on inmates. A small number of sadistic people may even be attracted to working in corrections because they think it will provide them the opportunity to physically abuse others. Pre-employment personality inventories, background checks, and face-to-face pre-employment interviews are all crucial in preventing such people from obtaining positions of authority in correctional facilities.

Contributing to the problem of corruption among correctional staff is low pay—especially in some jurisdictions. "If someone is desperate to make ends meet and someone offers them $2,100 to smuggle in a cell phone, it's a hell of a temptation," says Brian Olsen, executive director of a Texas labor union that represents Texas correctional officers.[58]

While all examples used in this chapter come from state correctional agencies, a look at statistics seems to show that corruption among federal correctional personnel is relatively rare. A 2008 Congressional report by the U.S. Department of Justice's (DOC) Office of the Inspector General (OIG), for example, found only 238 likely cases of criminal misconduct by BOP employees.[59] Given that the number of persons employed by the BOP in that year was approximately 36,000, BOP misconduct levels appear to be among the lowest in government.

THE IMPACT OF TERRORISM ON CORRECTIONS

In 2009, convicted terrorist Kevin James, 32, was sentenced in federal court in Santa Ana, California, to 16 years in prison. James had pleaded guilty in 2007 to conspiracy to wage war against the United States[60] and had been accused of plotting terrorist attacks on Jewish and military targets throughout California. Among those targets were Los Angeles International Airport, the Israeli Consulate, and Army recruiting centers.

Those who investigated James's background found that he had formed an Islamic terrorist group in California's Tehachapi Prison in 1997. While serving a 10-year sentence for robbery, James joined the Nation of Islam—a traditional American Islamic faith. Soon, however, he became engaged with a fringe group of Sunni Muslims at Tehachapi. The group, known as *Jamiyyat Ui Islam Is Saheeh* (the Assembly of Authentic Islam, or JIS), operates today throughout prisons in California where it is known as a radical Islamist prison gang, or STG. JIS advocates attacks on enemies of the Islamic faith, the U.S. government, Jews, "infidels," and supporters of Israel.

Convicted terrorist Kevin James answers questions put to him during an exclusive TV interview with producer and investigative journalist Eric Longabardi. James is the founder of Jamiyyat Ui Islam Is Saheeh *(the Assembly of Authentic Islam). Does terrorist recruiting take place in prison?*

Eventually, James took control of JIS and began distributing a handwritten manifesto known as the JIS Protocol, in which he justified the killing of infidels. Following transfer to the maximum-security California State Prison in Sacramento, James recruited more inmates to join JIS and used soon-to-be paroled inmates to recruit additional members outside of prison. Using smuggled letters and phone calls, James communicated his plans for terrorist attacks to recruits on the outside.

Mark Hamm, a criminal justice professor who studied the case of Kevin James, notes that "prisoner radicalization grows in the secretive underground of inmate subcultures through prison gangs and extremist interpretations of religious doctrines that inspire ideologies of intolerance, hatred and violence."[61] Hamm also learned that "prisoners are radicalized through a process of one-on-one proselytizing by charismatic leaders." Especially vulnerable, says Hamm, are those inmates who no longer have contact with their families and are angry and embittered by their circumstances. "I discovered," says Hamm, "that charismatic leadership was more important than other commonly cited factors associated with prisoner radicalization."[62]

Because of their marginal social status, inmates may be particularly vulnerable to recruitment by terrorist organizations. According to Chip Ellis, research and program coordinator for the National Memorial Institute for the Prevention of Terrorism, "Prisoners are a captive audience, and they usually have a diminished sense of self or a need for identity and protection. They're usually a disenchanted or disenfranchised group of people, [and] terrorists can sometimes capitalize on that situation."[63] Ellis points out that inmates can be radicalized in a variety of ways, including exposure to extremist literature and other radical inmates, as well as through anti-U.S. sermons delivered during religious services.

The FBI says that al-Qaeda continues to actively recruit followers inside American correctional institutions. Islamic terrorists are keenly aware of the 9,600 Muslims held in the federal prison system and see them as potential converts. "These terrorists seek to exploit our freedom to exercise religion to their advantage by using radical forms of Islam to recruit operatives," says FBI counterterrorism chief John Pistole.[64] "Unfortunately," notes Pistole, "U.S. correctional institutions are a valuable venue for such radicalization and recruitment."

Anti-Terrorism Planning

Not only must today's prison administrators be concerned about inmate involvement in terrorist activities, they must also think about and plan for the impact of the terrorism event within their facilities and within the communities in which their facilities are located. Moreover, incarcerating those who have been convicted of acts of terrorism presents new challenges for correctional administrators. For example, Sheik Omar Abdel-Rahman, spiritual leader for many terrorists, including Osama bin Laden, is now serving a life sentence in a U.S. federal penitentiary for conspiring to assassinate former Egyptian President Hosni Mubarak and blow up five New York City landmarks in the 1990s. Speculation that the sheik continues to motivate terrorist acts against the United States gained credibility when his attorney was sentenced to 28 months in prison in 2006 for passing illegal communications between Abdel-Rahman and an Egyptian-based terrorist organization known as the Islamic Group.[65] Another convicted terrorist, September 11 conspirator Zacarias Moussaoui, also known as the 20th hijacker, is serving a life sentence at the federal administrative maximum facility in Florence, Colorado. Moussaoui's fellow prisoners, housed on what has come to be known as "Bomber's Row," include al-Qaeda shoe bomber Richard Reid; Ramzi Yousef, mastermind of the 1993 World Trade Center bombing; seven of Yousef's accomplices; Ahmed Ressam, who was arrested at the Canadian border with explosives he intended to use to bomb Los Angeles International Airport; four men convicted in the 1998 bombing of U.S. embassies in Africa; and Abdul Hakim Murad, convicted in a 1995 al-Qaeda plan to bomb 12 airplanes during a two-day period.

Jess Maghan, former training director for the New York City Department of Corrections and now the director of the Forum for Comparative Corrections and professor of criminal justice at the University of Illinois at Chicago, points out that "the interaction of all people in a prison (staff, officers, and inmates) can become important intelligence sources."[66] Moreover, says Maghan, the flow of information between inmates and the outside world needs to be monitored in order to detect attack plans—especially when prisons house known terrorist leaders or group members. Covert information, says Maghan, can be passed through legal visits (where people conveying information may have no idea of its significance), sub rosa communications networks in prisons that can support communications between inmates and the outside world, and prison transportation systems.

In 2005, the Institute for the Study of Violent Groups at Sam Houston State University charged that Wahhabism—the most radical form of Islam—was being spread in American prisons by clerics approved by the Islamic Society of North America (ISNA). ISNA is one of two organizations that the Federal Bureau of Prisons uses to select prison chaplains to serve inmates in its facilities.[67] "Proselytizing in prisons," said the institute, "can produce new recruits with American citizenship." An example might be Chicago thug Jose Padilla, aka Abdulla al-Mujahir, who converted to Islam after exposure to Wahhabism while serving time in a Florida jail. Authorities claim Padilla intended to contaminate a U.S. city with a radiological dirty bomb. In 2007, Padilla was convicted of federal terrorism charges. Similarly, convicted shoe bomber Richard Reid converted to radical Islam while in an English prison before planning his attack on an American Airlines flight from Paris to Miami.[68]

A few years after the attacks of 9/11, the Office of the Inspector General of the U.S. Department of Justice released a review of the practices used by the Federal Bureau of Prisons in selecting Muslim clergy to minister to inmates in the bureau's facilities. The report concluded that the primary threat of radicalization came not from chaplains, contractors, or volunteers but from inmates. According to the

Muslim prisoners at prayer in a Virginia correctional facility. Radicalized inmates of any faith can represent a threat to facility security. What connection might exist between radicalized inmates and criminals or terrorist groups on the outside?

report, "Inmates from foreign countries politicize Islam and radicalize inmates, who in turn radicalize more inmates when they transfer to other prisons."[69] The report also identified a form of Islam unique to the prison environment called "Prison Islam."[70] The report said that Prison Islam is a form of Islam that is used by gangs and radical inmates to further unlawful goals. It adapts itself easily to prison values and promotes the interests of the incarcerated. Prison Islam was found to be especially common in institutions where religious services are led by lay *Mullahs* (spiritual leaders, who are often inmates)—a practice made necessary by a lack of Muslim chaplains. The report recommended that "the BOP can and should improve its process for selecting, screening, and supervising Muslim religious services providers. We recommend," said the report, that "the BOP take steps to examine all chaplains', religious contractors', and religious volunteers' doctrinal beliefs to screen out anyone who poses a threat to security." Echoing those sentiments is Mark Hamm, who says that the most significant thing that prison administrators can do to undercut terrorist recruitment in prison is to hire chaplains who have been properly vetted. "Without them," says Hamm, "radicalized prisoners are free to operate on their own, independent of religious authority to ensure moderation and tolerance."[71]

In 2006, the U.S. Justice Department's Office of the Inspector General released another report—this one critical of BOP inmate mail monitoring procedures, saying that "the threat remains that terrorist and other high-risk inmates can use mail and verbal communications to conduct terrorist or criminal activities while incarcerated." The report was based on findings that three convicted terrorists had been able to send 90 letters to Islamic extremists in the Middle East in 2005, praising Osama bin Laden. The report noted the fact that the BOP does not have the needed number of translators proficient in Arabic who are able to read inmate mail and said that budget restrictions do not allow for the reading of all incoming and outgoing mail.[72]

The threat of a terrorist act being carried out by inmates within a prison or jail can be an important consideration in facility planning and management. Of particular concern is the possibility of bioterrorism. A concentrated population such as exists within a prison or jail would be highly susceptible to rapid transmission of the ill effects from such an attack.[73]

Significant recommendations for addressing the terrorist threat within correctional institutions come from Y. N. Baykan, a management specialist with the Maryland Division of Correction. Baykan says that no successful strategies are being used today to control radical Islamist influences in American prisons and suggests the following:[74]

- Prison administrators must realize that the threat of transnational terrorism in American facilities is real.
- Radical Islamic groups should be seen as sophisticated social networks rather than gangs.
- Prison authorities must evaluate existing policies and strategies, looking closely at the roles and backgrounds of chaplains and volunteers and the rules governing religious conversions.

Indonesian terrorist Imam Samudra in prison in Bali awaiting execution. Samudra was convicted of masterminding terrorist bombings that killed 202 people in 2002 and was sentenced to death by firing squad. While imprisoned, Samudra wrote a jailhouse manifesto on the funding of terrorism through cyberfraud. He was executed by firing squad in 2008. How might incarcerated terrorists constitute a threat to the facilities in which they are housed? To the rest of society?

- Meetings of radicals should be closely monitored as should incoming propaganda.
- Prison staff should be taught to understand political Islam and should use information-management solutions that involve cutting-edge collection, storage, and analysis of data.
- Prison authorities must follow what is happening in other countries and learn from it.
- Threat information should be shared by all stakeholders, including state and federal systems and other law enforcement agencies.

As the United States faces more and more threats of terrorism, it is likely that the issues identified here will take on greater significance for correctional facilities throughout the nation and around the world.

REVIEW AND APPLICATIONS

SUMMARY

1 There is a hierarchy of staff positions from warden (or superintendent) at the top down to correctional officer and correctional officer trainee. A typical correctional staff includes (1) administrative staff, (2) clerical personnel, (3) program staff, (4) custodial staff, (5) service and maintenance staff, and (6) volunteers.

2 The types of power available to correctional officers are legitimate power, coercive power, reward power, expert power, and referent power. Correctional officer personality types discussed in this chapter are (1) the dictator, (2) the friend, (3) the merchant, (4) the turnkey, (5) the climber, (6) the reformer, and (7) the do-gooder.

3 The seven correctional officer assignments are (1) block officers, (2) work detail supervisors, (3) industrial shop and school officers, (4) yard officers, (5) administrative officers, (6) perimeter security officers (also called *wall post officers*), and (7) relief officers.

4 The five significant correctional staff issues discussed in this chapter are (1) gender-related concerns, (2) correctional officer stress, (3) staff safety, (4) job satisfaction among those working in corrections, and (5) professionalism.

5 Some correctional officers become corrupt, and serious corruption can threaten the security of the institution. Greed, the desire for sexual gratification, and a lack of professionalism can all contribute to corruption among corrections personnel.

6 Today's prison administrators and corrections personnel must be vigilant against the threat of terrorism and must guard against terrorist activities from within the institution and from outside.

KEY TERMS

roles, p. 311
staff roles, p. 311
custodial staff, p. 312
program staff, p. 312
gain time, p. 314
structured conflict, p. 315
subculture, p. 315
staff subculture, p. 315

correctional officer personalities, p. 317
block officers, p. 319
work detail supervisors, p. 320
industrial shop and school officers, p. 320
yard officers, p. 320
administrative officers, p. 320

perimeter security officers, p. 320
relief officers, p. 321
stress, p. 323
purpose, p. 329
mission, p. 329
vision, p. 329

QUESTIONS FOR REVIEW

1 What staff roles does the hierarchy of a typical correctional institution include?

2 According to John Hepburn, what are five bases of the power that correctional officers use to gain inmate compliance?

3 What are the seven correctional officer job assignments?

4 Five significant correctional staff issues discussed in this chapter are (1) officer gender; (2) stress; (3) staff safety; (4) job satisfaction; and (5) professionalism.

5 How might correctional officers become corrupt? What kinds of activities might corrupt officers engage in?

6 Briefly explain the impact that terrorism is having on prisons and prison administration.

THINKING CRITICALLY ABOUT CORRECTIONS

Prison Rape

James Gilligan, MD, contends that rape in prisons is "an intrinsic and universal part of the punishments that our government metes out to those whom it labels as 'criminal.' "[75] In essence, Gilligan suggests, prison administrators passively employ inmate-on-inmate rape as a management tool to control the prisoner population.

Dr. Gilligan bases his charge on three contentions:

First, the relevant legal authorities, from judges to prosecutors who send people to prison, to the prison officials who administer them, are all aware of the existence, the reality, and the near-universality of rape in the prisons. Indeed, this is one reason that many conscientious judges are extremely reluctant to send anyone to prison except when they feel compelled to, either by the violence of the crime or, as is increasingly true, by laws mandating prison sentences even for nonviolent crimes, such as drug offenses.

Second, the conditions that stimulate such rapes (the enforced deprivation of other sources of self-esteem, respect, power, and sexual gratification) are consciously and deliberately imposed upon the prison population by the legal authorities.

Third, all these authorities tacitly and knowingly tolerate this form of sexual violence, passively delegating to the dominant and most violent inmates the power and authority to deliver this form of punishment to the more submissive and nonviolent ones, so that the rapists in this situation are acting as the vicarious enforcers of a form of punishment that the legal system does not itself enforce formally or directly.

Given that rape is universally acknowledged as a crime, Dr. Gilligan's charge is tantamount to an accusation of criminal conspiracy of monumental proportions.

1. Do you believe there is merit to Gilligan's claims?
2. If so, how would you propose addressing this issue?

The Staff Subculture

The staff culture is generally instilled in correctional officer trainees by more experienced officers and by work experiences. Socialization into the staff subculture begins on the first day of academy training or the first day of work (whichever comes first). One of the most important beliefs of the staff subculture is that officers should support one another.

Some people argue that the staff subculture is dangerous because it can sustain improper and even illegal behavior while forcing correctional officers to keep to themselves what they know about such behavior. Others, however, suggest that the staff subculture is a positive element in the correctional world. It is important to correctional officer morale, they claim. They also suggest that it "fills the gaps" in formal training by establishing informal rules to guide staff behavior and decision making in difficult situations. The staff subculture can provide informal "workarounds" when the formal requirements of a correctional officer's position seem unrealistic.

1. Do you think the staff subculture contributes to or detracts from meeting the goals of institutional corrections? Why?

2. Do you think the staff subculture benefits or harms the lives and working environment of correctional officers? Explain.

3. What functions of the staff subculture can you identify? Rate each of those functions as positive or negative for its role in meeting the goals of institutional corrections.

ON-THE-JOB DECISION MAKING

Use of Force

You are an experienced correctional officer assigned to yard duty. As you patrol the prison yard, watching inmates milling around and talking, a fellow officer named Renée approaches you. Renée was hired only a week ago, and she has gained a reputation for being inquisitive—asking experienced correctional officers about prison work. Renée walks up and says, "You know, I'm wondering what I should do. Yesterday I saw an officer push an inmate around because the guy didn't do what he asked. I don't know if the inmate didn't hear what was being said, or if he was just ignoring the officer." Renée looks at the ground. "What am I supposed to do in a situation like that? Should I have said something right then? Should I talk to the officer privately? Should I suggest to the officer that maybe the inmate didn't hear him? He knows we aren't supposed to use force on inmates unless it's really necessary. If I see him do this kind of thing again, should I report him?" Looking up, Renée says, "I know we're supposed to support each other in here. But what would you do?" How would you respond to Renée's questions?

Former CO Inmate

For about four years, Alex Kaminsky was one of your fellow correctional officers at the McClellan Correctional Facility. During your service together, you developed a friendship close enough to include social occasions outside the job, and your wives became good friends.

Two years ago, Kaminsky was convicted of dealing controlled substances to inmates and received a 12- to 20-year sentence. Upon your recent transfer to the Brownley Correctional Facility, you discover that Kaminsky is one of the inmates incarcerated there. He resides in one of the cell blocks that falls in your area of responsibility and works on the maintenance crew that you supervise.

1. Should you seek assignment to another area of the prison or seek to have Kaminsky transferred out, to prevent the necessity of having contact with him? Explain.
2. If Kaminsky approaches you, should you permit the reestablishment of a relationship that might (or might not) prove beneficial to his rehabilitation?

For additional information, please see: www.mhhe.com/schmalleger6e

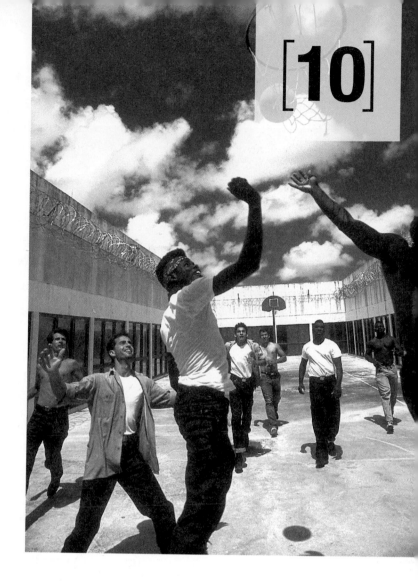

THE INMATE WORLD

Living Behind Bars

CHAPTER OBJECTIVES

After completing this chapter you should be able to do the following:

1 Explain what *inmate subculture* is and explain how it forms.

2 Know what is meant by the *prison code,* and be able to list some elements of it.

3 Explain what is meant by *prison argot.*

4 List some common roles that male inmates assume.

5 Describe some major differences between women's and men's prisons.

6 Compare some of the characteristics of female inmates with those of male inmates.

7 Explain how the social structure in women's prisons differs from that in men's prisons.

> *In prison, those things withheld from and denied to the prisoner become precisely what he wants most of all.*
>
> —Eldridge Cleaver, African-American author and activist

In 2011, sisters Jamie and Gladys Scott were set free from prison in Jackson, Mississippi, by Governor Haley Barbour, who suspended their life sentences for roles they played in a 1993 armed robbery that netted between $11 and $200.[1] One of the sisters, 38-year-old Jamie, was suffering from kidney failure, and her dialysis treatments were costing state taxpayers almost $200,000 a year—an issue that the governor said helped him reach a release decision. As a condition of the release, Gladys, 36, agreed to give her sister, Jamie, one of her kidneys in a transplant operation planned to occur after the release.

Evelyn Rasco, the sisters' mother, told reporters that she was excited about her daughters' homecoming. Rasco, who lives in Pensacola, Florida, the area to which the sisters will be paroled, said, "I just want to make sure everything's together for when my children get home." As the sisters' story demonstrates, not only do most prison inmates routinely interact with one another, attend classes and religious services, participate in skills-training programs, and even work behind bars but also they have family and personal relationships that extend beyond prison walls. This chapter will examine prison life, the inmate subculture, and the prison experience in general by looking first at men in prison and then at imprisoned women.

Gladys Scott, (left) and her sister Jamie Scott, confer with NAACP President Ben Jealous before a news conference in Jackson, Mississippi, in 2011. Why were the two released from prison?

MEN IN PRISON

As we have already seen, most state inmates are male, belong to racial or ethnic minority groups, are relatively young, and have been incarcerated for a violent offense. A recent Bureau of Justice Statistics study examined social, economic, and other characteristics of state inmates nationwide.[2] Highlights of that study are shown in Exhibit 10–1.

Prisons and other total institutions are small, self-contained societies with their own social structures, norms, and rules. While not entirely isolated, prison inmates are physically, emotionally, and socially restricted from anything more than minor participation in the surrounding society. As a consequence, they develop their own distinctive lifestyles, roles, and behavioral norms.

In his classic work *Asylums*, Erving Goffman used the phrase **total institution** to describe a place where the same people work, eat, sleep, and engage in recreation together day after day.[3] Life within total institutions is closely planned by those in control, and activities are strictly scheduled. Prisons, concentration camps, mental hospitals, and seminaries are all total institutions, said Goffman. They share many of the same characteristics—even though they exist for different purposes and house different kinds of populations. His words were echoed years later by Hans Toch, who noted that "prisons are 24-hour-a-day,

total institution

A place where the same people work, play, eat, sleep, and recreate together on a continuous basis. The term was developed by the sociologist Erving Goffman to describe prisons and other similar facilities.

EXHIBIT 10–1   National Profile of State Prison Inmates

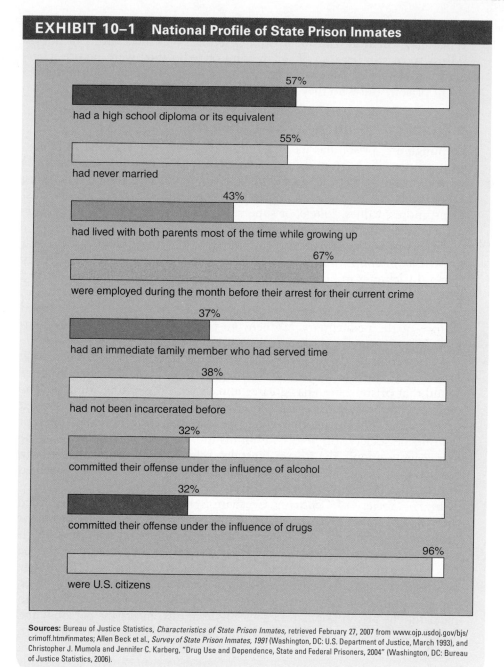

Sources: Bureau of Justice Statistics, *Characteristics of State Prison Inmates*, retrieved February 27, 2007 from www.ojp.usdoj.gov/bjs/crimoff.htm#inmates; Allen Beck et al., *Survey of State Prison Inmates, 1991* (Washington, DC: U.S. Department of Justice, March 1993), and Christopher J. Mumola and Jennifer C. Karberg, "Drug Use and Dependence, State and Federal Prisoners, 2004" (Washington, DC: Bureau of Justice Statistics, 2006).

year-in-and-year-out environments in which people are sequestered with little outside contact."[4]

Goffman also identified a number of modes of adaptation to prison life by which inmates attempt to adjust to the conditions around them. Some inmates, said Goffman, *convert* to life within institutions, taking on the staff's view of themselves and of institutional society. Others *withdraw*. Still others make attempts at *colonization*—meaning that they strike a balance between values and habits brought from home and those dictated by the social environment of the prison. Finally, some inmates *rebel*, rejecting the demands of their surroundings and often ending up in trouble with authorities. As Victoria R. Derosia of Castleton State College points out in her book *Living Inside Prison Walls*, some people "will make it through incarceration relatively unscathed and move on to a better life as a rehabilitated (or habilitated) citizen, while others will repeatedly fail at life outside prison. Offenders will successfully or poorly adjust to prison because of, or in spite of, who they were before incarceration, who they were while in prison, what they chose to do or not to do in prison, and who they want to become once released."[5]

What Is the Inmate Subculture?

Although any prison has its own unique way of life or culture, it is possible to describe a general inmate subculture that characterizes the lives of inmates in correctional institutions nationwide. The **inmate subculture** (also called the *prisoner subculture*) can be defined as "the habits, customs, mores, values, beliefs, or superstitions of the body of inmates incarcerated in correctional institutions."[6]

Prisoners are socialized into the inmate subculture through a process known as *prisonization*. The concept of **prisonization** was identified by Donald Clemmer in his book *The Prison Community*.[7] Clemmer defined *prisonization* as the process by which inmates adapt to prison society, and he described it as "the taking on of the ways, mores, customs, and general culture of the penitentiary." When the process of prisonization is complete, Clemmer noted, prisoners have become "cons."

In a further study of prisonization, Stanton Wheeler examined how prisoners adapted to life at the Washington State Reformatory.[8] Wheeler found that prisonization has greater impact with the passage of time. The prisonization of inmates, said Wheeler, can be described by a *U*-shaped curve. When an inmate first enters prison, the conventional values of the outside society still hold sway in his life. As time passes, however, he increasingly adopts the prison lifestyle. Wheeler also found that within the half-year before release, most inmates begin to demonstrate a renewed appreciation for conventional values.

In *The Society of Captives*,[9] Gresham Sykes described what he called the **pains of imprisonment**. According to Sykes, new inmates face major problems including the loss of liberty, a lack of material possessions, deprivation of goods and services, the loss of heterosexual relationships, the loss of personal autonomy, and a reduction in personal security. These deficits, Sykes noted, lead to self-doubts and reduced self-esteem. Prison society compensates for such feelings and reduces the pains of imprisonment for the prison population as a whole. It also meets the personal and social needs induced in inmates by the pains of imprisonment. In short, said Sykes, inmate society compensates for the losses caused by imprisonment, and it offers varying degrees of comfort to those who successfully adjust to it.

The inmate subculture can vary from one institution to another. Variations are due to differences in the organizational structure of prisons. Maximum-security institutions, for example, are decidedly more painful for inmates because security considerations require greater restriction of inmate freedoms and access to material items. As a result, the subcultures in maximum-security institutions may be much more rigid in their demands on prisoners than those in less secure institutions.

How Does an Inmate Subculture Form?

Early students of inmate subcultures, particularly Clemmer and Sykes, believed that such subcultures developed in response to the deprivations in prison life. This perspective is called **deprivation theory**. Shared deprivation gives inmates a basis for solidarity.[10]

---

inmate subculture (also *prisoner subculture*)

The habits, customs, mores, values, beliefs, or superstitions of the body of inmates incarcerated in correctional institutions; also, the inmate social world.

prisonization

The process by which inmates adapt to prison society; the taking on of the ways, mores, customs, and general culture of the penitentiary.

pains of imprisonment

Major problems that inmates face, such as loss of liberty and personal autonomy, lack of material possessions, loss of heterosexual relationships, and reduced personal security.

deprivation theory

The belief that inmate subcultures develop in response to the deprivations in prison life.

In some prisons, inmate subculture is fragmented as inmates form competing gangs and other groups along ethnic, racial, and geographic lines. How could the differences among such groups affect the order and stability of a prison?

A more recent perspective is that an inmate subculture does not develop in prison but is brought into prison from the outside world. Known as **importation theory**, this point of view was popularized by John Irwin and Donald R. Cressey.[11] It was further supported by the work of James Jacobs.[12] Importation theory holds that inmate society is shaped by factors outside prison—specifically, preprison life experiences and socialization patterns. Inmates who lived violent lives outside tend to associate with other violent inmates and often engage in similar behavior in prison.[13]

More realistic is the **integration model**, which acknowledges that both theories have some validity. According to the integration model, people undergo early socialization experiences. In childhood, some people develop leanings toward delinquent and criminal activity, acquiring—from peer groups, parents and other significant adults, television, movies, other mass media, and even computer and video games—values that support law-violating behavior. Those who become inmates are also likely to have experienced juvenile court proceedings and may have been institutionalized as juveniles. As a consequence, such people are likely to have acquired many of the values, much of the language, and the general behavioral patterns of deviant or criminal subcultures before entering adult prison.

The integration model also recognizes, however, the effects that the norms and behavioral standards of inmates in a particular prison have on those who are imprisoned. If a new inmate has already been socialized into a criminal lifestyle, the transition into the inmate subculture is likely to be easy. For some people, however—especially white-collar offenders with little previous exposure to criminal subcultures—the transition can be very difficult. The language, social expectations, and norms of prison society are likely to be foreign to them.

Norms and Values of Prison Society

Central to prison society is a code of behavior for all inmates. The **prison code** is a set of inmate rules antagonistic to the official administration and rehabilitation programs.[14] Violations of the code result in inmate-imposed

importation theory

The belief that inmate subcultures are brought into prisons from the outside world.

integration model

A combination of importation theory and deprivation theory. The belief that, in childhood, some inmates acquired, usually from peers, values that support law-violating behavior but that the norms and standards in prison also affect inmates.

prison code

A set of norms and values among prison inmates. It is generally antagonistic to the official administration and rehabilitation programs of the prison.

sanctions, ranging from ostracism to homicide. Sykes and Messinger have identified five main elements of the prison code:[15]

1. Don't interfere with the interests of other inmates. Never rat on a con. Don't have loose lips.
2. Don't lose your head. Don't quarrel with other inmates. Play it cool. Do your own time.
3. Don't exploit other inmates. Don't steal. Don't break your word. Pay your debts.
4. Don't whine. Be tough. Be a man.
5. Don't be a sucker. Don't trust the guards or staff. Remember that prison officials are wrong and inmates are right.

Prison Argot—The Language of Confinement

prison argot

The special language of the inmate subculture.

Prison argot is the special language of the inmate subculture. *Argot* is a French word meaning "slang." Prison society has always had its own unique language illustrated by the following argot-laden paragraph:

> The new con, considered fresh meat by the screws and other prisoners, was sent to the cross-bar hotel to do his bit. He soon picked up the reputation through the yard grapevine as a canary-bird. While he was at the big house, the goon squad put him in the freezer for his protection. Eventually, he was released from the ice-box and ordered to make little ones out of big ones until he was released to the free world. Upon release he received $100 in gate money, vowing never to be thrown in the hole or be thought of as a stool-pigeon again.[16]

Prison argot originated partly as a form of secret communication. Gresham Sykes, however, believed that it serves primarily as "an illustrative symbol of the prison community"—or as a way for inmates to mark themselves as outlaws and social outcasts.[17] Sykes's work brought prison argot to the attention of sociologists and criminologists. Since Sykes's time other authors have identified a number of words, terms, and acronyms in prison argot. Some of these terms are presented in Exhibit 10–2. Interestingly, rap musicians, many of whom have spent time in prison or deal with prison-related themes, have brought prison argot to a wider audience.

Social Structure in Men's Prisons

Inmate societies, like other societies, have a hierarchy of positions. Inmates assume or are forced into specific social roles, and some inmates—by virtue of the roles they assume—have more status and power than others.

Early writers often classified prisoners by the crimes they had committed or their criminal histories. Irwin, for example, divided prisoners into such categories as thieves (those with a culture of criminal values), convicts (time doers), square johns (inmates unfamiliar with criminal subcultures), and dope fiends (drug-involved inmates).[18]

inmate roles

Prison lifestyles; also, forms of ongoing social accommodation to prison life.

Other writers have identified **inmate roles**, defining them as prison lifestyles or as forms of ongoing social accommodation to prison life. Each role has a position in the pecking order, indicating its status in the prison society.

About a decade ago, Frank Schmalleger developed a typology of male inmate roles.[19] It is based on actual social roles found among inmates in prison, and it uses the prison argot in existence when it was created to name or describe each type. Each type can be viewed as a prison lifestyle either chosen by inmates or forced on them. Some of the types were previously identified by other writers. Although the terminology used in the typology sounds dated, the types of inmates it identifies are still characteristic of prison populations today. The 13 inmate types are discussed in the following paragraphs.

EXHIBIT 10–2   Prison Argot: The Language of Confinement

Argot in Men's Prisons

ace duce: best friend

back door parole: to die in prison

badge (or bull, hack, "the man," or screw): a correctional officer

ball busters: violent inmates

banger (or burner, shank, sticker): a knife

billys: white men

boneyard: conjugal visiting area

booty bandit: an imprisoned sexual predator who preys on weaker inmates

bug juice: antidepressant or antipsychotic medications provided by the medical staff

cantones: gang term for prisons

catch cold: to be killed

cat-J (or J-cat): a prisoner in need of psychological or psychiatric therapy or medication

cellie: cell mate

center men: inmates who are close to the staff

chester: child molester

chota: a correctional officer

croaker: a physician or a doctor

dancing on the blacktop: being stabbed

diaper sniper: child molester

diddler: a child molester or pedophile

dog: homeboy or friend

fag: a male inmate believed to be a natural (preprison) homosexual

fish: a newly arrived inmate

gorilla: an inmate who uses force to take what he wants from others

got stretched: became angry

grandma's: gang headquarters

hacks: correctional officers

hipsters: young, drug-involved inmates

homeboy: a prisoner from one's hometown or neighborhood

in the car: circle of friends

ink: tattoos

jointman: a prison inmate who behaves like a correctional officer

kite: a contraband letter

lemon squeezer: an inmate who has an unattractive "girlfriend"

lugger: an inmate who smuggles contraband into the facility

man walking: phrase used to signal that a guard is coming

merchant (or peddler): one who sells when he should give; or one who sells goods and services to other inmates illegally

nimby: not in my back yard

ninja turtles: correctional officers dressed in riot gear

punk: a male inmate who is forced into a submissive role during homosexual relations

rat (or snitch): an inmate who squeals (provides information about other inmates to the prison administration)

real men: inmates respected by other inmates

seed: the inmate's child

shank: a knife

schooled: knowledgeable in the ways of prison life

shakedown: search of a cell or a work area

shu (pronounced *shoe*): special housing unit

sleeved: covered with tatoos

slinging rock: selling crack

soda: cocaine

stainless-steel ride: lethal injection

toughs: those with a preprison history of violent crimes

tree jumper: rapist

turn out: to rape or make into a punk

veterano: a long-time gang member

wolf: a male inmate who assumes an aggressive role during homosexual relations

Argot in Women's Prisons

cherry (or cherrie): an inmate not yet introduced to lesbian activities

fay broad: a white inmate

femme (or mommy): an inmate who plays a female role during a lesbian relationship

lark: a woman who talks with the staff

safe: the vagina, especially when used for hiding contraband

stud broad (or daddy): an inmate who assumes a male role in a lesbian relationship

Sources: Gresham Sykes, *The Society of Captives* (Princeton, NJ: Princeton University Press, 1958); Rose Giallombardo, *Society of Women: A Study of Women's Prison* (New York: John Wiley, 1966); Richard A. Cloward et al., *Theoretical Studies in Social Organization of the Prison* (New York: Social Science Research Council, 1960). For a more contemporary listing of prison slang terms, see Reinhold Aman, *Hillary Clinton's Pen Pal: A Guide to Life and Lingo in Federal Prison* (Santa Rosa, CA: Maledicta Press, 1996); Jerome Washington, *Iron House: Stories from the Yard* (Ann Arbor, MI: QED Press, 1994); Morrie Camhi, *The Prison Experience* (Boston: Charles Tuttle, 1989); Harold Long, *Survival in Prison* (Port Townsend, WA: Loompanics Unlimited, 1990); insideprison.com (accessed March 24, 2009); Mother Jones, "A Glossary of Prison Slang" (July/August 2008), http://motherjones.com/politics/2008/07/glossary-prison-slang (accessed March 10, 2011).

Prison life is living in an insane world with insane rules. There's strength in numbers, and even the weak seem to "click up" in here. Everyone knows their own kind, it seems. Predators know one another immediately, as well as the bull queers, fags, and dudes just walking it down, keeping their nose clean. . . .

Here, these groups can set themselves apart quickly. Staff keeps track of high-profile inmates, and makes sure not to give them too much rope.

You definitely are classified by those you hang around with—labels are hard to shake in this environment. And the most important thing I've learned here is, there's plenty of dudes here who just love to hate on you and keep you here doing their digits with them. Misery loves company.

It's best to hook up with those that have the same objectives out of doing time as yourself. For me it's simply walking this time down to go home, and that's the type of dude I choose to hang with. Granted, he has to be solid, but first and foremost he has to be smart enough to choose which battles are worth dying over.

At any given time one group can have drama with another or trouble within its own ranks. So be sure that what you are willing to knuckle up over is well worth the repercussions, because you can be absolutely positive that staff will know what's happening almost as it's happening. This is a very small community—there are no secrets! Not even for staff.

You will hook up with dudes in here, and you feel some sort of bond grow between you and your bros. So you are there for them when they need you, and you can expect the same from them. Because even though this is prison, it's also where you live, and where they live.

Anonymous

The Real Man Real men do their own time, do not complain, and do not cause problems for other inmates. They see confinement as a natural consequence of criminal activity and view time spent in prison as an unfortunate cost of doing business. Real men know the inmate code and abide by it. They are well regarded within the institution and rarely run into problems with other inmates. If they do, they solve their problems on their own. They never seek the help of correctional officers or the prison administration. Although they generally avoid trouble within the institution, they usually continue a life of crime once released.

The Mean Dude Some inmates are notorious for resorting quickly to physical power. They are quick to fight and, when fighting, give no quarter. They are callous, cold, and uncaring. Mean dudes control those around them through force or the threat of force. The fear they inspire usually gives them a great deal of power in inmate society. At the very least, other inmates are likely to leave the mean dude alone.

The Bully A variation of the mean dude is the bully. Bullies use intimidation to get what they want. Unlike mean dudes, they are far more likely to use threats than to use actual physical force. A bully may make his threats in public so that others see the victim's compliance.

The Agitator The agitator, sometimes called a *wise guy*, is constantly trying to stir things up. He responds to the boredom of prison life by causing problems for others. An agitator may point out, for example, how a powerful inmate has been wronged by another inmate or that an inmate seen talking to a "rat" must be a snitch himself.

The Hedonist The hedonist adapts to prison by exploiting the minimal pleasures it offers. Hedonists always seek the easy path, and they plot to win the "cushiest" jobs. They may also stockpile goods to barter for services of various kinds. Hedonists live only in the now with little concern for the future. Their lives revolve around such activities as gambling, drug running, smuggling contraband, and exploiting homosexual opportunities.

The Opportunist The opportunist sees prison as an opportunity for personal advancement. He takes advantage of the formal self-improvement opportunities of the prison, such as schooling, trade training, and counseling. Other inmates generally dislike opportunists, seeing them as selfish *do-gooders*. Staff members, however, often see opportunists as model prisoners.

The Retreatist Some inmates, unable to cope with the realities of prison life, withdraw psychologically from the world around them. Depression, neurosis, and even psychosis may result. Some retreatists attempt to lose themselves in drugs or alcohol. Others attempt suicide. Isolation from the general prison population combined with counseling or psychiatric treatment may offer the best hope for retreatists to survive the prison experience.

The Legalist Legalists are known as *jailhouse lawyers*, or simply *lawyers*, in prison argot. They are usually among the better-educated prisoners, although some legalists have little formal education. Legalists fight confinement through the system of laws, rules, and court precedent. Legalists file writs with the courts, seeking hearings on a wide variety of issues. Although many legalists work to better the conditions of their own confinement or to achieve early release, most also file pleas on behalf of other prisoners.

The Radical Radicals see themselves as political prisoners of an unfair society. They believe that a discriminatory world has denied them the education and skills needed to succeed in a socially acceptable way. Most of the beliefs held by radical inmates are rationalizations that shift the blame for personal failure onto society. The radical inmate is likely to be familiar with contemporary countercultural figures.

The Colonist Colonists, also referred to as *convicts*, turn prison into home. Colonists know the ropes of prison, have many "friends" on the inside, and often feel more comfortable in prison than outside it. They may not look forward to leaving prison. Some may even commit additional offenses to extend their stay. Colonists are generally well regarded by other prisoners. Many are old-timers. Colonists have learned to take advantage of the informal opportunity structure in prisons, and they are well versed in the inmate code.

The Religious Inmate Religious inmates profess a strong religious faith and may attempt to convert both inmates and staff. Religious inmates frequently form prayer groups, request special meeting facilities and special diets, and may ask for frequent visits from religious leaders. Religious inmates are often under a great deal of suspicion from inmates and staff, who tend to think they are faking religious commitment to gain special treatment. Those judged sincere in their faith may win early release, removal from death row, or any number of other special considerations.

The Punk The punk is a young inmate, often small, who has been forced into a sexual relationship with an aggressive, well-respected prisoner. Punks are generally "turned out" through homosexual rape. A punk usually finds a protector among the more powerful inmates. Punks keep their protectors happy by providing them with sexual services.

Former Florida prison inmate Joe Murphy, who served time for murder, leads a prayer at the Okaloosa Correctional Institution in Crestview, Florida. What different kinds of inmates does this chapter identify?

The Gang-Banger Gang-bangers, or those affiliated with prison gangs, know that there is power in numbers. They depend upon the gang for defense and protection as well as for the procurement of desired goods and services. Gang-bangers are known by their tattoos and hand signs, which indicate gang affiliation and can be read by anyone familiar with prison society. Prison gangs, which are discussed in more detail in Chapter 13, often have links outside prison—leading to continued involvement in crime by those directing them from inside prison and to the creation of channels for the importation of banned items into correctional facilities.

Sexuality in Men's Prisons

Violence and victimization occur in men's prisons, and a good deal of prison violence has sexual overtones. The top of the sexual hierarchy in male prisons is occupied by inmates engaged in situational homosexuality who are called, quite simply, *Men.* They are heterosexual inmates who feel compelled to engage in homosexual behavior by the conditions of confinement.[20] Men with the power to own and control their own "punk" rise to the top of the inmate sexual hierarchy.

Punks are "owned" by powerful inmates who provide them protection from sexual violence and from other inmates. Many punks are forced to fill the traditional role of a wife and can often be found doing their Man's laundry, ironing, and making up the Man's bed. Although punks are usually seen as totally powerless and dependent upon their Man, punks can influence their "owners" in various ways. As one inmate observer[21] describes it, "There are punk wiles just as there are feminine wiles. A contented punk is much more desirable than a sullen and reluctant one, so there is a definite incentive for the Men to back off from a confrontation with their punks on an issue which they don't consider essential, though no Man will tolerate a rebellious punk." He adds, "A Man has a social obligation to share his wealth with his punk, much as a rich man on the outside is expected to keep his wife in furs and take her out to eat. As one Man put it: 'You punks have got it made; you don't have to fight, and you get all the dope and commissary from the men with the most money.'"[22]

The most powerful Men in prison society, cell block leaders, gang leaders, and so on, will "own" the most desirable punks. Punks, however, can be sold or given away. Once a person has become a punk, he can never again become a Man—at least not while still in prison. Not all punks, however, are outcasts. Punks belonging to Men who have high social status within the institution are treated with deference by other inmates. One rule of inmate society demands that Men must share what comforts they have accumulated in prison with their punks.

It is not uncommon for affectionate relationships to develop between Men and their punks. Some couples even "marry" in imitation ceremonies—many of which are followed by "parties" and attended by inmate "guests." As one writer explains it, "Imprisoned long enough, men can transfer any emotion they feel for women to their punks."[23]

One person who has contributed significantly to the study of sexual violence in men's prisons is Daniel Lockwood.[24] Using interviews and background data from prison files, Lockwood identified and studied 107 "targets" of aggressive sexual threats and 45 inmate "aggressors" in New York state male prisons. He also conducted a general survey that revealed that 28 percent of all male prisoners had been targets of sexual aggressors in prison at least once. Lockwood found that only one of the inmates he interviewed had actually been raped—an indication that the incidence of prison rape is quite low relative to other types of harm that may accompany sexual incidents, such as physical abuse, verbal abuse, threatening gestures, and threatening propositions.

Targets, when compared with nontargets, were found to be physically slight, young, white, nonviolent offenders from nonurban areas. They generally had a higher rate of psychological disturbance than other inmates and were more apt to attempt suicide while in prison. Exhibit 10–3 shows a note found by a new inmate in his cell at a New York state prison unit. The new inmate was young and not prison-wise. After discovering the note, the inmate asked to be moved to the prison's isolation area. His request was granted.[25]

The typical incident of sexual aggression, Lockwood found, is carried out by a group. About half the incidents Lockwood identified included physical violence, and another third involved threats. The incidents studied showed patterns of escalation from verbal abuse to physical violence.

Lockwood also found that prison rapes generally occur when gangs of aggressors circumvent security arrangements to physically control their victims. Fear, anxiety, suicidal thoughts, social disruption, and attitude changes develop in many victims of homosexual rape.

In 2003, in an effort to learn more about prison rape, Congress mandated the collection of prison rape statistics under the Prison Rape Elimination Act (PREA).[26] The PREA, which also established the federal Prison Rape Commission, calls for an evaluation of issues related to prison rape as well as for the development of national standards to help prevent prison rape.

Tasked by the PREA to gather data on prison rape, the Bureau of Justice Statistics completed its fourth annual national survey of administrative records and adult correctional facilities in 2011. The survey found that

Texas prison inmate Roderick Johnson, who claims that he was raped hundreds of times after his return to prison on charges of bouncing a $300 check while on parole for breaking and entering. In 2004, a federal lawsuit filed by Johnson, 33, an admitted homosexual, was allowed to go to trial. It names the head of the Texas Department of Criminal Justice, along with more than a dozen other officials at the James V. Allred Unit in Iowa Park, claiming that they failed to protect him from violent sexual attacks. What will the 2003 Prison Rape Elimination Act do for inmates like Johnson? Use the Internet to learn what happened to the civil suit filed on Johnson's behalf.

EXHIBIT 10–3   Inmate Note

> Yo S
> Check this out if you don't give me a peace
> of your ass I am going to take you off the
> count and that is my word.
> I be down a very long time So I need it Very
> Bad I will give you 5 Pack's of Smokes if
> you do it OK That is my word So if you
> Want to live you Better do it and get it over
> with there are Three of us who need it.
> OK...

reports of sexual violence varied significantly between prisons and across states, with every state prison system except Alaska and North Dakota reporting at least one allegation of sexual violence. Highlights from the most recent PREA survey reveal that an estimated 4.4 percent of prison inmates and 3.1 percent of jail inmates reported experiencing one or more incidents of sexual victimization at the hands of another inmate or facility staff member in the past 12 months.[27] An estimated 1.0 percent of prison inmates and 0.8 percent of jail inmates said they had nonconsensual sex with another inmate (the most serious type of acts), including unwilling manual stimulation and oral, anal, or vaginal penetration. Nationwide, these percentages suggest that approximately 88,500 adults held in prisons and jails at the time of the survey had been sexually victimized. In terms of numbers, correctional administrators reported 7,444 allegations of sexual victimization in 2008—slightly higher than the previous year.

About 2.1 percent of prison inmates and 1.5 percent of jail inmates reported an incident involving another inmate while approximately 2.8 percent of prison inmates and 2.0 percent of jail inmates reported having had sex or sexual contact with staff. At least half of the inmates who experienced staff sexual misconduct (1.8 percent in prison and 1.1 percent in jail) said that they willingly had sex or sexual contact with staff members. Sexual activity with facility staff was reported by 2.9 percent of male prisoners and 2.1 percent of male jail inmates compared to 2.1 percent of female prisoners and 1.5 percent of female jail inmates. Surprisingly, most victims of staff sexual misconduct were males while most perpetrators were females. Among male victims of staff sexual misconduct, 69 percent of those in prison and 64 percent of those in jails reported sexual activity with female staff. An additional 16 percent of prison inmates and 18 percent of jail inmates reported sexual activity with both female and male staff.

Female inmates were disproportionately victimized by both other inmates and staff in both federal and state prisons as well as in local jails. While females represent only 7 percent of sentenced prison inmates, they accounted for 21 percent of all victims of inmate-on-inmate sexual victimization in federal and state prisons. Similarly, females account for 13 percent of inmates in local jails but 32 percent of all victims.

In 2008, 931 allegations of sexual victimization (13 percent) were substantiated, that is, were determined to have occurred upon investigation.[28] About 54 percent of substantiated incidents of sexual victimization involved only inmates while 46 percent of substantiated incidents involved staff with inmates. Approximately 12 percent of substantiated incidents of inmate-on-inmate sexual victimization were committed by two or more perpetrators, but this varied by facility and incident type. Groups of two or more perpetrators committed a higher percentage of substantiated incidents in local jails (14 percent) than in prisons (9 percent). In addition, two or more perpetrators committed a higher percentage of nonconsensual sexual acts (16 percent) than abusive sexual contacts (7 percent).

Additional data from the survey show that a higher percentage of perpetrators in local jails were younger than 25 compared to perpetrators in prisons. Perpetrators of inmate-on-inmate sexual victimization in local jails were more likely to be under 25 (38 percent) than perpetrators in prisons (17 percent). Perpetrators in prisons were more likely than perpetrators in local jails to be ages 25–39 (48 percent in prisons compared to 39 percent in local jails) and 40 or older (35 percent compared to 23 percent).

Finally, injuries were reported in about 18 percent of incidents of inmate-on-inmate sexual victimizations and in less than 1 percent of incidents of staff-on-inmate sexual victimizations. Those numbers held true for both prisons and jails.

Official reports are unlikely to reflect the true incident of sexual violence. As BJS notes, "due to fear of reprisal from perpetrators, a code of silence among inmates, personal embarrassment, and lack of trust in staff, victims are often reluctant to report incidents to correctional authorities."[29] To circumvent such issues and to gather more reliable information, BJS has implemented a system of self-reports in which data are collected from incarcerated individuals as well as those recently released. Completed data will likely be used to assess existing policies and practices and to modify them as appropriate.

WOMEN IN PRISON

In America today, there are far fewer women's prisons than men's prisons, and men in prison outnumber women in prison 12 to 1.[30] As noted in Chapter 7, however, the number of women in prison is increasing much faster than that of men, and women represent the fastest-growing population in correctional facilities today.

A state usually has one women's prison housing a few hundred women. The size of a women's prison generally depends on the population of the state. Some small states house women prisoners in special areas of what are otherwise institutions for men.

Women's prisons are generally quite different from men's. Here's how one writer describes them:

> Often, there are no gun towers, no armed guards, and no stone walls or fences strung on top with concertina wire. Neatly pruned hedges, well-kept flower gardens, attractive brick buildings, and wide paved walkways greet the visitor's eye at women's prisons in many states. Often these institutions are located in rural, pastoral settings that may suggest tranquility and well-being to the casual observer.[31]

Such rural settings, however, make it hard for female inmates to maintain contact with their families who may live far from the correctional facility.

Many prisons for women are built on a cottage plan. Cottages dot the grounds of such institutions, often arranged in pods. A group of six or so cottages constitutes a pod. Each cottage is much like a traditional house, with individual bedrooms; a day room with a television, chairs, couches, and tables; and small personal or shared bathrooms.

Although there are far fewer women in prison than men, the number of women behind bars is growing steadily. What might account for the increasing number of imprisoned women?

Security in women's prisons is generally more relaxed than in men's, and female inmates may have more freedom within the institution than their male counterparts. Practically speaking, women—even those in prison—are seen as less dangerous than men and less prone to violence or escape.

Treatment, education, recreation, and other programs in women's prisons have often been criticized as inferior to those in men's prisons. Recent research has uncovered continuing disparities in many areas.[32] For example, men's institutions often have a much wider range of vocational and educational training programs and services and larger and better-equipped law libraries. Similarly, exercise facilities—including weight rooms, jogging areas, and basketball courts—are often better equipped and larger in men's institutions today than in women's.

Prison administrators have often found it impractical to develop and fund programs at the same level in women's and men's prisons because of differences in interest, participation, and space and the fact that relatively low numbers of women prisoners don't allow for the same economies of scale found in men's institutions. Nonetheless, it is important to strive for parity of opportunity as an ideal. The American Correctional Association, for example, through its *Guidelines for Women's Prison Construction and Programming,*[33] insists that the same level of services and opportunities be available in women's prisons as in men's prisons in the same jurisdiction.

In some instances, women may be placed in an institution housing inmates with a range of security levels. Consequently, women who are low security risks may have less personal freedom than their male counterparts. Women may also not have the opportunity to transfer to a less secure institution as their risk level drops.

Overcrowding, violence, and poor conditions are not unknown in prisons for women. By 2002, the Julia Tutwiler Prison for Women in Wetumpka, Alabama, for example, was home to more than 1,000 women. Built in 1942 with a capacity of only 364 inmates, it became the focus of a federal lawsuit brought by inmates to address extreme crowding.

Due largely to overcrowded conditions, the facility did not have the ability to separate dangerous prisoners from one another when its

Jack Osborn

Custody Utility Officer • Jefferson City Correctional Center
• Jefferson City, MO

Jack Osborn is a custody utility officer at the Jefferson City Correctional Center in Missouri. As a utility officer, he may be assigned to any area or department that needs an additional staff member.

Osborn advises knowing the inmates and being able to interpret behavioral changes. "Know what silence means. Communicate—listen," he says. "Learn who runs drugs and gambling, who the punks are. That's where your trouble will come from." Osborn believes that if you follow this advice and know the mechanics of the job, you should have a great career in corrections.

"What makes a good custody officer? Being honest goes far. If you don't know the answer, say so. If you say you will find out, do it. Learn to say no, too. You can change it to a yes easier than changing a yes to a no."

population was at its peak, nor did it have the resources to safely care for and separately house prisoners with mental illness and those with serious diseases. Meaningful programs for inmates were practically nonexistent, and most of the female prisoners spent endless idle hours in terribly hot dormitories crammed full of beds, sleeping pallets, and bunks.

The severe beating of a correctional officer in July 2002 brought problems with understaffing and crowded dorms into the spotlight. At the time there were, on average, only 12 officers at any given time responsible for supervising more than 1,000 prisoners—and at one point, there were as few as 9 officers on duty. Ninety-one assaults were recorded within the institution in 2002, making Alabama's only women's prison the most violent institution in the state.

The prisoner-brought lawsuit asked for, among other things, a reduction in crowding and the hiring of more corrections officers. Finally, under pressure from a federal judge, the state reduced the population at Tutwiler, sending hundreds of women to prisons out of state through contracts for prison space. Today, the Tutwiler prison has been expanded to a design capacity of 417 inmates but contains 743 beds. It's inmate population had fallen to 655 by the end of 2010—meaning that it was operating at 155 percent of its capacity.[34]

Characteristics of Women Inmates

Many of our conceptions of female inmates derive more from myth than reality. Recent BJS surveys provide a more realistic picture of female inmates.[35] At the start of 2011, women comprised 7.0 percent of sentenced prisoners in the nation. Since 2000, the female prison population has grown 28 percent,[36] a noticeably higher rate of growth than experienced in the male prison population, which had a 20 percent increase during the same period. As of January 1, 2010, there were 113,462 women under the jurisdiction of state and federal prison authorities.[37]

Female prisoners largely resemble male prisoners in race, ethnic background, and age. However, they are substantially more likely to be serving

An imprisoned woman. How do men's and women's prisons differ?

time for a drug offense and less likely to have been sentenced for a violent crime. Women are also more likely than men to be serving time for larceny or fraud.

Female inmates have shorter criminal records than male inmates. They generally have shorter maximum sentences than men. Half of all women receive a maximum sentence of 60 months or less while half of all men are sentenced to 120 months or less.

Significantly, more than 4 in 10 of the women prisoners responding to BJS surveys reported prior physical or sexual abuse. One of the major factors distinguishing male inmates from female inmates is that the women have experienced far more sexual and physical abuse than had the men. Interviews with incarcerated women have found that 70 percent of them report the occurrence of sexual molestation or severe physical abuse in childhood at the hands of parents or adolescent caregivers.[38] Fifty-nine percent report some form of sexual abuse in childhood or adolescence, and 75 percent of those interviewed report having been severely abused by an intimate partner as adults.

A report by the National Institute of Corrections found that women enter correctional institutions through different "pathways" than men. According to the report, most women offenders are typically nonviolent and their crimes are less threatening to community safety than those committed by male offenders. "Women's most common pathways to crime," said the report, "result from abuse, poverty, and substance abuse"—all of which, according to the report, are interconnected.[39] Exhibit 10–4 is a comparison of selected characteristics of female and male state prisoners.

Offenses of Incarcerated Women

Drug offenses account for the incarceration of a high percentage of the women behind bars. Twenty-seven percent of all women in state prisons are serving time on drug charges.[40] Some sources estimate that drug crimes and other crimes indirectly related to drug activities together account for the imprisonment of around 95 percent of today's women inmates. In short, drug use and abuse, or crimes stimulated by the desire for drugs and drug money, are what send most women to prison. This has been true for at least a decade. According to an ACA report, the primary reasons incarcerated women most frequently give for their arrest are (1) trying to pay for drugs, (2) attempts to relieve economic pressures, and (3) poor judgment.[41]

According to the BJS, before arrest, women in prison use more drugs than men and use those drugs more frequently.[42] About 54 percent of imprisoned women have used drugs in the month before the offense for which they were arrested compared with 50 percent of the men. Female inmates are also more likely than male inmates to have used drugs regularly (65 percent vs. 62 percent), to have used drugs daily in the month preceding their offense (41 percent vs. 36 percent), and to have been under the influence at the time of the offense (36 percent vs. 31 percent). Nearly one in four female inmates surveyed reported committing the offense to get money to buy drugs compared with one in six males.

EXHIBIT 10-4 Characteristics of Women and Men in State Prisons

Women in Prison

Criminal Offense

36% are in prison for violent offenses
27% are in prison for drug offenses
29% are in prison for property offenses
7% are in prison for public-order offenses
1% are in prison for other offenses

Criminal History

46% are nonviolent recidivists
28% have no previous sentence
26% are violent recidivists

Family Characteristics

78% have children
42% lived with both parents most of time growing up
33% had a parent/guardian who abused alcohol or drugs
17% were married at the time they committed the offense for which they were incarcerated
45% have never married
47% have a family member who had been incarcerated

Drug and Alcohol Use

59% used drugs daily in the month before the current offense
36% were under the influence of drugs at the time of the offense
12% were under the influence of alcohol at the time of the offense

Men in Prison

Criminal Offense

53% are in prison for violent offenses
18% are in prison for property offenses
18% are in prison for drug offenses
9% are in prison for public-order offenses
1% are in prison for other offenses

Criminal History

50% are violent recidivists
31% are nonviolent recidivists
19% have no previous sentence

Family Characteristics

64% have children
43% lived with both parents most of time growing up
26% had a parent/guardian who abused alcohol or drugs
18% were married at the time they committed the offense for which they were incarcerated
56% have never married
37% have a family member who had been incarcerated

Drug and Alcohol Use

56% used drugs daily in the month before the current offense
31% were under the influence of drugs at the time of the offense
18% were under the influence of alcohol at the time of the offense

Sources: Heather C. West, William J. Sabol, and Sarah J. Greenman, *Prisoners in 2009* (Washington, DC: Bureau of Justice Statistics, 2010); Allen Beck et al., *Survey of State Prison Inmates, 1991* (Washington, DC: U.S. Department of Justice, March 1993); and Christopher J. Mumola and Jennifer C. Karberg, "Drug Use and Dependence, State and Federal Prisoners, 2004" (Washington, DC: Bureau of Justice Statistics, 2006).

Female inmates who used drugs differed from those who did not in the types of crimes they committed. Regardless of the amount of drug use, users were less likely than nonusers to be serving a sentence for a violent offense.

Social Structure in Women's Prisons

As might be expected, the social structure and the subcultural norms and expectations in women's prisons are quite different from those in men's prisons. Unfortunately, however, relatively few studies of inmate life have been conducted in institutions for women.

One early study of women at the Federal Reformatory for Women in Alderson, West Virginia, was an effort to compare subcultural aspects of women's prisons with those of men's. Rose Giallombardo reached the conclusion that "many of the subcultural features of the institution are imported from the larger society."[43] Giallombardo believed that male and female inmate subcultures are actually quite similar except that women's prisons develop "a substitute universe," a world "in which inmates may preserve an identity which is relevant to life outside the prison."

Giallombardo was unable to find in the women's prison some of the values inherent in a male inmate subculture, such as "Do your own time."

The inmate subculture in a women's prison, she said, tends to encourage relationships rather than isolation. Hence, women are expected to share their problems with other inmates and to offer at least some support and encouragement to others. On the other hand, she observed, women prisoners tend to see each other as conniving, self-centered, and scheming. Hence, a basic tenet of the inmate subculture in a women's prison is "You can't trust other women." As Giallombardo put it, women prisoners tend to believe that "every woman is a sneaking, lying bitch."

Giallombardo concluded that the social structure of women's prisons and the social role assumed by each inmate are based on three elements:

1. the individual woman's level of personal dependence and her status needs (which are said to be based upon cultural expectations of the female role);
2. the individual's needs arising from incarceration combined with the institution's inability to meet female inmates' emotional needs; and
3. needs related to the individual's personality.

A more recent study was of inmates in the District of Columbia Women's Reformatory at Occoquan, Virginia.[44] Esther Heffernan identified three roles that women commonly adopt when adjusting to prison. According to Heffernan, women's roles evolve partly from the characteristics the women bring with them to prison and depend partly on the ways the women choose to adapt to prison life. The roles she described are discussed in the following paragraphs.

The Cool Inmate Cool women usually have previous records, are in the know, are streetwise, and do not cause trouble for other inmates while in prison. Cool women are seen as professional or semiprofessional criminals who work to win the maximum number of prison amenities without endangering their parole or release dates.

The Square Inmate Square women are not familiar with criminal lifestyles and have few, if any, criminal experiences other than the one for which they were imprisoned. They tend to hold the values and roles of conventional society.

The Life Inmate Life inmates are habitual or career offenders and are generally well socialized into lives of crime. They support inmate values and subculture. Life inmates typically have been in and out of prison from an early age and have developed criminal lifestyles dedicated to meeting their political, economic, familial, and social needs outside conventional society.

Recently, California State University (Fresno) criminologist Barbara Owens studied the culture of imprisoned women at Central California Women's Facility in Chowchilla, California, and found a "prison culture that is itself complex and diverse across numerous dimensions."[45] Owens identified a central component of that culture that she refers to as "the mix."

The mix, according to Owens, "is any behavior that can bring trouble and conflict with staff and other prisoners." It consists of fighting, doing drugs, prison-based lesbian activity ("homo-secting," in Owens's terms), and making trouble for the staff. It also involves continuing the kinds of behaviors that brought women to prison. Consequently, the mix is to be avoided by those who want to leave prison and not return. New women coming into the institution, Owens found, were advised to "stay out of the mix." The mix, says Owens, is also a state of mind, a way of thinking like a troublemaker.

One writer, summarizing the results of studies such as those discussed here, found that two primary features distinguish women's prisons from men's prisons:[46]

1. The social roles in women's prisons place greater emphasis on homosexual relations as a mode of adaptation to prison life.
2. The mode of adaptation a female inmate selects is best assessed by studying the inmate's preinstitutional experiences.

Pseudofamilies and Sexual Liaisons

A unique feature of women's prisons is pseudofamilies. **Pseudofamilies** are family-like structures, common in women's prisons, in which inmates assume roles similar to those of family members in free society. Pseudofamilies appear to provide emotional and social support for the women who belong to them. Courtship, marriage, and kinship ties formed with other women inmates provide a means of coping with the rigors of imprisonment. One inmate has explained pseudofamilies this way: "It just happens. Just like on the outside, you get close to certain people. It's the same in here—but we probably get even closer than a lot of families because of how lonely it is otherwise."[47]

Some authors suggest that pseudofamilies are to women's prisons what gangs are to men's.[48] Men establish social relationships largely through power, and gang structure effectively expresses such relationships. Women relate to one another more expressively and emotionally. Hence, family structures are one of the most effective reflections of women's relationships in prison, just as they are in the wider society. At least one study of prison coping behavior found that new female inmates, especially those most in need of support, advice, and assistance in adjusting to the conditions of incarceration, are the women most likely to become members of prison pseudofamilies.[49]

To a large extent, the social and behavioral patterns of family relationships in prison mirror their traditional counterparts in the community. Families in women's prisons come in all sizes and colors. They can be virtual melting pots of ethnicity and age. A member of a family may be young or old and may be black, white, or Hispanic. As in families in free society, there are roles for husbands and wives, sisters, brothers, grandmothers, and children. Roles for aunts and uncles do not exist, however.

"Stud broads," in prison argot, assume any male role, including that of husband and brother. Other inmates think of them as men. "Men" often assume traditional roles in women's prisons, ordering women around, demanding to be waited on, expecting to have their rooms cleaned and their laundry done, and so forth. Most women who assume masculine roles within prison are said to be "playing" and are sometimes called *players*. Once they leave, they usually revert to female roles. A "femme" or "mommy" is a woman who assumes a female role in a family and during homosexual activity.

Most women in prison, including those playing masculine roles, were generally not lesbians before entering prison. They resort to lesbian relations within prison because relationships with men are unavailable.

Although gender roles and family relationships within women's prisons appear to have an enduring quality, women can and sometimes do change role genders. When a woman playing a male role, for example, reverts to

pseudofamilies

Family-like structures, common in women's prisons, in which inmates assume roles similar to those of family members in free society.

The kinship of substitute families plays a major role in the lives of many female inmates, who take the relationships very seriously. How might these relationships supplant values such as "do your own time" commonly found in the subculture of men's prisons?

a female one, she is said to have "dropped her belt." A stud broad who drops her belt may wreak havoc on relationships within her own family and in families related to it.

Special Needs of Female Inmates

Rarely are the special needs of imprisoned women fully recognized—and even less frequently are they addressed. Many of today's prison administrators and correctional officers still treat women as if they were men. Nicole Hahn Rafter, for example, says that many prisons have an attitude akin to "just add women and stir."[50]

A recent report by the National Institute of Corrections (NIC) called for criminal justice agencies to acknowledge the "many differences between male and female offenders," and for the implementation of gender-responsive programming for treating the problems of imprisoned women.[51] *Gender-responsiveness* can be defined as "creating an environment . . . that reflects an understanding of the realities of women's lives and addresses the issues of the women."[52] Gender-responsive programming might, for example, strengthen policies against staff sexual misconduct in institutions that house women; provide more "safe and nurturing" drug treatment programs; and help inmate mothers to maintain strong relationships with their children. The NIC report concluded that "gender-responsive practice can improve outcomes for women offenders by considering their histories, behaviors, and life circumstances."[53]

Susan Cranford is division director of the Community Justice Assistance Division of the Texas Department of Criminal Justice. Rose Williams is warden of Pulaski State Prison in Hawkinsville, Georgia. Recently, Cranford and Williams suggested that "correctional staff should keep the unique needs of women offenders in mind."[54] They say that the effective running of a women's prison requires consideration of those needs.

A critical difference between male and female prisoners, say Cranford and Williams, is "the manner in which they communicate." Female offenders,

Oftentimes, my prison clients tell me that prison rehab providers like myself have few clues about the needs of people in prison rehabilitation programs. I think that many prisoners believe that educated people who have never used drugs have difficulty in developing and implementing drug rehab programs that really work. Many of my clients say they would design the program differently. I usually listen to their ideas, and sometimes I incorporate some of their thoughts in my work. But I realize that they would water a program down so much that other inmates who want to save themselves wouldn't have an opportunity to do so. Sometimes these clients argue that drug rehab providers should be former addicts—as if any knowledge gained in school, many years of experience, and dedication to helping others are worthless. I don't say that to them, but I do remind them that dentists don't need rotten teeth to be good dentists.

John McNerney
Correctional Counselor
Willard-Cybulski Correctional Institution
Enfield, Connecticut

they note, are usually much more open, more verbal, more emotional, and more willing to share the intimacies of their lives than men are. Male prisoners, like most men in free society, are guarded about the information they share and the manner in which they share it. "For men, information is power. For women, talking helps establish a common ground, a way to relate to others."

Gender-specific training is vital for COs who work in women's prisons, say Cranford and Williams. Proper training, they write, can head off the development of inappropriate relationships (especially initiated by male staff members), which could lead to sexual misconduct. Moreover, staff members who work with women should receive additional training in negotiating and listening skills.

An example of effective gender-specific training is the task-oriented curriculum titled *Working with the Female Offender* developed by Florida's Department of Corrections.[55] The program addresses unique aspects of managing female inmates and provides correctional staff training in the behaviors, actions, needs, and backgrounds presented by female offenders. A special segment examines how female offenders relate to supervision in various institutional or community corrections settings.

Moreover, say Cranford and Williams, it is important to realize that a woman's children are usually very important to her and that many imprisoned women have children on the outside. Hence, parenting skills should be taught to imprisoned mothers because most will rejoin and be with their children during critical stages in the children's development.

There are, however, those who feel that gender-responsive strategies won't work. The reason, they say, is because more and more women are being "convicted of crimes for which they would not previously have received a custodial sentence," and are being sent to prison "not because of the seriousness of their crimes, but mainly to receive psychological programming and reintegration training when, in fact, their main problems have stemmed from inadequate housing, poverty, and abusive men."[56] In other words, gender-responsive strategies assume that imprisonment can make a positive difference in women's lives, something that may not be true because such strategies often do little to address the problems women will again face upon release.

Mothers in Prison

According to one BJS study,[57] an estimated 6.7 percent of black women, 5.9 percent of Hispanic women, and 5.2 percent of white women are pregnant at the time of incarceration.

Talking about CORRECTIONS

INSTITUTIONAL CULTURE IN CORRECTIONS

Visit *Live Talk* at **Corrections .com (www.justicestudies .com/talking06)** and listen to the program "Institutional Culture in Corrections," which relates to ideas discussed in this chapter.

An estimated 4,000 women prisoners give birth each year, even though most women's prisons have no special facilities for pregnant inmates.[58] Some experts recommend that women's prisons should routinely make counseling available to pregnant inmates and that they should fully inform these women of the options available to them, including abortion and adoption.[59]

The ACA[60] recommends that institutions provide counseling for pregnant inmates, that "prenatal care" should be offered, and that deliveries should be made at community hospitals.[61] Similarly, the American Public Health Association's standards for health services in correctional institutions say that pregnant inmates should be provided with prenatal care, including medical exams and treatment, and that pregnant prisoners should be allowed a special program of housing, diet, vitamin supplements, and exercise.

Once inmates give birth, other problems arise—including the critical issue of child placement. Some states still have partial civil death statutes, which mean that prisoners lose many of their civil rights upon incarceration. In such states, women may lose legal custody of their children. Children either become wards of the state or are placed for adoption.

Although there is some historical precedent for allowing women inmates to keep newborns with them in the institutional setting, very few women's prisons permit this practice. Overcrowded prisons lack space for children, and the prison environment is a decidedly undesirable environment for children. A few women's prisons allow women to keep newborns for a brief period. Most, however, arrange for foster care until the mother is able to find relatives to care for the child or is released. Others work with services that put prison-born infants up for adoption. Some facilities make a special effort to keep mother and child together. Even relatively progressive prisons that allow mother–child contact usually do so only for the first year.

Many women are already mothers when they come to prison. BJS statistics[62] show that more than three-quarters of all women in prison in the United States have young children (i.e., under the age of 18). Black (69 percent) and Hispanic (72 percent) female inmates are more likely than white (62 percent) female inmates to have young children. Also, black women are more likely than other women to have lived with their young children before being imprisoned.

The children of 25 percent of women inmates with children under age 18 live with the other parent. More than a third of white female inmates report that their children are living with the children's fathers compared to a quarter of Hispanic women and less than a fifth of black women. Regardless of race, grandparents are the most common caregivers: 57 percent of imprisoned black mothers look to grandparents for child care as do 55 percent of imprisoned Hispanic mothers and 41 percent of imprisoned white mothers. Nearly 10 percent of the inmate mothers reported that their children are in a foster home, agency, or institution.

Worry about children affects female inmates' physical and emotional well-being. Although 78 percent of mothers (and 62 percent of fathers) report having at least monthly contact with their children, only 24 percent of mothers (and 21 percent of fathers) report personal visits from their children at least monthly.[63] A majority of both mothers (54 percent) and fathers (57 percent) report never having had a personal visit with their children since their imprisonment began.

According to BJS, nearly 90 percent of women with children under age 18 have had contact with their children since entering prison. Half of all women inmates surveyed have been visited by their children, four-fifths have corresponded by mail, and three-quarters have talked with children on the telephone. Female inmates with children under age 18 are more likely than those with adult children to make daily telephone calls to their children.

Understandably, inmate mothers frequently express concern about possible alienation from their children due to the passage of time associated with incarceration. They often worry that their children will develop strong bonds with new caretakers and be unwilling to return to them upon release.[64]

Finally, it is important to note that a number of women's prisons operate programs designed to develop parenting skills among inmates. Included are the Program for Caring Parents at the Louisiana Correctional Institute for Women; Project HIP (Helping Incarcerated Parents) at the Maine Correctional Center; and Neil J. Houston House, a program for nonviolent female offenders in Massachusetts.[65]

One 2011 study found that 1.7 million American children had a parent in prison.[66] Statistically speaking, 1 of every 43 American children has a parent in prison today, and ethnic variation in the numbers are striking. While only 1 out of every 111 white children has experienced the imprisonment of a parent, 1 out of every 15 black children has had that experience. Moreover, between 1991 and 2007, the number of incarcerated fathers rose 76 percent while the number of incarcerated mothers increased by 122 percent.

The effects of parental incarceration on children can be significant. A number of studies show that the children of incarcerated mothers experience alienation, hostility, anger, significant feelings of abandonment, and overall dysfunction. They are much less likely to succeed in school than their peers and far more likely to involve themselves in gangs, sexual misconduct, sexual abuse, and overall delinquency.[67]

In the federal population, 63.4 percent of male prisoners and 58.8 percent of female prisoners have minor children. The state data reverse this distribution, with 65.3 percent of female inmates and 54.7 percent of male inmates having minor children.

It is noteworthy that male inmates are, for the most part, rarely provided any special assistance for maintaining contact with their children during their incarceration. During the past decade, however, administrators in women's institutions across the country have implemented measures to foster stronger bonds between incarcerated mothers and their children. Ranging from the establishment of prison nurseries to the development of special visitation areas, these measures seek to facilitate the continued family contact that appears to be so important to female offenders.[68]

With 1 in 12 inmates pregnant at the time of admission[69] and 22 percent of all minor children with a parent in prison being under 5 years old,[70] correctional administrators need to address the unique problems presented by pregnant offenders and those with very young children. Some institutions have opted to create nurseries on site. At Nebraska's Correctional Center for Women, for example, inmates due for release before their children are 18 months old may keep the children with them in a specially designated floor of a standard prison building. The mothers are provided parenting and child-care classes, and they work only part time. While they work, other trained inmates provide child care.

Another example of programs designed to facilitate family bonding is the Ohio Reformatory for Women's annual three-day weekend camp, which brings children ages 6 to 12 from all over the state to spend days with their

Inmates in the Malachi Dads program at Louisiana State Penitentiary at Angola pray prior to a graduation ceremony at which they were recognized for their efforts to become better fathers. What are the problems faced by imprisoned parents? By their children?

inmate mothers. Originally pioneered at Bedford Hills Correctional Facility, New York's maximum-security prison for women, such camping visits have become more common in other facilities as well. Some states even allow overnight camping trips, both on and off the prison grounds.

Inmates apply for the program in January each year. Local churches and other community service groups support the program.[71] Selection criteria include a review of inmates' disciplinary records during incarceration, and those whose crimes involved their children are prohibited from participating. During the weekend, activities such as storytelling, softball, crafts, and meals facilitate bonding between mother and child. The inmates return to the prison to sleep at night, but the children "camp out" in sleeping bags at a local church.

Another innovative effort is Florida's "Reading Family Ties: Face to Face" program.[72] Begun in February 2000, it uses high-speed videoconferencing technology to permit weekly family visits between incarcerated mothers in two rural institutions and their children in the Miami area. Inmate mothers may sit before an Internet-linked camera to read to their children. Logistical limitations, of course, are significant, but administrators plan to expand the program to other major cities in Florida.

Perhaps the most family-centered efforts are being tried in California and Illinois. Oakland's Project Pride[73] permits mothers convicted of nonviolent offenses to serve the last portion of their sentences in residential community settings with their preschool-age children. Under the Family Foundations Program in Santa Fe Springs (CA), sentencing of convicted mothers with substance abuse histories can include treatment in residential centers where they can live with their children. Similarly, at Illinois's Decatur Correctional Center, infants live in separate rooms with their mothers. Books and toys are plentiful in the unit, and large day rooms are decorated with colorful murals. The program is intended to serve women whose children will be two years old or younger by the time they are released from prison.[74]

Prison programs to help fathers learn better parenting are also on the increase. The National Fatherhood Initiative, for example, started Inside Out Dad in 2004, and it now operates in more than 400 prisons and jails nationwide. The program's goal is to reduce recidivism through better fathering.[75]

Some hard-liners might decry such programs as unjustified coddling of convicted offenders. Few, however, can argue the benefits such programs provide to the children of incarcerated parents. Meanwhile, it remains to be seen whether the programs will serve to sustain family relationships, ease prisoners' return to the family environment after release, and, ultimately, reduce recidivism rates.

Cocorrectional Facilities

In 1971, a disturbance at the federal women's prison at Alderson, West Virginia, led to calls for ways to expand incarceration options for women. The Federal Bureau of Prisons responded by moving low-security female prisoners from the crowded Alderson institution to a federal minimum-security prison at Morgantown, West Virginia. The Morgantown facility had been built for young men but had not reached its design capacity. With this move, the modern era of coed prisons, or cocorrections, was born.

A **coed prison** is a facility housing both men and women, and **cocorrections** is the incarceration and interaction of female and male offenders under a single institutional administration.[76] It is estimated that as many as 52 adult correctional institutions in the United States are coed and that they confine almost 23,000 men and 7,000 women.[77]

coed prison
A prison housing both female and male offenders.

cocorrections
The incarceration and interaction of female and male offenders under a single institutional administration.

Since its inception, cocorrections has been cited as a potential solution to a wide variety of corrections problems. The rationales in support of cocorrections are that it:

1. reduces the dehumanizing and destructive aspects of incarceration by permitting heterosocial relationships;
2. reduces problems of institutional control;
3. creates a more "normal" atmosphere, reducing privation;
4. allows positive heterosocial skills to emerge;
5. cushions the shock of release;
6. increases the number of program offerings and improves program access for all prisoners; and
7. expands career opportunities for women.

An examination of the cocorrections literature from 1970 to 1990, however, found no evidence that cocorrections benefits female prisoners.[78] A former warden of a coed prison contends that "going coed" has often been done to appease male egos and smooth the running of men's prisons. Warden Jacqueline Crawford tells us that most women in prison have generally been exploited by the men in their lives. A coed prison, she says, furthers this experience because male prisoners continue the abuse women have come to expect from men.[79]

Others have found that some women's prisons have been turned into coed prisons, thus limiting correctional options for women. Overall, researchers have concluded, "Cocorrections offers women prisoners few, if any, economic, educational, vocational, and social advantages."[80] Whether prisoners released from coed prisons adjust better to the community or experience less recidivism has not been sufficiently studied.

Although literature related to single-sex prisons[81] has repeatedly shown poor overall performance in prisoner rehabilitation and public safety, correctional decision makers, policymakers, legislators, and the public are not calling for an end to one-sex imprisonment. If cocorrections is to become more than window dressing, however, it requires more attention to planning, implementation, and evaluation. Despite some early claims of success, coed prisons are not a quick fix for problems of prison administration.

REVIEW AND APPLICATIONS

SUMMARY

1 Prison inmates live their daily lives in accordance with the dictates of the inmate subculture. The inmate subculture consists of the customs and beliefs of those incarcerated in correctional institutions. *Deprivation theory* holds that prisoner subcultures develop in response to the pains of imprisonment. *Importation theory* claims that inmate subcultures are brought into prisons from the outside world. The integration model uses both theories to explain prisoner subcultures.

2 An important aspect of the male inmate subculture is the prison code. The prison code is a set of norms for the behavior of inmates. Central elements of the code include notions of loyalty (to prison society), control of anger, toughness, and distrust of prison officials. Because the prison code is a part of the inmate subculture, it is mostly opposed to official policies.

3 The inmate subculture also has its own language, called *prison argot*. Examples of prison argot are "fish" (a new inmate), "cellie" (cell mate), and "homeboy" (a prisoner from one's hometown).

4　Inmate roles are different prison lifestyle choices. They include the real man, the mean dude, the bully, the agitator, the hedonist, the opportunist, the retreatist, the legalist, the radical, the colonist, the religious inmate, the punk, and the gang-banger.

5　There are far fewer women's prisons than men's in the United States. Women's prisons often have no gun towers or armed guards and no stone walls or fences topped by barbed wire. They tend to be more attractive and are often built on a cottage plan. Security in most women's prisons is more relaxed than in institutions for men, and female inmates may have more freedom within the institution than do their male counterparts in their institutions. Other gender-based disparities favoring male prisoners exist. A lack of funding and inadequate training have been cited to explain why programs available to women inmates are often not on a par with those available to male prisoners.

6　Female prisoners largely resemble male prisoners in race, ethnic background, and age. However, they are substantially more likely to be serving time for drug offenses and less likely to have been sentenced for violent crimes.

7　While there are many similarities between men's and women's prisons, the social structure and the subcultural norms and expectations of women's prisons differ from those of men's prisons in a number of important ways. One important difference is that the prisoner subculture in a women's prison tends to encourage relationships rather than isolation. As a consequence, pseudofamilies arise, with fully developed familial relationships and roles.

KEY TERMS

total institution, p. 340

inmate subculture, p. 342

prisoner subculture, p. 342

prisonization, p. 342

pains of imprisonment, p. 342

deprivation theory, p. 342

importation theory, p. 343

integration model, p. 343

prison code, p. 343

prison argot, p. 344

inmate roles, p. 344

pseudofamilies, p. 357

coed prison, p. 362

cocorrections, p. 362

QUESTIONS FOR REVIEW

1　What is *inmate subculture,* and how is it central to understanding society in men's prisons?

2　What is the *prison code?* What are some of its key features? How does it influence behavior in men's prisons?

3　What is *prison argot?* Give some examples.

4　Explain what is meant by *inmate roles,* and give some examples.

5　In what ways do women's prisons differ from men's prisons?

6　Compare female and male inmates by their criminal histories, their family characteristics, and the offenses for which they are incarcerated.

7　How does the social structure of women's prisons differ from that in men's prisons? What are *pseudofamilies,* and why are they important to the society of women's prisons?

THINKING CRITICALLY ABOUT CORRECTIONS

Prison Birth

A woman who gives birth in prison may lose her child to state authorities or may have her parental rights severely restricted. In most cases, the child is removed from the inmate mother shortly after birth. Do you think this is fair? Why or why not?

Housing Assignments

Not surprisingly, state policies differ significantly on the question of housing assignments for prisoners. Some permit inmates to choose their cell mates while others enforce random cell assignments. What are the advantages and disadvantages of each policy style? Which style do you think is best?

ON-THE-JOB DECISION MAKING

Male Officers in Women's Prisons

You are a correctional officer assigned to a women's prison. Six months ago, the superintendent of your institution ordered an investigation to determine the proper role of male officers within the facility. The investigation centered on charges by a handful of inmates that they had been sexually harassed by male COs. The alleged harassment included requests for sexual favors in return for special privileges, observation of female inmates in various states of undress while in their rooms and in shower facilities, and inappropriate touching during cell and facility searches (policy allows only female COs to conduct body searches).

Although the investigation was inconclusive, the activities of male COs have been restricted. They are no longer permitted to have any physical contact with inmates unless an emergency demands that they restrain or search inmates. They have been reassigned to areas of the facility where they cannot view shower and toilet facilities. They are expected to announce their presence in living areas, and they have been ordered to take special classes on staff-inmate interaction.

Unfortunately, however, there are not enough female COs for all of the reassignments required by the recent shift in policy. As a result, the routines of female officers are being significantly disrupted. Female officers are being asked to work shifts that are inconvenient for their personal lives (many are mothers or college students and had come to count on predictable shift work). Most female COs also feel that their workload has increased because they have to cover areas of the institution and assume tasks that male officers would previously have handled.

A few female COs have already left for jobs elsewhere, citing difficulties created in the work environment by the new policies. The talk among the correctional staff is that many of the remaining female staff members might also soon leave. If more female COs leave the facility, it will be impossible for those who remain to keep the facility running under the new rules.

1. Did the superintendent make the right decision in limiting the activities of male COs? Why or why not?
2. Might there be other ways to resolve the issues raised by the investigation into sexual harassment? If so, what might they be?

Same-Sex Relationships

You are a chaplain working in a large state-run correctional facility. You take pride in your reputation among the inmates as a fair and reasonable counselor who treats them with courtesy and respect and never judges them for past transgressions or present problems.

Ronald, an inmate whom you know well, comes to you with a special request. He wants to marry Lawrence, another inmate, and he wants you to perform the ceremony in private. He also tells you that he knows that the "marriage" will have no legitimacy on the outside but says that the ceremony will be deeply moving for him and for Lawrence. Ronald's incarceration record is sterling. His disciplinary record shows no infractions, and there are numerous positive annotations regarding the obvious sincerity of his efforts to rehabilitate himself in preparation for his return to free society.

You are concerned that Ronald may actually be straight, and that his relationship with Lawrence may arise more from the pains of imprisonment than from any innate sexual orientation. You are uncertain what prison regulations might say about such a ceremony, but you suspect that, were you to inquire, the ceremony would be officially disallowed. Additionally, church elders in your denomination have condemned same-sex marriages like the one you are being asked to perform. Still, you think that Ronald is well-meaning in his efforts to form a more stable relationship with Lawrence, and you believe that such a relationship can help him adjust to the stresses of prison life.

1. What do you do? Is this an issue that you need time to think about, or do you answer right away?
2. Would you consider counseling Ronald in order to better assess his "true" sexual orientation?
3. Is his "true" sexual orientation an important consideration?
4. Would you further consider counseling Ronald and Lawrence, individually and jointly, regarding their desire to formalize their relationship?
5. Would you take the issue to the prison superintendent?

For additional information, please see: www.mhhe.com/schmalleger6e

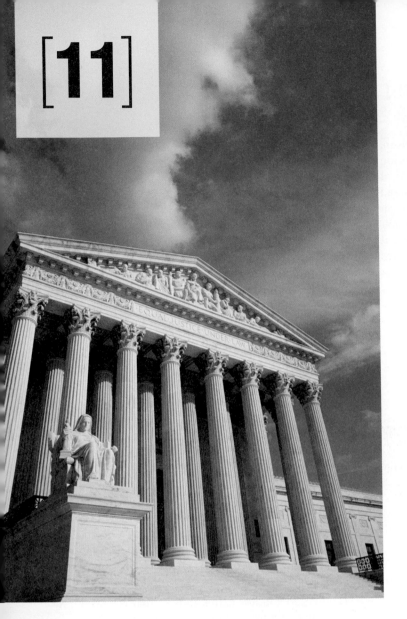

[11]

THE LEGAL WORLD

Prisoners' Rights

CHAPTER OBJECTIVES

After completing this chapter you should be able to do the following:

1 Explain what is meant by the *hands-off doctrine.*

2 Identify the key legal sources of prisoners' rights.

3 Recite the central question raised by the concern with the rights of prisoners.

4 List the five ways in which inmates can challenge their conditions of confinement.

5 Describe the major changes that took place during the prisoners' rights era.

6 List and explain the four amendments to the U.S. Constitution on which most prisoners' claims are based.

7 Explain how the development of rights for female prisoners has differed from that of rights for male prisoners.

> *All persons under any form of detention or imprisonment shall be treated in a humane manner and with respect for the inherent dignity of the human person.*
>
> —United Nations General Assembly Resolution 43/173, December 9, 1988

In 2011, the U.S. Supreme Court, in the case of *Brown* v. *Plata,* ordered the state of California to aggressively reduce its prison population by releasing as many as 58,000 inmates over the next two years.[1] The Justices held that overcrowded conditions throughout the state's prisons had significantly deprived inmates of their right to adequate health care and thereby violated the Eighth Amendment's ban on cruel and unusual punishment. The high Court's ruling upheld an earlier order by a three-judge federal panel intended to reduce the number of inmates supervised by the California Department of Corrections and Rehabilitation (CDCR) to around 120,000. At the time of the ruling, the CDCR was supervising around 160,000 inmates in 33 facilities originally designed to hold only 84,000. The rest of the state's prisoners were housed under contract in correctional facilities outside of the state, but the Supreme Court determined that the policy of transferring inmates inadequate to address California's overcrowding problem. In rendering the *Plata* ruling the Justices were drawing upon a legal tradition recognizing the rights of inmates that began in the United States more than 40 years earlier.

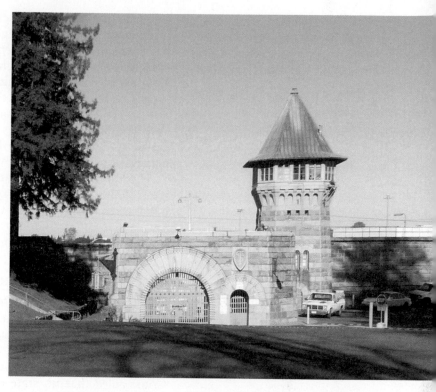

California's Folsom prison. In 2011, the U.S. Supreme Court ruled that California officials had to release as many as 58,000 inmates because of prison overcrowding. How did inmate rights figure into that decision?

THE HANDS-OFF DOCTRINE

In 1871, almost 140 years before the California order was issued, a Virginia judge declared the following: "A convicted felon . . . punished by confinement in the penitentiary instead of with death . . . is in a state of penal servitude to the State. He has, as a consequence of his crime, not only forfeited his liberty, but all his personal rights except those which the law in its humanity accords to him. He is for the time being the slave of the State. He is *civiliter mortuus;* and his estate, if he has any, is administered like that of a dead man. The Bill of Rights is a declaration of general principles to govern a society of freemen, and not of convicted felons and men civilly dead."[2]

In the case of *Ruffin* v. *Commonwealth,* the judge was voicing what had long been believed: that prisoners had no rights. It was this kind of thinking that long supported a "hands-off" approach to prisoners' rights. If inmates were really civilly dead, the federal government and the federal courts certainly had no cause to tell the states how to run their prisons.

hands-off doctrine

A historical policy of American courts not to intervene in prison management. Courts tended to follow the doctrine until the late 1960s.

Under the **hands-off doctrine,** U.S. courts for many decades avoided intervening in prison management. The doctrine was based on two rationales: (1) that under the *separation of powers* inherent in the U.S. Constitution, the judicial branch of government should not interfere with the running of correctional facilities by the executive branch and (2) that judges should leave correctional administration to correctional experts. For a very long time in our nation's history, states ran their prisons as they saw fit. Prison inmates were thought of as "nonpersons," and rights pertained only to persons. Pleas from prisoners based on allegations of deprivations of their rights were ignored.

The hands-off doctrine and the philosophy of the prisoner as a slave of the state began to change in the mid-1900s. Public attitudes about punishment versus rehabilitation changed, and more and more people became aware that inmates had *no* rights. As a result, the courts began to scrutinize the correctional enterprise in America.

Decline of the Hands-Off Doctrine

The 1941 case of *Ex parte Hull* began a dismantling of the hands-off doctrine. Prior to *Hull,* it had been common for corrections personnel to screen inmate mail, including prisoner petitions for writs of *habeas corpus.* Corrections officials often confiscated the petitions, claiming they were improperly prepared and not fit to submit to court. In *Hull,* the Supreme Court ruled that no state or its officers may interfere with a prisoner's right to apply to a federal court for a writ of *habeas corpus.* Thus, court officials, not corrections officials, have the authority to decide whether such petitions are prepared correctly.

Although this seemed like a small step at the time, it would facilitate a major leap in prisoners' rights. Three years later, in *Coffin v. Reichard* (1944), the Sixth Circuit Court of Appeals extended *habeas corpus* hearings to consider the conditions of confinement. Even more important, the *Coffin* case was the first in which a federal appellate court ruled that prisoners do not automatically lose their civil rights when in prison.[3] In the words of the Court, a prisoner "retains all the rights of an ordinary citizen except those expressly, or by necessary implication, taken from him by law."

San Quentin State Prison in Marin County, California. Opened in 1852, it is one of the state's oldest and best-known correctional institutions. Under the hands-off doctrine, American courts long refused to intervene in prison management. When did the hands-off doctrine end?

Another important development occurred in 1961 with the Supreme Court's ruling in *Monroe* v. *Pape*. Prior to *Pape,* it was believed that the phrase "under color of state law" in the Civil Rights Act of 1871 meant that a Section 1983 suit (explained in more detail on page 370) could involve only actions authorized by state law. In *Pape,* however, the Court held that for activities to take place *under color* of state law, they did not have to be *authorized* by state law. The statute, said the Court, had been intended to protect against "misuse of power, possessed by virtue of state law and made possible only because the wrongdoer is clothed with the authority of state law."

Officials "clothed with the authority of state law" seemed to include state corrections officials. Thus, state corrections officials who violated an inmate's constitutional rights while performing their duties could be held liable for their actions in federal court regardless of whether state law or policy supported those actions.[4]

A third important case establishing inmates' rights to access the courts was *Cooper* v. *Pate* (1964). In *Cooper,* a federal circuit court clarified the *Pape* decision, indicating that prisoners could sue a warden or another correctional official under Title 42 of the U.S. Code, Section 1983, based on the protections of the Civil Rights Act of 1871.

Commenting on the importance of *Cooper,* one observer noted,

> Just by opening a forum in which prisoners' grievances could be heard, the federal courts destroyed the custodian's absolute power and the prisoners' isolation from the larger society. The litigation itself heightened prisoners' consciousness and politicized them.[5]

With prisoners' access to the courts now established, cases challenging nearly every aspect of corrections were soon filed. The courts, primarily the federal district courts, began to review prisoners' complaints and intervene on prisoners' behalf.

The hands-off era is said to have ended in 1970 when a federal district court, in *Holt* v. *Sarver,* declared the entire Arkansas prison system "so inhumane as to be a violation of the Eighth Amendment bar on cruel and unusual punishment."[6] Robert Sarver, the Arkansas commissioner of corrections, admitted that "the physical facilities at both [prison units named in the suit] were inadequate and in a total state of disrepair that could only be described as deplorable." Additionally, he testified that inmates with trustee status, some of them serving life or long-term sentences, constituted 99 percent of the security force of the state's prison system.

Commissioner Sarver continued, testifying that "trustees sell desirable jobs to prisoners and also traffic in food, liquor, and drugs. Prisoners frequently become intoxicated and unruly. The prisoners sleep in dormitories. Prisoners are frequently attacked and raped in the dormitories, and injuries and deaths have resulted. Sleep and rest are seriously disrupted. No adequate means exist to protect the prisoners from assaults. There is no satisfactory means of keeping guns, knives, and other weapons away from the prison population."[7]

The *Holt* court declared in 1970,

> The obligation . . . to eliminate existing unconstitutionalities does not depend upon what the Legislature may do or upon what the Governor may do. . . . If Arkansas is going to operate a Penitentiary System, it is going to have to be a system that is countenanced by the Constitution of the United States.[8]

Prisoner litigation had brought sad conditions to light, and the court had intervened to institute reforms for the prisoners in Arkansas.

The case of *Holt v. Sarver* brought the hands-off era to a close and opened a new era of prisoners' rights. What were the issues involved in that case?

PRISONERS' RIGHTS

Legal Foundations

prisoners' rights

Constitutional guarantees of free speech, religious practice, due process, and other private and personal rights as well as constitutional protections against cruel and unusual punishments made applicable to prison inmates by the federal courts.

Prisoners' rights have four legal foundations: the U.S. Constitution, federal statutes, state constitutions, and state statutes. Most court cases involving prisoners' rights have involved rights claimed under the U.S. Constitution, even though state constitutions generally parallel the U.S. Constitution and sometimes confer additional rights. State legislatures and Congress can also confer additional prisoners' rights.

The U.S. Constitution The U.S. Constitution is the supreme law of our land. At the heart of any discussion of prisoners' rights lies one question: What does the Constitution have to say? As scholars began to search the Constitution, they could find no requirement that prisoners give up all of their rights as U.S. citizens (and human beings) after conviction.

constitutional rights

The personal and due process rights guaranteed to individuals by the U.S. Constitution and its amendments, especially the first 10 amendments, known as the *Bill of Rights*. Constitutional rights are the basis of most inmate rights.

It is important to remember, however, that **constitutional rights** are not absolute. Does freedom of speech mean that you have a protected right to stand up in a crowded theater and yell "fire"? It does not (at least not unless there *is* a fire). That is because the panic that would follow such an exclamation would probably cause injuries and would needlessly put members of the public at risk of harm. Hence, the courts have held that, although freedom of speech is guaranteed by the Constitution, it is not an absolute right; in other words, there are limits to it (*Schenck v. United States*, 1919).

So, the central issue raised by those interested in prisoners' rights seems to be the degree to which a person retains constitutional rights when convicted of a criminal offense and sentenced to prison. Addressing that issue has become a job of the courts. The positions on it dependent upon the courts' interpretation of the U.S. Constitution, state constitutions, and federal and state laws. Generally speaking, the courts have recognized four legitimate **institutional needs** that justify some restrictions on the constitutional rights of prisoners:

institutional needs

Prison administration interests recognized by the courts as justifying some restrictions on the constitutional rights of prisoners. Those interests are maintenance of institutional *order*, maintenance of institutional *security*, *safety* of prison inmates and staff, and *rehabilitation* of inmates.

1. maintenance of institutional *order;*
2. maintenance of institutional *security;*
3. *safety* of prison inmates and staff; and
4. *rehabilitation* of inmates.

According to the courts, *order* refers to calm and discipline within the institution, *security* is the control of individuals and objects entering or leaving the institution, *safety* means avoidance of physical harm, and *rehabilitation* refers to practices necessary for the health, well-being, and treatment of inmates.[9]

Federal Statutes Laws passed by Congress can confer certain rights on inmates in federal prisons. In addition, Congress has passed a number of laws that affect the running of state prisons. The Civil Rights Act of 1871, for example, was enacted after the Civil War to discourage lawless activities by state officials. Section 1983 reads as follows:

> Every person who, under color of any statute, ordinance, regulation, custom, or usage, of any State or Territory, subjects, or causes to be subjected, any citizen of the United States or other person within the jurisdiction thereof to the deprivation of any rights, privileges, or immunities secured by the Constitution and laws, shall be liable to the party injured in an action at law, suit in equity, or other proper proceeding for redress.

This section imposes **civil liability** (but not criminal blame) on any person who deprives another of rights guaranteed by the U.S. Constitution. The Civil Rights Act of 1871 allows state prisoners to challenge conditions of their imprisonment in federal court. Most prisoner suits brought under this act allege deprivation of constitutional rights. Another important piece of legislation is the Civil Rights of Institutionalized Persons Act (CRIPA),[10] which is discussed in more detail in Chapter 12.

State Constitutions Most state constitutions are patterned after the U.S. Constitution. However, state constitutions tend to be longer and more detailed than the U.S. Constitution and may contain specific provisions regarding corrections. State constitutions generally do not give prisoners more rights than are granted by the U.S. Constitution, except in a few states such as California and Oregon. Inmates in such states may challenge the conditions of their confinement in state court under the state's constitutional provision.

State Statutes Unlike the federal government, state governments all have inherent police power, which allows them to pass laws to protect the health, safety, and welfare of their citizens. A state legislature can pass statutes to grant specific rights beyond those conferred by the state constitution. Often such legislation specifies duties of corrections officials or standards of treatment for prisoners. Prisoners who can show failure of officials to fulfill state statutory obligations may collect money damages or obtain a court order compelling officials to comply with the law.

Mechanisms for Securing Prisoners' Rights

Inmates today have five ways to challenge the legality of their confinement, associated prison conditions, and the practices of correctional officials: (1) a state *habeas corpus* action, (2) a federal *habeas corpus* action after state remedies have been exhausted, (3) a state tort lawsuit, (4) a federal civil rights lawsuit, and (5) a petition for injunctive relief.[11]

Writ of *Habeas Corpus* A **writ of habeas corpus** is an order from a court to produce a prisoner in court so that the court can determine whether the prisoner is being legally detained. *Habeas corpus* is Latin for "you have the body." A prisoner, or someone acting for a prisoner, files a *habeas corpus* petition asking a court to determine the lawfulness of the imprisonment. The petition for the writ is merely a procedural tool. If a writ is issued, it has no bearing on any issues to be reviewed. It guarantees only a hearing on those issues.

Federal and state prisoners may file *habeas corpus* petitions in federal courts. State prisoners must first, however, exhaust available state *habeas corpus* remedies. In 2000, of 11,880 petitions that inmates filed in *federal* courts, 3,870 (33 percent) were *habeas corpus* actions; of 46,371 petitions that inmates filed in *state* courts, 21,345 (46 percent) were *habeas corpus* actions.[12]

civil liability
A legal obligation to another person to do, pay, or make good something.

A writ of habeas corpus is a court order requiring that a prisoner be brought before the court so that the court can determine whether the person is being legally detained. What is required of a state prisoner who wants to bring a habeas corpus action in federal court?

writ of *habeas corpus*
An order that directs the person detaining a prisoner to bring him or her before a judge, who will determine the lawfulness of the imprisonment.

tort

A civil wrong, a wrongful act, or a wrongful breach of duty, other than a breach of contract, whether intentional or accidental, from which injury to another occurs.

nominal damages

Small amounts of money a court may award when inmates have sustained no actual damages, but there is clear evidence that their rights have been violated.

compensatory damages

Money a court may award as payment for actual losses suffered by a plaintiff, including out-of-pocket expenses incurred in filing the suit, other forms of monetary or material loss, and pain, suffering, and mental anguish.

punitive damages

Money a court may award to punish a wrongdoer when a wrongful act was intentional and malicious or was done with reckless disregard for the rights of the victim.

injunction

A judicial order to do or refrain from doing a particular act.

Tort Action in State Court State inmates can file a tort action in state court. A **tort** is a civil wrong, a wrongful act, or a wrongful breach of duty, other than a breach of contract, whether intentional or accidental, from which injury to another occurs. In tort actions, inmates commonly claim that a correctional employee, such as the warden or a correctional officer, or the correctional facility itself failed to perform a duty required by law regarding the inmate. Compensation for damages is the most common objective. Tort suits often allege such deficiencies as negligence, gross or wanton negligence, or intentional wrong.

Federal Civil Rights Lawsuit Federal and state inmates can file suit in federal court alleging civil rights violations by corrections officials. Most of these suits challenge the conditions of confinement, under Section 1983 of the Civil Rights Act of 1871, which is now part of Title 42 of the U.S. Code. Lawsuits may claim that officials have deprived inmates of their constitutional rights, such as adequate medical treatment, protection against excessive force by correctional officers or violence from other inmates, due process in disciplinary hearings, and access to law libraries. According to the Bureau of Justice Statistics, 1 of 10 civil cases filed in U.S. district courts is *Section 1983 litigation* as it is commonly called.

When such suits seek monetary damages from federal agents for violation of constitutional rights, they are often referred to as *Bivens* actions, recalling the 1971 case in which the U.S. Supreme Court articulated inmates' entitlement to sue. In subsequent rulings (e.g., *FDIC* v. *Meyer*, 1994), the Court specified that "a *Bivens* action may only be maintained against an individual," not the federal agency by which he or she is employed, and it declined to extend the damage action authority of *Bivens* to permit suits against private entities operating correctional facilities under federal contract (*Correctional Services Corporation, Petitioner* v. *John E. Malesko*, 2001).

If inmates are successful in their civil suits, in state or federal courts, the courts can award three types of damages. **Nominal damages** are small amounts of money that may be awarded when inmates have sustained no actual damages, but there is clear evidence that their rights have been violated.

Compensatory damages are payments for actual losses, which may include out-of-pocket expenses the inmate incurred in filing the suit, other forms of monetary or material loss, and pain, suffering, and mental anguish. Some years ago, for example, a federal appeals court sustained an award of $9,300 against a warden and a correctional commissioner. The amount was calculated by awarding each inmate $25 for each day he had spent in solitary confinement (a total of 372 days for all the inmates) under conditions the court found cruel and unusual (*Sostre* v. *McGinnis*, 1971).

Punitive damages are awarded to punish the wrongdoer when the wrongful act was intentional and malicious or was done with reckless disregard for the rights of the inmate.

Request for Injunctive Relief An **injunction** is a judicial order to do or refrain from doing a particular act. A request for an injunction might claim adverse effects of a health, safety, or sanitation procedure and might involve the entire correctional facility. It is important for anyone working in corrections to realize that a lack of funds cannot justify failure to comply with an injunction (*Smith* v. *Sullivan*, 1977).

EXHIBIT 11–1 **Criminal Court Structure in the United States**

The Criminal Court System There is a dual court system in the United States; the federal and state court systems coexist (see Exhibit 11–1). The federal court system is nationwide with one or more federal courts in each state. These courts coexist with state court systems. Whether a defendant is tried in a federal court or a state court depends on which court has jurisdiction over the particular case.

The **jurisdiction** of a court is the power or authority of the court to act with respect to a case before it. The acts involved in the case must have taken place or had an effect in the geographic territory of the court, or a statute must give the court jurisdiction.

District courts are the trial courts of the federal system. They have original jurisdiction over cases charging defendants with violations of federal criminal laws. Each state has at least one U.S. district court, and some, like New York and California, have as many as four. There are also federal district courts in Puerto Rico, the District of Columbia, and the U.S. territories. There are currently 11 U.S. courts of appeals, arranged by circuit, a District of Columbia circuit, and one federal circuit (see Exhibit 11–2).

Each state has its own court system. Most state court structures are similar to the federal court structure—with trial courts, intermediate appellate courts, and a top appellate court. In most states, the trial courts are organized by county.

Although federal offenses are prosecuted in federal court and state offenses are prosecuted in state courts, the federal courts have supervisory jurisdiction over the administration of criminal justice in the state courts. The U.S. Supreme Court has ruled that constitutional requirements for criminal procedure in federal courts also apply to the states. Violation of these constitutional requirements can be the subject of both state appeals and federal suits by prisoners.

jurisdiction

The power, right, or authority of a court to interpret and apply the law.

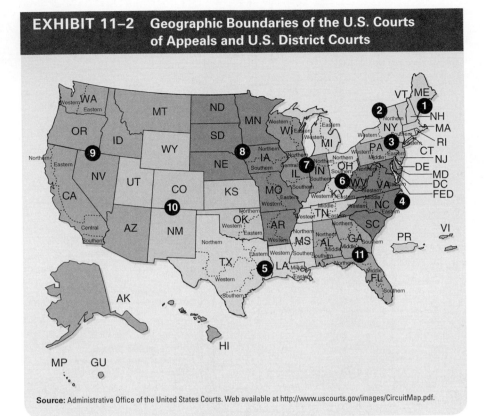

EXHIBIT 11–2 Geographic Boundaries of the U.S. Courts of Appeals and U.S. District Courts

Source: Administrative Office of the United States Courts. Web available at http://www.uscourts.gov/images/CircuitMap.pdf.

Inmate Grievance Procedures

Inmate grievance procedures are formal institutional processes for hearing inmate complaints. Grievance procedures, which typically employ internal hearing boards, are the method most frequently used by inmates to enforce the protections afforded to them by law.[13] Most inmate grievances concern discipline, program assignments, medical issues, personal property, and complaints against staff members. Only about 1 in 12 inmate grievances is approved or results in some action being taken by prison administrators to correct the problem.

The creation of formal mechanisms for the hearing of inmate grievances was encouraged by the comptroller general of the United States following the riot at New York's Attica Prison. The comptroller's report, published in 1977,[14] listed a number of reasons for establishing grievance mechanisms, including (1) promoting justice and fairness, (2) providing opportunities for inmates to voice complaints, (3) reducing the number of court cases filed by inmates, (4) assisting correctional administrators in the identification of institutional problems, and (5) reducing violence.

Today most correctional systems use a three-step process for resolving grievances. First, a staff member or committee in each institution receives complaints, investigates them, and makes decisions. Second, if a prisoner is dissatisfied with that decision, the case may be appealed to the warden. Third, if the prisoner is still dissatisfied, the complaint may be given to the state's commissioner of corrections or the state's corrections board. This three-step procedure satisfies the requirements for U.S. Department of Justice certification.

Inmate lawsuits are common. However, with the advent of more advanced grievance systems, the number of lawsuits drops, because through the grievance system some disputes can be resolved. But we still have lawsuits, and some of them are pretty outlandish. Just because someone files a lawsuit doesn't mean that it ever goes to trial.

We see quite a few filings or attempts at lawsuits on our grooming policy. It's pretty strict, because of our fears of inmates being able to change their appearance and being able to hide contraband in long hair. So male inmates have to have their hair above their collar and above their ears and no facial hair except if there are medical reasons. Males may have a neatly trimmed mustache. Females can have their hair shoulder length.

We get people saying that they have taken a vow of the Nazarite and that having a razor or scissors touch their hair would violate their beliefs. So far they have yet to prevail in court, because we have a genuine security interest. And inmates are always going to challenge issues of confinement, and some of those get pretty outlandish. We had one inmate file a lawsuit because he wanted to wear women's underwear. He did not win.

A couple of years ago we instituted a ban on all tobacco products, because of the fears of secondhand smoke and the cost of our health care. There have been some filings regarding that. They think it's their freedom—pursuit of happiness—and that it's cruel and unusual punishment not to have tobacco products. Those cases haven't gone anywhere yet either.

If a lawsuit is truly frivolous, it won't get to court—the judge will stop them before they get to that. Lawsuits I see without merit? Most of them.

Generally inmates have to exhaust the grievance process before they can file—which is good. It gives them a voice—last year we had more than 49,000 grievances filed by inmates in this system. Of those, about 1,300 were found to have merit, which is a small percentage—but it's still 1,300 cases where something wasn't quite right. And if that's the case, we need to know.

Dina Tyler
Assistant to the Director
Arkansas Department of Correction

THE PRISONERS' RIGHTS ERA (1970–1991)

Many refer to the era following *Holt* v. *Sarver* (1970) as the *prisoners' rights era*. As some have observed, "The prisoners' rights movement must be understood in the context of a 'fundamental democratization' that has transformed American society since World War II, and particularly since 1960."[15] Over the past 40 years, an increasing number of once-marginal groups, including African Americans, Hispanics, gays, and those who are economically disenfranchised and physically and mentally challenged, have acquired social recognition and legal rights that were previously unavailable to those outside the American social mainstream. Seen in this context, the prisoners' rights era was but a natural outgrowth of an encompassing social movement that recognized the existence and potential legitimacy of a wide number of group grievances.

Although the phrase *prisoners' rights era* might give the impression that prisoners won virtually every case brought during that period, such is not the case. Although prisoners did win some significant court battles, it was the turnaround in legal attitudes toward prisoners that was most remarkable. As we shall see, courts went from practically ignoring prison systems to practically running those systems. It might be more appropriate to refer to the period as the "court involvement era." We will now review some of the most important cases won *and* lost by inmates, presented in order of the constitutional amendments on which they were based.

When we speak of prisoners' rights, we are generally speaking of the rights found in four of the amendments to the U.S. Constitution. Three of these—the First (free expression), Fourth (privacy), and Eighth Amendments (cruel and unusual punishment)—are part of the Bill of Rights (the

EXHIBIT 11-3   Selected U.S. Supreme Court Cases Involving Prisoners' Rights

Case Name	Year	Decision
Brown v. Plata (Eighth Amendment)	2011	Found that seriously overcrowded conditions in California prisons are a violation of the Eighth Amendment's ban on cruel and unusual punishment.
U.S. v. Georgia	2006	Under the Americans with Disabilities Act, a state may be liable for rights deprivations suffered by inmates held in its prisons who are disabled.
Johnson v. California	2005	The decision invalidated the California Department of Corrections and Rehabilitation's unwritten policy of racially segregating prisoners in double cells each time they entered a new correctional facility.
Wilkinson v. Austin	2005	The Court upheld an Ohio policy allowing the most dangerous offenders to be held in "supermax" cells following several levels of review prior to transfer.
Overton v. Bazzetta	2003	The decision upheld the Michigan Department of Corrections' visitation regulation that denies most visits to prisoners who commit two substance abuse violations while incarcerated.
Porter v. Nussle (Eighth Amendment)	2002	The "exhaustion requirement" of the Prison Litigation Reform Act of 1995 (PLRA) applies to all inmate suits about prison life, whether they involve general circumstances or particular episodes and whether they allege excessive force or some other wrong.
Hope v. Pelzer (Eighth Amendment)	2002	The Court found an Eighth Amendment violation in the case of a prisoner who was subjected to unnecessary pain, humiliation, and risk of physical harm.
Booth v. Churner (Eighth Amendment)	2001	The decision upheld a requirement under the PLRA that state inmates must "exhaust such administrative remedies as are available" before filing a suit over prison conditions.
Lewis v. Casey	1996	Earlier cases do not guarantee inmates the wherewithal to file any and every type of legal claim. All that is required is "that they be provided with the tools to attack their sentences."
Sandin v. Conner (Fourteenth Amendment)	1995	Perhaps signaling an end to the prisoners' rights era, this case rejected the argument that disciplining inmates is a deprivation of constitutional due process rights.
Wilson v. Seiter (Eighth Amendment)	1991	The case clarified the totality of conditions notion, saying that some conditions of confinement "in combination" may violate prisoners' rights when each would not do so alone.
Washington v. Harper (Eighth Amendment)	1990	An inmate who is a danger to self or others as a result of mental illness may be treated with psychoactive drugs against his or her will.
Turner v. Safley (First Amendment)	1987	A Missouri ban on correspondence between inmates was upheld as "reasonably related to legitimate penological interests."
O'Lone v. Estate of Shabazz (First Amendment)	1987	An inmate's right to practice religion was not violated by prison officials who refused to alter his work schedule so that he could attend Friday afternoon services.

precedent

A previous judicial decision that judges should consider in deciding future cases.

first 10 amendments to the Constitution). The fourth is the Fourteenth Amendment (deprivation of life, liberty, and property). Keep in mind that what we call *inmates' rights* today are largely the result of federal court decisions that have interpreted constitutional guarantees and applied them to prisons and prison conditions. Often such a case sets a **precedent,** serving as an example or authority for future cases. Rulings in cases that find violations of inmates' rights must be implemented by the administrators of affected correctional systems and institutions. (See Exhibit 11–3 for more U.S. Supreme Court cases involving prisoners' rights.)

EXHIBIT 11–3	Selected U.S. Supreme Court Cases Involving Prisoners' Rights *(continued)*	
Case Name	**Year**	**Decision**
Whitley v. *Albers* (Eighth Amendment)	1986	The shooting and wounding of an inmate was not a violation of that inmate's rights, because "the shooting was part and parcel of a good-faith effort to restore prison security."
Ponte v. *Real*	1985	Inmates have certain rights in disciplinary hearings.
Hudson v. *Palmer* (Fourth Amendment)	1984	A prisoner has no reasonable expectation of privacy in his prison cell that entitles him to protections against "unreasonable searches."
Block v. *Rutherford* (First Amendment)	1984	State regulations may prohibit inmate union meetings and use of mail to deliver union information within the prison. Prisoners do not have a right to be present during searches of cells.
Rhodes v. *Chapman* (Eighth Amendment)	1981	Double-celling of inmates is not cruel and unusual punishment unless it involves the wanton and unnecessary infliction of pain or conditions grossly disproportionate to the severity of the crime committed.
Ruiz v. *Estelle* (Eighth Amendment)	1980	The Court found unconstitutional conditions in the Texas prison system—including overcrowding, understaffing, brutality, and substandard medical care.
Cooper v. *Morin*	1980	Neither inconvenience nor cost is an acceptable excuse for treating female inmates differently from male inmates.
Jones v. *North Carolina Prisoners' Labor Union, Inc.* (First Amendment)	1977	Inmates have no inherent right to publish newspapers or newsletters for use by other inmates.
Bounds v. *Smith*	1977	The case resulted in the creation of law libraries in many prisons.
Estelle v. *Gamble* (Eighth Amendment)	1976	Prison officials have a duty to provide proper inmate medical care.
Wolff v. *McDonnell* (Fourteenth Amendment)	1974	Sanctions cannot be levied against inmates without appropriate due process.
Procunier v. *Martinez* (First Amendment)	1974	Censorship of inmate mail is acceptable only when necessary to protect legitimate governmental interests.
Pell v. *Procunier* (First Amendment)	1974	Inmates retain First Amendment rights that are not inconsistent with their status as prisoners or with the legitimate penological objectives of the corrections system.
Cruz v. *Beto* (First Amendment)	1972	Inmates have to be given a "reasonable opportunity" to pursue their religious faiths. Also, visits can be banned if such visits constitute threats to security.
Johnson v. *Avery*	1968	Inmates have a right to consult "jailhouse lawyers" when trained legal assistance is not available.
Monroe v. *Pape*	1961	Individuals deprived of their rights by state officers acting under color of state law have a right to bring action in federal court.

First Amendment

Congress shall make no law respecting an establishment of religion, or prohibiting the free exercise thereof; or abridging the freedom of speech, or of the press; or the right of the people peaceably to assemble, and to petition the government for a redress of grievances.

First Amendment guarantees are important to members of a free society. It is no surprise, then, that some of the early prisoners' rights cases concerned those rights. For example, in 1974, in *Pell* v. *Procunier,* four California prison inmates and three journalists challenged the constitutionality of regulation 415.071 of the California Department of Corrections

Tammy Waldrop

Inspector of Correctional Facilities • Palm Beach County, Florida

Tammy Waldrop is an inspector with the Palm Beach County (Florida) Sheriff's Office, assigned to Corrections Administration. Quarterly, Waldrop inspects all four correctional facilities in Palm Beach County to verify that each one complies with agency, local, state, and American Correctional Association standards. She investigates staff and inmate grievances and works with the Legal Advisors' office to resolve conflicts.

Waldrop received her bachelor's degree in criminal justice from Florida Atlantic University in Boca Raton. She remembers that the undergraduate course that influenced her the most was a sociology course titled "Social Conflict." She says, "This course changed my perspective on life and my views on crime. It was the best preparation for my current job. It helped me understand the importance of changing conflict into occasions for problem solving."

In the future, Waldrop would like to build on her present career, attend law school, concentrate on corrections law, and work in the Legal Advisors' office.

"In corrections, the words care, custody, *and* control *are repeatedly stated as your primary tasks. But remember three additional words in your interactions with inmates:* fair, firm, *and* consistent. *And never, never lie to an inmate."*

---

legitimate penological objectives

The realistic concerns that correctional officers and administrators have for the integrity and security of the correctional institution and the safety of staff and inmates.

balancing test

A method the U.S. Supreme Court uses to decide prisoners' rights cases, weighing the rights claimed by inmates against the legitimate needs of prisons.

and Rehabilitation (CDCR). That regulation specified that "press and other media interviews with specific individual inmates will not be permitted." The rule had been imposed after a violent prison episode that corrections authorities attributed at least in part to a former policy of free face-to-face prisoner-press interviews. Such interviews had apparently resulted in a relatively small number of inmates gaining disproportionate notoriety and influence with other prisoners.

The U.S. Supreme Court held that "in light of the alternative channels of communication that are open to the inmate appellees, [regulation] 415.071 does not constitute a violation of their rights of free speech." Significantly, the Court went on to say, "A prison inmate retains those first amendment rights that are not inconsistent with his status as prisoner or with the *legitimate penological objectives* of the corrections system" (emphasis added). **Legitimate penological objectives** are the permissible aims of a correctional institution. They include the realistic concerns that correctional officers and administrators have for the integrity and security of the correctional institution and the safety of staff and inmates. The *Pell* ruling established a **balancing test** that the Supreme Court would continue to use, weighing the rights claimed by inmates against the legitimate needs of prisons.

Freedom of Speech and Expression Visits to inmates by friends and loved ones are forms of expression. But prison visits are not an absolute right. In *Cruz* v. *Beto* (1972), the Supreme Court ruled that all visits can be banned if they threaten security. Although *Cruz* involved short-term confinement facilities, the ruling has also been applied to prisons.

Another form of expression is correspondence. As a result of various court cases, prison officials can (and generally do) impose restrictions on inmate mail. Inmates receive mail not directly from the hands of postal carriers but from correctional officers. They place their outgoing mail not in U.S. Postal Service mailboxes but in containers provided by the correctional institution.

Corrections officials often read inmate mail—both incoming and outgoing—in an effort to uncover escape plans. Reading inmate mail, however, is different from censoring it. In 1974, in *Procunier* v. *Martinez,* the U.S. Supreme Court held that the censoring of inmate mail is acceptable only when necessary to protect legitimate government interests. The case turned upon First Amendment guarantees of free speech.

Under a 1979 federal appeals court decision, in *McNamara* v. *Moody,* prison officials may not prohibit inmates from writing vulgar letters or those that make disparaging remarks about the prison staff. Similarly, while correctional administrators have a legitimate interest in curbing inmates' deviant sexual behavior, courts have held that viewing nudity is not deviant sexual behavior. Hence, prison officials may not ban mailed nude pictures of inmates' wives or girlfriends (*Peppering* v. *Crist,* 1981) although restrictions against posting them on cell walls have generally been upheld. Similarly, officials may not prevent inmates from receiving, by mail direct from publishers, publications depicting nudity unless those publications depict deviant sexual behavior (*Mallery* v. *Lewis,* 1983).

In 1989, in the case of *Thornburgh* v. *Abbott,* in an effort to clear up questions raised by lower court rulings concerning mailed publications, the U.S. Supreme Court ruled as follows:

> Publications which may be rejected by a warden include but are not limited to publications which meet one of the following criteria: (1) it depicts or describes procedures for the construction or use of weapons, ammunition, bombs, or incendiary devices; (2) it depicts, encourages, or describes methods of escape from correctional facilities or contains blueprints, drawings, or similar descriptions of Bureau of Prisons institutions; (3) it depicts or describes procedures for the brewing of alcoholic beverages or the manufacture of drugs; (4) it is written in code; (5) it depicts, describes, or encourages activities which may lead to the use of physical violence or group disruption; (6) it encourages or instructs in the commission of criminal activities; (7) it is sexually explicit material which by its nature or content poses a threat to the security, good order, or discipline of the institution or facilitates criminal activity.

Unless at least one of these standards is met, restrictions on the receipt of published materials—especially magazines and newspapers that do not threaten prison security—are generally not allowed. In the 2006 U.S. Supreme Court case of *Beard* v. *Banks,* however, the justices held that Pennsylvania prison officials could legitimately prohibit the state's most violent inmates from having access to newspapers, magazines, and photographs. Prison officials had argued that the policy helped motivate better behavior on the part of particularly difficult prisoners. The Court agreed, noting that "prison officials have imposed the deprivation only upon those with serious prison-behavior problems; and those officials, relying on their professional judgment, reached an experience-based conclusion that the policies help to further legitimate prison objectives."

Similarly, in the case of *Turner* v. *Safley* (1987), the Supreme Court upheld a Missouri ban on correspondence among inmates. Such a regulation is valid, the Court said, if it is "reasonably related to legitimate penological interests." *Turner* established that officials had to show only that a regulation was reasonably *related* to a legitimate penological interest. No clear-cut damage to legitimate penological interests had to be shown.

The U.S. Supreme Court sided with corrections officials in its 1977 decision in *Jones* v. *North Carolina Prisoners' Labor Union, Inc.* In *Jones,* the Court upheld regulations established by the North Carolina Department of Correction that prohibited prisoners from soliciting other inmates to join the union and barred union meetings and bulk mailings concerning the union from outside sources. Citing *Pell* v. *Procunier,* the Court went on

Inmate rights are not absolute but are limited by legitimate penological objectives. What does the phrase "legitimate penological objectives" mean?

to say, "The prohibition on inmate-to-inmate solicitation does not unduly abridge inmates' free speech rights. If the prison officials are otherwise entitled to control organized union activity within the confines of a prison, the solicitation ban is not impermissible under the First Amendment, for such a prohibition is both reasonable and necessary."

Freedom of Religion Lawsuits involving religious practices in prison have been numerous for at least 40 years. In 1962, for example, in *Fulwood* v. *Clemmer,* the court of appeals for the District of Columbia ruled that the Black Muslim faith must be recognized as a religion and held that officials may not restrict members of that faith from holding services.

In 1970, the U.S. Supreme Court refused to hear an appeal from inmate Jack Gittlemacker, who wanted the state of Pennsylvania to provide him with a clergyman of his faith. The Court held that although states must give inmates the opportunity to practice their religions, they are not required to provide clergy for that purpose.

In *Cruz* v. *Beto* (mentioned earlier), the Supreme Court also decided that inmates had to be given a "reasonable opportunity" to pursue their religious faiths. Later federal court decisions expanded this decision, requiring officials to provide such a "reasonable opportunity" even to inmates whose religious faiths were not traditional.

In 1975, the U.S. Court of Appeals for the Second Circuit ruled in *Kahane* v. *Carlson* that an Orthodox Jewish inmate has the right to a kosher diet unless

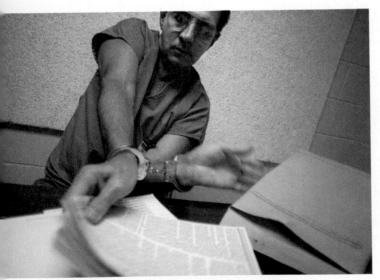

Inmates have limited rights to send and receive mail. Restrictions on inmates' mail focus on maintaining institutional security. Judicial interpretations of which constitutional amendment have led to inmates' rights to send and receive mail?

the government can show good cause for not providing it. Similarly, the courts have held that "Muslims' request for one full-course pork-free meal once a day and coffee three times daily is essentially a plea for a modest degree of official deference to their religious obligations" (*Barnett* v. *Rodgers,* 1969).

On the other hand, courts have determined that some inmate religious demands need not be met. In the 1986 Fifth Circuit Court of Appeals case of *Udey* v. *Kastner*, for example, Muslim prisoners had requested raw milk, distilled water, and organic fruits, juices, vegetables, and meats. The special diet was so costly that a federal court allowed the prison to deny the inmates' request.

In 2000, the Religious Land Use and Institutionalized Persons Act (RLU-IPA) became law. RLUIPA says, "No government shall impose a substantial burden on the religious exercise of a person residing in or confined to an institution even if the burden results from a rule of general applicability unless the government demonstrates that imposition of the burden on that person (1) is in furtherance of a compelling governmental interest; and (2) is the least restrictive means of furthering that compelling governmental interest." Because RLUIPA is a federal law, it is especially relevant to prison programs and activities that are at least partially supported with federal monies. In 2005, in the case of *Benning* v. *State*, the Eleventh Circuit Court of Appeals found in favor of a Georgia state prison inmate who claimed that RLUIPA supported his right as a "Torah observant Jew" to eat only kosher food and wear a yarmulke (or skullcap) at all times. Also in 2005, in the case of *Cutter* v. *Wilkinson*, the U.S. Supreme Court ruled in favor of past and present Ohio inmates who claimed that the state's correctional system failed to accommodate their nonmainstream religious practices.

Fourth Amendment

The right of the people to be secure in their persons, houses, papers, and effects, against unreasonable searches and seizures, shall not be violated, and no Warrants shall issue, but upon probable cause, supported by Oath or affirmation, and particularly describing the place to be searched, and the persons or things to be seized.

The right to privacy is at the heart of the Fourth Amendment. Clearly, unreasonable searches without warrants are unconstitutional. Does this mean that an inmate has a right to privacy in his or her cell? When is it reasonable

Correctional officers preparing for a cell search at Rikers Island Jail in New York City. One of the officers is carrying an electric stun shield for protection from aggressive inmates. Prisoners do not retain the right to privacy in their cells or possessions because institutional interests of safety and security supersede constitutional guarantees of privacy. Under which amendment to the Constitution does the right to be free from unreasonable searches and seizures fall?

My name is Brian Pierce. I'm an ex-con.

Let me tell you about myself. I grew up in a small southern Minnesota river town. In an effort to bring our family closer together, my parents purchased a small family-run tourist business they hoped we could eventually run as a family. My parents have always been hard workers and Christians. I am not sure what got me started really, but by the time I was 14 I was using drugs heavily and starting to spin the revolving door of Minnesota's illustrious correctional system.

First, I was court-ordered into a drug treatment center called the Cannon Valley Center in Cannon Falls, Minnesota. From there I went to a halfway house in Winona named the East House. When the county ran out of funding, they told me I could leave, despite the fact that the counselors did not think I was ready. Not long after getting home I was on the way to the Minnesota Correctional Facility at Red Wing, the end of the line for juveniles in Minnesota.

When I turned 18, I was moving too fast to slow down and was soon on my way to the Minnesota Correctional Facility at St. Cloud. I was sentenced to 38 months for third-degree burglary and received two shorter sentences that ran concurrently for theft charges. Under Minnesota's guidelines, I had to serve two-thirds of that sentence inside and the remaining one-third on parole.

St. Cloud is relatively old and made predominately out of dark gray granite. The wall is solid granite and somewhere around 20 feet high and several feet thick. It encompasses over 50 acres, including several cell houses, factories, maintenance facilities, and a yard for recreation. There are armed guard towers spaced evenly around the top of the wall.

Like most of my friends there, I got out and quickly got back into the same old routine. An Olmstead County judge gave me the option of pleading guilty to possession of a controlled substance but getting a stay of adjudication pursuant to Minnesota Statute Section 152.18 and being sentenced to treatment rather than a prison term. If I completed the recommended treatment, follow-up, and aftercare, the charge would not appear on my record. Although it sounded good, I had already been in prison once and thought I would screw it up in the treatment program and end up doing the time anyway. I asked to have my sentence executed.

A few months after being released from St. Cloud for the second time in four years, I jumped my parole and began wandering around the country with a group of misfits selling Dunn-EZ, a homemade chemical cleaner, to small businesses. Eventually, we ended up in Atlanta, Georgia, where I met my wife. She was a single mother with two young boys and was as wild as I was. Together, my wife, the boys, and I traveled the country treading water for the next several months until we found ourselves in the Lowndes County, Georgia, jail for credit card fraud. It was the most miserable time I have ever had in jail—first, because the woman I loved was in with me and, second, because the conditions were unbelievable. I slept on the floor of a very small one-man cell with two other guys. At night the guards would come by and for a Little Debbie snack or two, they would sell you a full bottle of Nyquil. One of my cell mates would drink it and get high.

With the help of my parents, my new wife and I rode the Greyhound back to Minnesota. I had to finish up about 30 days' worth of my last Minnesota sentence so that my parole would expire. Because the time left on my sentence was so short, Minnesota refused to extradite me from Georgia for the parole violation (leaving the state) but was ready and willing to incarcerate me for every day I had coming if I returned to Minnesota.

Once released and working odd jobs, I enrolled in the University of Minnesota, Duluth. I received my B.A. *magna cum laude* in criminology, with a minor in psychology, almost four years later. Graduating from college felt so unbelievably good to me. I was energized and committed to going on to law school. I applied to the University of Minnesota's law school, where I received my Juris Doctorate *cum laude,* May 10, 1997. Midway through my first year I hooked up with a law professor interested in computers, as I was. Together we created the Human Rights Library on the World Wide Web.

I completed a one-year judicial clerkship with a judge on the Court of Appeals, and I am currently clerking for my second year with the Chief Judge of the Court of Appeals. In addition, I develop Web sites for law firms and nonprofit human rights organizations, and I am writing a book. I also do public speaking about drugs, crime, corrections, and rehabilitation.

Brian Pierce

to search a cell without a warrant? Some suggest that the needs of institutional security prohibit privacy for inmates. Others argue that a prison cell is the equivalent of an inmate's house. Over the years, the courts have been fairly consistent in deciding that the privacy rights implied in this amendment must be greatly reduced in prisons to maintain institutional security.

In *United States* v. *Hitchcock* (1972), an inmate claimed that his Fourth Amendment rights had been violated by a warrantless search and seizure of documents in his prison cell. Previously, courts had generally held that "constitutionally protected" places—such as homes, motel rooms, safe-deposit boxes, and certain places of business—could not be searched without a warrant. In *Hitchcock*, however, the U.S. Court of Appeals for the Ninth Circuit created a new standard: "first, that a person have exhibited an actual (subjective) expectation of privacy and second, that the expectation be one that society is prepared to recognize as reasonable." The court concluded that, although Hitchcock plainly expected to keep his documents private, his expectation was not reasonable. In the words of the court,

> It is obvious that a jail shares none of the attributes of privacy of a home, an automobile, an office, or a hotel room. In prison, official surveillance has traditionally been the order of the day. . . . [Hence], we do not feel that it is reasonable for a prisoner to consider his cell private.

In *Hudson* v. *Palmer* (1984), a Virginia inmate claimed a correctional officer had unreasonably destroyed some of his permitted personal property during a search of his cell. The inmate also claimed that under the Fourth Amendment, the cell search was illegal. Echoing *Hitchcock*, the U.S. Supreme Court ruled that "a prisoner has no reasonable expectation of privacy in his prison cell entitling him to the protection of the Fourth Amendment against unreasonable searches." Similarly, in *Block* v. *Rutherford* (1984), the Court ruled that prisoners do not have the right to be present during searches of their cells.

In 1985, the Ninth Circuit Court of Appeals decided a case involving inmates at San Quentin State Prison (*Grummett* v. *Rushen*). The inmates had brought a class action lawsuit against prison administrators, objecting to the policy of allowing female correctional officers to view nude or partly clothed male inmates. Women officers, complained the inmates, could see male inmates while they were dressing, showering, being strip-searched, or using toilet facilities. Such viewing, said the inmates, violated privacy rights guaranteed by the U.S. Constitution.

At the time of the suit, approximately 113 of the 720 correctional officers at San Quentin were female. Both female and male correctional officers were assigned to patrol the cell block tiers and gun rails. Both were also assigned to supervise showering from the tiers and from the gun rails, but only male officers were permitted to accompany inmates to the shower cells and lock them inside to disrobe and shower. Female officers were allowed to conduct pat-down searches that included the groin area.

The court found that prison officials had "struck an acceptable balance among the inmates' privacy interests, the institution's security requirements, and the female guards' employment rights." According to the court,

> The female guards are restricted in their contact with the inmates, and the record clearly demonstrates that at all times they have conducted themselves in a professional manner, and have treated the inmates with respect and dignity. . . . Routine pat-down searches, which include the groin area, and which are otherwise justified by security needs, do not violate the Fourteenth Amendment because a correctional officer of the opposite gender conducts such a search.

Eighth Amendment

Excessive bail shall not be required, nor excessive fines imposed, nor cruel and unusual punishments inflicted.

Many prisoners' rights cases turn upon the issue of **cruel and unusual punishment**. Defining such punishment is not easy. A working definition, however, might be "punishments that are grossly disproportionate to the offense as well as those that transgress today's broad and idealistic concepts of dignity, civilized standards, humanity, and decency."[16] Cases concerning constitutional prohibition of cruel and unusual punishment have centered on prisoners' need for decent conditions of confinement. In the case that began this chapter, *Brown* v. *Plata* (2011), for example,

cruel and unusual punishment
A penalty that is grossly disproportionate to the offense or that violates today's broad and idealistic concepts of dignity, civilized standards, humanity, and decency (*Estelle* v. *Gamble,* 1976, and *Hutto* v. *Finney,* 1978). In the area of capital punishment, cruel and unusual punishments are those that involve torture, a lingering death, or unnecessary pain.

overcrowded conditions in California prisons were found to have violated the Eighth Amendment by making it impossible for adequate health care to be delivered to most inmates. Inmates' rights cases involving the Eighth Amendment cover areas as diverse as medical care, prison conditions, physical insecurity, psychological stress, and capital punishment.

Medical Care The history of inmates' rights in the health care area can be traced to the 1970 case of *Holt* v. *Sarver*[17] in which a federal district court declared the entire Arkansas prison system inhumane and found that it was in violation of the Constitution's Eighth Amendment's ban on cruel and unusual punishment.

In a related case, medical personnel in state prisons had given inmates injections of apomorphine without their consent in a program of "aversive stimuli." The drug caused vomiting, which lasted from 15 minutes to an hour. The state justified it as "Pavlovian conditioning." The federal courts, however, soon prohibited the practice (*Knecht* v. *Gillman*, 1973).

Another decision, that of *Estelle* v. *Gamble* (1976), spelled out the duty of prison officials to provide inmates with medical care. The Court held that prison officials could not lawfully demonstrate **deliberate indifference** to the medical needs of prisoners. In the words of the Court, "Deliberate indifference to serious medical needs of prisoners constitutes the 'unnecessary and wanton infliction of pain' proscribed by the Eighth Amendment." A serious medical condition is one that "causes pain, discomfort, or threat to good health" (*Rufo* v. *Inmates of Suffolk County Jail*, 1992). The mental health needs of prisoners are governed by the same constitutional standard of deliberate indifference as those described in court opinions dealing with the physical health of inmates.[18]

Prison Conditions The 1976 federal court case of *Pugh* v. *Locke* introduced the **totality of conditions** standard. That standard, said the court, is to be used in evaluating whether prison conditions are cruel and unusual. The *Pugh* court held that "prison conditions [in Alabama] are so debilitating that they necessarily deprive inmates of any opportunity to rehabilitate themselves or even maintain skills already possessed." The totality of conditions approach was also applied in a 1977 federal case,

deliberate indifference

Intentional and willful indifference. Within the field of correctional practice, the term refers to calculated inattention to unconstitutional conditions of confinement.

totality of conditions

A standard to be used in evaluating whether prison conditions are cruel and unusual.

A Newark, NJ, prison inmate takes tuberculosis medication as a nurse watches. A number of Eighth Amendment cases have established that prison officials have a duty to provide adequate medical care to inmates in their charge. How does the concept of "deliberate indifference" relate to that requirement?

Battle v. *Anderson,* in which officials in overcrowded Oklahoma prisons had forced inmates to sleep in garages, barbershops, libraries, and stairwells. Oklahoma prison administrators were found to be in violation of the cruel and unusual punishment clause of the U.S. Constitution.

The U.S. Supreme Court ruled on the use of solitary confinement in *Hutto* v. *Finney* (1978). The Court held that confinement in Arkansas's segregation (solitary confinement) cells for more than 30 days was cruel and unusual punishment. It then went on to exhort lower courts to consider the totality of the conditions of confinement in future Eighth Amendment cases. Where appropriate, it said, a court should specify the changes needed to remedy the constitutional violation.

In the 1991 case of *Wilson* v. *Seiter,* the U.S. Supreme Court clarified the totality of conditions standard. The Court noted,

> Some conditions of confinement may establish an Eighth Amendment violation "in combination" when each would not do so alone, but only when they have a mutually enforcing effect that produces the deprivation of a single, identifiable human need such as food, warmth, or exercise—for example, a low cell temperature at night combined with a failure to issue blankets. . . . To say that some prison conditions may interact in this fashion is a far cry from saying that all prison conditions are a seamless web for Eighth Amendment purposes. Nothing so [shapeless] as "overall conditions" can rise to the level of cruel and unusual punishment when no specific deprivation of a single human need exists.

Several rulings have addressed inmate claims that overcrowding was cruel and unusual punishment. A U.S. Supreme Court case, *Rhodes* v. *Chapman* (1981), decided the issue of double-celling (housing two inmates in a cell designed for one) in long-term correctional facilities. In response to rising prison populations, Ohio authorities had begun double-celling. There was no evidence that Ohio authorities had wantonly inflicted pain through the practice, and double-celling had not resulted in food deprivation, a lower quality of medical care, or a decrease in sanitation standards. For those reasons, the Court denied the inmates' claims.

In *Rhodes,* the Court also emphasized that the Eighth Amendment prohibition of cruel and unusual punishment is a fluid concept that "must draw its meaning from the evolving standards of decency that mark the progress of a maturing society." In other words, what is considered cruel and unusual changes as society evolves.

In 1982, the U.S. Court of Appeals for the Seventh Circuit ruled, in *Smith* v. *Fairman,* that double-celling in a short-term facility (a jail) was not cruel and unusual punishment. The court said that government officials did not intend to punish inmates by double-celling. The double-celling was innocent overcrowding required by circumstances.

Many conditions of confinement that violate prisoners' Eighth Amendment rights can be remedied by changes in prison rules, by special training for correctional personnel, or by educational programs for prisoners. The remedies can be implemented through everyday administrative policies in the prison once prisoners' court petitions have brought violations to light. Relief of overcrowding, however, is not always within the power of prison administrators. Prison officials have little control over the sizes of their prisons or the numbers of inmates the courts assign to them. New prison facilities are expensive and take time to build.

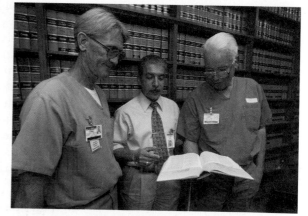

The Eighth Amendment's prohibition of cruel and unusual punishment has been tied to prisoners' need for decent conditions of confinement. In determining whether conditions such as overcrowding and inadequate diet constitute a denial of such protection, courts have used the concept of totality of conditions. What is meant by the totality of conditions?

Fourteenth Amendment

No State shall make or enforce any law which shall abridge the privileges or immunities of citizens of the United States; nor shall any State deprive any person of life, liberty, or property, without due process of law; nor deny to any person within its jurisdiction the equal protection of the laws.

When the Constitution and the Bill of Rights became law, the people of many states thought the document applied only to federal courts and to federal law. This attitude prevailed at least until the end of the Civil War. After the war, to clarify the status of the newly freed slaves and to apply the Bill of Rights to state actions, the Fourteenth Amendment was passed. The just-quoted portion of the Fourteenth Amendment is relevant to our discussion.

Most cases involving prisoners' rights and the Fourteenth Amendment deal with issues of **due process.** Due process requires that laws and legal procedures be reasonable and that they be applied fairly and equally. The right to due process is a right to be fairly heard before being deprived of life or liberty.

By 1987, long after the hands-off doctrine had eroded, U.S. Supreme Court justice Sandra Day O'Connor summarized the thrust of earlier opinions, holding that "prison walls do not form a barrier separating prison inmates from the protections of the Constitution" (*Turner* v. *Safley*). Without access to the courts, O'Connor said, inmates have no due process opportunities.

To bring their cases to court, however, prisoners need access to legal materials, and many of them need legal assistance. What if one inmate understands how to file cases with the court, but a second inmate does not? Does the second inmate have a right to enlist the aid of the first? "Yes," said the U.S. Supreme Court in *Johnson* v. *Avery* (1968). Inmates have a right to consult "jailhouse lawyers" (other inmates knowledgeable in the law) when trained legal advisers are not available.

The case of *Wolff* v. *McDonnell* (1974) expanded the concept of due process by applying it to disciplinary actions within prisons. Prior to *Wolff*, prison administrators had the discretion to discipline inmates who broke prison rules. Disciplinary procedures were often tied to vague or nonexistent rules of conduct and were exercised without challenge. A prisoner might be assigned to solitary confinement or might have good-time credits reduced because of misconduct. Because the prisoner was physically confined and lacked outside communication, there was no opportunity for the prisoner to challenge the charge. The *Wolff* Court concluded that sanctions (disciplinary actions) could not be levied against inmates without appropriate due process, saying,

> [The state of Nebraska] asserts that the procedure for disciplining prison inmates for serious misconduct is a matter of policy raising no constitutional issue. If the position implies that prisoners in state institutions are wholly without the protection of the Constitution and the Due Process Clause, it is plainly untenable. Lawful imprisonment necessarily makes unavailable many rights and privileges of the ordinary citizen, a retraction justified by the consideration underlying our penal system. . . . But though his rights may be diminished by the needs and exigencies of the institutional environment, a prisoner is not wholly stripped of constitutional protections when he is imprisoned for a crime.

The *Wolff* Court imposed minimal due process requirements on prison disciplinary proceedings that could lead to solitary confinement or reduction of good-time credits. The requirements included (1) advance notice by means of a written statement of the claimed violation, (2) a written

due process

A right guaranteed by the Fifth, Sixth, and Fourteenth Amendments to the U.S. Constitution and generally understood, in legal contexts, to mean the expected course of legal proceedings according to the rules and forms established for the protection of persons' rights.

statement by an impartial fact finder of the evidence relied on and the reasons for imposing punishment, and (3) an opportunity to testify and call witnesses unless the fact finder concluded such proceedings would undermine institutional security.

In 1976, inmates lost three due process appeals. First, in *Baxter* v. *Palmigiano*, the Supreme Court decided that due process for an inmate in a disciplinary hearing does not include a right to counsel even when the consequences are potentially "serious." In a second opinion issued that year (*Meacham* v. *Fano*), the Court held that prisoners have no right to be in any particular prison and therefore have no due process protections before being transferred from one prison to another. A third case (*Stone* v. *Powell*) denied prisoners the right in most instances to seek federal review of state court Fourth Amendment search-and-seizure decisions.

Inmates' right to legal materials was formally recognized in 1977 in the U.S. Supreme Court decision in *Bounds* v. *Smith*. In *Bounds*, the Court held,

> The fundamental constitutional right of access to the courts requires prison authorities to assist inmates in the preparation and filing of meaningful legal papers by providing prisoners with adequate law libraries or adequate assistance from persons trained in the law.

As a result of the *Bounds* decision, law libraries were created in prisons across the nation.

As we saw in Chapter 9, one challenge facing corrections personnel is to find safe, humane ways to manage inmate populations. Inmates often have grievances regarding conditions of confinement or disciplinary actions for infractions. Those grievances must be dealt with to maintain the safety and security of the institution. The Supreme Court's decision in *Jones* v. *North Carolina Prisoners' Labor Union, Inc.* (1977) required prisons to establish and maintain formal opportunities for the airing of inmate grievances. *Ponte* v. *Real* (1985) required prison officials to explain to inmates why their requests to have witnesses appear on their behalf at disciplinary hearings were denied.

The due process clause protects against unlawful deprivation of life or liberty. When a prisoner sued for damages for injuries (*Daniels* v. *Williams*, 1986), the Supreme Court ruled that prisoners could sue for damages in federal court only if officials had inflicted injury intentionally. According to the Court, "The due process clause is simply not implicated by a negligent act of an official causing unintended loss or injury to life, liberty, or property."

A 2001 ruling by a panel of federal judges in the case of *Gerber* v. *Hickman* addressed a unique claim of unlawful deprivation of life. Gerber wanted to impregnate his wife. He was, however, serving a life sentence in a California Department of Corrections and Rehabilitation (CDCR) prison, and CDCR regulations prohibit conjugal visits for life-term prisoners. Consequently, the Gerbers could not employ the usual method for creating the child they desired.

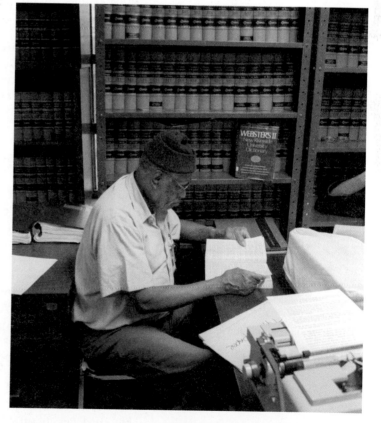

Inmates must be allowed access to the courts and assistance in preparing their cases. To meet that requirement, most states stock law libraries in each correctional institution. Under which clause of the Fourteenth Amendment does inmates' access to the courts fall?

Undeterred, Gerber sought permission to artificially inseminate his wife. CDCR officials denied his request, citing the facts that (1) impregnating his wife was not medically necessary for Gerber's physical well-being and (2) Gerber had failed to show that denial of the request would violate his constitutional rights.

In a civil suit, however, Gerber alleged that the CDCR regulation violated the due process clause by denying him his constitutional right to procreate. On a defendant's motion, the suit was dismissed in federal district court. Gerber appealed to the U.S. Court of Appeals for the Ninth Circuit where a three-judge panel initially held "that the right to procreate survives incarceration." The panel reversed the district court's dismissal and reinstated Gerber's claim, mandating further review of the case. Upon review, however, the full Ninth Circuit Court of Appeals ruled that prison inmates do not have a constitutional right to fatherhood. The appellate court's majority opinion cited the 1984 U.S. Supreme Court case of *Hudson* v. *Palmer* (mentioned earlier in this chapter), which held that "while persons imprisoned . . . enjoy many protections of the Constitution, it is also clear that imprisonment carries with it the . . . loss of many significant rights."

As we have seen, federal and state inmates can file suits in federal court alleging civil rights violations by corrections officials. In 1988, the U.S. Supreme Court (in *West* v. *Atkins*) decided that private citizens who contracted to do work for prisons could be sued for civil rights violations against inmates. The Court found that such contractors were acting "under color of state law," as required by Section 1983 of the Civil Rights Act of 1871.

As a result of Supreme Court decisions, most prisons now have rules that provide for necessary due process when prisoners appear before disciplinary committees. The makeup of disciplinary committees varies among institutions. The committees may include both inmates and free citizens.

End of the Prisoners' Rights Era

By the late 1980s, the prisoners' rights era was drawing to a close. Following a change in the composition of the Supreme Court, the justices sitting on the Court had become less sympathetic to prisoners' civil rights claims. As discussed earlier, the 1986 case of *Daniels* v. *Williams* helped establish the notion that due process requirements were intended to prevent abuses of power by correctional officials, not to protect against mere carelessness. Furthermore, judicial and legislative officials began to realize that inmates frequently abused what had previously been seen as their right of access to the courts. As state costs of defending against **frivolous lawsuits** by inmates began to grow, federal courts began to take a new look at prisoners' rights.

Examples of abuse of the court system by prison inmates abound. One inmate sued the state of Florida because he got only one bread roll with dinner. He sued two more times because he did not get a salad with lunch and because prison-provided TV dinners did not come with drinks. He sued yet again because his cell was not equipped with a television. Another inmate claimed prison officials were denying him freedom of religion. His religion, he said, required him to attend prison chapel services in the nude. Still another inmate, afraid that he could get pregnant through homosexual relations, sued because prison officials would not give him birth control pills.

frivolous lawsuits

Lawsuits with no foundation in fact. They are generally brought for publicity, political, or other reasons not related to law.

As early as 1977, the U.S. Supreme Court refused to hear an appeal from Henry William Theriault, founder of the Church of the New Song (or CONS).[19] Theriault, an inmate at the federal penitentiary in Atlanta, had a mail-order divinity degree. Members of CONS celebrated communion every Friday night. They claimed that prison officials must supply them with steak and Harvey's Bristol Cream sherry for the practice. Although "Bishop Theriault" admitted that he had originally created CONS to mock other religions, he claimed that he became a serious believer as the religion developed and acquired more followers. The U.S. Supreme Court dismissed that argument and held that the First Amendment does not protect so-called religions that are obvious shams.

The Cases One of the important cases setting the stage for a review of prisoners' claimed rights was that of *Turner* v. *Safley,* decided in 1987. In *Turner,* the U.S. Supreme Court established a four-pronged test for determining the reasonableness of prison regulations. In order for a prison regulation to be acceptable, said the Court, there must first be a "valid, rational connection" between the prison regulation and the "legitimate governmental interest" offered to justify it. A second factor relevant in determining the reasonableness of a prison restriction, especially one that limits otherwise established rights, is whether alternative means of exercising that right remain available to prison inmates. If they do, then the restriction is more acceptable. A third consideration is the impact that accommodating an asserted constitutional right would have on officers and other inmates and on the allocation of scarce prison resources. If accommodation makes the job of correctional officers more dangerous or if it is unduly expensive, then it need not be granted. Finally, the fourth prong holds that prisoners have no recourse if there are no readily available alternatives that might permit exercise of claimed rights without compromising penological goals. In other words, if inmates or their attorneys cannot suggest a workable alternative to meet an asserted right, then accommodations need not be made.

In *Wilson* v. *Seiter* (1991), the U.S. Supreme Court sided with prison officials in a way uncharacteristic of the previous two decades. In *Wilson,* the Court found that overcrowding, excessive noise, insufficient locker space, and similar conditions did not violate the Constitution if the intent of prison officials was not malicious. The Court ruled that the actions of officials did not meet the "deliberate indifference" standard defined in *Estelle* v. *Gamble* (1976).

After *Wilson,* inmates won very few new cases. The courts either reversed themselves or tightened the conditions under which inmates could win favorable decisions. Decisions supporting freedom of religion had been among the earliest and most complete victories during the prisoners' rights era. Even in that area, however, things began to change. The courts held that crucifixes and rosaries could legally be denied to inmates because of their possible use as weapons (*Mark* v. *Nix,* 1993, and *Escobar* v. *Landwehr,* 1993). Although some jurisdictions had previously allowed certain Native American religious items within prisons (*Sample* v. *Borg,* 1987), the courts now ruled that prohibiting ceremonial pipes, medicine bags, and eagle claws did *not* violate the First Amendment rights of Native American inmates (*Bettis* v. *Delo,* 1994).

In the 1992 Supreme Court case of *Hudson* v. *McMillan,* the "deliberate indifference" standard was interpreted as requiring both actual knowledge *and* disregard of the risk of harm to inmates or others. This tighter definition allowed federal courts to side more easily with state prison officials in cases in which prisoners claimed there was deliberate indifference. In 1994, in the case of *Farmer* v. *Brennan*, the Supreme Court ruled that even when a prisoner is harmed and even when prison officials knew that the risk of harm existed, officials cannot be held liable if they took appropriate steps to mitigate that risk.

If there was any question that the prisoners' rights era had ended, that question was settled in 1995 by the case of *Sandin* v. *Conner*. In *Sandin*, the Supreme Court rejected the argument that, by disciplining inmates, a state deprived prisoners of their constitutional right not to be deprived of liberty without due process. "The time has come to return to those due process principles that were correctly established and applied in earlier times," said the Court. A year later, the decision in *Lewis* v. *Casey* overturned portions of *Bounds* v. *Smith*. The *Bounds* case had been instrumental in establishing law libraries in prisons. The Court in *Lewis* held, however, that "*Bounds* does not guarantee inmates the wherewithal to file any and every type of legal claim but requires only that they be provided with the tools to attack their sentences."

In *Edwards* v. *Balisok* (1997), the Supreme Court made it even harder to successfully challenge prison disciplinary convictions. The Court held that prisoners cannot sue for monetary damages under Section 1983 of the U.S. Code for loss of good-time credits until they are able to sue successfully in state court to have their disciplinary conviction set aside.

In 2003, in the case of *Overton* v. *Bazzetta*, the Court upheld visitation regulations established by the Michigan Department of Corrections that denied most visits to prisoners who had committed two substance abuse violations while incarcerated. In its ruling, the Court said that "the regulations bear a rational relation to legitimate penological interests [sufficient] to sustain them." Wording taken directly from the Court's opinion is shown in Exhibit 11–4. It provides a summary of the factors used by the courts to decide whether prison regulations meet constitutional requirements.

Finally, in 2008, in a somewhat different kind of case, the U.S. Supreme Court found that federal correctional officers are "law enforcement officers" within the meaning of federal law—and that they are therefore immune from claims alleging injury or loss of property "caused by negligence or a wrongful act or omission" when acting within their scope of employment. The case, *Ali* v. *Federal Bureau of Prisons*,[20] involved a federal prisoner who claimed that some of his personal belongings had disappeared when he was transferred between prisons.

The Legal Mechanisms Changes in state and federal statutes have also slowed the pace of prisoners' rights cases. In 1980, Congress modified the Civil Rights of Institutionalized Persons Act.[21] It now requires a state inmate to exhaust all state remedies before filing a petition for a writ of *habeas corpus* in federal court. In effect, a state prisoner must give the state an opportunity to correct alleged violations of its prisoners' federal rights (*Duncan* v. *Henry*, 1995). Inmates in federal prisons may still file *habeas corpus* petitions directly in federal court. In their petitions, federal inmates are now required to show (1) that they were deprived of some right to which they were entitled despite the confinement and (2) that the deprivation of this right made the imprisonment more burdensome.

The Prison Litigation Reform Act of 1995[22] (PLRA) was another legislative response to the ballooning number of civil rights lawsuits filed by prisoners. It restricts the filing of lawsuits in federal courts by:

EXHIBIT 11–4 *Overton v. Bazzetta (2003)*

Responding to concerns about prison security problems caused by the increasing number of visitors to Michigan's prisons and about substance abuse among inmates, the Michigan Department of Corrections (MDOC) promulgated new regulations limiting prison visitation. . . .

The fact that the regulations bear a rational relation to legitimate penological interests suffices to sustain them regardless of whether respondents have a constitutional right of association that has survived incarceration. This Court accords substantial deference to the professional judgment of prison administrators, who bear a significant responsibility for defining a corrections system's legitimate goals and determining the most appropriate means to accomplish them. The regulations satisfy each of four factors used to decide whether a prison regulation affecting a constitutional right that survives incarceration withstands constitutional challenge.

First, the regulations bear a rational relationship to a legitimate penological interest. The restrictions on children's visitation are related to MDOC's valid interests in maintaining internal security and protecting child visitors from exposure to sexual or other misconduct or from accidental injury. They promote internal security, perhaps the most legitimate penological goal, by reducing the total number of visitors and by limiting disruption caused by children. It is also reasonable to ensure that the visiting child is accompanied and supervised by adults charged with protecting the child's best interests. Prohibiting visitation by former inmates bears a self-evident connection to the State's interest in maintaining prison security and preventing future crime. Restricting visitation for inmates with two substance-abuse violations serves the legitimate goal of deterring drug and alcohol use within prison.

Second, respondents have alternative means of exercising their asserted right of association with those prohibited from visiting. They can send messages through those who are permitted to visit, and can communicate by letter and telephone. Visitation alternatives need not be ideal; they need only be available.

Third, accommodating the associational right would have a considerable impact on guards, other inmates, the allocation of prison resources, and the safety of visitors by causing a significant reallocation of the prison system's financial resources and by impairing corrections officers ability to protect all those inside a prison's walls.

Finally, [complainants] have suggested no alternatives that fully accommodate the asserted right while not imposing more than a [minimum] cost to the valid penological goals.

Source: *Overton* v. *Bazzetta,* 539 U.S. 126 (2003), Syllabus.

1. requiring state prisoners to exhaust all local administrative remedies prior to filing suit in federal court;
2. requiring inmates to pay federal filing fees unless they can claim pauper status;[23]
3. limiting awards of attorneys' fees in successful lawsuits;
4. requiring judges to screen all inmate lawsuits and immediately dismiss those they find frivolous;
5. revoking good-time credit toward early release if inmates file malicious lawsuits;
6. barring prisoners from suing the federal government for mental or emotional injury unless there is an accompanying physical injury;
7. allowing court orders to go no further than necessary to correct the particular inmate's civil rights problem;
8. requiring some court orders to be renewed every two years or be lifted; and
9. ensuring that no single judge can order the release of federal inmates for overcrowding.

In May 2001, the U.S. Supreme Court further restricted inmate options under the PLRA. The ruling mandates that inmates must complete prison administrative processes that could provide some relief before suing over prison conditions even if that relief would *not include a monetary payment* (*Booth* v. *Churner*, 2001).

A 2005 study of the PLRA's effectiveness conducted by the National Council for State Courts (NCSC), found that the PLRA "achieved its intended effects" and significantly lowered the number of frivolous filings by inmates in federal courts.[24]

FEMALE INMATES AND THE COURTS

The prisoners' rights movement has been largely a male phenomenon. While male inmates were petitioning the courts for expansion of their rights, female inmates frequently had to resort to the courts simply to gain rights that male inmates already had.

The Cases

One early state case, *Barefield* v. *Leach* (1974), demonstrated that the opportunities and programs for female inmates were clearly inferior to those for male inmates. In that case, a court in New Mexico spelled out one standard for equal treatment of male and female inmates. The court said that the equal-protection clause of the Constitution requires equal treatment of male and female inmates but not identical treatment. *Barefield*, however, was a state case—not binding on other states or the federal government.

In 1977, in *State, ex rel. Olson* v. *Maxwell*, the Supreme Court of North Dakota ruled that a lack of funds was not an acceptable justification for unequal treatment of male and female prisoners. Although this decision also came in a state court case, it would later be cited as a legal authority in a similar federal court case.

Many claims of female inmates have focused on the failure of correctional institutions to provide them with educational opportunities and medical care comparable to those provided male inmates. The equal-protection clause of which amendment guarantees female inmates conditions of confinement comparable to those of male inmates?

In *Glover* v. *Johnson* (1979), a U.S. district court case, a group of female prisoners in the Michigan system filed a class action lawsuit claiming that they were denied access to the courts and constitutional rights to equal protection. The prisoners demanded educational and vocational opportunities comparable to those for male inmates. At trial, a prison teacher testified that, although men were allowed to take shop courses, women were taught remedial courses at a junior high school level because the attitude of those in charge was "Keep it simple, these are only women." The court found that "the educational opportunities available to women prisoners in Michigan were substantially inferior to those available to male prisoners." Consequently, the court ordered a plan to provide higher education and vocational training for female prisoners in the Michigan prison system. *Glover* was a turning point in equal treatment for imprisoned women. Since 1979, female inmates have continued to win the majority of cases seeking equal treatment and the elimination of gender bias.

In the 1980 case of *Cooper* v. *Morin*, the U.S. Supreme Court accepted neither inconvenience nor cost as an excuse for treating female jail inmates differently from male inmates. Female inmates at a county jail in New York had alleged that inadequate medical attention in jail violated their civil rights. Later that same year, a federal district court rejected Virginia's claims that services for female prison inmates could not be provided at the same level as those for male inmates because of cost-effectiveness issues (*Bukhari* v. *Hutto,* 1980). Virginia authorities said that the much smaller number of women in prison raised the cost of providing each woman with services. The appellate court ordered the state of Virginia to provide equitable services for inmates, regardless of gender.

An action challenging the denial of equal protection and the conditions of confinement in the Kentucky Correctional Institution for Women was the basis of *Canterino* v. *Wilson*, decided in U.S. district court in 1982. The district court held that the "levels system" used to allocate privileges to female prisoners, a system not applied to male prisoners, violated both the equal-protection rights and the due process rights of female inmates. The court also held that female inmates in Kentucky's prisons must have the same opportunities as men for vocational education, training, recreation, and outdoor activity.

In 1982, in *McMurray* v. *Phelps*, a district court in Louisiana ordered an end to the unequal treatment of female inmates in that state's jails. (Recall that the federal courts have supervisory jurisdiction over state courts.) The next year, the Seventh Circuit Court of Appeals found that strip searches of female misdemeanor offenders awaiting bond in a Chicago lockup were unreasonable under the Fourth Amendment (*Mary Beth G.* v. *City of Chicago,* 1983). In addition, the court found that a policy of subjecting female arrestees to strip searches while subjecting similarly situated males only to hand searches violated the equal-protection clause of the Constitution.

In 1994, in a class action suit by female inmates, a federal district court held the District of Columbia Department of Corrections liable under the Eighth Amendment for inadequate gynecological examinations and testing, inadequate testing for sexually transmitted diseases, inadequate health education, inadequate prenatal care, and an inadequate overall prenatal protocol (*Women Prisoners of the District of Columbia Department of Corrections* v. *District of Columbia,* 1994).

Court oversight of OB-GYN services at the District of Columbia Department of Corrections ended in 2004, following an agreement in which the department promised to continue to provide adequate services for women inmates. The agreement ended 33 years of court oversight of the DC department—involving a total of 15 class action lawsuits filed by inmate groups or their representatives during that time.[25]

Also in 2004, U.S. district judge Myron Thompson approved a settlement in a class action lawsuit centered on concerns about medical care and general conditions at three Alabama women's prisons. Thompson said that the settlement, which required lowering the number of prisoners held at three locations, would not make the facilities "comfortable or pleasant" but would "afford class members the basic necessities mandated by the United States Constitution."[26] Affected were the Julia Tutwiler Prison for Women, the Tutwiler Annex, and the Birmingham Work Release Facility—all operated by the Alabama Department of Corrections. The lawsuit, filed by the Southern Center for Human Rights, had complained of "intensely overcrowded" and "unbearably hot and poorly ventilated dormitories." Tutwiler Prison had been built in the 1940s to hold no more than 364 inmates but was filled with more than 1,000 inmates at the time of the lawsuit. Under the agreement, the population was lowered to 700 by sending some inmates to prisons in Louisiana and by releasing others under community supervision.

REVIEW AND APPLICATIONS

SUMMARY

1 The hands-off doctrine was a working philosophy of the courts in this country until 1970. It allowed corrections officials to run prisons without court intervention. The hands-off doctrine existed because courts were reluctant to interfere with activities of the executive branch and because judges realized that they were not experts in corrections.

2 The key legal sources of prisoners' rights are the U.S. Constitution, federal statutes, state constitutions, and state statutes.

3 The central question about prisoners' rights is not whether prisoners have them, but rather, to what extent they retain or forfeit them by virtue of incarceration.

4 Inmates can challenge the legality of their confinement, associated prison conditions, and the practices of correctional officials through (1) a state *habeas corpus* action, (2) a federal *habeas corpus* action, (3) a state tort lawsuit, (4) a federal civil rights lawsuit, and (5) an injunction to obtain relief.

5 During the prisoners' rights era (1970–1991), inmates won many court cases based on claims that conditions of their confinement violated their constitutional rights. Court decisions affected inmate rights to freedom of expression, including free speech; personal communications; access to the courts and legal services; religion; assembly and association; the voicing of grievances about disciplinary procedures; protection from personal and cell searches; health care, including diet and exercise; protection from violence; adequate physical conditions of confinement; and rehabilitation.

6 Most prisoners' claims focus on denial of constitutional rights guaranteed by the First (freedom of expression and religion), Fourth (freedom from unlawful search and seizure), Eighth (freedom from cruel and unusual punishment), and Fourteenth (due process and equal protection of the law) Amendments.

7 The prisoners' rights movement has been largely a male phenomenon. More recently, female inmates have had to petition the courts to gain rights that male inmates already had.

KEY TERMS

hands-off doctrine, p. 368

prisoners' rights, p. 370

constitutional rights, p. 370

institutional needs, p. 370

civil liability, p. 371

writ of *habeas corpus*, p. 371

tort, p. 372

nominal damages, p. 372

compensatory damages, p. 372

punitive damages, p. 372

injunction, p. 372

jurisdiction, p. 373

precedent, p. 376

legitimate penological
   objectives, p. 378

balancing test, p. 378

cruel and unusual
   punishment, p. 383

deliberate indifference, p. 384

totality of conditions, p. 384

due process, p. 386

frivolous lawsuits, p. 388

QUESTIONS FOR REVIEW

1 Why was the hands-off doctrine so named? What was the basis for the doctrine?

2 What are the key legal sources of prisoners' rights?

3 What is the central question identified by this chapter with regard to prisoners' rights?

4 What are the legal mechanisms through which inmates can challenge the legality of their confinement and associated prison conditions?

5 What rights were won by inmates during what the book calls the *prisoners' rights era?*

6 What constitutional amendments are most often cited by prisoners claiming rights? What claimed rights are associated with each of these amendments?

7 Do the rights accorded male inmates correspond to the rights of female inmates? Why or why not?

THINKING CRITICALLY ABOUT CORRECTIONS

Freedom of Nonverbal Expression

The right to freedom of nonverbal expression is said to be implied in the First Amendment. Hence, how people wear their hair and how they dress are expressions that some believe are protected by the First Amendment.

1. Might there be modes of dress that interfere with a correctional institution's legitimate goals?

2. If so, what might they be?

Checks and Balance

On January 11, 2003, in a dramatic legal move shortly before leaving office, former Illinois governor George Ryan commuted the sentences of every one of the state's 167 death row inmates. Four of the sentences were reduced to 40-year terms; the remaining 163 sentences were commuted to life in prison. Governor Ryan based his action on his

determination of inherent arbitrariness and unfairness in the application of capital punishment and on the high risk of executing an innocent person.

While the scope of his action is unusual, the commutations typify the power placed in the hands of each state's chief executive. Essentially, this means that, within the respective states and based solely on personal opinion, a single individual is empowered to overturn sentencing decisions and attendant legal rulings on those decisions made at any level up to and including the nation's most powerful court, the U.S. Supreme Court.

1. Should this be the case?

2. Does the lack of a legal mechanism to counter a governor's decision regarding a pardon or a commutation violate the principle of checks and balances so intricately woven into America's state and federal governmental structures?

ON-THE-JOB DECISION MAKING

Inmate Communications

You are a prison administrator. The prison where you work has a rule that inmates may write letters in English only. This rule seems sensible. After all, if inmates could write in languages not understood by correctional officers, they could discuss plans to escape, riot, or smuggle drugs or weapons into the prison. The courts allow the censoring of outgoing inmate mail; what good is that power if corrections personnel cannot read the mail?

You realize, however, that inmates who cannot write in English will have difficulty communicating with the outside world and with their families. Inmates unable to write in English will not even be able to write to their attorneys. You also wonder what might happen if an inmate can write in English but his parents can read only a foreign language. If the inmate and his parents cannot afford long-distance phone calls, they will not be able to communicate with each other at all. You begin to consider how the English-only rule might be changed to facilitate wholesome communications while still preventing communications that might endanger the safety of the institution and the inmate population.

1. Can the English-only rule be amended to meet the inmate needs discussed here while still being consistent with legitimate institutional concerns? If so, how?

2. Does an inmate have a constitutionally protected right to communicate with his or her parents?

3. What if that right conflicts with prison policy?

Law Libraries

The Supreme Court's ruling in *Bounds* v. *Smith* (1977) led to the establishment of law libraries for prisoner use in correctional facilities throughout the nation. Numerous subsequent prisoner civil suits resulted in follow-on rulings mandating the need to maintain these libraries with up-to-date reference materials in serviceable condition.

You are an advisor on correctional issues on the staff of your state's attorney general. In the past few weeks, she has repeatedly complained that these rulings impose excessive financial demands on the state's already nearly impoverished correctional system. In particular, she says, routine vandalism by inmates who tear pages from law books and take the pages back to their cells—or simply discard them—is especially costly. It also creates a circumstance in which another inmate could threaten another civil suit upon finding a book to be "unserviceable" when attempting to use it, a threat to which the system can respond only by immediately purchasing a replacement book.

This, the attorney general says, typifies a cycle that causes an extraordinary drain on limited financial resources. She rants about the "ludicrous" fact that the reference material in her own office is so out of date as to be virtually unusable, but she cannot fix the problem because she spends that portion of her budget on repeatedly restoring the prisoners' law libraries in the various institutions throughout the state.

The attorney general has tasked you to resolve this issue.

1. What will you do?

2. Might advances in information technology be the key to a solution?

For additional information, please see: www.mhhe.com/schmalleger6e

SPECIAL PRISON POPULATIONS

Prisoners Who Are Elderly, Mentally Challenged, and Who Have HIV/AIDS

[12]

CHAPTER OBJECTIVES

After completing this chapter you should be able to do the following:

1 Define the term *inmate with special needs.*

2 Report on the management needs of special population inmates.

3 Report on the impact of substance abusers on the corrections system.

4 Discuss why treating HIV in prison is difficult.

5 Discuss the five essential elements of cost-effective management of HIV/AIDS inmates.

6 Explain why so many inmates have mental illnesses.

7 Describe ways to divert persons with mental illness from the criminal justice system.

8 List the cost and health issues associated with older inmates.

9 Review the legal issues surrounding special population inmates.

> *The democratic principle that 'all men are created equal' implies that persons with disabilities are entitled like everyone else to equal access and fair treatment appropriate to their context, whether the context is a prison, church, or place of employment.*
>
> —Marca Bristo, former chairperson, National Council on Disability, letter to the editor
>
> of the *Washington Times*, July 27, 1998

Prisoners who are elderly are creating a new phenomenon in correctional policy—*an over-50 institution* to house older inmates, provide round-the-clock nursing care, and offer hospice care for dying prisoners.

Since 1995, there has been an 85 percent increase in prisoners who are elderly. The issue of inmates who are elderly is a hidden problem that is going to grow into a dinosaur soon. Consider these cases.[1]

Dennis Whitney was condemned to die when he was 17 for a double murder. He spent 12 years on death row at the Florida State Prison (renamed Union Correctional Institution in 1973) near Raiford. His sentence was commuted to life in prison in 1972 when the U.S. Supreme Court declared Florida's death penalty law unconstitutional.

By age 61, Whitney had undergone two angioplasties at state expense to clear blocked blood vessels, and he still needed a third. The first two cost $9,000. Whitney was denied parole every time he appeared before the Florida parole commission. "If they turn me down, I'm just going to let the state take care of me for the rest of my life. I'm well fed, well clothed, and well taken care of." Whitney died a prisoner in 2005.

Seventy-three-year-old Robert Doyle is also serving a life sentence at Union Correctional Institution. He describes his prison experience as struggling to survive. There is "absolutely nothing for us to do," Doyle told a reporter. "You see people go downhill. They actually give up. This is a warehousing institution."

Today, prisoners who are elderly have an average of three chronic illnesses (an illness or condition that affects an individual's well-being for an extended interval and is usually not curable but can be controlled to provide a reasonable level of physical and psychological functioning), and incarcerating one prisoner who is elderly costs taxpayers an estimated $80,000 per year. What can or should correctional policymakers do about prisoners who are elderly? This chapter raises the issue of prisoners who are elderly, mentally ill, drug addicted, or afflicted with a communicable disease. Such prisoners are inmates with special needs and corrections professionals are responding to their incarceration in unique and innovative ways.

Dennis Whitney, shown here at age 61, had been incarcerated for 44 years in Florida for the 1960 murder of seven people. During his time in prison, Whitney received two angioplasties at state expense to clear blocked blood vessels. He was eligible for parole after serving 30 years, but the Florida Parole Commission turned him down. Just before his last parole hearing in 2004 Whitney said, "If they turn me down, I'm just going to let the state take care of me for the rest of my life. I'm well fed, well clothed, and well taken care of." And that is what happened. Whitney died a prisoner in 2005. Today the prisoners who are elderly are the fastest-growing segment of the prison population and are creating a new phenomenon in correctional policy—an over-50 institution to house older inmates, provide round-the-clock nursing care, and offer hospice care for dying inmates. Do prisoners who are elderly threaten public safety? Could they be paroled? Should they be held in nursing-home-like facilities away from the general population? What are the implications for housing a population of prisoners who are elderly?

inmates with special needs
Those prisoners who exhibit unique physical, mental, social, and programmatic needs that distinguish them from other prisoners and to whom jail and prison management and staff have to respond in nontraditional and innovative ways.

INMATES WITH SPECIAL NEEDS

Increasingly, prisons and jails are dealing with a growing population of inmates with special needs. **Inmates with special needs** are "those prisoners who exhibit unique physical, mental, social, and programmatic needs that distinguish them from other prisoners and for whom jail and prison management and staff have to respond to in nontraditional and innovative ways."[2] These special populations suffer from mental illness; chemical dependency (drug or alcohol); communicable diseases (especially HIV/AIDS and tuberculosis); chronic diseases (e.g., diabetes, heart disease, seizures, and detoxification); the general problems of people who are elderly; the special concern of managing young female offenders in correctional settings; the problems that arise when youthful offenders are housed in adult institutions; and the issues arising from sexual identity, prisoner victimization, transgender prisoners, and the management of sex offenders within correctional settings.

Such inmates present operational and administrative problems for correctional staff—it is often difficult for the staff to know what they are observing or, once they recognize an inmate's special needs, how to address the situation. Louisiana addresses the issue by partnering with the Louisiana State University health care system to provide inmate health care.[3] A plan is under review in California that would put the University of California in charge of state prison inmates' medical needs that some say could save the state $12 billion over the next decade.[4] And the majority of states now use telemedicine for medical and mental health services, staff training, and other health education programs.[5] States are finding that society benefits when correctional administrators and health professionals work together to provide regular medical care and better prevention programs.

A statewide research study on jail management in New Mexico indicated that inmates with special needs require extra attention from jail staff.[6] For example, they must be watched closely for possible suicide. Almost 9 of 10 such inmates disrupt normal jail activities; 7 of 10 require an excess of scarce medical resources; 4 of 10 engage in acts of violence; and almost 3 of 10 are abused by other inmates. The characteristics of inmates with special needs, the treatment programs offered, and the policies for dealing with those inmates depend on the type of special need.

The American Correctional Association urges correctional agencies to develop and adopt procedures for the early identification of inmates with special needs, to provide the services that respond to those needs, and to monitor and evaluate the delivery of services in both community and institutional settings (see Exhibit 12–1). This chapter reviews the management and treatment of the five largest groups of inmates with special needs: substance-abusing inmates, HIV-positive and AIDS inmates, inmates with mental illness, inmates with tuberculosis, and older inmates.

Substance-Abusing Inmates

Alcohol and other drug problems are the common denominator for most offenders in the criminal justice system, and untreated substance-abusing offenders are more likely to relapse to drug abuse and return to criminal behavior. A **substance-abusing inmate** is an incarcerated person suffering from dependency on one or more substances including alcohol and a wide range of drugs.

Substance abuse takes a toll on users, the community, and the criminal justice system. The National Center on Addiction and Substance Abuse at Columbia University (CASA) estimates that 65 percent of all U.S. jail and prison inmates (some 1.5 million) meet the medical criteria for substance abuse addiction, but only 11.2 percent receive any treatment while incarcerated.[7] Another 458,000, while not meeting the strict medical criteria for alcohol and drug abuse and addiction nevertheless were either under

substance-abusing inmate

An incarcerated individual suffering from dependency on one or more substances including alcohol and a wide range of drugs.

EXHIBIT 12–1   American Correctional Association

Public Correctional Policy on Offenders with Special Needs

Introduction:

The provision of humane and gender-responsive programs and services for the accused and adjudicated requires addressing the special needs of juvenile, youthful and adult offenders. To meet this goal, correctional agencies should develop and adopt procedures for the early identification of offenders with special needs. Agencies should provide the services that respond to these needs and monitor and evaluate the delivery of services in both confined and community settings.

Policy Statement:

Correctional systems must assure provision of specialized services, programs and conditions of confinement to meet the special needs of offenders. To achieve this, correctional systems should:

A. Identify the juvenile, youthful and adult offenders who require special care or programs including:

- Offenders with psychological needs, developmental disabilities, psychiatric disorders, behavioral disorders, disabling conditions, neurological impairments, and substance abuse disorders;
- Offenders who have acute or chronic medical conditions, are physically disabled or terminally ill;
- Older offenders;
- Offenders with social and/or educational deficiencies, learning disabilities, or language barriers;
- Offenders with special security or supervision needs;
- Sex offenders; and
- Female offenders.

B. Provide services and programs in a manner consistent with professional standards and nationally-accepted exemplary practices. Such services and programs may be provided within the correctional agency itself, by referral to another agency that has the necessary specialized resources, or by contracting with private or volunteer agencies or individuals that meet professional standards;

C. Provide appropriately trained, licensed and/or certified, staff, contractors and volunteers for the delivery of, care, programs, and services and provide incentives to attend the continuing education and training necessary to maintain credentials and state-of-the-art, knowledge and mastery-level skills;

D. Maintain professionally appropriate records of all delivered services and programs;

E. Conduct evaluations of service delivery adherence to program standards, while also evaluating the effectiveness of the services, with regular feedback to administrators and service providers for continuous quality improvement; and

F. Provide leadership and advocacy for legislative and public support to obtain the resources needed to meet these special needs.

Source: Copyright © American Correctional Association.

the influence of alcohol or other drugs at the time of their offense, stole money to buy drugs, are substance abusers, violated the alcohol or drug laws, or share some combination of these characteristics. Consider these startling statistics reported by CASA. In 2006, alcohol and drugs were involved in

- 78 percent of violent crimes;
- 83 percent of property crimes; and
- 77 percent of public order, immigration or weapons offenses, and probation/parole violations.

As this chapter points out, we know how to reduce the costs of incarceration and the crimes committed by substance-involved offenders. However, the barriers to action include the setting of mandatory sentences that eliminate the possibilities of alternative sentencing such as drug courts or parole, the lack of a clear mandate to provide treatment, the economic interests in prison expansion, and the failure of public policy to reflect the science of addiction and changing public attitudes about addiction and justice. But there is some good news. A number of states (and the federal government) have either reversed mandatory sentencing or are considering doing so. There are more examples of evidence-based practices informing correctional policy today as evidenced across these chapters. And the public doesn't think treatment is bad. An ABC news poll found that two-thirds of Americans support state laws requiring treatment—not jail time for first- and second-time drug offenders.[8] Tight budgets, however, might force states to cut back on treatment. Kansas and Pennsylvania have already done so and California and Texas are considering it.

Drug Use and Dependence If inmates are any indication, the war on drugs is not affecting persons who commit prison-bound offenses. In October 2006, the U.S. Department of Justice reported its findings on drug use and dependence among state and federal prisoners in 1997 and 2004.[9] That survey found that in 1997 and 2004, nearly one-third of state inmates and one-fourth of federal inmates committed their offenses under the influence of drugs. Drug use in the month before the offense by state prisoners remained unchanged from 1997 (stable at 56–57 percent), but drug use in the month before the offense by federal prisoners rose from 45 to 50 percent. Today 18 percent of state prisoners and 51 percent of federal prisoners are incarcerated for drug offenses.

Drug Use Among state inmates, one-third said they had committed their current offense while under the influence of drugs. Most reported using marijuana, hashish, cocaine, heroine, and other opiates. However, more than one-half reported using drugs in the month before their offense. The profile of a state prisoner using drugs in the month before the offense is male (56 percent), white (58 percent), and 24 years old or younger (66 percent).

Among federal inmates, one-fourth said they had committed their current offense while under the influence of drugs. Most reported using marijuana, hashish, cocaine, heroine, and stimulants including amphetamines and methamphetamines. In the month before their offense, one-half (up from 45 percent in 1997) reported drug use. The profile of a federal prisoner using drugs in the month before the offense is either male or female (female use jumped from 37 percent in 1997 to 48 percent in 2004), white (58 percent), and 24 years old or younger (62 percent).

The survey also reported that state drug offenders reported more serious criminal records than federal prisoners. Among state drug offenders, 50 percent were on probation, parole, or escape at the time of their arrest; 78 percent had a prior sentence to incarceration or probation; 22 percent had a prior violent offense; and 16 percent reported that all prior sentences were for drug offenses. Among federal prisoners, only 24 percent were on a criminal justice status at the time of their arrest, 62 percent had a prior sentence, 16 percent had a prior violent offense, and 15 percent reported prior sentences for only drug offenses.

An interesting finding in the government's survey is that prior drug use grew most quickly among middle-age inmates. Although drug use in the month before the offense is still highest among the youngest inmates (24 or younger), the largest increase in prior drug use since 1997 was reported by middle-age inmates. Among state prisoners ages 45 to 54, drug use in the month before the offense rose from 40 to 47 percent.

Almost two-thirds of all U.S. jail and prison inmates (some 1.5 million) meet the medical criteria for substance abuse addiction but only 11.2 percent receive any treatment while incarcerated. What should jails and prisons do to control the revolving door of drug and alcohol abusers and addicts in and out of prison?

Drug Dependence and Abuse The same Department of Justice survey reported on drug dependence and abuse among state and federal prisoners and compared those results with drug dependence and abuse in the U.S. adult resident population. Overall, 53 percent of state inmates, 46 percent of federal inmates, and 68 percent of jail inmates met the *Diagnostic and Statistical Manual of Mental Disorders (DSM-IV)* criteria for drug dependence or abuse. The national prevalence of drug dependence or abuse in the U.S. adult resident population is 2 percent. These statistics signal the importance of drug treatment for inmates. Yet, as this chapter will show, only 11 percent of prisoners who need drug treatment actually receive it.

Abuse symptoms included repeated drug use in hazardous situations such as driving, swimming, or using machinery or recurrent occupational, educational, legal, or social problems related to drug use. Recurrent social problems (for example, arguments or physical fights with spouse, intimate, family, or friends) due to drug use were the most commonly reported abuse symptom (45 percent of state and 34 percent of federal inmates).

Drug dependence covered a range of symptoms including increased tolerance for drugs and more drug use; compulsive use; bad aftereffects from cutting down or stopping drug use; neglect of work, school, and family activities; and continued use even though it was causing emotional or psychological problems. Continued use even though it was causing emotional or psychological problems was the most common symptom reported by both state and federal inmates (36 and 28 percent, respectively) followed by increasing tolerance (34 percent state and 28 percent federal).

According to the National Institute of Justice's Arrestee Drug Abuse Monitoring Program (ADAM), which tracks drug use among arrestees in 35 cities, the percentage of men testing positive for drugs when arrested ranges from 49 percent in Laredo, Texas, to 84 percent in Chicago. Among women, percentages range from 35 percent in Laredo to 81 percent in New York City.[10]

Drug Treatment Programs Why should prisoners receive drug treatment? According to Jeremy Travis, president of John Jay College of Criminal Justice, former senior fellow at the Urban Institute and former director of the National Institute of Justice, there are two powerful reasons.[11]

First, drug offenders consume a staggering volume of illegal drugs, and any reduction in their drug use represents a significant reduction in the nation's demand for illegal drugs. About 60 percent of the cocaine and heroin consumed by the entire nation in a year is consumed by individuals arrested in that year. Drug treatment has the potential for significantly reducing the nation's demand for illegal drugs.

Second, we now know from the evidence-based literature that we can reduce drug use in the offender population. Drug abuse treatment improves outcomes for drug-abusing offenders and has beneficial effects for public health and safety. There is ample, consistent, and cumulative evidence that substance abuse treatment for incarcerated populations is an effective intervention for drug abusers even if the motivation for entering treatment is coerced.[12] The National Treatment Improvement Evaluation Study found that prison-based treatment programs produced reductions in criminal behavior and in arrests.[13] Participation in correctional substance abuse treatment is also associated with enhanced mental health and physical health. Ideally, treatment programs should begin the moment a person enters prison. Research shows that treatment programs that start nine months to a year before prison release, provide community-based aftercare services (housing, education, employment, and health care), attract and retain staff who demonstrate concern for the offender's welfare, and give offenders a clear understanding of the program's rules and the penalties for breaking them provide the greatest chances for success.[14] Such programs have success rates as high as 80 to 90 percent. Community aftercare services are particularly important for substance abusers because they tend to have medical problems such as cirrhosis of the liver, diabetes, and HIV/AIDS.

The criminal justice system has become the largest source of mandated, or coerced, drug treatment in the United States.[15] Contrary to what some believe, research consistently indicates that offenders' motivations for entering drug treatment (voluntary or coerced) are not as important in treatment outcome as their ultimate length of stay in treatment. The longer inmates participate in treatment, the more likely they are to adopt

EVIDENCE-BASED CORRECTIONS

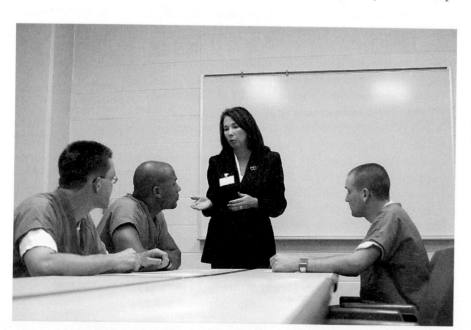

Many inmates enter prison addicted to illegal drugs. Although there's evidence that drug and alcohol treatment in prison reduces recidivism, only 13 percent of inmates who need substance abuse treatment actually receive it. Should correctional facilities be required to provide substance abuse treatment? What are the benefits of substance abuse treatment?

prosocial attitudes and overcome their initial resistance. (Generally, better outcomes are associated with treatment that lasts longer than 90 days with the greatest reductions in drug abuse and criminal behavior occurring to those who complete treatment.) This point is important because treatment in a prison always involves an element of coercion.

With 2,000 inmates returning to the general population every day, correctional health and public health are becoming increasingly intertwined. Health care and disease prevention in correctional facilities must become a top priority for correctional managers and all correctional personnel.

Drug treatment programs provide evidence that rehabilitation is more likely to succeed for those offenders who complete drug treatment programs, and reducing drug-seeking behavior aids in management of jail facilities. A recent NIJ-sponsored research study found that the greatest benefit of drug treatment programs in jails was that they provided a "behavioral management tool" that controlled inmates' behavior and helped lower the incidence of inmate violence.[16]

The study evaluated five drug treatment programs in California and New York. At all five sites, substance abuse inmates in drug treatment programs had lower rates of serious physical violence and other behavioral problems (e.g., insubordination and possession of nondrug contraband) than those not in the programs. During a one-year follow-up, 83 percent of the inmates in drug treatment and 77 percent of the control group were not convicted of another offense.

Therapeutic Community One successful prison-based substance treatment program is the therapeutic community. A **therapeutic community (TC)** is a residential treatment program in which inmates are housed in a separate unit within a prison or jail facility and is characterized by highly structured treatment involving resocialization, intensive counseling, and an increasing level of responsibility as the inmate progresses through the program. TC relies on interactions within the peer group to help members confront their addictions and to commit to lifestyle changes that will enable them to remain drug free and crime free.[17]

Postrelease Outcomes Evaluations of prison-based TC programs conducted in several states and the federal prison system have provided empirical support for the effectiveness of these programs in reducing recidivism and relapse to drug use, especially when combined with continuity of care in the community following release from prison to parole.

In September 2000, the federal BOP published the results of a three-year evaluation of its residential drug abuse treatment programs that are designed for inmates with moderate to severe substance abuse problems.[18] The study assessed the postrelease outcomes of 1,842 men and 473 women released from 20 different federal prisons with residential drug treatment programs between August 1992 and December 1997. The evaluation revealed that male inmates who completed residential drug abuse treatment were 16 percent less likely to be rearrested or have their supervision revoked than were inmates who did not receive such treatment; the comparable figure for female inmates was 18 percent. This reduction in recidivism was coupled with a 15 percent reduction in drug use by male participants and an 18 percent reduction in drug use by female participants. The study also found improved employment for women after release. The research strongly suggests that residential drug abuse treatment can make a significant difference in the lives of inmates following

therapeutic community (TC)

A residential treatment program in which substance abuse inmates are housed in a separate unit within a prison or jail facility.

their release from prison and return to the community. Similar results have been reported in Delaware where researchers conducted a longitudinal study of inmates who completed in-prison and work-release TC treatment.[19] They were more drug free and arrest free than their control groups at 18-month and three- and five-year follow-up periods. The Delaware research demonstrates the importance of treatment continuing during the transition stage to work and the free community.

Drug abuse treatment is cost-effective in reducing drug abuse and bringing about associated health care, crime, and incarceration cost savings. Positive net economic benefits are consistently found for drug abuse treatment across various settings and populations. For example, in 1996, the people of Arizona led the way in drug reform by passing the Drug Medicalization, Prevention and Control Act. The act requires drug users to be placed on probation and to participate in appropriate drug treatment. In the second year of operation, 62 percent of the probationers complied with treatment. Probation supervision and community treatment cost approximately $1.1 million. Based on prison costs of almost $53 per day, Arizona saved an estimated $6.7 million in incarceration costs.[20] Four years later, 61 percent of California voters passed Proposition 36—the Substance Abuse and Crime Prevention Act. It requires that first- and second-time nonviolent drug offenders convicted of drug possession, use, or transportation be offered substance abuse treatment instead of incarceration. However, the legislation authorized $120 million per year for only five years, and as the state's budget crisis worsened, the legislature declined to fund Prop 36 past 2011. Many have questioned why the law guaranteed only five years of funding for a mandate that would continue indefinitely. At its peak, Prop 36 was helping 36,000 people a year, and a UCLA study said that every $1 invested in Prop 36 treatment saved the state between $2.50 and $4 in incarceration costs—some $2 billion in savings—enough some say that should have won more budget support.[21]

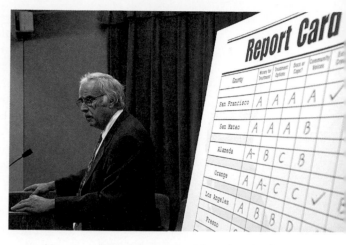

California Proposition 36 requires that first- and second-time nonviolent simple drug possession offenders be placed on probation instead of being sentenced to time behind bars. On Wednesday, June 27, 2001, California state senate president pro tem John Burton held a news conference on the Lindesmith Center Drug Policy Foundation's grading of how 11 counties plan to implement Proposition 36. How do such new laws save taxpayers' money and rehabilitate drug offenders?

What Works? Principles of Drug Abuse Treatment for Criminal Justice Populations Controlling the revolving door of drug and alcohol abusers and addicts in the criminal justice population is an important aspect of management for corrections officials. The National Institute on Drug Abuse (NIDA) looked at all the research that had been published on drug abuse treatment for the last 40 years and discovered 13 principles that constitute effective drug treatment.[22] They are:

1. Drug addiction is a brain disease that affects behavior and the brain's anatomy and chemistry, and these changes can last for months or years after the individual has stopped using drugs.

2. Effective drug abuse treatment engages participants in a therapeutic process, retains them in treatment for an appropriate length of time, and helps them learn to maintain abstinence over time.

3. Effective drug abuse treatment must last long enough to produce stable behavioral changes.

4. A comprehensive assessment of the nature and extent of an individual's drug problems and mental health evaluation is the first step in effective drug abuse treatment.

EVIDENCE-BASED CORRECTIONS

5. Tailoring services to fit the needs of the individual is an important part of effective drug abuse treatment because individuals differ in terms of age, gender, ethnicity, problem severity, recovery stage, and level of supervision needed.

6. Effective drug abuse treatment programs carefully monitor drug use through urinalysis or other objective methods because individuals trying to recover from drug addiction may experience a relapse, or return, to drug use.

7. Effective drug abuse treatment programs target feelings that are associated with criminal behavior. These can include feeling entitled to have things one's own way; feeling that one's criminal behavior is justified; failing to be responsible for one's actions; and constantly failing to anticipate or appreciate the consequences of one's behavior.

8. Effective drug abuse treatment programs incorporate treatment planning for drug-abusing offenders, and treatment providers are aware of correctional supervision requirements as treatment goals.

9. Effective drug abuse treatment programs recognize that continuity of care helps offenders deal with problems at reentry such as learning to handle situations that could lead to relapse, learning how to live drug free in the community, and developing a drug-free peer support network.

10. Effective drug abuse treatment programs recognize that a balance of rewards and sanctions encourages prosocial behavior and treatment participation.

11. Effective drug abuse treatment programs recognize that offenders with co-occurring drug abuse and mental health problems require an integrated approach that combines drug abuse treatment with psychiatric treatment, including the use of medication to address depression, anxiety, and other mental health problems.

12. Effective drug abuse treatment programs recognize that medications are an important part of treatment for many drug-abusing offenders and can be instrumental in enabling offenders with co-occurring mental health problems to function successfully in society.

13. Effective drug abuse treatment programs understand that rates of infectious diseases such as tuberculosis and HIV/AIDS are higher in drug abusers, incarcerated offenders, and those under community correctional supervision than in the general population.

HIV (human immunodeficiency virus)

A group of retroviruses that infect and destroy helper T cells of the immune system, causing the marked reduction in their numbers that is diagnostic of AIDS.

AIDS (acquired immunodeficiency syndrome)

A disease of the human immune system that is characterized cytologically, especially by reduction in the numbers of CD4-bearing helper T cells to 20 percent or less of normal, rendering a person highly vulnerable to life-threatening conditions. The disease is caused by infection with HIV commonly transmitted in infected blood and bodily secretions (as semen), especially during sexual intercourse and intravenous drug use.

HIV-Positive and AIDS Inmates

HIV/AIDS is the fourth leading cause of death worldwide. **HIV** is the acronym for **human immunodeficiency virus,** which is any of a group of retroviruses that infect and destroy helper T cells of the immune system. When enough of a person's T cells have been destroyed by HIV, he or she is diagnosed with **AIDS,** or **acquired immunodeficiency syndrome.** The AIDS virus attacks the body's natural immune system, making it unable to fight off diseases. In this state, a person is highly vulnerable to life-threatening conditions, which people with healthy immune systems can fight off easily.

Corrections professionals should be concerned with treating communicable diseases in the inmate population for at least four reasons:

1. Sexually transmitted diseases, HIV/AIDS, hepatitis B and C, and tuberculosis can be transmitted to other inmates.
2. Correctional employees and prison visitors are at risk of becoming infected from inmates with communicable diseases if appropriate precautions are not implemented.
3. Almost 2,000 prisoners are released every day from prison. Unless they are effectively treated, they may transmit their diseases into the community, threatening public health.
4. Unless prisoners are treated in prison, they become a financial burden on community health care systems.[23]

Recently, the Bureau of Justice Statistics reported on HIV in prison.[24] The major finding is that the number of HIV-positive state and federal inmates continues to decline as shown in Exhibit 12–2.

1. At year-end 2008, a reported 20,449 state prisoners and 1,538 federal prisoners were HIV positive or had confirmed AIDS, accounting for 1.5 percent of the total custody population. There's been a steady decline every year since 2000.
2. Three states, Florida (3,626), New York (3,500), and Texas (2,450), continue to house nearly one-half (46 percent) of all inmates known to be infected with HIV or to have confirmed AIDS in state prisons at year-end 2008.
3. At year-end 2008, an estimated 5,733 state and federal inmates had confirmed AIDS, down from 5,977 in 2006.
4. At year-end 2008, the rate of confirmed AIDS in state and federal prisoners was more than 2½ times higher than in the U.S. population. About 41 in 10,000 prison inmates were estimated to have confirmed AIDS, compared to 17 per 10,000 persons in the general population.
5. During 2007 (the most recent year for which data on inmate deaths are available for state prisons), 120 state inmates and 13 federal inmates died from AIDS-related causes, down from an estimated 143 in 2006. Florida (14), New York (11), and Texas (10) reported 10 or more AIDS-related deaths during 2007.

Treating HIV in prison is difficult for at least five reasons.[25] The first is the issue of privacy. People infected with HIV usually do not want to disclose their condition. The therapeutic regimen often involves taking multiple drugs several times a day, and going to the prison medication line often compromises a prisoner's privacy and increases the risk of stigmatization by other inmates and staff. Stigmatization can range from isolation and shunning to more overt forms of abuse. This is true even when high-quality health care is available. Anti-retroviral therapies (ART) can effectively treat HIV but only if corrections officials help inmates overcome the obstacles to obtaining the treatment.

A second reason involves the frequency of taking medication and the prison routine. Some drugs must be taken with food and others in a fasting state. As the therapeutic regimen increases to five or six times a day, it strains the routine of most prisons to dispense medication frequently and to provide food as required.

The third reason is distrust of the medical and legal system. Not surprisingly, many inmates do not trust the legal and health care systems. This may be especially true for women and minorities who have a

EXHIBIT 12–2   HIV and AIDS in Correctional Institutions, 1995, 2000–2008

Total HIV/AIDS cases

(Percentage of custody population)

Year	Cases
1995	24,256
2000	25,088
2002	23,864
2004	22,936
2006	21,980
2008	21,987

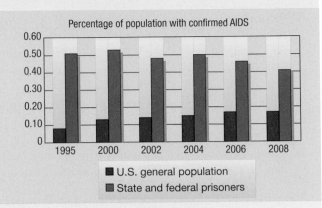

Percentage of population with confirmed AIDS

- U.S. general population
- State and federal prisoners

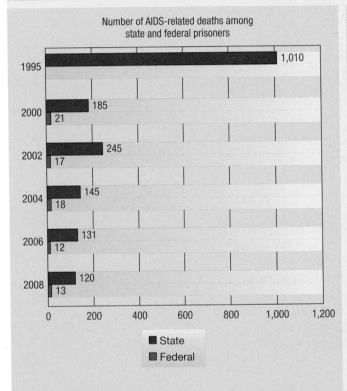

Number of AIDS-related deaths among state and federal prisoners

Year	State	Federal
1995	1,010	
2000	185	21
2002	245	17
2004	145	18
2006	131	12
2008	120	13

- State
- Federal

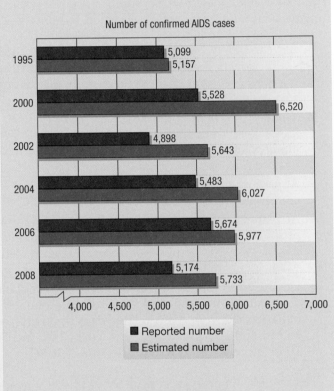

Number of confirmed AIDS cases

Year	Reported number	Estimated number
1995	5,099	5,157
2000	5,528	6,520
2002	4,898	5,643
2004	5,483	6,027
2006	5,674	5,977
2008	5,174	5,733

- Reported number
- Estimated number

Sources: Adapted from Laura M. Maruschak, *HIV in Prisons, 2004* (November 2006); Laura M. Maruschak, *HIV in Prison 2006* (April 2008); Laura M. Maruschak, *HIV in Prisons, 2007–08* (December 2009); "Rate of Confirmed AIDS in Prison 2.5 Times the Rate in the U.S. General Population," U.S. Department of Justice, Office of Justice Programs, Press Release, January 28, 2010; and Christopher J. Mumola and Margaret E. Noonan, *Deaths in Custody Statistical Tables* (n.d.). (all Washington, DC: U.S. Department of Justice, Bureau of Justice Statistics). Data reported for 2007–08 carried these footnotes: some previous counts may have been revised; some data from Alaska, Illinois, Indiana, and Oregon were excluded due to incomplete reporting; and counts for 2008 may not be comparable to previous year counts due to the implementation of a new record-keeping system.

documented history of being experimented on without consent and being denied appropriate legal and medical care.

The fourth reason is fear of side effects. The HIV drug regimen is known to make patients feel worse than they already do. Consequently, inmates will be less likely to adhere to the strict dosages and timing.

The final reason is that the courts have rejected the idea that the level and quality of health care available to prisoners must be the same as is available to society at large.[26] This falls under the principle of least eligibility—the belief that prison conditions, including the delivery of health care, be a step below those of the working class and people on welfare. Thus,

I am serving a life without parole sentence under Alabama's Habitual Offender Act. All 17 years of my incarceration have been spent here at W. C. Holman Correctional Facility in Atmore, Alabama. When I first came to Holman prison, life was hard. There was a lot of violence and very little hope. Most of my effort was spent just trying to get through each day with my sanity intact. The institution offered little if any opportunity for self-betterment. The guilt for my crime and the feelings for the people I had hurt, both my victim and my family, weighed heavily upon me.

The stress of prison life, however, gave me little time to reflect upon these areas. Consequently, I gave in to the temptation of doing drugs and gambling as a means of dealing with prison life. This ultimately led me down a path that left me more depressed and guilt ridden than I was to begin with. Facing life without parole and turning 40 years old caused me to ask some serious questions of myself. I wanted my life to be worth something, even if I never was allowed to reenter society.

That is why restorative justice is such a refreshing concept to me. It puts crime back into a human perspective and believes that all the parties involved are worthwhile and important. When the honor dorm was started at Holman, I was skeptical at first, but the chaplain convinced me that I should give it a try. Since becoming a part of the dorm, I have learned to live in a community setting where positive growth and respect for others is promoted. This has been such a drastic change here at Holman because there has never been a program or movement like the honor dorm before now.

With the implementation of restorative justice principles, I have learned a new way to deal with conflict. I have had the opportunity to focus on the crime that brought me to prison and reflect on its impact to my victim and my family, from whom I've been separated. My experience in the dorm allows me to take on responsibility and feel as if my life is of more value. It helps me to have a sense that the choices I make in life are important because I can see how they affect others in a community environment.

If I am to expect society to trust me again as a citizen, then I must earn that trust and what better way to do that than to work hard, help others, and believe that the time I'm spending in prison is meaningful and not wasted.

Anonymous

---

prisoners are denied access to medical specialists, timely delivery of medical services, technologically advanced diagnostic techniques, the latest medication and drug therapies, up-to-date surgical procedures, and second opinions.

Overcoming these obstacles will not be easy. If an inmate undergoes complex drug therapy in prison but cannot obtain the same therapy upon release, his or her health is compromised. In addition, he or she may transmit the virus to others. The key is developing trust between HIV-infected prisoners and the prison health care team, extending the regimen when inmates are discharged, and building collaboration between correctional institutions and public health agencies.

Cost-effective management of such inmates with HIV has at least five essential elements:

1. early detection and diagnosis through medical and mental health screening of each new jail inmate upon admission;

2. medical management and treatment by health specialists, including regular reevaluation and assessment;

3. inmate classification and housing to discourage intravenous drug use and homosexual intercourse or to provide private rooms for terminally ill inmates;

4. education and training of staff and inmates in the cause of AIDS, the stages of the disease, transmission methods, preventive measures, available treatment and therapies, testing issues and policies, confidentiality issues and policies, classification and program assignment policies, and supervision issues, including transportation and inmate movement; and

5. adequate funds to provide increasingly costly treatment to inmates with HIV or AIDS.

Dealing with HIV/AIDS Inmates Most correctional systems test their inmates for HIV, but testing policies vary widely:

- All states (except Kentucky, Missouri, New Hampshire, and Utah) and the federal BOP test inmates if the inmates request a test.
- All states (except Georgia, Massachusetts, Michigan, Oregon, and West Virginia) and the federal BOP test inmates if they have HIV-related symptoms.
- 42 states and the federal BOP test inmates after they are involved in an incident.
- 23 states test all inmates who enter their facilities.
- 18 states and the federal BOP test inmates who belong to specific "high-risk groups."
- 6 states (Alabama, Arkansas, Delaware, Missouri, Nevada, and Texas) test inmates upon their release.
- 3 states (Alabama, Arkansas, and New York) test inmates selected at random.
- 5 states (Idaho, Iowa, Missouri, Nevada, and North Dakota) test all inmates currently in custody.[27]

Today's corrections professionals need a network of medical experts—university medical school faculty, state health department staff, federal health officials, and local health care providers—to consult about HIV and AIDS. Such consultation will give corrections professionals reliable information and familiarize the noncorrectional medical community with the problems facing jails. The ACA recommends that all correctional staff adopt universal precautions when dealing with inmates. This means the staff should assume that all inmates are carrying the virus because, without testing, there is no way to know who is infected and who is not.[28]

Education and Prevention Education and prevention programs are becoming more common in correctional facilities. Incarceration offers opportunities for high-risk inmates to learn basic disease information, safer sex practices, tattooing risks, and triggers for behavior relapse, and they may develop more accurate risk self-perceptions. Such programs benefit not only the inmate but also the health and well-being of the community to which the inmate returns. (Canadian officials estimate that 45 percent of inmates acquire a tattoo while in prison. Believing that stopping tattooing isn't going to happen, Canadian correctional officials set up safe tattoo studios in 6 of its 51 federal prisons.)[29]

The types of education and prevention programs provided vary among correctional systems but may include instructor-led programs, pretest/posttest counseling, multisession prevention counseling, and audiovisual and written materials.

Another method of reducing high-risk behavior among incarcerated populations is peer-led counseling. Besides providing information about HIV/AIDS in formal settings, the informal interactions that incarcerated peer educators have with other inmates in the yard or other locations around the institution offer opportunities for ongoing dialogue about HIV/AIDS. Peer-led counseling is also cost-effective because most peer educators are volunteers and therefore provide HIV/AIDS education to others at no additional cost to the correctional facility.

Research on peer-led counseling has shown that peer educators report significant improvement in their self-esteem, may become paid employees of

Talking about CORRECTIONS

MENTAL HEALTH REENTRY

Visit *Live Talk* at **Corrections**.com (**www.justicestudies**.com/talking06**) and listen to the program "Mental Health Reentry," which relates to ideas discussed in this chapter.

community-based organizations following release from prison as a result of the skills acquired in peer education training, and are influential in encouraging other inmates to volunteer for HIV testing. However, only 13 percent of state and federal prisons and 3 percent of jails in the United States offer peer-led HIV/AIDS education programs.

A little bit of charm and persuasion also works. In August 2001, the Reverend Jesse Jackson visited the Cook County Jail in Chicago. He, along with 177 jail inmates and 25 ministers, took a two-minute HIV test.[30] "We're here to save your lives," Reverend Jackson told the inmates. He talked with them about the psychological barrier, the "taboo," that prevents at-risk people from testing themselves for HIV infection. He told the inmates, "Regardless of the results, people who take the test can't lose. Those who test negative should view themselves as lucky—they can get out of the way of AIDS through their knowledge, behavior, and commitment. HIV-positive detainees, on the other hand, can take solace in the fact that early detection leads to correction." Results were reported within two weeks, with only two tests coming back positive. Those persons received counseling and referrals.

HIV/AIDS is a serious problem for our nation's correctional facilities. To overcome the taboo that prevents at-risk people from testing themselves for HIV, the Reverend Jesse Jackson took an HIV test with Cook County (Chicago) jail inmates. Should HIV-positive inmates be treated any differently then other inmates? Should they be isolated?

However, what is done in prison may be undone in the community if ex-prisoners do not continue their treatment after they leave prison. A Texas study found that only about 30 percent of former inmates had filled a prescription for their medication within two months of release.[31] Halting treatment and reverting to dangerous behaviors such as drug use and unprotected sex diminishes the benefits inmates received while they were under direct prison supervision, which poses a public health challenge for all of us. Some states such as New York focus on educating prisoners about their treatment and aftercare options. When inmates are near their release, they are connected with community organizations that help them plan for their continued HIV care. Appointments are arranged for inmates to visit a clinic or doctor upon release, and each inmate leaves prison with a 30-day supply of medications and necessary prescriptions. Researchers don't know how well community groups and clinics follow through with former inmates or how well former prisoners follow through with their care. Hugh Potter, director of research at the University of Central Florida's department of criminal justice, believes that early intervention—making HIV/AIDS care and education available to those on probation—is the key and not waiting until offenders progress all the way to prison.[32]

Inmates with Mental Illness

Mental health is fundamental to a person's overall health, indispensable to personal well-being, and instrumental in leading a balanced and productive life. Every day, our nation's 3,365 local jails face the challenge of dealing with offenders who are not only suffering from schizophrenia, bipolar disorders, and major depression, among other illnesses but also from co-occurring substance abuse and dependence disorders and require close monitoring, medication, and other services. It is estimated that 16 percent of the nation's incarcerated are mentally ill and their per inmate cost is twice that of the rest of the jail and prison population, and that is only for security, not treatment.[33] Jails are the largest provider of mental health services in the United States.

More than half of all prison and jail inmates have a mental health problem such as schizophrenia, major depression, bipolar disorder, or post-traumatic stress disorder, and about 40 percent do not receive mental health treatment while incarcerated.[34] Significant as these numbers are, many experts believe that because of underreporting by people who do not want to disclose the information or are unaware of their illness, the numbers are actually higher. A coalition of law enforcement officers, judges, and social service officials in Michigan believe the true number of mentally ill persons in Michigan prisons and jails is more than 50 percent.[35]

As special needs inmates, people who are mentally ill do not do well in prison. They are perceived as disruptive, unpredictable, and sometimes dangerous. They are stigmatized, neglected, and easy prey for inmate assaults and robberies. The stress of incarceration can worsen their symptoms, leading to acute psychiatric disturbances, including harm to self or others, and adjustment and disciplinary problems such as refusal to leave one's cell or destruction of property. Behaviors that are characteristic of mental illness such as neglecting personal hygiene, ignoring orders, screaming, and banging against walls oftentimes are met with discipline, which can mean being placed in isolation where the conditions worsen.

Is corrections being asked to shoulder the burden of the nation's failure to diagnose properly and care for those with mental or emotional disorders? You be the judge: It is estimated that there are nearly eight times more people who are mentally ill in the nation's jails and prisons (nearly 478,000) than there are in mental hospitals (60,000).[36] Six to 8 percent of the 10 to 12 million people who enter the nation's jails annually have severe mental illness. The three largest de facto psychiatric hospitals in the United States are now the Los Angeles County Jail, Rikers Island Jail in New York City, and Cook County Jail in Chicago. The L.A. County Jail spends $10 million a year on psychiatric medication![37]

Suggesting that these facilities replace mental hospitals altogether overstates their treatment capacity and the function of these facilities—the mental health care required is far beyond what most correctional facilities are equipped to offer. Correctional officers are not therapists and correctional facilities are not mental hospitals. Corrections personnel are not trained to facilitate mental health treatment and, according to Dr. David Satcher, U.S. surgeon general from 1998 to 2002, "they should not have to."[38]

All jails have a constitutional mandate to provide at least minimum mental health or psychiatric care to detainees, yet 2 of 10 jails have no access to mental health services, 8 of 10 jail officers receive little or no training in mental health issues, and record numbers of jail inmates with mental illness are released into the community without any discharge planning, increasing the probability they will relapse and return to incarceration. Dr. Satcher noted that treating mental health rather than incarcerating those affected by mental illness could save $3 billion.

Why So Many? Why are there so many people who are mentally ill in the nation's jails and prisons? The reasons include failure to differentiate who should be in jail and who shouldn't, failure to treat people before they enter the criminal justice system, deinstitutionalization (moving the mentally ill from hospitals to nonsecure residential community settings), stricter commitment laws, less stringent discharge criteria, reductions or curtailment of public funding, lack of adequate insurance coverage, and three-strikes laws because those with mental illness may, when the illness is not effectively treated, be less able to follow the rule of law.[39] Former mental patients as well as people whose bizarre behavior might have landed them in a hospital bed a few years ago are now being arrested and are ending up in jail. While 40 state mental hospitals have closed in the last decade, more than 400 new prisons have opened,[40] state spending for treatment of people who are mentally ill is one-third less today than it was in 1950,[41] and changes in mental health laws have made involuntary commitment more difficult. As a result, jails and prisons have become the institutions most likely to house those with mental illness.

In addition, offenders often live as transients or in crowded conditions, increasing their levels of stress, which can precipitate mental illness. Offenders also tend to be economically disadvantaged, meaning they are less likely to get mental health treatment. Finally, they have high rates of substance abuse, which is correlated with mental illness.

Correctional facilities have an opportunity to provide prevention and treatment interventions to a seriously underserved and needy population. Policies and programs for prisoners help them return to our communities as better citizens, in better health, under treatment for their medical and mental health conditions, and better equipped and motivated to protect themselves and others, while possibly reducing the cost to taxpayers of future health care and reincarceration. Good health care is also an integral part of institutional security. Investments in prisoner health care result in fewer correctional disturbances, disciplinary actions, and inmate injuries and in less negative publicity for the institution.[42]

Given that a significant expansion of resources for state mental health care systems is highly unlikely, the key to curbing recidivism of people who are mentally ill is to expand public health services into the jails and prisons so that inmates can begin therapy the moment they walk into custody. When that happens, correctional institutions can provide offenders a better "hand off" from the institution to the community. Unless correctional policy moves in this direction, mental illness will continue to worsen in isolation and, for some inmates, lead to suicide.

What will it take for corrections policy to shift in that direction? Dean Aufderheide, director of Mental Health Services for the Florida Department of Corrections, believes we need to think of mental illness as a chronic illness. When we do that, we'll develop new strategies for dealing with it in prison and after release. He wrote, "By conceptualizing mental illness as a chronic illness, one that waxes and wanes, and like diabetes, is the manifestation of dynamic combinations of genetic and congenital vulnerabilities, environmental influences, and individual behavior, public health and safety officials can collaborate in seizing the opportunity to develop more and effective and efficient strategies for managing inmates with mental illness in prison and after release."[43]

There are more people who are mentally ill in U.S. jails and prisons than there are in mental hospitals, but correctional officers are not therapists and correctional facilities are not mental hospitals. Why are there so many people who are mentally ill in U.S. jails and prisons and what are the innovative strategies for keeping people with mental illness out of correctional facilities?

About 13 years ago, we began what's called the Maryland Community Criminal Justice Treatment Program. I developed this in partnership with the Maryland Correctional Administrators Association, because we were seeing numbers of people with mental illness coming into the local detention centers. So we developed comprehensive programs that provided each detention center—there are 23—with mental health services case management. The case managers' role is to try to connect people to community services upon release.

As we started understanding the population more, we started seeing that it wasn't just about mental health and corrections—it was about poverty and homelessness and substance abuse. So we had to try to develop community-based systems of support that brought together all of the different publicly based entities. We're very holistic—housing is crucial. You're not going to get someone to leave and "be compliant" while they're living under a bridge. We all start with "what would we want? What would we need?"

It's never just one thing. Our latest thing we're seeing is pregnant women—pregnant, incarcerated women. What started out as a program to meet the needs of mentally ill folks in the jail has branched into this program that addresses needs across the board.

Our project is an interesting blend of federal, state, and private money. With the leadership of both correctional administration and mental hygiene coming together, you realize these are all of our folks, and just because they rotate from system to system doesn't mean we drop them. We also believe these are the highest users of public services. You look at how many of them go into jails, how many of them are using the ER without insurance, using homeless shelters, using court time—it's a myriad of different public services that separately, at different times, provide for their needs. We believe if we can have one coordinated effort, we're not only serving the client better but reducing the need for them to be rotating from system to system.

Recidivism? Last year we only had 4.9 percent go back to jail.

Joan Gillece
Director of Special Needs Populations
Maryland Mental Hygiene Administration

Innovative Alternatives There are many successful and innovative ways to divert persons with mental illnesses from the criminal justice system, including the creation of law enforcement–mental health liaison programs, increased training of law enforcement personnel, and a general improvement in the funding and effectiveness of community mental health services. Three innovative strategies are presented next.

The Memphis Police Crisis Intervention Team (CIT) has won widespread national acclaim for the cooperative relationships that developed between the police and the mental health system. CIT officers, dispatchers, and other key police personnel receive intensive training about the signs and symptoms of serious mental illnesses, crisis intervention and deescalation techniques, and community mental health resources and options. A specialized mental health triage unit at the University of Memphis medical center was created to respond specifically to individuals referred by the police. Memphis police now know they have options available to them other than arrest and incarceration. So far there have been fewer arrests, better treatment outcomes, and reduced officer injuries.[44] CIT has been emulated in more than 50 communities across the United States, and other communities have developed alternative law enforcement–mental health triage capabilities.

A second innovative strategy for keeping people with mental illness out of jail and prison is mental health court, an extremely recent phenomenon. The term *mental health court* is most often used to refer to a specialized docket for defendants with mental illness that provides the opportunity to participate in court-supervised treatment. A court team, composed of a judge, court personnel, and treatment providers, defines the terms of participation, provides ongoing status assessments with individualized sanctions and rewards, and determines resolution of cases upon successful completion of court-ordered treatment plans. In 1997, there were four

Career Profile

Jon Wood

Family Counselor • Kandiyohi County Community Corrections • Kandiyohi, Minnesota

Jon Wood is a family counselor with the Kandiyohi County Community Corrections office in Kandiyohi, Minnesota. He has held that position for the past 11 years, after working in a similar position as a contractor for two years. Prior to that he received a master's degree in community counseling and a bachelor's degree in applied psychology from St. Cloud State University in St. Cloud, Minnesota.

Wood says the bulk of his time is spent providing counseling to first-time offenders, either in a one-on-one capacity or in a family setting. He specializes in dealing with juveniles with mental health issues, many of which are just emerging or have not even been diagnosed yet. He also works with schools, collaborates with other mental health professionals who might be dealing with the same individuals, and deals with social service agencies and probation agents.

Most of his clients are very young—according to Wood, the problems start to show up around age 10. "They're showing some behaviors at school, and I try to coordinate treatment with psychologists and psychiatrists, so we can figure out what to do for them," he says. "And a big challenge is trying to talk parents into making it happen, given the stigma that is attached to mental health issues."

Wood says his goal is to help both parents and children understand the illnesses that they are facing and help them develop methods of dealing with them. This means developing new cognitive skills and learning problem-solving and negotiation skills. "It's trying to help them find other ways to think," he says, "so they don't have to always be fighting each other or some authority figure.

"About once every two years I'll get a letter from a parent saying thanks. It doesn't happen very often but once in a while. And every now and then I'll run into an old client in a grocery store, and he tells me that he's going to college. So I know that something that we talked about made sense to him."

> *"So often parents who are dealing with the juvenile justice system get to a point where they freak out, they don't want to have anything to do with it, and they throw their hands up in the air and give up."*

mental health courts in the United States. Today more than 150 have been established and dozens more are being planned.[45] Two rationales underlie mental health courts: (1) to protect the public by addressing the mental illness that contributed to the criminal act, thereby reducing recidivism, and (2) to recognize that criminal sanctions, whether intended as punishments or deterrents, are neither effective nor morally appropriate when mental illness is a significant cause of the criminal act. Very little research is available on the effectiveness of mental health courts, but early findings on such courts in Broward County, Florida, point to relative success. Defendants were twice as likely to receive services for their mental illness and were no more likely to commit a new crime despite spending 75 percent fewer days in jail than did comparable defendants.[46] Congress has promoted the development of mental health courts with the passage of the Law Enforcement and Mental Health Project Act in 2000, which makes federal funds available to local jurisdictions seeking to establish or expand mental health courts and diversion programs, and the Mentally Ill Offender Treatment and Crime Reduction Act of 2004, which authorizes federal funds for jail diversion, mental health treatment for inmates with mental illnesses, community reentry services, and training. The acts recognize that states and communities are best able to develop their own innovative approaches to reduce the criminalization of people with mental illnesses.

There are eight times more people with mental illness in jail and prison than there are in mental hospitals. What are some ways the needs of women correctional clients with mental disorders can be met?

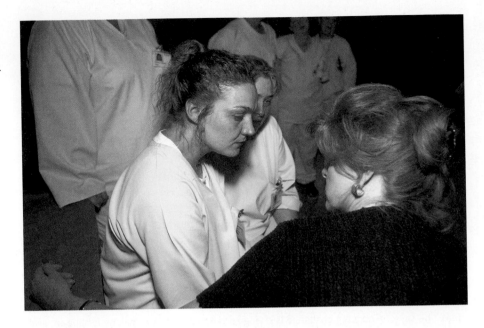

A third strategy to keep people who are mentally ill out of jail and prison is the Assertive Community Treatment (ACT) Program. ACT programs are teams of social service professionals who provide a broad and integrated range of services to individuals diverted from jails or reentering communities following incarceration with severe and persistent mental illnesses. The services include medication and medication management, housing assistance, case management, substance abuse treatment, vocational supports, and mobile crisis management. ACT teams emphasize preventing people in crisis from "falling through the cracks." Today there are approximately 15 ACT programs in the United States, 3 of them in the Ohio Department of Rehabilitation and Corrections, for individuals with severe and persistent mental illnesses reentering their communities after completing prison sentences.

The American Association for Community Psychiatrists Committee on the Mentally Ill Behind Bars developed a list of recommendations to keep people with mental illness out of jail:[47]

1. Address the lack of access to community mental health and other diagnostic services in order to improve early diagnosis and treatment.

2. Create alternatives to incarceration for as many nonviolent offenders with mental illness as possible. For example, have a center to which police can take people who are experiencing a mental crisis.

3. Improve jail conditions that have negative effects on the mental health of inmates. For example, researchers are finding that serious bullying is a cause of suicide.[48] Suicide is the leading cause of death in jail and ranks third in prison.[49]

4. Establish vigorous programs designed to reintegrate inmates with mental illness into the community, with specific attention paid to their housing needs.

5. Create oversight boards to prevent human rights abuses and to guarantee that adequate physical and mental health services are available upon release.

Developing innovative alternatives for keeping people with mental illness out of jail and prison requires staff who are educated and trained in multidisciplinary perspectives. Consult the Appendix: Careers in Corrections at the Online Learning Center Web site www.mhhe.com/schmalleger6e for the steps involved in career planning, developing employability and job readiness, and finding the right job.

Inmates with Tuberculosis

Although not extremely common among the general U.S. population, **tuberculosis** has traditionally been more common in correctional facilities.[50] It is estimated that the risk of incurring a tuberculosis infection is 4 to 17 times higher for those incarcerated than for those who live in the general population because of very close living quarters, overcrowding, poor sanitation, and the large number of inmates with a high risk of having TB, such as HIV-positive detainees, intravenous drug users, and immigrants.[51] This was underscored by the 1999–2001 institutional outbreak of TB among 33 HIV-infected inmates in a segregated housing unit for HIV-infected inmates in South Carolina. TB is considered to be the most common cause of death among the world's prisoners.[52]

When a person who has TB coughs, sneezes, or laughs, tiny droplets of fluid containing TB bacteria are released into the air, which are then inhaled by others. The TB germ becomes active in people when their immune system becomes weak. It multiplies and causes active TB. If left untreated, active TB can cause the infected person to literally waste away.

In 2009, all states reported testing their inmates for TB at intake and tracking identified cases. States also report using more than one testing policy.

- 31 states test inmates annually.
- 29 states test inmates upon a physician's request.
- 11 states test inmates upon their request.[53]

Experts concerned about TB in correctional facilities have indicated that the most important issues for corrections professionals are to understand the causes and control of TB, to implement appropriate and cost-effective screening programs, and to develop close working relationships with local health authorities. Public health departments can provide correctional facilities access to expert TB medical consultation and laboratory services. Health department staff can also train correctional personnel in performing, interpreting, and recording tuberculin skin tests, identifying signs and symptoms of tuberculosis disease, initiating and observing therapy, monitoring medication side effects, collecting specimens, educating inmates, and maintaining record systems.

Older Inmates

The special circumstances surrounding the incarceration of older inmates also create new challenges for correctional institutions. Bureau of Justice Statistics figures for 2008 indicate that there were nearly 2.4 million inmates under the jurisdiction of the nation's prisons and jails, representing an increase of 9 percent (200,000) over the previous 12 months. Problems that were manageable two decades ago now threaten to overwhelm state and federal corrections systems. One issue that is being addressed by

tuberculosis (TB)

A highly variable communicable disease that is characterized by toxic symptoms or allergic manifestations that in humans primarily affect the lungs.

Carol Finkes, 67, is 1 of 600 women in the United States over 65 years of age serving a prison sentence. She is serving a sentence of 20 years to life at the Ohio Reformatory for Women in Marysville for aggravated murder that she committed when she was 59. She sews book bags that are donated to children in the Ohio foster care system. What are the options states are looking at to save money and respond to the needs of older inmates who pose no threat outside prison?

administrators across the nation is the aging of the prison population, the issue we turn to next in this chapter.

The Aging of the Prison Population Most of us imagine prisoners as young and aggressive. However, *people who are elderly* and *passive* describe a significant portion of the prison population. The definition of *elderly* is subject to debate. Some define *elderly* as 65 years of age and older, some suggest 60 years, others suggest 55, and still others 50. There are some who do not consider chronological age at all. Rather, they believe that, because of the impact of prison lifestyle, including lower socioeconomic status and limited access to medical care, a prisoner's physiological age may be higher than his or her chronological age. In addition, some say that a lengthy prison stay can age an inmate 10 years beyond her or his chronological age.

Despite the differences among definitions of *elderly*, it is possible to establish a common chronological starting point to define *older* inmates for purposes of comprehensive planning, programming, evaluation, and research within and among prison systems. After careful study of the issue, the National Institute of Corrections recommended that correctional agencies nationwide adopt age 50 as the chronological starting point for defining *older inmates*.[54] On January 1, 2010, almost 11 percent of state and federal prisoners were 50 years of age or older.[55] Some prison officials predict that by 2025, people 50 and older will constitute one-fourth of the prison population.[56] Still others predict that by 2030, about one-third of the U.S. prison population will be 55 years of age and older.[57]

In an examination of the impact of California's three-strikes law,[58] Ryan King and Marc Mauer of The Sentencing Project found that the law has significantly altered the demographics of that state's prison population in just the 7 years since its inception. They estimate that, within 25 years, 30,000 prisoners will be incarcerated in California under sentences of 25 years to life. King and Mauer project this burgeoning population of older prisoners will place an extraordinary burden on the penal system's resources. Of particular concern is the increased cost of housing older inmates, who typically have high need of costly medical care.

Geriatric Prison Facilities Recently, a number of scholars and policymakers have argued in favor of age-segregated prisons for four reasons.[59] First, age segregation allows correctional authorities to relocate older prisoners from institutions that are largely oriented toward the care and needs of younger inmates to institutions designed to care for the specific and specialized health care needs of older prisoners. Second, the financial costs of making physical and program changes in every prison in the United States in order to comply with the Americans with Disabilities Act of 1990 would be prohibitive. Advocates of age-segregated prisons argue that age-segregated prisons could reduce a correctional system's civil liabilities if they centralize disability services in age-segregated institutions that fully comply with ADA requirements. Third, age-segregated prisons advance prisoner safety. Kerbs and Jolley report four key findings from studies of older prisoners' safety in non-age-segregated prisons: Older prisoners are victimized by younger prisoners; they feel vulnerable to attack by younger prisoners; they prefer to live with inmates in their own age bracket; and at times they choose to live in age-segregated protective custody units. Why not then, they

COMMISSION ON SAFETY AND ABUSE IN AMERICA'S PRISONS: HEALTH CARE

"Much of the public imagines jails and prisons as sealed institutions, where what happens inside remains inside. In the context of disease and illness, which can travel naturally from one environment to another, that view is clearly wrong. Protecting the public health, reducing human suffering, fulfilling our constitutional obligation to those we incarcerate, and addressing the financial cost of untreated illness depends on good and adequately funded correctional health care.

—The Commission on Safety and Abuse in America's Prisons

Every year, more than 1.5 million people are released from jail and prison carrying a life-threatening infectious disease. At least 300,000 to 400,000 prisoners have a serious mental illness—a number three times the population of state mental hospitals nationwide. And prisoners on average require significantly more health care than most Americans because of poverty, substance abuse, and because they most often come from underserved communities.

Many corrections leaders are struggling to provide quality care without adequate resources and often without frontline staff who understand and share their goal. The consequences for individuals and families can be tragic. In California, where control of health care in state prisons has been ceded to a federal judge, one prisoner was dying needlessly from medical malpractice or neglect every six to seven days as recently as October 2005.

Correctional facilities have a constitutional obligation to provide health care—and some fulfill that obligation with vigor. They also have a tremendous opportunity: to protect the public health and to use precious health care resources efficiently through disease prevention, early detection, and appropriate treatment. But corrections cannot do this alone, and legislatures chronically underfund correctional health care.

The following six recommendations suggest ways to improve correctional health care:

Partner with Health Providers from the Community

Departments of corrections and health providers from the community should join together in the common project of delivering high-quality health care that protects prisoners and the public.

Build Real Partnerships Within Facilities

Corrections administrators and officers must develop collaborative working relationships with those who provide health care to prisoners.

Commit to Caring for Persons with Mental Illness

Legislators and executive branch officials, including corrections administrators, need to commit adequate resources to identify and treat prisoners who are mentally ill and, simultaneously, to reduce the number of people with mental illness in prisons and jails.

Screen, Test, and Treat for Infectious Disease

Every U.S. prison and jail should screen, test, and treat for infectious diseases under the oversight of public health authorities and in compliance with national guidelines and ensure continuity of care upon release.

End Copayments for Medical Care

State legislatures should revoke existing laws that authorize prisoner copayments for medical care.

Extend Medicaid and Medicare to Eligible Prisoners

Congress should change the Medicaid and Medicare rules so that correctional facilities can receive federal funds to help cover the costs of providing health care to eligible prisoners. Until Congress acts, states should ensure that benefits are available to people immediately upon release.

Source: Excerpts from *Confronting Confinement: A Report of the Commission on Safety and Abuse in America's Prisons* by John J. Gibbons and Nicholas de B. Katzenbach, June 2006. Copyright © 2006, Vera Institute of Justice. Note: The full 126-page report, *Confronting Confinement: A Report of the Commission on Safety and Abuse in America's Prisons,* can be accessed on the Internet at www.prisoncommission.org.

ask, provide age-segregated correctional institutions to enhance the safety of older inmates while decreasing the risk of civil liabilities when older inmates are mainstreamed with younger inmates? And fourth, age-segregated facilities can promote rehabilitation by advancing age-specific treatment opportunities.

Today we find age-segregated prisons in Alabama, Arizona, Georgia, Illinois, Kansas, Kentucky, Maryland, Michigan, Minnesota, Mississippi,

North Carolina, New Jersey, Ohio, Pennsylvania, South Carolina, Tennessee, Texas, Virginia, West Virginia, and Wisconsin. Few stairs, reduced distances, geriatric chairs and beds, walkers, wheelchairs, handrails, more crafts and leisure activities, and staff trained in gerontological issues make these facilities unique. The majority confine only male prisoners who are elderly. Older female prisoners, who constitute close to 6 percent of the total population of prisoners who are elderly, are generally kept in a state's only women's prison.

hospice

An interdisciplinary, comfort-oriented care facility that helps seriously ill patients die with dignity and humanity in an environment that facilitates mental and spiritual preparation for the natural process of dying.

Prison Hospice Programs Before the onset of AIDS and the increased numbers of prisoners who are elderly, few prisoners died while incarcerated. Inmate deaths occur more frequently now, and correctional administrators have taken measures to address the unique problems associated with helping prisoners who are terminally ill through their passing. A **hospice** is an interdisciplinary, comfort-oriented care facility that helps patients who are seriously ill die with dignity and humanity in an environment that facilitates mental and spiritual preparation for the natural process of dying. Hospice programs provide a wide array of services, including pain management, spiritual support, and psychological counseling, as well as grief counseling for bereaved families. In 2007, the American Correctional Association reported that hospice care or similar services were offered in nearly all state prison systems.[60]

Often one of the challenges in starting a prison hospice is educating the prison staff in caring for prisoners who are terminally ill and making a psychological adjustment to get over the resentment that prisoners are getting this level of care. According to Elizabeth Craig, executive director of the National Prison Hospice Association (NPHA) in Boulder, Colorado, "In my view, inmates are being punished by being incarcerated; we don't need to create more suffering for them."[61]

The nation's best-known prison hospice program is the one at the Louisiana State Penitentiary (LSP) at Angola. LSP Angola is the nation's largest state prison. Of its nearly 5,200 inmates, over 90 percent are expected to die while incarcerated.[62]

LSP Angola's hospice program has five core goals:

1. Provide quality end-of-life care regardless of a patient's criminal charge or personal history.
2. Honor the patient's support system, including his family (as defined by him).
3. Address the patient's needs holistically with emphasis on palliation of physical, social, spiritual, and emotional suffering.
4. Assist the patient with activities that he considers life affirming.
5. Maintain an end-of-life care system consistent with "free-world" standards.

A fundamental part of hospice care at LSP Angola is the emphasis on family. Each inmate patient is allowed to designate two inmates from Angola's general prisoner population as "family," and within the constraints of security, these inmates are treated like the inmate's biological family members. Angola's staff provides whatever considerations are possible within the constraints of security to ensure that the patient's final days are as meaningful as possible for all involved.

Other options states are looking at to save money and respond to the needs of prisoners who are terminally ill include releasing terminally ill, disabled, and dying inmates who pose no threat outside prison, providing volunteer inmate aides as in the program at Angola, and increasing family visitation.[63] Approximately 34 states now release seriously ill or dying inmates. Family visitations for inmates who are terminally ill or dying are permitted 24 hours a day in South Dakota. These new forms of release are not without their critics, however. Some argue it's like a shell game and there is no real cost savings: You shift the expense of medical care from one state agency to another, mostly Medicaid, which is funded partly by federal money. Others are troubled by the fact that convicted criminals are released into adult care homes in the community used by the rest of the population. North Carolina state senator Debbie Clary asked, "Do you want your grandmother in the same room beside a convicted felon?"[64]

Health Issues The physical, mental, and medical health care needs of older inmates have implications for prison policymakers, administrators, and staff. Older, sicker inmates challenge health care systems.

It is estimated that a prisoner who is elderly suffers from an average of three chronic illnesses. Additionally, men and women who are elderly require screening for colon cancer, prostate cancer, breast cancer, and many other conditions that become more prevalent as people age.

Researchers in California found that almost 70 percent of the women prisoners who are geriatric said that at least one prison activity was very difficult for them: 59 percent reported difficulties hearing orders, 57 percent said it was very difficult for them to drop to the floor for alarms, 35 percent said it was very difficult for them to stand in line for head counts, 14 of the 35 women who were assigned to upper bunks said it was very difficult for them to climb on and off a top bunk, and 61 percent said they had been given jobs that were too difficult to perform, including janitorial and yard crew work.[65] Incarcerating older prisoners with impaired eyesight, physical disabilities, cancer, arthritis, diabetes, heart disease, hypertension, or Alzheimer's disease and treating these illnesses raise many concerns. For example, how ethical is it for prisons to provide surgery, physical therapy, and daily medication to prisoners who are elderly when people outside prison are unable to afford similar medical treatment? However, if left untreated, might these inmates be less likely to provide for themselves upon release and more likely to become a health care burden to society?

Another issue that must be considered is the effect of health-related legislation. For example, the Americans with Disabilities Act (ADA) affects not only mainstream society but also prisons and jails. Designing prison spaces that are accessible for prisoners who are elderly with ramps, handrails, good lighting, and subtle grades, is now law under ADA. In *Goodman & U.S.* v. *Georgia* (2006), the Supreme Court ruled that prisoners with disabilities may sue for monetary damages if the violation of ADA is so serious as to also constitute a violation of civil rights.[66]

Cost Issues The economic consequences of incarcerating older prisoners are huge. The estimated national cost per year to confine an inmate over 55 is $70,000.[67] If a 55-year-old inmate lives to 80, this figure would project to $1.75 million. In North Carolina, it costs $37,000 per year to keep prisoners who are elderly at the McCain Correctional Facility. The average annual cost for such an inmate in Maryland is $69,000. In California, it is $80,000.

Get-tough-on-crime policies have led to an increased number of inmates serving longer periods of time behind bars. The Colorado Territorial Correctional Facility in Cañon City includes a 32-bed infirmary for prisoners who are elderly with cancer, heart disease, diabetes, and respiratory problems and highlights the public health costs associated with prisoners who are elderly. What are some of the special needs of inmates who are geriatric?

It is doubtful that, when mandatory sentencing laws, three-strikes laws, and truth-in-sentencing laws were enacted, the economic impact of incarcerating prisoners who are elderly for long periods of time was actually considered. Unless legislatures give courts and prison administrators more leeway to interchange prison sentences with community sentences, states will find themselves in economic crises as they attempt to provide for the 33 percent of the inmate population that is projected to be elderly by the year 2030.

SEXUALLY TRANSMITTED DISEASES IN JAIL

Most studies on infectious diseases in correctional facilities focus on prison. The problem of sexually transmitted diseases (STDs) in jail is addressed less frequently even though some believe that STDs are more common in jail than in prison.[68] However, rapid turnover and frequent movement of inmates make jails difficult settings in which to study the prevalence of various diseases. But recently, the Society of Correctional Physicians published a report by Dr. Karl Brown, infectious disease supervisor at New York City's Rikers Island Jail, on the increase of STDs in jail and the difficulties diagnosing and treating four of the most common STDs found in jail today: syphilis, gonorrhea, chlamydia, and genital herpes. **Syphilis** is caused by the bacteria *Treponema pallidum*. Syphilis is passed from person to person through direct contact with a syphilis sore. Transmission of the bacteria occurs during sexual contact. **Gonorrhea** is caused by *Neisseria gonorrhea*, a bacteria that grows and multiplies in mucous membranes of the body. Gonorrhea bacteria grows in the warm, moist areas of the reproductive tract, including the cervix, uterus, and fallopian tubes in women and in the urethra (urine canal) in women and men. The bacteria can also grow in the mouth, throat, and anus. Gonorrhea is spread through sexual contact. **Chlamydia** is the most frequently reported STD in the United States. It is caused by the bacteria *Chlamydia trachomatis*. Chlamydia is transmitted through sexual contact. **Genital herpes** is a lifelong infection caused by the herpes simplex viruses type 1 (HSV-1) and type 2 (HSV-2). A person can get HSV-1 by coming into contact with the saliva of an infected person. HSV-1 causes infections of the mouth and lips, so-called fever blisters. A person almost always gets HSV-2 infection during sexual contact with someone who has a genital HSV-2 infection. According to Brown, after declining for many years, the rates of syphilis, gonorrhea, and chlamydia began increasing in jails and juvenile detention centers in 2000, especially among female prisoners.

The jail environment may be the key to controlling STDs, but less than half of the nation's jails have a policy of routine screening, and even in those jails with routine screening, less than half of the inmates were tested for syphilis, gonorrhea, or chlamydia. Brown also found another problem: Approximately half of arrestees were released within 48 hours, but most jails received the inmates' test results more than 48 hours after admission.

The type of screening for STDs in jail should be based on the prevalence of STDs as measured by the population served. For example, gonorrhea and chlamydia are four times higher in northern Florida than they are in northern California. The key to controlling STDs is to continuously collect, monitor, and analyze information and then to discuss the results with public health officials. Diagnosis also requires a thorough nonjudgmental sexual history and a careful genital exam.

syphilis

A sexually transmitted disease caused by the bacteria *Treponema pallidum*. If left untreated, syphilis can cause serious heart abnormalities, mental disorders, blindness, other neurological problems, and death. Syphilis is transmitted when an infected lesion comes in contact with the soft skin of the mucous membrane.

gonorrhea

The second most common sexually transmitted disease. Often called *the clap*, gonorrhea is caused by the *Neisseria gonorrhea* bacteria found in moist areas of the body. Infection occurs with contact to any of these areas.

chlamydia

The most common sexually transmitted disease. Caused by the bacteria *Chlamydia trachomatis*, it can affect the eyes, lungs, or urogenital (urinary-genital) area, depending on the age of the person infected and how the infection is transmitted.

genital herpes

A sexually transmitted disease caused by the herpes simplex virus, or HSV. It is one of the most common STDs in the United States.

LEGAL ISSUES

Providing inmates adequate health care is of concern to the courts and professional associations. As we discussed in Chapter 7, in 1976, the U.S. Supreme Court ruled in *Estelle* v. *Gamble*[69] that inmates have a constitutional right to reasonable, adequate health services for serious medical needs. However, the Court also made clear that such a right did not mean that prisoners have unqualified access to health care. Lower courts have held that the Constitution does not require that medical care provided to prisoners be perfect, the best obtainable, or even very good.[70] Nevertheless, health care professionals and inmate advocates—such as the American Medical Association, the American Correctional Health Services Association, and the National Commission on Correctional Health Care—insist on alleviating the pain and suffering of all persons, regardless of their status. They believe that no distinction should be made between inmates and free citizens.

Another important piece of legislation affecting inmate health care is the Civil Rights of Institutionalized Persons Act (CRIPA).[71] This law places prisoners in a class with others confined in government institutions, such as people with disabilities and elderly people in government-run nursing homes.

Prisoners in wheelchairs and others with special needs place an extraordinary strain on prison resources. Inmates with disabilities are protected under the federal Americans with Disabilities Act (ADA) of 1990. What does the act require of correctional facilities? What are the alternatives to incarceration for inmates with disabilities?

Inmates with Disabilities

Inmates with special needs face numerous difficulties. Consider the case of Ronald Yeskey. Yeskey was sentenced to 18 to 36 months in a Pennsylvania correctional facility. He was recommended for a motivational boot camp, which would have shortened his sentence to six months. He was, however, refused admission to the boot camp because of a physical disability—hypertension. He sued, claiming that the **Americans with Disabilities Act (ADA)** of 1990 prohibits any "public entity" from discriminating against a "qualified individual with a disability" because of that disability.

In 1998 in a unanimous opinion, the U.S. Supreme Court held that state prisons fall squarely within the ADA's definition of a "public entity."[72] Reacting to the decision, Yeskey's attorney noted, "The court's ruling means that prison officials cannot discriminate against prisoners with disabilities and must make reasonable modifications to prison operations so that these prisoners will have reasonable access to most prison programs;"[73] otherwise, prisoners can sue for monetary damages.

Americans with Disabilities Act (ADA)

Public Law 101-336, enacted July 26, 1990, which prohibits discrimination and ensures equal opportunity for people with disabilities in employment, state and local government services, public accommodations, commercial facilities, and transportation. It also mandates the establishment of TDD/telephone relay services.

Inmates with HIV/AIDS

Most suits by prisoners with HIV/AIDS are claims that officials have violated a prisoner's rights by revealing the condition or by segregating the prisoner because of the condition. In 1988, officials in Erie County, New York, placed an HIV-positive female prisoner in a segregated prison wing reserved for inmates with mental illness. They also placed on her possessions red stickers revealing her HIV-positive status. The inmate sued, claiming denial of her rights to privacy and due process. The district court agreed (*Nolley* v. *County of Erie*, 1991). In the same year, however, the Eleventh Circuit Court of Appeals held that an Alabama policy of isolating all HIV-positive inmates did not violate the Fourth or Eighth Amendments (*Harris* v. *Thigpen* and *Austin* v. *Pennsylvania Dept. of Corr.*).

Other legal issues relate to the work assignments of HIV/AIDS inmates. In 1994 in *Gates* v. *Rowland*, the Ninth Circuit Court of Appeals ruled that California correctional officials could continue to bar HIV-positive inmates from working in prison kitchens. The court made it clear that its decision was based more on the anticipated reactions of prisoners receiving the food than on any actual risk of infection. The court agreed that food service "has often been the source of violence or riots" because inmates "are not necessarily motivated by rational thought and frequently have irrational suspicions or phobias that education will not modify" and because prisoners "have no choice of where they eat." Correctional officials had based their policy, the court said, on "legitimate penological concerns."

Inmates with Mental Illness

The federal courts have recognized the right of inmates who are mentally ill to treatment. According to a district court in Illinois, this right is triggered when it becomes reasonably certain that (1) the prisoner's symptoms demonstrate a serious mental disease or brain injury, (2) the disease or injury is curable or at least treatable, and (3) delaying or denying care would cause substantially more harm to the inmate (*Parte* v. *Lane*, 1981). In 1990, in *Washington* v. *Harper*, the U.S. Supreme Court ruled that inmates who are dangerous to themselves or others as a result of mental illness may be treated with psychoactive drugs against their will. Such involuntary drug treatment, however, has to be in the best interest of the inmate's mental health, not just for the convenience of the correctional institution.

REVIEW AND APPLICATIONS

SUMMARY

1 Some inmates require special treatment or care because they suffer from mental illness, chemical dependency, a communicable disease, or typical problems associated with people who are elderly. These inmates present unique problems for correctional staff and administrators.

2 Inmates with special needs present significant management problems because they are typically more violent and prone to be disruptive, require close monitoring as suicide risks, tax-scarce medical resources, and are often targets of abuse by other inmates.

3 A tenfold increase in prison populations over the past 25 years caused a commensurate increase in the number of inmates with substance abuse problems. These inmates tremendously drain finite resources, are disruptive to daily life within the walls, and create unique management problems in all areas of prison life.

4 Special difficulties related to HIV/AIDS among prison populations include privacy issues, disruption of the prison routine due to the frequency of taking medication, inmate distrust of the medical and legal systems, fear of side effects, and the legal dilemma embodied in the principle of least eligibility.

5 The five essential elements of cost-effective management of HIV/AIDS inmates are early detection and diagnosis, medical management and treatment, inmate classification and housing, education and training of staff and inmates, and funding.

6 The increase in the number of inmates with mental illness is attributable to several factors: the deinstitutionalization of persons who are mentally ill to nonsecure residential environments; stricter commitment laws; failure to know who should and should not be in jail; failure to treat them before they enter the criminal justice

system; less stringent discharge criteria; reduction or elimination of public funding; lack of adequate insurance coverage; and three-strikes laws because those with mental illness may, when the illness is not effectively treated, be less able to follow the rule of law.

7 Ways to divert persons with mental illnesses from the criminal justice system include the creation of law enforcement–mental health liaison programs, increased training of law enforcement personnel, and a general improvement in the funding and effectiveness of community health services.

8 Estimates are that, on average, each older inmate is afflicted with three chronic illnesses that require ongoing and expensive medical treatment. Some question the equity of providing such free treatment to criminal offenders when the same free treatment is not provided to the public at large. The annual cost of incarcerating an inmate who is elderly is significantly higher than the average per inmate cost of incarceration.

9 In 1976, the U.S. Supreme Court ruled in *Estelle* v. *Gamble* that inmates have a constitutional right to reasonable, adequate health services for serious medical needs. However, the Court also made clear that such a right did not mean that prisoners have unqualified access to health care. The Civil Rights of Institutionalized Persons Act (CRIPA) places prisoners in a class with others confined in government institutions. In 1998, the U.S. Supreme Court held that state prisons fall squarely within the ADA's definition of a "public entity" and prohibits them from discriminating against a "qualified individual with a disability" because of that disability. Federal courts have ruled differently on whether segregation of inmates with HIV violates the inmate's rights to privacy and due process. A district court agreed, a circuit court of appeals disagreed. The federal courts have also recognized the right of inmates who are mentally ill to treatment.

KEY TERMS

inmates with special needs, p. 398

substance-abusing inmate, p. 399

therapeutic community (TC), p. 404

HIV (human immunodeficiency virus), p. 406

AIDS (acquired immunodeficiency syndrome), p. 406

tuberculosis (TB), p. 417

hospice, p. 420

syphilis, p. 422

gonorrhea, p. 422

chlamydia, p. 422

genital herpes, p. 422

Americans with Disabilities Act (ADA), p. 423

QUESTIONS FOR REVIEW

1 What defines an inmate with special needs?

2 Summarize the management problems that special-needs inmates pose for corrections officials.

3 What criteria would you use to assess the impact that substance abusers have on the corrections system?

4 How would you design a system that makes it easier to treat HIV in prison?

5 What ideas can you add to the five essential elements of providing cost-effective management of HIV/AIDS inmates?

6 What evidence explains why there are so many inmates with mental illness in prison?

7 Suggest additional strategies for diverting persons with mental illness from the criminal justice system.

8 What should corrections do about the cost and health issues associated with older inmates?

9 Why is it important to understand the legal issues surrounding special population inmates?

THINKING CRITICALLY ABOUT CORRECTIONS

Aging Prison Population and Costs

As the prison population ages, the costs of incarcerating large numbers of older inmates will skyrocket. This, in turn, will strain correctional budgets and adversely impact correctional administrators' ability to provide essential services to the general prisoner population. Should inmates who are elderly be released from incarceration? Could services provided by other public agencies be tapped to meet the needs of inmates who are elderly? If so, which services might be invoked?

The Principle of Least Eligibility

Discussions of the principle of least eligibility invariably fire emotions. Should inmates rate free medical care that is not available to law-abiding citizens? Why or why not? Would you support a ballot proposal to formalize the principle of least eligibility as law in your state? Why or why not? If such a law were adopted, do you think it would withstand challenge through the state and federal court systems? Why or why not?

ON-THE-JOB DECISION MAKING

How to Use Personal Experience to Advance Correctional Training in HIV/AIDS

You are the warden of a state prison and on record as a supporter of the principle of least eligibility. Walter Edmunds is one of your most dependable correctional officers. Mature, calm, and unfailingly professional, Edmunds can be counted on in every crisis. You have come to rely on his leadership as a positive element among the correctional staff. Unfortunately, Edmunds has a young son dying of AIDS, which he contracted through a blood transfusion during an appendectomy.

Yesterday your medical staff conducted training for your correctional officers on procedures for handling inmates suffering from HIV and AIDS. About 10 minutes into the training session, Edmunds apologized for interrupting and then asked why the prisoners received top-notch medical treatment for free treatment that ordinary law-abiding citizens can't afford.

From that single question, things quickly deteriorated, and Edmunds became increasingly agitated. Before long, the training room was in turmoil as Edmunds's questions and angry comments whipped up the sympathy and anger of his fellow correctional officers.

Clearly out of his depth, the medical officer canceled the remainder of the training session and then bolted to your office. By the time he finished relating the incident, one of your correctional lieutenants appeared to report that the unionized correctional staff was in an uproar and threatening to walk off the job. What would you do to defuse this situation? Once you contained the crisis, how would you handle Edmunds?

Deciding Legitimate Penological Concerns

You are a correctional lieutenant at a state prison that has a conjugal visitation program. Carl Packard, one of your inmates, was recently diagnosed as HIV-positive. During an interview with a member of the medical staff, Packard acknowledged recent illicit drug use during which he shared a needle with other inmates. He and the medic believe this needle sharing to be the source of Packard's HIV infection.

Yesterday, Packard applied for a conjugal visit with his wife. You summoned him to your office and asked if he had advised his wife of his infection. Packard stated he had not and that he had no intention of "tellin' that bitch nothin'." This morning, you sought guidance from the prison's legal advisor and the warden. They informed you that infection with HIV did not prohibit an inmate's participation in the conjugal visitation program and that privacy policies prohibit you from informing Mrs. Packard of her husband's physical condition. You strongly believe that the threat to Mrs. Packard's health and safety outweighs what you consider to be ill-advised rules and policies.

1. What do you do?
2. What is your reasoning?

For additional information, please see: www.mhhe.com/schmalleger6e

Issues in Corrections

Part Five focuses on some of the most controversial debates

in contemporary corrections. Prison overcrowding became a problem shortly after a wing of the Walnut Street Jail was converted into the world's first prison in 1790, and it continues to be a problem today. When prisons are overcrowded, safety is compromised and conditions for disturbances and riots ripen.

One way to control prison overcrowding is to build more prisons. Today, the federal government and some states are building supermax prisons to deal

with inmates whose violent behavior makes it impossible for them to live among the general prison population. Other options to control prison overcrowding are accreditation, which mandates acceptable staff-inmate ratios; privatization, the goal of which is to turn institutions into cost-effective private businesses; and technology, which can reduce the number of people required to supervise a given inmate population.

The increase in attention to victims' rights has also changed the corrections landscape. Today, all states and the federal government have laws that establish, protect, and enforce victims' rights. However, as you will learn, victims' rights laws are unevenly applied and sometimes partially ignored. Would a constitutional amendment, as recommended by Congress and the president, result in more even application and enforcement?

Possibly no other corrections issue has received more attention than capital punishment. The watershed U.S. Supreme Court case *Furman* v. *Georgia* (1972) changed the way judges and juries impose the death penalty. Since 1977, 1,242 people have been executed in the United States, and 3,261 are on death row today. New research on defendant–victim racial characteristics, execution of the innocent, and social consensus is sharpening the debate over capital punishment.

The face of juvenile corrections is also changing. The first juvenile court established in Cook County (Chicago, Illinois) in 1899 had high hopes for controlling and preventing delinquency. However, today society's response to rare yet high-profile juvenile offending means that the needs of the vast majority of juveniles who are arrested for nonviolent offenses are virtually ignored. There is no magic bullet to prevent delinquency, but there are correctional strategies and "best practices" that work. Implementing them will be up to you, the next generation of correctional professionals.

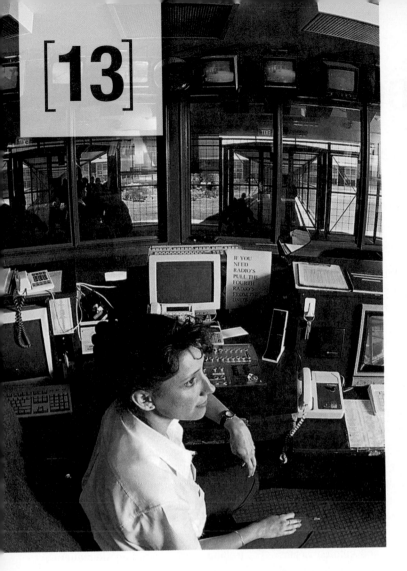

[13]

PRISON ISSUES AND CONCERNS

Overcrowding, Security, Accreditation, Privatization, and Technology

CHAPTER OBJECTIVES

After completing this chapter you should be able to do the following:

1 List the four main reasons prisons are overcrowded.

2 Identify six methods of controlling prison overcrowding.

3 Explain how prisons control the influence of security threat groups (STGs).

4 Identify five causes of prison riots.

5 Describe what can be done to prevent prison riots.

6 Outline the emergence of supermax housing and its impact on prisoners and staff.

7 Describe "no-frills" jails and prisons and their impact on corrections.

8 List the reasons that correctional agencies and facilities should be accredited.

9 List the arguments for and against privatization.

10 Discuss the impact of technology on corrections.

> *It's not about rehabilitation here. It's about the consequences of your choices.*
> —Lt. Steve Perez, Correctional Officer, Pelican Bay State Prison,
> Security Housing Unit, Crescent City, California

A flip of the switch activated the electromagnetic field between the inmates' metallic boots and the prison floor and stopped the prison disturbance in the film *Face/Off* starring Nicolas Cage and John Travolta. Sound far out? It may not be that unimaginable. Imagine reporting a crime to a "software agent" police officer at your local police department via the Internet. Imagine probation officers monitoring electronically transmitted smells to keep track of the lifestyles of convicted drug offenders. Imagine virtual courtrooms, digitally displayed evidence, and virtual tours of crime scenes. Imagine a 6-foot assault intervention device (a robot) that stops a prison disturbance by blasting millimeter waves that simulate intense heat under the skin where pain receptors are located. You do not even have to imagine. The technology is already here.

But what are the issues and concerns of the prison environment today? In this chapter, we shall consider seven aspects of the prison environment: overcrowding, riots and violence, supermax housing, "no-frills" prisons and jails, accreditation, privatization, and technocorrections.

Detection technology, like the magnetic field and the principles of geographical information systems that stopped the prison disturbance in Face/Off, starring Nicolas Cage and John Travolta, is changing corrections. How can technology address correctional health, safety, and security issues?

OVERCROWDING

In the past, a prison was often referred to as "the big house." Today, however, a more appropriate description is "the full house." Over the past 25 years, prison population has increased sixfold—from 240,000 to more than 1.6 million. Some say that prisons are "capacity driven"; that is, if you cut the ribbon, they are full. Saying exactly how full, though, is difficult because each state has its own method for measuring prison capacity. Three states and the federal BOP use rated capacity only (the number of beds in a facility), 10 states use operational capacity only (the number of inmates that can be accommodated based on a facility's staff and existing programs and services), and 2 use design capacity only (the number of inmates that planners intended the facility to house).[1] The problem is compounded because 32 jurisdictions use more than one definition, and some have their own definitions. In spite of the differences, by any measure today's prisons are overcrowded.

On January 1, 2010, state prisons taken as a whole were operating between full capacity and 40 percent above capacity while federal prisons were operating at 36 percent above capacity.[2] That would suggest that as many as 562,249 (40 percent) of the 1,405,622 persons held in state prison and 74,922 (36 percent) of the 208,118 persons held in federal prison were housed in overcrowded facilities. Eliminating the present overcrowding would require building 425 new prisons, each at a cost of $75 million (assuming that each has a capacity of 1,500 cells and each cell costs conservatively $50,000 to build) and then staffing and maintaining each new facility at an average annual cost of $42.7 million each per year (1,500 cells multiplied by $28,466, the average of state and federal annual incarceration costs). Even if this were possible, the relief from overcrowding would be short term because the prisoner population grows continually.

Why Are Prisons Overcrowded?

Prisons are overcrowded for four main reasons. The first is a continuous increase in the number of people sent to prison. In 2000, 1,391,261 persons were in state and federal prisons. On January 1, 2010, that number had increased to more than 1.6 million, an average annual increase of 1.8 percent.

The second reason is that offenders now serve a larger portion of their sentences. The amount of time served has increased from an average of 22 months for prisoners released in 1990 to 57 months for those released in 2004.[3] Sentencing laws changed, reducing the difference between the sentence imposed and the actual time served and restricting the possibility of early release from prison. Jurisdictions began to depart from the prevailing approach, known as *indeterminate sentencing* (broad authorized sentencing ranges, parole release, and case-by-case decision making), in the mid-1970s (see Chapter 3). Today the trend in many jurisdictions is toward determinate sentencing—a fixed term of incarceration and no possibility of parole. In addition, most jurisdictions have adopted one or more of the following sentencing approaches: mandatory minimum sentences, three-strikes laws, or truth-in-sentencing laws requiring offenders to serve mandated percentages of imposed sentences (see Chapter 3).

The third reason prisons are overcrowded is that many incoming prisoners are drug users, not the drug dealers the tougher drug laws were designed to capture. The goal of tougher drug laws was to arrest and convict drug dealers, thereby reducing drug use and the drug-related crime rate. This goal has not been achieved. As we pointed out in Chapter 12, the majority of persons sentenced to prison for drug offenses are low-level, nonviolent offenders, primarily street-level dealers and couriers, not the kingpins or major traffickers the laws were written for. One in four drug offenders sentenced to prison in New York has been convicted of simple possession.[4]

Today almost 350,000 people are behind bars for drug crimes. According to an article in *The New York Times,* Americans do not use more drugs than people in other nations, but the United States is virtually alone among Western democracies in choosing the path of incarceration for drug offenders.[5]

The fourth reason prisons are overcrowded is a trend some people call the "prison industrial complex." Private corporations have a real estate investment in the prisons they build and operate. Correctional officers' unions are expanding in many states and securing the use of incarceration into the future. Rural communities such as Del Norte, California—a remote, impoverished county in the northwest corner of the state with an unemployment rate of more than 20 percent and all of its industries severely depressed since the 1980s—negotiated successfully with the California Department of Corrections to build Pelican Bay State Prison, one of the nation's largest state prisons. States have an incentive to incarcerate because the 1994 crime bill provides matching funds to states to keep violent offenders in prison longer by denying them parole and requiring that they serve at least 85 percent of their sentence. There is no reason to believe that the nation's prison population will decrease even though crime has declined every year since 1991. To quote Dr. Allen Beck, the Department of Justice's lead statistician on criminal justice issues, "We've got crime going in one direction (down), and prison policy going in the other (up)."[6]

Do you want to know why Louisiana has the highest incarceration rate in this country? Our sentences are too long, our sentences are too tough! You're doing more time for every crime than you do in most any other state. The problem with Louisiana? We don't ever let 'em go. Once you break the law, you don't get another chance. If it were up to me I'd say let's not keep dying old men in prison. They're too old to pull an armed robbery or be a ski-mask rapist. They ought to do about 20 years on most any serious crime and when they turn about 50 years old—when those two come together on a graph—they pretty well should have a good shot at going free.

Burl Cain
Warden
Louisiana State Penitentiary at Angola

How Can Prison Overcrowding Be Controlled?

In most jurisdictions across the United States today, we find at least six methods of controlling prison overcrowding:

1. Reduce the number of people going to prison.
2. Release the less dangerous to make room for the more dangerous.
3. Change prison or jail sentences to community-related sentences.
4. Increase the number of releases.
5. Expand existing prison capacity or build new prisons.
6. Implement an overall program of structured sentencing.

The first four methods are referred to as *front-end, trap-door, side-door,* and *back-end* strategies, respectively (see Chapter 5).

The fifth method of controlling prison overcrowding is the most commonly considered—build more prisons. For the past 25 years, political leaders have addressed public concerns about crime by devoting unprecedented financial resources to the construction of prisons. The number of prisons increased from 1,160 in 1995 to 2,236 today. In 1990, the nation's prisons cost $12 billion.[7] Today it's more than $52 billion.[8]

However, the fiscal crisis that began in 2007 is changing the face of corrections. To balance their budgets, governors are looking at corrections—the fastest-growing segment of state budgets, second only to Medicaid. Ten years ago, it would have been unthinkable for governors to propose slowing prison growth, closing institutions, or putting a moratorium on building new ones, but today all areas of public spending are being looked at for possible savings. Many people today are echoing what Ryan Sherman, a spokesperson for the powerful California corrections officer union said on January 3, 2011, "The state cannot build its way out of the overcrowding prison problem. If they build more beds, we will fill up more beds and continue to be overcrowded. Until we figure out how to reform and reorganize the department so it's efficient and accountable, and take into consideration the limited budget and what's best for the state, I don't anticipate anything improving a great deal."[9]

Instead of new construction, the majority of states today are engaged with one or more of the following ways to reduce corrections spending:

- making more use of use evidence-based corrections;
- applying justice reinvestment (an approach to reduce corrections spending and reinvest savings in strategies that can decrease crime and strengthen neighborhoods);
- sentencing reform;
- creating alternatives for "prison bound" offenders;
- reducing time served in prison;

- speeding early release;
- adopting risk assessment instruments to aid parole boards in considering release issues;
- reducing revocations;
- reducing personnel costs;
- downsizing or eliminating programs;
- closing and/or selling facilities;
- changing food services;
- implementing new technology;
- exploring strategies to save on energy costs;
- diverting more offenders to drug courts;
- establishing medical parole for terminally ill prisoners;
- considering parole for aging people;
- instituting more "good time" policies;
- implementing or expanding work release, intermediate sanctions, and community corrections; and
- reducing barriers to successful reentry.

Many states are looking closely at what Texas—a state known for its "tough on crime" approach and its "lock 'em up and throw away the key" attitude—has done to reduce its prison population and halt plans for prison expansion. Texas addressed three key areas:

1. **In prison.** Knowing that many prison sentences and repeat offenses result from drug crimes, Texas offered substance-abuse treatment in jail and prison and put some prisoners in treatment after being released.
2. **During parole and probation.** Many inmates who commit minor infractions while on parole end up back in prison. Texas created detention centers to provide supervised housing to punish those offenders without sending them to prison.
3. **After prison.** Many former inmates fail to adjust successfully to life outside and end up committing more crimes. Texas built residential treatment centers and halfway houses to help former prisoners with the transition.

Texas spent several hundred million dollars to develop these programs initially. The changes are expected to avoid the costs of building more prisons, reduce the correctional budget by $210 million, and result in an additional savings of $233 million.[10]

The sixth method of controlling prison overcrowding is the use of sentencing guidelines that are designed to save prison beds for more serious crimes and violent offenses. Structured sentencing is a compromise between indeterminate sentencing and mandatory determinate sentencing (see Chapter 3). Guidelines were conceived as a way to guide judicial discretion in sentencing.

structured sentencing

A set of guidelines for determining an offender's sentence.

Under **structured sentencing,** a commission creates a set of guidelines that consider both the severity of a current offense and a few personal characteristics of the offender (notably, a prior criminal record). Sentencing commissions take a wide range of forms from mere advisory panels to bodies that have the full, legislatively delegated force of law to establish a state's sentencing guidelines. The commissions gather facts and figures on whom their states are incarcerating, why, and for how long. The stronger commissions use the information to develop guidelines and grid charts that seek to prioritize prison bed space for the most serious offenders and require judges to spell out their reasons if they depart from the sentencing recommendations. Today 21 states, the federal government, and the District of Columbia have sentencing commissions.[11]

A jurisdiction establishing structured sentencing might consider implementing nonprison options such as interchangeability of punishments, also called **exchange rates.** A sentencing commission might, for example, decide that three days under house arrest or 40 community service hours is equivalent to one day of incarceration or that three years under intensive supervision is equivalent to one year in prison.[12]

exchange rates

An approach to sentencing that emphasizes interchangeability of punishments; for example, three days under house arrest might be considered equal to one day of incarceration.

What Are the Consequences of Prison Overcrowding?

Researchers and prison administrators routinely observe the consequences of prison overcrowding. These include increases in idleness, drug trafficking, predatory sexual behavior, safety risks, gang confrontations, arguments, fights, assaults, murders, suicides, riots, medical and mental health problems, staff turnover, and stress. Other consequences include decreases in program opportunities, inappropriate housing assignments, judicial intervention to counteract illegal conditions, fines by state governments for operating over capacity, excessive wear and tear on prison facilities and equipment, and negative publicity about conditions in overcrowded facilities. Researchers have also linked overcrowding to higher rates of recidivism and inmate assaults on staff.[13] Phil Glover, a federal BOP union official, told the House Judiciary subcommittee on crime, terrorism, and homeland security that federal prisons, which are currently operating at 36 percent above capacity, have become increasingly dangerous places to work because of serious correctional officer understaffing and overcrowding. Glover told the subcommittee that inmate-on-staff violence rose 6 percent and inmate-on-inmate violence jumped 16 percent in federal prisons in 2006 compared to 2005. Comparable data for the states is not available. The federal courts, U.S. Congress, Attorney General, and Secretary of Health and Human Services are also weighing in on the consequences of prison overcrowding, and we turn our attention to those concerns.

Prisons Under Court Order In 2005, there were fewer public and private prisons under federal court order than there had been in 2000. The number of prisons under federal court order or consent decree to limit the size of their inmate population declined from 145 in 2000 to 44 in 2005, from 119 public and 26 private prisons in 2000 to 21 public and 23 private in 2005. Prisons under federal court order or consent decree for specific conditions also declined from 320 to 218, from 303 public and 17 private prisons in 2000 to 190 public and 28 private prisons in 2005.[14]

Among the reasons prisons are under federal court order are to reduce crowding; improve inmate visiting, mail, and telephone privileges; accommodate prisoners who are physically challenged; permit religious expression; and offer mental health treatment.

Although new prison facilities are being built, crowding continues to be an issue in many places. The auditorium of the Deuel Vocational Institution in Tracy, California, is converted into a dormitory to house prisoners. The prison has a design capacity of 1,681 but an operating capacity of 3,748. How can prison crowding be controlled?

Prison Sexual Violence Another serious consequence of prison overcrowding is sexual violence, which includes nonconsensual sexual acts (considered the most serious form of sexual assault), abusive sexual assault, staff sexual misconduct, and staff sexual harassment.

The Prison Rape Elimination Act (PREA) of 2003 discussed in Chapter 10 requires the Bureau of Justice Statistics to perform a comprehensive statistical review and analysis of the incidents and effects of sexual victimization for each calendar year. In 2008–2009, the BJS surveyed 81,566 inmates ages 18 or older at 463 state and federal prisons, jails, and special confinement facilities operated by Immigration and Customs Enforcement (ICE), the U.S. military, and correctional institutions in Indian territories. Approximately 88,500 prison and jail inmates reported being sexually victimized by another inmate or facility staff in the past 12 months or since admission to the facility.[15] Circumstances surrounding victimization include:

- Thirteen percent of male prison inmates and 19 percent of male jail inmates said they were victimized within the first 24 hours after admission compared to 4 percent of female inmates in prison and jail.
- Inmate-on-inmate victimization in prisons and jails was most commonly reported to have occurred between 6 p.m. and midnight.
- Most victims of staff sexual misconduct were males; most perpetrators were females.
- Among inmates who reported staff sexual misconduct, nearly 16 percent of male victims in prison and 30 percent of male victims in jail said they had been victimized by staff within the first 24 hours of their incarceration compared to 5 percent of female victims in prison and 4 percent of female victims in jail.

The BJS report also provides a list of prisons and jails according to the prevalence of sexual victimization, but that list is not provided here. The researchers say that many incidents of sexual victimization go unreported due to inmates' fear of repercussions by perpetrators, embarrassment, lack of trust in facility administrators, and a "code of silence" among inmates.[16]

In September 2008, after nine days of public hearings, a federal review panel released a list of 32 best practices for preventing sexual assaults in correctional facilities.[17] Attorney General Eric Holder was required by law to enact the new guidelines and practices by June 23, 2010, but as that date came and went, Holder wrote, "I believe that it is essential that the Department take the time necessary to craft regulations that will endure."[18] Holder expressed concern that prisons and jails do not have enough funding to implement the new standards, which include staff training and inmate education; medical and mental health treatment for sexual abuse victims; and regular, independent, external audits to hold agencies accountable for failures to keep inmates safe from abuse. Among the recommendations are:

1. Make prevention of sexual assault a high and unequivocal priority and institute a zero tolerance policy conveyed from the top down.
2. Consider the risk of sexual predation or victimization of the inmate when making inmate housing assignments.
3. Install video cameras in places where assaults are likely to occur.
4. Have independent investigators conduct or at least oversee any investigation of sexual victimization.

5. Limit those who participate in or observe strip searches of inmates to correctional officers of the same sex as the inmate.

6. Train staff members in how childhood abuse, sexual abuse, and other trauma affect and ultimately surface among male and female inmates.

7. Train staff in the requirements of the PREA and the prison system's sexual assault policies.

8. Offer higher pay to prison staff in order to better attract and retain recruits and to retain experienced staff.

9. Establish a telephone hotline for inmates to report threats and sexual victimization confidentially and directly to the office of prosecutor or system inspector general.

10. Implement a peer training program in which appropriately selected and trained inmates teach new inmates about how to avoid sexual victimization and how to report threats and assaults.

11. Ban pornography, especially for those inmates who have a history of sexual assault or are assessed as being at a high risk of becoming sexual predators.

12. Reduce prison overcrowding.

13. Replace inmate idleness with work and programming.

PRISON SECURITY

For prisoners, staff, and their families on the outside, nothing is more frightening than a prison gang confrontation, a prison riot, or a natural disaster involving a prison.

Prison Gangs—Security Threat Groups

Prison gangs are among the most significant developments in American prisons since the existence of the Gypsy Jokers Motorcycle Club was first recorded at the Walla Walla, Washington, penitentiary in 1950. To eliminate any publicity that gang members may draw about their gang or its activities and to describe accurately how these gangs negatively impact the security of prison operations, experts refer to them as **security threat groups (STGs)**. An STG is an inmate group, gang, organization, or association that has a name or identifying signs, colors, clothing, shoes, hair, tatoos, hand signs, associations, scars, language/codes, or symbols and whose members or associates engage in a pattern of gang activity or departmental rule violation to pose a threat to the staff, to public safety, to the secure and orderly operation of a correctional institution, or to other inmates. Most STGs were founded along racial and ethnic lines to offer inmates protection, but today many of them have joined alliances with other STGs to conduct organized criminal activity such as drug trafficking, prostitution, assault, or extortion. Research shows that STG members are five times more likely to incite or be involved in prison violence than are nonmembers and twice as likely to perpetuate assault within the first three years of incarceration when compared to inmates not affiliated with an STG. STG activity is a reflection of the intricacies that corrections professionals must contend with on a daily basis.[19]

Recently, Mark Pitcavage, a historian and expert on race-based STGs, conducted a study of contemporary prison STGs. His interview with the Southern Poverty Law Center's *Intelligence Report* is presented in Exhibit 13–1.

security threat groups (STGs)

The current term for prison gangs that describes how they negatively impact the security of prison operations.

| EXHIBIT 13–1 | "Behind the Walls: An Expert Discusses the Role of Race-Based Gangs in America's Prisons" |

An Interview with Mark Pitcavage

Intelligence Report (IR): Why do prisoners join gangs?

Mark Pitcavage (MP): Prison gangs offer protection—and money and drugs. Some offer ideology, racial or otherwise, but protection is the key.

IR: Is virtually every prisoner affiliated?

MP: No, no. A lot of prisoners never become affiliated. It all depends on the prison. If you're talking about a minimum security prison, you're not going to see much of that. In maximum security prisons, you see much more gang activity.

In state prisons, where many inmates are serving long sentences, there is a great deal of gang activity. There are gangs in federal prisons, too. Some gangs even have federal and state prison chapters. But even in state prison, where there is generally more activity, a minority of prisoners will belong.

IR: What are the largest prison gangs?

MP: The most prominent white supremacist gangs are the Aryan Brotherhood, the Aryan Circle, the Nazi Low Riders, and the Peckerwoods. There are racist black groups, like the Black Guerilla Family, the Five Percenters, and the Moorish Science Temple. And major Hispanic gangs include the Mexican Mafia (known as "la eme," for its first letter) and La Nuestra Familia. And basically apolitical street gangs like the Crips and the Bloods are inside the prisons, too.

IR: Did something occur to help promote these gangs' growth?

MP: Many prison populations were desegregated during the 1960s, and one result was that many inmates felt they had to join a race-based gang for protection. If white prisoners and black prisoners were separated, then that would not be an issue. [*IR Editor's note: Some states have actually resegregated certain cell blocks as a security measure meant to weaken race-based gangs.*]

But the key to the Aryan Brotherhood—and the key to understanding virtually all prison gangs—is that ideology often takes a back seat to organized criminal activity. The Aryan Brotherhood is an organized crime group—that is the primary dynamic behind it. It's all about drugs, protection rackets, prostitution, extortion, witness intimidation, assaults, etc.

In many prisons, the Aryan Brotherhood actually makes alliances with gangs of other races. If they were ideological white

supremacists, they wouldn't do that. That is why a lot of people who join race-based prison gangs while in prison don't stay with them once they're out or join other white supremacist groups. They just aren't primarily ideologically motivated.

IR: There was a major federal bust of 40 members of the Aryan Brotherhood, 30 in prison and 10 on the outside, in October 2002. A central allegation was that members killed or attempted to kill people inside and outside the prisons in order to control drug trafficking, gambling, and extortion. How do prisoners reach outside the walls to control or influence activity that involves the free world?

MP: There are a lot of ways you can pass on information from the prisons. Wives and girlfriends of prisoners often play an important role. The Aryan Circle, for example, uses its female supporters on the outside, who they call *sisters,* to conduct business operations and spread racist propaganda. And you can always meet privately with your attorney, who may be willing to carry messages to someone else on the outside. There are ways. If you are in a maximum-security prison or in administrative isolation, it obviously is more difficult.

IR: You note in your report that the men who murdered James Byrd Jr. in the Jasper, Texas, truck-dragging incident had developed their racial beliefs while behind bars. What is the link between incarceration and politicization?

MP: Exactly what dynamic occurs varies with each particular individual, but there are some universals. Prisoners have a lot of time on their hands, and as a result they are desperate for reading materials. They are desperate for stimulation. Some of them are just fine with pumping weights, but others aren't and seek out extremist publications as well as nonextremist publications. You see prisoners asking for free subscriptions, for correspondence, for people to send them materials, anything. They may not be ideological at that point, but they want something—and the material they get can lead to their politicization.

Another thing is that many prisoners want to justify or rationalize what they have done or what has happened to them. They don't want to say they did something wrong or deserved what they got. This is true whether you are black or white. By adopting a particular ideological slant, you can rationalize that you are not a simple criminal, that you are in jail for political reasons.

In 2002, the National Major Gang Task Force (NMGTF) surveyed all adult prison systems in the United States, Guam, Puerto Rico, the U.S. Virgin Islands, and Canada. With almost 80 percent responding, NMGTF identified more than 1,600 STGs with a total estimated membership of almost 114,000 inmates. By 2009, the percentage of known STG membership had spiked to more than 356,000 inmates. Montana reports the lowest percentage of STGs (less than 1 percent), and Oklahoma reports the highest (70 percent). States with more than

EXHIBIT 13–1	"Behind the Walls: An Expert Discusses the Role of Race-Based Gangs in America's Prisons" *(continued)*

Left-wing extremists have rationalized bank robberies as expropriations from the state. A right-wing prisoner rationalizes his crime as fighting back against ZOG [or "Zionist Occupied Government," a term used by many neo-Nazis]—and he will be backed up morally by white supremacist publications.

The ideologies offer an excuse and a sense of empowerment that allows someone in jail to be transformed from a criminal into a "prisoner of war" or "political prisoner."

IR: Are there other benefits for prisoners?

MP: If you join a movement, you can receive all kinds of benefits from outside people in the movement. A lot of left-wing groups do serious prisoner support, sending you gifts or money, raising funds for your defense. They may write you letters, put up Web pages about you, and so on. Many right-wing groups do the same, setting up "prison ministries." Often young women are encouraged to write to male prisoners, something that is seen as a terrifically important benefit.

This can play out well for prisoners who get out. They enter a world where they are heroes. They are ex-"POWS," liberated "political prisoners" who can tell the youngsters outside what it's all about. As such, they have access to women, drugs, all kinds of things.

IR: How do outside groups recruit in the prisons?

MP: Sending materials and writing letters are the most common ways. Sometimes visits are used. Prisoners are lonely and have often been abandoned by their friends and family. Extremists capitalize on those feelings.

IR: Who decides what literature gets into prison?

MP: They're called security threat group analysts. The federal level has a whole bunch of them. On the state level, they may be substantial or sometimes just a few who monitor activities in all the prisons in a given state. They look at all the materials coming in and out of prison to see if they are allowable or if they are linked to extremism, street gangs, organized crime, violence and so on. If they identify a prisoner as a member of one of these groups, they may be able to take additional measures against him, such as placing him in administrative segregation. They have fairly wide latitude.

IR: Is there a relationship between getting recruited into these racist groups and then committing hate crimes or other violence after leaving prison?

MP: My suspicion is that there is probably not a huge link, because a lot of these people just join the gangs while they are in prison, and then leave them when they get out. But the fact is that some prisoners do get genuinely politicized, and on top of that, prison gives them an education in violence. It's a mess. I think that is what happened in Texas (with the murderers of James Byrd Jr.), and the result was one of the most inhumane acts ever perpetrated in modern America.

IR: Is there a significant distinction between those who come into prison without much racial awareness, like the men who killed James Byrd, and extremists who enter prison already highly politicized?

MP: People who are already ideologically extreme don't stop their activities in prison—some of them see prison as a great opportunity for recruiting. Take Leroy Schweitzer, the Montana Freeman (a form of "sovereign citizen") leader who's in federal prison in South Carolina serving a 22-year sentence for various financial scams. He's teaching prisoners how to engage in "paper terrorism," how to file bogus liens against public officials, attorneys, and others. He even showed one jewel dealer serving a 40-year sentence on money laundering charges how to file a (bogus) $1.5 billion lien against the judge in his case.

Other imprisoned ideologues try to influence followers outside of prison. Craig "Critter" Marshall, environmental extremist serving a five-year sentence for conspiracy to commit arson, told *Earth First!* readers last year that the only form of solidarity he wants is more arsons. He wrote something like, "When someone picks up a bomb, instead of a pen, is when my spirits really soar."

IR: How much of a threat do these gangs pose to prison staff?

MP: Prisons are dangerous. I don't know whether the violence from gang members is greater than that of nongang members, although obviously there is a greater potential for planned or organized violence. But there is a lot of training for this sort of thing now—prisons in general have better control mechanisms, whether it is cameras, doors that can automatically shut, or special training. But that doesn't stop prisoners from killing each other all the time—and it doesn't stop guards from being assaulted. Let's face it, prisons are nasty places.

Source: Excerpt from Mark Pitcavage, "Behind the Walls: An Expert Discusses the Role of Race-Based Gangs in America's Prisons," *Intelligence Report,* vol. 108, Winter 2002, pp. 24–27. Copyright © 2002 Southern Poverty Law Center.

10 percent STGs include Arkansas (17 percent), Colorado (15 percent), Delaware (11 percent), Florida (18 percent), Hawaii (20 percent), Maryland (13 percent), Massachusetts (20 percent), Minnesota (26 percent), Mississippi (26 percent), Nebraska (24 percent), New Jersey (17 percent), New Mexico (36 percent), North Dakota (13 percent), Ohio (16 percent), Rhode Island (15 percent), Tennessee (22 percent), Washington (18 percent), and Wisconsin (25 percent). On average, 14 percent of a state's prison population is STG.[20]

Six major STGs in the United States are recognized nationally for their participation in organized crime and violence. They are:[21]

1. *Aryan Brotherhood:* Originated in 1967 in California's San Quentin Prison, its racial makeup is white.
2. *Black Guerilla Family:* Founded in 1966 at San Quentin Prison and considered the most politically oriented of the major state prison STGs, its racial makeup is black.
3. *Mexican Mafia:* Formed in the late 1950s in California's youth facility at Duel, its racial makeup is Mexican American/Hispanic.
4. *La Nuestra Familia:* Originated in the California state prison at Soledad in the mid-1960s, its racial makeup is Mexican American/Hispanic.
5. *Neta:* Established in 1970 in the Rio Piedras Prison, Puerto Rico, its racial makeup is Puerto Rican American/Hispanic.
6. *Texas Syndicate:* Originated in California's Folsom prison in the early 1970s in direct response to the other California prison gangs (notably the Aryan Brotherhood and the Mexican Mafia), which were attempting to prey on native Texas inmates, its racial makeup is Mexican American/Hispanic.

New among the STGs is an influx of street gangs, such as Mara Salvatrucha 13 (MS-13) composed mostly of Salvadorans, Hondurans, Guatemalans, and Nicaraguans, Miami's "112 Avenue Boys," and Boston's "Franklin Field Pistons," that have less national organization than traditional STGs and do not easily fit into standard prison gang categories because of their smaller numbers, fewer cohesive ties, and less organized methods of operation.

STGs have a profound impact on prison security, and many prisons today have a security threat group unit that is responsible for the identification and overall coordination of all STG-related information at their facilities. In an attempt to control STG influence, some prison administrators have transferred known STG members from one institution to another only to find that this practice actually increased STG organization and activity—it extended the STG's influence throughout a state's prison system. Other states enacted "gang enhancement" statutes that imposed severe sentences on STG activity. Today, many states are adopting a new strategy, segregating known STG members to highly restrictive supermax housing, correctional facilities that are designed to house the "worst of the worst" prisoners under complete lockdown and total isolation. Advocates of this approach contend that removing STG leaders from the general prison population reduces the amount of control that STG leaders exert. Critics of the approach argue that violence actually may increase because conditions within supermax housing are so harsh that they emotionally damage inmates who may one day be returned to the general prison population or released or paroled into the community.

Two explanations for STG development are deprivation and importation. As noted in Chapter 10, the basic premise of deprivation theory is that inmates develop a social system as a way to adapt to the pains of imprisonment. Because inmates are deprived of liberty, autonomy, goods and services, sexual relations, and security, they develop a culture that helps them get back what imprisonment has taken away. Importation theory, on the other hand, emphasizes that inmates' preprison attitudes and values guide their reactions and responses to the internal conditions of prison. Both theories are valid; most major STGs can be traced to preprison attitudes and values, but prison conditions influence when and to what extent STG activity and violence occur.

Besides STGs, there is another kind of threat to prison security today. It's the threat posed by radicalized prisoners. For example, Sheikh Omar Abdel Rahman, the blind sheikh who is serving a life sentence in New York for conspiring to bomb a number of New York landmarks, was accused of sending messages from prison through visiting attorneys to members of Gama'a al-Islamiyya, Egypt's largest militant group.

Mark Hamm, professor of criminology at Indiana State University, recently completed a study for the National Institute of Justice on prisoner radicalization and profiled the case of Kevin Lamar James.[22] James and three other men pleaded guilty to conspiracy to wage war against the United States for plotting to attack U.S. military facilities, Israeli government facilities, and Jewish synagogues in Los Angeles. As a teenager, James was a member of the 76th Street Crips in Los Angeles. When he was 21, he was sentenced to 10 years in prison for robbery. In prison, he followed the beliefs of the Nation of Islam. Finding those beliefs uninteresting, he embraced the teachings of Jam'iyyat Ul-Islam Is-Saheed (the Assembly of Authentic Islam), or JIS, whose message says it is the duty of Muslims to violently attack enemies of Islam, including the U.S. government.

By 2004, James had several dozen followers. One of those, Levar Washington, was ready for parole. James directed Washington to recruit five people without felony records from the community, acquire firearms, and find people with explosives expertise. James's plan was to attack a target of the Iraq war—a U.S. Army recruiting office—on September 11, 2005, four years to the day after the 9/11 attacks. James directed the attack from his prison cell even though the outside group lived in an apartment in Los Angeles. However, when one of the outside members dropped his cell phone at a gas station robbery, it led to the indictment of James and the three men.

Professor Hamm found that moving from religious radicalization to terrorism can be prevented by hiring prison chaplains, diversifying corrections personnel, training staff on the recruitment activities of gangs, and increasing our research base on prison culture that leads to radicalization and terrorist recruitment. "When there is a shortage of chaplains to provide religious guidance, into that void comes inmates with exotic religious messages," says Hamm.[23]

Can gang members change? Gabriel Morales, founder of Gang Prevention Services in Seattle, says "yes." In November 2008, he told a reporter with the *Seattle Post-Intelligencer* that his brother, a former gang member, changed at age 40.[24] "He was a gang member," Morales told the reporter. "He had no teeth—his bones were brittle. He looked a lot older than me though he was younger. He got tired of it. He had a kid, and he got tired of his kid seeing him when he was locked up and crying and missing Daddy. It broke his heart. He had to change his heart before he changed his mind."

Men and women prisoners have tattoos. How would you identify those who are STG members from those who aren't?

EVIDENCE-BASED CORRECTIONS

The evidence-based literature confirms Morales's point. Researchers James Byrne and Don Hummer remind us that "changing" inmate behavior rather than simply "controlling" it is key.[25] Classification systems that are control based may predict STG involvement, but they will not reduce criminal activity. Classification systems that focus on offenders' participation in prison programming and treatment are the most effective prison violence reduction strategies. Finding the optimal "tipping point" in oneself is the key. For Morales's brother, it happened when he saw his kid unhappy at seeing his dad locked up. That changed his heart and his thinking about criminal gang activity.

Jail Gangs—Security Threat Groups

Most of our knowledge about STGs is based on research conducted in state or federal prisons. Comparatively little is known about the extent of STGs in jails and for that reason we report on it here.

In 2004, researchers from California State University, Chino; the University of Missouri, St. Louis; and the National Youth Gang Center examined the perceptions of jail administrators about the problems that STG members cause in their facilities, the prevalence of these populations, methods of classifying gang membership, and approaches that may reduce the disruption or violence associated with these groups.[26] In spite of the methodological limitations of the study (e.g., jails in the northeast and small jails were underrepresented), the results shed some light on the influence of STGs in jails.

Jail administrators said designation of gang membership by another law enforcement agency along with tattoos, clothing/gang colors, hand signs, and an individual's self-declaration was commonly used to define STG membership. They estimated STG membership at 13.2 percent. Extrapolating this estimate to the June 2009 national jail population (837,833), for example, would result in 110,594 STG members held in jail on any given day.

When asked about the problems that STG members cause in their facilities, jail administrators reported that gang members are less disruptive than inmates with severe mental illnesses but are more likely to assault other inmates. Their most important tools to control STG harm were the gathering and dissemination of gang intelligence within the facility and to other law enforcement agencies. Segregation of STG members was also effective in large jails, but small jails were unlikely to have the ability or resources to segregate inmates. A prime example of jail monitoring of STGs is the Broward County Sheriff's Department (Ft. Lauderdale, Florida, the second most populous county in Florida) where persons suspected of being involved with an STG are interviewed, information is collected, activity documented, and paraphernalia managed.

According to Ruddell, Decker, and Egley, researchers from California State University, the University of Missouri, and the National Youth Gang Center study, the benefits of controlling STGs in jails are twofold. First, jails will be safer and as a result there will be less need for inmates to join gangs in search of safety. And second, information sharing may enhance the effectiveness of prison-based STG intervention.

Prison Riots and Disturbances

Each prison disturbance and riot is unique. The precipitating conditions, resolutions, and aftermath are shaped by the characteristics of the institution, its staff, its administration, and its inmate population as well as the state or federal agency to which it belongs. No amount of comprehensive planning can prevent all disturbances and riots because, as one expert contends, some have no root causes.[27] It is impossible to predict where and when they will occur. Still, understanding prison disturbances and riots can help correctional administrators avoid some problems, take steps to prevent certain events from launching into full-fledged riots, limit the extent of damage, and terminate disturbances and riots in the least costly way.

In May 2002 and again in July/August 2006, the American Correctional Association (ACA) published the results of a survey of prison disturbances, riots, assaults, and escapes. ACA defined **disturbance** as an altercation involving three or more inmates, resulting in official action beyond summary sanctions, and for which there is an institutional record. Most prison disturbances were fights, stabbings, assaults, shouting obscenities at staff, refusal to follow orders (e.g., clean cell area and return to cell), hostage taking, and cell extraction. A **riot** is any action by a group of inmates that constitutes a forcible attempt to gain control of a facility or area within a facility.

The ACA recorded a decrease in prison disturbances from 2,674 in 2000 to 405 in 2006 and reported a similar decrease in riots from 2000 to 2006. In 2000, there were two riots. In 2006, there were no riots.[28] From 2000 to 2006, there were also decreases in the number of inmates killed by inmates and staff, staff and officers assaulted, inmate suicide attempts and deaths, inmates injured by staff, and escapees and walkaways.

What some states call a *riot*, others downplay and call a *disturbance*. For example, in 1993 there were more than 186 disturbances in 21 corrections systems—but only 7 were classified as riots.[29] In Connecticut, a gang fight involving more than 300 inmates and causing more than $100,000 in damage was called a *riot*. At Leavenworth, a racial fight involving 427 inmates that caused significant damage to the prison's auditorium, chapel, and industry buildings was called a *disturbance*. Correctional administrators label most incidents *disturbances* because the term is less sensational.

How many prison riots have there been in the United States? Nobody knows for sure. Not only do we have different opinions as to what constitutes a riot, but wardens and state officials are also reluctant to publicize loss of control. Scholars estimate that almost 500 prison riots have taken place in the United States since 1855.[30]

Prison violence and riots are as old as prisons themselves. There were riots and mass escapes at the Walnut Street Jail in Philadelphia, at Newgate Prison in New York, and almost everywhere from the beginning of prisons in this country. One particularly eventful year was 1952 when riots erupted in 25 of the 152 U.S. prisons. Although no lives were lost, prison staff and inmates were in danger, and damage ran into the millions. Reasons for the riots included absence of inmate programs and work, idleness, unqualified staff who were poorly trained and poorly paid, old facilities (one-third were more than 70 years old), absence of procedures for hearing inmate grievances, overcrowding, insufficient prison budgets, absence of inmate classification, philosophical conflicts about the nature of prisoners (treat them as human beings who will one day rejoin society or "treat them rough"), and the presence of a new generation of prisoners.[31]

In 1953, reformers advocated overhauling and modernizing prison programs, replacing old prisons, hiring more and better staff, and developing an integrated state system. They advocated the creation of:

- professionally staffed classification centers;
- prison size restricted to no more than 500 beds;
- professionally trained, well-paid correctional officers;

disturbance

An altercation involving three or more inmates, resulting in official action beyond summary sanctions and for which there is an institutional record.

riot

Any action by a group of inmates that constitutes a forcible attempt to gain control of a facility or area within a facility.

- inmate self-governance;
- procedures that allow inmate grievances to be aired;
- prison work programs with fair wages paid to prisoners;
- periodic review of sentencing patterns and parole board decisions;
- dissemination of statistics on commitments and releases;
- prerelease orientation and job-finding assistance for discharged prisoners; and
- statewide prison leadership headed by nonpolitical, nationally recruited, and professionally trained individuals.[32]

The New Mexico Penitentiary riot, which took place on February 2 and 3, 1980, is considered one of the world's five largest prison riots. Thirty-three inmates died and hundreds more were treated for injuries. None of the 12 corrections officers taken hostage were killed, but seven were treated for injuries caused by beatings and rapes. What are some of the causes of prison riots, and how can they be prevented?

Despite reformers' appeals for overhauls of prison programs and management, violence-provoking conditions continue to exist in many prisons. One might wonder whether anything has changed since the storm of prison riots in 1952. Three of the bloodiest and most violent prison riots in the United States occurred in severely overcrowded prisons in New York in 1971, in New Mexico in 1980, and in Ohio in 1993.

In the 1971 riot at the Attica Correctional Facility, New York where 2,225 inmates were incarcerated in a prison designed for 1,200, 43 lives were lost: Four inmates were killed during the riot as part of inmate "justice," and when police stormed in to retake the prison, they killed 10 civilian hostages and 29 prisoners. The New York State Special Commission that investigated the riot wrote, "With the exception of Indian massacres in the late 19th century, the State Police assault which ended the four-day prison uprising was the bloodiest one-day encounter between Americans since the Civil War."[33]

In the 1980 riot at the Penitentiary of New Mexico in Santa Fe where 1,136 inmates were confined in a space designed for 900 inmates, the taking of human life was brutal. Thirty-three inmates were tortured, dismembered, decapitated, burned alive, and killed by fellow inmates. Although staff were held hostage, none were killed.

The longest prison riot in U.S. history occurred at the Southern Ohio Correctional Facility in Lucasville in 1993 where 1,820 inmates were held in a prison built for 1,540. Inmates killed nine of their fellow inmates and one correctional officer in the 11-day siege.

The riot at Lucasville cost an estimated $15 million in property damage. At Santa Fe, the estimate was $28.5 million. At Attica, the cost was more than $3 million. A new chapter in the cost of prison riots was written on August 28, 2000, when, after three decades of waiting, federal district court judge Michael A. Telesca accepted New York State's agreement to set aside $12 million (the largest amount ever in a prisoners' rights case) to compensate more than 500 inmates and relatives for the abuse that the prisoners suffered. Four million dollars was set aside for lawyer fees, and $8 million was divided among 502 inmates and relatives of the inmates who died in the uprising. After the riot ended, inmates were stripped naked and threatened with castration, forced to crawl naked in the mud with an X on their backs as if to make them a target, severely beaten, and shot. After hearing the inmates' stories, Judge Telesca described the aftermath as littered with "brutal beatings and acts of torture" and unlimited racial epithets.

Causes of Prison Riots According to sociology professor Burt Useem at Purdue University, there are five theoretical explanations for the causes of prison riots.[34]

The first is random chance. Useem says that some prison riots have no root causes. It is impossible to predict where and when they will occur.

The second explanation is bad conditions. This explanation tells us that overcrowding, antiquated facilities, low staffing levels, insufficient staff training, lack of programs for inmates, lack of funding, and poor implementation of correctional policy account for prison riots. Overcrowding is the most important of these. It causes heightened prison tension and potential violent disruption. Overcrowding is responsible for curtailing or even eliminating opportunities for education, vocational training, and recreation. When the ratio of correctional officers to inmates becomes too low, something has to give. At Attica, Santa Fe, and Lucasville, overcrowding raised tensions, interfered with prisoner classification, reduced living space, and restricted access to programs. Restlessness and boredom grew.

The third explanation involves rebellious inmates and racial antagonism. This includes gang members and violent or aggressive inmates. Riots tend to occur in higher-security facilities. Outside prison, the ratio of racial minorities to whites is about one to five. In prison, however, whites are the minority. That different ratio, in addition to overcrowding, close living quarters, and lack of space, adds to racial antagonism. Antagonism is heightened when inmates separate themselves along racial or ethnic lines for self-protection. Researchers have discovered that as inmates' perception of overcrowding increases, their antagonism toward other racial and ethnic groups also increases. Prisoners at Attica, Santa Fe, and Lucasville were young, violence prone, and poorly classified. Most were undereducated, underemployed, and uncommitted to society's means for achieving social goals. The racial and ethnic minority imbalance together with these individual factors prompted many inmates to adopt tough attitudes and join STGs for self-protection.

The fourth explanation focuses on institutional structure and readiness. Riots occur when a prison's infrastructure wears thin and authorities fail to plan and prepare. At Attica, a faulty weld joint in a metal gate gave way and allowed prisoners access to most areas of the institution. At Santa Fe, inmates pounded on "shatterproof" glass with a fire extinguisher until the glass fell out of the frame. At Lucasville, inmates collected master keys from staff hostages and opened cell doors.

The fifth explanation focuses on administrative factors. Poor prison management and administration are linked to prison riots. Poor management can result from frequent staff turnover, low correctional officer qualifications, inadequate training, poor staff–inmate communication, and low staff pay. At Attica, Santa Fe, and Lucasville, inmates' complaints about living conditions, lack of programs, and officers' excessive use of force and harassment went unheard by administration. Rumors of riots were not taken seriously.

Preventing Prison Riots Prison violence provokes more violence. Measures to prevent prison riots must become a national priority, and change must occur. Three years before the Attica riot, the U.S. National

Advisory Commission on Civil Disorders (the Kerner Commission) warned that the only effective way to prevent riots, whether in or out of prison, was to eliminate sources of tension by making good "the promises of American democracy to all citizens, urban and rural, white and black, Spanish surname, American Indian, and every minority group."[35] While that change is long range, corrections officials can implement immediate measures to reduce the likelihood of inmate aggression, including the following:

- formal inmate grievance procedures;
- ombudsmen to mediate disputes;
- an improved classification system;
- smaller institutions;
- meaningful prison school and work programs;
- alternatives to incarceration;
- professional corrections staff who are trained and well paid;
- administrators who are visible and available to staff and inmates; and
- clearly written and understood policies on the use of force when necessary.

To ensure that the use of force is appropriate and justifiable, the ACA recommends establishing policies and procedures that govern its use (see Exhibit 13–2).

SUPERMAX HOUSING AND "NO-FRILLS" PRISONS AND JAILS

In an effort to control the behavior of violence-prone inmates, two new types of prisons are emerging—supermax housing and "no-frills" prisons and jails. Both alter the conditions of confinement for thousands of U.S. prisoners, raising important issues for the prisoners and staff who must live and work in them and the society that must accept the prisoners when they are released.

Supermax Housing

Prison systems have always needed a way to deal with inmates whose violent behavior makes it impossible for them to live with the general prison population. Generally such measures involve separating such inmates and are called *segregation* or *solitary confinement*. Prisoners who are dangerous or chronically violent, have escaped or attempted to escape from a high-security correctional facility, have incited or attempted to incite disruption in a correctional facility, or who have preyed on weaker inmates are removed from the general population. You may recall from Chapter 7 that, in 1829, the Eastern State Penitentiary in Cherry Hill, Pennsylvania, was built on the principle of solitary confinement. However, in 1913 the Pennsylvania legislature dropped "solitary" from sentencing statutes, and housing arrangements at Eastern State became congregate. From that point forward, specialized housing units were developed for management and control of troublesome inmates.

The Federal Bureau of Prisons (BOP) returned to the idea of controlling the most violent and disruptive inmates in indefinite solitary confinement when it opened Alcatraz in 1934. Alcatraz, which had a capacity of 275, did not offer any treatment program; its sole purpose was to incarcerate and punish

| EXHIBIT 13–2 | Public Correctional Policy on Use of Force |

Introduction

Correctional agencies are responsible for ensuring the safety in correctional programs. To achieve this goal, it may be necessary for correctional staff to use legally authorized force in certain situations.

Policy Statement

Correctional agencies are committed to exercising an appropriate use of force consistent with statutory requirements and the needs of the situation. Use of force consists of physical contact with an offender in a confrontational situation to promote safety, control behavior and enforce order. Use of force includes use of restraints (other than for routine transportation and movement), chemical agents, electronic devices, and weapons. Force is justified only when required to maintain or regain control, or when there is imminent danger of escape, injury to self, others or damage to property. To ensure that the use of force is appropriate and justifiable, correctional agencies should establish and maintain policies and procedures that:

A. Establish strategies to reduce and prevent the necessity of use of force, that authorize force only when no reasonable alternative is possible, that advocate the minimum force necessary, and that prohibit the use of force as a retaliatory or disciplinary measure;

B. Define the range of methods for and alternatives to the use of force, and that specify the conditions under which each is permitted. These policies must assign responsibility for authorizing the use of force; outline the steps for appropriate implementation of the use of force; provide for close monitoring of the person while in restraints; and require proper documentation, administrative review, investigation and remedial action;

C. Establish and maintain procedures that limit the use of deadly force to those instances where it is legally authorized and where there is an imminent threat to human life or to public safety;

D. Prohibit restraint techniques which cause or could cause partial or complete impairment of respiratory exchange (positional asphyxia) such as the hogtie position or certain restraints on the neck, or those that cause or could cause partial or complete paralysis;

E. Whenever possible, assure that age, gender, health and mental health status are considered prior to initiating the use of force and that the least restrictive and/or least likely type to cause impairment/harm is utilized. Electronic devices, chemical agents and other types of restraints should not be used on pregnant offenders or those with respiratory and other debilitating conditions;

F. Provide ongoing specialized staff training designed to teach staff to anticipate, stabilize and diffuse situations that might give rise to conflict, confrontation and violence and that ensures staff's competency in the use of all methods and equipment in the use of force.

Source: Copyright © American Correctional Association.

the federal prison system's most desperate criminals and worst troublemakers. Alcatraz was "America's Devil's Island, 'Hellcatraz'—a place where convicts slowly went insane from the tedium and hopelessness of endless years on 'the Rock.'"[36] By 1963, Alcatraz was judged an expensive failure; it symbolized a penal philosophy that was outdated in an era that espoused rehabilitation, not punishment, as the goal of incarceration. Alcatraz closed in the early 1960s under orders from U.S. Attorney General Robert Kennedy. During the era of rehabilitation that followed the Alcatraz closing, prison officials used the *dispersal model*—problem prisoners were distributed to a

Several states are considering closing prison gun towers as a cost-cutting move. But that's not under consideration at the federal supermax prison in Florence, Colorado, where three mirrored-glass gun towers define the maximum-security level of heightened confinement. Officially known as the United States Penitentiary Florence Administrative Maximum (ADMAX), 25 percent of the 400 prisoners there will remain in confinement for the rest of their lives. What are the pros and cons of such facilities?

supermax housing

A freestanding facility, or a distinct unit within a facility, that provides for management and secure control of inmates who have been officially designated as exhibiting violent or serious and disruptive behavior while incarcerated.

number of prisons. Prison officials hoped that dispersal among populations of generally law-abiding inmates would dilute the influence of problem prisoners. Inmates from Alcatraz were moved to federal prisons in Atlanta and Leavenworth.

By the 1970s, the goal of incarceration had shifted back to punishment. Disturbances, violence, and riots at state and federal prisons convinced the BOP to try again to control the most troublesome federal inmates in one location. The BOP reverted to the *concentration model*—all problem prisoners would be housed together in a separate facility. The federal prison at Marion, Illinois, was chosen for this purpose. The construction features at Marion, however, made it difficult for staff to maintain complete control over recalcitrant inmates. Open cell fronts were a major limitation in Marion's design to control the toughest prisoners. Through their cell bars, inmates threw trash, urine, and feces at corrections officers; passed contraband; set fires; and verbally harassed and lunged at staff and other prisoners as they walked by. Tension, hostility, violence, and murder were all too common. On October 23, 1983, a state of emergency was declared after two corrections officers and one prisoner were murdered by inmates, and two other officers were seriously injured. The Marion facility was placed on lockdown status until September 2006. Over the next few years, the BOP conceived plans to build a supermax facility that would implement construction features for controlling difficult inmates.

In 1994, the BOP opened its first **supermax housing** facility at Florence, Colorado, a rural community of about 3,800 residents 110 miles south of Denver. Officially known as United States Penitentiary Florence Administrative Maximum (ADMAX), the prison houses the 450 most dangerous, violent, escape prone, and STG federal inmate leaders. More than 25 percent will never be released from federal custody and will remain in confinement for the rest of their lives. Among the prisoners at ADX are Zacarias Moussaoui, confessed 9/11 conspirator; Olympic Park bomber Eric Rudolph; "Unabomber" Ted Kaczynski; Robert Hanssen, American FBI agent-turned Soviet spy; Oklahoma City bombing conspirator Terry Nichols; would-be "shoe bomber" Richard Reid; and 1993 World Trade Center bombing conspirator Ramzi Yousef. Thomson, Illinois, about 150 miles east of Chicago and home to about 600 residents, could become the location to house detainees from Guantanamo Bay, Cuba. Like Florence, Colorado, some 20 years ago, Thomson is desperate for jobs and is seeking a federal prison to keep it alive. The residents even collected about $130,000 to buy 600 acres that they then donated to the federal BOP to entice it to build a prison.

Construction cost for the federal supermax prison in Florence, Colorado, totaled $60 million ($150,000 per cell). Annual operating cost per cell per year is another $40,000, or $19.2 million total annually. According to Mears and Watson, a low-end estimate of the typical life course of a supermax prison (35 years) is close to $1 billion.[37]

Supermax prisons are significantly more expensive to build than traditional prisons due in part to the enhanced and extensive high-security features on locks, doors, and perimeters; heavily reinforced walls, ceilings, and floors; and incorporation of advanced electronic systems and technology. Providing meals and other services at individual cell fronts, having multiple-officer escorts, and maintaining elaborate electronic systems contribute to the high cost.

Cell design at the federal supermax prison in Florence, Colorado, resists vandalism. Each prisoner's bed, desk, stool, and bookcase are made of reinforced concrete and anchored in place. Each 7 by 12-foot cell has a shower stall with flood-proof plumbing and a 12-inch black-and-white television set. Cell windows deny prisoners all views of the outside except the sky above. A simple hole-in-the-wall apparatus for lighting cigarettes has replaced matches and cigarette lighters. Meals are dispensed through cell slots in separate heated trays from airline-style carts pulled by small tractors. Cells are staggered so that inmates cannot make eye contact with other inmates. There are no congregate activities of any kind. Each cell has a double-entry door: an interior barred cage door backed up by a windowed steel door that prevents voice contact among prisoners. Visits are noncontact, and inmates are allowed out of their cells for an hour a day of solitary exercise.

The new prison has 1,400 electronically controlled gates, 168 television monitors, and three mirror-glass gun towers. The 400 cells are subdivided among nine units—each unit is self-contained and includes a sick-call room, law library, and barber chair. After three years of good behavior, an inmate gradually regains social contact. "What puts a man in is his behavior, and what gets a man out is his behavior," said John M. Vanyur, former associate warden.[38]

This type of supercontrolled environment is taking hold across the United States. Forty-four states, the District of Columbia, and the BOP now operate one or more supermax prisons that collectively house more than 25,000 inmates.[39] Despite the fact that supermax prisons typically cost two to three times more to build and operate than traditional maximum-security prisons, the facilities are politically and publicly attractive. "Supermax prisons have become political symbols of how 'tough' a jurisdiction has become."[40]

California opened Pelican Bay State Prison in Crescent City in 1990 for 1,600 inmates in an X-shaped windowless bunker. Construction cost was $133,653 per cell. All inmates are denied access to prison work and group exercise yards. Pelican Bay, like the federal supermax housing facility in Florence, Colorado, is entirely automated. Inmates in the supermax housing unit have no face-to-face contact with staff or other inmates. Cell doors are solid stainless steel with slots for food trays. Cell doors open and close electronically. Officers can talk with or listen in on inmates through a speaker system. These inmates do not work. They have no recreational equipment. They do not mix with other inmates. They are not permitted to smoke. They eat all meals in their cells. They leave their cells only for showers and 90 minutes of daily exercise in small cement areas enclosed by 20-foot cement walls. Visits with family and friends are noncontact behind glass partitions. Prisoners are strip searched and handcuffed whenever they are removed from their cells and placed in full shackles with waist and hobble chains.

The National Institute of Corrections (NIC) studied supermax prisons nationwide and described the supermax prison as "a highly restrictive, high-custody housing unit within a secure facility, or an entire secure facility, that isolates inmates from the general population and from each other due to grievous crimes, repetitive assaultive or violent institutional behavior, the threat of escape or actual escape from high-custody facility(s), or inciting or threatening to incite disturbances in a correctional institution."[41] Supermax housing does not include maximum or close custody facilities that are designated for routine housing of inmates with high-custody needs, inmates in disciplinary segregation or protective custody, or other inmates requiring segregation or separation for other routine purposes. In fact, NIC opined that as comforting as it might be to prison staff to send nuisance inmates who continuously test the limits, frequently break minor rules, consume an inordinate amount of staff time, are situationally assaultive, or cannot control their behavior due to mental illness to supermax facilities, it is inappropriate to do so. Use of extended control housing for nuisance inmates is inefficient, consumes expensive high-security beds, has little overall operational impact, and is arguably overkill. And according to some, use of supermax for nonviolent inmates happens all too often. Marianne McNabb, former regional administrator for the Washington State Department of Corrections said, "People have a notion that behind the supermax facilities are all psychopathic serial killers. But many are low-level criminals who, because of the inability to manage their behavior in the open institutional population, and how they are dealt with by staff, are kept in virtual lockdown."[42]

NIC found that a universal definition of supermax housing is problematic and states vary considerably in their criteria for the placement in and release of inmates from these facilities. The many states that provided information had different reasons and needs for supermax housing. Some supermax prisons house inmates who could not be controlled in traditional administrative segregation units, including prisoners who are uncontrollable due to mental illness. Others are an extension or expansion of segregation and house protective custody and/or disciplinary segregation inmates. Still others house inmates who would reside in close custody among the general population in most other jurisdictions. As these prisons have increased in number, been reported on by the media, and gained popularity with the public, a variety of names have emerged to describe them: *special housing unit, extended control unit, maxi-maxi, maximum control facility, secured housing unit, intensive housing unit, intensive management unit,* and *administrative maximum penitentiary*. The term *supermax* is the one heard most frequently in the media and in the field of corrections. Yet, as the NIC survey indicates, the term is applied to a wide variety of facilities and programs handling an equally wide variety of inmate populations. NIC's conclusion is, "Supermax as defined in the survey may exist in relatively few agencies."[43]

To date, research on super-maximum-security prisons is minimal despite the rapid increase in and costs of such facilities nationally. Criminologists, psychiatrists, lawyers, and the courts who have studied the effects of long-term solitary confinement report evidence of acute sensory deprivation, paranoid delusion belief systems, irrational fears of violence, resentment, little ability to control rage, and mental breakdowns. Forty-five percent of prisoners in Washington's supermax units were diagnosed as seriously mentally ill.[44]

The vast majority of inmates in long-term solitary confinement remain anxious, angry, depressed, insecure, and confused. Some commit suicide. For example, 69 percent of the 41 suicides committed in California prisons in 2005 occurred in units where inmates are isolated for 23 hours a day. Most of the 24 prisoner suicides in Texas in 2005 were in some form of solitary confinement, leaving many to link the increase in prisoner suicides to the rising number of inmates kept in solitary confinement.[45]

Some inmates in supermax prison will have been so deprived of human contact that it will be hard for them to cope with social situations. If the

"Supermax" prisons are ultra-high-security correctional facilities. Here, an empty day room at the Northern Correctional Institution at Somers, Connecticut (Connecticut's only level 5 maximum security) can be seen with prisoner cells above as a correctional officer escorts a prisoner out of a shower, top left. What kinds of inmates should be held in such facilities?

correctional staff cannot confidently assess what the inmate will do when supermax restrictions are lifted, members revisit the risks that have been avoided by placing an inmate in a supermax facility when the inmate is released, either back into the general prison population or into society.

The impact of supermax facilities on staff is also a subject of much discussion. Having to deal on a daily basis with inmates who have proven to be the most troublesome—in an environment that prioritizes human control and isolation—presents staff with extraordinary challenges. Correctional administrators with experience in operating supermax prisons talk about the potential for creating a "we/they syndrome" between staff and inmates. The nature and reputation of the inmate and frequently the inmate's behavior, combined with ultracontrol and rigidity, magnify the tension between inmates and staff. When there is little interaction except in control situations, the adversarial nature of the relationships tends to be one of dominance and, in return, resistance on both sides. Stuart Grassian, a physician and expert on prison control units, believes that people who work in supermax facilities lose their capacity to be shocked by the kinds of things they see. "It may put money in your pocket," Dr. Grassian notes, "but over time it destroys you psychologically and brings out rage and sadism and violence and brutality."[46]

One piece of academic research that examined what the goals of supermax prison are, how they ought to be assessed, what the unintended effects are, and what political, moral, and economic factors enter the decision to build or not was published in 2006.[47] Mears and Watson reviewed the literature; visited three supermax prisons where they conducted focus groups and interviews with corrections policymakers, officials, and practitioners; and interviewed similar individuals in eight other states. They concluded, "no solid empirical foundation exists to say with confidence that they [supermax prisons] are either effective or ineffective."[48] The fact that Mears and Watson found a wide range of goals and impacts from increasing prison safety and order to controlling and improving prisoners' behavior, reducing the influence of gangs, increasing public safety, and increasing efficiencies throughout correctional systems makes cross-state evaluations of supermax prisons a challenge, and how goals should be measured remains unclear.

Mears and Watson's analysis also pointed to a wide range of potential unintended impacts, some positive (for example, increasing the quality of life among general population prison staff and inmates and improving the economy in the communities where supermax prisons are located) and some negative (for example, decreasing the quality of inmate–staff relations and increasing mental illness among supermax-confined inmates). But how common these unintended impacts are, nobody knows; and until we do know, we can't conclude that supermax prisons merit support.

So far, only one study used a powerful type of research design to assess whether supermax prisons contribute to a decrease in prison violence, and the results are at best mixed. The study focused on four states, three of which had supermax prisons (Arizona, Illinois, and Minnesota) and one that did not (Utah). Researchers studied inmate-on-inmate and inmate-on-staff assaults and found that the opening of a supermax prison did not reduce the level of inmate-on-inmate violence although in Illinois there was a reduction in assaults on staff. The finding in Illinois suggested support for supermax prisons, but it raised this question: Why would a supermax prison reduce inmate-on-staff assaults but not inmate-on-inmate assaults?[49]

In recent years, the controversies surrounding super-maximum-security prisons have reached the U.S. courts. Inmates in supermax housing facilities have challenged the conditions of their confinement and the selection procedures by which inmates are transferred to supermax prisons.

COMMISSION ON SAFETY AND ABUSE IN AMERICA'S PRISONS: LIMITING SEGREGATION

"Separating dangerous or vulnerable individuals from the general prison population is a necessary part of running a safe correctional facility. In some systems around the country, however, the drive for safety, coupled with public demand for tough punishment, has had perverse effects: Prisoners who should be housed at safe distances from particular individuals or groups of prisoners end up locked in their cells 23 hours a day, every day, with little opportunity to engage in programming to prepare them for release. People who pose no real threat to anyone and also the mentally ill are languishing for months or years in high-security units and supermax prisons. And in some places, the environment in segregation is so severe that people end up completely isolated, living in what can only be described as torturous conditions. There is also troubling evidence that the distress of living and working in this environment actually causes violence between staff and prisoners."

—The Commission on Safety and Abuse in America's Prisons

On June 30, 2000, when the federal Bureau of Justice Statistics last collected data from state and federal prisons, approximately 80,000 people were confined in segregation units. BJS also found that from 1995 to 2000 the growth rate in the number of prisoners housed in segregation outpaced the growth rate of the overall prison population, 40 percent compared to 28 percent. There are no similar data for local jails.

The commission concluded that the overreliance on and inappropriate use of segregation hurts individual prisoners and officers. Furthermore, the misuse of segregation works against the process of rehabilitating people and threatens public safety.

Walter Dickey, former secretary of the Wisconsin Department of Corrections, told the commission that his state's supermax prison was filled with the wrong people, "the young, the pathetic, the mentally ill," and at twice the cost of incarceration in a maximum-security prison.

The following three recommendations focus on limiting segregation in America's prisons and jails:

Make Segregation a Last Resort and a More Productive Form of Confinement, and Stop Releasing People Directly from Segregation to the Streets

Tighten admissions criteria and safely transition people out of segregation as soon as possible. And go further: To the extent that safety allows, give prisoners in segregation opportunities to fully engage in treatment, work, study, and other productive activities, and to feel part of a community.

End Conditions of Isolation

Ensure that segregated prisoners have regular and meaningful human contact and are free from extreme physical conditions that cause lasting harm.

Protect Prisoners Who Are Mentally Ill

Prisoners with a mental illness that would make them particularly vulnerable to conditions in segregation must be housed in secure therapeutic units. Facilities need rigorous screening and assessment tools to ensure the proper treatment of prisoners who are both mentally ill and difficult to control.

Source: Excerpts from *Confronting Confinement: A Report of the Commission on Safety and Abuse in America's Prisons* by John J. Gibbons and Nicholas de B. Katzenbach, June 2006. Copyright © 2006, Vera Institute of Justice. Note: The full 126-page report, *Confronting Confinement: A Report of the Commission on Safety and Abuse in America's Prisons,* can be accessed on the Internet at www.prisoncommission.org.

In 1995, inmates at Pelican Bay's supermax unit challenged the constitutionality of extreme isolation and environmental deprivation. They claimed that the degree of segregation was so extreme and the restrictions so severe that the inmates confined there were psychologically traumatized and, in some cases, deprived of sanity. The federal court agreed. The court ruled in *Madrid* v. *Gomez* (1995) that "conditions in security housing unit did impose cruel and unusual punishment on mentally ill prisoners" and "those who were at particularly high risk for suffering very serious or severe injury to their mental health."[50] The court declared that the state of California could not continue to confine inmates who were already mentally ill or those who were at an unreasonably high risk of suffering serious mental illness in the supermax unit. The court also appointed a **special master** (a person appointed to act as the representative of the court) to work with the state of California to develop a satisfactory remedial plan and provide a progress report to the court.

In 2005, the U.S. Supreme Court ruled on a case from Ohio that challenged the constitutionality of the "process" by which inmates were sent to supermax prisons. The Court said in *Wilkinson* v. *Austin* that Ohio's revised classification process that gave the inmate advanced notice of the impending action, an informal administrative hearing in which the inmate speaks on his or her behalf, and a statement of reasons after the decision is made provided the basic elements of due process that were sufficient to protect inmates against arbitrary or erroneous placement in supermax conditions.[51] What the Supreme Court said in *Wilkinson* is that because supermax conditions are so much more stringent than those in more "typical" prisons, inmates have a liberty interest in not being sent there and must, therefore, be afforded procedural protections before that decision is made.

However, not everyone agrees that the conditions of supermax confinement exacerbate symptoms of mental illness and create mental illness where none previously existed, and these findings may impact future court decisions. In January 2011, the U.S. Department of Justice released the results of a one-year longitudinal study of the psychological effects of supermax confinement conducted by the Colorado Department of Corrections.[52] Colorado houses 6.2 percent (1,413) of its 23,000-inmate population in supermax confinement. The researchers found that psychological disturbances were not unique to prisoners in supermax confinement. Elevated psychological disturbances were present among prisoners in the general population as well. The researchers also noted that there was initial improvement in psychological well-being for both groups at the first two testing sessions followed by relative stability for the remainder of the year. They also reported that contrary to expected findings, offenders with mental illness did not deteriorate over time in supermax confinement at a rate more rapid and more extreme than those without mental illness. They conclude that although inmates in supermax confinement possessed traits believed to be associated with long-term segregation, those features could not be attributed to supermax confinement alone because they were present at the time of placement and occurred in the comparison study group.

As you can imagine, however, the study has its critics. Among them is Dr. Stuart Grassian, Boston psychiatrist who is internationally recognized for describing the crippling effects of supermax confinement. Dr. Grassian described the report as "garbage in, garbage out. Their approach and methodology are fatally flawed."[53] Grassian and others argue that the research was flawed from the start because the researchers started with inmates experiencing mental health crises at the beginning of their study. Hence, their baseline data were slanted. They also question the truthfulness of the inmates' responses. Will inmates, they ask, admit to mental health problems if they are trying to earn their way out of supermax confinement? They also question the results of the study by raising the issue of the so-called Hawthorne Effect, a form of reactivity whereby subjects improve or modify an aspect of their behavior being experimentally measured simply in response to the fact that they are being studied, not in response to any particular experimental manipulation. The critics point out that two inmates were thrown out of the

special master

A person appointed by the court to act as its representative to oversee remedy of a violation and provide regular progress reports.

study because they made sexual advances to one of the female graduate students conducting the interviews.

No-Frills Prisons and Jails

The image of prisons and jails as "country clubs" and "miniresorts" is not new, and it continues to make for great speeches, but it is erroneous. It ignores the harsh realities of imprisonment. Having only the information that appears on television and in newspapers and magazines, the public still believes that inmates are living the good life, lounging on recliners and channel surfing. In 1995, an NBC television poll found that 82 percent of Americans felt that prison life was too easy.[54] In March 1998, the *Atlanta Journal-Constitution* published a story on the elimination of sports from Georgia's prisons.[55] The article said the reason that sports programs in prison were cut back was public resentment toward criminals who have it too easy behind bars. However, there has been very little systematic empirical evidence to support this claim. Available research shows that public views on prison amenities are not as harsh as many assume. The public does not want luxurious prisons, but they want prisons to be productive, humane places that try to improve inmates during their incarceration. The public is willing to provide and retain amenities if these items are useful for inmate management and rehabilitation.[56]

Public perception has influenced reality because corrections reform has focused on the conditions of confinement. **No-frills prisons and jails** that take away prisoner amenities and privileges are part of the corrections landscape. New policies are designed to make jail and prison life as unpleasant as possible in the belief that such conditions deter even the most hardened criminals.

Proponents of no-frills jails and prisons argue that the only incentives offenders should have is the opportunity to straighten out their lives. They further argue that incentives such as smoking, use of weight equipment and electronic equipment, and wearing personal clothing encourage offenders only to fake their way through incarceration to get the privileges. Pleasures of any kind, they claim, contribute to the crime rate by making prison a tolerable way of life. Reducing or eliminating amenities and privileges is what inmates deserve. This is not vindictive revenge—the offender committed a serious crime that warrants incarceration, and incarceration is meant to be punitive.

From Alaska to Mississippi to Massachusetts, states are gearing up to pass no-frills legislation. Alaska passed the No-Frills Prison Act in 1997, which removed or prohibited premium cable television, cassette tape players, tobacco use, pornographic material, and weight-lifting equipment. Former Alaska senator Dave Donley sponsored the bill and defended the legislation by observing that "this law will make people think twice before committing a crime in Alaska."[57] In Mississippi, former representative Mark McInnis said it clearly: "The people who run the prisons want happy prisoners. I want prisoners to be so miserable that they won't even think of coming back."[58] And in April 1998, former Massachusetts governor William Weld said that life in prison should be "akin to a walk through the fires of hell," where inmates should learn only the joys of busting rocks.[59] At the federal level, the No-Frills Prison Act was enacted in 1996. It prohibits in-cell television viewing (except for prisoners who are segregated from the general population for their own safety), coffee pot, hot plate, or heating element; R-, X-, or NC-17 rated movies; boxing, wrestling, judo, Karate, or any other martial art; any bodybuilding or

no-frills prisons and jails
Correctional institutions that take away prisoner amenities and privileges.

weight-lifting equipment; and use or possession of any electric or electronic musical instrument in all federal prisons.

Often the public favors taking away prison amenities because it assumes they are paid for by tax dollars. States that permit in-cell television and electric equipment do not pay for them. They are purchased by the inmates or their families. Political rhetoric contributes to the public misconception regarding who pays for prison amenities. Would the public be more supportive of prison amenities if it knew the inmates paid for them? According to a citizens' survey in Tampa Bay, Florida, the answer is yes. "Respondents who were informed that prisoners pay for their privileges were more likely to support inmate access to all of the amenities except air-conditioning than were those who were told tax dollars are used to finance inmate privileges. . . . It is only when citizens are informed that taxpayers absorb the cost that they become unsupportive. . . . This finding suggests that educating people that inmates pay for the more 'luxurious' items will result in higher levels of support for them."[60]

Arguably, proponents of no-frills jails and prisons have a point. Privileges, if not handled properly, can undermine rehabilitation. On the other hand, without privileges, offenders may not take advantage of the opportunity for rehabilitation in the first place. In a perfect world, prison would make offenders realize that their mistakes have caused them pain and deprived them of their freedom, and they would gratefully volunteer for rehabilitation programs to gain back their freedom. However, in a perfect world, these people would most likely not be incarcerated to start with because they would have realized that their behaviors were causing them unwanted consequences and would have taken corrective measures outside prison. Most offenders do not think this way; they do not think about the consequences beforehand. They think they will never get caught. The eventual consequences for their lack of responsibility are arrest and incarceration.

In August 2002, *Corrections Compendium*, the peer-reviewed journal of the American Correctional Association, published the results of a survey on inmate privileges in U.S. prison systems.[61] Comparing the results of that survey with one taken four years earlier, the *Compendium* concluded, "The trend for decreased privileges has continued for a variety of reasons [to reduce the coddling of inmates, to control the problems of overcrowding and lack of resources, or for practical reasons such as elimination of secondhand smoke] . . . and will likely continue in the future."[62] Some of the results of the survey follow:

1. Smoking is prohibited in 53 percent of U.S. prisons.
2. Free weights are prohibited in 38 percent of U.S. prisons.
3. Electronic equipment (for example, television, radio, CD or cassette players, calculators, electric shavers, typewriters, coffee/hot pots, clocks, musical instruments, fans, desk lamps, hair dryers/curlers, and video games) is prohibited in the District of Columbia. All other facilities attach restrictions to their use.

No-frills prisons and jails take away prisoner amenities and privileges. What are the arguments for and against no-frills prisons and jails?

Tammie Booker

Chief • Escambia County, Florida • Department of Community Corrections

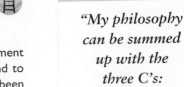

Tammie Booker is the chief for the Escambia County Department of Community Corrections. She serves as second in command to the director of the department for 53 employees. She has been employed with the department since 1984. Over the last 25 years, Booker has worked in various positions within the department: probation assistant, probation officer, senior probation officer, criminal justice program coordinator, and pretrial services administrator. She is a member of numerous professional and community organizations and has received numerous awards and recognition for leadership and public speaking. She also supervises internship placements for local colleges and universities.

Booker received her bachelor of science degree from the College of Arts and Sciences at Alabama State University and her master of criminal justice degree from the University of Alabama. She attributes her professional leadership style to the quality and relevance of the course curriculum provided by those universities. Booker is a strong advocate for continued learning and achievement. It is her desire to take advantage of every excellent learning opportunity, and she shares this sentiment with her staff. She encourages the employees within her department to attend available and applicable training sessions and workshops. She also notes that knowledge of community resources, professional networking, and staying abreast of technological advances and research are imperative in order for rehabilitation and/or punishment to be effectively and efficiently implemented.

Booker's desire is to continue to exhibit a style of leadership and management that will inspire others to work with open and free-flowing communication, to exhibit commitment to their criminal justice profession, and to provide consistency in implementing a fair and just decision-making process for the customers whom they serve. She believes that a teamwork approach in the workplace coupled with integrity and professionalism allow the staff to willingly support the department's mission.

> *"My philosophy can be summed up with the three C's: communication, commitment, and consistency."*

4. R-rated movies are prohibited in 58 percent of U.S. facilities.
5. Books and magazines are restricted everywhere by content, quantity, space considerations, who sends them, and custody level.

To date, no court case has been heard on no-frills prisons and jails. Unless the eliminated or reduced amenity or privilege results in serious harm to the inmate, the no-frills movement will continue.

At present, there is no evidence that making prisons and jails more unpleasant has any effect on crime. Legislators claim that inmates will not want to be incarcerated or reincarcerated under such harsh conditions. However, more than 200 years of prison history has not proved that making a prison austere deters offenders. State wardens, corrections experts, and attorneys do not believe that eliminating privileges will reduce crime.[63] They cringe at the idea of trying to maintain civility without amenities and privileges. "What some outside the corrections profession perceive as privileges, we in the profession see as vital prison and jail management tools to insure the safety of the facility," said Bobbie Huskey, former president of the ACA.[64]

Others have wondered what impact no-frills incarceration may have on institutional security. Eliminating frills might "increase disturbances, either in the short term if inmates react violently to the loss or in the long term if inmates have more idle time, resent the perceived vindictiveness of corrections managers, or conclude they have nothing more to lose by misbehaving."[65] A corrections official in Florida concluded, "From a correctional administrator's standpoint, there is a point at which further reductions create an undue risk to a safe and orderly operation." A 27-year veteran corrections administrator in the New Jersey Department of Corrections fears that the "take-back trend," as he calls it, might result in inmate retaliation on staff.[66] Sufficient time has not passed to study the long-term impact of no-frills incarceration. However, there is concern that eliminating privileges (such as weight lifting, television, and recreation) that keep inmates busy may encourage inmates to spend more time planning or causing trouble.

If privileges are eliminated, what positive incentives will correctional staff have with which to motivate appropriate inmate behavior? A survey of 823 wardens of state adult prisons indicates that programs and amenities serve a critical control function.[67] Correctional officers can grant access to privileges and amenities in exchange for adherence to rules and restrict access as punishment for rule violation. "The entire prison disciplinary structure is founded on punishments that amount to restriction of privileges," report the survey's authors. Chances are that prison administrators will not completely eliminate or abolish privileges or amenities; they will curtail availability and offer the privileges or amenities as a reward for good behavior.

ACCREDITATION

We introduced the issue of accreditation in Chapter 6. Here we expand on that discussion. *Accreditation* is a process through which correctional facilities and agencies can measure themselves against nationally adopted standards and through which they can receive formal recognition and accredited status. Besides accreditation, some correctional agencies use the evidence-based standards introduced throughout this text. However, here the focus is on accreditation.

ACA standards are the national benchmark for the effective operation of correctional systems throughout the United States and are necessary to ensure that correctional agencies and facilities operate professionally. The ACA administers the only national accreditation program for all components of adult and juvenile corrections. For that reason, the federal courts have increasingly relied on ACA's standards to decide whether correctional agencies and facilities meet constitutional standards. The ACA's policy on accreditation is shown in Exhibit 13–3.

Founded in 1870 as the National Prison Association, the ACA is the oldest association specifically developed for practitioners in the corrections profession. Today, the ACA has more than 20,000 active members. The ACA initiated correctional accreditation in 1974 when it created the Commission on Accreditation for Corrections (CAC). CAC continually revises the standards based on changing practices, current case law, and agency experience. CAC is governed by 25 corrections professionals, architects, doctors, and legal experts.

Correctional accreditation is available for 21 different kinds of juvenile and adult correctional agencies and facilities, including institutions and community residential programs for adults and juveniles, jails and detention centers, probation and parole agencies, health care programs, and remote-location monitoring. The standards cover administrative and fiscal concerns, staff training and development, the physical plant, safety and emergency procedures, sanitation, food service, and rules and discipline. Standards are divided into two categories. To be accredited, an agency

Public Correctional Policy on Standards
and Accreditation

Introduction

Adult and juvenile correctional agencies should provide community and institutional programs and services that offer a full range of effective, just, humane, and safe dispositions and sanctions for accused and adjudicated offenders. To assure accountability and professional responsibility, these programs and services should meet accepted professional and performance-based standards and obtain accreditation. The use of standards and the accreditation process provides a valuable mechanism for self-evaluation, stimulates improvement of correctional management and practice, and provides recognition of acceptable programs and facilities. The American Correctional Association and the Commission on Accreditation for Corrections have promulgated national standards and a voluntary system of national accreditation for correctional agencies. The beneficiaries of such a process are the staff of correctional agencies, offenders, and the public.

Policy Statement

All adult and juvenile detention and correctional facilities, institutional services, and community programs should be operated in accordance with the standards established by the American Correctional Association. These facilities and programs should be accredited through the Commission on Accreditation for Corrections. To fulfill this objective, correctional agencies should:

- A. implement improvement to comply with appropriate correctional standards;
- B. seek and maintain accreditation through the process developed by the Commission on Accreditation for Corrections in order that, through self-evaluation and peer review, necessary improvements are made, programs and services come into compliance with appropriate standards, and professional recognition is obtained.

Source: Copyright © American Correctional Association. August 15, 2007.

or facility must have 100 percent compliance with *mandatory* standards and 90 percent compliance with *nonmandatory* standards. As of February 2, 2011, 622 of the 2,236 state, federal, and private adult correctional institutions and 131 of the 3,365 local adult detention facilities have been awarded ACA accreditation.[68]

Why Should Correctional Agencies and Facilities Be Accredited?

There are at least eight reasons that correctional agencies and facilities should be accredited:[69]

1. Accreditation Improves Staff Training and Development Accreditation requires having written policy and procedures to establish a training and staff development program for all categories of personnel. The professional growth of employees is developed through training plans that annually identify current job-related training needs in relation to position requirements, current correctional issues, new theories, techniques, and technologies.

2. Accreditation Assesses Program Strengths and Weaknesses Accreditation assesses issues and concerns that affect the quality of life at a facility such as staff training, adequacy of medical services, sanitation, use of segregation and detention, incidents of violence, crowding, offender activity levels, programs, and provisions of basic services that may impact the life, safety, and health of inmates and staff.

3. Accreditation Is a Defense Against Lawsuits

Accredited agencies and facilities have a stronger defense against litigation through documentation and the demonstration of a "good faith" effort to improve conditions of confinement. For example, in *Grayson v. Peed* (1999), the U.S. Supreme Court said, "The appellant's own expert penologist conceded that [Sheriff] Peed's policies met the standards of both the Virginia Board of Corrections and the American Correctional Association. . . . Appellant's claims that [Sheriff] Peed provided inadequate training for his employees must also fail. At the time of the incident, the jail had been accredited for more than ten years . . . by the American Correctional Association . . . whose training requirements often surpass minimal constitutional standards."

4. Accreditation Establishes Measurable Criteria for Upgrading Operations

Through the standards and accreditation process, agencies continuously review their policies and procedures and have the ability to make necessary improvements when deficiencies are recognized.

5. Accreditation Improves Staff Morale and Professionalism

Accreditation is awarded to the "best of the best" in the corrections field. Staff have a better understanding of policies and procedures, and this contributes to improved working conditions for staff.

6. Accreditation Offers a Safer Environment for Staff and Offenders

Staff and offenders benefit from increased accountability and attention to physical plant issues and security procedures. Whether for an agency or facility, the accreditation process ensures assessment of strengths and weaknesses.

7. Accreditation Reduces Liability Insurance Costs

Insurance companies offer a reduction on liability insurance premiums to accredited agencies and facilities. Adherence to nationally recognized standards for fire, safety, health, and training reduces claim expenses, allowing up to a 10 percent credit on liability insurance premiums.

8. Accreditation Offers Performance-Based Benefits

Performance-based standards provide data that can be used to gauge the day-to-day management of the facility, thereby providing agencies with a cost-effective, proactive approach to offender care. They can also be used to justify requests for additional funding.

Traditionally, correctional agencies have sought accreditation for one of three reasons: first, to ensure that the organization is in compliance with national standards; second, to demonstrate to interested parties that the organization is operating at acceptable professional levels; and third, to comply with court orders. Consult the Appendix Careers in Corrections at the Online Learning Center Web site for the steps involved in career planning, developing employability and job readiness, and finding the right job.

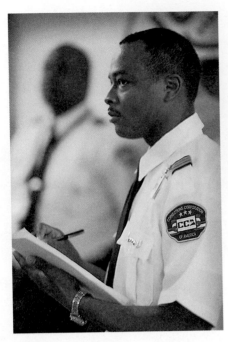

More than 129,300 adults are held in 107 private prisons across the United States. Still the debate over privatization continues. Why do state governments contract with for-profit companies for such services?

PRIVATIZATION

According to Malcolm Feeler, the involvement of the private sector in corrections began shortly after the first English colonists arrived in Virginia in 1607.[70] Convicted felons were transported by private entrepreneurs to America, as a condition of pardon, to be sold into servitude. During the 18th century, jails and prisons emerged in the American colonies as alternatives to servitude or the death penalty. Privately operated facilities copied from English custom became popular. Private contractors claimed they could both manage prisons and employ convicts in labor, arguing that the practice would be both rehabilitative and financially rewarding. San Quentin was the first U.S. prison constructed and operated by a private provider in the 1850s. However, after a number of major scandals surfaced surrounding the mismanagement of the facility by the private provider, California turned San Quentin prison over to the control of state government. By 1885, 13 states had contracts with private enterprises to lease out prison labor.

As discussed in Chapter 6, *privatization* is defined as a contract process that shifts public functions, responsibilities, and capital assets, in whole or in part, from the public sector to the private sector. In corrections, privatization is generally one of three types: contracting out, private sector development, or private management.

Contracting out of specific services entails a competition among private bidders to perform governmental activities such as providing medical and mental health services, educational and vocational programming, food preparation, maintenance, work, and industry. Contracts for specialized services generate little controversy.

Private sector development refers to the private sector developing, designing, and financing or arranging for the financing of correctional facilities. This often involves owning the facility and leasing it back to the jurisdiction through a lease/purchase contract, which serves as an alternative to a public bond or tax increase.

The third type of privatization is full-scale *private management* of jails and prisons. Because it involves government transfer of assets, commercial enterprises, and management responsibilities to the private sector, this option is controversial. In 1976, RCA Services assumed control of the Weaversville Intensive Treatment Unit in North Hampton, Pennsylvania, marking the modern beginning of privatization in corrections. The trend toward privately operated correctional facilities has continued with 129,366 adults now housed in 107 privately operated prisons and 22,847 adults in privately operated halfway houses and residential drug treatment centers in 33 states, the District of Columbia, and the federal government.[71]

The catalyst for privatizing correctional institutions today is prison overcrowding and the economic downturn that began in 2007. Even though the recession has also affected the private sector, industry analysts believe that the private prison business will rebound. This will be especially so as states (e.g., California with huge budget deficits and prisons already under federal court order to reduce its inmate population by more than 30,000 before July 2013) scramble to find housing for prisoners. As noted earlier, on January 1, 2010, state prisons, taken as a whole, were operating between full capacity and 40 percent above capacity while federal prisons were operating at 36 percent above capacity. Other reasons for the growth in private corrections are the public's lack of confidence in the ability of correctional services provided by federal, state, and local governments to rehabilitate offenders and a reluctance to provide more funding for rising correctional costs. The enthusiasm for privatization is fueled by the prospect for more innovative, cost-effective prison management, including the involvement of the private sector in the financing of new prison construction. This enthusiasm is not shared by all, however.

The Debate

Largely because there has been no conclusive research, arguments continue to rage over the merits of privately run correctional facilities. The overriding reason supporting privatization in corrections is the desire of state and local governments to rapidly increase bed space, save taxpayers money by providing correctional services traditionally supplied by government at less cost, improve the quality of correctional services, and reduce crime and recidivism.

Most advocates of privatization also suggest that allowing facilities to be operated by the private sector could result in cost reductions of 20 percent. Most studies, however, report more modest savings. In fact, researchers at the University of Cincinnati looked at 33 cost-effectiveness evaluations of public and private prisons and concluded that prison size, age, and security level, not prison ownership (public vs. private), predict prison costs: "Relinquishing the responsibility of managing prisons to the private sphere is unlikely to alleviate much of the financial burden on state correctional budgets."[72] There are very few studies comparing the quality of inmate confinement between public and privately operated correctional institutions. Some report that private prisons outperform their public counterparts. Others do not.

In possibly the most carefully controlled comparative recidivism study of releasees from private and public prisons, researchers at the University of Florida matched 198 inmates from private prisons with 198 inmates from public prisons on the basis of offense, race, age, and prior record.[73] The researchers tracked the inmates for 12 months after each inmate's respective date of release and recorded any new rearrest, any technical violation, resentencing, and reincarceration. The researchers also measured the severity of recidivism (technical violation, misdemeanor offense, drug or weapon possession felony, property felony, or violent or personal felony). Releasees from private prisons had lower recidivism rates than did their public prison matches for all indicators of recidivism except technical violations.

Proponents also argue that public prisons are not without their problems, and unlike state and federal governments, private firms are free from politics, cumbersome bureaucracies, and costly union contracts. Proponents also suggest that privately run correctional facilities can be economic boons for the areas in which they are located, providing many jobs and feeding public coffers with increased tax revenues. ACA's support of private sector involvement in corrections is shown in Exhibit 13–4.

Opponents of privatization, on the other hand, build their arguments on mostly philosophical grounds. One writer says that the fundamental issue is a moral one: Should private parties make a profit from inflicting pain on others?[74] Will private prisons, in their pursuit for profits, find ways to keep cells filled, prison construction booming, and more offenders under private supervision? The notion that convicted offenders should be the responsibility of private entrepreneurs motivated by profit is contradictory to the public function of offender apprehension and conviction. Most opponents of privatization argue that the practice is inherently flawed by the profit motive of private corporations.[75] The corporate interest in maximizing profits, they claim, can have numerous negative consequences for inmates, correctional employees, and society. Some claim, for example, that the need to maintain healthy profit margins may preclude the cost of

Talking about CORRECTIONS

PRIVATIZATION SAVINGS OR NOT?

Visit *Live Talk* at **Corrections .com** (**www.justicestudies .com/talking06**) and listen to the program "Privatization Savings or Not?" which relates to ideas discussed in this chapter.

EXHIBIT 13–4   **American Correctional Association**

Public Correctional Policy on Private Sector Involvement in Corrections

Introduction

Historically correctional programs have been operated by public agencies, but there is ongoing use of public-nonprofit and/or profit partnerships (hereafter referred to as the private sector). Private sector organizations may have resources for the delivery of services that often differ from the public correctional agency.

Policy Statement

Government has the ultimate authority and responsibility for corrections. For its most effective operation, corrections should use all appropriate resources, both public and private. Government should consider use of private sector correctional services and programs only when such programs or services:

- are needed;
- meet professional standards;
- ensure necessary public safety;
- provide the best value to the taxpayer; and
- are equivalent to or better than those offered by the public sector.

While government retains the ultimate responsibility, authority and accountability for the offenders under its jurisdiction as well as for actions of private agencies and individuals under contract, it is consistent with good correctional policy and practice to consider outsourcing services that support the mission of correctional operations by:

- **A.** enhancing service delivery systems by contracting with the private sector when justified in terms of cost, quality, availability, effectiveness, and ability to meet program objectives;
- **B.** using private sector organizations to develop, fund, build, operate, and/or provide services, programs, and facilities

when such an approach has a cost benefit; is effective as well as efficient; is gender- and culturally responsive; and is safe and consistent with the public interest and sound correctional practice;

- **C.** using the private sector to gather information and provide independent evaluation of process and performance measures of programs and services provided by or contracted for by public agencies; and
- **D.** using the private sector to enhance staff development, competency, and professionalism through training, certification, and continuing education of correctional practitioners.

Correctional agencies also should:

- **A.** continue to engage members of the private sector in an advisory role in the development and implementation of correctional programs and policies;
- **B.** ensure the appropriate level of service delivery and compliance with recognized standards through professional contract preparation and vendor selection, as well as effective evaluation and monitoring by the responsible government agency;
- **C.** indicate clearly in any contract for services, facilities, or programs the responsibilities and obligations of both government and contractor, including but not limited to liability of all parties, performance bonding, and causal factors and procedures for contract termination;
- **D.** share information about successful public–private sector partnerships with other corrections practitioners; and
- **E.** evaluate the effectiveness of services, facilities, and programs.

Source: Copyright © American Correctional Association.

---

rehabilitation and recreational programs for inmates. Other opponents of privatization say that privately run companies save money by paying lower wages and benefits than states do.[76] Among the groups opposing privatization are the American Jail Association, the National Sheriffs' Association, and the American Federation of State, County, and Municipal Employees.

Recently, the National Council on Crime and Delinquency (NCCD) reviewed the literature on privatization and conducted a national survey of private correctional management firms. NCCD found that, rather than the projected 20 percent savings, the average saving from privatization was only about 1 percent, and most of that was achieved through lower labor costs.[77] "In summary," wrote NCCD, "the cost benefits of privatization have not materialized to the extent promised by the private sector. Although there are examples of cost savings, there are other examples in which such benefits have not been realized. Moreover, it is probably too early to determine if the initial cost savings can be sustained over a long time period."[78]

And when the National Institute of Justice compared two cost and performance analyses of the same four prisons—one privately operated and

EXHIBIT 13–5	**Arguments For and Against Private Prisons**

For Private Prisons

1. Private operators can provide construction financing options that allow the government client to pay only for capacity as needed in lieu of accumulating long-term debt.
2. Private companies offer modern state-of-the-art correctional facility designs that are efficient to operate and that are built according to value-engineering specifications.
3. Private operators typically design and construct a new correctional facility in half the time required for a comparable government construction project.
4. Private vendors provide government clients with the convenience and accountability of one entity for all compliance issues.
5. Private corrections management companies are able to mobilize rapidly and to specialize in unique facility missions.
6. Private corrections management companies provide economic development opportunities by hiring locally and, to the extent possible, purchasing locally.
7. Government can reduce or share its liability exposure by contracting with private corrections companies.
8. The government can retain flexibility by limiting the contract function and by specifying facility mission.
9. Adding other service providers injects competition among both public and private organizations.

Against Private Prisons

1. There are certain responsibilities that only the government should meet, such as safety and environmental protection. To provide incarceration, the government has legal, political, and moral obligations. Major constitutional competition among both public and private issues revolves around the deprivation of liberty, discipline, and preserving the constitutional rights of inmates. Related issues include the use of force, loss of time credit, and segregation.
2. Few private companies are available from which to choose.
3. Private operators may be inexperienced with key correctional issues.
4. Operators may become monopolies through political ingratiation, favoritism, and so on.
5. Government may lose the capability to perform the function over time.
6. The profit motive will inhibit the proper performance of duties. Private prisons have financial incentives to cut corners and offer lower wages, pensions, benefits, and staffing levels.
7. The procurement process is slow, inefficient, and open to risks.
8. Creating a good, clear contract is a daunting task.
9. Lack of enforcement remedies in contracts leaves only termination or lawsuits as recourse.

Source: Dennis Cunningham, *Public Strategies for Private Prisons*, paper presented at the Private Prison Workshop, January 29–30, 1999, at the Institute on Criminal Justice, University of Minnesota Law School.

three publicly operated—in 2008, the results were different.[79] One analysis found it was 14.8 percent cheaper to operate the private prison than the three publicly operated ones. The other analysis found it was only 2.2 percent cheaper. Why the difference? NIJ tells us that cost comparisons are not as simple as might be presumed. Inmate population sizes and what is included in overhead costs are reasons that the cost analyses were different.

Some critics note that, although the administration of punishment may be delegated in part to the private sector, the government retains ultimate responsibility for it. Indeed, the courts have held government responsible for actions taken by a private provider that violate an inmate's constitutional rights or that put the prison staff, inmates, or surrounding community in harm's way. Today, private–public contracts include performance standards and monitoring procedures. Writing a good, clear contract that outlines the roles, responsibilities, and consequences for the private provider and government sector is key. Proponents note that governments almost always renew contracts with private operators—proving such contracts worthwhile. In spite of the arguments for and against privatization, "The core theme is that properly conceptualized, properly managed, and properly monitored privatization initiatives can serve the public interest."[80] Exhibit 13–5 summarizes the reasons to accept or reject the privatization concept.

Privatizing Community Supervision

There is also movement toward privatization in community corrections, including offender assessment, drug testing and treatment, electronic monitoring, halfway house management, and probation field services. There is no census on the number of persons who are under private community supervision. However, in searching the Internet, we find that a number of states that have privatized community supervision include Connecticut, Colorado, Georgia, Missouri, Tennessee, and Utah. In most states, the impetus for privatizing community supervision was similar: Staffing and resources were not keeping pace with increasing caseloads. Community supervision officials felt they had exhausted the use of interns and volunteers, and obtaining funding for new staff was not possible. States partnered with the private sector to monitor the low-risk offender population, a group that generally has few needs, whose past records reflect little or no violence, and that successfully completes probation about 90 percent of the time.

In Connecticut, for example, the privatization initiative to monitor low-risk offender populations by the private sector allowed scarce resources to be used to better monitor offenders with higher levels of risk. Private case management responsibilities in Connecticut included sending an introductory letter to the probationer, monitoring restitution payments and compliance with conditions of probation, responding to probationer's inquiries, preparing standardized reports for probation officers, providing verification of conditional compliance, and providing statistical reports.

The situation in Colorado was similar. When Colorado officials adopted risk management and looked at how treatment and supervision were matched with levels of risk, they found more probation officers were needed than the Colorado General Assembly would fund. The result was a directive that allowed probation departments to contract with private agencies for the supervision of low-risk probationers. Thirteen of Colorado's 22 judicial districts have entered into such contracts. The private agencies directly bill the probationers for their supervision services, eliminating public expenditures for community supervision.

However, the debate over privatizing community supervision has its critics. Consider the situation in Georgia. In 2003, Georgia passed SB 474 that transferred supervision of 25,000 convicted misdemeanants from the state Department of Corrections to individual counties and permitted each county to contract with a for-profit probation agency to supervise these misdemeanants. Today, approximately 40 private probation agencies are registered in Georgia; they employ 850 probation officers and serve 640 courts.[81]

In Georgia, every person who cannot pay his or her misdemeanor fine on the day of court is placed on probation under the supervision of a private, for-profit company until he or she pays the fine. For example, assume you are ordered to pay $200 for a traffic fine. If you have enough money to pay it on the day you go to court, you can avoid probation. If you can't you must pay your fine and a monthly supervision fee in the range of $35–$44 to a private company in weekly or biweekly installments over a period of three months to a year. By the time your probation is over, you may have paid more than twice or three times the amount that the judge had ordered. In Americus, Georgia, just 10 miles from where President Jimmy Carter was raised, one high school student convicted of violating the terms of his learner's permit served seven months on probation and paid $505 in court fines and probation fees. Had he been able to pay the fine the day he was sentenced, he would have paid only $155.[82]

Critics argue that for-profit probation is unfair to poor people, needlessly supervises persons who are not a threat to society, and carries the risk of unnecessary incarceration because persons on probation can be arrested for technical violations such as missing a meeting with a probation officer. How often all this happens is unknown because in 2006, the Georgia Assembly passed a law that permits for-profit probation companies to keep their records secret. In the summer of 2008, a reporter with *Mother Jones* visited the offices of Middle Georgia Community Probation Services and was politely told, "We don't talk to reporters."[83]

In 2007, the Private Probation Association of Georgia (PPAG) attempted to expand the reach of private probation and lobbied the General Assembly to allow it to supervise people convicted of more than 90 types of felonies ranging in seriousness from child molestation to shoplifting to credit card fraud and for a new law that would allow it to charge every misdemeanor probation a minimum monthly fee of $50 (in contrast, felony probationers were paying the state $23 per month for probation supervision). A coalition of Georgia judges, sheriffs, and others strongly opposed the bill, and it was defeated. PPAG pledged it would continue its efforts to enter the business of felony probation supervision.

The absence of systematic research on for-profit probation supervision means that we don't know how private community supervision is working elsewhere.

Future Trends

According to Reginald A. Wilkinson, former director of the Ohio Department of Rehabilitation and Correction,

> The next ten years will reveal whether the privatization of prisons will succeed. If so, the evolution from public to private management may prove to be painful to correctional traditionalists. Debate on the pros and cons, rights and wrongs, of "punishment for profit" will rage back and forth. In the end, the profit margin and public opinion may be the determining factors on how much of the corrections profession will be outsourced to for-profit providers.[84]

Other trends may include the following:

1. The number of private prisons is likely to increase, especially in the overseas market, but not at the pace exhibited during the past two decades.
2. The number of companies operating privatized prisons is likely to decrease as competition and the costs of doing business increase, thus forcing a consolidation of firms within the industry.
3. Important inroads can be expected for specialty prisons, for example, for the geriatric inmate population.

TECHNOCORRECTIONS

The technological forces that made the use of cell phones commonplace is converging with corrections to create "technocorrections." Technological changes have impacted communication, offender and officer tracking and recognition, and detection. "While technology alone cannot overcome the myriad challenges (facing corrections), it will most certainly play a major role."[85]

Communication

Information is crucial to a well-run correctional system. Knowing what is happening gives correctional administrators the power not only to react to problems promptly but also to anticipate and prevent them. In recent

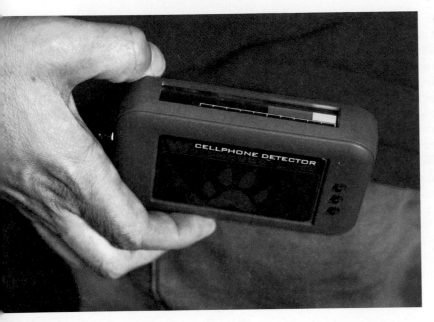

Whereas "managed access" (a network of antennas that intercept cell phone communications within a prison) in Mississippi allows prison staff to use authorized cell phones and detects inmates' use of unauthorized ones, other states such as New Jersey have banned all cell phones from state prisons. New technology similar to the Wolfhound contraband cell phone detection device can detect when cell phones are turned on or transmitting data. A directional antenna then helps locate the phone. New Jersey is experimenting with 24 of these detection devices. Why is inmate access to cell phones a threat to public safety? Are there any advantages in allowing inmates to have cell phones? Is it possible for corrections to control the disadvantages while allowing the advantages?

contraband

Any item that represents a serious threat to the safety and security of the institution.

decades, communication technology has undergone significant changes. Correctional officers can now keep in touch by e-mail and can share information in electronic databases in management information systems, Facebook, and on Web pages. The majority of corrections departments now have online searchable prisoner registries, including photographs, and some post schedules of upcoming parole hearings on the Internet.

Several years ago, the Federal Bureau of Prisons set up e-mail programs that allow inmates to send and receive e-mails.[86] According to the BOP, the program cuts down on the amount of paper mail (which can conceal drugs and other contraband), helps prisoners connect regularly with their families, and helps inmates build computer skills they can use when they return to the community. The BOP uses proceeds from prison commissaries and charges inmates 5 cents a minute to compose and read e-mails. Messages are screened for key words, are read by correctional officers before they are sent, and can be sent only to contacts who agree beforehand to receive e-mail from specific inmates.

Technology has also produced the newest prison **contraband**: cell phones.[87] We used to think of prison contraband as a file inside a cake. Now it's a smartphone hidden under a mattress. Visitors smuggle them in. Inmates returning from work release smuggle them in. And staff sell them to inmates for as much as $1,000, depending on the type of phone and service plan. In 2010, the number of cell phones confiscated by officials was 9,000 in California and about 1,200 in Texas. California prison authorities even found an LG flip phone under Charles Manson's mattress. The Federal BOP staff discovered almost 1,200 cell phones. Inmates are using smuggled cell phones to threaten victims, conduct drug deals, order killings, and plot escapes. In December 2010, Georgia prisoners used cell phones to coordinate work stoppages with inmates at other prisons. They sent text messages, created e-mail distribution lists, and publicized their complaints about visitation, food, and living conditions on Facebook and Twitter. In response, some states have passed new laws making inmate phone possession a felony, have trained dogs to detect cell phones, and have added high-tech security equipment, much like machines used at airports. In August 2010, President Obama signed a bill making inmate possession of a cellphone or a wireless device in federal prison a felony punishable by up to a year of additional sentence.

The solution may be a new system introduced in Mississippi. Called *managed access*, the system establishes a network around the prison that detects every call and text message. Callers using cell phones that are not on an approved list receive a message saying the device is illegal and will no longer function. In the last six months of 2010, more than 216,000 texts and cell phone calls were blocked from being delivered inside the Mississippi State Penitentiary at Parchman. However, finding the actual cell phones inside a prison is another issue, and this is where states such as Maryland, New Jersey, and Rhode Island are spending as much as $7,000 to train one dog to sniff out the ionization of cell phone batteries. Other states would like the Federal Communications Commission to grant them authority to overpower the signal with a stronger one (called

I got out of prison April 22, 1996, after being locked up for 10 years for robbing a bank at gunpoint. For three weeks, I just hung out, reacclimating to society. I got restless the fourth week and tried to get a job, but nobody called me back. My parole officer kept asking me, "Have you gone to RIO yet?" I thought the program would get me only menial jobs, like heavy cleanup work, but finally I went just to appease my parole officer. After I completed RIO's five-day job preparation course I got the first job I interviewed at, a sales agent at a hotel.

Project RIO Participant
RIO (Reintegration of Offenders) is a job-placement program for offenders.

jamming) or "trick" the cell phone to react as if a "no service" signal is received (called *spoofing*). However, the Communications Act of 1934 prohibits the manufacture, importation, marketing, sale, or operation of jamming or spoofing devices because they would "bleed" over into the public broadcast area.

Videoconferencing Videoconferencing is another way to share thoughts and ideas in the correctional community. Meetings and lectures that once required expensive travel can now be "attended" from the comfort of one's office or from a local teleconference site. In addition, satellite TV and video technology have enhanced distance learning for both officers and inmates.

Prison systems across the country are using videoconferencing for arraignments, interrogations, and visitation. Until Connecticut installed videoconferencing in all of its 18 prisons, it sometimes cost as much as $1,800 to transport an inmate from prison to a courtroom. Connecticut and other states report using videoconferencing between judges and inmates to improve public safety and save money.[88]

One of the largest videoconferencing correctional facilities in the United States is the Douglas County Corrections Center in Omaha, Nebraska. Taylor Dueker, one of the center's architects, reports that the videoconference visitation facility has already produced a number of benefits for staff, inmates, and family and friends of prisoners, including:

- increasing the number of visitations conducted each day;
- reducing staff time in checking in visitors;
- reducing the staff time previously needed to escort inmates to a centralized visitation area or courtroom for arraignments and other preliminary proceedings;
- reducing inmate movement, thereby increasing safety for staff and inmates;
- reducing space requirements and construction and operating costs on visitation areas; and
- eliminating contraband that was formerly passed by visitors in face-to-face contact.[89]

Videoconferencing can be especially helpful in high-profile cases for which security is tighter and exposure to the public needs to be minimized. Dueker sees the day when equipped with a simple Web cam, visitation will take place from the comfort of home under certain supervisory conditions.

Telemedicine Telemedicine, one of the newest advances in medicine, is providing prisoners adequate, cost-effective health care. Taking a prisoner to a specialist outside the prison poses a danger to correctional officers and the community by giving the prisoner an opportunity to escape or to have contact with other people in a less-controlled environment. Telemedicine allows physicians to consult with on-site medical personnel through videoconferencing and compatible medical devices, such as medical microcameras. Health care in correctional settings is improved, and the substantial savings on in-prison consultations and on trips to local providers can offset the costs of introducing this technology. Arizona, for example, saved $237,000 in 2008 by using telemedicine in nine correctional facilities.[90] Those states that have implemented telemedicine technology equally divide use between medical and mental health services. Several systems use telemedicine for staff training and education.[91] However, some critics question the quality of medicine inmates receive via telemedicine, and point out that inmates need practice interacting effectively with people outside of prison.

Offender and Officer Tracking and Recognition

Automated kiosks, also discussed in Chapter 5, are on the way to replacing routine visits to probation and parole officers. Offenders are instructed to report to a kiosk at a specified location. There they are electronically interviewed and in some cases tested for alcohol by means of a breath analysis attachment. Using the kiosks, offenders can also e-mail their parole officers to schedule personal meetings. The system identifies the offender by reading a magnetic card and using a biometric fingerprint scanner. **Biometrics** is the automated identification or verification of human identity through measurable physiological and behavioral traits such as iris, retinal, and facial recognition; hand and finger geometry; fingerprint and voice identification; and dynamic signature. The biometrics of the future are body odor, ear shape, facial thermography, and thermal imagery.

Remote-location monitoring of offenders, discussed in Chapter 5, is steadily improving and is likely to be used far more in the future. However, remote-location monitoring is not just for inmates. Correctional officers can also wear personal alarm and location units that allow a computer to track their locations and respond to distress signals by sending the closest officers to the site of the emergency.

Fairly new in the field of corrections is the Global Positioning System (GPS). Already used in airplanes, automobiles, and PDAs (personal digital assistants), GPS is now also used for monitoring offenders under community supervision. The GPS tracking unit worn by an offender allows computers to pinpoint the offender's location at any time to the precise street address. The device can be programmed to send a signal if an offender enters a forbidden zone or even a spoken warning emanating from the device itself instructing the offender to leave the area or face the consequences. In the field of inmate monitoring, there is also some discussion about implanting chips in offenders' bodies that would alert officials to unacceptable behavior. In some cases, when criminal activity was detected, the chip might give an electric shock that would temporarily shut down the offender's central nervous system.

A new technological tool designed to track an offender's alcohol consumption is the continuous transdermal alcohol monitoring device. An electrostatic pad presses against the offender's upper arm, chemically "tasting" sweat for signs of alcohol. A continuous transdermal alcohol monitor was used on Lindsay Lohan after she violated her probation stemming from DUI charges.[92]

Administrators are also relying on new telecommunications technology to help track inmates and former inmates. Speaker ID technology identifies

biometrics

The automated identification or verification of human identity through measurable physiological and behavioral traits.

a speaker even if he or she has a cold, just woke from a deep sleep, or has a poor telephone connection. Systems using speaker ID can be used to keep track of who calls inmates in prison and to monitor criminal activity such as escape plans, gang activity, and smuggling contraband. Speaker ID can also be used for low-risk offenders granted early parole as an alternative to incarceration. The system can make random calls and positively identify the speaker from his or her response. The offenders never know when or how they will receive calls. When no one answers the phone or the speaker is not identified, the system alerts authorities to a possible violation.

To increase the efficiency of inmate monitoring and cut administrative costs, a smart card, a plastic card embedded with a computer chip, can be used to store all types of information about the inmate—from medical care to meals eaten.

The use of facial recognition technology is also on the increase in corrections. All 300 employees of the Prince George County Correctional Center in Upper Marlboro, Maryland, swipe picture-image ID cards across a scanner. The swipe alerts the system that an employee is entering the facility. The system verifies the image from a database and using the biometrics of the employee's face, compares it to the one captured by the camera. Eventually, Prince George County will use biometric-based access control technology to screen visitors to determine whether they are ex-inmates.

The principles of geographic information systems (GISs) are also changing corrections.[93] GIS links graphics with tabular information to produce a graphical, layered, spatial interface or map that can help prison management in many ways. For example, in 2004 Congress approved a $3 million expenditure for a high-tech prison training program known as simulated prison environment crisis aversion tools (SPECAT) whose aim is to help corrections officials deal with inmate disturbances by providing a three-dimensional computer modeling of prison interiors and preparation for confronting particular scenarios.[94]

Proponents foresee a time when corrections mapping can be used to do the following:

1. track and display inmate location and movement;
2. indicate whether a housing unit is balanced with regard to religion, group affiliation, age, race, and ethnicity;
3. pinpoint the locations of gang members and link them to each inmate's behavioral and criminal history as well as the inmate's rank in the hierarchy of the group;
4. pinpoint areas in a prison that are potentially dangerous such as hallways or blind corners where a number of assaults may have occurred;
5. incorporate aerial photos of a facility to check for possible security breaches and potential escape routes;
6. provide a basis for proactive investigation and enforcement, for example, mapping the flow of money in and out of prison and then linking it to data about visitation, telephone calls, and correspondence addresses to show a potential drug problem; and
7. link inmate data to the names, telephone numbers, and addresses of all the people the inmate had contact with during incarceration, in case of an escape.

Prison medical staff videoconference with an offsite physician about a prisoner's physical health. Advances in technology have helped make prisons and jails safer and more secure, while facilitating innovations such as telemedicine. What promises might tomorrow's technologies hold for correctional institutions?

Detection

To maintain prison security, researchers have developed new detection technologies. One is ground-penetrating radar (GPR), which can be used to locate underground escape tunnels. Another is heartbeat monitoring. Using the same technology employed by geologists to detect earthquakes, geophone machines can detect the heartbeat of an inmate trying to escape in a laundry or trash truck leaving the prison. In 1999, heartbeat monitoring prevented the escape of a prisoner in Tennessee. X-rays and magnetic resonance imaging scan the body for concealed weapons, eliminating the necessity for a physical search. Noninvasive drug detection technology places a swab or patch on the skin, which absorbs perspiration and signals the presence of illegal drugs. Pupillometry (a binocular-like device that flashes a light to stimulate pupil contraction) can also measure drug or alcohol use. Another technological tool for drug testing has inmates look through a viewfinder. Ion scans can also detect drug particles on visitors to correctional facilities. In addition, correctional officers can now control prison riots and disturbances using a joystick and monitor that directs an "assault intervention device," a 6-foot robot to blast millimeter waves that simulate intense heat under the skin where pain receptacles are located.

Implementation

Despite the increase in such technology, obstacles must still be overcome. Corrections personnel have been slow to embrace new technology, in part because new systems can be unreliable and difficult to maintain and have high life cycle costs. Ethical concerns about the rights of offenders might be another barrier to implementing new technology. Through a program sponsored by the Department of Justice—Staff and Inmate Monitoring (SAINT)—the Navy's Space and Naval Warfare System Center in Charleston, South Carolina, is systematically addressing biometric and smart card technology through development, testing, and evaluation of a prototype system in the Navy Consolidated Brig in Charleston.[95] There is no question, however, that new technologies are playing an increasingly important role in correctional institutions as a means to address critical health, safety, and security issues.

REVIEW AND APPLICATIONS

SUMMARY

1 Prisons are overcrowded for four main reasons. First, over the past decade, there has been an increase in imprisonment. Second, changes in federal and state sentencing laws require more offenders to serve longer periods. Third, there has been an increase in imprisonment for drug and violent offenses. Fourth, a prison industrial complex has emerged.

2 This chapter examined six methods of controlling prison overcrowding. First, reduce the number of people who go to prison by making more use of *front-end strategies* such as diversion, community corrections, and intermediate sanctions. Second, put a cap or ceiling on the prison population, sometimes called a *trap-door strategy.* Third, use what are called *side-door strategies,* such as giving sentenced offenders the opportunity to apply to the sentencing court for release to intensive community corrections programs, usually six months after imprisonment. Fourth, use more parole and halfway houses, called *back-door strategies.* Fifth, build more

prisons and/or expand existing facilities. Sixth, use structured sentencing guidelines that are designed to save prison space for serious crimes and violent offenses, while using community corrections and intermediate sanctions for lesser offenses.

3 Prisons control the influence of security threat groups by referring to them as STGs rather than "gangs." Some prisons have security threat group units that are responsible for the identification and overall coordination of all STG-related information at their facilities. Some prisons transfer known STG members from one institution to another. Some states have enacted "gang enhancement" statutes that impose severe sentences on STG activity. And some states have built supermax prisons that house STG members in complete lockdown and isolation.

4 Prison riots occur for a number of reasons. Sometimes they result from spontaneous outburst. Most experts believe that the primary causes of prison riots are bad conditions (overcrowding, antiquated facilities, low staffing levels, insufficient staff training, lack of programs for inmates, lack of funding, and poor implementation of correctional policy), rebellious inmates and racial antagonism, institutional structure and readiness, and administrative factors (for example, frequent staff turnover, low correctional officer qualifications, inadequate training, poor staff–inmate communication, and low staff pay).

5 Preventing prison riots requires changes both outside and inside the prison. Outside prison it is important for other social institutions to reduce sources of tension that contribute to crime. Inside prison experts recommend implementing formal inmate grievance procedures, ombudsmen, improved classification systems, smaller institutions, meaningful educational and work programs, alternatives to incarceration, professional prison staff who are well trained and well paid, and clearly written and well-understood policies on the use of force.

6 A supermax housing facility is a freestanding facility or a distinct unit within a facility that provides for management and secure control of inmates who have been officially designated as violent or who exhibit serious and disruptive behavior while incarcerated. Some experts who have studied the effects of long-term solitary confinement report evidence of acute sensory deprivation, paranoid delusion belief systems, irrational fears of violence, resentment, little ability to control rage, and mental breakdowns. Others believe the conditions of supermax confinement do not exacerbate symptoms of mental illness or create mental illness where none previously existed. They tell us that psychological disturbances are present among prisoners in the general population as well. Supermax prisons also present extraordinary challenges for staff, possibly creating a "we/they syndrome" and magnifying tensions between inmates and staff.

7 No-frills prisons and jails eliminate prisoner privileges and amenities in the belief that this process will deter criminals from future criminal activity. It appears, however, that no-frills correctional facilities may actually produce the results they were designed to avert, thereby increasing the number of prison disturbances and making it difficult for corrections staff to motivate appropriate inmate behavior. Corrections professionals tell us that they consider what outsiders perceive as privileges and amenities to be important management tools. Research from Florida shows that public views on prison amenities are not as harsh as many assume. The public is willing to provide and retain amenities if they are useful for inmate management and rehabilitation.

8 Correctional facilities and agencies should be accredited for eight reasons. Accreditation improves staff training and development, assesses program strengths and weaknesses, is a defense against lawsuits, establishes measurable criteria for upgrading operations, improves staff morale and professionalism, offers a safer environment for staff and offenders, reduces liability insurance costs, and offers performance-based benefits.

9 Arguments in favor of privatization include construction financing options that allow government clients to pay only for capacity as needed in lieu of accumulating long-term debt; modern state-of-the-art correctional facility designs that are efficient to operate; less time to build than comparable government construction projects; convenience and accountability of one entity for all compliance issues; rapid mobilization and specialization in unique facility missions; and economic development opportunities from hiring and purchasing locally. Reasons not to privatize include the moral issue of the government's responsibility for public safety; a lack of private companies from which to choose; private contractor inexperience with corrections issues; the potential for private vendors to become a monopoly through political ingratiation and favoritism; the potential for

government to lose the capability to perform the function over time; the potential for the profit motive to inhibit proper performance of duties; slow procurement processes that are open to risks; the difficulty of creating a contract with a private vendor; and the potential for a lack of enforcement to result in termination or expensive lawsuits as the only recourse.

10 Technology has affected corrections in the areas of communication, offender and officer tracking and recognition, and detection.

KEY TERMS

structured sentencing, p. 432

exchange rates, p. 433

security threat groups (STGs), p. 435

disturbance, p. 441

riot, p. 441

supermax housing, p. 446

special master, p. 451

no-frills prisons and jails, p. 452

contraband, p. 464

biometrics, p. 466

QUESTIONS FOR REVIEW

1 Debate the four reasons that prisons are overcrowded.

2 Which method of controlling prison crowding do you believe is most important?

3 What do you believe is the most effective solution for controlling the influence of security threat groups (STGs)?

4 Rank the five causes of prison riots in order from most to least important.

5 Speculate what can be done to prevent prison riots.

6 Summarize the emergence of supermax housing and its impact on prisoners and staff.

7 What do you think about no-frills jails and prisons and their impact on corrections?

8 What ideas can you add to the reasons correctional agencies and facilities should be accredited?

9 Critique the arguments for and against privatization.

10 Debate the pros and cons of using technology in corrections.

THINKING CRITICALLY ABOUT CORRECTIONS

The Politics of Defining Prison Overcrowding

Think about the three ways to discuss prison overcrowding. Which definition of *capacity* is the most conservative? Which one is the most liberal? Explain. If you were a warden of a prison operating at 40 percent over capacity but you didn't believe your prison was overcrowded in the strict sense of the word, and a reporter asked you if your facility was overcrowded, which definition would you offer and why? How do the politics of corrections, your job, and the definition of *overcrowding* influence your response and shape the public debate on prison overcrowding?

No-Frills Jails and Prisons and the Politics of Misinformation

The public favors taking away prison amenities in part because it believes they are paid for by tax dollars. However, in this chapter you learned that a survey of Orlando, Florida, residents indicates that they supported inmate access to prison amenities when they learned that the prisoners, not the taxpayers, paid for their privileges. If most jurisdictions require inmates to pay for their amenities, why is the public misinformed? Can the politics of misinformation both harm and help corrections? Explain.

ON-THE-JOB DECISION MAKING

Overcoming Opposition to Privatization

It is 2015 and you are the director of your state's Department of Corrections and Rehabilitation. Your predecessors contracted with several private vendors to perform government activities such as food preparation and inmate programming. You signed contracts for full-scale private management of two state prisons. So far, your experience with privatization has been successful. Predictions from a decade ago that your state would not privatize the entire state department of corrections might be wrong. Your prisons continue to operate above capacity, and you believe that you spend more time in court than you do in your office. You need more bed space, but the public refuses to spend more on prisons. You are thinking seriously about a proposal that would turn over the management of all your state's adult prisons to the public sector. How will you overcome the opposition of your state's correctional officer association?

What Inmates Need to Know to Work Their Way out of Supermax Prison

Morris Thigpen, director of the National Institute of Corrections, tells us, "It is imperative that all inmates placed in supermax be fully aware of how they can work their way out." Assume that your state is planning a supermax prison. You remember Thigpen's words. What will you propose as opportunities for inmates to demonstrate positive behavior to work their way out?

For additional information, please see: www.mhhe.com/schmalleger6e

DEATH

The Ultimate Sanction

[15]

CHAPTER OBJECTIVES

After completing this chapter you should be able to do the following:

1 Discuss the history of capital punishment.

2 Describe the characteristics of people executed in the United States since 1977 and on death row today.

3 Discuss the politics influencing capital punishment.

4 List and summarize the major U.S. Supreme Court decisions that influenced capital punishment legislation.

5 Summarize the arguments for and against the death penalty.

6 Describe the death penalty appeals process.

7 Summarize Liebman's findings on the frequency of errors in capital punishment cases.

8 Discuss the Supreme Court's reasoning for banning the execution of offenders with mental retardation and juveniles.

> " *Whatever you think about the death penalty, a system that will take life must first give justice.* "
>
> —John J. Curtin Jr., president, American Bar Association, 1990–1991

Do innocent people get sentenced to die? That is the fundamental question being asked in places such as the Center for Wrongful Convictions at Northwestern University, the Innocence Project at Yeshiva University's Benjamin N. Cardozo School of Law, and the U.S. Congress. Northwestern's Center for Wrongful Convictions and Yeshiva's Innocence Project are dedicated to identifying and rectifying wrongful convictions and other serious miscarriages of justice. Congress aided the effort in 2004 by passing the Justice for All Act. Among the provisions of the act is Title IV, the Innocence Protection Act, which provides access to postconviction DNA testing in federal cases, helps states improve the quality of legal representation in capital cases, and increases compensation in federal cases of wrongful convictions from a flat $5,000 to $50,000 per year in noncapital cases and $100,000 per year in capital cases. The Innocence Protection Act also established the Kirk Bloodsworth (the first person in the United States cleared by DNA testing) Post-Conviction DNA Testing Program, which authorizes $25 million over five years to defray the costs of postconviction DNA testing.

Kirk Bloodsworth spent nine years on death row before he was pardoned by the governor of Maryland for a crime he did not commit. He was the first person in the United States cleared by DNA testing. How is it possible that innocent people can be convicted—and even sentenced to die—under our system of justice?

exonerate

To clear of blame and release from death row.

DNA testing is now a major factor in changing the criminal justice system. It provides scientific proof that our system convicts and sentences innocent people—and that wrongful convictions are not isolated or rare events. According to the Death Penalty Information Center,[1] of the 138 people in 26 states whose innocence has been established after they were sent to death row since 1973, DNA testing played a substantial role in establishing the innocence and freedom of 17 of them. Exhibit 15–1 lists the **exonerations** by year and state. Each exoneree served an average of 9.8 years on death row before exoneration.

The first person in the United States cleared by DNA testing was Kirk Bloodsworth.[2] He was 24, with neither a criminal history nor a deviant past, when a Baltimore County judge ordered his execution following a conviction for the brutal rape, beating, and strangling death of 9-year-old Dawn Hamilton. Bloodsworth maintained his innocence and sounded so sincere that famed singer Willie Nelson and hundreds of other people wrote to him offering support.

After reading a book by crime novelist Joseph Wambaugh about genetic fingerprinting, Bloodsworth asked his attorney to have DNA

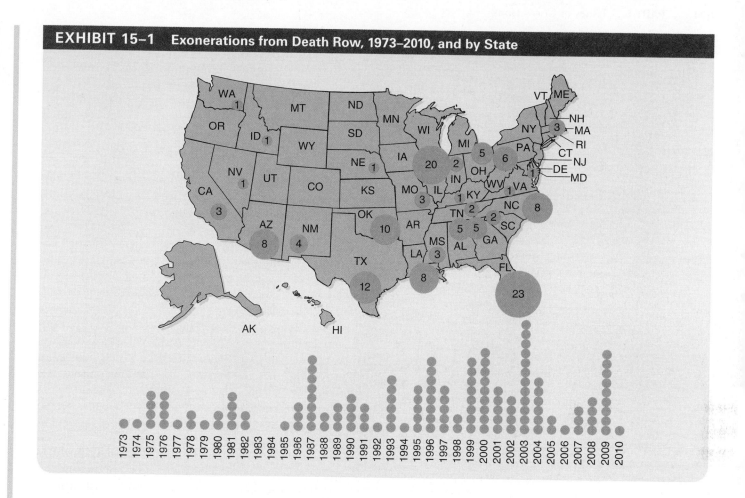

EXHIBIT 15–1   Exonerations from Death Row, 1973–2010, and by State

experts analyze semen stains that had been found on the victim's underwear. The new analysis, undertaken independently by a private company and the FBI, conclusively cleared Bloodsworth of the crime. In 1993, he was released from prison. A few months later, the governor of Maryland granted him a pardon.[3] Not until 2004 was the real killer identified by DNA tests.

Bloodsworth, who had served almost nine years behind bars, thought that his nightmare had ended when he was released from prison. Far from it. His reentry into free society has been difficult and painful. After his release, people telephoned him in the night shouting, "They never should have let you out." He once found the words "child killer" scrawled across his windshield. His first night off death row, sleeping in his father's house, he relieved himself in the corner of the bedroom—thinking in the darkness that he was standing in front of his urinal in his death row cell. He suffers from recurring dreams of execution, and that dream still haunts him—still grabs him in the night and drags him down the long hallway toward death. Right before the end, he says, he wakes up, drenched in sweat and choking to breathe.

HISTORY OF CAPITAL PUNISHMENT

capital punishment
Lawful imposition of the death penalty.

Capital punishment was once common throughout the world and imposed for many crimes, including murder, rape, stealing, witchcraft, piracy, desertion, sodomy, adultery, concealing the birth or death of an infant, aiding runaway slaves, counterfeiting, and forgery. Death, however, was not the harshest punishment—torture was. Torture, so cruel that death came as a relief, sometimes lasted for days. Death was a form of leniency. Criminals were boiled, burned, roasted on spits, drawn and quartered, broken on wheels, disemboweled, torn apart by animals, gibbeted (hung from a post with a projecting arm and left to die), bludgeoned (beaten to death with sticks, clubs, or rocks), or pressed (crushed under a board and stones).

Capital punishment began changing in the 18th century during the Enlightenment. This philosophical movement led to many new theories on crime and punishment. One of these theories proposed that punishment should fit the crime. Penalties involving torture began to disappear, and the use of the death penalty diminished.

At the turn of the 20th century, some states began to ban capital punishment and others began to limit its use. After World War I, as socialists challenged capitalism, a number of states reinstated the death penalty in order to deter threats of revolution. Around the same time, criminologists argued that capital punishment was a necessary social measure, and as the United States suffered through Prohibition and the Great Depression in the 1930s, there were more executions, an average of 167 per year, than in any other decade in American history.

By 1950, as prosperity followed World War II, public sentiment for capital punishment faded. The number of executions dropped. Support for capital punishment was at its lowest in 1966 (42 percent), and constitutional challenges were starting to surface. In the late 1960s, the U.S. Supreme Court began "fine-tuning" the way the death penalty was administered. In 1968 in *U.S.* v. *Jackson*,[4] the Court held that the provision of the federal kidnapping statute requiring that the death penalty be imposed only upon the recommendation of a jury was unconstitutional because it encouraged

On September 30, 1283, Dafydd ap Gruffydd, the last native prince of Wales, was condemned to die for plotting the death of King Edward I. On October 3, 1283, Dafydd was dragged through the streets behind a horse, hanged and then revived, disemboweled (his stomach was cut open, and his intestines were removed and thrown into a fire as he watched), beheaded, and then drawn and quartered. Drawing-and-quartering was officially abolished as a method of execution in Britain in 1870. Why did penalties involving torture disappear?

defendants to waive their right to a jury trial to ensure they would not receive a death sentence. Later that year in *Witherspoon* v. *Illinois*,[5] the Court held that a potential juror's mere reservations about the death penalty were insufficient grounds to prevent that person from serving on the jury in a death penalty case. Jurors could be disqualified only if the prosecutors showed that the juror's attitude toward capital punishment would prevent him or her from making an impartial decision about punishment. The watershed case in capital punishment took place in 1972 when the Court decided *Furman* v. *Georgia*.[6] In brief, the Court held that Georgia's death penalty statute, which gave the sentencing authority (judge or trial jury) complete sentencing discretion without any guidance as to how to exercise that discretion, could result in arbitrary sentencing and was therefore in violation of the Eighth Amendment's ban against cruel and unusual punishment.

On June 29, 1972, the Court voided 40 death penalty statutes because they were no longer valid. Four years later, in *Gregg* v. *Georgia*, the Supreme Court upheld guided discretionary capital statutes, opining that "such standards do provide guidance to the sentencing authority and thereby reduce the likelihood that it will impose a sentence that fairly can be called capricious and arbitrary." Thirty years later, the trends in capital punishment are these: Death sentences are down, executions are down, and public support for capital punishment is falling. This chapter will explore these issues.

Amir Karbalaei (right), Payam Amini (center), and Majid Qasemi (left), are seen hanging with ropes around their necks in the northeastern Lavizan district of Tehran, Iran, on Sunday, September 29, 2006, five days after their death verdict was approved by the Iranian Supreme Court. The men were convicted of abducting, raping, and robbing women. How would you describe the international use of capital punishment?

Capital Punishment Around the World

In 2010, Amnesty International documented 527 executions in 23 countries, but the total did not include figures from China, which executes more people than the rest of the world combined. The five countries that reported the most executions in 2009 were Iran (252), North Korea (60), Yemen (53), United States (46), and Saudi Arabia (27).[7]

As of March 2010, the majority of countries (139) had abolished the death penalty in law or in practice.[8] Fifty-eight countries still retain it. Retentionist and abolitionist countries are shown in Exhibit 15–2.

CAPITAL PUNISHMENT IN THE UNITED STATES

The face of capital punishment is changing in the United States. On Wednesday, March 9, 2011, Illinois became the 16th state to abolish capital punishment and commuted the sentences of 15 death row inmates to life without parole. Governor Pat Quinn told reporters, "This is the most difficult decision I've made as governor. It was made after many days and nights of reflection and review…I studied everything to the best of my ability and followed my conscience. I made this decision today to sign the law passed by the members of the general assembly and it became law today with my signature."[9]

Although 34 states, the U.S. military, and the federal government allow capital punishment and 16 states and the District of Columbia do not (see Exhibit 15–3), public opinion, grassroots lobbying, political and legislative changes, judicial rulings, and the current economic crisis are reshaping the capital punishment debate.

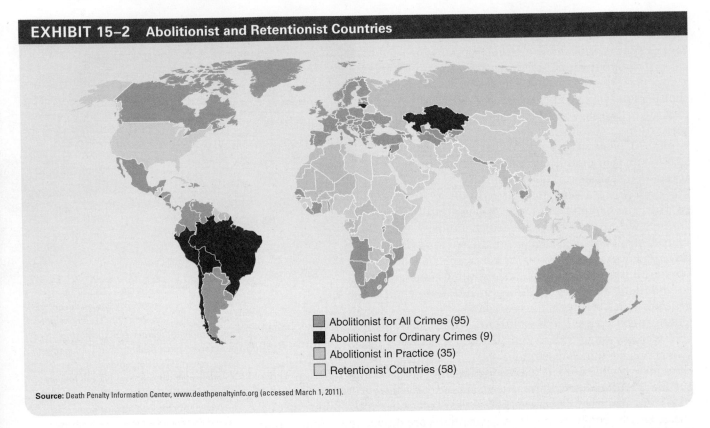

EXHIBIT 15-2 Abolitionist and Retentionist Countries

Abolitionist for All Crimes (95)
Abolitionist for Ordinary Crimes (9)
Abolitionist in Practice (35)
Retentionist Countries (58)

Source: Death Penalty Information Center, www.deathpenaltyinfo.org (accessed March 1, 2011).

Today the death penalty is under attack because it costs too much. Both New Jersey and New Mexico abolished the death penalty in 2007 and 2009, respectively, citing cost as a primary reason. Consider the following:[10]

- **$508,000.** Cost in Kansas for a death penalty trial (2003).
- **$32,000.** Cost in Kansas for a nondeath penalty trial (2003).
- **$2.16 million.** Estimated cost per execution in North Carolina (1993).
- **$250 million.** Estimated cost per execution in California (2005).
- **$71 million.** Cost in Maryland for all capital cases that did not result in a death sentence (2008).
- **$620,932.** Average cost for the defense in a federal death penalty case (2008).
- **$192,333.** Average cost of legal representation in federal death penalty cases that resulted in a plea bargain (1998).
- **$55,772.** Average cost of representation in federal cases that were eligible for the death penalty but in which the death penalty was not sought (1998).
- **$51 million.** Cost to Florida taxpayers per year for keeping inmates on death row more than holding them for life without parole.
- **$186 million.** Cost to Maryland taxpayers for pursuing five capital cases between 1978 and 1999.

The high cost of crime scene investigations, pretrial preparations and motions, expert witness investigations, jury selection, the necessity for two trials—one on guilt and one on sentencing—appeals, and heightened death row security and maintenance costs are pushing officials to limit the number of capital murder cases that can be prosecuted in hope of reducing costs. Lawmakers in Colorado, Kansas, Maryland, Montana, Nebraska, and New Hampshire have introduced bills, albeit unsuccessfully, to replace capital punishment with life in prison. They argued that the money spent on death rows could be better spent on police officers, courts, prison cells, social services, health care, schools, and parks. An editorial in *The New York Times* summed it up this way: "It's an economic drain on governments with already badly depleted budgets."[11]

While Colorado, Kansas, Maryland, Montana, Nebraska, and New Hampshire are considering eliminating the death penalty or sharply limiting its use, other states are trying to reinstate or expand it. Alaska, which abolished the death penalty in 1957, is considering reestablishing it. California legislators approved $356 million to construct a new 768-cell death row unit to replace the current one holding 670 death row inmates. Georgia lawmakers are considering legislation to allow death sentences even if juries do not unanimously agree on such a sentence. Nebraska lawmakers are promoting legislation that would establish lethal injection as the state's method of execution and allow death sentences to be carried out again following the state Supreme Court's ruling that the electric chair was unconstitutional. And Virginia's General Assembly wants to expand capital punishment by allowing the state to execute those who assist in a murder but do not personally carry it out.

After having a decade-long moratorium on executions and examining the state justice system, its record on wrongful convictions, and the cost of conducting executions, on Wednesday, March 9, 2011, Illinois Governor Pat Quinn signed legislation abolishing capital punishment, making Illinois the 16th state to do so. Governor Quinn told reporters, "This is the most difficult decision I've made as governor. It was made after many days and nights of reflection and review ... I studied everything to the best of my ability and followed my conscience. I made this decision today to sign the law passed by the members of the general assembly and it became law today with my signature." Do you think Illinois will be the "bellwether" of the American death penalty?

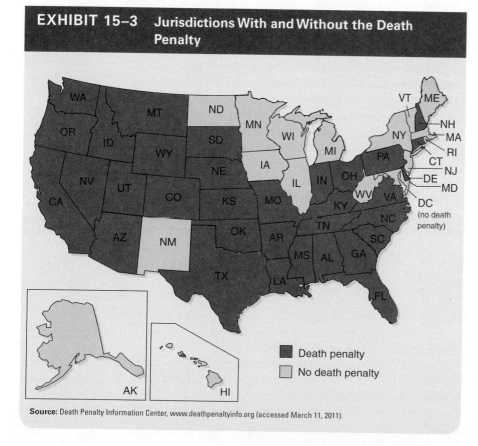

EXHIBIT 15–3 **Jurisdictions With and Without the Death Penalty**

Death penalty
No death penalty

Source: Death Penalty Information Center, www.deathpenaltyinfo.org (accessed March 11, 2011).

EXHIBIT 15–4   People Executed, 1976–2010

Sources: Bureau of Justice Statistics, "Key Facts at a Glance—Executions," http://bjs.ojp.usdoj.gov (accessed February 28, 2011).

Although research on executions in the United States has been hampered by a lack of official records, more than 15,000 executions, beginning in the 1600s, have been confirmed.[12]

Executions were halted in 1968 pending a U.S. Supreme Court decision on the constitutionality of certain aspects of capital punishment. By 1977, the Court had ruled that capital punishment itself was not unconstitutional and did not violate the Eighth Amendment to the U.S. Constitution, thus paving the way for executions to resume. The first person to be executed after the moratorium ended was Gary Gilmore, who gave up his right to appeal and was executed by firing squad on January 17, 1977, by the state of Utah. See Exhibit 15–4 for the number of executions from 1976 through 2010.

Today in the United States, what constitutes a **capital crime**—a crime that is punishable by death—is defined by law. This definition varies among jurisdictions. In Delaware, for example, first-degree murder with at least one statutory aggravating circumstance is a capital crime. In Nevada, first-degree murder with at least 1 of 15 aggravating circumstances is a capital crime. In Texas, criminal homicide with one of nine aggravating circumstances is a capital offense.[13]

capital crime

A crime for which the death penalty may but need not necessarily be imposed.

The Federal Death Penalty

The Constitution of the United States does not mention the death penalty, but it does permit the federal government to deprive citizens of life after giving due process. In 1790, the first Congress mandated the death penalty for several offenses, including treason, willful murder on federal property, forgery, piracy, counterfeiting, and several crimes on the high seas; the first federal death penalty was used on June 25, 1790, when Thomas Bird was hanged for murder in Maine. By the end of the 19th century, the number of federal capital crimes had expanded to include kidnapping, spying, all murders, and arson of a dwelling or a fort.

Since 1790, the federal government has executed 336 men and 4 women. Of these, 134 (39 percent) were white, 118 (35 percent) were black, 63 (19 percent) were Native American, and 25 (7 percent) were Hispanic or of unknown origin. Methods of execution in federal cases have included hanging, electrocution, and the gas chamber. Today the federal government uses lethal injection.

EXHIBIT 15–5   Federal Laws Providing for the Death Penalty

- Assassination or kidnapping resulting in the death of the president or vice president
- Bank-robbery-related murder or kidnapping
- Civil rights offenses resulting in death
- Death resulting from aircraft hijacking
- Death resulting from offenses involving transportation of explosives, destruction of government property, or destruction of property related to foreign or interstate commerce
- Destruction of aircraft, motor vehicles, or related facilities resulting in death
- Espionage
- First-degree murder
- Genocide
- Mailing of injurious articles with intent to kill or resulting in death
- Murder by a federal prisoner
- Murder by an escaped federal prisoner already sentenced to life imprisonment
- Murder by the use of a weapon of mass destruction
- Murder committed at an airport serving international civil aviation
- Murder committed by the use of a firearm during a crime of violence or a drug-trafficking crime
- Murder committed during a drug-related drive-by shooting
- Murder committed during an offense against maritime navigation
- Murder committed during an offense against a maritime fixed platform
- Murder committed in a federal government facility
- Murder during a hostage taking
- Murder during a kidnapping
- Murder for hire
- Murder involved in a racketeering offense
- Murder involving torture
- Murder of a court officer or juror
- Murder of a federal judge or law enforcement official
- Murder of a foreign official
- Murder of a member of Congress, an important executive official, or a Supreme Court Justice
- Murder of a state correctional officer
- Murder of a state or local law enforcement official or other person aiding in a federal investigation
- Murder of a U.S. national in a foreign country
- Murder related to a carjacking
- Murder related to rape or child molestation
- Murder related to sexual exploitation of children
- Murder related to the smuggling of aliens
- Murder related to a continuing criminal enterprise or related murder of a federal, state, or local law enforcement officer
- Murder with the intent of preventing testimony by a witness, victim, or informant
- Retaliatory murder of a member of the immediate family of law enforcement officials
- Retaliatory murder of a witness, victim, or informant
- Terrorist murder of a U.S. national in another country
- Treason
- Willful wrecking of a train resulting in death

Source: Adapted from Tracy L. Snell, *Capital Punishment, 2007* (Washington, DC: U.S. Department of Justice, December 2008).

From 1972, the year of the Supreme Court's *Furman* decision (discussed later in this chapter), until the late 1980s, federal capital prosecutions were rare. In 1988, President Reagan signed the Anti–Drug Abuse Act, which authorized capital punishment for murder committed by people involved in certain drug trafficking activities.

In 1994, President Clinton signed into law the Violent Crime Control and Law Enforcement Act. Title VI is the Federal Death Penalty Act. It dramatically expanded the number of federal offenses punishable by death (see Exhibit 15–5).

In addition to incorporating the Supreme Court law ban on execution of offenders with mental retardation and juveniles, the Federal Death Penalty Act also exempts women while they are pregnant. The act permits federal employees who oppose the death penalty to opt out of participating in executions, and it restricts the federal government's ability to seek the death penalty for Native Americans whose offense occurred within the boundaries of Indian country.

The last three federal executions were:

- Timothy McVeigh, white, executed June 11, 2001.
- Juan Raul Garza, Hispanic, executed June 19, 2001.
- Louis Jones Jr., black, executed March 18, 2003.

Procedures in Federal Capital Cases Federal prosecutors who wish to file capital charges are required by the Department of Justice to first obtain authorization from the attorney general. The request is reviewed by the assistant attorney general, by the deputy attorney general, and ultimately by the attorney general.

For example, on Monday, November 17, 2003, lawyers for serial bomber Eric Rudolph met with then attorney general John Ashcroft's death penalty committee. The committee's job was to listen, review evidence, and recommend to the attorney general whether Rudolph should be added to the list of 124 people tried under the federal death law since it was reinstated in 1988. On Friday, December 13, 2003, the attorney general authorized prosecutors to seek the death penalty against Rudolph. However, in April 2005, Rudolph pleaded guilty and was sentenced to four life terms in exchange for avoiding a trial and a potential death sentence. Rudolph is confined at the federal supermax prison in Florence, Colorado (read more about supermax confinement in Chapter 13).

The new Federal Death Penalty Act changes an offender's right to counsel in three ways. First, it requires that a minimum of two lawyers be appointed to represent federal capital defendants. Second, at least one of the two lawyers must have experience in capital work. And third, the federal court must consider the federal public defender's recommendation regarding which counsel are qualified for appointment in capital cases.

Federal Death Row The federal death row is at the U.S. Penitentiary, Terre Haute, Indiana. It is called the Special Confinement Unit (SCU). It opened in 1999 because of the increasing number of federal defendants sentenced to death. On March 1, 2011, 60 people were on federal death row in Terre Haute.

SCU is a two-story renovated housing unit. It includes 120 single cells, upper-tier and lower-tier corridors, an industrial workshop, indoor and outdoor recreation areas, a property room, a food preparation area, attorney and family visiting areas, and a video-teleconferencing area that is used to facilitate inmate access to the courts and to their attorneys.

When Timothy McVeigh was executed in 2001 for the murder of 168 people in the Oklahoma City bombing, the U.S. Department of Justice instituted an elaborate process to handle any last-minute legal interruptions that might prevent or delay his execution. Two hours before McVeigh's execution, prison officials ended his visiting privileges to give him one final opportunity to seek a stay from the courts or President Bush. Forty-five minutes before the execution—and again at 10 minutes before the execution—the White House was contacted by telephone. In the event of a delay, a U.S. marshal was ready to instruct the executioner to step away from the execution equipment and to notify McVeigh and everyone present that the execution had been delayed or stayed. McVeigh received no stays.

Race and the Federal Death Penalty In 2000, the Justice Department released its findings on the question of racial and geographic disparities in federal death penalty prosecutions forwarded to the Justice Department for review between 1995 and 2000. It reported that 80 percent of the defendants were from minorities.[14] The study found that minorities are overrepresented in the federal death penalty system as both victims and defendants relative to the general population. Then attorney general Janet Reno said, "This should be of concern to all of us."[15]

The study confirmed an internal Justice Department report on racial disparities that found that between 1988, when President Reagan signed the Anti–Drug Abuse Act into law, and October 1993, the attorney general authorized federal prosecutors to seek the death penalty against 30 defendants. Over 70 percent were black, and one-half of the remaining defendants were Mexican American.[16] Later in this chapter, we will examine the debate over such statistics.

DEATH ROW TODAY

Characteristics of People Executed Since 1977

As of February 23, 2011, 1,242 people have been executed in the United States since Gary Gilmore's execution in January 1977. Like Gilmore, 133 other death row inmates asked the court to drop their appeals and carry out the death sentence. Each time, the inmate either fired the defense lawyer or told him or her to stop filing appeals. Their reasons are similar—mainly remorse, a desire for atonement, and not wanting to spend their lives in prison.[17]

The peak year for executions in the United States since they resumed in 1977 was 1999, when 98 people were executed. By 2010, the number of executions had declined to 46. Thirty-eight percent (466) of all executions have taken place in Texas. Has the death penalty affected the murder rate in Texas? You be the judge: From 2000 through 2009 (the last year for which complete *Uniform Crime Reports* data are available), the murder rate in the United States averaged 5.5 per year per 100,000 population. In Texas, the average was almost 6.0 per year per 100,000 population, 0.09 percent more than the national average. In 2009, in states with the death penalty the murder rate was 4.9 while the average in states without the death penalty was 2.8, close to one-half of the national average.

From the time of Gary Gilmore's execution in 1977 through January 1, 2010, the South led the United States in executions with 1,022. In 2010, all but 11 of the 46 executions took place in the South. Only 1.0 percent of all the people executed since 1977 have been female; 56 percent were white, 35 percent black, 7 percent Hispanic, and 2 percent other background.[18]

Few issues generate more public controversy than that of the death penalty. In some states there are movements to end the death penalty while in others the move is to speed up death row appeals and complete the sentence of execution. Do demonstrations such as these influence the public policy implemented by state legislatures?

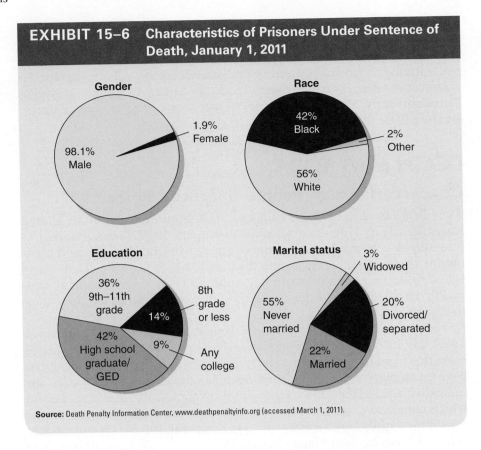

EXHIBIT 15–6 Characteristics of Prisoners Under Sentence of Death, January 1, 2011

Gender

98.1% Male

1.9% Female

Race

42% Black

2% Other

56% White

Education

36% 9th–11th grade

8th grade or less

14%

42% High school graduate/GED

9%

Any college

Marital status

3% Widowed

55% Never married

20% Divorced/separated

22% Married

Source: Death Penalty Information Center, www.deathpenaltyinfo.org (accessed March 1, 2011).

Inmates executed in 2010 had been on death row an average of 14 years. In 1990 by comparison, the average time to execution was about 7 years.

Characteristics of Prisoners Under Sentence of Death

Today 3,261 persons are awaiting execution, a decrease of 332 from one decade earlier. At the time of Gary Gilmore's execution on January 17, 1977, there were 423 people on death row. Ten years later, the number was 1,984. After more than 20 years of continued increase in the number of people sentenced to die in the United States, the number on death row peaked in 2000 to 3,593 and has been decreasing ever since.

Today, U.S. juries are imposing fewer death sentences than they did on average during the 1990s. In the 1990s, an average of almost 300 people were sentenced to death each year. Since 2001, the average has been 137, a drop of more than 50 percent.

Forty-four percent of the nation's death row population is in three states: California (697), Florida (398), and Texas (337). Exhibit 15–6 shows additional characteristics of inmates under sentence of death.

Victim Race, Gender, Geography, and the Death Penalty

Defendant–victim racial combinations have been the subject of considerable debate.[19] Recognizing that whites and minorities are murder victims in approximately equal numbers, why is it that 78 percent of the victims in cases resulting in executions since 1977 have been white? This disparity

Chris Summers

Chaplain • W. C. Holman Correctional Facility
• Atmore, Alabama

I received an M.A. degree in Christian Theological Studies from the University of Mobile. I am an evangelical Christian, ordained Southern Baptist, and believe in the saving grace of Jesus Christ by faith.

The maximum-security prison where I now work is W. C. Holman Correctional Facility in Atmore, Alabama. I have worked with the Alabama Department of Corrections for 30 years. I began working in this system in 1981 as a full-time Chaplain's Assistant through a Christian mission organization. I was hired by the state as a full-time Chaplain in 1990. In 1997 I began work at W. C. Holman Correctional Facility, where death row is housed and sentences are carried out. This is where I began my early work in prison ministry and have known many men on death row and those who have mitigated sentences from the death penalty since 1981.

At W. C. Holman Correctional Facility I minister to the entire institution, which includes a 617-man population, 211 single-cell segregation unit, and 174-man death row unit. I am also a regional chaplaincy coordinator who is a member of the Religious Activities Review Committee, which develops policies and confirms acceptable religious expressions within the state correctional institutions of Alabama.

Among many other chaplaincy programming responsibilities, I weekly perform duties on the death row unit. Some of my responsibilities are to visit each man once a week, administrate and coordinate weekly volunteer services, and schedule periodic special events. During a two-week period prior to an execution, my responsibilities involve close practical and spiritual engagement with the offender's family and friends and the execution team officers and spiritual assistance or direct spiritual guidance for the offender. In the execution chamber as the sentence is being carried out, I am the only person in the room with the condemned. This responsibility was created and detailed by the current Warden, Tony Patterson. The offender then has the spiritual assistance and personal comfort of the Chaplain available while the sentence is being carried out. I oftentimes hold the offender's hand and pray with him until the first stage of execution, sleep, is performed. On several occasions, responsibilities of death row ministry include the privilege of conducting funerals for the aged or those executed.

At this time, I have witnessed 37 executions, 10 by electrocution and 27 by lethal injection. In 2002 Alabama first employed the use of lethal injection and still has the option of electrocution according to the offender's preference.

Out of my experience, it is my belief that restorative justice epistemology and practice is the answer to our current criminal justice crisis. I use every given opportunity to communicate its practical and viable application, even for those victims and offenders who incur *Death: the Ultimate Sanction*. It has been my message to the men on death row and my experience that true closure for wrongs committed come through restorative accountability for all involved in the harms of crime.

> "It has been my message to the men on death row and my experience that true closure for wrongs committed come through restorative accountability for all involved in the harms of crime."

---

is confirmed even in studies that control for similar crimes by comparing defendants with similar backgrounds. Does it imply that white victims are considered more important by the criminal justice system? Former U.S. attorney general John Ashcroft argued that blacks and Hispanics are more likely than whites to be sentenced to death and executed because they are more likely to be arrested on facts that can support a capital charge and because whites are more likely to negotiate plea bargains that spare their lives. Others disagree, citing consistent patterns of racial bias.[20] A study of more than 1,500 homicide cases in North Carolina between 1990 and 2009 found that defendants of all races were more than twice as

Reporters observe the execution chair in which Gary Gilmore sat when facing a Utah firing squad on January 17, 1977. Upper right on the chair back are the bullet holes. Draped over the back of the chair is the corduroy material hood that Gilmore wore during the execution. On March 15, 2004, Utah repealed its use of the firing squad, leaving lethal injection as the only option. Should condemned inmates be permitted to choose the method of their execution if, when they were sentenced to die, state law allowed the choice?

likely to be sentenced to death if at least one of their alleged victims was white. Another study concluded that in the cases of the 159 people then on death row in North Carolina, prosecutors had removed blacks from juries at more than twice the rate that they struck prospective nonblack jurors. A new law in North Carolina might change that, however. In 2009, North Carolina lawmakers passed the Racial Justice Act. For the first time, the law allows judges to consider statistical evidence that suggests that race was a significant factor in the prosecutor's seeking or the court's imposing the death sentence on a disproportionate number of people from a minority group. A similar bill passed in Kentucky and is being considered by lawmakers in California, Pennsylvania, and other states.

Researchers have also asked if location is related to whether or not someone is sentenced to die. All things considered, how can a capital murder on one side of a county or city line result in a death sentence and, on the other side, life in prison? But according to a review of Virginia's system of capital punishment by the Virginia General Assembly in 2001, "Location, more than any other factor impacted the probability that prosecutors would actually seek the death penalty for capital murder cases."[21] The lawmakers studied 215 capital punishment-eligible cases in Virginia from 1995 to 1999 and found that statewide, prosecutors in high-density, urban areas sought the death penalty for only 16 percent of their capital-eligible cases. In comparison, prosecutors in medium-density, mostly suburban areas sought the death penalty in approximately 45 percent of the cases and prosecutors in low-density, mostly rural areas sought execution in 34 percent of the cases. Some argue that differences among communities is a positive factor. Jury pools are different, and they speak for the community. Others disagree, pointing to the U.S. Supreme Court mandate that the death penalty be reserved for the worst crimes committed by the worst offenders. If a rural county has few murders, then a relatively unaggravated homicide may appear to be the worst of the worst. If the crime is put on a continuum in an urban area, it may not be considered this way. The issue the Virginia lawmakers asked of themselves is whether these disparate outcomes are acceptable in a system in which the ultimate sanction is death and prosecutors are vested with discretionary authority to prosecute difficult and troubling cases.

Location can also change the outcome in federal death penalty prosecutions.[22] Whereas a state homicide is prosecuted in the county of offense, a federal homicide is prosecuted in one of 94 federal districts. Consider the federal Eastern District of Louisiana, for example. It consists of 12 parishes (counties) including Orleans Parish (New Orleans). If a federal homicide happens in New Orleans, a jury pool is chosen from the federal district pool of all 12 parishes, not just Orleans Parish. The outcome can be affected by incorporating more white and more conservative jurors from other areas than the predominant minority and more liberal community members of Orleans Parish who may be unfazed by the murder. Critics of this approach, including conservative Supreme Court Justice Antonin Scalia, have called for the abolition of the federal death penalty and the selection of the jury from the county of offense to prosecute federally.[23]

More recently, researchers at Bowling Green State University examined the data on almost 6,000 homicides in Ohio that occurred between 1981 and

EXHIBIT 15–7   Method of Execution

States in which lethal injection is the sole method of execution
States that authorize lethal injection and electrocution
States that authorize lethal injection and lethal gas
States that authorize lethal injection and hanging
States that authorize lethal injection and firing squad
State that authorizes lethal injection, electrocution, and firing squad
Jurisdictions without capital punishment

Note: The U.S. government and U.S. military authorize lethal injection.

Source: Death Penalty Information, www.deathpenaltyinfo.org (accessed March 1, 2011); and Tracy L. Snell, *Capital Punishment 2007* (Washington, DC: U.S. Department of Justice, Bureau of Justice Statistics, December 2008).

1997. They found that even after controlling for several legally relevant factors, analyses revealed that homicides with white female victims were more likely to result in a death sentence than others. "In fact," the researchers wrote, "homicides with white female victims are the only statistically distinct victim dyad. This is consistent with the view that black female victims do not have the same status as white female victims. In other words, it appears that decision making in homicides is not influenced by the same factors in all cases, and that white female victim homicides may be substantively unique."[24]

Methods of Execution

Five methods of execution are used in the United States: (1) lethal injection, (2) electrocution, (3) lethal gas, (4) hanging, and (5) firing squad. As you can see in Exhibit 15–7, lethal injection is the predominant method of execution, used in 34 states. In 1977, Oklahoma became the first state to adopt lethal injection as a means of execution. Today nine states authorize electrocution; five states, lethal gas; two states, hanging; and three states, firing squad. Some states authorize more than one method. For example, Arizona uses lethal injection for people sentenced after November 15, 1992; those sentenced before that date may select lethal injection or lethal gas. Oklahoma authorizes electrocution if lethal injection is ever held unconstitutional and firing squad if both lethal injection and electrocution are held unconstitutional. The federal government authorizes a different method of execution under each of two different laws; the method of execution for federal prisoners prosecuted under the *Code of Federal Regulations*, Volume 28, Part 26, is lethal injection; for those offenses prosecuted under the Violent Crime Control and Law Enforcement Act of 1994, the method used is that in the state in which the person was convicted. If the state has no death penalty, the inmate is transferred to another state that has one.

When lethal injection is used, the condemned person is strapped to a gurney, and several heart monitors are positioned on his or her chest. Two needles (one is a backup) are inserted into arm veins. Long tubes connect the needle through a hole in a wall to several intravenous drips. A saline solution is started immediately. At the warden's signal, a curtain is raised, exposing the inmate to the witnesses in an adjoining room. In most states, the inmate is then injected with three drugs generally administered over a five-minute period. The first is 60 cc of sodium thiopental or pentothal to kill pain and cause unconsciousness. Next flows 60 cc of pavulon or pancuronium bromide, which paralyzes the entire muscle system and stops the inmate's breathing. Finally, the flow of 60 cc of potassium chloride stops the heart. The three injections are delivered separately and the lines cleaned out with saline solution after each drug injection; otherwise, the chemicals could become erosive and damage the IV lines. Death results from anesthetic overdose and respiratory and cardiac arrest while the condemned person is unconscious.[25]

For lethal injections, most states use the drug sodium thiopental, which renders the condemned person unconscious before he or she is given two other drugs that cause death. However, three states used only one drug, sodium thiopental, for executions. Ohio and Washington passed laws allowing for its use in large enough doses to kill the prisoner. How much of the drug Ohio and Washington have available is not known. A shortage of sodium thiopental is now delaying executions, causing states to look for other execution options. In November 2010, the California Department of Corrections and Rehabilitation paid a British distributor more than $36,000 for 521 grams of sodium thiopental, enough to execute about 90 condemned persons and for backup and training purposes. After the drug was shipped, however, Britain came under fire from the other European nations for providing the drug for executions; therefore Britain barred its future export to the United States for executions.[26] The Italian firm that makes sodium thiopental in its North Carolina plant announced in January 2011 that the Italian Parliament had demanded that the company ensure the drug would be used only for medical purposes.[27]

After two anesthesiologists convinced a federal court in November 2010 that 5,000 milligrams of pentobarbital—the drug widely used to euthanize animals—would cause unconsciousness and death within minutes, Oklahoma replaced sodium thiopental with pentobarbital. That state has executed three inmates with pentobarbital since December 2010. In January 2011, Ohio also switched drugs, replacing sodium thiopental with pentobarbital. It used a single-drug method for the first time Thursday, March 10, 2011, to execute Johnnie Batson, 37, for the 1994 killing of Chong Mah, 53, a Toledo store owner. H. Lundbeck of Copenhagen, the Danish company that distributes pentobarbital in the United States, criticized Ohio's use of the drug for executions. "It's against everything we stand for," said a spokesperson for the Danish company. "We invent and develop medicine with the aim of alleviating people's burden. This is the direct opposite of that."[28]

Changing drugs for lethal injections is not easy. Adopting a new protocol for them requires formal proposals, public comment, and often challenges in court, a process that can takes months and years. States adopted the three-drug cocktail only after lengthy court challenges, and changing to another drug would trigger new lawsuits and appeals. One expert said, "If you start to change the drugs, you at least have to make a showing that this has been vetted and tested. What evidence do you have that this isn't going to be severely painful and unreliable?"[29]

What Is Death Row Like?

Prisoners who are sentenced to death are held on **death row**, a prison within a prison. All states except Missouri and Tennessee segregate death row inmates from the general prison population. According to George Lombardi, director of the Missouri Department of Corrections, mainstreaming death row prisoners with the general population saves money; provides death row inmates more access to recreation, visitation, and prison programs and services; benefits non-death-row inmates because, before mainstreaming, even non-death-row prisoner movement was restricted due to security concerns over the segregated death row unit; and facilitates staff management of prisoners because recreation, visitation, and prison programs and services are seen as privileges that can be taken away. Mainstreaming in Missouri has also decreased inmate violence and disciplinary actions that surface when inmates feel they have nothing to lose.[30] Otherwise, according to Lombardi and others, the conditions among death rows in the majority of states are virtually indistinguishable. Inmates receive few, if any, rehabilitation, treatment, or work programs, and they leave their individual cells for an average of one hour a day. About one-half of the states allow contact visitation; the other half restrict it to inmates' attorneys. For that reason, death row existence has been called "living death" to convey a prisoner's loneliness, isolation, boredom, and loss of privacy.[31]

What many people forget is that a death row inmate's living environment is a correctional officer's workplace. Prison is a loud place, and sound can cause the most torment. The concrete and steel construction materials and furnishings that guarantee security and durability in death row amplify normal sounds within its hard walls. It takes little effort to imagine what effect shouting, flushing toilets, opening and closing steel doors, janitorial work, the blaring of televisions and radios, and voices wailing has not only on those who live there but also on those who work there. In summer the oppressive heat and in winter the freezing cold are trapped by walls of steel and concrete. The quality of life experienced by inmates depends on the work environment created by the corrections officers who guard them, but even the corrections officers are affected by the surroundings. Consult the Appendix: Careers in Corrections at the Online Learning Center Web site for the steps involved in career planning, developing employability and job readiness, and finding the right job.

Death row cells usually have steel bunks, toilets, and sinks. These are bolted to concrete floors and cinder block walls. Small lockers or

death row

A prison area housing inmates who have been sentenced to death.

Prisoners who are sentenced to death are held on death row. Do most death-sentenced prisoners need to be separated from the general prison population? Why or why not?

I am definitely sorry for all of the suffering I've caused people, especially the victims; I just wish there was a way to make things right. I wish I could let people know how genuinely I've had to deal with it for the eight years I've been in prison and had to look in the mirror every day. . . . I want to continue to help troubled teens, as I once was, and I presently get the opportunity to be in a Youth Enlightenment Program (Y.E.P.) that

we have here at this prison. . . . I came to death row a very messed up, drug-addicted, 17-year-old runaway that had to grow up here in the worst of prison realities. I've had to wake up every day facing the pain and suffering I've caused others.

Christopher Simmons
Seventeen-year-old Missouri youth convicted of murder and sentenced to die, wrote this

when he was on death row. On March 1, 2005, his case persuaded the U.S. Supreme Court that the Eighth and Fourteenth Amendments forbid the execution of offenders who were under the age of 18 when their crimes were committed.

wall shelves hold prisoners' personal property, which may include toiletries, books, pictures, a clock, and usually a television. The television is the death row inmate's most valued possession, not only because of its entertainment value but also because it makes available the world that the death row inmate has lost. Sometimes correctional officers use the threat of revoking television or telephone privileges to control behavior on death row. However, corrections officers say that death row inmates seldom exhibit disciplinary problems. One death row warden described death row inmates as "the group who causes the least trouble."[32] Researchers in Indiana examined the disciplinary records of 39 death row inmates who were transferred to the general prison population following modification of their sentences from death to capital life between 1972 and 1999. The researchers found that, despite the heinousness of their capital offenses, the majority of these former death row inmates did not commit acts of serious violence on death row or after their transfer to the general prison population. Most presented little persistent disciplinary management difficulty in the general prison population.[33] The reasons, researchers suggest, are aging, prior adjustment to institutionalization while on death row, restrictive death row conditions, and higher levels of supervision.

Most death row inmates spend 22 to 23 hours a day in five-by-eight- or six-by-nine-foot cells, about the size of a bathroom. They are counted once an hour. They receive their meals through slots in the cell doors. Generally twice a week, they are handcuffed, escorted to, and locked in shower stalls for 5- or 10-minute showers. In some jurisdictions, death row inmates may visit the prison library; in others, books are taken to them. In Florida, death row inmates may receive mail every day except holidays and weekends. They may have cigarettes, snacks, radios, and a 13-inch television in their cells. They do not have cable television or air-conditioning and they are not allowed to be with each other in a common room. They can watch religious services on closed-circuit television. They wear orange T-shirts and blue pants.

Most death row inmates slowly lose their ties with the outside world. Although some states permit contact visits, most allow only noncontact visits. Every time death row inmates leave death row for visits—whether contact or noncontact—they are strip-searched before and after. Over the years, visitors and mail come less frequently, and they sometimes cease altogether. Corrections officers assigned to death row are instructed not to establish relationships with inmates because it may make it more difficult to carry out their duties. Pennsylvania's policy manual for death row corrections officers reads, "Employees must not be too familiar or discuss personal items of interest with the inmates."[34]

Preparing for an execution is a correctional officer's toughest job. "We begin to dread electrocutions weeks before they take place," says former corrections officer Lynch Alford Sr. "We're almost glad when someone is commuted, regardless of what crime he committed. We just sit around and wait. We drink coffee. We don't talk about anything. We don't talk about the electrocution. We just get it over with as soon as possible and then go home immediately." A death row inmate who refuses to walk to the death chamber is carried by corrections officers, sometimes screaming and kicking. "Guards have been known to go all to pieces during episodes such as these. Their nerves just don't hold up. In my opinion it is something you never become accustomed to. It's the most gruesome job I've come in contact with during my 35 years with the department. The more you see, the more you hate it."[35] Texas law governing execution is presented in Exhibit 15–8. At one time, Texas death row inmates had more freedom, worked in a prison garment factory, enjoyed group recreation, participated in education programs, and had an occasional contact visit. But in 1999, seven condemned prisoners escaped. After they were captured, prison officials moved death row from Huntsville to Livingston, eliminated the work and education programs, put inmates in permanent solitary confinement, and eliminated television.

Public Opinion, Politics, and Capital Punishment

According to the Gallup Poll, public support for capital punishment in the United States was at its lowest in 1966 when only 42 percent of Americans supported it. It reached its highest level (80 percent) in 1994. Most recently, the AngusReid public opinion poll found that 83 percent of Americans support the death penalty in murder cases.[36] However, as the number of innocent people released from death row increases and news of their innocence makes headlines, the empirical evidence demonstrates that attitudes regarding capital punishment are changing in the United States. A 15-year decline in death sentences (from 315 in 1996 to 112 in 2009), a 53 percent drop in executions (from 98 in 1999 to 46 in 2010), a shrinking death row population (from 3,593 in 2000 to 3,261 in 2009), and waning support for capital punishment have marked a significant turnaround in the use of the death penalty.

Death penalty researchers across the country are finding that while the public may accept the use of capital punishment, it may actually prefer other punishment options such as life without the possibility of parole (LWOP) when given the opportunity. There is now a significant body of research showing that support for the death penalty drops considerably when it is compared with alternatives such as a sentence of life in prison with no parole. A national poll of 1,500 registered voters in May 2010 conducted by Lake Research Partners found a clear majority of voters

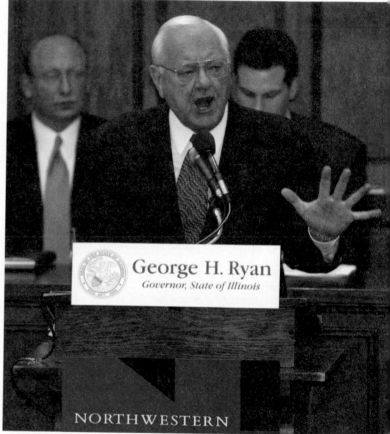

In January 2003, Illinois governor George Ryan commuted 164 death row inmates' sentences to life in prison, commuted 3 other death row inmates' sentences to 40 years in prison, and pardoned 4 other death row inmates because of mounting evidence that the death penalty was not being applied fairly in Illinois. Eight years later, on March 9, 2011, Illinois governor Pat Quinn signed legislation that abolished capital punishment. Wrongful convictions and executions harm not only the accused but also the victim, the family and friends of the accused and the victim, the criminal justice system, and society. How can we prevent the wrongful conviction and execution of innocent people?

EXHIBIT 15–8   Capital Punishment in Texas

Execution of Convict

Whenever the sentence of death is pronounced against a convict, the sentence shall be executed at any time after the hour of 6 P.M. on the day set for the execution, by intravenous injection of a substance or substances in a lethal quantity sufficient to cause death and until such convict is dead, such execution procedure to be determined and supervised by the Director of the institutional division of the Texas Department of Criminal Justice.

Warrant of Execution

Whenever any person is sentenced to death, the clerk of the court in which the sentence is pronounced, shall within ten days after the court enters its order setting the date for execution, issue a warrant under the seal of the court for the execution of the sentence of death, which shall recite the fact of conviction, setting forth specifically the offense, the judgment of the court, the time fixed for his or her execution, and directed to the Director of the Department of Corrections at Huntsville, Texas, commanding him to proceed, at the time and place named in the order of execution, to carry the same into execution, as provided in the preceding Article, and shall deliver such warrant to the sheriff of the county in which such judgment of conviction was had, to be by him delivered to the said Director of the Department of Corrections, together with the condemned person if he or she has not previously been so delivered.

Taken to Department of Corrections

Immediately upon the receipt of such warrant, the sheriff shall transport such condemned person to the Director of the Department of Corrections, if he or she has not already been so delivered, and shall deliver him or her and the warrant aforesaid into the hands of the Director of the Department of Corrections and shall take from the Director of the Department of Corrections his receipt for such person and such warrant, which receipt the sheriff shall return to the office of the clerk of the court where the judgment of death was rendered. For his services, the sheriff shall be entitled to the same compensation as is now allowed by law to sheriffs for removing or conveying prisoners under the provisions of Section 4 of Article 1029 or 1030 of the Code of Criminal Procedure of 1925, as amended.

Upon the receipt of such condemned person by the Director of the Department of Corrections, the condemned person shall be confined therein until the time for his or her execution arrives, and while so confined, all persons outside of said prison shall be denied access to him or her, except his or her physician, lawyer, and clergyperson, who shall be admitted to see him or her when necessary for his or her health or for the transaction of business,

and the relatives and friends of the condemned person, who shall be admitted to see and converse with him or her at all proper times, under such reasonable rules and regulations as may be made by the Board of Directors of the Department of Corrections.

Executioner

The Director of the Texas Department of Corrections shall designate an executioner to carry out the death penalty provided by law.

Place of Execution

The execution shall take place at a location designated by the Texas Department of Corrections in a room arranged for that purpose.

Present at Execution

The following persons may be present at the execution: the executioner, and such persons as may be necessary to assist him in conducting the execution; the Board of Directors of the Department of Corrections; two physicians, including the prison physician; the spiritual advisor of the condemned; the chaplains of the Department of Corrections; the county judge and sheriff of the county in which the Department of Corrections is situated; and any of the relatives or friends of the condemned person that he or she may request, not exceeding five in number, shall be admitted. No convict shall be permitted by the prison authorities to witness the execution.

Body of Convict

The body of a convict who has been legally executed shall be embalmed immediately and so directed by the Director of the Department of Corrections. If the body is not demanded or requested by a relative or bona fide friend within forty-eight hours after execution then it shall be delivered to the Anatomical Board of the State of Texas, if requested by the Board. If the body is requested by a relative, bona fide friend, or the Anatomical Board of the State of Texas, such recipient shall pay a fee not to exceed twenty-five dollars to the mortician for his or her services in embalming the body for which the mortician shall issue to the recipient a written receipt. When such receipt is delivered to the Director of the Department of Corrections, the body of the deceased shall be delivered to the party named in the receipt or his or her authorized agent. If the body is not delivered to a relative, bona fide friend, or the Anatomical Board of the State of Texas, the Director of the Department of Corrections shall cause the body to be decently buried, and the fee for embalming shall be paid by the county in which the indictment which resulted in conviction was found.

Source: Excerpted from Texas Code of Criminal Procedure, Chapter 43, Articles 43.15–43.26.

(61 percent) would choose a punishment other than the death penalty for murder, including life with no possibility of parole and with restitution to the victims' family (39 percent), life with no possibility of parole (13 percent), or life with the possibility of parole (9 percent).[37]

The men in the red jumpsuits—dead men walking! I don't judge them, I don't disrespect them, I just protect them from other inmates and themselves. I work on death row and have for a lot of years. Death row inmates sleep in cell blocks which consist of 16 individual cells with solid electronic steel doors. Some talk to everybody all the time, some don't talk to anyone, and others act as if they have multiple personalities. If they aren't talking, they're playing cards or checkers or doing push-ups. They get outside two times a day to exercise. Law says they can't work.

Some act like they are your buddies, and some act as if they can't stand you. For the most part, the ones that act like your buddy are usually trying to get you to do something for them. As a group, they are very manipulative in every exchange they have with everyone, including each other.

Most of the inmates say they are innocent. A few say they actually committed the crime, and others say they were framed.

I know a lot about most of their cases and it seems to me that they belong here—on death row. But a few of the cases seem questionable. That's a private thought, and I don't let it change the way I deal with these offenders in red jumpsuits.

John Juehrs
Correctional Officer
Death Row
Central Prison
Raleigh, North Carolina

Similar shifts are taking place in the judicial and political arenas. Jurors and judges are now imposing fewer death penalties. As mentioned earlier, the number of persons sentenced to die dropped by two-thirds in the past decade, from 315 in 1996 to 112 in 2009.

Professional organizations and the judiciary are also weighing in on the question of capital punishment. The American Medical Association's Code of Ethics prohibits physicians from participating in a lethal injection and recently, the 40,000-member American Board of Anesthesiologists decided to revoke the certification of any member who participates in executing a prisoner by lethal injection. Mark Rockoff, the board's secretary said, "We are healers, not executioners."[38]

In 1997, the American Bar Association called for a death penalty moratorium until jurisdictions implement policies and procedures that ensure that death penalty cases are administered fairly and impartially, in accordance with due process, and with minimum risk of executing innocent people. The ABA reiterated that call in 2000 and again in 2003. And a survey of the world's leading criminologists published in 2009 that asked their expert opinions on whether the empirical research supports the contention that the death penalty is a superior deterrent concluded that the death penalty does not add deterrent effects above those already achieved by long-term imprisonment.[39]

Voices from the bench are also speaking out. In rare public statements, four past and present U.S. Supreme Court Justices have spoken out against the death penalty. "If statistics are any indication," said former U.S. Supreme Court Justice Sandra Day O'Connor, "the system may well be allowing some innocent defendants to be executed." She suggested that "perhaps it's time to look at minimum standards for appointed counsel in death cases and adequate compensation for appointed counsel when they are used."[40] Justice Ruth Bader Ginsburg added that she has "yet to see a death penalty case among the dozens coming to the Supreme Court on eve-of-execution stay applications in which the defendant was well-represented at trial" and that "people who are well represented at trial do not get the death penalty."[41] In 1994, when the U.S. Supreme Court denied review in the Texas death penalty case of Bruce Edwin Callins, Justice Harry A. Blackmun wrote in his dissent opinion, "From this day forward, I no longer shall tinker with the machinery of death. For more than 20 years I have endeavored to develop rules that would lend more than the mere appearance of fairness to the death penalty endeavor. Rather than continue

Six months after President Gerald Ford appointed John Paul Stevens to the U.S. Supreme Court, he joined the conservative majority of Justices and allowed the use of the death penalty in the United States. He wrote it is possible to ensure "evenhanded, rational and consistent imposition of death sentences under law" with careful and narrow use. Thirty-two years later, Justice Stevens reversed course. He said personnel changes on the court, coupled with "regrettable judicial activism," had created a system of capital punishment that is shot through with racism, skewed toward conviction, infected with politics, tinged with hysteria, hopelessly flawed, and unconstitutional. If you were a U.S. Supreme Court Justice, what would you say?

EXHIBIT 15–9 | **Arguments Favoring and Opposing the Death Penalty**

PRO

- It deters people from crime through fear of punishment; it exerts a positive moral influence by stigmatizing crimes of murder and manslaughter.
- It is a just punishment for murder; it fulfills the "just deserts" principle of a fitting punishment; life in prison is not a tough enough punishment for a capital crime.
- It is constitutionally appropriate; the Eighth Amendment prohibits cruel and unusual punishment, yet the Fifth Amendment implies that, with due process of law, one may be deprived of life, liberty, or property.
- It reduces time spent on death row to reduce costs of capital punishment and the attendant costs of postconviction appeals, investigations, and searches for new evidence and witnesses.
- It protects society from the most serious and feared offenders; it prevents the reoccurrence of violence.
- It is more humane than life imprisonment because it is quick; making the prisoner suffer by remaining in prison for the rest of his or her life is more torturous and inhumane than execution.
- It is almost impossible for an innocent person to be executed; the slow execution rate results from the process of appeals, from sentencing to execution.

CON

- It does not deter crime; no evidence exists that the death penalty is more effective than other punishments.
- It violates human rights; it is a barbaric remnant of an uncivilized society; it is immoral in principle; and it ensures the execution of some innocent people.
- It falls disproportionately on racial minorities; those who murdered whites are more likely to be sentenced to death than are those who murdered blacks.
- It costs too much; $2 million to $5 million are poured into each execution while other criminal justice components such as police, courts, and community corrections lack funding.
- It boosts the murder rate; this is known as the *brutalizing effect;* the state is a role model, and when the state carries out an execution, it shows that killing is a way to solve problems.
- Not everyone wants vengeance; many people favor alternative sentences such as life without parole.
- It is arbitrary and unfair; offenders who commit similar crimes under similar circumstances receive widely differing sentences; race, social and economic status, location of crime, and pure chance influence sentencing.

to coddle the court's delusions that the desired level of fairness has been achieved, I feel obligated simply to concede that the death penalty experiment has failed."[42]

In 1976, just six months after being appointed to the U.S. Supreme Court by President Gerald Ford, Justice John Paul Stevens voted to reinstate capital punishment. He did not join the most liberal Justices at the time—William Brennan and Thurgood Marshall—who insisted that any execution violated the Eighth Amendment ban on cruel and unusual punishment. Instead, he joined the conservative majority and wrote that it is possible to ensure "evenhanded, rational and consistent imposition of death sentences under law." Thirty-two years and 1,100 executions later, Justice Stevens reversed course and said the death penalty is hopelessly flawed and unconstitutional. He framed the question this way: It's not whether you believe in a death penalty, it's whether you believe in *this* death penalty, the one the U.S. is currently using. He wrote that personnel changes on the

Court, coupled with "regrettable judicial activism," had created a system of capital punishment that is shot with racism, skewed toward conviction, infected with politics, and tinged with hysteria. He added, "That the murder of black victims is treated as less culpable than the murder of white victims provides a haunting reminder of once-prevalent Southern lynchings." Justice Stevens said that he and the other Justices voted to continue capital punishment in 1976, arguing for a careful and narrow use of capital punishment, but since then, the Supreme Court has made its use increasingly less careful and less narrow. He also commented on the unreliability of capital punishment, pointing out that more than 130 people have been exonerated and released from death row since 1973.[43]

There are many arguments favoring capital punishment and many arguments opposing it. Some of the arguments—pro and con—are summarized in Exhibit 15–9. Where do you stand?

THE COURTS AND THE DEATH PENALTY

"Death is different [from other punishments]," said U.S. Supreme Court Justice William Brennan. For that reason, every phase of a capital crime proceeding, from jury selection to sentencing instructions, has been influenced by court rulings. The legal history of today's death penalty can be traced through several landmark cases. In the June 29, 1972, decision in *Furman* v. *Georgia*,[44] the U.S. Supreme Court ruled by a vote of five to four that the death penalty, as imposed and carried out under the laws of Georgia, was cruel and unusual punishment in violation of the Eighth and Fourteenth Amendments. According to the Court, Georgia's death penalty statute gave the sentencing authority (judge or trial jury) complete freedom to impose a death or life imprisonment sentence without standards or guidelines; the death penalty had been imposed arbitrarily, discriminatorily, and selectively against minorities. The Supreme Court voided 40 death penalty statutes, thereby commuting the death sentences of all 629 death row inmates around the United States, and suspended the death penalty because existing statutes were no longer valid. It is important to note that the Court majority did *not* rule that the death penalty itself was unconstitutional but that only the way in which it was administered at that time.

States responded to the *Furman* decision by rewriting their capital punishment statutes to limit discretion and avoid arbitrary and inconsistent results. The new death penalty laws took two forms. Some states imposed a **mandatory death penalty** for certain crimes, and others permitted **guided discretion,** which sets standards for judges and juries to use when deciding whether to impose the death penalty.

In 1976, the U.S. Supreme Court rejected mandatory death penalty statutes in *Woodson* v. *North Carolina* and *Roberts* v. *Louisiana,* but it approved guided discretion statutes in *Gregg* v. *Georgia* and two companion cases.[45]

In *Gregg,* the Court approved automatic appellate review, a proportionality review whereby state appellate courts compare a sentence with those of similar cases, and a **bifurcated trial,** or special two-part trial. The first part of a bifurcated trial, the *guilt phase,* decides the issue of guilt. If the defendant is found guilty, the second part of the trial, the *penalty phase,* takes place. The penalty phase includes presentation of facts that mitigate or aggravate the circumstances of the crime. **Mitigating circumstances** are factors that may reduce the culpability of the offender (make the defendant less deserving of the death penalty). **Aggravating circumstances** are factors that may increase the offender's culpability (make the defendant more

mandatory death penalty

A death sentence that the legislature has required to be imposed upon people convicted of certain offenses.

guided discretion

Decision making bounded by general guidelines, rules, or laws.

bifurcated trial

Two separate hearings for different issues in a trial, one for guilt and the other for punishment.

mitigating circumstances

Factors that, although not justifying or excusing an action, may reduce the culpability of the offender.

aggravating circumstances

Factors that may increase the culpability of the offender.

EXHIBIT 15–10   The Florida Death Penalty Statute

921.141 Sentence of death or life imprisonment for capital felonies; further proceedings to determine sentence.

(1) SEPARATE PROCEEDINGS ON ISSUE OF PENALTY. Upon conviction or adjudication of guilt of a defendant of a capital felony, the court shall conduct a separate sentencing proceeding to determine whether the defendant should be sentenced to death or life imprisonment as authorized by s. 775.082. The proceeding shall be conducted by the trial judge before the trial jury as soon as practicable. If, through impossibility or inability, the trial jury is unable to reconvene for a hearing on the issue of penalty, having determined the guilt of the accused, the trial judge may summon a special juror or jurors as provided in chapter 913 to determine the issue of the imposition of the penalty. If the trial jury has been waived or if the defendant pleaded guilty, the sentencing proceeding shall be conducted before a jury impaneled for that purpose, unless waived by the defendant. In the proceeding, evidence may be presented as to any matter that the court deems relevant to the nature of the crime and the character of the defendant and shall include matters relating to any of the aggravating or mitigating circumstances enumerated in subsections (5) and (6). Any such evidence that the court deems to have probative value may be received, regardless of its admissibility under the exclusionary rules of evidence, provided the defendant is accorded a fair opportunity to rebut any hearsay statements. However, this subsection shall not be construed to authorize the introduction of any evidence secured in violation of the Constitution of the United States or the Constitution of the State of Florida. The state and the defendant or his counsel shall be permitted to present argument for or against sentence of death.

(2) ADVISORY SENTENCE BY THE JURY. After hearing all the evidence, the jury shall deliberate and render an advisory sentence to the court, based upon the following matters:

(a) whether sufficient aggravating circumstances exist as enumerated in subsection (5);

(b) whether sufficient mitigating circumstances exist that outweigh the aggravating circumstances found to exist; and

(c) based on these considerations, whether the defendant should be sentenced to life imprisonment or death.

(3) FINDINGS IN SUPPORT OF SENTENCE OF DEATH. Notwithstanding the recommendation of a majority of the jury, the court, after weighing the aggravating and mitigating circumstances, shall enter a sentence of life imprisonment or death, but if the court imposes a sentence of death, it shall set forth in writing its findings upon which the sentence of death is based as to the facts:

(a) that sufficient aggravating circumstances exist as enumerated in subsection (5), and

(b) that there are insufficient mitigating circumstances to outweigh the aggravating circumstances.

In each case in which the court imposes the death sentence, the determination of the court shall be supported by specific written findings of fact based upon the circumstances in subsections (5) and (6) and upon the records of the trial and the sentencing proceedings. If the court does not make the findings requiring the death sentence, the court shall impose sentence of life imprisonment in accordance with s. 775.082.

(4) REVIEW OF JUDGMENT AND SENTENCE. The judgment of conviction and sentence of death shall be subject to automatic review by the Supreme Court of Florida within 60 days after certification by the sentencing court of the entire record, unless the time is extended for an additional period not to exceed 30 days by the Supreme Court for good cause shown. Such review by the Supreme Court shall have priority over all other cases and shall be heard in accordance with rules promulgated by the Supreme Court.

(5) AGGRAVATING CIRCUMSTANCES. Aggravating circumstances shall be limited to the following:

(a) The capital felony was committed by a person under sentence of imprisonment or placed on community control.

(b) The defendant was previously convicted of another capital felony or of a felony involving the use or threat of violence to the person.

(c) The defendant knowingly created a great risk of death to many people.

(d) The capital felony was committed while the defendant was engaged, or was an accomplice, in the commission of, or an attempt to commit, or flight after committing or attempting to commit, any robbery, sexual battery, arson, burglary, kidnapping, or aircraft piracy or the unlawful throwing, placing, or discharging of a destructive device or bomb.

(e) The capital felony was committed for the purpose of avoiding or preventing a lawful arrest or effecting an escape from custody.

(f) The capital felony was committed for pecuniary gain.

(g) The capital felony was committed to disrupt or hinder the lawful exercise of any governmental function or the enforcement of laws.

(h) The capital felony was especially heinous, atrocious, or cruel.

(i) The capital felony was a homicide and was committed in a cold, calculated, and premeditated manner without any pretense of moral or legal justification.

(j) The victim of the capital felony was a law enforcement officer engaged in the performance of his official duties.

(k) The victim of the capital felony was an elected or appointed public official engaged in the performance of his official duties if the motive for the capital felony was related, in whole or in part, to the victim's official capacity.

EXHIBIT 15–10 **The Florida Death Penalty Statute** *(continued)*

(6) MITIGATING CIRCUMSTANCES. Mitigating circumstances shall be the following:

(a) The defendant has no significant history of prior criminal activity.

(b) The capital felony was committed while the defendant was under the influence of extreme mental or emotional disturbance.

(c) The victim was a participant in the defendant's conduct or consented to the act.

(d) The defendant was an accomplice in the capital felony committed by another person and his participation was relatively minor.

(e) The defendant acted under extreme duress or under the substantial domination of another person.

(f) The capacity of the defendant to appreciate the criminality of his conduct or to conform his conduct to the requirements of law was substantially impaired.

(g) The age of the defendant at the time of the crime.

(7) VICTIM IMPACT EVIDENCE. Once the prosecution has provided evidence of the existence of one or more aggravating circumstances as described in subsection (5), the prosecution may introduce, and subsequently argue, victim impact evidence. Such evidence shall be designed to demonstrate the victim's uniqueness as an individual human being and the resultant loss to the community's members by the victim's death. Characterizations and opinions about the crime, the defendant, and the appropriate sentence shall not be permitted as a part of victim impact evidence.

(8) APPLICABILITY. This section does not apply to a person convicted or adjudicated guilty of a capital drug trafficking felony under s. 893.135.

Source: Florida Statute 921.141.

deserving of death). Florida's death penalty statute, including its list of mitigating and aggravating circumstances (subsections 5 and 6), is shown in Exhibit 15–10.

In 2002, the U.S. Supreme Court handed down another decision that shaped capital sentencing. In *Ring* v. *Arizona*,[46] the Court held that only juries, not judges, can determine the presence of "aggravating factors" to be weighed in the capital sentencing process. Although judges may still reduce sentences, the Court held that a defendant may not receive a penalty that exceeds the maximum penalty that he or she would have received if punished according to the facts in the jury verdict. Two years later in *Schriro* v. *Summerlin*,[47] the U.S. Supreme Court determined that its 2002 decision in *Ring* v. *Arizona* was not retroactive, thereby denying new sentencing hearings for dozens of death row inmates in Arizona, Idaho, Montana, and Nebraska whose sentences were originally handed down by judges. With their decision in *Summerlin*, the Justices decided that their original decision in *Ring* was a procedural rule and thus was not retroactive.

Appealing the Death Penalty

Death penalty cases may pass through as many as 10 courts across 3 stages: trial and direct review, state postconviction appeals, and federal *habeas corpus* appeals (see Exhibit 15–11).

In stage one, trial and direct review, a death sentence is imposed. As a consequence of the *Furman* decision, the laws of all states require that legal issues about the trial and sentence automatically be appealed to the state appellate courts. Alabama and Ohio have two rounds of appeals in the direct review process; this means that the legal issues may be heard first in the state court of criminal appeals (court 1) before reaching the state supreme court (court 2). These courts evaluate the trial for legal or constitutional errors and determine whether the death sentence is consistent with sentences imposed in similar cases. State appellate courts seldom overturn a conviction or change a death sentence. The defendant then

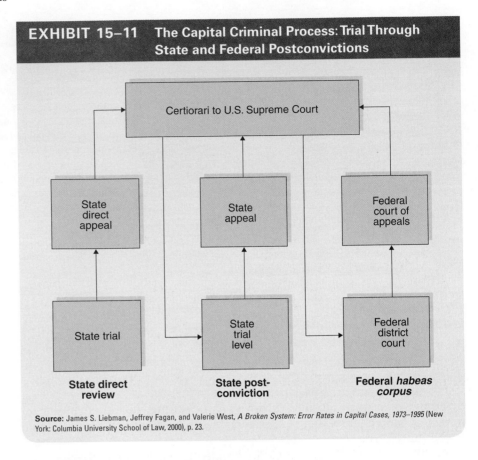

EXHIBIT 15–11   The Capital Criminal Process: Trial Through State and Federal Postconvictions

Certiorari to U.S. Supreme Court

State direct appeal

State appeal

Federal court of appeals

State trial

State trial level

Federal district court

State direct review

State postconviction

Federal *habeas corpus*

Source: James S. Liebman, Jeffrey Fagan, and Valerie West, *A Broken System: Error Rates in Capital Cases, 1973–1995* (New York: Columbia University School of Law, 2000), p. 23.

serious error

Error that substantially undermines the reliability of the guilt finding or death sentence imposed at trial.

petitions the U.S. Supreme Court (court 3) to grant a petition for a writ of *certiorari*—a written order to the lower court whose decision is being appealed to send the records of the case forward for review. Stage one, direct review, consumes about five years—half of the time required for the entire appeals process. Nationally, the rate of **serious error** (error that substantially undermines the reliability of the guilt finding or death sentence imposed at trial) discovered on direct review is 41 percent. States with the highest rate of serious error found on direct review are Wyoming (67 percent), Mississippi (61 percent), North Carolina (61 percent), Alabama (55 percent), and South Carolina (54 percent).[48]

If the defendant's direct appeals are unsuccessful and the Supreme Court denies review, stage two—state postconviction appeals—begins. At this point, many death row inmates allege ineffective or incompetent trial counsel, and new counsel is engaged or appointed. The new counsel petitions the trial court (court 4) with newly discovered evidence; questions about the fairness of the trial; and allegations of jury bias, tainted evidence, incompetence of defense counsel, and prosecutorial or police misconduct. If the trial court denies the appeals, they may be filed with the state's appellate courts (either directly to the state supreme court or, if there exists a dual level of appellate review, through a petition first to the state court of criminal appeals (court 5) followed by a petition to the state supreme court (court 6). Most often, the state appellate courts deny the petition. Defendant's counsel then petitions the U.S. Supreme Court (court 7). If the U.S. Supreme Court denies the petition for a writ of *certiorari*, stage two ends and stage three begins. The rate of serious error found on state postconviction appeals is 10 percent. State postconviction reversals are highest in Maryland (52 percent), Wyoming (33 percent), Indiana (25 percent), Utah (23 percent), and Mississippi (20 percent).

In stage three, the federal *habeas corpus* stage, a defendant files a petition in U.S. district court (court 8) in the state in which the defendant was convicted and is incarcerated and alleging violations of constitutional rights. Such rights include the right to due process (Fourteenth Amendment), prohibition against cruel and unusual punishment (Eighth Amendment), and effective assistance of counsel (Sixth Amendment). If the district court denies the petition, defense counsel submits it to the U.S. court of appeals (court 9) for the circuit representing the jurisdiction. If the court of appeals denies the petition, defense counsel asks the U.S. Supreme Court (court 10) to grant a writ of *certiorari*. If the U.S. Supreme Court denies *certiorari*, the office of the state attorney general asks the state supreme court to set a date for execution. Federal courts find serious error in 40 percent of the capital cases they review. The highest rate of serious error is found in California (80 percent), Montana (75 percent), Mississippi (71 percent), Idaho (67 percent), and Georgia (65 percent). The Eleventh Circuit—the nation's most active capital appeals circuit with jurisdiction over Alabama, Georgia, and Florida—finds serious error in 50 percent of the death cases it reviews.

In 1996, in an effort to reduce the time people spend on death row and the number of federal appeals, the U.S. Congress passed the Antiterrorism and Effective Death Penalty Act (AEDPA). The AEDPA defines filing deadlines and limits reasons for second, or successive, federal appellate reviews to (1) new constitutional law, (2) new evidence that could not have been discovered at the time of the original trial, or (3) new facts that, if proven, would be sufficient to establish the applicant's innocence. Under the AEDPA, if the U.S. Supreme Court denies the petition for a writ of *certiorari* in the final federal *habeas corpus* appeal, defense counsel may once again petition the federal courts; however, before a second, or successive, application for a writ of *habeas corpus* may be filed in a U.S. district court, defense counsel must petition the appropriate U.S. court of appeals for an order authorizing the district court to consider the application. The petition to the U.S. court of appeals is decided by a three-judge panel; the panel must grant or deny the authorization to file the second, or successive, application within 30 days after the petition is filed. If the panel approves the petition, the district court must render a decision regarding the application within 180 days. If the motion is appealed to the court of appeals representing the jurisdiction, the court must render its decision within 120 days. If the petition is filed with the U.S. Supreme Court, the Court may grant the petition for *certiorari* or let the lower court's decision stand.

DEATH PENALTY ISSUES IN THE 21ST CENTURY

Of all the reforms that capital punishment has gone through since *Furman*, perhaps none has been as significant as those that have occurred in the 21st century. We have already discussed how the cost of capital punishment, the current budget crisis, and the shortage of sodium thiopental are shaping the debate on capital punishment. We add three more issues for you to consider: wrongful convictions, the banning of executions of offenders who have mental retardation, and juveniles.

Wrongful Convictions: The Liebman Study

According to some scholars, Americans seem to be of two minds about the death penalty. One is the fear that capital trials put people on death row who do not belong there. The other is that capital appeals take too

On Friday, January 19, 2003, former Illinois death row inmate LeRoy Orange was pardoned by Governor George Ryan after spending 19 years on death row for a crime he did not commit. Since 1983, 138 persons have been released from death row, and news of their innocence has set off a new debate over capital punishment in the United States. How has the Liebman report shaped the debate?

long. The two sides are not as oppositional as it might appear, however. It may be that capital sentences spend too much time under appellate review and they are fraught with unacceptable levels of error. At least that is the conclusion of one of the most controversial studies of appellate reviews of capital sentences ever undertaken in the United States, known as the *Liebman study.*

Possibly because four times as many people had their death sentences overturned or received clemency than were executed since 1977, the Judiciary Committee of the U.S. Senate asked Columbia law professor James Liebman to calculate the frequency of error in capital cases.[49] Liebman and his colleagues studied 4,578 appeals between 1973 and 1995. Their conclusion is powerful: The overall rate of prejudicial error in the U.S. capital punishment system is 68 percent. More than two of every three capital judgments reviewed by the courts during the 23-year study period were found to be seriously flawed. Ten states (Alabama, Arizona, California, Georgia, Indiana, Maryland, Mississippi, Montana, Oklahoma, and Wyoming) have overall error rates of 75 percent or higher. Almost 1,000 of the cases sent back for retrial ended in sentences less than death, and 87 ended in *not guilty* verdicts.

Liebman and his colleagues found two types of serious error. The first is incompetent defense lawyering (accounting for one-third of all state postconviction appeals). The second is prosecutorial suppression of evidence that the defendant is innocent or does not deserve the death penalty (accounting for almost 20 percent). When the errors were corrected through the stages already discussed, 8 of 10 people on retrial were found to deserve a sentence less than death and 7 percent were found innocent of the capital crime. Exhibit 15–12 shows the flow of 100 death sentences imposed and reviewed between 1973 and 1995. It shows that for every 100 death sentences imposed, 41 were turned back at the trial and direct review phase because of serious error. Of the 59 that passed to the state postconviction stage, 10 percent—6 of the original 100—were turned back due to serious flaws. Of the 53 that passed to the next stage of federal *habeas corpus,* 40 percent—an additional 21 of the original 100—were turned back because of serious error. Together, 68 of the original 100 were thrown out after 9 to 10 years had passed because of serious flaws. Of the 68 individuals whose death sentences were overturned for serious

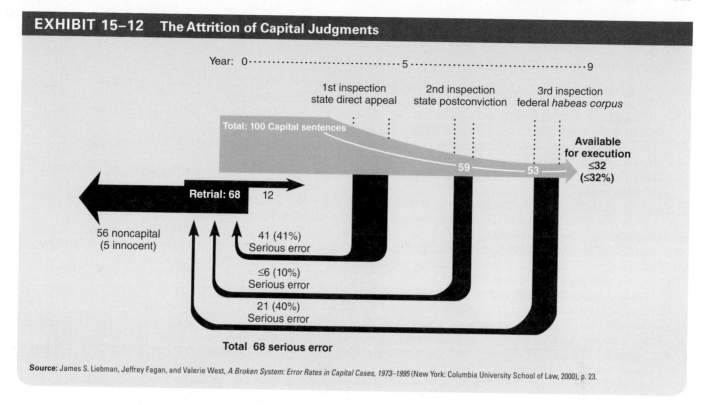

EXHIBIT 15–12   **The Attrition of Capital Judgments**

Year: 0 ·· 5 ·· 9

1st inspection
state direct appeal

2nd inspection
state postconviction

3rd inspection
federal *habeas corpus*

Total: 100 Capital sentences

Available
for execution
≤32
(≤32%)

59 ——— 53 ——→

Retrial: 68   12

56 noncapital
(5 innocent)

41 (41%)
Serious error

≤6 (10%)
Serious error

21 (40%)
Serious error

Total 68 serious error

Source: James S. Liebman, Jeffrey Fagan, and Valerie West, *A Broken System: Error Rates in Capital Cases, 1973–1995* (New York: Columbia University School of Law, 2000), p. 23.

error, 82 percent (56) were found on retrial not to deserve the death penalty, including 5 who were found innocent of the offense. Each one had spent an average of nine years and two months on death row.

What if a death sentence is imposed today in the United States? What could the defendant, relative, lawyer, or judge expect? Liebman and his colleagues answer this way: "The capital conviction or sentence will probably be overturned due to serious error. It'll take 9 or 10 years to find out, given how many other capital cases being reviewed for likely error are lined up ahead of this one. If the judgment is overturned, a lesser conviction or sentence will probably be imposed."[50]

If death sentences are not reliable and persons are wrongfully convicted and sentenced, the error has serious consequences for the wrongly convicted, for the family of the victim whose search for justice is incomplete, for the family of the person wrongly convicted in terms of the prolonged and distorted grief they suffer, for subsequent victims of the real offender still at large, and for the public in terms of lost confidence in the criminal justice system. A report in the *Chicago Tribune* on October 26, 2003, revealed that police and prosecutors rarely pursue new leads and suspects after a wrongly convicted defendant has been released from death row.[51] The actual perpetrators remain in society to commit additional crimes, and many death row exonerees remain under a cloud of police suspicion because law enforcement failed to find the true offender.

Another consequence of wrongful convictions not often discussed is the cost of serious errors. On January 25, 2005, a federal jury in Chicago found two FBI agents liable for framing Steve Manning, former Chicago police officer and awarded Manning $6.6 million.[52] Jurors said the FBI agents induced witnesses to make false statements against Manning in the murder investigation of trucking firm owner James Pellegrino. Manning was convicted of the murder and sent to Illinois' death row in 1993. In 2000, he was exonerated and released from death row. Eddie Lowery

---

EXHIBIT 15–13 | **When Justice Fails: Exonerated Compensation by State**

Compensation by State

- Alabama has a minimum of $50,000 for each year of wrongful incarceration.
- California has a maximum of $100 per day (or $36,500 per year) for wrongful incarceration.
- Connecticut bases compensation on claims for loss of liberty, loss of earning capacity, physical and mental pain, attorney's fees, and other expenses related to such person's wrongful conviction.
- The District of Columbia asks the court to determine what amount fairly and reasonably compensates the exonerated person.
- Florida provides for $50,000 annually for wrongful incarceration with a maximum of $2 million.
- Illinois allows for $85,350 for those who served up to 5 years, $170,000 for those who served between 5 and 14 years, and $199,150 for those who served more than 14 years.
- Iowa provides $50 per day (or $18,250 per year) of wrongful incarceration plus lost wages up to $25,000 a year plus attorney's fees.
- Louisiana provides $15,000 per year of wrongful incarceration with a maximum of $150,000.
- Maine has a maximum of $300,000.
- Maryland's Board of Public Works determines compensation packages for pardoned persons who were wrongfully convicted and may grant a reasonable amount for any financial or other appropriate counseling for the individual.
- Massachusetts has a maximum of $500,000.
- Mississippi allows $50,000 for each year of wrongful incarceration with a maximum of $500,000.
- Missouri provides $50 per day (or $18,250 per year) of postconviction confinement.
- Nebraska allows $25,000 per year with a maximum of $500,000.
- New Hampshire provides a maximum of $20,000 for the entirety of the wrongful incarceration.
- New Jersey allows twice the amount of the exoneree's income in the year prior to incarceration or $20,000 per year of incarceration, whichever is greater.
- New York, whose Court of Claims determines what amount will fairly and reasonably compensate the wrongfully convicted person, has no maximum amount.
- North Carolina provides $50,000 for each year of wrongful incarceration with a maximum of $750,000.
- Ohio allows $40,330 per year in addition to lost wages, costs, and attorney's fees.
- Oklahoma provides $175,000 for the entirety of the wrongful incarceration.
- Tennessee has a maximum of $1,000,000 for the entirety of a wrongful incarceration.
- Texas allows $80,000 per year of a wrongful incarceration, as well as $25,000 per year spent on parole or as a registered sex offender, plus an annuity.
- United States (federal) allows $50,000 per year in noncapital cases and $100,000 per year in capital cases.
- Utah provides the monetary equivalent of the nonagricultural payroll wage in the state to a wrongfully convicted person for each year of incarceration up to a maximum of 15 years.
- Vermont gives between $30,000 and $60,000 per year the person was incarcerated if a request is filed within 3 years of exoneration.
- Virginia provides 90% of the Virginia per capita personal income for up to 20 years.
- West Virginia does not specify a maximum amount.
- Wisconsin provides $5,000 for each year in prison with a maximum of $25,000 plus attorney's fees.

Source: Innocence Project, *Making Up For Lost Time: What the Wrongfully Convicted Endure and How to Provide Fair Compensation* (New York: Benjamin N. Cardozo School of Law, Yeshiva University, 2010).

---

received a $7.5 million settlement along with apologies from officials in Riley County, Kansas, where he was arrested in 1981 for the rape of an elderly woman. He served 10 years in prison and registered as a sex offender after he was paroled. In 2003, the original rape kit was sent for DNA testing. It showed that Lowery couldn't have committed the rape. DNA testing pointed to a suspect who is now awaiting trial. Illinois death row inmate Dennis Williams received $13 million from Cook County (Chicago) after he was exonerated. Today, 26 states, the District of Columbia, and the federal government have passed laws that compensate people wrongfully convicted (see Exhibit 15–13). However, research in California shows how difficult it is for the exonerated to receive compensation. Since 2000, 132 people have been released from prison in California after a court declared them factually innocent. California can award $100 a day for each day spent behind bars for a wrongful conviction. Of the 132 claims, 7 were withdrawn, 56 were rejected by the Victim Compensation and Government Claims Board, 14 have a hearing pending, and of the 55 who went to a hearing, 11 were approved for compensation. Critics charge that exonerees are asked to prove things far beyond what is reasonable. For example, one exoneree who had been declared factually innocent by a Santa Clara County Superior Court judge was told by the three-member board that his claim was rejected because the victim of the robbery still believed he was guilty. The claimant filed a civil lawsuit and was eventually awarded $1 million, not from the Victim Compensation and Government Claims Board, but from Santa Clara county.[53] Nobody knows the exact amount that has been paid out, but it is reasonable to believe that prejudicial error is costly. It includes money lost on education, health and human services, community protection, and economic growth and development.

How can we reduce serious capital error? Liebman identifies two options. The first is to end the death penalty entirely. The second is to curb the scope of the death penalty to reach only the small number of offenses on which there is broad social consensus that only the death penalty will serve. The reforms he suggests follow:[54]

1. Require proof beyond any doubt that the defendant committed the capital crime.
2. Require that aggravating factors substantially outweigh mitigating ones before a death sentence may be imposed.
3. Bar the death penalty for people with extenuating circumstances such as juveniles.
4. Make life imprisonment without parole an alternative to the death penalty and clearly inform juries of the option.
5. Abolish judge overrides of jury verdicts imposing life sentences.
6. Use comparative review of murder sentences to identify what counts as the "worst of the worst."
7. Base charging decisions in potentially capital cases on full and informed deliberations.
8. Make all police and prosecution evidence bearing on guilt versus evidence and on aggravation versus mitigation available to the jury at trial.
9. Insulate capital sentencing and appellate judges from political pressure.
10. Identify, appoint, and compensate capital defense counsel in ways that attract an adequate number of well-qualified lawyers to do the work.

Today 10 states require videotaping of at least some interrogations such as those in crimes that carry the death penalty, and seven state supreme courts have required or strongly encouraged recording.[55]

Banning the Juvenile Death Penalty

The first recognized juvenile execution in the United States occurred in 1642 when Thomas Graunger was hanged in Plymouth, Massachusetts, for committing the crime of buggery (having sex with an animal) when he was 16 years old.[56] Since then, the United States has executed 365 people for offenses they committed when children. In the current era of capital punishment (1976 through March 2, 2005), 22 people were executed for offenses they committed as juveniles.[57] The last was Scott Allen Hain on April 3, 2003, by lethal injection in Oklahoma. Four months after his 17th birthday, Hain and an accomplice committed murder. He was sentenced to die in May 1988.

On March 2, 2005, Christopher Simmons's case led the U.S. Supreme Court to bar the execution of juveniles for crimes they committed before turning age 18 as cruel and unusual punishment prohibited by the Eighth Amendment. Simmons and 71 others on death row will wind up receiving life sentences. What were the court's rationales in deciding Atkins and Simmons?

The U.S. Supreme Court first addressed the constitutionality of applying the death penalty to juvenile offenders in 1988 in *Thompson* v. *Oklahoma*.[58] The Court ruled in a 5–4 opinion that it was unconstitutional to sentence a 15-year-old to death. The following year, in *Stanford* v. *Kentucky*[59] and *Wilkins* v. *Missouri*,[60] the Court held that the Eighth Amendment's prohibition against cruel and unusual punishment did not forbid imposition of the death penalty for crimes committed by people at 16 and 17 years of age. Justice Antonin Scalia's majority opinion reasoned that, because a majority of the 37 states that had death penalty statutes at the time allowed capital punishment for juveniles, the practice did not violate evolving standards of decency.

However on March 2, 2005, the U.S. Supreme Court, by a narrow 5–4 vote in *Roper* v. *Simmons*,[61] reversed itself and said that it was unconstitutional and in violation of the Eighth Amendment's ban on cruel and unusual punishment to execute people for crimes they committed before turning age 18. The Court's ruling vacated the death sentences of 72 people on death rows across the United States. Most of these offenders will wind up with life sentences, many without parole.

In deciding *Roper* v. *Simmons*, the justices reasoned several things. First, since their 1987 decisions in *Stanford* v. *Kentucky* and *Wilkins* v. *Missouri*, 5 states had banned capital punishment for juveniles, making the practice illegal in 30 states. The justices said that the trend toward banning capital punishment for juveniles reflected "evolving standards of decency that mark the progress of a maturing society."

Second, the justices cited scientific literature from the American Academy of Child and Adolescent Psychiatry, the American Medical Association, and the American Psychological Association showing that adolescents lack mature judgment, are less aware of the consequences of their decisions and actions, are more vulnerable than adults to peer pressure, and have a greater tendency toward impulsiveness and lesser reasoning skills, regardless of how big they are or how tough they talk. Or, as one person put it, "They may look like, talk like, act like and even shoot like adults, but they think like kids. . ... Juveniles are not the same as adults even though the crimes might be the same."[62]

Third, the justices cited overseas legal practices and pointed out that the death penalty for juvenile offenders has become a uniquely American practice. The death penalty for juveniles has been abandoned by nations everywhere else in large part due to the express provisions of the United Nations Convention on the Rights of the Child and of several other international treaties and agreements. Since 1990, juvenile offenders are known to have been executed in only eight countries: China, Democratic Republic of Congo, Iran, Nigeria, Pakistan, Yemen, Saudi Arabia, and the United States. The justices said that the United States' practice of executing juvenile criminals was out of line with other developed countries.

Banning the Execution of People with Mental Retardation

In 1989, the U.S. Supreme Court held that executing people with mental retardation was not a violation of the Eighth Amendment. But on June 19, 2002, the Court held in *Atkins* v. *Virginia* that execution of offenders with mental retardation is cruel and unusual punishment prohibited by the Eighth Amendment. The Court argued that a national consensus has developed against executing this group of people. At that time, 12 states banned executions altogether. However, beginning in 1988 Arizona, Arkansas,

Colorado, Connecticut, Florida, Georgia, Indiana, Kansas, Kentucky, Maryland, Missouri, Nebraska, New Mexico, New York, North Carolina, South Dakota, Tennessee, Washington, and the federal government passed statutes banning the execution of offenders with mental retardation. The Court argued that it was not so much the number of states that had passed similar statutes but the consistency of the direction of change. In the words of the Court, "Given the well-known fact that anticrime legislation is far more popular than legislation providing protections for persons guilty of violent crime, the large number of states prohibiting the execution of people with mental retardation (and the complete absence of states passing legislation reinstating the power to conduct such executions) provides powerful evidence that today our society views these offenders as categorically less culpable than the average criminal. The evidence carries even greater force when it is noted that the legislatures that have addressed the issue have voted overwhelmingly in favor of the prohibition."[63]

School records and the results of an IQ test confirmed that Daryl Renard Atkins, the Virginia inmate whose case persuaded the U.S. Supreme Court to exclude murderers with mental retardation from executions, had an IQ of 59 (a score of 70 or below is generally considered an indicator of mental retardation). However, in its 2002 ruling, the Supreme Court left it to the states to define mental retardation and returned Atkins's case to the Virginia Supreme Court, which then passed it down to the York County Circuit Court. Virginia's definition of mental retardation requires "significant subaverage intellectual functioning" at the onset of adulthood.

Daryl Atkins, whose case led the U.S. Supreme Court on June 19, 2002, to bar the execution of people with mental retardation as cruel and unusual punishment prohibited by the Eighth Amendment, sits in a York-Poquoson Courtroom in Yorktown, Virginia. In 2008, his sentence was commuted to life in prison. What are the criteria in Virginia to prove mental retardation?

In July 2005, a jury decided that Atkins was intelligent enough to be executed on the basis that the constant contact he had with his lawyers had intellectually stimulated him and raised his IQ above 70, making him competent to be put to death under Virginia law. However, two and one-half years later, evidence of prosecutorial misconduct surfaced that would have stricken the testimony of Atkins' codefendant William Jones. Without Jones' testimony being admissible the judge ruled to commute Atkins sentence to lifes and the Virginia Supreme Court agreed.

The California Supreme Court said that offenders must meet three criteria in order to prove mental retardation: significant subaverage general intellectual functioning, which means an IQ score that is approximately 70 or below; proof of significant deficits in adaptive behavior (everyday functioning); and proof that these deficits arose before age 18. Today 30 of California's almost 650 death row inmates are asking the state Supreme Court to review their cases according to these criteria."[64]

REVIEW AND APPLICATIONS

SUMMARY

1 Capital punishment has been imposed throughout history for crimes ranging from horse stealing and witchcraft to crimes against humanity and murder. Before the 18th century, torture often preceded death. In the 18th century, use of the death penalty diminished as philosophers argued that punishment should fit the crime. After World War I, states reinstated use of the death penalty to deter threats to capitalism, and criminologists argued that capital punishment was a necessary social measure. After World War II, however, sentiment for capital punishment faded, and constitutional challenges surfaced, culminating in the Supreme Court decision of *Furman* v. *Georgia* in 1972.

2   As of February 23, 2011, 1,242 people had been executed in the United States since Gary Gilmore's execution in January 1977. The peak year was 1999, when 98 people were executed. Thirty-eight percent (466) of all executions have taken place in Texas. The South leads the United States with 1,022 executions. Only 1.0 percent of all the people executed since 1977 were female; 56 percent were white, 35 percent black, and 7 percent Hispanic. Today, 3,261 prisoners are on death row. Forty-four percent of the nation's death row population is in three states: California (697), Florida (398), and Texas (337). Ninety-nine percent of all prisoners on death row are male, with whites predominating (56 percent). Inmates executed in 2010 had been on death row an average of 14 years.

3   Among the influences on capital punishment are public opinion; executive, legislative, and judicial changes; and professional organizations. Public opinion continues to support capital punishment with more people choosing life imprisonment as an option. In the wake of the Illinois moratorium on capital punishment in 2000, professional organizations and legislatures across the country are calling for death penalty moratoriums, funding studies of capital punishment, granting death row inmates access to DNA testing, affording extra assistance to lawyers handling capital cases, raising the amount of financial compensation that states provide innocent people found to have been erroneously convicted, allowing prosecutors to seek life without parole instead of the death penalty, and barring the execution of juveniles and offenders with mental retardation.

4   The landmark cases that influenced capital punishment were *Furman* v. *Georgia* (1972), *Gregg* v. *Georgia* (1976), *Ring* v. *Arizona* (2002), *Atkins* v. *Virginia* (2002), and *Roper* v. *Simmons* (2005). In *Furman* v. *Georgia*, the U.S. Supreme Court ruled that capital punishment, as imposed by Georgia, constituted cruel and unusual punishment—Georgia's death penalty statute gave the sentencing authority (judge or trial jury) complete freedom to impose a death sentence without standards or guidelines. As a result of the *Furman* ruling, state death penalty statutes took two forms—mandatory death penalty or sentencing based on guided discretion. In *Woodson* v. *North Carolina* and *Roberts* v. *Louisiana,* the Court rejected mandatory statutes. However, in *Gregg* v. *Georgia,* the Court ruled that Georgia's new guided discretion death penalty legislation was not unconstitutional. In *Ring* v. *Arizona,* the Court held that only juries, not judges, can determine the presence of aggravating factors to be weighed in the capital sentencing process. The Court held that a defendant may not receive a penalty that exceeds the maximum penalty that he or she would have received if punished according to the facts in the jury verdict. In *Atkins* v. *Virginia* (2002) and *Roper* v. *Simmons* (2005), the Court ruled that it was unconstitutional to execute persons with mental retardation or who commit capital crimes before turning age 18.

5   Arguments in favor of the death penalty include the following: It deters rational people from becoming habitual killers; it is "just" punishment for taking someone's life; it is constitutional as long as it is achieved with due process of law; it reduces the amount of time a person spends on death row; it protects society from feared offenders; it is more humane than life imprisonment; and it is almost impossible for an innocent person to be executed. Arguments against the death penalty include the following: It violates human rights; it does not deter violent crime; it is implemented arbitrarily and unfairly; it falls disproportionately on racial minorities; it actually boosts the murder rate by promoting homicides in the months following an execution; not everyone wants vengeance; and it costs too much to support a capital trial, appeals, and execution.

6   Death penalty cases may pass through as many as 10 courts and across 3 stages: trial and direct review, state postconviction appeals, and federal *habeas corpus* appeals.

7   Liebman found that the frequency of errors in capital punishment cases is 68 percent. More than two of every three capital judgments reviewed by the courts during a 23-year study period were found to be seriously flawed. Ten states (Alabama, Arizona, California, Georgia, Indiana, Maryland, Mississippi, Montana, Oklahoma, and Wyoming) had overall error rates of 75 percent or higher. Almost 1,000 of the cases sent back for retrial ended in sentences less than death, and 87 ended in *not guilty* verdicts.

8   In 2002, the Court held in *Atkins* v. *Virginia* that execution of offenders with mental retardation is cruel and unusual punishment prohibited by the Eighth Amendment because a national consensus has developed against executing these offenders. In 2005, the Court held in *Roper* v. *Simmons* that execution of persons for crimes they committed before turning age 18 was also unconstitutional and in violation of the Eighth Amendment. The Court's reasoning

in both cases was similar: The large number of states banning the execution of people with mental retardation and of persons who committed capital crimes before turning age 18 provided evidence that our society views offenders with mental retardation and juveniles as categorically less culpable than the average criminal.

KEY TERMS

exonerate, p. 502

capital punishment, p. 504

capital crime, p. 508

death row, p. 517

mandatory death penalty, p. 523

guided discretion, p. 523

bifurcated trial, p. 523

mitigating circumstances, p. 523

aggravating circumstances, p. 523

serious error, p. 526

QUESTIONS FOR REVIEW

1 Trace the history of capital punishment inside and outside the United States noting, in particular, the number of U.S. jurisdictions with and without the death penalty, the changes brought on by former Illinois governor George Ryan, the Supreme Court rulings that first halted and then resumed executions, the number of persons executed since 1977, and what constitutes a capital crime.

2 What are the characteristics of people executed in the United States since 1977 and on death row today?

3 Illustrate the politics influencing capital punishment.

4 What major U.S. Supreme Court decisions influenced capital punishment legislation?

5 Prioritize the arguments for and against the death penalty.

6 Evaluate the death penalty process.

7 Debate Liebman's findings on the frequency of errors in capital punishment cases.

8 What is the Supreme Court's reasoning for banning the execution of juveniles and offenders with mental retardation?

THINKING CRITICALLY ABOUT CORRECTIONS

Murder Rates and the Death Penalty

According to the Death Penalty Information Center, in 2009, death penalty states recorded higher murder rates than non-death-penalty states. The average murder rate among death penalty states was 4.9 per 100,000 population; for non-death-penalty states, the rate was 2.8. The South executes the largest percentage of offenders who are convicted of a capital crime (82 percent) and records the highest murder rate (6.0 murders per 100,000 people); the Northeast executes the fewest (less than one-half of 1 percent) and records the lowest murder rate, 3.8. What conclusions might you draw from these data?

Cost of Execution

Research shows that execution costs more than life imprisonment. Do you think there is a point at which the economic consequence of execution outweighs its value to the public? Explain.

ON-THE-JOB DECISION MAKING

Should the Cost of a Capital Trial Be a Factor in a Prosecutor's Decision to Seek the Death Penalty?

Capital murder trials are longer and more expensive at every step than other murder trials. The irreversibility of the death sentence requires courts to follow heightened due process in the preparation and course of the trial. Defendants are much more likely to insist on a trial when they are facing a possible death sentence. Crime investigations, pretrial preparations and motions, expert witness investigations, jury selection, and the necessity for two trials—one on guilt and one on sentencing—make capital cases extremely costly even before the appeals process begins. After conviction, there are constitutionally mandated appeals that involve both prosecution and defense costs. Even if a jury recommends life over death or ends as a hung jury or if the condemned person's sentence is commuted after he or she has served time on death row, the state has already paid the cost of a capital trial. Assume that you are the prosecuting attorney in a rural county of 7,500 people in a southern state. A capital case is coming up for trial. Estimates of costs for the case begin at $500,000. How will you justify paying for the prosecution of the case?

Does Maintaining Innocence Put Innocent People at Risk?

Why would a person confess to a crime he or she didn't commit and possibly face the death penalty? Professor Saul Kassin wrote an interesting article on the psychology of confessions. His thesis is innocence puts people at risk. Innocence does not protect people in a number of critical stages in criminal justice. In interrogation, police presume suspects are guilty. However, innocent people believe that everyone can see the transparency of their innocence and will naively waive their rights. Because their resistance to admitting guilt is seen as resistance and further evidence of their guilt, interrogations become more confrontational. Torture techniques like those used in the Abu Ghraib prisoner torture scandal show, for example, that extreme tactics such as excessive interrogation time and no rest is accompanied by the suspect's stress, fatigue, and feeling of helplessness. A similar study was conducted by Brandon Garrett, University of Virginia professor of law.

Read Kassin's article "On the Psychology of Confessions: Does Innocence Put Innocents at Risk?" *American Psychologist*, vol. 60, no. 3, pages 215–228. (If you're not sure how to access *American Psychologist* online at your library, consult your librarian.) Listen to Professor Garrett explain his research on why some kinds of people are induced to confess at http://www.law.virginia.edu/html/news/2009_spr/garrett.htm.

Think about the issues Kassin and Garrett raise. How can we prevent these harms to innocent people?

For additional information, please see: www.mhhe.com/schmalleger6e

ENDNOTES

Chapter 1

1. Kevin McCoy, "Inmates Stole $39 million from the IRS in 2009," *USA Today*, (February 15, 2001), p 1A.

2. "The New Wolfhound-PRO Contraband Cell Phone Detector to be 'Unleashed' at the American Correctional Association Winter Conference," PRNewswire, January 25, 2011, http://www.prnewswire.com/news-releases/the-new-wolfhound-pro-contraband-cell-phone-detector-to-be-unleashed-at-the-american-correctional-association-winter-conference-114559409.html (accessed March 15, 2011).

3. The word *outlawed* is used loosely. While some states have outlawed inmate possession of working cell phones and some others are moving in that direction, such possession is more often a violation of administrative regulations.

4. For an in-depth discussion of this issue, see Steven Raphael and Michael A. Stoll (eds.), *Do Prisons Make Us Safer? The Benefits and Costs of the Prison Boom* (New York: Russell Sage Foundation, 2010).

5. Fox Butterfield, "Crime Keeps on Falling, but Prisons Keep on Filling," *New York Times* News Service, September 28, 1997.

6. John P. Conrad, "The Pessimistic Reflections of a Chronic Optimist," *Federal Probation*, vol. 55, no. 2 (1991), p. 4.

7. Ibid., p. 8.

8. See, for example, Jory Farr, "A Growth Enterprise," www.press-enterprise.com/focus/prison/html/agrowthindustry.html (accessed March 28, 2002).

9. Timothy A. Hughes et al., *Trends in State Parole, 1990–2000* (Washington, DC: U.S. Department of Justice, 2001).

10. Margaret Werner Cahalan, *Historical Corrections Statistics in the United States, 1850–1984* (Washington, DC: U.S. Department of Justice, 1986).

11. Heather C. West, William J. Sabol, and Sarah J. Greenman, *Prisoners in 2009* (Washington, DC: Bureau of Justice Statistics, 2010).

12. Lauren E. Glaze, *Correctional Populations in the United States, 2009* (Washington, DC: Bureau of Justice Statistics, 2010).

13. Cahalan, *Historical Corrections Statistics.*

14. American Correctional Association, *Vital Statistics in Corrections* (Lanham, MD: American Correctional Association, 2000).

15. Kristen A. Hughes, *Justice Expenditure and Employment in the United States, 2003* (Washington, DC: Bureau of Justice Statistics, 2006), p. 6.

16. The figure may be somewhat misleading, however, because an offender who commits a number of crimes may be prosecuted for only one.

17. Much of the following material is adapted from Bureau of Justice Statistics, *Report to the Nation on Crime and Justice*, 2nd ed. (Washington, DC: Bureau of Justice Statistics, 1988), pp. 56–58.

18. President's Commission on Law Enforcement and Administration of Justice, *The Challenge of Crime in a Free Society* (Washington, DC: U.S. Government Printing Office, 1967), p. 159.

19. National Advisory Commission on Criminal Justice Standards and Goals, *Corrections* (Washington, DC: U.S. Government Printing Office, 1975), p. 2.

20. Bureau of Justice Statistics, *Correctional Populations in the United States, 1995* (Washington, DC: U.S. Government Printing Office, 1997).

21. Bob Barrington, "Corrections: Defining the Profession and the Roles of Staff," *Corrections Today*, August 1987, pp. 116–120.

22. Arlin Adams, *The Legal Profession: A Critical Evaluation*, 93 Dick. L. Rev. 643 (1989).

23. Harold E. Williamson, *The Corrections Profession* (Newbury Park, CA: Sage, 1990), p. 79.

24. Adams, *The Legal Profession.*

25. Williamson, *The Corrections Profession*, p. 20.

26. P. P. Lejins, "ACA Education Council Proposes Correctional Officer Entry Tests," *Corrections Today*, vol. 52, no. 1 (February 1990), pp. 56, 58, 60.

27. Mark S. Fleisher, "Teaching Correctional Management to Criminal Justice Majors," *Journal of Criminal Justice Education*, vol. 8, no. 1 (Spring 1997), pp. 59–73.

28. See Robert B. Levinson, Jeanne B. Stinchcomb, and John J. Greene III, "Corrections Certification: First Steps Toward Professionalism," www.aca.org/development/doc_certification firststeps.pdf (accessed March 23, 2003).

29. See the ACA's Professional Certification Program Web page at www.corrections.com/aca/development/certification.htm (accessed September 10, 2011) for more information.

30. The AJA defines a jail manager as "a person (sworn or civilian) who directs, administers, and/or is in charge of the operations of an adult jail facility, division, bureau, department, program, and/or shift; and/or a person (sworn or civilian) who supervises the work and performance of an employee or employees in an adult jail facility." See AJA, *CJM: Handbook for Candidates*, www.corrections.com/aja/cjm_handbook.pdf (accessed March 25, 2007).

31. Lawrence W. Sherman et al., *Preventing Crime: What Works, What Doesn't, What's Promising* (Washington, DC: National Institute of Justice, 1997).

32. National Institute of Corrections, "A Framework for Evidence-Based Decision Making in Local Criminal Justice Systems" (Center for Effective Public Policy, 2010), http://www.cepp.com/documents/EBDM Framework.pdf (accessed September 10, 2011).

33. Office of Justice Programs, "Justice Resource Update" (Washington, DC: U.S. Department of Justice, 2010).

34. The University of California, Irvine, Center for Evidence-Based Corrections, http://ucicorrections.seweb.uci.edu (accessed June 6, 2009).

35. Public Safety Performance Project, Pew Center on the States, *One in 31: The Long Reach of American Corrections* (Philadelphia: Pew, 2009), pp. 23–24.

36. Michale Omi and Howard Winant, *Racial Formation in the United States: From the 1960s to the 1980s* (New York: Routledge and Kegan Paul, 1986), p. 145.

37. National Center for Women and Policing, *Equality Denied: The Status of Women in Policing, 2001* (Beverly Hills, CA: NCWP, 2002), p. 11.

38. Dianne Carter, "The Status of Education and Training in Corrections," *Federal Probation*, vol. 55, no. 2 (June 1991), pp. 17–23.

39. Williamson, *The Corrections Profession.*

Chapter 2

1. *Gazette d'Amsterdam*, April 1, 1757. Cited by Michel Foucault, *Discipline & Punish: The Birth of the Prison*, trans. Alan Sheridan (New York: Vintage Books, 1995).

2. Edward M. Peters, "Prison Before the Prison: The Ancient and Medieval Worlds," in Norval Morris and David J. Rothman (eds.), *The Oxford History of the Prison* (New York: Oxford University Press, 1995), p. 6.

3. James Hastings et al., *Dictionary of the Bible*, vol. 1 (New York: Scribner; 1905), pp. 523 ff. Cited in Arthur Evans Wood and John Barker Waite, *Crime and Its Treatment: Social and Legal Aspects of Criminology* (New York: American Book Company, 1941), p. 462.

4. Foucault, *Discipline & Punish*, p. 8.

5. See Peters, "Prison Before the Prison," pp. 14–15.

6. Wood and Waite, *Crime and Its Treatment*, p. 462.

7. Pieter Spierenburg, "The Body and the State: Early Modern Europe," in Norval Morris and David J. Rothman (eds.), *The Oxford History of the Prison* (New York: Oxford University Press, 1995), pp. 52–53.

8. Ibid., p. 53.

9. Harry Elmer Barnes and Negley K. Teeters, *New Horizons in Criminology*, 3rd ed. (Englewood Cliffs, NJ: Prentice Hall, 1959), p. 290.

10. Some of the information in this section comes from Harry Elmer Barnes, *Story of Punishment* (Montclair, NJ: Patterson Smith, 1930); and George Ives, *A History of Penal Methods* (London: Stanley Paul, 1914).

11. Barnes and Teeters, *New Horizons*, p. 349.

12. Ives, *A History of Penal Methods*, p. 53.

13. Henry Burns Jr., *Corrections: Organization and Administration* (St. Paul, MN: West, 1975), p. 86.

14. Barnes and Teeters, *New Horizons*, p. 292.

15. Ives, *A History of Penal Methods*, p. 56.

16. John Howard, *The State of the Prisons* (London: J. M. Dent, 1929).

17. Spierenburg, "The Body and the State," p. 53.

18. Burns, *Corrections*, p. 87.

19. Spierenburg, "The Body and the State," p. 62.

20. See Abbott Emerson Smith, *Colonists in Bondage* (Chapel Hill: University of North Carolina Press, 1947).

21. For a good account of the practice, see Robert Hughes, *The Fatal Shore: The Epic of Australia's Founding* (New York: Vintage Books, 1988).

22. James Trager, *The People's Chronology* (New York Henry Holt, 1994).

23. See Aleksandr Solzhenitsyn, *The Gulag Archipelago, 1918–1956* (1974) and *The Gulag Archipelago* 2 and 3 (1975, 1978).

24. Barnes and Teeters, *New Horizons*, p. 293.

25. Norman Johnson, "Evolving Function: Early Use of Imprisonment as Punishment," *The Prison Journal*, Supplement to vol. 89, no. 1 (March 2009), pp. 10S–34S.

26. Peters, "Prison Before the Prison," p. 7.

27. Johnson, "Evolving Function: Early Use of Imprisonment as Punishment," p. 14S.

28. Spierenburg, pp. 49–77.

29. Ibid., p. 67.

30. Johnson, "Evolving Function: Early Use of Imprisonment as Punishment," p. 14S.

31. Ibid., p. 72.

32. Randall McGowen, "The Well-Ordered Prison," in Norval Morris and David J. Rothman (eds.), *The Oxford History of the Prison* (New York: Oxford University Press, 1995), p. 83.

33. Foucault, *Discipline & Punish*, p. 11.

34. See Wood and Waite, *Crime and Its Treatment*, p. 463.

35. Harry Elmer Barnes, *The Repression of Crime* (New York: Doran, 1926), p. 101.

36. John Howard, *The State of the Prisons in England and Wales* (London: William Eyres, 1777).

37. Spierenburg, "The Body and the State," pp. 49–77.

38. McGowen, "The Well-Ordered Prison," p. 86.

39. "Enlightenment, Age of," *Microsoft Encarta 96, CD-ROM* (Redmond, WA: Microsoft Corporation, 1995).

40. Ibid.

41. Some of the information in this section comes from The Nanaimo Region John Howard Society (of Canada) at http://jhsnr.org (accessed October 30, 2011).

42. Howard, *The State of the Prisons*.

43. Randall McGowen, "The Well-Ordered Prison: England 1780–1865," in Norval Morris and David J. Rothman (eds.), *The Oxford History of the Prison* (New York: Oxford University Press, 1995), p. 87.

44. Some of the information in this section comes from *The Internet Encyclopedia of Philosophy*, www.utm.edu/research/iep/ (accessed June 26, 2007).

45. Some of the information in this section comes from the Bentham Project at University College, London, www.ucl.ac.uk/Bentham–Project (accessed October 30, 2011).

46. For further information, see Frank E. Hagan, "Panopticon," in Marilyn D. McShane and Frank P. Williams III (eds.), *Encyclopedia of American Prisons* (New York: Garland, 1996), pp. 341–342.

47. Wood and Waite, *Crime and Its Treatment*, p. 456.

48. From "The Secret of Great Workers," *The Penny Magazine*, vol. 1, no. 1 (March 31, 1832), citing M. Dumont, "Recollections of Mirabeau."

49. See Margaret Wilson, *The Crime of Punishment* (New York: Harcourt Brace, 1931), p. 165.

50. See the All Saints Project, www.klis.com/allsaints/pnotes.htm (accessed October 30, 2011). This site includes input from the Royal Canadian Mounted Police and the Nova Scotia Crime Prevention Association.

51. See Lucia Zedner, "Wayward Sisters: The Prison for Women," in Norval Morris and David J. Rothman (eds.), *The Oxford History of the Prison* (New York: Oxford University Press, 1995).

52. Ibid., p. 333.

53. Ibid., p. 336.

54. Ibid.

55. Sanford Bates, *Prisons and Beyond* (New York: Macmillan, 1936).

56. Rodney Henningson, "Sanford Bates," in Marilyn D. McShane and Frank P. Williams (eds.), *Encyclopedia of American Prisons* (New York: Garland, 1996), pp. 51–53.

57. David M. Horton and George R. Nielsen, *Walking George: The Life of George John Beto and the Rise of the Modern Texas Prison System* (Denton: University of North Texas Press, 2006).

58. Dan Richard Beto, review of Jeremy Travis and Michelle Waul (eds.), *Prisoners Once Removed: The Impact of Incarceration and Reentry on Children, Families, and Communities* (Washington, DC: Urban Institute Press, 2003), in *Federal Probation*, vol. 68, no. 2 (2004), www.uscourts.gov/fedprob/September_2004/bookshelf.html (accessed January 10, 2007).

59. Charles Jeffords and Jan Lindsey, "George J. Beto," in Marilyn D. McShane and Frank P. Williams (eds.), *Encyclopedia of American Prisons* (New York: Garland, 1996), pp. 58–61.

Chapter 3

1. Nicole D. Porter, *The State of Sentencing 2010* (Washington, DC: The Sentencing Project, 2011).

2. John P. Conrad, "The Pessimistic Reflections of a Chronic Optimist," *Federal Probation*, vol. 55, no. 2 (1991), p. 7.

3. Sigmund Freud, *Totem and Taboo*, trans. and ed. by James Strachey (New York: Norton, 1990).

4. Lisa Kennedy, "The Miseducation of Nushawn Williams," *POZ online*, August 2000, www.poz.com/archive/august2000/

inside/nushawnwilliams.html (accessed June 20, 2002); Jackie Cooperman, "AIDS Scare Triples in Scope," ABCNEWS.com, October 28, 1997.

5. "'AIDS Monster' Denied Parole in New York," *Austin Chronicle,* August 31, 2001, www.austinchronicle.com/issues/dispatch/2001-08-31/cols_aboutaids.html (accessed June 20, 2002).

6. Andrew von Hirsch, *Doing Justice: The Choice of Punishments* (New York: Hill and Wang, 1976), pp. 48–49.

7. Morgan O. Reynolds, *The Reynolds Report: Crime and Punishment in the U.S.,* NCPA Policy Report No. 209 (Dallas, TX: National Center for Policy Analysis, 1997), www.public-policy.org/~ncpa/studies/s209/s209.html (accessed August 30, 2007).

8. Edwin Zedlewski, *Making Confinement Decisions,* Research in Brief (Washington, DC: National Institute of Justice, 1987).

9. John J. DiIulio, "Crime and Punishment in Wisconsin," *Wisconsin Policy Research Institute Report,* vol. 3, no. 7 (1990), pp. 1–56; see also William Barr, *The Case for More Incarceration* (Washington, DC: U.S. Department of Justice, Office of Policy Development, 1992).

10. Washington State Institute for Public Policy, *Evidence-Based Public Policy Options to Reduce Future Prison Construction, Criminal Justice Costs, and Crime Rates* (Olympia, WA: The Institute, October 2006), p. 10. For a national overview of such data, see William Spelman, "What Recent Studies Do (and Don't) Tell Us About Imprisonment and Crime," in Michael Tonry (ed.), *Crime and Justice: A Review of Research,* vol. 27 (Chicago: University of Chicago Press, 2002), p. 422.

11. R. A. Liedka and B. Useem, "The Crime-Control Effect of Incarceration: Does Scale Matter?" *Criminology and Public Policy,* vol. 5, no. 2 (2006), pp. 245–276. Cited in Howard N. Snyder and Jeanne B. Stinchcomb, "Do Higher Incarceration Rates Mean Lower Crime Rates?" *Corrections Today,* vol. 68 (October 2006), p. 92.

12. Francis T. Cullen and Paul Gendreau, "Assessing Correctional Rehabilitation: Policy, Practice, and Prospects," in Julie Horney (ed.), *Criminal Justice 2000,* vol. 3 (Washington, DC: National Institute of Justice, 2000).

13. Robert Martinson, "What Works? Questions and Answers About Prison Reform," *Public Interest,* vol. 35 (Spring 1974), pp. 22–54.

14. Cullen and Gendreau, "Assessing Correctional Rehabilitation."

15. Edgardo Rotman, *Beyond Punishment: A New View on the Rehabilitation of Criminal Offenders* (Westport, CT: Greenwood, 1990), p. 11.

16. Jack Leonard and Megan Garvey, "Users Kicking Prop. 36, Not Drugs," *Los Angeles Times,* April 01, 2007, page A-1.

17. Christie Gardiner, "Diverted, or Not? A Preliminary Analysis of California's Proposition 36," paper presented at the annual meeting of the American Society of Criminology (ASC), Los Angeles Convention Center, Los Angeles, CA, November 01, 2006.

18. Marty Price, "Crime and Punishment: Can Mediation Produce Restorative Justice for Victims and Offenders?" www.vorp.com/articles/crime.html (accessed February 9, 1999).

19. United Nations, *Restorative Justice: Report of the Secretary-General* (Vienna, Austria: United Nations Commission on Crime Prevention and Criminal Justice, 2002).

20. Graeme Newman, *The Punishment Response* (Philadelphia: Lippincott, 1978), p. 104.

21. See, for example, Andrew R. Klein, *Alternative Sentencing: A Practitioner's Guide* (Cincinnati, OH: Anderson, 1988).

22. Much of what follows is derived from Bureau of Justice Assistance, *National Assessment of Structured Sentencing* (Washington, DC: Bureau of Justice Assistance, 1996).

23. S. A. Shane-DuBow, A. P. Brown, and E. Olsen, *Sentencing Reform in the U.S.: History, Content and Effect* (Washington, DC: U.S. Department of Justice, 1985).

24. J. Cohen and M. H. Tonry, "Sentencing Reforms and Their Impacts," in A. Blumstein et al. (eds.), *Research on Sentencing:*

The Search for Reform (Washington, DC: National Academy Press, 1983), pp. 305–459.

25. State of Washington, Sentencing Guidelines Commission, *Adult Sentencing Manual 2000,* www.sgc.wa.gov/adult_sentencing_manual_2000.htm (accessed October 30, 2011).

26. The materials in this section are derived from the Web site of the United States Sentencing Commission, www.ussc.gov.

27. Title II of the Comprehensive Crime Control Act of 1984; 18 U.S.C. § 3551–3626 and 28 U.S.C. § 991–998.

28. 21 U.S.C. 841(b)(1)(C).

29. *Rita* v. *United States,* U.S. Supreme Court, 551 U.S. 338 (2007).

30. United States Sentencing Commission, Office of Research and Data, "Memorandum: Analysis of the Impact of Amendment to the Statutory Penalties for Crack Cocaine Offenses Made by the Fair Sentencing Act of 2010," January 28, 2011.

31. USSG §1B1.10, comment.

32. Ibid., p. 15.

33. M. Tonry, *Sentencing Matters* (Oxford, UK: Oxford University Press, 1995).

34. U.S. Department of Justice, *Mandatory Sentencing* (Washington, DC: Office of Justice Programs, 1997).

35. In 1999, California's three-strikes law was upheld by the U.S. Supreme Court in the case of *Riggs* v. *California,* 525 U.S. 1114 (1999) cert. denied.

36. G. L. Pierce and W. J. Bowers, "The Bartley-Fox Gun Law's Short-Term Impact on Crime in Boston," *Annals of the American Academy of Political and Social Science,* vol. 455 (1981), pp. 120–132.

37. C. Loftin, M. Heumann, and D. McDowall, "Mandatory Sentencing and Firearms Violence: Evaluating an Alternative to Gun Control," *Law and Society Review,* vol. 17 (1983), pp. 287–318.

38. C. Loftin and D. McDowall, "The Deterrent Effects of the Florida Felony Firearm Law," *Journal of Criminal Law and Criminology,* vol. 75 (1984), pp. 250–259.

39. D. McDowall, C. Loftin, and B. Wierseman, "A Comparative Study of the Preventive Effects of Mandatory Sentencing Laws for Gun Crimes," *Journal of Criminal Law and Criminology,* vol. 83, no. 2 (Summer 1992), pp. 378–394.

40. Joint Committee on New York Drug Law Evaluation, *The Nation's Toughest Drug Law: Evaluating the New York Experience,* a project of the Association of the Bar of the City of New York, the City of New York, and the Drug Abuse Council, Inc. (Washington, DC: Government Printing Office, 1978).

41. Much of what follows is taken from John Clark, James Austin, and D. Alan Henry, *Three Strikes and You're Out: A Review of State Legislation* (Washington, DC: National Institute of Justice, 1997).

42. Bureau of Justice Assistance, *National Assessment of Structured Sentencing* (Washington, DC: U.S. Department of Justice, February 1996).

43. Elizabeth A. King, "Inter Alia," *Corrections Compendium,* April 2002, p. 22.

44. Several states have had such laws on the books for many years. For example, South Dakota has had three-strikes–type legislation since 1877.

45. James Austin, "'Three Strikes and You're Out': The Likely Consequences on the Courts, Prisons, and Crime in California and Washington State," *St. Louis University Public Law Review,* vol. 14, no. 1 (1994).

46. The Washington law does permit the governor to grant a pardon or clemency, but it also recommends that no person sentenced under this law to life in prison without parole be granted clemency until he or she has reached 60 years of age and is judged no longer a threat to society.

47. *Andrade* v. *Attorney General of the State of California,* 270 F.3d 743 (2001).

48. *Lockyer* v. *Andrade,* 538 U.S. 63 (2003).

49. *Ewing v. California*, 538 U.S. 11 (2003).

50. Austin, "'Three Strikes and You're Out.'"

51. Countywide Criminal Justice Coordination Committee, *Impact of the "Three Strikes Law" on the Criminal Justice System in Los Angeles County* (Los Angeles: CCJCC, November 15, 1995).

52. Center for Urban Analysis, Santa Clara County Office of the County Executive, *Comparing Administration of the "Three-Strikes Law" in the County of Los Angeles with Other Large California Counties* (Santa Clara, CA: Center for Urban Analysis, Santa Clara County Office of the County Executive, May 1996).

53. Los Angeles County Sheriff's Department, *"Three Strikes" Law— Impact on Jail: Summary Analysis* (Los Angeles: Los Angeles County Sheriff's Department, August 31, 1996).

54. John Clark et al., *Three Strikes and You're Out: A Review of State Legislation* (Washington, DC: National Institute of Justice, 1997).

55. The California State Auditor, *California Department of Corrections and Rehabilitation: Inmates Sentenced Under the Three Strikes Law and a Small Number of Inmates Receiving Specialty Health Care Represent Significant Costs* (Sacramento, CA: May 2010), p. 1.

56. Ryan S. King and Marc Mauer, *Aging Behind Bars: "Three Strikes" Seven Years Later* (Washington, DC: Sentencing Project, 2001).

57. Ibid.

58. Fox Butterfield, "States Ease Laws on Time in Prison," *The New York Times*, Sept. 2, 2001, http://www.nytimes.com/2001/09/02/us/states-ease-laws-on-time-in-prison.html (accessed June 25, 2011).

59. Ibid.

60. Ryan S. King, *The State of Sentencing 2008: Developments in Policy and Practice* (Washington: The Sentencing Project, 2009).

61. Connecticut House Bill 5933 (2008); Iowa HF 2393 (2008).

62. The Sentencing Project, "Iowa Governor Signs Nation's First Racial Impact Sentencing Bill" (Washington: The Sentencing Project, 2007), p. 2.

63. Edith E. Flynn et al., "Three-Strikes Legislation: Prevalence and Definitions," in National Institute of Justice, *Task Force Reports From the American Society of Criminology* (Washington, DC: National Institute of Justice, 1997).

64. Paula M. Ditton and Doris J. Wilson, *Truth in Sentencing in State Prisons* (Washington, DC: Bureau of Justice Statistics, 1999), p. 1.

65. Robin I. Lubitz and Thomas W. Ross, "Sentencing Guidelines: Reflections on the Future," *Sentencing and Corrections: Issues for the 21st Century,* no. 10 (Washington, DC: National Institute of Justice, 2001).

66. Edgardo Rotman, *Beyond Punishment: A New View on the Rehabilitation of Criminal Offenders* (Westport, CT: Greenwood Press, 1990), p. 3.

Chapter 4

1. Sources consulted include Melissa Grace, "Alleged Tyra Banks Stalker Threatened TV Aide, Prosecutor Charges," *Daily News* (New York), April 17, 2009, www.nydailynews.com; TMZ Staff, "Tyra Banks Takes a Stand Against Alleged Stalker," April 29, 2009, www.tmz.com; Sewell Chan and John Eligon, "Man Convicted of Stalking Tyra Banks," *The New York Times*, April 29, 2009, www.nytimes.com; TMZ Staff, "Tyra's Stalker Sentenced to Learn How Not to Stalk," June 18, 2009, www.tmz.com; Gina Serpe, "Tyra's Alleged Stalker Goes on Trial," Eonline!, April 17, 2009, www.eonline.com; Melissa Grace, "Tyra Banks Will Be Facing Her Accused Stalker," *Daily News (New York)*, April 26, 2009, www.nydailynews.com (all sources accessed November 30, 2010).

2. B. J. George, "Screening, Diversion and Mediation in the United States," *New York Law School Law Review*, vol. 29 (1984), pp. 1–38.

3. Doris Layton MacKenzie, *What Works in Corrections: Reducing the Criminal Activities of Offenders and Delinquents* (New York: Cambridge University Press, 2006).

4. National Association of Pretrial Services Agencies, *Pretrial Diversion in the 21st Century: A National Survey of Pretrial Diversion Programs and Practices* (Washington, DC: National Association of Pretrial Services Agencies, 2009).

5. Bradley Schaffer, "Veterans Courts and Diversion Alternatives," *American Jails*, vol. 23, no. 6 (February 2010), pp. 21–24.

6. Thomas E. Ulrich, "Pretrial Division in the Federal Court System," *Federal Probation*, vol. 66, no. 3 (December 2002), pp. 30–38.

7. M. D. Anglin and Y. Hser, "Treatment of Drug Abuse," in Michael Tonry and James Q. Wilson (eds.), *Drugs and Crime: Crime and Justice: A Review of Research*, vol. 13 (Chicago: University of Chicago Press, 1990), pp. 393–460; D. N. Nurco, T. W. Kinlock, and T. E. Hanlon, "The Nature and Status of Drug Abuse Treatment," *Maryland Medical Journal*, vol. 43 (January, 1994), pp. 51–57; D. D. Simpson et al., "A National Evaluation of Treatment Outcomes for Cocaine Dependence," *Archives of General Psychiatry*, vol. 56, no. 6 (1999), pp. 507–514.

8. Edward W. Sieh, "A Theoretical Basis for Handling Technical Violations," *Federal Probation*, vol. 67, no. 3 (December 2003), pp. 28–33.

9. John Augustus, *A Report of the Labors of John Augustus, for the Last Ten Years, in Aid of the Unfortunate* (Boston: Wright and Hasty, 1852); reprinted as *John Augustus, First Probation Officer* (New York: National Probation Association, 1939), p. 26.

10. Ibid., pp. 4–5, 78–79.

11. Ibid, pp. 78–79.

12. Robert Panzarella, "Theory and Practice of Probation on Bail in the Report of John Augustus," *Federal Probation*, vol. 66, no. 3 (December 2002), pp. 38–43.

13. Sanford Bates, "The Establishment and Early Years of the Federal Probation System," *Federal Probation*, vol. 14 (1950), pp. 16–21; Joel R. Moore, "Early Reminiscences," *Federal Probation*, vol. 14 (1950), pp. 21–29; Richard A. Chappell, "The Federal Probation System Today," *Federal Probation*, vol. 14 (1950), pp. 30–40.

14. Lauren E. Glaze and Thomas P. Bonczar, *Probation and Parole in the United States, 2009* (Washington, DC: Bureau of Justice Statistics, December 2010).

15. Sean Rosenmerkel, Matthew Durose, and Donald Farole, *Felony Sentences in State Courts, 2006—Statistical Tables* (Washington, DC: U.S. Department of Justice, Bureau of Justice Statistics, December 2009), Table 2.4, p. 14.

16. Caroline Wolf Harlow, *Prior Abuse Reported by Inmates and Probationers* (Washington, DC: Department of Justice, Bureau of Justice Statistics, April 1999).

17. "States Imposing More Fees on Inmates and Probationers," *Corrections Journal*, January 23, 2006, p. 7.

18. Barbara Krauth and Larry Link, *State Organizational Structures for Delivering Adult Probation Services* (Washington, DC: U.S. Department of Justice, National Institute of Corrections, June 1999), pp. 3–5.

19. Kathy L. Waters, "Probation, Parole and Community Corrections: A Difficult Topic to Understand?" *Corrections Today*, vol. 65, no. 1 (February 2003), p. 10.

20. Institute for Court Management, *Private Probation in Georgia: A New Direction, Service and Vigilance* (Atlanta: Administrative Office of Courts, May 2001), pp. 24–37; see also Rick Neale, "Brevard to Privatize Probation Services," www.floridatoday.com, December 20, 2010 (accessed December 24, 2010).

21. Steve Aos, Marna Miller, and Elizabeth Drake, *Evidence-Based Adult Corrections Programs: What Works and What Does Not* (Olympia, WA: Washington State Institute for Public Policy,

2006); and Jennifer L. Sheem and Sarah Monchak, "Back to the Future: From Klocklar's Model of Effective Supervision to Evidence-Based Practice in Probation," *Journal of Offender Rehabilitation*, vol. 47, no. 3 (2008), pp. 220–247.

22. Mario Paparozzi and Matthew DeMichele, "Probation and Parole: Overworked, Misunderstood, and Under-Appreciated: But Why?" *The Howard Journal*, vol. 47, no. 3 (July 2008), pp. 275–296.

23. James A. Gondles Jr., "The Probation and Parole System Needs Our Help to Succeed," *Corrections Today*, vol. 65, no. 1 (February 2003), p. 8.

24. Peter Finn and Sarah Kuck, *Stress Among Probation and Parole Officers and What Can Be Done About It* (Washington, DC: U.S. Department of Justice, National Institute of Justice, 2005).

25. Jeff Holcomb, "The Carrying of Firearms by Probation Officers," paper presented at the annual meeting of the Academy of Criminal Justice Sciences, Cincinnati, Ohio, March 2008; see also Brian Freskos, "Probation Officers' Role Evolving as Law Has Shifted Parole's Focus," *Star News Online* (Wilmington, North Carolina), November 17, 2010, www.starnewsonline.com (accessed November 30, 2010).

26. Emily Gaarder, Nancy Rodriguez, and Marjorie Zatz, "Criers, Liars, and Manipulators: Probation Officers' Views of Girls," *Justice Quarterly*, vol. 21, no. 3 (September 2004), p. 572.

27. Mark Sanders, "Building Bridges Instead of Walls: Effective Cross-Cultural Counseling," *Corrections Today*, vol. 65, no. 1 (February 2003), pp. 58–59.

28. Kathleen M. Carroll, Charla Nich, and Bruce J. Rounsaville, "Contribution of the Therapeutic Alliance to Outcome in Active Versus Control Psychotherapies," *Journal of Consulting and Clinical Psychology*, vol. 65, no. 3 (1997), pp. 510–514.

29. Brad Bogue, *The Framework Behind the COMBINES Curriculum* (Boulder, CO: unpublished manuscript).

30. Aos, Miller, and Drake, *Evidence-Based Adult Corrections Programs: What Works and What Does Not*.

31. Ann M. Schlarb, "A Comparison of the Effects of the MRT Cognitive Behavioral Program Between Male and Female Parolees," *Cognitive-Behavioral Treatment Review*, vol. 19, no. 1 (First Quarter 2010), pp. 10–13.

32. Mario A. Paparozzi and Paul Gendreau, "An Intensive Supervision Program that Worked: Service Delivery, Professional Orientation, and Organizational Supportiveness," *The Prison Journal*, vol. 85, no. 4 (December 2005), pp. 445–466.

33. "Missouri Considers New Sentencing System," *Corrections Compendium*, vol. 29, no. 6 (November/December 2004), p. 39.

34. Michael D. Norman and Robert C. Wadman, "Probation Department Sentencing: Recommendations in Two Utah Counties," *Federal Probation*, vol. 64, no. 2 (December 2000), pp. 47–51.

35. Michael D. Norman and Robert C. Wadman, "Utah Presentence Reports: User Group Perceptions of Quality and Effectiveness," *Federal Probation*, vol. 64, no. 1 (June 2000), pp. 8–9.

36. Michael D. Norman and Robert C. Wadman, "Utah Presentence Reports: User Group Perceptions of Quality and Effectiveness."

37. Patricia M. Harris, Raymond Gingerich, and Tiffany A. Whittaker, "The 'Effectiveness' of Differential Supervision," *Crime & Delinquency*, vol. 50, no. 2 (April 2004), pp. 235–271.

38. Steven Kreytak, "Probationers Getting in Less Trouble Under New Program: First Measure of Probation Department Overhaul Shows It's Working," *Austin American Statesman*, March 30, 2009, www.statesman.com (accessed April 1, 2011).

39. American Bar Association, *Standards Relating to Sentencing Alternatives and Procedures* (Chicago: American Bar Association, n.d.).

40. Mike Gangloff, "Federal Sentences Are not Clear-cut," *Roanoke News* (Roanoke, VA), www.roanoke.com/news (accessed November 1, 2011).

41. Ibid.

42. Ibid.

43. Finn and Kuck, *Stress Among Probation and Parole Officers.*

44. Thomas G. Ogden, "Pagers, Digital Audio, and Kiosk: Office Assistants," *Federal Probation*, vol. 65, no. 2 (September 2001), pp. 35–37.

45. American Probation and Parole Association, *Caseload Standards for Probation and Parole* (Lexington, KY: APPA, September 2006), www.appa-net.org (accessed January 17, 2011).

46. Michelle Gaseau, *Mapping to Improve Supervision and Community Corrections*, October 23, 2000, www.corrections.com (accessed October 10, 2011); Jaishankar Karuppannan, "Mapping and Corrections: Management of Offenders with Geographic Information Systems," *Corrections Compendium*, vol. 30, no. 1 (January/February 2005), pp. 7–9, 31–33.

47. Peggy Burke, "Probation and Parole Violations: An Overview of Critical Issues," in Madeline M. Carter (ed.), *Responding to Probation and Parole Violators* (Washington, DC: National Institute of Corrections, April 2001), p. 6.

48. Joan Petersilia, "Probation in the United States," in Michael Tonry, *Crime and Justice: A Review of Research*, vol. 22 (Chicago: University of Chicago Press, 1997), p. 151.

49. "Leading Officials Issue Plan for 'Reinventing' Probation," *Criminal Justice Newsletter*, vol. 30, no. 7 (April 1, 1999), pp. 1–2.

50. *HOPE in Hawaii: Swift and Sure Changes in Probation* (Washington, DC: National Institute of Justice, June 2008); see also Angela Hawken and Mark Kleiman, *Managing Drug-Involved Probationers with Swift and Certain Sanctions: Evaluating Hawaii's HOPE* (Washington, DC: U.S. Department of Justice, National Institute of Justice, December 2009).

51. Meghan Fay, "Effective Ways to Manage Parole and Probation Violations," The Corrections Connection Network News (CCNN), Eye on Corrections, June 19, 1999, www.corrections.com (accessed June 24, 2011).

52. As cited in Fay, "Effective Ways to Manage Parole."

53. Burke, "Probation and Parole Violations," pp. 5–6.

54. Ibid, p. 5

55. Glaze and Bonczar, *Probation and Parole in the United States, 2009.*

Chapter 5

1. Bill Poovey, "Sarah Palin Hacker Trial Begins, Defendant David Kernell Fears Palin Will Dazzle Jurors," *The Huffington Post* (New York City, NY), April 20, 2010, www.huffingtonpost.com (accessed January 5, 2011); Mike Harvey, "Student David Kernell Denies Hacking into Sarah Palin's Personal E-mail," *The Times* (London, England), March 10, 2009, technology.timesonline.co.uk (accessed January 5, 2011); "Judge Sentences David Kernell to Year in Custody For Hacking Sarah Palin's E-Mail," *The Commercial Appeal* (Memphis, TN), www.commercialappeal.com (accessed January 5, 2011).

2. United States Sentencing Commission, *Proceedings from the Symposium on Alternatives to Incarceration* (July 14–15, 2008), http://www.ussc.gov/SYMPO2008/NSATI_0.htm (accessed October 20, 2011); Patrick Marley, "Doyle's Proposal to Free Some Inmates Early Stirs Controversy," *Journal Sentinel*, Milwaukee, Wisconsin, February 24, 2009, www.jsonline.com (accessed February 24, 2011).

3. Linh Vuong, Christopher Hartney, Barry Krisberg, and Susan Marchionna, *The Extravagance of Imprisonment Revisited* (Oakland, CA: NCCD, January 2010).

4. See, for example, "Changing Public Attitudes Toward the Criminal Justice System" http://www.soros.org/initiatives/usprograms/focus/justice/articles_publications/publications/hartpoll_20020201

(accessed June 10, 2011); Marc Mauer, *Race to Incarcerate* (New York: Free Press, 2006), p. 13; Frank T. Cullen and Brenda A. Vose, "Public Support for Early Intervention: Is Child Saving a Habit of the Heart?" *Victims and Offenders,* vol. 2, no. 2 (2007), pp. 109–124; "The UConnPoll: Prison Crowding," University of Connecticut, Center for Survey Research and Analysis, March 8, 2004.

5. William H. DiMascio, *Seeking Justice: Crime and Punishment in America* (New York: Edna McConnell Clark Foundation, 1997), p. 43.

6. Pew Center on the States, "Public Attitudes on Crime and Punishment," www.pewcenteronthestates.org, September 2010 (accessed January 5, 2011).

7. "California Lawmakers Battle over Prison Budget," *Corrections Today,* vol. 65, no. 3 (June 2003), p. 20.

8. Michael Tonry and Mary Lynch, "Intermediate Sanctions," in Michael Tonry (ed.), *Crime and Justice: A Review of Research,* vol. 20 (Chicago: University of Chicago Press, 1996), pp. 102–103.

9. Camille Graham Camp and George M. Camp, *Adult Corrections Yearbook* (Middletown, CT: Criminal Justice Institute, 2001), p. 170.

10. Betsy A. Fulton, Susan Stone, and Paul Gendreau, *Restructuring Intensive Supervision Programs: Applying What Works* (Lexington, KY: American Probation and Parole Association, 1994).

11. Doris Layton MacKenzie, "Evidence-Based Corrections: Identifying What Works," *Crime & Delinquency,* vol. 46, no. 4 (October 2000), pp. 457–472.

12. Doris Layton MacKenzie, *What Works in Corrections: Reducing the Criminal Activities of Offenders and Delinquents* (New York: Cambridge University Press, 2006), p. 322; and Steve Aos, Marna Miller, and Elizabeth Drake, *Evidence-Based Public Policy Options to Reduce Future Prison Construction, Criminal Justice Costs, and Crime Rates* (Olympia, WA: State Institute for Public Policy, 2006), p. 6.

13. Joan Petersilia, Arthur J. Lurigio, and James M. Byrne, "Introduction," in James M. Byrne, Arthur J. Lurigio, and Joan Petersilia (eds.), *Smart Sentencing: The Emergence of Intermediate Sanctions* (Newbury Park, CA: Sage, 1992), pp. ix–x; Elizabeth Deschenes, Susan Turner, and Joan Petersilia, *Intensive Community Supervision in Minnesota: A Dual Experiment in Prison Diversion and Enhanced Supervised Release* (Washington, DC: National Institute of Justice, 1995); Joan Petersilia and Susan Turner, *Evaluating Intensive Supervision Probation/Parole: Results of a Nationwide Experiment* (Washington, DC: National Institute of Justice, May 1993).

14. Aos, Miller, and Drake, *Evidence-Based Public Policy Options.*

15. "Washington State Researchers Rates What Works in Treatment," *Criminal Justice Newsletter,* September 1, 2006, p. 2.

16. Ibid.

17. National Association of Drug Court Professionals, www.nadcp .org/whatis/ (accessed January 15, 2011).

18. Ibid.

19. John S. Goldcamp, "What We Know About the Impact of Drug Courts: Moving Research from 'Do They Work?' to 'When and How They Work,'" testimony before the Senate Judiciary Subcommittee on Youth Violence, October 3, 2000, p. 1.

20. "Types of Drug Courts," National Association of Drug Court Professionals, www.nadcp.org (accessed January 15, 2011).

21. Ibid.

22. Aos, Miller, and Drake, *Evidence-Based Public Policy Options;* Christopher T. Lowenkamp, Alexander M. Holsinger, and Edward J. Latessa, "Are Drug Courts Effective: A Meta-Analytic Review," *Journal of Community Corrections,* vol. 28 (Fall 2005), pp. 5–10; Deborah Koetzle Shaffer, *Reconsidering Drug Court Effectiveness: A Meta-Analytic Review* (Las Vegas, NV: Department of Criminal Justice, University of Nevada, 2006); David B. Wilson, Ojmarrh Mitchell, and Doris Layton MacKenzie, "A Systematic Review of Drug Court Effects on Recidivism," *Journal of Experimental Criminology,* vol. 2, no. 4 (November 2006), pp. 459–487; Doris Layton MacKenzie, *What Works in Corrections: Reducing the Criminal Activities of Offenders and Delinquents,* pp. 221–240.

23. Shannon M. Carey, Michael Finigan, Dave Crumpton, and Mark Waller, "California Drug Courts: Outcomes, Costs and Promising Practices: An Overview of Phase II in a Statewide Study," *Journal of Psychoactive Drugs, SARC Supplement 3* (November 2006), pp. 345–356.

24. William Rhodes, Ryan Kling, and Michael Shively, *Suffolk County Court Evaluation* (Cambridge, MA: Abt Associates, 2006).

25. Michael W. Finigan, Shannon M. Carey, and Anton Cox, *The Impact of a Mature Drug Court over 10 Years of Operation: Recidivism and Costs* (Portland, OR: NPC Research, Inc., 2007).

26. Aos, Miller, and Drake, *Evidence-Based Public Policy Options.*

27. Carey, Finigan, Crumpton, and Waller, "California Drug Courts."

28. Finigan, Carey, and Cox, *The Impact of a Mature Drug Court.*

29. "Drug Courts Unavailable to Most," *Corrections Today,* vol. 71, no. 6 (December 2009), p. 16; and Sam Hananel, "Drug Courts Successful for Few Who Get It," *The Washington Post,* November 30, 2009, www.washingtonpost.com (accessed November 30, 2010).

30. Douglas B. Marlowe, David S. DeMatteo, and David S. Festinger, "A Sober Assessment of Drug Courts," *Federal Sentencing Reporter,* vol. 16, no. 2 (December 2003), pp. 113–128.

31. Bureau of Justice Assistance, *How to Use Structured Fines (Day Fines) as an Intermediate Sanction* (Washington, DC: Department of Justice, November 1996).

32. "Finn's Speed Fine Is a Bit Rich," MSNBC online, http://news .bbc.co.uk/2/hi/business/3477285.stm (accessed January 6, 2011); "Sentencing Law and Policy," May 12, 2009 and December 1, 2009, sentencing.typepad.com (accessed January 6, 2011).

33. Bureau of Justice Assistance, *How to Use Structured Fines.*

34. Susan Turner and Joan Petersilia, *Day Fines in Four U.S. Jurisdictions* (Santa Monica, CA: Rand, 1996); and Susan Turner and Judith Greene, "The FARE Probation Experiment: Implementation and Outcomes of Day Fines for Felony Offenders in Maricopa County," *Justice System Journal,* vol. 21, no. 1 (1999), pp. 1–21.

35. Aos, Miller, and Drake, *Evidence-Based Public Policy Options,* p. 9.

36. Morris and Tonry, *Between Prison and Probation,* p. 152.

37. Julie C. Martin, "Community Service for Offenders," in Tara Gray (ed.), *Exploring Corrections* (Boston: Allyn & Bacon, 2002), pp. 311–318.

38. Michael Tonry, "Parochialism in U.S. Sentencing Policy," *Crime & Delinquency,* vol. 45, no. 1 (1999), p. 58.

39. DiMascio, *Seeking Justice,* pp. 43–45.

40. Warren Young, *Community Service Orders* (London: Heinemann, 1979); Gill McIvor, *Sentenced to Serve: The Operation and Impact of Community Service by Offenders* (Aldershot, UK: Avebury, 1992); Peter J. O. Tak, "Netherlands Successfully Implements Community Service Orders," *Overcrowded Times,* vol. 6 (1995), pp. 16–17.

41. DiMascio, *Seeking Justice,* p. 37.

42. *David King,* "Fewer Prisoners, Fewer Prisons," *Gotham Gazette,* March 17, 2010, www.gothamgazette.com (accessed January 6, 2011).

43. Dale G. Parent, "Day Reporting Centers: An Evolving Intermediate Sanction," *Federal Probation,* vol. 60, no. 4 (December 1996), pp. 51–54; George Mair, "Day Centres in England and Wales," *Overcrowded Times,* vol. 4 (1993), pp. 5–7.

44. Charles Bahn and James R. Davis, "Day Reporting Centers as an Alternative to Incarceration," *Journal of Offender Rehabilitation,* vol. 27, no. 3/4 (1998), pp. 139–150.

45. Dale G. Parent et al., *Day Reporting Centers* (Washington, DC: National Institute of Justice, 1995).

46. *Sedgwick County Day Reporting Center Helps Alleviate Jail Overcrowding, Reduce Criminogenic Risk and Reduce Repeat Offenses* (Boulder, CO: BI Incorporated, n.d.); Jeff Shields, "Would Day Reporting Be Better for Nonviolent Offenders?" *The Philadelphia Inquirer*, April 21, 2010, www.philly.com (accessed April 21, 2011).

47. Dale Parent, "Day Reporting Centers: An Emerging Intermediate Sanction," *Overcrowded Times*, vol. 2 (1991), pp. 6, 8; Jack McDevitt and Robyn Miliano, "Day Reporting Centers: An Innovative Concept in Intermediate Sanctions," in James M. Byrne, Arthur J. Lurigio, and Joan Petersilia (eds.), *Smart Sentencing: The Emergence of Intermediate Sanctions* (Newbury Park, CA: Sage, 1992).

48. Liz Marie Marciniak, "The Addition of Day Reporting to Intensive Supervision Probation: A Comparison of Recidivism Rates," *Federal Probation*, vol. 64, no. 1 (June 2000), pp. 34–39.

49. Ibid., p. 37.

50. Roy Sudipto, "Adult Offenders in a Day Reporting Center—A Preliminary Study," *Federal Probation*, vol. 66, no. 1 (June 2002), pp. 44–51.

51. Christine Martin, Arthur J. Lurigio, and David E. Olson, "An Examination of Rearrests and Reincarcerations Among Discharged Day Reporting Center Clients," *Federal Probation*, vol. 67, no. 1 (June 2003), pp. 24–31.

52. "New Study Reveals Franklin County Day Reporting Center Reaps Rewards for Counties," Franklin County, PA, January 6, 2011, www.co.franklin.pa.us (accessed February 15, 2011).

53. Interview with Joe Russo, program manager at the National Law Enforcement and Corrections Technology Center, in Dana Razzano, "Strides Made in Electronic Monitoring: Improving Accuracy and Lowering Price," Corrections.com, www.corrections.com (accessed April 17, 2002); Robert S. Gable and Kirkland R. Gable, "The Practical Limitations and Positive Potential of Electronic Monitoring, *Corrections Compendium*, vol. 32, no. 5 (September/October 2007), pp. 6–8, 40–42.

54. Kathrine Johnson, "States' Use of GPS Offender Tracking Systems," *Journal of Offender Monitoring*, vol. 15, no. 2 (Summer/Fall 2002), pp. 15, 21–22, 26; Katharine Mieszkowski, "Tracking Sex Offenders with GPS," www.salon.com/news/feature/2006/12/19/offenders/index_np.htm (accessed December 31, 2006).

55. Gable and Gable, "The Practical Limitations and Positive Potential of Electronic Monitoring," p. 6.

56. Pew Charitable Trusts, *Public Safety, Public Spending: Forecasting America's Prison Population 2007–2011* (Philadelphia, PA: Pew Charitable Trusts, 2007).

57. Robert S. Gable and Kirkland R. Gable, "The Practical Limitations and Positive Potential of Electronic Monitoring," p. 6.

58. Tracy M. L. Brown, Steven A. McCabe, and Charles Welford, *Global Positioning System (GPS) Technology for Community Supervision: Lessons Learned* (Washington, DC: National Institute of Justice, 2007).

59. Darren Gowen, "Remote Location Monitoring—A Supervision Strategy to Enhance Risk Control," *Federal Probation*, vol. 65, no. 2 (September 2001), pp. 38–41.

60. Darren Gowen, "Overview of the Federal Home Confinement Program, 1988–1996," *Federal Probation*, vol. 64, no. 2 (December 2000), pp. 11–18; see also Brian K. Payne and Randy R. Gainey, "The Electronic Monitoring of Offenders Released from Jail or Prison: Safety, Control, and Comparisons to the Incarceration Experience," *The Prison Journal*, vol. 84, no. 4 (December 2004), pp. 413–435.

61. William Bales, Karen Mann, Thomas Blomberg, Gerry Gaes, Kelle Barrick, Karla Dhungana, and Brian McManus, *A Quantitative and Qualitative Assessment of Electronic Monitoring* (Washington, DC: U.S. Department of Justice, National Institute of Justice, January 2011).

62. Layton MacKenzie, *What Works in Corrections*, p. 322.

63. Ibid., p. 335; see also William D. Burrell and Robert S. Gable, "From B.F. Skinner to Spiderman to Martha Stewart: The Past, Present and Future of Electronic Monitoring of Offenders," *Journal of Offender Rehabilitation*, vol. 46, no. 3/4 (2008), pp. 101–118.

64. Nancy Hicks, "A New Relationship: Halfway Houses and Corrections," *Corrections Compendium*, vol. 12, no. 4 (October 1987), pp. 1, 5–8.

65. Camp and Camp, *Adult Corrections Yearbook*, p. 124.

66. "Weekly Population Report," www.bop.gov (accessed January 19, 2011)

67. "Director Addresses Change Within BOP," *The Third Branch*, vol. 38, no. 3 (March 2006), www.uscourts.gov/ttb/03-06/interview/index.html (accessed January 1, 2007).

68. Dan Morse, "Arenas Arrives at Halfway House to Serve Sentence," *The Washington Post*, April 11, 2010, www.washingtonpost.com (accessed January 7, 2011); and A. J. Perez, "Gilbert Arenas Sentenced to 30 days in Halfway House," *NBA Fanhouse*, March 29, 2010, nba.fanhouse.com (accessed January 7, 2011).

69. Division of Criminal Justice, Office of Research and Statistics, *Executive Summary: 2000 Community Corrections Study Results* (Denver: State of Colorado, Division of Criminal Justice, Office of Research and Statistics, March 22, 2001), www.cdpsweb.state.co.us/ors/docs.htm (accessed May 18, 2001).

70. Christopher T. Lowenkamp and Edward J. Latessa, "Developing Successful Reentry Programs: Lessons Learned from the 'What Works' Research," *Corrections Today*, vol. 67, no. 2 (April 2005), pp. 72–77; and "Halfway Houses Seen as Way to Cut Prison Costs in Ohio," www.cleveland.com/metro (accessed May 21, 2009).

71. Kurt D. Siedschlaw and Beth A. Wiersma, "Costs and Outcomes of a Work Ethic Camp: How Do They Compare to a Traditional Prison Facility?" *Corrections Compendium*, vol. 30, no. 6 (November/December 2005), pp. 1–5, 28–30.

72. Aos, Miller, and Drake, *Evidence-Based Public Policy Options*.

73. Steve Schultze, "Clarke Drops Plan for Early Prisoner Release," *Journal Sentinel* (Milwaukee, WI), January 27, 2010, www.jsonline.com; and Steve Schultze, "Milwaukee County's Inmate Training Program Raising Concerns," *Journal Sentinel* (Milwaukee, WI), December 5, 2010, www.jsonline.com (accessed December 8, 2010).

74. Doris L. MacKenzie and Eugene E. Hebert (eds.), *Correctional Boot Camps: A Tough Intermediate Sanction* (Washington, DC: National Institute of Justice, 1996).

75. Dale G. Parent, *Correctional Boot Camps: Lessons from a Decade of Research* (Washington, DC: U.S. Department of Justice, National Institute of Justice, June 2003).

76. Doris Layton MacKenzie et al., "Boot Camps as an Alternative for Women," in Doris L. MacKenzie and Eugene E. Hebert (eds.), *Correctional Boot Camps: A Tough Intermediate Sanction* (Washington, DC: National Institute of Justice, 1996).

77. Doris L. MacKenzie and A. Rosay, "Correctional Boot Camps for Juveniles," in *Juvenile and Adult Boot Camps* (Laurel, MD: American Correctional Association, 1996).

78. Sheldon X. Zhang, *Evaluation of the Los Angeles County Juvenile Drug Treatment Boot Camp, Executive Summary* (Washington, DC: U.S. Department of Justice, National Institute of Justice, 2000).

79. Merry Morash and Lila Rucker, "Critical Look at the Ideal of Boot Camp as Correctional Reform," *Crime & Delinquency*, vol. 36 (1990), pp. 204–222; DiMascio, *Seeking Justice*, p. 41.

80. Doris L. MacKenzie and J. W. Shaw, "The Impact of Shock Incarceration on Technical Violations and New Criminal Activities," *Justice Quarterly*, vol. 10, no. 3 (1993), pp. 463–486.

81. Dionne T. Wright and G. Larry Mays, "Correctional Boot Camps, Attitudes, and Recidivism: The Oklahoma Experience," *Journal of Offender Rehabilitation*, vol. 28, no. 1/2 (1998), pp. 71–87.

82. Jeanne B. Stinchcomb and W. Clinton Terry III, "Predicting the Likelihood of Rearrest Among Shock Incarceration Graduates: Moving Beyond Another Nail in the Boot Camp Coffin," *Crime & Delinquency*, vol. 47, no. 2 (April 2001), pp. 221–242.

83. As cited in Dan Herbeck, "Schumer Urges Ashcroft to Reconsider Closure of Shock Prison Camps," *Buffalo News*, January 16, 2005, p. A12.

84. Ibid.

85. See, for example Cheryl L. Clark and David W. Aziz, "Shock Incarceration in New York State: Philosophy, Results, and Limitations," in Doris L. MacKenzie and Eugene E. Hebert (eds.), *Correctional Boot Camps: A Tough Intermediate Sanction* (Washington, DC: National Institute of Justice, 1996), pp. 38–68; MacKenzie and Hebert, *Correctional Boot Camps*; Parent, *Correctional Boot Camps*.

86. Dale Parent, "Boot Camps Failing to Achieve Goals," *Overcrowded Times*, vol. 5 (1994), pp. 8–11; Doris Layton MacKenzie, "Boot Camps: A National Assessment," *Overcrowded Times*, vol. 5 (1994), pp. 14–18; Philip A. Ethridge and Jonathan R. Sorensen, "An Analysis of Attitudinal Change and Community Adjustment Among Probationers in a County Boot Camp," *Journal of Contemporary Criminal Justice*, vol. 13, no. 2 (May 1992), pp. 139–154.

87. W. J. Dickey, *Evaluating Boot Camp Prisons* (Washington, DC: National Institute of Justice, 1994); Peter Katel and Melinda Liu, "The Bust in Boot Camps," *Newsweek*, February 21, 1994, p. 26; Parent, "Boot Camps Failing to Achieve Goals."

88. Doris L. MacKenzie and Claire Souryal, *Multi-Site Evaluation of Shock Incarceration: Executive Summary* (Washington, DC: National Institute of Justice, 1994); see also Doris L. MacKenzie and A. Piquero, "The Impact of Shock Incarceration Programs on Prison Crowding," *Crime & Delinquency*, vol. 40 (1994), pp. 222–249.

89. Wilson Ring, "Study: Novel Sentencing Program Really Works," www.rulandherald.com (accessed February 1, 2011).

90. Pew Center on the States, *One in 31: The Long Reach of American Corrections* (New York: Pew Charitable Trusts, March 2009), p. 3.

91. Ibid., pp. 23–30.

92. Christopher Hartney and Susan Marchionna, *Attitudes of U.S. Voters Toward Nonserious Offenders and Alternatives to Incarceration* (Oakland, CA: National Council on Crime and Delinquency, June 2009).

93. George F. Cole et al., *The Practice and Attitudes of Trial Court Judges Regarding Fines as a Criminal Sanction* (Washington, DC: National Institute of Justice, 1987).

Chapter 6

1. Sources include "Former Mayor of Detroit Goes to Jail," *USA Today*, October 29, 2008, p. 3A; George Hunter and Charlie LeDuff, "Ex-Mayor Heads to Jail Tuesday: Room 14J-4 Is Kilpatrick's New Home," www.detnews.com (accessed October 28, 2008); M. J. Stephey, "Kwame Kilpatrick," www.time.com (accessed October 29, 2008); Sara Bonisteel, "Detroit Mayor Kwame Kilpatrick Resigns in Plea Deal," www.foxnews.com (accessed September 5, 2008); "Manoogian Mansion," en.wikipedia.org (accessed January 26, 2009); and Paul Egan, "Kilpatrick Has Air-Conditioned Cell with Private Bath in Prison," *The Detroit News*, June 25, 2010, www.detnews.com (accessed June 14, 2010).

2. Michael O'Toole, "Jails and Prisons: The Numbers Say They Are More Different Than Generally Assumed," *American Jails*, www.corrections.com/aja/mags/articles/toole.html (accessed May 9, 2011); see also Daron Hall, "Jails vs. Prisons," *Corrections Today*, vol. 68, no. 1 (February 2006) p. 8.

3. Todd D. Minton, *Jail Inmates at Midyear 2009—Statistical Tables* (Washington, DC: Bureau of Justice Statistics, June 2010).

4. Doris J. James, *Profile of Jail Inmates, 2002* (Washington, DC: U.S. Department of Justice, Bureau of Justice Statistics, July 2004); and Allen J. Beck, "What Do We Know About Jails at the National Level?" Presentation at the Jail Reentry Roundtable, Urban Institute, Washington, DC June 27, 2006.

5. National Advisory Commission on Criminal Justice Standards and Goals, *Corrections* (Washington, DC: U.S. Government Printing Office, 1973), p. 273.

6. Marilyn D. McShane and Frank P. Williams III (eds.), *Encyclopedia of American Prisons* (New York: Garland, 1996), p. 494.

7. Ibid., p. 496.

8. Ronald L. Goldfarb, *Jails: The Ultimate Ghetto* (Garden City, NY: Doubleday, 1975), p. 29.

9. John Irwin, *The Jail: Managing the Underclass in American Society* (Berkeley: University of California Press, 1986).

10. Randall G. Shelden and William B. Brown, "Correlates of Jail Crowding: A Case Study of a County Detention Center," *Crime & Delinquency*, vol. 37, no. 3 (1991), pp. 347–362.

11. David M. Parrish, "The Evolution of Direct Supervision in the Design and Operation of Jails," *Corrections Today*, www.corrections.com/aca/cortoday/october00/parrish.html (accessed October 26, 2011).

12. Linda Zupan, *Jails: Reform and the New Generation Philosophy* (Cincinnati, OH: Anderson, 1991); see also Richard Wener, "The Invention of Direct Supervision," *Corrections Compendium*, vol. 30, no. 2 (March/April, 2005), pp. 4–7, 32–34.

13. Brandon K. Applegate and Eugene A. Paoline III, "Jail Officers' Perceptions of the Work Environment in Traditional Versus New Generation Facilities," *American Journal of Criminal Justice*, vol. 31 (2007), pp. 64–80.

14. Dennis McCave, "Testing the Seams: When the Limits Are Pushed in Direct Supervision," *American Jails*, vol. 16, no. 1 (2002), pp. 51–56.

15. Peter Perroncello, "Direct Supervision: A 2001 Odyssey," *American Jails*, vol. 15, no. 6 (2001), p. 25. See also Constance Clem et al., *Direct Supervision Jails: 2006 Sourcebook* (Longmont, CO: National Institute of Corrections Information Center, September 2006); Christine Tartaro, "Are They Really Direct Supervision Jails? A National Study," *American Jails*, vol. 20, no. 5 (November/December 2006), pp. 9–17.

16. Ray Coleman, former facility commander of the King County Regional Justice Center in Kent, Washington, and past president of the American Jail Association, and Chuck Oraftik, director of justice architecture at Hellmuth, Obata, and Kassabaum, San Francisco, CA (personal communication, December 15, 2006).

17. Ken Kerle, "Jail Statistics: The Need for Public Education," *American Jails* (September/October 2006), p. 5.

18. Doris J. James, *Profile of Jail Inmates, 2002* (Washington, DC: U.S. Department of Justice, Bureau of Justice Statistics, July 2004).

19. James Austin, Luiza Chan, and Williams Elms, *Women Classification Study—Indiana Department of Corrections* (San Francisco, CA: National Council on Crime and Delinquency, 1993).

20. James, *Profile of Jail Inmates, 2002*; see also Gail Elias and Kenneth Ricci, *Women in Jail: Facility Planning Issues* (Washington, DC: U.S. Department of Justice, National Institute of Corrections, March 1997).

21. Tim Brennan and James Austin, *Women in Jail: Classification Issues* (Washington, DC: U.S. Department of Justice, National Institute of Corrections, March 1997).

22. Merry Morash, Timothy S. Bynum, and Barbara A. Koons, *Women Offenders: Programming Needs and Promising Approaches* (Washington, DC: U.S. Department of Justice, National Institute of Justice, August 1998).

23. Nastassia Walsh, *When More Is Less: How a Larger Women's Jail in Baltimore Will Reduce Public Safety and Diminish Resources for Positive Social Investments* (Washington, DC: Justice Policy Institute, January 2011).

24. William C. Collins and Andrew W. Collins, *Women in Jail: Legal Issues* (Washington, DC: U.S. Department of Justice, National Institute of Corrections, December 1996).

25. Linda Zupan, "The Persistent Problems Plaguing Modern Jails," in Tara Gray (ed.), *Exploring Corrections* (Boston: Allyn & Bacon, 2002), pp. 37–62.

26. Kenneth Kerle, "Women in the American World of Jails: Inmates and Staff," *Margins: Maryland's Law Journal on Race, Religion, Gender, and Class*, vol. 2, no. 1 (Spring 2002), pp. 41–61.

27. Barbara Bloom, Barbara Owen, and Stephanie Covington, *Gender-Responsiveness Strategies Research, Practice, and Guiding Principles for Women Offenders* (Washington, DC: U.S. Department of Justice, National Institute of Corrections, June 2003).

28. Todd D. Minton, *Jails in Indian Country, 2007* (Washington, DC: U.S. Department of Justice, Bureau of Justice Statistics, November 2008).

29. U.S. Department of the Interior, Office of Inspector General, *Neither Safe Nor Secure—An Assessment of Indian Detention Facilities* (Washington, DC: U.S. Department of the Interior, Office of Inspector General, September 2004).

30. Ibid., pp. 1–2.

31. Samuel Walker, Cassia Spohn, and Miriam DeLone, "Corrections: A Picture in Black and White," in Tara Gray (ed.), *Exploring Corrections* (Boston: Allyn & Bacon, 2002), pp. 13–24.

32. Michael Tonry, *Malign Neglect* (New York: Oxford University Press, 1995); *Targeting Blacks: Drug Law Enforcement and Race in the United States* (New York: Human Rights Watch, 2008); and Ryan S. King, *Disparity by Geography: The War on Drugs in America's Cities* (Washington, DC: The Sentencing Project, 2008).

33. Walker, Spohn, and DeLone, "Corrections," p. 16.

34. Doris J. James and Lauren E. Glaze, *Mental Health Problems of Prison and Jail Inmates* (Washington, DC: U.S. Department of Justice, Bureau of Justice Statistics, September 2006).

35. Henry J. Steadman, Fred C. Osher, Pamela Clark Robbins, Brian Case, and Steven Samuels, "Prevalence of Serious Mental Illness Among Jail Inmates," *Psychiatric Services*, vol. 60, no. 6 (June 2009), pp. 761–765.

36. Ibid.; see also Liz Lipton, "Few Safeguards Govern Elimination of Psychiatric Beds," *Psychiatric News*, vol. 36, no. 15 (August 3, 2001), p. 9, http://pn.psychiatriconline.org/cgi/content/full/36/15/9 (accessed January 13, 2011).

37. Sally Satel, "Out of the Asylum, Into the Cell," *The New York Times*, November 1, 2003, www.psychlaws.org/GeneralResources/article199.htm (accessed January 13, 2007); Bazelon Center for Mental Health Law, "Lawsuit Alleges Civil Rights Violations in Cook County Jail," August 12, 2003, www.bazelon.org/newsroom/archive/2003/8-12-03cookcounty (accessed January 13, 2011).

38. Amanda Petterati and Nastassia Walsh, *Moving Target: A Decade of Resistance to the Prison Industrial Complex* (Washington, DC: Justice Policy Institute, 2008), p. 4.

39. James A. Gondles, "The Mentally Ill Don't Belong in Jail," *Corrections Today*, vol. 67, no. 2 (April 2005), p. 6.

40. Lance Couturier, Frederick Maue, and Catherine McVey, "Releasing Inmates with Mental Illness and Co-occurring Disorders into the Community," *Corrections Today*, vol. 67, no. 2 (April 2005).

41. United States House of Representatives, Committee on Government Reform—Minority Staff Special Investigations Division, *Incarceration of Youth Who Are Waiting for Community Mental Health Services in the United States* (Washington, DC: U.S. House of Representatives, July 2004).

42. Kenneth E. Kerle, *Exploring Jail Operations* (Hagerstown, MD: American Jail Association, 2003), p. 31.

43. Ray Bynum, Gerald Milan, Daniel W. Phillips III, and Barbara Weber, "Mental Health Education and Corrections," *American Jails*, vol. 22, no. 4 (September/October, 2008), pp. 23–29.

44. Christopher G. Mumola, *Suicide and Homicide in State Prisons and Local Jails* (Washington, DC: U.S. Department of Justice, Bureau of Justice Statistics, August 2005); Christopher J. Mumola and Margaret E. Noonen, *Deaths in Custody Statistical Tables: Local Jail Deaths 2000–2006* (Washington, DC: Bureau of Justice Statistics, 2008); and Margaret Noonan, *Mortality in Local Jails, 2000–2007* (Washington, DC: U.S. Department of Justice, Bureau of Justice Statistics, July 2010).

45. Connie Milligan and Ray Sabbatine, "From Public Crisis to Innovation—The Mental Health Crisis Network," *American Jails*, vol. 21, no. 6 (January/February 2008), pp. 9–14.

46. Noonan, *Mortality in Local Jails, 2000–2007*; Christina Tartaro and Rick Ruddell, "Trouble in Mayberry: A National Analysis of Suicides and Attempts in Small Jails," *American Journal of Criminal Justice*, vol. 31, no. 1 (2006), pp. 81–100; see also Rick Ruddell and G. Larry Mays "Expand or Expire: Jails in Rural America," *Corrections Compendium*, vol. 31, no. 6 (November/December 2006) pp. 1–2, 4–5, 20–21, 27.

47. Allen J. Beck and Paige M. Harrison, *Sexual Victimization in Prisons and Jails Reported by Inmates, 2008–09* (Washington, DC: U.S. Department of Justice, Bureau of Justice Statistics, August 2010).

48. Allen J. Beck and Paige M. Harrison, *Sexual Victimization in Local Jails Reported by Inmates, 2007* (Washington, DC: U.S. Department of Justice, Bureau of Justice Statistics, June 2008), p. 2.

49. James J. Stephan, *Census of Jails, 1999* (Washington, DC: U.S. Department of Justice, Bureau of Justice Statistics, August 2001).

50. Minton, *Jail Inmates at Midyear 2009—Statistical Tables*.

51. Ibid.

52. American Correctional Association, *Vital Statistics in Corrections*, p. 26.

53. Niyi Awofeso, "Measuring and Evaluating Quality of Health Care Services in Prisons and Jails," *American Jails*, vol. 22, no. 3 (July/August, 2008), pp. 35–38.

54. Michael L. Birzer and Delores Craig-Moreland, "Why Do Jails Charge Housing Fees?" *American Jails*, vol. 20, no. 1 (March/April 2006), pp. 63–68; Laura Bauer, "Some Inmates Pay for Their Crimes and Jail Stays," www.kansascity.com (accessed April 28, 2011); Tracy Loew, "Debt to Society Costs Some Inmates $60 a Night," www.usatoday.com (accessed May 27, 2011).

55. Joann Brown Morton, "Providing Gender-Responsiveness Services for Women and Girls," *Corrections Today*, vol. 69, no. 4 (August 2007), pp. 6, 12.

56. Stephanie Simon, "Jailbirds Order Up Hot Wings," *Wall Street Journal*, April 27, 2010, http://online.wsj.com (accessed April 28, 2011).

57. Jennifer Steinhauer, "For $82 a Day, Booking a Cell in a 5-Star Jail," *The New York Times*, April 29, 2007, www.nytimes.com (accessed April 30, 2011); Jennifer Steinhauer, "Some Jails Let Prisoners Pay to Stay in Nicer Surroundings," *The San Diego Union-Tribune*, April 29, 2007, www.signonsandiego.com (accessed April 30, 2011); Larry Welborn and Eric Carpenter, "Jaramillo Wants to Pay for Jail," *The Orange County Register*, March 3, 2007, www.ocregister.com (accessed May 10, 2011). See also the Web sites of the Huntington Beach (CA) police department, Torrence (CA) police department, and Santa Ana (CA) police department. Beverly Hills Police Department opened its pay to stay jail in late 2009.

58. Alex Doobuzinskis, "$85-a-Night Jail a Hit With L.A.'s Celebrity Convicts," www.prisonlegalnews.org (accessed February 1, 2011).

59. National Sheriff's Association, *The State of Our Nation's Jails, 1982* (Washington, DC: National Sheriff's Association, 1982).

60. Kerle, "Women in the American World of Jails."

61. Stephan, *Census of Jails, 1999.*

62. National Sheriff's Association, *The State of Our Nation's Jails.*

63. Ibid., p. 231.

64. Ibid., p. 151.

65. Jeanne B. Stinchcomb and Susan W. Campbell, *Jail Leaders Speak: Current and Future Challenges to Jail Operations and Administration* (Washington, DC: U.S. Department of Justice, Bureau of Justice Statistics, 2008).

66. As cited in National Institute of Corrections, *Briefing Paper: Trends in Jail Privatization* (Boulder, CO: National Institute of Corrections Information Center, February 1992).

67. Mark Nadler, "Reentry for a Jail Audience," *American Jails,* vol. 19, no. 4 (September/October 2005), pp. 13–24.

68. Richard P. Seiter and Karen R. Kadela, "Prisoner Reentry: What Works, What Does Not, and What Is Promising," *Crime & Delinquency,* vol. 49, no. 3 (2003), pp. 360–388.

69. Holly Ventura and J. Mitchell Miller, "Community In-Reach Through Jail Reentry: Findings from a Quasi-Experimental Design," *Justice Quarterly,* vol. 27, no.6 (December 2010), pp. 893–910.

70. Deborah Dennis and Daniel J. Abreu, "SOAR: Access to Benefits Enables Successful Reentry," *Corrections Today,* vol. 72, no. 2 (April 2010), pp. 82–85.

71. Paula M. Ditton, *Mental Health and Treatment of Inmates and Probationers* (Washington, DC: U.S. Department of Justice, Bureau of Justice Statistics, July 1999), p. 1.

72. Caroline Wolf Harlow, *Profile of Jail Inmates, 2002,* p. 3.

73. Rod Miller, "When Jail Inmates Work Everyone Wins," *American Jails,* vol. 24, no 3 (July/August 2010), pp. 8–16.

74. Pat Nolan, "Prison Fellowship and Faith-Based Initiatives," *On the Line,* vol. 25, no. 5 (November 2002), p. 2.

75. Bryon R. Johnson, David B. Larson, and Timothy C. Pitts, "Religious Programs, Institutional Adjustment, and Recidivism Among Former Inmates in Prison Fellowship Programs," *Justice Quarterly,* vol. 14, no. 1 (March 1997), pp. 145–166; Bryon R. Johnson, "Religious Programs and Recidivism Among Former Inmates in Prison Fellowship Programs: A Long-Term Follow-Up Study," *Justice Quarterly,* vol. 21, no. 2 (June 2004), pp. 329–354.

76. Sheldon Crapo, "Breaking the Cycle of Crime . . . One Life at a Time," *American Jails,* vol. 11, no. 1 (March/April 1997), p. 24.

77. Kenneth E. Kerle, *Exploring Jail Operations,* p. 128.

78. Anthony Colarossi and Willoughby Mariano, "If All Central Florida Jails Rate an A, Is It Deserved?" *Orlando Sentinel,* May 15, 2010, www.orlandosentinel.com (accessed May 20, 2011).

79. American Bar Association, Criminal Justice Section, Report to the House of Delegates, August 21, 2008, www.abanet.org/crimjust/policy/am08104b.pdf-2008-08-21 (accessed January 20, 2011).

80. Kathy Black-Dennis, director of Standards and Accreditation, American Correctional Association (personal communication, February 25, 2011).

81. As posted on the American Correctional Association Web site, www.aca.org/standards/testimonials (accessed January 20, 2011).

82. Peter D. Friedman, Faye S. Taxman, and Craig E. Handerson, "Evidence-Based Treatment Practices for Drug-Involved Adults in the Criminal Justices System," *Journal of Substance Abuse Treatment*, vol. 32, no. 3 (April 2007), pp. 267–277.

Chapter 7

1. Sources consulted include Christopher Reed, "Prison a Rite of Passage for Los Angeles Gangster," *Sunday Age* (Melbourne, Australia), June 2, 1996, www.lexisnexis.com, www.ask.com/wiki/Sanyika_Shakur, and www.fantasticfiction.co.uk/e/ (accessed January 23, 2011).

2. Heather West, William J. Sabol, and Sarah J. Greenman, *Prisoners in 2009* (Washington, DC: U.S. Department of Justice, Bureau of Justice Statistics, December 2010).

3. Ibid.

4. Marc Mauer, executive director of the public safety performance project of the Pew Center on the States, quoted in John Schwartz, "Report Finds States Holding Fewer Prisoners," *New York Times,* March 16, 2010, www.nytimes.com (accessed March 17, 2011).

5. Ibid.

6. Roy Walmsley, *World Prison Population List,* 8th ed. (London: Kings College, University of London, January 2009), www.risonstudies.org (accessed January 24, 2011); and Adam Liptak, "Inmate Court in U.S. Dwarfs Other Nations," www.nytimes.com (accessed April 23, 2011).

7. Federal Bureau of Investigation, "Crime in the United States 2007," www.fbi.gov (accessed February 7, 2009); West Sabol, and Greenman, *Prisoners in 2009.*

8. Andrew Coyle, "The Use and Abuse of Prison Around the World," *Corrections Today* (December 2004), pp. 64–67; see also David A. Bowers and Jerold L. Waltman, "Do More Conservative States Impose Harsher Felony Sentences? An Exploratory Analysis of 32 States," *Criminal Justice Review,* vol. 18, no.1 (Spring 1993), pp. 61–70.

9. West, Sabol, and Greenman, *Prisoners in 2009;* James J. Stephan and Jennifer C. Karberg, *Census of State and Federal Facilities, 2000* (Washington, DC: U.S. Department of Justice, Bureau of Justice Statistics, October 2003); and James J. Stephen, *Census of State and Federal Correctional Facilities, 2005* (Washington, DC: U.S. Department of Justice, Bureau of Justice Statistics, October 2008).

10. Beth R. Richie, "Challenges Incarcerated Women Face as They Return to Their Communities: Findings from Life History Interviews," *Crime & Delinquency,* vol. 47, no. 3 (July 2001), pp. 368–389; and Elaine A. Lord, "The Challenges of Mentally Ill Offenders in Prison," *Criminal Justice and Behavior,* vol. 35, no. 8 (August 2008), pp. 928–942.

11. Meda Chesney-Lind, "Putting the Breaks on the Building Binge," *Corrections Today,* vol. 54, no. 6 (August 1992), p. 30.

12. Marc Mauer and Ryan S. King, *Uneven Justice: State Rates of Incarceration by Race and Ethnicity* (Washington, DC: The Sentencing Project, July 2007), p. 3.

13. Thomas P. Bonczar, *Prevalence of Imprisonment in the U.S. Population, 1974–2001* (U.S. Department of Justice, Bureau of Justice Statistics, 2003).

13. West, Sabol, and Greenman, *Prisoners in 2009;* Steve Miletich, "Two State Supreme Court Justices Stun Some Listeners with Race Comments," *The Seattle Times,* October 22, 2010, seattletimes.nwsource.com (accessed October 27, 2011).

15. Cassia Spohn, *Thirty Years of Sentencing Reform: The Quest for a Racially Neutral Sentencing Process* (Washington, DC: U.S. Department of Justice, National Institute of Justice, 2000); Phillip Beatty, Amanda Petteruti, and Jason Ziedenberg, *The Vortex: The Concentrated Racial Impact of Drug Imprisonment and the Characteristics of Punitive Counties* (Washington, DC: Justice Policy Institute, 2007); and Ryan S. King, *Disparity by Geography: The War on Drugs in America's Cities* (Washington, DC: The Sentencing Project, May 2008).

16. Steve Aos, Marna Miller, and Elizabeth Drake, *Evidence-Based Public Policy Options to Reduce Future Prison Construction, Criminal Justice Costs, and Crime Rates* (Olympia, WA: State Institute for Public Policy, 2006).

17. Kathleen A. Gnall and Gary Zajac, "Assessing for Success in Offender Reentry," *Corrections Today,* vol. 67, no. 2 (April 2005), p. 94.

18. Niyi Awofeso, "Evolution of Prisoner Classification Systems," *American Jails* (September/October 2006), pp. 87–91.

19. Carl B. Clements, "The Future of Offender Classification: Some Cautions and Prospects," *Criminal Justice and Behavior,* vol. 8 (1981), pp. 15–16.

20. Carl B. Clements, "Offender Classification: Two Decades of Progress," *Criminal Justice and Behavior,* vol. 23 (1996), p. 123.

21. Patricia L. Hardyman, James Austin, and Johnette Peyton, *Prisoner Intake Systems: Assessing Needs and Classifying Prisoners* (Washington, DC: U.S. Department of Justice, National Institute of Corrections, February 2004), p. viii.

22. J. Alexander et al., *Internal Prison Classification Systems: A Field Test of Three Approaches* (San Francisco, CA: National Council on Crime and Delinquency, 1997).

23. Ibid., p. ix.

24. Clements, "Offender Classification."

25. Ibid.

26. Robert B. Levinson, *Unit Management in Prisons and Jails* (Lanham, MD: American Correctional Association, 1999).

27. Melvina Sumter, "Editorial Introduction: Faith Based Prison Programs," *Criminology & Public Policy,* vol. 5, no. 3 (August 2006), pp. 523–528.

28. National Institute of Corrections, *Report of the National Institute of Corrections Advisory Board Hearings: Faith-Based Approach to Correctional Issues* (Washington DC: U.S. Department of Justice, National Institute of Corrections, June 2005).

29. "Free Faith-Based Television Gaining Ground in U.S. Prisons," *American Jails,* vol. 22, no. 6 (January/February 2009), p. 90.

30. Daniel P. Mears, "Faith-Based Reentry Programs: Cause for Concern or Showing Promise," *Corrections Today,* vol. 69, no. 2 (April 2006), p. 32; see also D. P. Mears et al., "Faith-Based Efforts to Improve Prisoner Reentry: Assessing the Logic and Evidence," *Journal of Criminal Justice,* vol. 34, no. 4 (2006), pp. 351–367.

31. Thomas P. O'Connor, "What Works, Religion as a Correctional Intervention: Part II," *Journal of Community Corrections,* vol. 14 (2005), pp. 4–6, 20–26; "Faith-Based Prison Program Struck Down by Federal Judge," *Criminal Justice Newsletter,* June 1, 2006, pp. 1–2; and Mears, "Faith-Based Reentry Programs," and Mears et al., "Faith-Based Efforts to Improve Prisoner Reentry."

32. Nancy La Vigne, Diana Brazzell, and Kevonne Small, *Evaluation of Florida's Faith- and Character-Based Institutions* (Washington, DC: The Urban Institute, October 2007), www.urban.org (accessed February 9, 2011).

33. As discussed in Sumter, "Editorial Introduction."

34. Camille Powell, "Ravens' Lewis Out of Prison," *The Washington Post,* June 4, 2005, p. E5; Bill Montgomery, "Pro Football: Freed, Lewis Has No Bitter Feelings," *The Atlanta Journal-Constitution,* June 4, 2005, p. 8.

35. Aos, Miller, and Drake, *Evidence-Based Public Policy Options.*

36. Barry Krisberg and Susan Marchionna, *Attitudes of U.S. Voters Toward Prisoner Rehabilitation and Reentry Policies* (San Francisco CA: National Council on Crime and Delinquency, April 2006), www.nccd-crc.org (accessed February 11, 2007).

37. Bureau of Justice Assistance, *Prison Industry Enhancement Certification Program,* www.ojp.usdoj.gov/BJA/grant/piecp.html (accessed January 28, 2011).

38. Cindy J. Smith et al., *Correctional Industries Preparing Inmates for Re-entry: Recidivism and Post-Release Employment* (Washington, DC: U.S. Department of Justice, June 2006).

39. Kevin Johnson, "Prison Workforce Feels Pinch," *USA TODAY,* July 19, 2010, www.usatoday.com (accessed July 19, 2011).

40. W. Saylor and G. Gaes, *Study of "Rehabilitating" Inmates Through Industrial Work Participation, and Vocational and Apprenticeship Training* (Washington, DC: Federal Bureau of Prisons, 1996); Joseph Summerill, "Congress Continues to Dismantle UNICOR," *Corrections Today,* vol. 67, no. 4 (July 2005) pp. 26–27, 30.

41. Karl O. Haigler et al., *Executive Summary of Literacy Behind Prison Walls: Profiles of the Prison Population from the National Adult Literacy Survey* (Washington, DC: U.S. Department of Education, National Center for Education Statistics, 1994).

42. Caroline Wolf Harlow, *Education and Correctional Populations* (Washington, DC: U.S. Department of Justice, Bureau of Justice Statistics, January 2003).

43. Marcia Gelbart, "City Prisoners' Low Reading and Math Levels Surprise Officials," www.philly.com, November 24, 2010 (accessed September 1, 2011).

44. "Inmate Education Programs," *Corrections Compendium,* vol. 33, no. 3 (May/June 2008), p. 9.

45. Anne F. Parkinson and Stephen J. Steurer, "Overcoming the Obstacles in Effective Correctional Instruction," *Corrections Today,* vol. 66, no. 2 (April 2004), pp. 88–91.

46. Stephen J. Steuer, Alice Tracy, and Linda Smith, *Three State Recidivism Study* (Lanham, MD: Correctional Education Association, 2001).

47. Aos, Miller, and Drake, *Evidence-Based Public Policy Options;* and Doris Layton MacKenzie, *What Works in Corrections: Reducing the Criminal Activities of Offenders and Delinquents* (New York: Cambridge, 2006).

48. Quoted in "Prisoners Less Educated, Less Literate, Study Finds," press release, U.S. Department of Education, Office of Public Affairs, December 2, 1994; Alison Lawrence, *Cutting Corrections Costs: Earned Time Policies for State Prisoners* (Denver, CO: National Conference of State Legislatures, July 2009).

49. West, Sabol, and Greenman, *Prisoners in 2009.*

50. Ryan S. King and Marc Mauer, *State Sentencing and Corrections Policy in an Era of Fiscal Constraint* (Washington, DC: The Sentencing Project, 2002).

51. Michael S. Vaughn and Leo Carroll, "Separate and Unequal: Prison Versus Free-World Medical Care," *Justice Quarterly,* vol. 15 (1998), pp. 3–40.

52. Claire Cooper, "Federal Judge Takes over State Prisons' Health Care System," *The Press Democrat,* July 1, 2005, pp. A1, A13.

53. Plaintiffs Trial Exhibit 1012A, *Coleman v. Schwarzenegger,* No. CIV S-90-0520 LKK JFM P, 2009 WL 2430820 (E.D. Cal. August 4, 2009) as cited in Donald Specter, "Everything Revolves Around Overcrowding: The State of California's Prisons," *Federal Sentencing Reporter,* vol. 22, no. 3 (February 2010), pp. 194–199.

54. Amanda Gardner, "Many in U.S. Prisons Lack Good Health Care: Report Finds High Rate of Chronic Disease that Often Goes Untreated," www.health.usnews.com (accessed February 3, 2011).

55. "Inmate Health Care and Communicable Diseases," *Corrections Compendium,* vol. 34, no. 4 (Winter 2009), pp. 13–35.

56. The Rebecca Project for Human Rights and the National Women's Law Center, *Mothers Behind Bars: A State-by-State Report Card and Analysis of Federal Policies on Conditions of Confinement for Pregnant and Parenting Women and the Effect on their Children* (Washington, DC: The Rebecca Project for Human Rights and the National Women's Law Center, October 2010).

57. James J. Stephan, *Census of State and Federal Correctional Facilities, 2005* (Washington, DC: U.S. Department of Justice, Bureau of Justice Statistics, October 2008).

58. Excerpted from California and South Dakota's departments of corrections Web sites (accessed February 1, 2011).

59. Stephan, *Census of State and Federal Correctional Facilities 2005*, p. 12.; Jon Ortiz, "Fiscal Changes Hit Prison Officers Union Hard," *The Sacramento Bee*, June 28, 2009, www.sacbee.com (accessed July 1, 2010).

60. American Correctional Association, "Correctional Officer Wages and Benefits," *Corrections Compendium*, vol. 35, no. 2 (Summer 2010), pp. 21–39.

61. *The Continuing Fiscal Crisis in Corrections: Setting a New Course* (New York: Vera Institute of Justice, October 2010), p. 7.

62. Jennifer Gonnerman, "An Expert Analyzes the Prison Population Boom" *Village Voice*, February 22, 2000, p. 56; and Pew Center on the States, *One in 31: The Long Reach in American Corrections* (New York: Pew Charitable Trusts, March 2009), p. 20.

63. Pew Charitable Trusts, *Public Safety, Public Spending: Forecasting America's Prison Population 2007–2011* (Philadelphia: Pew Charitable Trusts, 2007).

64. Linh Vuong, Christopher Hartney, Barry Krisberg, and Susan Marchionna, *The Extravagance of Imprisonment Revisited*, p. 9.

65. "Prison System in Need of Correction," http://blog.nj.com (accessed December 18, 2010).

66. Pew Charitable Trusts, *Public Safety, Public Spending*.

67. Sources consulted include "States Reduce Prison Spending," *Corrections Compendium*, vol. 34, no 3 (Fall 2009), p. 32; Judith Greene and Marc Mauer, *Downscaling Prisons: Lessons from Four States* (Washington, DC: The Sentencing Project, 2010); Len Engel, John Larivee, and Richard Luedman, "Reentry and the Economic Crisis: An Examination of Four States and Their Budget Efforts," *Corrections Today*, vol. 71, no. 6 (December 2009), pp. 42–45; *The Continuing Fiscal Crisis in Corrections: Setting a New Course*; Les Zaitz, "Oregon to Close Prison, Lay off 63 Workers in $2.5 Million Budget Cut," www.oregonlive.com, September 30, 2010 (accessed October 1, 2011); Mark Hornbeck, "Michigan Prisons Focus on Released Inmates: Curb Inmate Count, Help Inmates Return to Society, Leader Urges," *Detroit News*, April 27, 2010, www.detnews.com (accessed April 7, 2011); and Tom Beyerlein, "Probation, Parole for Nonviolent Crime Could Save States $15B," *Dayton Daily News*, June 10, 2010, www.daytondailynews.com (accessed June 14, 2011).

68. Greene and Mauer, *Downscaling Prisons: Lessons from Four States*, p. 61.

69. Stephan, *Census of State and Federal Correctional Facilities*, 2005.

70. Ibid.

71. Ibid.

72. Devlin Barrett, "Budget Cutting Starts at Justice Department," *The Wall Street Journal*, January 27, 2011, online.wsj.com (accessed January 27, 2011).

73. Shawn Mansfield, Federal Bureau of Prisons, Research and Evaluation (personal communication, January 26, 2011).

74. Patrick A. Langan and David J. Levin, *Recidivism of Prisoners Released in 1994* (Washington, DC: Bureau of Justice Statistics, June 2002).

75. As quoted in Nick Wilson, "Prisons Swollen by Foreigners, Druggies," *Courthouse News Service*, March 18, 2010, www.courthousenews.com (accessed March 24, 2011).

76. Scott Shane, "U.S. Tops World in Prison Population; Overtakes Russia for Dubious Honor," *Arizona Republic*, June 8, 2003, p. A 14.

77. See, for example, series of three articles in *Criminology & Public Policy*, vol. 5, no. 2 (2006), pp. 213–298.

78. Bruce Western, *Punishment and Inequality in America* (New York: Russell Sage Foundation, 2006).

79. Paul Gendreau, Tracy Little, and Claire Goggin, "A Meta-Analysis of Adult Offender Recidivism: What Works!" *Criminology*, vol. 34, no. 3 (1996), pp. 575–607.

80. Layton MacKenzie, *What Works in Corrections: Reducing the Criminal Activities of Offenders and Delinquents*, p. 340.

Chapter 8

1. Sources consulted include Carrie Johnson, "As Bush's Term Ends, Some Big Names Seek Pardons," *The Washington Post*, November 1, 2011 www.washingtonpost.com (accessed November 1, 2011); Kathy Gill, "Controversial Presidential Pardons—An Overview," http://uspolitics.about.com, January 3, 2009 (accessed November 1, 2011); "A Need for Mercy," *The Washington Post*, November 1, 2011, www.washingtonpost.com (accessed November 1, 2011); "Presidential Clemency Actions, 1789–2001," *Jurist*, http://jurist.law.pitt.edu (accessed November 1, 2011); "Presidential Clemency Actions by Fiscal Year (1900 to 1945 and 1945 to Present)," Office of the Pardon Attorney, U.S. Department of Justice, www.usdoj.gov (accessed November 1, 2011); "Presidential Pardons: Legal Guidelines," http://usgovinfo.about.com (accessed November 1, 2011); "Pardon Information and Instructions," Office of the Pardon Attorney, U.S. Department of Justice, www.usdoj.gov (accessed November 1, 2011); and Erica Werner, "Obama Pardons 9 People," *Washington Post*, December 3, 2010, www.washingtonpost.com (accessed November 1, 2011); and Debra Cassens Weiss, "Editorial Criticizes Obama as a 'No-Pardon' President," *ABA Journal*, November 1, 2011, www.abajournal.com (accessed November 1, 2011).

2. Charles L. Newman, *Sourcebook on Probation, Parole and Pardons*, 3rd ed. (Springfield, IL: Charles C. Thomas, 1970), pp. 30–31; see also Norval Morris, *Maconochie's Gentlemen: The Story of Norfolk Island and the Roots of Modern Prison Reform* (New York: Oxford University Press, 2002).

3. Philip Klein, *Prison Methods in New York State* (New York: Columbia University Press, 1920), p. 417. Cited in U.S. Department of Justice, *Attorney General's Survey of Release Procedures*, vol. 4 (Washington, DC: U.S. Government Printing Office, 1939–1940), p. 5.

4. M. W. Calahan, *Historical Corrections Statistics in the United States, 1850–1984* (Washington, DC: Bureau of Justice Statistics, 1986).

5. G. W. Wickersham, *Reports of the United States National Commission on Law Observance and Enforcement: Wickersham Commission, Report on Penal Institutions, Probation and Parole* (Washington, DC: U.S. Government Printing Office, 1930–1931), p. 324.

6. Ibid., p. 325.

7. Edwin H. Sutherland and Donald R. Cressey, *Principles of Criminology* (Chicago: Lippincott, 1955), p. 568.

8. David J. Rothman, *Conscience and Convenience: The Asylum and Its Alternatives in Progressive America* (Boston: Little Brown, 1980), pp. 159–161.

9. Douglas R. Lipton, Robert Martinson, and Judith Wilks, *The Effectiveness of Correctional Treatment: A Survey of Treatment Evaluation Studies* (New York: Praeger, 1975).

10. Peggy McGarry, *Handbook for New Parole Board Members* (Philadelphia: Center for Effective Public Policy, 1989), p. 4.

11. Patrick A. Langan and David J. Levin, *Recidivism of Prisoners Released in 1994* (Washington, DC: U.S. Department of Justice, Bureau of Justice Statistics, July 2002); see also Pew Charitable Trusts, *Public Safety, Public Spending: Forecasting America's Prison Population 2007–2011* (Philadelphia: Pew Charitable Trusts, 2007).

12. Heather West and William J. Sabol, *Prisoners in 2007* (Washington, DC: U.S. Department of Justice, Bureau of Justice Statistics, December 2008), Appendix Table 5, p. 17.

13. The Council of State Governments, *The Report of the Re-Entry Policy Council: Charting the Safe and Successful Return of Prisoners to the Community* (Lexington, KY: The Council of State Governments, 2005).

14. Nancy G. La Vigne et al., *Prisoner Reentry and Community Policing Strategies for Enhancing Public Safety* (Washington, DC: Urban Institute, 2006); Marc Mauer and Meda Chesney-Lind (eds.), *Invisible Punishment: The Collateral Consequences of Mass Imprisonment* (New York: The New Press, 2002).

15. Beth E. Richie, "Challenges Incarcerated Women Face as They Return to Their Communities: Findings from Life History Interviews," *Crime & Delinquency*, vol. 47, no. 3 (July 2001), p. 370.

16. Geneva Brown, *The Intersectionality of Race, Gender, and Reentry: Challenges for African-American Women* (Washington, DC: American Constitution Society, November 2010).

17. See, for example, Kamala Mallik-Kane and Christy A. Visher, *Health and Prisoner Reentry: How Physical, Mental, and Substance Abuse Conditions Shape the Process of Reintegration* (Washington, DC: Urban Institute, February 2008); Catherine H. Conly, *Helping Inmates Obtain Federal Disability Benefits: Serious Medical and Mental Illness, Incarceration and Federal Disability Entitlement Programs* (Washington, DC: U.S. Department of Justice, National Institute of Justice, November 2005); Christy Visher and Pamela Lattimore, "Study Examines Prisoners' Reentry Needs," *Corrections Today*, vol. 70, no. 2 (April 2008), pp. 146–147; and Beth E. Richie, "Challenges Incarcerated Women Face as They Return to Their Communities: Findings from Life History Interviews," *Crime and Delinquency*, vol. 47, no. 3 (July 2001), p. 370.

18. Tracey Meares, Andrew V. Papachristos, and Jeffrey Fagan, *Review of Research: Homicide and Gun Violence in Chicago: Evaluation and Summary of the Project Safe Neighborhood Program*. Available at www.psnchicago.org/PDFs/2009-PSN-Research-Brief_v2.pdf (accessed January 7, 2011).

19. The Pew Charitable Trusts, *Collateral Costs: Incarceration's Effect on Economic Mobility* (Washington, DC: The Pew Charitable Trusts, 2010), p. 25; and Josh Farley, "Will the State Bring Back Half-Off Sentences for Good Behavior?" *Kitsap Sun* (Bremerton, WA), October 9, 2010, www.kitsapsun.com (accessed November 1, 2011).

20. Camille Graham Camp and George M. Camp, *The Corrections Yearbook 1997* (Middletown, CT: Criminal Justice Institute, 1997), p. 181.

21. Nancy M. Campbell, *Comprehensive Framework for Paroling Authorities in an Era of Evidence-Based Practices* (Washington, DC: U.S. Department of Justice, National Institute of Corrections, 2008), p. 21.

22. Ronald Burns et al., "Perspectives on Parole: The Board Members' Viewpoint," *Federal Probation*, vol. 63, no. 1 (June 1999), pp. 16–22.

23. Mary West-Smith, Mark R. Pogrebin, and Eric D. Poole, "Denial of Parole: An Inmate Perspective," *Federal Probation*, vol. 64, no. 2 (December 2000), p. 5.

24. A. M. Heinz et al., "Sentencing by Parole Boards: An Evaluation," *Journal of Criminal Law and Criminology*, vol. 67 (1976), pp. 1–31.

25. West-Smith, Pogrebin, and Poole, "Denial of Parole."

26. West-Smith, Pogrebin, and Poole, "Denial of Parole."

27. Belinda Goldsmith, "John Lennon's Killer Refused Parole for Sixth Time," *ABC News*, September 8, 2010, www.abcnews.com (accessed November 1, 2011).

28. "Non-Revocable Parole," California Department of Corrections and Rehabilitation, www.cdcr.ca.gov/Parole/Non_Revocable_Parole/index.html (accessed February 8, 2011); Sam Stanton, "Critics Say New California Parole Policy Is Costly, Dangerous," *The Sacramento Bee*, April 12, 2010, www.sacbee.com (accessed November 1, 2011); and John Wilkens, "Inmates Released Under New Law," *The San Diego Union Tribune*, January 26, 2010, www.signonsandiego.com (accessed November 1, 2011).

29. Lauren E. Glaze and Thomas P. Bonczar, *Probation and Parole in the United States, 2009* (Washington, DC: U.S. Department of Justice, Bureau of Justice Statistics, December 2010).

30. Thomas P. Bonczar, *Characteristics of State Parole Supervising Agencies, 2006* (Washington, DC: U.S. Department of Justice, Bureau of Justice Statistics, August 2008).

31. Joan Petersilia, *When Prisoners Return to the Community: Political, Economic, and Social Consequences* (Washington, DC: U.S. Department of Justice, National Institute of Justice, November 2000).

32. Harry J. Holzer, *What Employers Want: Job Prospects for Less Educated Workers* (New York: Russell Sage Foundation, 1996).

33. Devah Pager, "Evidence-Based Policy for Successful Prisoner Reentry," *Criminology & Public Policy*, vol. 5, no. 3 (August 2006), pp. 505–514.

34. John Christoffersen, "Some Cities Look Other Way in Hiring of Former Inmates," *St. Louis Post-Dispatch*, January 6, 2009, www.stltoday.com (accessed January 6, 2009); and Amos Maki, "Memphis Council Removes Criminal-Record Notation from City Applications," *The Commercial Appeal*, June 23, 2010, www.commercialappeal.com (accessed June 28, 2011).

35. Robert F. Kronick, Dorothy E. Lambert, and E. Warren Lambert, "Recidivism Among Adult Parolees: What Makes the Difference?" *Journal of Offender Rehabilitation*, vol. 28, no. 1–2 (1998), pp. 61–69.

36. Amy L. Solomon, Vera Kachnowski, and Avinash Bhati, *Does Parole Work? Analyzing the Impact of Postprison Supervision on Rearrest Outcomes* (Washington, DC: Urban Institute, March 2005).

37. Glaze and Bonczar, *Probation and Parole*: "FY 2000 Cooperative Agreement: Transition from Prison to the Community," *Federal Register*, May 12, 2000; and "California Budget Held Captive by State Prisons," *National Public Radio*, www.npr.org, July 23, 2009.

38. Arthur J. Lurigio, "Effective Services for Parolees with Mental Illnesses," *Crime & Delinquency*, vol. 47, no. 3 (July, 2006), p. 457; Justice Policy Institute, *Pruning Prisons: How Cutting Corrections Can Save Money and Protect Public Safety* (Washington, DC: Justice Policy Institute, May 2009).

39. Peggy B. Burke, *Abolishing Parole: Why the Emperor Has No Clothes* (Lexington, KY: American Probation and Parole Association, 1995).

40. Jeffrey Lin, Ryken Grattet, and Joan Petersilia, "'Back-End Sentencing' and Reimprisonment: Individual, Organizational, and Community Predictors of Parole Sanctioning Decisions," *Criminology*, vol. 48, no. 3 (2010), pp. 759–795.

41. Peggy C. Giordano, Stephen A. Cernkovich, and Jennifer L. Rudolph, "Gender, Crime, and Desistance: Towards a Theory of Cognitive Transformation," *American Journal of Sociology*, vol. 107, no. 4 (2002), 990–1064.

42. Nicole D. Porter, *Expanding the Vote: State Felony Disenfranchisement Reform, 1997–2010* (Washington, DC: The Sentencing Project, October 2010).

43. Erika Wood and Rachel Bloom, *DeFacto Disenfranchisement* (Washington, DC: The Sentencing Project, 2008).

44. John F. Timoney, "Two More Issues for President Obama, With Implications for Justice and Race," *Subject to Debate: A*

Newsletter of the Police Executive Research Forum, vol. 22, no. 11 (November 2008), p. 2.

45. *Reentry Courts: Managing the Transition from Prison to Community* (Washington, DC: Office of Justice Programs, September, 1999).

46. Ibid., p. 9.

47. Jeffrey Spelman, "An Initial Comparison of Graduates and Terminated Clients in America's Largest Re-Entry Court," *Corrections Today,* vol. 65, no. 2 (August 2003), pp. 74–83; Erik Shilling, "Ohio Court's Re-entry Program Helps Felons Adjust," *USA Today,* February 13, 2010, www.usatoday.com (accessed February 15, 2011); Jeffrey Spelman, Ashland University (personal communication, February 15, 2011) corrected the information reported in the *USA Today* article.

48. Susan Herman and Cressida Wasserman, "A Role for Victims in Offender Reentry," *Crime & Delinquency,* vol. 47, no. 3 (July 2001), pp. 428–445.

49. Andrew von Hirsch, *Doing Justice: The Choice of Punishments, Report of the Committee for the Study of Incarceration* (New York: Hill and Wang, 1976).

50. Jessica Fargan, "Herald Eyes Parole Votes, Turns to Court for Records' Release," *Boston Herald,* November 13, 2008 www.bostonherald.com (accessed November 1, 2011).

51. La Vigne, Solomon, Beckman, and Dedel, *Prisoner Reentry and Community Policing,* p. 16.

52. Justin Jones and Edward Flynn, "Cops and Corrections: Reentry Collaborations for Public Safety," *Corrections Today,* vol. 70, no. 2 (April 2008), pp. 26–29; and Ashbel T. Wall II and Tracy Z. Poole, "Partnerships with Local Law Enforcement and Community Agencies: A Critical Component to Successful Prison Reentry Initiatives," *Corrections Today,* vol. 70, no. 2 (April 2008), pp. 30–37.

53. Kevin Johnson, "Unlikely Mentors Give Felons Hope," *USA Today,* June 21, 2010, www.usatoday.com (accessed June 28, 2011).

54. Donald G. Evans, "Community-Focused Parole," *Corrections Today,* vol. 68, no. 7 (December 2006), pp. 90–91.

55. *Swarthout v. Cooke,* 562 U.S. _____ (2011).

56. Ibid, p. 4.

57. Ibid, p. 5.

58. Ibid.

Chapter 9

1. James A. Gondles Jr., "*Guard* Must Go," *Corrections Today,* August 2006, p. 9.

2. See Sylvia G. McCollum, "Excellence or Mediocrity: Training Correctional Officers and Administrators," *The Keeper's Voice,* vol. 17, no. 4 (Fall 1996).

3. Anthony R. Martinez, "Corrections Officer: The 'Other' Prisoner," *The Keeper's Voice,* vol. 18, no. 1 (Spring 1997).

4. Don A. Josi and Dale K. Sechrest, *The Changing Career of the Correctional Officer: Policy Implications for the 21st Century* (Boston: Butterworth-Heinemann, 1998), p. 11.

5. Ibid., p. 12.

6. John Hepburn, "The Exercise of Power in Coercive Organizations: A Study of Prison Guards," *Criminology,* vol. 23, no. 1 (1985), pp. 145–164.

7. Gresham Sykes, *The Society of Captives* (Princeton, NJ: Princeton University Press, 1958).

8. See, for example, James B. Jacobs and Lawrence J. Kraft, "Integrating the Keepers: A Comparison of Black and White Prison Guards in Illinois," *Social Problems,* vol. 25, no. 3 (1978), pp. 304–318.

9. Adapted from John J. Macionis, *Society: The Basics,* 2nd ed. (Englewood Cliffs, NJ: Prentice Hall, 1994), p. 405.

10. Kelsey Kauffman, *Prison Officers and Their World* (Cambridge, MA: Harvard University Press, 1988), pp. 85–86.

11. American Correctional Association, *Vital Statistics in Corrections* (Lanham, MD: ACA, 2000), p. 143; James J. Stephan and Jennifer C. Karberg, *Census of State and Federal Correctional Facilities, 2000* (Washington, DC: Bureau of Justice Statistics, 2003).

12. U.S. Bureau of the Census, *The Population Profile of the United States: 2000 (Internet Release),* www.census.gov/population/www/pop-profile/profile2000.html (accessed June 29, 2002).

13. ACA, *Vital Statistics in Corrections.*

14. Ibid.

15. See, for example, E. Poole and R. M. Regoli, "Work Relations and Cynicism Among Prison Guards," *Criminal Justice and Behavior,* vol. 7 (1980), pp. 303–314.

16. Adapted from Frank Schmalleger, *Criminal Justice Today: An Introductory Text for the 21st Century,* 9th ed. (Upper Saddle River, NJ: Prentice Hall, 2007).

17. Lucien X. Lombardo, *Guards Imprisoned: Correctional Officers at Work,* 2nd ed. (Cincinnati, OH: Anderson, 1989).

18. Adapted from Dora B. Schriro, "Women in Prison: Keeping the Peace," *The Keeper's Voice,* vol. 16, no. 2 (Spring 1995).

19. Ibid.

20. M. I. Cadwaladr, "Women Working in a Men's Jail," *FORUM,* vol. 6, no. 1 (1994).

21. Ibid.

22. N. C. Jurik and J. Halemba, "Gender, Working Conditions, and the Job Satisfaction of Women in a Non-Traditional Occupation: Female Correctional Officers in Men's Prisons," *Sociological Quarterly,* vol. 25 (1984), pp. 551–566.

23. Joseph R. Rowan, "Who Is Safer in Male Maximum Security Prisons?" *The Keeper's Voice,* vol. 17, no. 3 (Summer 1996).

24. Ibid.

25. See, for example, Stephen Walters, "Changing the Guard: Male Correctional Officers' Attitudes Toward Women as Co-workers," *Journal of Offender Rehabilitation,* vol. 20, no. 1 (1993), pp. 47–60.

26. Cadwaladr, "Women Working in a Men's Jail."

27. Ibid.

28. Public Service Commission (of Canada), "Stress and Executive Burnout," *FORUM,* vol. 4, no. 1 (1992). Much of the material in this section is taken from this work.

29. B. M. Crouch, "The Guard in a Changing Prison World," in B. M. Crouch (ed.), *The Keepers: Prison Guards and Contemporary Corrections* (Springfield, IL: Charles C. Thomas, 1980).

30. Shannon Black, "Correctional Employee Stress & Strain," *Corrections Today,* October 2001, p. 99.

31. Lombardo, *Guards Imprisoned.*

32. Eric G. Lambert, "Work-Family Conflict: An Unexplored Stressor for Correctional Staff," *Corrections Compendium,* vol. 26, no. 5 (May 2001).

33. Public Service Commission, "Stress and Executive Burnout."

34. For an excellent overview of the literature on correctional officer stress, see Tammy L. Castle and Jamie S. Martin, "Occupational Hazard: Predictors of Stress Among Jail Correctional Officers," *American Journal of Criminal Justice,* vol. 31, no. 1 (Fall 2006), pp. 65–80.

35. "Not Stressed Enough?" *FORUM,* vol. 4, no. 1 (1992). Adapted from C. C. W. Hines and W. C. Wilson, "A No-Nonsense Guide to Being Stressed," *Management Solutions,* October 1986, pp. 27–29.

36. J. T. Dignam, M. Barrera, and S. G. West, "Occupational Stress, Social Support, and Burnout Among Correctional Officers," *American Journal of Community Psychology,* vol. 14, no. 2 (1986), pp. 177–193.

37. M. C. W. Peeters, B. P. Buunk, and W. B. Schaufeli, "Social Interactions and Feelings of Inferiority Among Correctional Officers:

A Daily Event-Recording Approach," *Journal of Applied Social Psychology,* vol. 25, no. 12 (1995), pp. 1073–1089.

38. Jessie W. Doyle, "6 Elements That Form a Context for Staff Safety," *Corrections Today,* October 2001, pp. 101–104.

39. Terry L. Stewart and Donald W. Brown, "Focusing on Correctional Staff Safety," *Corrections Today,* October 2001, pp. 90–93.

40. Ibid.

41. David Robinson, Frank Porporino, and Linda Simourd, "Do Different Occupational Groups Vary on Attitudes and Work Adjustment in Corrections?" *Federal Probation,* vol. 60, no. 3 (1996), pp. 45–53. See also Francis T. Cullen et al., "How Satisfying Is Prison Work? A Comparative Occupational Approach," *The Journal of Offender Counseling Services and Rehabilitation,* vol. 14, no. 2 (1989), pp. 89–108.

42. Timothy J. Flanagan, Wesley Johnson, and Katherine Bennett, "Job Satisfaction Among Correctional Executives: A Contemporary Portrait of Wardens of State Prisons for Adults," *Prison Journal,* vol. 76, no. 4 (1996), pp. 385–397.

43. Lombardo, *Guards Imprisoned.*

44. Martinez, "Corrections Officer."

45. Thomas Gillan, "The Correctional Officer: One of Law Enforcement's Toughest Positions," *Corrections Today,* October 2001, p. 113.

46. Black, "Correctional Employee Stress & Strain," p. 99.

47. Andrew Metz, "Life on the Inside: The Jailers," in Tara Gray (ed.), *Exploring Corrections* (Boston: Allyn & Bacon, 2002), p. 65.

48. Ibid., p. 64.

49. Black, "Correctional Employee Stress & Strain," p. 99.

50. Stephen Walters, "The Determinants of Job Satisfaction Among Canadian and American Correctional Officers," *Journal of Crime and Justice,* vol. 19, no. 2 (1996), pp. 145–158.

51. John R. Hepburn and Paul E. Knepper, "Correctional Officers as Human Services Workers: The Effect on Job Satisfaction," *Justice Quarterly,* vol. 10, no. 2 (1993), pp. 315–337.

52. Stephen Walters, "Gender, Job Satisfaction, and Correctional Officers: A Comparative Analysis," *The Justice Professional,* vol. 7, no. 2 (1993), pp. 23–33.

53. Dana M. Britton, "Perceptions of the Work Environment Among Correctional Officers: Do Race and Sex Matter?" *Criminology,* vol. 35, no. 1 (1997), pp. 85–105.

54. Adapted from William Sondervan, "Professionalism in Corrections," in Frank Schmalleger and John Smykla (eds.), *Corrections in the Twenty-First Century,* 5e (New York: McGraw-Hill, 2011), p. 572.

55. Ibid.

56. Justin Fenton, "Indictments Reveal Prison Crime World," *Baltimore Sun,* April 18, 2009.

57. Jack Dolan, "California Prison Guards Union Called Main Obstacle to Keeping Cell Phones Away from Inmate," *Los Angeles Times,* February 4, 2011. Web posted at http://www.latimes.com/news/local/la-me-prison-guards-20110204,0,2785860.story (accessed February 21, 2011).

58. Mike Ward, "Low Pay May Make Prison Guards Ripe for Smugglers," *American Statesman,* October 24, 2008.

59. U.S. Department of Justice, Office of the Inspector General, *Semiannual Report to Congress: April 1, 2008–September 30, 2008* (Washington, DC: USGPO, 2008).

60. International Herald Tribune, "Man Behind U.S. Terrorism Plot Gets 16 Years," March 6, 2009. Web posted at http://www.iht.com/articles/ap/2009/03/06/america/NA-US-Terrorism-Probe.php (accessed March 27, 2009).

61. Mark S. Hamm, "Prisoner Radicalization: Assessing the Threat in U.S. Correctional Institutions," *NIJ Journal* (No. 261), p. 17.

62. Ibid., p. 18.

63. Quoted in Meghan Mandeville, "Information Sharing Becomes Crucial to Battling Terrorism Behind Bars," Corrections.com, December 8, 2003, http://database.corrections.com/news/results2.asp?ID_8988 (accessed August 1, 2005).

64. "FBI: Al-Qaida Recruiting in U.S. Prisons," United Press International wire service, January 7, 2004, http://database.corrections.com/news/results2.asp?ID_9148 (accessed August 1, 2005).

65. "Lawyer Sentenced to 28 Months in Prison on Terrorism Charge," Court TV News, October 16, 2006, www.courttv.com/news/2006/1016/cynne_Stewart_ap.html.

66. Jess Maghan, *Intelligence-Led Penology: Management of Crime Information Obtained from Incarcerated Persons,* paper presented at the Investigation of Crime World Conference, 2001, p. 6.

67. Institute for the Study of Violent Groups, "Land of Wahhabism," *Crime and Justice International,* March/April 2005, p. 43.

68. Office of the Inspector General, *A Review of the Federal Bureau of Prisons' Selection of Muslim Religious Services Providers* (Washington, DC: U.S. Department of Justice, 2004).

69. Ibid., p. 8.

70. Ibid.

71. Mark S. Hamm, "Terrorist Recruitment in American Correctional Institutions: An Exploratory Study of Non-Traditional Faith Groups," nonpublished paper, December 2007.

72. U.S. Department of Justice, Office of the Inspector General, *The Federal Bureau of Prisons' Monitoring of Mail for High-Risk Inmates* (Washington, DC: U.S. Government Printing Office, 2006).

73. Keith Martin, "Corrections Prepares for Terrorism," (Corrections Connection News Network, January 21, 2002, www.corrections.com (accessed July 10, 2005).

74. Y. N. Baykan, "The Emergence of Sunni Islam in America's Prisons," *Corrections Today,* February 2007, pp. 49–51.

75. James Gilligan, *Violence: Reflections on a National Epidemic* (New York: Vintage Books, 1997), p. 165.

Chapter 10

1. Elizabeth Crips and Molly Parker, "Scott Sisters to Leave Mississippi Prison Today," Join Families, *USA Today,* January 7, 2001, p. 3A.

2. Allen Beck et al., *Survey of State Prison Inmates, 1991* (Washington, DC: U.S. Department of Justice, March 1993), www.ojp.usdoj.gov/bjs/pub/ascii/sospi91.txt.

3. Erving Goffman, *Asylums: Essays on the Social Situation of Mental Patients and Other Inmates* (Garden City, NY: Anchor Books, 1961).

4. Hans Toch, *Living in Prison: The Ecology of Survival,* reprint ed. (Washington, DC: American Psychological Association, 1996), p. xv.

5. Victoria R. DeRosia, *Living Inside Prison Walls: Adjustment Behavior* (Westport, CT: Praeger, 1998).

6. "Inmate Subculture," in Virgil L. Williams (ed.), *Dictionary of American Penology: An Introductory Guide* (Westport, CT: Greenwood, 1979).

7. Donald Clemmer, *The Prison Community* (Boston: Holt, Rinehart & Winston, 1940).

8. Stanton Wheeler, "Socialization in Correctional Communities," *American Sociological Review,* vol. 26 (October 1961), pp. 697–712.

9. Gresham M. Sykes, *The Society of Captives: A Study of a Maximum Security Prison* (Princeton, NJ: Princeton University Press, 1958).

10. Stephen C. Light, *Inmate Assaults on Staff: Challenges to Authority in a Large State Prison System*, dissertation, State University of New York at Albany (Ann Arbor, MI: University Microfilms International, 1987).

11. John Irwin and Donald R. Cressey, "Thieves, Convicts and the Inmate Culture," *Social Problems*, vol. 10 (Fall 1962), pp. 142–155.

12. James Jacobs, *Stateville: The Penitentiary in Mass Society* (Chicago: University of Chicago Press, 1977).

13. Miles D. Harer and Darrell J. Steffensmeier, "Race and Prison Violence," *Criminology*, vol. 34, no. 3 (1996), pp. 323–355.

14. John M. Wilson and Jon D. Snodgrass, "The Prison Code in a Therapeutic Community," *Journal of Criminal Law, Criminology, and Police Science*, vol. 60, no. 4 (1969), pp. 472–478.

15. Gresham M. Sykes and Sheldon L. Messinger, "The Inmate Social System," in Richard A. Cloward et al. (eds.), *Theoretical Studies in Social Organization of the Prison* (New York: Social Science Research Council, 1960), pp. 5–19.

16. Peter M. Wittenberg, "Language and Communication in Prison," *Federal Probation*, vol. 60, no. 4 (1996), pp. 45–50.

17. Sykes, *The Society of Captives*.

18. John Irwin, *The Felon* (Englewood Cliffs, NJ: Prentice Hall, 1970).

19. Adapted from Frank Schmalleger, *Criminal Justice Today*, 7th ed. (Upper Saddle River, NJ: Prentice Hall, 2003).

20. See, for example, Donald Tucker, *A Punk's Song: View from the Inside* (AMS Press, 1981), from which some of the information here is adapted.

21. Ibid.

22. Ibid.

23. Ibid.

24. Daniel Lockwood, *Sexual Aggression Among Male Prisoners*, dissertation, State University of New York at Albany (Ann Arbor, MI: University Microfilms International, 1978); Daniel Lockwood, "Issues in Prison Sexual Violence," *The Prison Journal*, vol. 58, no. 1 (1983), pp. 73–79.

25. Adapted from Toch, *Living in Prison*, p. 274.

26. Pub. L. No. 108-79.

27. Paul Guerino and Allen J. Beck, *Sexual Victimization Reported by Adult Correctional Authorities, 2007-2008* (Washington, DC: Bureau of Justice Statistics, 2011).

28. Allen J. Beck and Paige M. Harrison, *Sexual Victimization in Prisons and Jails Reported by Inmates, 2008–09* (Washington, DC: Bureau of Justice Statistics, 2010).

29. Allen J. Beck and Timothy A. Hughes, *Sexual Violence Reported by Correctional Authorities, 2004* (Washington, DC: Bureau of Justice Statistics, 2005).

30. Heather C. West, William J. Sabol, and Sarah J. Greenman, *Prisoners in 2009* (Washington, DC: Bureau of Justice Statistics, 2010).

31. Phyllis J. Baunach, "Critical Problems of Women in Prison," in Imogene L. Moyer (ed.), *The Changing Roles of Women in the Criminal Justice System* (Prospect Heights, IL: Waveland Press, 1985), pp. 95–110.

32. See John W. Palmer and Stephen E. Palmer, *Constitutional Rights of Prisoners*, 6th ed. (Cincinnati, OH: Anderson, 1999).

33. American Correctional Association, *Standards for Adult Correctional Institutions* (Lanham, MD: ACA, 1990).

34. Alabama Department of Corrections, *Monthly Statistical Report for November 2010* (Montgomery, Alabama; Alabama Department of Corrections, 2011), p. 3.

35. Lawrence A. Greenfeld and Tracy L. Snell, *Women Offenders*, Bureau of Justice Statistics Special Report (Washington, DC: Bureau of Justice Statistics, December 1999, revised October 3, 2000); West, Sabol, and Greenman, *Prisoners in 2009*.

36. West, Sabol, and Greenman, *Prisoners in 2009*.

37. Ibid.

38. Angela Browne, Brenda Miller, and Eugene Maguin, "Prevalence and Severity of Lifetime Physical and Sexual Victimization Among Incarcerated Women," *International Journal of Law and Psychiatry*, vol. 22, no. 3–4 (1999), pp. 301–322.

39. Bloom et al., *Gender-Responsive Strategies: Research, Practice, and Guiding Principles for Women Offenders* (Washington, DC: National Institute of Corrections, 2003).

40. West, Sabol, and Greenman, *Prisoners in 2009*.

41. American Correctional Association, *Female Offenders: Meeting Needs of a Neglected Population* (Laurel, MD: ACA, 1993).

42. Tracy Snell, *Women in Prison* (Washington, DC: Bureau of Justice Statistics, 1994).

43. Rose Giallombardo, *Society of Women: A Study of a Women's Prison* (New York: John Wiley, 1966).

44. Esther Heffernan, *Making It in Prison: The Square, the Cool, and the Life* (New York: Wiley-Interscience, 1972).

45. Barbara Owens, "The Mix: The Culture of Imprisoned Women," in Mary K. Stohr and Craig Hemmens (eds.), *The Inmate Prison Experience* (Upper Saddle River, NJ: Prentice Hall, 2004), pp. 152–172.

46. Williams, "Inmate Subculture." p. 109.

47. Kathryn Watterson, *Women in Prison: Inside the Concrete Tomb*, 2nd ed. (Boston: Northeastern University Press, 1996), p. 291.

48. For example, see John Gagnon and William Simon, "The Social Meaning of Prison Homosexuality," in David M. Petersen and Charles W. Thomas (eds.), *Corrections: Problems and Prospects* (Englewood Cliffs, NJ: Prentice Hall, 1980).

49. Doris Layton MacKenzie, James Robinson, and Carol Campbell, "Long-Term Incarceration of Female Offenders: Prison Adjustment and Coping," *Criminal Justice and Behavior*, vol. 16, no. 2 (1989), pp. 223–238.

50. Nicole Hahn Rafter, *Partial Justice: Women, Prisons and Social Control* (New Brunswick, NJ: Transaction, 1990).

51. Bloom et al., *Gender-Responsive Strategies*.

52. Barbara Bloom and Stephanie Covington, *Gendered Justice: Programming for Women in Correctional Settings*, paper presented at the American Society of Criminology annual meeting, San Francisco, November 2000, p. 11.

53. Bloom et al., *Gender-Responsive Strategies*.

54. Susan Cranford and Rose Williams, "Critical Issues in Managing Female Offenders," *Corrections Today*, vol. 60, no. 7 (December 1998), pp. 130–135.

55. John DeBell, "The Female Offender: Different . . . Not Difficult," *Corrections Today*, vol. 63, no. 1 (February 2001), pp. 56–61.

56. Pat Carlen, "Analyzing Women's Imprisonment: Abolition and Its Enemies," *Women, Girls & Criminal Justice*, vol. 7, no. 6 (October/November 2006), p. 85.

57. Tracy L. Snell, "Women in Prison," *Bureau of Justice Statistics Bulletin* (Washington, DC: Bureau of Justice Statistics, March 1994).

58. As estimated by Vesna Markovic, "Pregnant Women in Prison: A Correctional Dilemma?" *The Keepers' Voice*, Summer 1995.

59. Ibid.

60. American Correctional Association, *Standards for Adult Correctional Institutions*, 3rd ed. (ACA, January 1990).

61. Gerald Austin McHugh, "Protection of the Rights of Pregnant Women in Prison and Detention Facilities," *New England Journal of Prison Law*, vol. 6, no. 2 (Summer 1980), pp. 231–263.

62. Snell, "Women in Prison."

63. National Institute of Corrections, *Services for Families of Prison Inmates* (Washington, DC: NIC, 2002), p. 3.

64. Phyllis Jo Baunach, "Critical Problems of Women in Prison," in Imogene L. Moyer (ed.), *The Changing Roles of Women in the*

Criminal Justice System (Prospect Heights, IL: Waveland Press, 1985), p. 16.

65. John J. Sheridan, "Inmates May Be Parents, Too," *Corrections Today,* vol. 58, no. 5 (August 1996), p. 100.

66. Patricia Allard and Judith Greene, *Children on the Outside: Voicing the Pain and Human Costs of Parental Incarceration* (New York; Justice Strategies, 2011).

67. L. Wright and C. Seymour, *Working with Children and Families Separated by Incarceration: A Handbook for Child Welfare Agencies* (Washington, DC: Child Welfare League of America, 2000).

68. Kelsey Kauffman, "Mothers in Prison," *Corrections Today* (February 2001), pp. 62–65.

69. Harrison and Beck, *Prisoners in 2006.*

70. Christopher J. Mumola, *Incarcerated Parents and Their Children,* Bureau of Justice Statistics Special Report (Washington, DC: Bureau of Justice Statistics, August 2000), p. 1.

71. Suzanne Hoholik, "Weekend Camp Lets Mother, Kids Bond," *The Columbus Dispatch,* July 22, 2000, pp. A1–A2.

72. Rini Bartlett, "Helping Inmate Moms Keep in Touch," *Correctional Compass* (Tallahassee, FL: Department of Corrections, February 2001), www.dc.state.fl.us/pub/compass/0102/page07.html (accessed June 2, 2007).

73. Kauffman, "Mothers in Prison," p. 62.

74. Huey Freeman, "Illinois Prison Program Guides New Mothers," Pantagraph.com, http://www.pantagraph.com/news/state-and-regional/illinois/article_ab1d5106-4631-11df-97d4-001cc4c002e0.html (accessed March 12, 2011).

75. Rick Jervis, "Prison Dads Learn Meaning of 'Father,'" *USA Today,* June 18, 2010, http://www.usatoday.com/news/nation/2010-06-17-prison-dads_N.htm (accessed March 15, 2011).

76. John Ortiz Smykla, "Coed Prison: Should We Try It (Again)?" in Charles B. Fields (ed.), *Controversial Issues in Corrections* (Boston: Allyn & Bacon, 1999), pp. 203–218.

77. John Ortiz Smykla and Jimmy J. Williams, "Co-Corrections in the United States of America, 1970–1990: Two Decades of Disadvantages for Women Prisoners," *Women & Criminal Justice,* vol. 8, no. 1 (1996), pp. 61–76.

78. Ibid.

79. Jacqueline K. Crawford, "Two Losers Don't Make a Winner: The Case Against the Co-correctional Institution," in John Ortiz Smykla (ed.), *Coed Prison* (New York: Human Sciences Press, 1980), pp. 263–268.

80. Smykla and Williams, "Co-corrections in the United States," p. 61.

81. Lawrence W. Sherman et al., *Preventing Crime: What Works, What Doesn't, What's Promising* (Washington, DC: NIJ, 1997).

Chapter 11

1. Rich Pedroncelli, "Judges Back a One-Third Reduction in State Prison Population," *Los Angeles Times,* February 10, 2009.

2. *Ruffin* v. *Commonwealth,* 62, Va. 790, 1871.

3. Frances Cole, "The Impact of *Bell* v. *Wolfish* Upon Prisoners' Rights," *Journal of Crime and Justice,* vol. 10 (1987), pp. 47–70.

4. D. J. Gottlieb, "The Legacy of *Wolfish* and *Chapman:* Some Thoughts About 'Big Prison Case' Litigation in the 1980s," in I. D. Robbins (ed.), *Prisoners and the Law* (New York: Clark Boardman, 1985).

5. James B. Jacobs, *New Perspectives on Prisons and Imprisonment* (Ithaca, NY: Cornell University Press, 1983).

6. *Holt v. Sarver,* 442 F.2d 304 (1971).

7. Ibid.

8. *Holt v. Sarver,* 309 F.Supp. 362 (E.D.Ark.1970), aff'd, 442 F.2d 304 (8th Cir. 1971).

9. Todd Clear and George F. Cole, *American Corrections,* 4th ed. (New York: Wadsworth, 1997).

10. Civil Rights of Institutionalized Persons Act, 42 U.S.C. § 1997 et seq. (1976 ed., Supp. IV), as modified 1980. (Current through P.L. 104-150, approved June 3, 1996.)

11. R. Hawkins and G. P. Alpert, *American Prison Systems: Punishment and Justice* (Englewood Cliffs, NJ: Prentice Hall, 1989).

12. John Scalia, *Prisoner Petitions Filed in U.S. District Courts, 2000, with Trends 1980–2000* (Washington, DC: U.S. Department of Justice, December 2001).

13. Florida Department of Corrections, Office of the Inspector General, *Annual Report 1994–1995,* www.dc.state.fl.us/pub/IGannual/19941995/page6.html (accessed May 30, 2002).

14. *Report of the Comptroller General of the United States: Grievance Mechanisms in State Correctional Institutions and Large-City Jails* (Washington, DC: U.S. Government Printing Office, June 17, 1977), Appendix I.

15. James B. Jacobs, "The Prisoners' Rights Movement and Its Impacts," in Edward J. Latessa, Alexander Holsinger, James W. Marquart, and Jonathan R. Sorensen, *Correctional Contexts: Contemporary and Classical Readings,* 2nd ed. (Los Angeles: Roxbury, 2001), p. 211. Reprinted from James B. Jacobs, *Crime and Justice,* vol. II (Chicago: University of Chicago Press, 1980).

16. See *Estelle* v. *Gamble,* 429 U.S. 97 (1976), and *Hutto* v. *Finney,* 437 U.S. 678 (1978).

17. *Holt v. Sarver,* 309 F. Supp 362 (1970), aff'd. 442 F.2d 304 (8th Cir. 1974).

18. American Civil Liberties Union, *ACLU Position Paper: Prisoners' Rights* (Fall 1999), www.aclu.org/library/PrisonerRights.pdf (accessed March 2, 2011).

19. In 1977, Theriault's appeal to the U.S. Supreme Court was denied (see 434 U.S. 953, November 14, 1977).

20. *Ali* v. *Federal Bureau of Prisons,* 552 U.S. 214 (2008).

21. In Section 1997e, Congress created a specific, limited exhaustion requirement for adult prisoners bringing actions pursuant to section 1983.

22. Prison Litigation Reform Act, Pub. L. No. 104-134, § 801-10, 110 Stat. 1321 (1995).

23. If a prisoner wishes to proceed as an indigent on appeal, the prisoner must file in the district court, with the notice of appeal, a motion for leave to proceed as an indigent, a certified copy of a prison trust account statement, and Form 4 from the Appendix of Forms found in the *Federal Rules of Appellate Procedure.*

24. Fred L. Cheesman, Brian J. Ostrom, and Roger A. Hanson, *A Tale of Two Laws Revisited: Investigating the Impact of the Prison Litigation Reform Act and the Antiterrorism and Effective Death Penalty Act* (Williamsburg, VA: National Center for State Courts, 2005).

25. "Court Intervention Ends for D.C. DOC," *Corrections Today,* December 2004, p. 12.

26. "Judge Approves Settlement in Alabama Prison Lawsuit," *Corrections Journal,* August 9, 2004, p. 1.

Chapter 12

1. Excerpted from Ron Word, "Elderly Inmates Swell Nation's Prisons," www.angelfire.com/fl13/starke/elderlyswell.html (accessed October 3, 2011).

2. Stan Stojkovic (ed.), *Managing Special Populations in Jails and Prisons* (Kingston, NJ: Civic Research Institute, 2005), p. xv.

3. "Inmate Health Care and *Communicable Diseases,*" *Corrections Compendium,* vol. 34, no. 4 (Winter 2009), p. 13.

4. Michael Rothfeld, "UC Could Oversee Prison Health," *Los Angeles Times,* March 19, 2010, www.latimes.com (accessed March 24, 2011).

5. "Inmate Health Care and Communicable Diseases," pp. 32–33.

6. G. Larry Mays and Daniel L. Judiscak, "Special Needs Inmates in New Mexico Jails," *American Jails*, vol. 10, no. 2 (1996), pp. 32–41.

7. National Center on Addiction and Substance Abuse, *Behind Bars II: Substance Abuse and America's Prison Population* (New York: National Center on Addiction and Substance Abuse, Columbia University, February 2010).

8. Kate Miltner, "Treatment over Jail Time Poll: Most Favor Efforts to Combat Addiction over Punishment," http://abcnews.go.com/sections/politics/dailynews/poll010606.html (accessed July 12, 2011).

9. Christopher J. Mumola and Jennifer C. Karberg, *Drug Use and Dependence, State and Federal Prisoners, 2004* (Washington, DC: U.S. Department of Justice, Bureau of Justice Statistics, October 2006).

10. National Institute of Justice, *Annualized Site Reports 2001* (Washington, DC: U.S. Department of Justice, National Institute of Justice, June 2003).

11. Jeremy Travis, *Framing the National Agenda: A Research and Policy Perspective.* Speech to National Corrections Conference on Substance Abuse, April 23, 1997.

12. M. D. Anglin and Y. Haer, "Treatment of Drug Abuse," in Michael Tonry and James Q. Wilson (eds.), *Drugs and Crime: Crime and Justice: A Review of Research*, vol. 13 (Chicago: University of Chicago Press, 1990), pp. 393–460; D. N. Nurco, T. W. Kislock, and T. E. Hanlon, "The Nature and Status of Drug Abuse Treatment," *Maryland Medical Journal*, vol. 43 (January 1994), pp. 51–57; D. D. Simpson et al., "A National Evaluation of Treatment Outcomes for Cocaine Dependence," *Archives of General Psychiatry*, vol. 56, no. 6 (1999), pp. 507–514; and Doris Layton MacKenzie, *What Works in Corrections: Reducing the Criminal Activities of Criminals and Delinquents* (NewYork: Cambridge University Press, 2006).

13. Center for Substance Abuse Treatment, *NTIES: The National Treatment Improvement Study—Final Report* (Rockville, MD: U.S. Department of Health and Human Services, Substance Abuse and Mental Health Services Administration, 1997).

14. Marcia R. Chaiken, *Prison Programs for Drug-Involved Offenders* (Washington, DC: National Institute of Justice, October 1989); D. A. Andrews et al., "Does Correctional Treatment Work? A Clinically Relevant and Psychologically Informed Meta-Analysis," *Criminology*, vol. 28, no. 3 (1990), pp. 369–404; Donald Lipton and Frank Pearson, *The CDATE Project: Reviewing Research on the Effectiveness of Treatment Programs for Adults and Juvenile Offenders*, paper presented at the annual meeting of the American Society of Criminology, Chicago, IL, 1996.

15. Lana D. Harrison, "The Revolving Prison Door for Drug-Involved Offenders: Challenges and Opportunities," *Crime & Delinquency*, vol. 47, no. 3 (July 2001), pp. 462–485.

16. Sandra Tunis et al., *Evaluation of Drug Treatment in Local Corrections* (Washington, DC: U.S. Department of Justice, 1997).

17. Steven S. Martin, James A. Inciardi, and Daniel J. O'Connell, "Treatment Research in *Oz*—Is Randomization the Ideal or Just Somewhere Over the Rainbow?" *Federal Probation*, vol. 67, no. 2 (September 2003), pp. 53–60.

18. Bernadette Pelissier et al., *TRIAD Drug Treatment Evaluation Project Final Report of Three-Year Outcomes: Part I* (Washington, DC: Federal Bureau of Prisons, Office of Research and Evaluation, September 2000).

19. James A. Inciardi et al., "An Effective Model of Prison-Based Treatment for Drug-Involved Offenders," *Journal of Drug Issues*, vol. 27, no. 2 (Spring 1997), pp. 261–278; James A. Inciardi, Steven S. Martin, and Clifford A. Butzin, "Five-Year Outcomes of Therapeutic Community Treatment of Drug-Involved Offenders After Release from Prison," *Crime & Delinquency*, vol. 50, no. 1 (January 2004), pp. 88–107.

20. *Administrative Office of Courts, Drug Treatment and Education Fund, Annual Report, Fiscal Year 1999*, Arizona Supreme Court, November 2001.

21. Josh Richman, "Money Is Gone, But Proposition 36's Drug-Treatment Mandate Remains," *Oakland Tribune* (Oakland, CA), February 22, 2011, www.contracostatimes.com (accessed February 22, 2011); and Scott Ehlers and Jason Ziedenberg, *Proposition 36: Five Years Later* (Washington, DC: Justice Policy Institute, April 2006).

22. National Institute on Drug Abuse, *Principles of Drug Abuse Treatment for Criminal Justice Populations—A Research-Based Guide* (Washington, DC: U.S. Department of Health and Human Services, 2006).

23. National Commission on Correctional Health Care, *The Health Status of Soon-to-Be-Released Inmates: A Report to Congress*, Vol. I (Washington, DC: U.S. Department of Justice, September 2004), p. ix.

24. Laura M. Maruschak, *HIV in Prisons, 2007–08* (Washington, DC: U.S. Department of Justice, Bureau of Justice Statistics, December 2009).

25. *Management of the HIV-Positive Prisoner* (New York: World Health CME, n.d.).

26. Michael S. Vaughn and Leo Carroll, "Separate and Unequal: Prison Versus Free-World Medical Care," *Justice Quarterly*, vol. 15, no. 1 (March 1998), pp. 3–40.

27. Maruschak, *HIV in Prison 2007–08*.

28. American Correctional Association, *Managing Special Needs Offenders* (Lanham, MD: American Correctional Association, 2004).

29. Theodore M. Hammett, Cheryl Roberts, and Sofia Kennedy, "Health-Related Issues in Prisoner Reentry," *Crime & Delinquency*, vol. 47, no. 3 (July 2001), pp. 390–409; Abe Macher, "Clinical Management of HIV Disease in Correctional Facilities," in Stan Stojkovic (ed.), *Managing Special Populations in Jails and Prisons*, pp. 4–1 to 4–57; "Jailhouse Tatooing" (New York: Civic Reaserch Institute, 2006), *American Jails*, vol. 20, no. 4 (September/October 2006), pp. 96–98.

30. Jaime Shimkus, "Side by Side, Ministers and Detainees Test for HIV Infection," *CorrectCare*, Fall 2001, p. 16.

31. Christina Hernandez, "HIV Prisoners: What Happens When They Get Out?" *The Crime Report*, October 29, 2009, www.thecrimereport.com (accessed October 26, 2011).

32. Ibid.

33. Mike Israel, *Criminal Justice Washington Letter*, October 15, 2004.

34. Doris J. James and Lauren E. Glaze, *Mental Health Problems of Prison and Jail Inmates* (Washington, DC: U.S. Department of Justice, Bureau of Justice Statistics, September 2006); and "Offenders with Health Problems Found to Fare Poorly After Prison," *Criminal Justice Newsletter*, March 17, 2008, pp. 6–7.

35. "Michigan Coalition Calls for Mental Health Solutions," *Corrections Compendium*, vol. 33, no. 2 (March/April 2008), p. 10.

36. Thomas N. Faust, "Shift the Responsibility of Untreated Mental Illness out of the Criminal Justice System," *Corrections Today*, April 2003, pp. 6–7; see also Liz Lipton, "Few Safeguards Govern Elimination of Psychiatric Beds," *Psychiatric News*, vol. 36, no. 15 (August 3, 2001), p. 9, http://pn.psychiatriconline.org/cgi/content/full/36/15/9 (accessed January 13, 2011); James and Glaze, *Mental Health Problems of Prison and Jail Inmates*.

37. Michael P. Maloney, Michael P. Ward, and Charles M. Jackson, "Study Reveals That More Mentally Ill Offenders Are Entering Jail," *Corrections Today*, April 2003, pp. 100–103.

38. Phillip Comey, "Health Care and Prisons: Considering the Connection," *On the Line* (Lanham: MD. American Correctional Association, November 2005), p. 1.

39. Risdon N. Slate et al., "Doing Justice for Mental Illness and Society: Federal Probation and Pretrial Service Officers as Mental Health Specialists," *Federal Probation*, vol. 67, no. 3 (December 2003).

40. Maloney, Ward, and Jackson, "Study Reveals."

41. The Bazelon Center for Mental Health Law, *Position Statement on Involuntary Commitment, 1999.* As cited in The Sentencing Project, *Mentally Ill Offenders in the Criminal Justice System: An Analysis and Prescription* (Washington, DC: The Sentencing Project, January 2002), p. 4.

42. John M. Greacen, "Then & Now: Reflections on 25 Years of Correctional Health Care," *CorrectCare,* vol. 16, no.1 (Winter 2002), pp. 9, 22.

43. Dean H. Aufderheide, "The Mentally Ill in America's Prisons," *Corrections Today,* vol. 67, no. 1 (2005), pp. 30–33.

44. Randy M. Bourn et al., "Police Perspectives on Responding to Mentally Ill People in Crisis: Perceptions of Program Effectiveness," *Behavioral Sciences and the Law,* vol. 16, no. 4 (1998), pp. 393–402.

45. Michael Thompson, Fred Osher, and Denise Tomasini-Joshi, *Improving Responses to People with Mental Illness: The Essential Elements of a Mental Health Court* (Washington, DC: U.S. Department of Justice, Bureau of Justice Assistance, 2007).

46. Roger A. Boothroyd et al., "The Broward Mental Health Court: Process, Outcomes and Service Utilization," *International Journal of Law and Psychiatry,* vol. 26 (2003), pp. 55–71.

47. American Association for Community Psychiatrists, *Position Statement on Persons with Mental Illness Behind Bars, 1999,* www.wpic.pitt.edu/aacp/finds/mibb.html (accessed May 16, 2003). See also Arthur J. Lurigio, "Effective Services for Parolees with Mental Illnesses," *Crime & Delinquency,* vol. 47, no. 3 (July 2001), pp. 446–461; other recommendations can be found in Elaine A. Lord, "The Challenges of Mentally Ill Female Offenders in Prison," *Criminal Justice and Behavior,* vol. 35, no. 8 (August 2008), pp. 928–942, and Kenneth Adams and Joseph Ferrandino, "Managing Mentally Ill Inmates in Prison," *Criminal Justice and Behavior,* vol. 35, no. 8 (August 2008), pp. 913–927.

48. Eric Blaauw, Frans Willem Winkel, and Ad J. F. M. Kerkhof, "Bullying and Suicidal Behavior in Jails," *Criminal Justice and Behavior,* vol. 28, no. 3 (June 2001), pp. 279–299.

49. J. Richard Goss, "Characteristics of Suicide Attempts in a Large Urban Jail System with an Established Suicide Prevention Program," *Psychiatric Services,* vol. 53 (2002), pp. 574–579; Lance Couturier and Frederick R. Maue, "Suicide Prevention Initiatives in a Large Statewide Department of Corrections: A Full Court Press to Save Lives," *Jail Suicide/Mental Health Update,* vol. 9, no. 4 (2000), pp. 1–8.

50. Mason R. Goodman, "An Overview of Tuberculosis in Jails in the United States for Health Care and Administrative Corrections Professionals," *American Jails,* vol. 10, no. 4 (1996), pp. 45–50.

51. Paula J. Moynihan, "The Role of Diet and Nutrition in the Etiology and Prevention of Oral Disease," *Bulletin of the World Health Organization,* vol. 83, no. 9 (2005), pp. 641–720.

52. American Correctional Association, *Managing Special Needs Offenders;* Abe Macher, "Tuberculosis in Correctional Facilities," in Stan Stojkovic (ed.), *Managing Special Populations in Jails and Prisons* (New York: Civic Research Institute, 2006), pp. 6–1 to 6–55.

53. "Inmate Health Care and Communicable Diseases," *Corrections Compendium,* vol. 32, no. 5 (September/October 2007), pp. 9–31. Eight correctional systems did not respond to the survey.

54. Joann B. Morton, *An Administrative Overview of the Older Inmate* (Washington, DC: National Institute of Corrections, August 1992), www.nicic.org.

55. Heather C. West, William J. Sabol, and Sarah J. Greenman, *Prisoners in 2009* (Washington, DC: U.S. Department of Justice, Bureau of Justice Statistics, December 2010), p. 27.

56. Sheila McLaughlin, "Prison Population Graying," *Cincinnati Enquirer,* February 9, 2009, www.cincinnati.com (accessed February 11, 2011).

57. John J. Kerbs and Jennifer M. Jolley, "A Commentary on Age Segregation for Older Prisoners: Philosophical and Pragmatic Considerations for Correctional Systems," *Criminal Justice Review,* vol. 34, no. 1 (March 2009), pp. 119–139.

58. Ryan S. King and Marc Mauer, *Aging Behind Bars: "Three Strikes" Seven Years Later* (Washington, DC: The Sentencing Project, August 2001).

59. Ibid.

60. "Inmate Health Care and Communicable Diseases," p. 9.

61. Anne Seidlitz, "National Prison Hospice Association Facilities Deal with Inmate Deaths," *CorrectCare,* vol. 12, no. 1 (Spring 1998), p. 10; see "Appendix" in Statement of Professor Jonathan Turley before a Joint Hearing of the Senate Subcommittee on Aging and Long Term Care, Senate Committee on Public Safety, and Senate Select Committee on the California Correctional System, February 25, 2003.

62. Michael J. Osofeky, Philip J. Zimbardo, and Burl Cain, "Revolutionizing Prison Hospice: The Interdisciplinary Approach of the Louisiana State Penitentiary at Angola," *Corrections Compendium,* vol. 29, no. 4 (2004), pp. 5–7.

63. "Inmate Health Care and Communicable Diseases," pp. 9–10; "N.C. and Ala. Join States that Release Dying Inmates," *Corrections Compendium,* vol. 33, no. 5 (September/October 2008), p. 35; Mark Johnson, "No-Risk Inmates' 'Release Debated: Dying, Disabled, Aged Are Eligible," *The News and Observer,* January 22, 2009, www.newsobserver.com (accessed January 27, 2011).

64. As quoted in Mark Johnson, "No-Risk Inmates' Release Debated."

65. Ronald H. Aday, "Golden Years Behind Bars: Special Programs and Facilities for Elderly Inmates," *Federal Probation,* vol. 58, no. 2 (June 1994), pp. 47–54; Brie A. Williams et al., "Being Old and Doing Time: Functional Impairment and Adverse Experiences of Geriatric Female Prisoners," *Journal of the American Geriatric Society,* vol. 54, no. 2 (April 2006), pp. 702–707.

66. *Goodman & United States* v. *Georgia,* 546 U.S. 126 (2006).

67. Jurgen Neffe, "The Old Folks' Slammer: Aging Prison Population in the United States," *World Press Review,* vol. 44, no. 6 (June 1997), pp. 30–32; Irina R. Soderstrom and W. Michael Wheeler, "Is It Practical to Incarcerate the Elderly Offender? Yes and No," in Charles B. Fields (ed.), *Controversial Issues in Corrections* (Boston: Allyn & Bacon, 1999), pp. 72–89; Patricia S. Corwin, "Senioritis—Why Elderly Federal Inmates Are Literally Dying to Get Out of Prison," *Journal of Contemporary Health, Leisure and Policy,* vol. 17 (2001), pp. 687–688; Barry Holman, "Old Men Behind Bars," *Washington Post,* July 25, 1999, p. 88.

68. Karl Brown, "Managing Sexually Transmitted Diseases in Jails," *HEPP Report,* vol. 6, no. 9 (September 2003), pp. 1–3.

69. *Estelle* v. *Gamble,* 429 U.S. 97 (1976).

70. Vaughn and Carroll, "Separate and Unequal," pp. 3–40.

71. Civil Rights of Institutionalized Persons Act, 42 U.S.C. 1997 et seq. (1976 ed., Supp. IV), as modified 1980. (Current through P.L. 104-150, approved June 3, 1996.)

72. *Pennsylvania Department of Corrections* v. *Yeskey,* 524 U.S. 206 (1998).

73. Associated Press, "Supreme Court Upholds Rights of Disabled Inmates," June 15, 1998; *Goodman &United States* v. *Georgia.*

Chapter 13

1. Heather C. West, William J. Sabol, and Sarah J. Greenman, *Prisoners in 2009* (Washington DC: U.S. Department of Justice, Bureau of Justice Statistics, December 2010).

2. Ibid.

3. *State Court Sentencing of Convicted Felons, 2004 Statistical Tables.* Electronic format only, www.ojp.usdoj.gov/bjs/abstract/scscfst.htm (accessed March 2, 2011).

4. Human Rights Watch, *Targeting Blacks: Drug Law Enforcement and Race in the United States* (New York: Human Rights Watch, 2008).

5. Timothy Egan, "Less Crime, More Criminals," *The New York Times*, March 7, 1999.

6. http://www.nytimes.com/1999/03/07/weekinreview/the-nation-hard-time-less-crime-more-criminals.html?pagewanted=4

7. James J. Stephan, *State Prison Expenditures, 1996* (Washington, DC: U.S. Department of Justice, Bureau of Justice Statistics, August 1999).

8. Pew Charitable Trusts, *Public Safety, Public Spending: Forecasting America's Prison Population 2007–2011* (Philadelphia: Pew Charitable Trusts, 2007); Jennifer Warren, *One in 100: Behind Bars in America 2008* (Washington, DC: Pew Charitable Trusts 2009); and The Pew Center on the States, *One in 31: The Long Reach of American Corrections* (New York: Pew Charitable Trusts, March 2009).

9. As quoted in Marisa Lagos, "CA State Prison Projects Funded But Not Completed," *San Francisco Chronicle*, January 3, 2011, www.sfgate.com (accessed January 11, 2011).

10. J. J. Hensley, "Arizona Aims to Cut Prison Costs; In Texas, a New Approach," *The Arizona Republic*, April 18, 2010, www.azcentral.com (accessed April 25, 2011)

11. National Association of State Sentencing Commissions, www.ussc.gov/states.htm (accessed Feb 23, 2011).

12. David C. May, Peter B. Wood, and Amy Eades, "Lessons Learned from Punishment Exchange Rates: Implications for Theory, Research, and Correctional Policy," paper presented at the annual meeting of the American Society of Criminology, Atlanta, Georgia, November 2007.

13. David P. Farrington and C. P. Nuttal, "Prison Size, Overcrowding, Prison Violence, and Recidivism," *Journal of Criminal Justice*, vol. 8, no. 4 (1980), pp. 221–231; and Joe Davidson, "Crowded Prisons Endanger Workers, Union Says," *Washington Post*, July 22, 2009, www.washingtonpost.com (accessed July 23, 2011); and John Wooldredge and Benjamin Steiner, "Comparing Methods for Examining Relationships Between Prison Crowding and Inmate Violence," *Justice Quarterly*, vol. 26, no 4 (December 2009), pp. 795–826.

14. James J. Stephan, *Census of State and Federal Correctional Facilities, 2005* (Washington, DC: U.S. Department of Justice Statistics, October 2008).

15. Allen J. Beck, Paige M. Harrison, Marcus Berzoksky, Rachel Caspar, and Christopher Krebs, *Sexual Victimization in Prisons and Jails Reported by Inmates, 2008–09* (Washington, DC: U.S. Department of Justice, Bureau of Justice Statistics, August 2010).

16. Janine M. Zweig, Rebecca L. Naser, John Blackmore, and Megan Schaffer, *Addressing Sexual Violence in Prisons: A National Snapshot of Approaches and Highlights of Innovative Strategies* (Washington, DC: Urban Institute, Justice Policy Center, October 2006).

17. Steven T. McFarland and Carroll Ann Ellis, *Report on Rape in Federal and State Prisons in the U.S.: Findings and Best Practices* (Washington, DC: U.S. Department of Justice, September 24, 2008).

18. Cara Tabachnik, "Sexual Violence Behind Bars," *The Crime Report*, August 26, 2010, thecrimereport.org (accessed August 26, 2011).

19. Mary E. Pelz, "Gangs," in Marilyn D. McShane and Frank P. Williams III (eds.), *Encyclopedia of American Prisons* (New York: Garland, 1996), p. 213; and Marie L. Griffin and John R. Hepburn, "The Effect of Gang Affiliation on Violent Misconduct Among Inmates During the Early Years of Confinement," *Criminal Justice and Behavior*, vol. 33, no. 4 (2006), pp. 419–448.

20. Keith L. Martin, "Staying Ahead of Gangs/STGs in Corrections," Corrections.com, www.corrections.com/news/feature/index.html (accessed October 29, 2011); Melinda Rogers, "Jailed Gang Members Still a Potent Threat," *The Salt Lake Tribune*, February 15, 2009, www.sltrib.com (accessed February 17, 2011); "Gangs/Security Threat Groups," *Corrections Compendium*, vol. 34, no. 1 (Spring 2009), pp. 23–37 and "Gangs/Security Threat Groups," *Corrections Compendium*, vol. 34, no 1 (Spring 2009), pp. 25–37.

21. Excerpted from Florida Department of Corrections, "Gang and Security Threat Group Awareness," www.dc.state.fl.us/pub/gangs/prison.html (accessed November 3, 2011).

22. Mark S. Hamm, *Terrorist Recruitment in American Correctional Institutions: An Exploratory Study of Non-Traditional Faith Groups* (Washington, DC: U.S. Department of Justice, National Institute of Justice, December 2007).

23. As quoted in Michael B. Farrell, "Are America's Prisons Incubating Radical Islamists?" *The Christian Science Monitor*, October 19, 2009, www.csmonitor.com (accessed November 1, 2011).

24. Hector Castro, "A Moment with Gabriel Morales, a Local Gang Specialist," *Seattle Post-Intelligencer*, November 27, 2008, http://seattlepi.nwsource.com (accessed December 1, 2010).

25. James Byrne and Don Hummer, "In Search of the 'Tossed Salad Man' (and Others Involved in Prison Violence): New Strategies for Predicting and Controlling Violence in Prison," *Aggression and Violent Behavior*, vol. 12 (2007), pp. 531–541.

26. Rick Ruddell, Scott H. Decker, and Arlen Egley Jr., "Gang Intervention in Jails: A National Analysis," *Criminal Justice Review*, vol. 31, no. 1 (March 2006), pp. 33–46.

27. Burt Useem and Peter Kimball, *States of Siege: U.S. Prison Riots, 1971–1986* (New York: Oxford University Press, 1991).

28. "Prison Violence and Escapes," *Corrections Compendium*, vol. 31, no. 4 (July/August 2006); American Correctional Association, "Riots, Disturbances, Violence, Assaults and Escapes," *Corrections Compendium*, vol. 27, no. 5 (May 2002), pp. 6–19.

29. J. Lillis, "Prison Escapes and Violence Remain Down," *Corrections Compendium*, vol. 19, no. 6 (1994), pp. 6–21.

30. Vernon B. Fox, *Violence Behind Bars: An Explosive Report on Prison Riots in the United States* (New York: Vantage, 1956); Reid H. Montgomery Jr., "Bringing the Lessons of Prison Riots into Focus," *Corrections Today*, vol. 59, no. 1 (February 1997), pp. 28–33.

31. "Prison Riots . . . Why?" *The Prison Journal*, vol. 33, no. 1 (April 1953); "Aftermath of Riot," *The Prison Journal*, vol. 34, no. 1 (April 1954).

32. Negley K. Teeters, "The Dilemma of Prison Riots," *The Prison Journal*, vol. 33, no. 1 (April 1953), pp. 19–20.

33. New York State Special Commission on Attica (McKay Commission), *Attica: The Official Report of the New York State Special Commission on Attica* (New York: Bantam, 1972), p. xi; for a good discussion of prison violence, see James M. Byrne, Don Hummer, and Faye S. Taxman, *The Culture of Violence* (Boston, MA: Pearson, 2008).

34. Bert Useem and Anne Morrison Piehl, *The Challenge of Mass Incarceration* (New York: Cambridge University Press, 2008), Bert Useem, Camille Camp and George Camp, *Resolution of Prison Riots: Strategy and Policies* (New York: Oxford University Press, 1996), Bert Useem and Peter A. Kimball, *States of Siege: U.S. Prison Riots, 1971–1986* (New York: Oxford University Press, 1989), and Bert Useem and Jack A. Goldstone, "Forging Social Order and Its Breakdown: Riot and Reform in U.S. Prisons," *American Sociological Review*, vol. 67, pp, 499–525.

35. U.S. National Advisory Commission on Civil Disorders (Kerner Commission), *Report* (Washington, DC: Kerner Commission, 1968), p. 2.

36. David A. Ward and Allen F. Breed, *The U.S. Penitentiary, Marion, Illinois: Consultants' Report Submitted to the Committee on the Judiciary, U.S. House of Representatives, Ninety-Eighth Congress, Second Session* (Washington, DC: U.S. Government Printing Office, 1985), p. 1.

L

37. Daniel P. Mears and Jamie Watson, "Towards a Fair and Balanced Assessment of Supermax Prisons," *Justice Quarterly,* vol. 23, no. 2 (June 2006), pp. 231–270.

38. As quoted in Francis X. Clines, "A Futuristic Prison Awaits the Hard-Core 400," *The New York Times,* October 17, 1994, p. A1.

39. Daniel P. Mears, "An Assessment of Supermax Prisons Using an Evaluation Research Framework," *The Prison Journal,* vol. 88, no. 1 (March 2008), pp. 43–68.

40. Chase Riveland, *Supermax Housing: Overview and General Considerations* (Washington, DC: National Institute of Corrections, January 1999), p. 5. See also Gerald Berge, Jeffrey Geiger, and Scot Whitney, "Technology Is the Key to Security," *Corrections Today,* July 2001, pp. 105–109.

41. Chase Riveland, *Supermax Housing: Overview and General Considerations,* p. 5.

42. As quoted in Jules Verdone, "Second Thoughts About Prison Isolation," *Just 'Cause,* vol. 17, no. 3 (Fall 2010), p. 3.

43. Chase Riveland, *Supermax Housing: Overview and Considerations,* p. 4.

44. See, for example, Richard H. McCleery, "Authoritarianism and the Belief System of Incorrigibles," in Donald R. Cressy (ed.), *The Prison: Studies in Institutional Organization and Change* (New York: Holt, Rinehart & Winston, 1961), pp. 260–306; *Wright v. Enomoto* (July 23, 1980), pp. 5, 15; *Madrid v. Gomez,* 889 F. Supp. 1146 (N.D. Cal. 1995); Craig Haney, "Infamous Punishment: The Psychological Consequences of Isolation," *National Prison Project Journal* (Spring 1993); Craig Haney, "A Culture of Harm: Taming the Dynamics of Cruelty in Supermax Prisons," *Criminal Justice and Behavior,* vol. 35, no. 8 (August 2008), pp. 956–984; and David Lovell, "Patterns of Disturbed Behavior in a Supermax Population," *Criminal Justice and Behavior,* vol. 35, no. 8 (August 2008), pp. 985–1004.

45. Kevin Johnson, "Inmate Suicides Linked to Solitary," *USA Today,* December 28, 2006, p. 1A.

46. As quoted in Corey Weinstein, "Even Dogs Confined to Cages for Long Periods of Time Go Berserk," in May and Pitts, *Building Violence,* p. 122.

47. Mears and Watson, "Towards a Fair and Balanced Assessment of Supermax Prisons."

48. Ibid., p. 261.

49. Chad S. Briggs, Jody L. Sundt, and Thomas C. Castellano, "The Effect of Supermaximum Security Prisons on Aggregate Levels of Institutional Violence," *Criminology,* vol. 41, no. 4 (March 2006), pp. 1341–1376.

50. *Madrid v. Gomez,* 889 F. Supp. 1146 (N.D. Cal. 1995).

51. *Wilkinson v. Austin,* 545 U.S._(2005).

52. Maureen L. O'Keefe, Kelli J. Klebe, Alysha Stucker, Kristin Sturm, and William Leggett, *One Year Longitudinal Study of the Psychological Effects of Administrative Segregation* (Washington, DC: U.S. Department of Justice, National Institute of Justice, October 2010).

53. Susan Greene, "Questioning Study that Showed Inmates in Solitary Get Better," *Denver Post,* November 7, 2010, www.denverpost.com (accessed November 16, 2010).

54. Mark Curriden, "Hard Time: Chain Gangs Are In and Exercise Rooms Are Out in the Prisons of the 90s," *ABA Journal,* vol. 81 (July 1995), pp. 72–76.

55. "Sports in Prison," *Atlanta Journal-Constitution,* March 22, 1998, pp. E9–E12.

56. Brandon K. Applegate, "Penal Austerity: Perceived Utility, Desert, and Public Attitudes Toward Prison Amenities," *American Journal of Criminal Justice,* vol. 25, no. 2 (2001), pp. 253–268.

57. As quoted in Nygel Lenz, "'Luxuries' in Prison: The Relationship Between Amenity Funding and Public Support," *Crime & Delinquency,* vol. 48, no. 4 (October 2002), p. 501.

58. As quoted in Garry Boulard, "What's Tough Enough?" *State Legislatures,* vol. 21, no. 10 (December 1995), p. 26.

59. Keynote speech, U.S. Attorney General's Summit on Corrections, April 27, 1998.

60. Lenz, "'Luxuries' in Prison," p. 519.

61. "Inmate Privileges and Fees for Service," *Corrections Compendium,* vol. 27, no. 8 (August 2002), pp. 4–26.

62. Ibid., pp. 8–9.

63. "5 Florida County Jails Make It Real Hard Time: No Television," *The New York Times,* August 14, 1994, p. L27; Richard Tewksbury and Elizabeth Ehrhardt Mustaine, "Insiders' Views on Prison Amenities: Beliefs and Perceptions of Correctional Staff Members," *Criminal Justice Review,* vol. 30, no. 2 (September 2005), pp. 174–188.

64. As quoted in Brett Pulley, "Always a Good Sound Bite: The 'Good Life' Behind Bars," *The New York Times,* September 22, 1996, Section 13, p. 2.

65. "5 Florida County Jails."

66. John J. Rafferty, "Prison Industry: The Next Step," *Corrections Today,* vol. 60, no. 4 (July 1998), p. 22.

67. W. Wesley Johnson, Katherine Bennett, and Timothy J. Flanagan, "Getting Tough on Prisoners: Results from the National Corrections Executive Survey, 1995," *Crime & Delinquency,* vol. 43, no. 1 (January 1997), pp. 24–41.

68. Kathy Black-Dennis, Director of Standards, Accreditation and Professional Development, American Correctional Association (personal communication, February 25, 2011).

69. Adapted from the Web site of the American Correctional Association, www.corrections.com/aca/standards/benefits.htm (accessed June 15, 2011).

70. Malcolm M. Feeler, "The Privatization of Prisons in Historical Perspective," *Criminal Justice Research Bulletin,* vol. 6, no. 2 (1991), pp. 1–10.

71. Stephan, *Census of State and Federal Correctional Facilities 2005.* and Heather C. West, William J. Sabol, and Sarah J. Greenman, *Prisoners in 2009* (Washington, DC: U.S. Department of Justice, Bureau of Justice Statistics, December 2010)

72. Travis C. Pratt and Jeff Maahs, "Are Private Prisons More Cost-Effective Than Public Prisons? A Meta-Analysis of Evaluation Research Studies," *Crime & Delinquency,* vol. 45, no. 3 (July 1999), pp. 358–371.

73. Lonn Lanza-Kaduce, Karen F. Parker, and Charles W. Thomas, "A Comparative Recidivism Analysis of Releases from Private and Public Prisons," *Crime & Delinquency,* vol. 45, no. 1 (January 1999), pp. 28–47.

74. David Shichor, *Punishment for Profit: Private Prisons/Public Concerns* (Thousand Oaks, CA: Sage, 1995).

75. Joel Caplan, "Policy for Profit: The Private-Prison Industry's Influence over Criminal Justice Legislation," *ACJS Today,* vol. 26, no. 1 (January/February 2003).

76. Curtis Blakely and John Ortiz Smykla, "Correctional Privatization and the Myth of Inherent Efficiency," in Robert E. Bohm and Jeffrey T. Walker (eds.), Demystifying Crime and Criminal Justice (Los Angeles, CA: Roxbury, 2007), pp. 214–220 and Maeve McMahon, review of *Punishment for Profit: Private Prisons/Public Concerns,* by David Shichor, *Canadian Journal of Criminology,* vol. 39, no. 1 (January 1997), p. 115.

77. James Austin and Gary Coventry, *Emerging Issues on Privatized Prisons* (Washington, DC: U.S. Department of Justice, Bureau of Justice Statistics, February 2001).

78. Ibid., p. 29.

79. Gerry Gaes, "Cost, Performance Studies Look at Prison Privatization," *NIJ Journal,* issue 259 (March 2008), pp. 32–36.

80. Charles W. Thomas, *Testimony Regarding Correctional Privatization,* presented before the Little Hoover Commission of the State of California, Sacramento, CA, 1997. As quoted in Austin and Coventry, *Emerging Issues on Privatized Prisons,* p. 21.

81. Private Probation Association of Georgia, www.ppagonline.com (accessed February 26, 2011).

82. Southern Center for Human Rights, *Profiting From the Poor* (Atlanta, GA: Southern Center for Human Rights, 2008), p. 5.

83. Celia Perry, "Probation Profiteers," *Mother Jones,* July/August 2008, motherjones.com (accessed February 27, 2011).

84. Reginald A. Wilkinson, "The Future of Adult Corrections," *Corrections Management Quarterly,* vol. 1, no. 1 (Winter 1997).

85. James A. Gondles Jr., "A Changing Reality," *Corrections Today,* vol. 65, no. 4 (July 2003), p. 6.

86. "Federal Prisons Set Up E-mail Programs," *Corrections Compendium,* vol. 33, no. 5 (September/October 2008), p. 35.

87. Sarah Wheaton, "Inmates in Georgia Prisons Use Contraband Phones to Protest," *The New York Times,* December 12, 2010, www.nytimes.com (accessed January 11, 2011); Kim Severson and Robbie Brown, "Outlawed, Cellphones Are Thriving in Prisons," *The New York Times,* January 2, 2011, www.nytimes .com (accessed January 11, 2011); Steve Kanigher, "Prisons Face Threat of Smuggled Cell Phones," *Las Vegas Sun,* December 17, 2010, www.lasvegassun.com (accessed December 20, 2010); Brian Haas, "Dogs To Help Sniff Out TN Inmates' Cell Phones," *The Tennessean,* July 26, 2011, www.tennessean.com (accessed July 26, 2011); Jack Dolan, "Charles Manson Had a Cellphone? California Prisons Fight Inmate Cellphone Profileration," *Los Angeles Times,* December 2, 2010, www.latimes.com (accessed December 3, 2010); Therese Apel, "State's Prisons Test Technology: Cell Phones Blocked Behind Bars," *The Clarion-Ledger* (Jackson, MS), September 9, 2010, www.clarionledger.com (accessed September 15, 2011).

88. Susan Haigh, "Prisons Beef Up Teleconferencing to Save Money," *USA Today,* November 23, 2008, www.usatoday.com (accessed January 15, 2009).

89. Taylor T. Dueker, "Video Visitation a Boom in Omaha," *American Jails,* vol. 18, no. 5 (November/December 2004), pp. 65–67.

90. "Telemedicine Expanding in Ohio Prison System," *TECHbeat,* Spring 2002, p. 10; and "More States Turn to Videoconferencing," *Corrections Today,* vol. 71, no. 3 (June 2009), p. 14.

91. "Inmate Health Care and Communicable Diseases," *Corrections Compendium,* vol. 34, no. 4 (Winter 2009), pp. 13–35.

92. Graeme Wood, "Prison Without Walls," *The Atlantic,* September 2010, www.theatlantic.com (accessed August 24, 2010), p. 5.

93. "CORMAP It," *TECHbeat,* Summer 2002, p. 5.

94. Sean Reilly, "Earmarking Doles Out Pork in Billions," *Mobile Register,* August 15, 2004, pp. 1A, 6A.

95. Christopher A. Miles and Jeffrey P. Cohn, "Tracking Prisoners in Jail with Biometrics: An Experiment in a Navy Brig," *NIJ Journal,* no. 253 (January 2006), pp. 6–9.

Chapter 14

1. Details for this story come from Glen Puit, "1978 Mutilation: Family Relieved by Singleton's Death," *Las Vegas Review-Journal,* January 6, 2002.

2. Section 28(e) of Article I of the California Constitution.

3. Much of the material in this chapter is adapted from Office for Victims of Crime, *New Directions from the Field: Victims Rights and Services for the 21st Century* (Washington, DC: U.S. Department of Justice, 1998).

4. National Organization for Victim Assistance, *1988 NOVA Legislative Directory* (Washington, DC: National Organization for Victim Assistance, 1988), p. 191.

5. Victim and Witness Protection Act of 1982, Pub. L. No. 97-291.

6. Office of Justice Programs, *President's Task Force on Victims of Crime: Four Years Later* (Washington, DC: U.S. Government Printing Office, May 1986), p. 4.

7. Office for Victims of Crime, *The Crime Victim's Right to Be Present* (Washington, DC: OVC Legal Series Bulletin no. 3, November 2001).

8. National Victim Center, *1996 Victims' Rights Sourcebook: A Compilation and Comparison of Victims' Rights Laws* (Arlington, VA: National Victim Center, 1997).

9. National Victims' Constitutional Amendment Passage, http:// www.nvcap.org (accessed January 9, 2010).

10. Victim and Witness Protection Act of 1982, Pub. L. No. 97-291, Section 2(b).

11. Crime Control Act of 1990, Pub. L. No. 101-647.

12. Ibid., Title V, Section 502–503.

13. Violent Crime Control and Law Enforcement Act of 1994, Pub. L. No. 103-322.

14. Megan's Law amendment to the Jacob Wetterling Crimes Against Children and Sexual Violent Offender Act, 42 U.S.C. Section 14071.

15. S.2329.

16. NVCAN was created following a meeting sponsored by the National Organization for Victim Assistance (NOVA) and Mothers Against Drunk Driving (MADD) in 1985.

17. See the National Victims' Constitutional Amendment Network (NVCAN), *1996 Constitutional Amendment Action Kit.*

18. National Victims' Constitutional Amendment Network, *President Bush Announces Support for Bi-partisan Victims' Rights Amendment,* www.nvcan.org/home.htm (accessed June 24, 2002).

19. National Institute of Justice, *Victim Costs and Consequences: A New Look* (Washington, DC: NIJ, January 1996).

20. Kathryn E. McCollister, Michael T French, and Hai Fang, "The Cost of Crime to Society: New Crime-specific Estimates for Policy and Program Evaluation," *Drug and Alcohol Dependence* (January, 2010).

21. Ibid.

22. Much of the material in this section comes from Office for Victims of Crime, *New Directions.*

23. Anne Seymour, "Promoting Victim Justice Through Corrections-Based Victim Services," *Corrections Today,* July 2000, pp. 140–142.

24. Office of Victims of Crime, Archive, *Corrections,* Chapter 5, https://www.ncjrs.gov/ovc_archives/directions/chap5.htm (accessed August 6, 2011).

25. A. Seymour, *National Victim Services Survey of Adult and Juvenile Correctional Agencies and Paroling Authorities, 1996* (Arlington, VA: National Victim Center, April 1997).

26. Office for Victims of Crime, *New Directions.*

27. Seymour, *National Victim Services Survey,* p. 5.

28. Megan's Law, Pub. L. No. 104-145, 110 Stat. 1345.

29. Information in this paragraph comes from the National Center for Victims of Crime Public Policy Issues page, www.ncvc.org/law/ issues/community.htm (accessed November 25, 2007).

30. See Office for Victims of Crime, *New Directions.*

31. See Dorothy Mercer, R. Lord, and J. Lord, *Sharing Their Stories: What Are the Benefits? Who Is Helped?* paper presented at the Annual Meeting of the International Society for Traumatic Stress Studies, Chicago, IL, November 8, 1994.

32. Office for Victims of Crime, *New Directions.*

33. Dean G. Kilpatrick, David Beatty, and Susan Smith Howley, *The Rights of Crime Victims—Does Legal Protection Make a Difference?* (Washington, DC: NIJ, December 1998).

34. Ibid.

35. Office for Victims of Crime, *New Directions*.

36. Seymour, *National Victim Services Survey*.

37. Seymour, *Promising Practices and Strategies for Victim Services in Corrections* (Washington, DC: Office for Victims of Crime, 1999).

38. Office for Victims of Crime, *State Crime Victim Compensation and Assistance Grant Programs* (Washington, DC: OVC Fact Sheet, January 2002).

39. Office for Victims of Crime, *New Directions*.

40. President's Task Force on Victims of Crime, *Final Report* (Washington, DC: U.S. Government Printing Office, December 1982), p. 39.

41. National Association of Crime Victim Compensation Boards, *Crime Victim Compensation: An Overview* (Washington, DC: National Association of Crime Victim Compensation Boards, 1997), p. 1; Office for Victims of Crime, *State Crime Victim Compensation and Assistance Grant Programs*.

42. Office for Victims of Crime, *Nationwide Analysis, Victims of Crime Act: 1996 Victims of Crime Act Performance Report, State Compensation Program* (Washington, DC: U.S. Department of Justice, Office of Justice Programs, Office for Victims of Crime, April 14, 1997).

43. Victims of Crime Act of 1984, Pub. L. No. 104-235.

44. Office for Victims of Crime, *Victims of Crime Act Crime Victims Fund* (Washington, DC: OVC Fact Sheet, January 2002).

45. Office for Victims of Crime, *State Crime Victim Compensation and Assistance Grant Programs*.

46. President's Task Force on Victims of Crime, *Final Report*.

47. Much of the material in this section is taken from the Office for Victims of Crime fact sheet, www.ncjrs.org/ovcfs.htm (accessed September 1, 2003).

48. Victim and Witness Protection Act of 1982, Pub. L. No. 97-291, Sec. 4.

49. President's Task Force on Victims of Crime, *Final Report* (Washington, DC: U.S. Government Printing Office, December 1982), p. 72.

50. The Mandatory Victim Restitution Act, Title II of the Antiterrorism and Effective Death Penalty Act of 1996, Pub. L. No. 104-132 (1996), 18 U.S.C. Section 3663A (1996).

51. P. A. Langan and M. A. Cunniff, *Recidivism of Felons on Probation, 1986–89* (Washington, DC: U.S. Department of Justice, Bureau of Justice Statistics, February 1992).

52. R. L. Cohen, *Probation and Parole Violators in State Prison, 1991* (Washington, DC: Bureau of Justice Statistics, 1995).

53. Kilpatrick, Beatty, and Howley, *The Rights of Crime Victims*, p. 5.

54. Cohen, *Probation and Parole Violators*.

55. Office for Victims of Crime, *OVC Fact Sheet: What Is the Office for Victims of Crime?* (Washington, DC: OVC, 2004), from which much of the material in this section is taken.

56. Office for Victims of Crime, *What You Can Do If You Are a Crime Victim* (Washington, DC: OVC Fact Sheet, April 2002).

57. The National Victim Center, "INFOLINK: Victim Impact Statements," www.nvc.org/infolink/info72.htm (accessed January 2, 1999).

58. See Ellen K. Alexander and Janice Harris Lord, *Impact Statements: A Victim's Right to Speak, A Nation's Responsibility to Listen* (Washington, DC: Office for Victims of Crime, 1994).

59. *Payne* v. *Tennessee*, 501 U.S. 808, 111 S. Ct. 2597, 115 L. Ed. 2d 720.

60. National Victim Center, *1996 Victims' Rights Sourcebook*.

61. Office for Victims of Crime, *Vision 21: Transforming Victim Services,* Web available at http://ovc.ncjrs.gov/vision21 (accessed March 5, 2011).

62. Office for Victims of Crime, *New Directions*.

Chapter 15

1. www.deathpenaltyinfo.org (accessed March 1, 2011).

2. Excerpted from Susan Levine, "10 Years After Being Freed by DNA Evidence, His Life Is Still Trying," *Pittsburgh Post-Gazette*, March 2, 2003, p. A-12.

3. Details for this story come from Edward Connors et al., *Convicted by Juries, Exonerated by Science: Case Studies in the Use of DNA Evidence to Establish Innocence after Trial, Issues in Child Abuse Accusations*, vol. 10 (1998), www.ipt-forensics.com/journal/volume10/j10_3_6_2.htm (accessed March 20, 2011).

4. *U.S.* v. *Jackson*, 390 U.S. 570 (1968).

5. *Witherspoon* v. *Illinois*, 391 U.S. 510 (1968).

6. *Furman* v. *Georgia*, 408 U.S. 238 (1972).

7. Death Penalty Information Center, www.deathpenaltyinfo.org (accessed August 11, 2011).

8. www.deathpenaltyinfo.org (accessed February 28, 2011) and Amnesty International, *Death Sentences and Executions 2009* (London, England: Amnesty International, 2010).

9. Ray Long, "Quinn Signs Death Penalty Ban, Commutes 15 Death Row Sentences to Life," *Chicago Tribune*, March 9, 2011, www.chicagotribune.com (accessed March 11, 2011).

10. Ron Sylvester, "From a Budget Standpoint, Is Death Row Worth It?" *The Wichita Eagle* (Kansas), October 20, 2009, www.kansas.com (accessed October 21, 2011).

11. Editorial, "High Cost of Death Row," *The New York Times*, September 27, 2009, www.nytimes.com (accessed October 1, 2011).

12. M. Watt Espy and John Ortiz Smykla, "Executions in the U.S. 1608–2003: The Espy File" (Inter-University Consortium for Political and Social Research, 1994).

13. Tracy L. Snell, *Capital Punishment, 2007* (Washington, DC: U.S. Department of Justice, Bureau of Justice Statistics, December 2008).

14. United States Department of Justice, *The Federal Death Penalty System: A Statistical Survey* (Washington, DC: U.S. Department of Justice, September 12, 2000).

15. As cited in Marc Lacey and Raymond Bonner, "Reno Troubled by Death Penalty Statistics," *New York Times*, September 12, 2000, p. A17.

16. www.deathpenaltyinfo.org (accessed March 10, 2011).

17. Brett Barrouquere, "Lawyers Face Ethics Dilemma When Inmates Seek Death," *USA Today*, November 20, 2008, www.usatoday.com (accessed October 22, 2011).

18. www.deathpenaltyinfo.org (accessed March 1, 2011).

19. Robert M. Bohm, *Deathquest III: An Introduction to the Theory and Practice of Capital Punishment in the United States*, 3rd ed. (Cincinnati, OH: Anderson, 2007); Raymond Paternoster, Robert Brame, and Sarah Bacon, *The Death Penalty: America's Experience with Capital Punishment* (New York: Oxford University Press, 2008).

20. John Boger, "Landmark North Carolina Death Penalty Study Finds Dramatic Racial Bias," www.deathpenaltyinfo.org (accessed April 1, 2011).

21. Joint Legislative Audit and Review Commission, The Virginia General Assembly, *Review of Virginia's System of Capital Punishment* (Richmond, VA: Joint Legislative Audit and Review Commission, December 2001).

22. G. Ben Cohen and Robert J. Smith, "The Racial Geography of the Federal Death Penalty," *Washington Law Review*, vol. 45 (2010), pp. 425–492.

23. *Atkins v. Virginia,* 536 U.S. 304, 353 (202) (Scalia, J., dissenting).

24. Jefferson E. Holcomb, Marion R. Williams, and Stephen Demuth, "White Female Victims and Death Penalty Disparity Research," *Justice Quarterly,* vol. 21, no. 7 (December 2004), pp. 877–902.

25. J. Weisberg, "This Is Your Death," *The New Republic,* July 1, 1991.

26. Rob Stein, "Company to Stop Making Drug Commonly Used in Executions," *The Washington Post,* January 22, 2011, www.washingtonpost.com (accessed January 25, 2011).

27. Carol J. Williams, "California Got Lethal Injection Drug from Britain," *Los Angeles Times,* December 8, 2010, www.latimes.com (accessed December 8, 2010).

28. Rob Stein, "Ohio Executes Inmate Using New, Single-drug Method for Death Penalty," *Washington Post,* March 11, 2011, www.washingtonpost.com (accessed March 11, 2011).

29. Richard Dieter with the Death Penalty Information Center as quoted in Kathy Lohr, "States Delay Executions Owing to Drug Shortages," National Public Radio, September 16, 2010.

30. George Lombardi, Richard D. Sluder, and Donald Wallace, *The Management of Death-Sentenced Inmates: Issues, Realities, and Innovative Strategies,* paper presented at the annual meeting of the Academy of Criminal Justice Sciences, Las Vegas, Nevada, March 1996.

31. Robert Johnson, "Under Sentence of Death: The Psychology of Death Row Confinement," *Law and Psychology Review,* vol. 5 (Fall 1979), pp. 141–192.

32. As quoted in Bonnie Bartel Latino and Bob Vale, "Welcome to Death Row," *The Birmingham News,* January 16, 2000, pp. 1C, 4C.

33. Thomas J. Reidy, Mark D. Cunningham, and Jon R. Sorensen, "From Death to Life: Prison Behavior of Former Death Row Inmates in Indiana," *Criminal Justice and Behavior,* vol. 28, no. 1 (February 2001), pp. 62–82.

34. Mark Costanzo, *Just Revenge: Costs and Consequences of the Death Penalty* (New York: St. Martin's Press, 1997), p. 51.

35. As quoted in John Ortiz Smykla, "The Human Impact of Capital Punishment," *Journal of Criminal Justice,* vol. 15, no. 4 (1987), pp. 331–347.

36. "Americans Support Punishing Murder with the Death Penalty," AngusReid Public Opinion, November 9, 2010, www.angus-reid.com (accessed February 15, 2011).

37. For example, see John K. Cochran, Denise Paquette Boots, and Kathleen M. Heide, "Attribution Styles and Attitudes Toward Capital Punishment for Juveniles, the Mentally Incompetent, and the Mentally Retarded," *Justice Quarterly,* vol. 20, no. 1 (March 2003), pp. 65–93; J. A. Fox, M. L. Radelet, and J. L. Bonsteel, "Death Penalty Opinion in the Post-Furman Years," *New York University Review of Law and Social Change,* vol. 28 (1991), pp. 499–528; M. Sandys and E. F. McGarrell, "Attitudes Toward Capital Punishment Among Indiana Legislators: Diminished Support in Light of Alternative Sentencing Options," *Justice Quarterly,* vol. 11 (1994), pp. 651–677; H. Zeisel and A. Gallup, "Death Penalty Sentiment in the United States," *Journal of Quantitative Criminology,* vol. 5 (1989), pp. 285–296; and "Poll Shows Growing Support for Alternatives to the Death Penalty; Capital Punishment Ranked Lowest Among Budget Priorities," www.deathpenaltyinfo.org (accessed November 16, 2010).

38. As quoted in Rob Stein, "Group to Censure Physicians Who Play Role in Lethal Injections," *The Washington Post,* May 2, 2010, www.washingtonpost.com (accessed May 4, 2010).

39. As cited in Robert M. Bohm, "The Future of Capital Punishment in the United States," *ACJS Today,* vol. 22, no. 4 (November/December 2000), p. 4; Michael L. Radelet and Traci L. Lacock, "Do Executions Lower Homicide Rates? The Views of Leading Criminologists," *Journal of Criminal Law and Criminology,* vol. 99, no. 2 (2009), pp. 489–508.

40. "O'Connor Questions Death Penalty Fairness," ABC News, Minneapolis, July 3, 2003, abcnews.go.com (accessed August 1, 2003).

41. "Justice Backs Death Penalty Freeze," CBS News, February 11, 2009, www.cbsnews.com (accessed March 1, 2011).

42. *Callins v. Collins,* 510 U.S. 1141 (1994).

43. John Paul Stevens (December 23, 2010). "On the Death Sentence" [Review of the book *Peculiar Institutions: America's Death Penalty in an Age of Abolition,* by David Garland]. *The New York Review of Books.*

44. *Furman v. Georgia,* 408 U.S. 238 (1972).

45. *Woodson v. North Carolina,* 428 U.S. 280 (1976); *Roberts v. Louisiana,* 428 U.S. 325 (1976); *Gregg v. Georgia,* 428 U.S. 153 (1976); *Jurek v. Texas,* 428 U.S. 262 (1976); *Proffitt v. Florida,* 428 U.S. 242 (1976).

46. *Ring v. Arizona,* 122 U.S. 2428 (2002).

47. *Schriro v. Summerlin,* 542 U.S. 348 (2004).

48. James Liebman, Jeffrey Fagan, and Valerie West, *A Broken System: Error Rates in Capital Cases, 1973–1995* (New York: Columbia University School of Law, 2000), p. i.; Barry Latzer and James N. G. Cauthen, *Justice Delayed? Time Consumption in Capital Appeals: A Multistate Study* (Washington, DC: U.S. Department of Justice, March 2007). The authors found a median of 966 days to complete direct appeals across 14 states from 1992 to 2002. Processing direct appeals was fastest in Virginia (295 days) and slowest in Ohio, Tennessee, and Kentucky (1,388, 1,350, and 1,309 days, respectively).

49. Ibid. See also Timothy G. Poveda, "Estimating Wrongful Convictions," *Justice Quarterly,* vol. 18, no. 3 (September 2001), pp. 689–708; Talia Roitberg Harmon, "Predictors of Miscarriages of Justice in Capital Cases," *Justice Quarterly,* vol. 18, no. 4 (December 2001), pp. 949–968.

50. Liebman, Fagan, and West, *A Broken System,* p. 18.

51. Steve Mills and Maurice Possley, "After Exonerations, Hunt for Killer Rare," *Chicago Tribune,* October 27, 2003, p. 1A, www.deathpenaltyinfo.org (accessed June 15, 2007).

52. Matt O'Connor, "Jury Believes Ex-Chicago Cop Framed by FBI," *Chicago Tribune,* January 25, 2005; and Shaun Hittle, "10 Years Later, Eddie Lowery's Name is Clear and the Man Accused of the Rape for Which Lowery Was Convicted Is Behind Bars," *Channel 49 News,* February 11, 2010, www.ktka.com (accessed March 2, 2011).

53. Marie C. Baca, "Wrongly Convicted Rarely Compensated," *San Francisco Chronicle,* March 7, 2011, www.sfgate.com (accessed March 8, 2011).

54. James S. Liebman et al., *A Broken System, Part II: Why There Is So Much Error in Capital Cases, and What Can Be Done About It* (New York: Columbia University School of Law, 2002), pp. 391–428.

55. John Schwartz, "Confessing to Crime, But Innocent," *The New York Times,* September 13, 2010, www.nytimes.com (accessed September 15, 2010).

56. Espy and Smykla, "Executions in the U.S."

57. Does not include Jose High, executed November 6, 2001, in Georgia. He may have been 17 years old at the time of the crime. Records concerning his age are disputed.

58. *Thompson v. Oklahoma,* 487 U.S. 815 (1988).

59. *Stanford v. Kentucky,* 492 U.S. 361 (1989).

60. Consolidated with *Stanford.*

61. *Roper v. Simmons,* 543 U.S._(2005).

62. James Alan Fox as cited in Meghan Mandeville, "Supreme Court Puts an End to Juvenile Death Penalty," Juvenile Info Network online, www.juvenilenet.org/news.html (accessed March 22, 2011).

63. *Atkins* v. *Virginia,* 536 U.S. (2002).
64. Richard Gonzales, "Death-Row Inmates Seek Low-IQ Exception," *National Public Radio,* March 21, 2005.

Chapter 16

1. Excerpt from Tom Sheehan, "Buddy Testifies Teen Didn't Like His Stepmother," *The Columbus Dispatch,* February 2, 2000, p. 1B. Copyright © 2000 Columbus Dispatch, used with permission.
2. "Teen Admits Killing Father, Stepmother," *The Cincinnati Enquirer,* Tristate Digest, March 25, 2000, http://enquirer.com/editions/2000/03/25/loc_tristate_digest.html (accessed June 13, 2003).
3. See, for example, Jeff Armour and Sarah Hammond, *Minority Youth in the Juvenile Justice System: Disproportionate Minority Contact* (Washington, DC: National Conference of State Legislatures, 2009).
4. Ken Wooden, *Weeping in the Playtime of Others* (New York: McGraw-Hill, 1976), pp. 23–24.
5. *People ex rel. O'Connell* v. *Turner,* 55 Ill.280, 8 Am. Rep. 645.
6. R. M. Mennel, *Thorns and Thistles: Juvenile Delinquency in the United States, 1825–1940* (Hanover, NH: University Press of New England, 1973), p. 131.
7. *Kent* v. *United States,* 383 U.S. 541 (1966).
8. *In re Gault,* 387 U.S. 1, 55 (1967).
9. *In re Winship,* 397 U.S. 358 (1970).
10. *McKeiver* v. *Pennsylvania,* 403 U.S. 528 (1971).
11. *Breed* v. *Jones,* 421 U.S. 519 (1975).
12. This paragraph is adapted from Howard N. Snyder and Melissa Sickmund, *Juvenile Offenders and Victims: 1999 National Report* (Washington, DC: Office of Juvenile Justice and Delinquency Prevention, 1999), p. 99.
13. Melissa Sickmund, *Juveniles in Court* (Washington, DC: Office of Juvenile Justice and Delinquency Prevention, June 2003), p. 5.
14. FBI, *Crime in the United States, 2010* (Washington, DC: U.S. Department of Justice, 2011).
15. Charles Puzzanchera et al., *Juvenile Court Statistics 2006–2007* (Washington, DC: Office of Juvenile Justice and Delinquency Prevention, December 2008).
16. Josephson Institute Press Release, "Largest Study Ever Shows Half of All High School Students were Bullies and Nearly Half Were the Victims of Bullying During Past Year," October 25, 2010, http://charactercounts.org/pdf/reportcard/2010/press-release_bullying-violence.pdf (accessed March 7, 2011).
17. U.S. Department of Education, Office for Civil Rights, "Dear Colleague Letter Harassment and Bullying: Background, Summary, and Fast Facts," (October 26, 2010), http://www2.ed.gov/about/offices/list/ocr/docs/dcl-factsheet-201010.pdf (accessed March 8, 2011).
18. Josephson Institute Press Release, op. cit.
19. Ibid., p. 6.
20. Ibid., p. 9.
21. Gerald Bayens, *Assessing the Impact of Judicial Waiver Laws in Kansas: Implications for Correctional Policy* (Ann Arbor, MI: University Microfilms International, 1998).
22. E. J. Loughran et al., *CJCA Yearbook 2006: A National Perspective of Juvenile Corrections* (Braintree, MA: Council of Juvenile Correctional Administrators, 2007), from which parts of this section are derived.
23. Charles Puzzanchera, et al, Juvenile Court Statistics, *2006–2007* (Pittsburgh, PA: National Center for Juvenile Justice, 2010).
24. Howard N. Snyder and Melissa Sickmund, *Juvenile Offenders and Victims: 2006 National Report* (Washington, DC: Office of

Juvenile Justice and Delinquency Prevention, 2006), from which some of the material in this section is adapted.
25. Melissa Sickmund, *Juvenile Residential Facility Census, 2002: Selected Findings* (Washington, DC: Office of Juvenile Justice and Delinquency Prevention, 2006), p. 2.
26. R. Hare and C. Richards, *Blazing the Trail: A New Direction in Youth Development & Leadership* (Washington, DC: National Collaborative on Workforce and Disability for Youth, Institute for Educational Leadership 2007), p. 2.
27. Ibid., p. 3.
28. J. C. Gagnon and C. Richards, *Making the Right Turn: A Guide about Improving Transition Outcomes of Youth Involved in the Juvenile Corrections System* (Washington, DC: National Collaborative on Workforce and Disability for Youth, Institute for Educational Leadership, 2008), p. 25.
29. S. Zavlek, "Planning Community-Based Facilities for Violent Juvenile Offenders as Part of a System of Graduated Sanctions," *Juvenile Justice Bulletin* (August 2005).
30. Gagnon and Richards. *Making the Right Turn,* p. 34.
31. Benjamin Adams and Sean Addie, *Delinquency Cases Waived to Criminal Court, 2007* (Washington, DC: Office of Juvenile Justice and Delinquency Prevention, 2010).
32. Tammy Hawkins (personal communication, September 21, 1998).
33. Youth Court Guidebook Advisory Committee, *Youth Cases for Youth Courts: Desktop Guide* (Chicago: American Bar Association, 2005), from which a number of the paragraphs that follow have been adapted.
34. Sarah S. Pearson and Sonia Jurich, *Youth Court: A Community Solution for Embracing At-Risk Youth—A National Update* (Washington, DC: American Youth Policy Forum, 2005).
35. Ibid., p. 13.
36. Jeffrey A. Butts and Janeen Buck, *Teen Courts: A Focus on Research* (Washington, DC: Office of Juvenile Justice and Delinquency Prevention, October 2000).
37. Tammy Hawkins (personal communication, September 21, 1998).
38. Much of the information in this section comes from the National Gang Center Web site, http://www.nationalgangcenter.gov. (accessed October 31, 2011).
39. Arlen Egley, Jr., James C. Howell, and John P. Moore, *Highlights of the 2008 National Youth Gang Survey* (Washington, DC: Office of Juvenile Justice and Delinquency Prevention, 2010), and other years.
40. Federal Bureau of Investigation, *Kids Crime Prevention Page,* www.fbi.gov, 2002 (accessed June 20, 2003).
41. Candice M. Kane, *Prosecutor: Technical Assistance Manual* (Washington, DC: OJJDP, 1992).
42. Ibid.
43. Office of Juvenile Justice and Delinquency Prevention, *1998 National Youth Gang Survey* (Washington, DC: U.S. Department of Justice, November 2000).
44. Jeff Ferrell, "Criminological Verstehen: Inside the Immediacy of Crime," *Justice Quarterly,* vol. 14, no. 1 (1997), pp. 3–23.
45. Janeen Buck Willison, Daniel P. Mears, Tracey Shollenberger, Colleen Owens, and Jeffrey A. Butts, *Past, Present, and Future of Juvenile Justice: Assessing the Policy Options (APO): Final Report* (The Urban Institute).
46. Reagan Daly, Tarika Kapur, and Margaret Elliott, *Capital Change: A Process Evaluation of Washington, DC's Secure Juvenile Placement Reform* (New York: The Vera Institute of Justice, 2011), p. iii.
47. Ania Dobrzanska, "ACA's Certification Program Extends to Juvenile Corrections," *Corrections Today,* June 2005, p. 20.
48. James Turpin, "Juvenile Justice in the Spotlight," *Corrections Today,* vol. 59, no. 3 (1997), p. 124.

GLOSSARY

Numbers in parentheses indicate the pages on which the terms are defined.

A

absconding Fleeing without permission of the jurisdiction in which the offender is required to stay. (123)

accreditation The process through which correctional facilities and agencies can measure themselves against nationally adopted standards and through which they can receive formal recognition and accredited status. (206)

adjudication The process by which a court arrives at a final decision in a case; or the second stage of the juvenile justice process in which the court decides whether the offender is formally responsible for (guilty of) the alleged offense. (12)

administrative officers Those who control keys and weapons and sometimes oversee visitation. (320)

aggravating circumstances Factors that may increase the culpability of the offender. (523)

AIDS (acquired immunodeficiency syndrome) A disease of the human immune system that is characterized cytologically, especially by reduction in the numbers of CD4-bearing helper T cells to 20 percent or less of normal, rendering a person highly vulnerable to life-threatening conditions. The disease is caused by infection with HIV commonly transmitted in infected blood and bodily secretions (as semen), especially during sexual intercourse and intravenous drug use. (406)

Americans with Disabilities Act (ADA) Public Law 101-336, enacted July 26, 1990, which prohibits discrimination and ensures equal opportunity for people with disabilities in employment, state and local government services, public accommodations, commercial facilities, and transportation. It also mandates the establishment of TDD/telephone relay services. (423)

arraignment An appearance in court prior to trial in a criminal proceeding. (12)

Auburn system The second historical phase of prison discipline, implemented at New York's Auburn prison in 1815. It followed the Pennsylvania system and allowed inmates to work silently together during the day, but they were isolated at night. (216)

average daily population (ADP) The sum of the number of inmates in a jail or prison each day for a year, divided by the total number of days in the year. (174)

B

back-end programs Sanctions that move offenders from higher levels of control to lower ones for the final phase of their sentences. (132)

balancing test A method the U.S. Supreme Court uses to decide prisoners' rights cases, weighing the rights claimed by inmates against the legitimate needs of prisoners. (378)

best efforts standard A requirement of the federal Victims' Rights and Restitution Act of 1990 (also known as the *Victims' Rights Act*) that mandates that federal law enforcement officers, prosecutors, and corrections officials use their best efforts to ensure that victims receive basic rights and services during their encounter with the criminal justice system. (475)

bifurcated trial Two separate hearings for different issues in a trial, one for guilt and the other for punishment. (523)

biometrics The automated identification or verification of human identity through measurable physiological and behavioral traits. (466)

blended sentencing A two-part (juvenile and adult) sentence in which the adult sentence may be waived if the offender complies with all provisions of the juvenile sentence. (551)

block officers Those responsible for supervising inmates in housing areas. (319)

boot camp A short institutional term of confinement that includes a physical regimen designed to develop self-discipline, respect for authority, responsibility, and a sense of accomplishment. (156)

bridewell A workhouse. The word came from the name of the first workhouse in England. (42)

C

capital crime A crime for which the death penalty may but need not necessarily be imposed. (508)

capital punishment Lawful imposition of the death penalty. (504)

case investigation The first major role of probation officers, consisting of interviewing the defendant and preparing the presentence report (PSR). (110)

certification A credentialing process, usually involving testing and career development assessment, through which the skills, knowledge, and abilities of correctional personnel can be formally recognized. (21)

chlamydia The most common sexually transmitted disease. Caused by the bacteria *Chlamydia trachomatis*, it can affect the eyes, lungs, or urogenital (urinary-genital) area, depending on the age of the person infected and how the infection is transmitted. (422)

chronological résumé A résumé that organizes information in reverse time sequence and emphasizes work history. (A-7)

citation A type of nonfinancial pretrial release similar to a traffic ticket. It binds the defendant to appear in court on a future date.

civil liability A legal obligation to another person to do, pay, or make good something. (371)

classification The process of subdividing the inmate population into meaningful categories to match offender needs with correctional resources. (232)

clemency   Kindness, mercy, forgiveness, or leniency, usually relating to criminal acts. (267)

cocorrections   The incarceration and interaction of female and male offenders under a single institutional administration. (362)

coed prison   A prison housing both female and male offenders. (362)

cognitive-behavioral treatment   A problem-focused intervention that emphasizes skill training. (109)

community corrections   A philosophy of correctional treatment that embraces (1) decentralization of authority, (2) citizen participation, (3) redefinition of the population of offenders for whom incarceration is most appropriate, and (4) emphasis on rehabilitation through community programs. (131)

community corrections acts (CCAs)   State laws that give economic grants to local communities to establish community corrections goals and policies and to develop and operate community corrections programs. (114)

community notification   Notification to the community of the release or pending release of convicted offenders. (487)

community service   A sentence to serve a specified number of hours working in unpaid positions with nonprofit or tax-supported agencies. (145)

commutation   A change of a legal penalty to a lesser one (e.g., from death to life imprisonment). (264)

compensatory damages   Money a court may award as payment for actual losses suffered by a plaintiff, including out-of-pocket expenses incurred in filing the suit, other forms of monetary or material loss, and pain, suffering, and mental anguish. (372)

concurrent sentences   Sentences served together. (69)

conditional diversion   Diversion in which charges are dismissed if the defendant satisfactorily completes treatment, counseling, or other programs ordered by the justice system. (95)

conditional release   Pretrial release under minimum or moderately restrictive conditions with little monitoring or compliance. It includes ROR, supervised pretrial release, and third-party release.

consecutive sentences   Sentences served one after the other. (69)

consent decree   A written compact, sanctioned by a court, between parties in a civil case, specifying how disagreements between them are to be resolved. (377)

constitutional rights   The personal and due process rights guaranteed to individuals by the U.S. Constitution and its amendments, especially the first 10 amendments, known as the Bill of Rights. Constitutional rights are the basis of most inmate rights. (370)

contraband   Any item that represents a serious threat to the safety and security of the institution. (464)

contract system   A system of prison industry in which the prison advertised for bids for the employment of prisoners, whose labor was sold to the highest bidder. (218)

convict lease system   A system of prison industry in which a prison temporarily relinquished supervision of its prisoners to a lessee. The lessee either employed the prisoners within the institution or transported them to work elsewhere in the state. (221)

corporal punishments   Physical punishments, or those involving the body. (32)

correctional clients   Prison inmates, probationers, parolees, offenders assigned to alternative sentencing programs, and those held in jails. (8)

correctional econometrics   The study of the cost-effectiveness of various correctional programs and related reductions in the incidence of crime. (62)

correctional officer personalities   The distinctive personal characteristics of correctional officers, including behavioral, emotional, and social traits. (317)

corrections   All the various aspects of the pretrial and post-conviction management of individuals accused or convicted of crimes. (15)

corrections professional   A dedicated person of high moral character and personal integrity who is employed in the field of corrections and takes professionalism to heart. (20)

counterperformance   The defendant's participation, in exchange for diversion, in a treatment, counseling, or educational program aimed at changing his or her behavior. (92)

crime   A violation of the criminal law. (3)

crime rate   The number of major crimes reported for each unit of population.

criminal justice   The process of achieving justice through the application of the criminal law and through the workings of the criminal justice system. Also, the study of the field of criminal justice. (8)

criminal justice system   The collection of all the agencies that perform criminal justice functions, whether these are operations or administration or technical support. The basic divisions of the criminal justice system are police, courts, and corrections. (8)

criminal law   (also called *penal law*) That portion of the law that defines crimes and specifies criminal punishments. (16)

cruel and unusual punishment   A penalty that is grossly disproportionate to the offense or that violates today's broad and idealistic concepts of dignity, civilized standards, humanity, and decency (*Estelle v. Gamble*, 1976, and *Hutto v. Finney*, 1978). In the area of capital punishment, cruel and unusual punishments are those that involve torture, a lingering death, or unnecessary pain. (383)

custodial staff   Those staff members most directly involved in managing the inmate population. (312)

D

day fine   A financial penalty scaled both to the defendant's ability to pay and to the seriousness of the crime. (141)

day reporting center (DRC)   A community correctional center to which an offender reports every day or several days a week for supervision and treatment. (148)

death row   A prison area housing inmates who have been sentenced to death. (517)

deliberate indifference   Intentional and willful indifference. Within the field of correctional practice, the term refers to calculated inattention to unconstitutional conditions of confinement. (384)

delinquent offenses   Acts committed by juveniles that, if committed by adults, could result in criminal prosecution. (547)

deprivation theory The belief that inmate subcultures develop in response to the deprivations in prison life. (342)

deserts See **just deserts.** (179)

design capacity The number of inmates that planners or architects intend for the facility. (250)

detention hearing A judicial review of the intake officer's detention decision. (549)

determinate sentence (also called *fixed sentence*) A sentence of a fixed term of incarceration, which can be reduced by good time. (71)

deterrence The discouragement or prevention of crimes through the fear of punishment. (60)

direct file provisions Provisions under which the prosecutor determines whether to initiate a case against a juvenile in juvenile court or in adult criminal court. (556)

direct-supervision jail See **third-generation jail.** (179)

discretionary release Early release based on the paroling authority's assessment of eligibility. (268)

disposition The third stage of the juvenile justice process in which the court decides the disposition (sentence) for a juvenile case. (550)

disturbance An altercation involving three or more inmates, resulting in official action beyond summary sanctions and for which there is an institutional record. (441)

diversion The halting or suspension, before conviction, of formal criminal proceedings against a person, conditioned on some form of counterperformance by the defendant. (92)

drug court A special court that is given responsibility to treat, sanction, and reward drug offenders with punishment more restrictive than regular probation but less severe than incarceration. (137)

due process A right guaranteed by the Fifth, Sixth, and Fourteenth Amendments to the U.S. Constitution and generally understood, in legal contexts, to mean the expected course of legal proceedings according to the rules and forms established for the protection of persons' rights. (386)

E

equity The sentencing principle that similar crimes and similar criminals should be treated alike. (82)

evidence-based corrections (also called *evidence-based penology*) The application of social scientific techniques to the study of everyday corrections procedures for the purpose of increasing effectiveness and enhancing the efficient use of available resources. (23)

exchange rates An approach to sentencing that emphasizes interchangeability of punishments; for example, three days under house arrest might be considered equal to one day of incarceration. (433)

exonerate To clear of blame and release from death row. (502)

external classification Interinstitutional placement of an inmate that determines an inmate's security level. (233)

F

fair sentencing Sentencing practices that incorporate fairness for both victims and offenders. *Fairness* is said to be achieved by implementing principles of proportionality, equity, social debt, and truth in sentencing. (82)

Federal Prison Industries (FPI) A federal, paid inmate work program and self-supporting corporation. (244)

felony A serious criminal offense; specifically, one punishable by death or by incarceration in a prison facility for more than a year. (7)

fine A financial penalty used as a criminal sanction. (141)

first-generation jail Jail with multiple-occupancy cells or dormitories that line corridors arranged like spokes. Inmate supervision is intermittent; staff must patrol the corridors to observe inmates in their cells. (178)

fixed sentence See **determinate sentence.** (71)

flat sentences Those that specify a given amount of time to be served in custody and allow little or no variation from the time specified. (69)

folkways Time-honored ways of doing things. Although they carry the force of tradition, their violation is unlikely to threaten the survival of the social group. (15)

fourth-generation jail Jail that incorporates natural light into the dayroom where staff members work and inmates spend most of their day, and brings program services, staff, volunteers, and visitors to the housing unit. (182)

frivolous lawsuits Lawsuits with no foundation in fact. They are generally brought for publicity, political, or other reasons not related to law. (388)

front-end programs Punishment options for initial sentences more restrictive than traditional probation but less restrictive than jail or prison. (132)

functional résumé A résumé that emphasizes abilities over work history, organizing information according to skills, results, contributions, or functions. (A-8)

G

gain time Time taken off an inmate's sentence for participating in certain positive activities such as going to school, learning a trade, and working in prison. (314)

gang A criminal enterprise having an organizational structure, acting as a continuing criminal conspiracy, that employs violence and any other criminal activity to sustain itself. (560)

general deterrence The use of the example of individual punishment to dissuade others from committing crimes. (60)

genital herpes A sexually transmitted disease caused by the herpes simplex virus or HSV. It is one of the most common STDs in the United States. (422)

gonorrhea The second most common sexually transmitted disease. Often called *the clap,* gonorrhea is caused by the *Neisseria gonorrhea* bacteria found in moist areas of the body. Infection occurs with contact to any of these areas. (422)

good time The number of days or months prison authorities deduct from a sentence for good behavior and for other reasons. (71)

group home A nonsecure residential facility for juveniles. (551)

guardian *ad litem* A person appointed by the juvenile court, often defense counsel, to serve as a special guardian for the youth being processed through the juvenile justice system. (550)

guided discretion Decision making bounded by general guidelines, rules, or laws. (523)

H

habitual offender statute   A law that (1) allows a person's criminal history to be considered at sentencing or (2) makes it possible for a person convicted of a given offense and previously convicted of another specified offense to receive a more severe penalty than that for the current offense alone. (79)

hands-off doctrine   A historical policy of the American courts not to intervene in prison management. Courts tended to follow the doctrine until the late 1960s. (368)

hedonistic calculus   The idea that people are motivated by pleasure and pain and that the proper amount of punishment can deter crime. (48)

HIV (human immunodeficiency virus)   Any of a group of retroviruses that infect and destroy helper T cells of the immune system, causing the marked reduction in their numbers that is diagnostic of AIDS. (406)

hospice   An interdisciplinary, comfort-oriented care facility that helps seriously ill patients die with dignity and humanity in an environment that facilitates mental and spiritual preparation for the natural process of dying. (420)

I

importation theory   The belief that inmate subcultures are brought into prison from the outside world. (343)

incapacitation   The use of imprisonment or other means to reduce an offender's capability to commit future offenses. (61)

indeterminate sentence   A sentence in which a judge specifies a maximum length and a minimum length, and an administrative agency, generally a parole board, determines the actual time of release. (70)

industrial shop and school officers   Those who ensure efficient use of training and educational resources within the prison. (320)

informational interviewing   Talking to people who are currently employed in a career field of interest. (A-4)

infraction   A minor violation of state statute or local ordinance punishable by a fine or other penalty, but not incarceration, or by a specified, usually very short term of incarceration. (8)

injunction   A judicial order to do or refrain from doing a particular act. (372)

inmate roles   Prison lifestyles; also, forms of ongoing social accommodation to prison life. (344)

inmate subculture   (also called *prisoner subculture*) The habits, customs, mores, values, beliefs, or superstitions of the body of inmates incarcerated in correctional institutions; also, the inmate social world. (342)

institutional corrections   That aspect of the correctional enterprise that "involves the incarceration and rehabilitation of adults and juveniles convicted of offenses against the law, and the confinement of persons suspected of a crime awaiting trial and adjudication." (14)

institutional needs   Prison administration interests recognized by the courts as justifying some restrictions on the constitutional rights of prisoners. Those interests are maintenance of institutional *order*, maintenance of institutional *security, safety* of prison inmates and staff, and *rehabilitation* of inmates. (370)

intake   The first stage of the juvenile justice process. A court-appointed officer reviews the case and recommends a course of action—dismissal, informal disposition, formal disposition, or transfer to adult criminal court. (549)

intangible losses   Costs such as fear, pain, suffering, and reduced quality of life that accrue to victims as a result of their victimization. (478)

integration model   A combination of importation theory and deprivation theory. The belief that, in childhood, some inmates acquired, usually from peers, values that support law-violating behavior but that the norms and standards in prison also affect inmates. (343)

intensive supervision probation (ISP)   Control of offenders in the community under strict conditions, by means of frequent reporting to a probation officer whose caseload is generally limited to 30 offenders. (136)

intermediate sanctions   New punishment options developed to fill the gap between traditional probation and traditional jail or prison sentences and to better match the severity of punishment to the seriousness of the crime. (131)

internal classification   Intrainstitutional placement that determines, through review of an inmate's background, assignment to housing units or cellblocks, work, and programming based on the inmate's risk, needs, and time to serve. (233)

J

jail accreditation   Formal approval of a jail by the American Correctional Association and the Commission on Accreditation. (206)

jails   Locally operated correctional facilities that confine people before or after conviction. (174)

job interview   A meeting with a prospective employer in which a job applicant projects his or her most impressive qualities. (A-13)

job shadow   A career exploration activity where persons observe the day-today activities of a professional currently working in a person's career field of interest. (A-4)

jurisdiction   The power, right, or authority of a court to interpret and apply the law. (373)

just deserts   Punishment deserved. A just deserts perspective on criminal sentencing holds that criminal offenders are morally blameworthy and are therefore *deserving* of punishment. (60)

justice reinvestment   The practice of reducing spending on prisons and investing a portion of the savings into infrastructure and civic institutions located in high-risk neighborhoods. (254)

juvenile court   Any court that has jurisdiction over matters involving juveniles. (550)

juvenile detention facility   A facility for keeping juvenile offenders in secure custody, as necessary, through various stages of the juvenile justice process. (549)

L

legitimate penological objectives   The realistic concerns that correctional officers and administrators have for the integrity and security of the correctional institution and the safety of staff and inmates. (378)

M

mandatory death penalty A death sentence that the legislature has required to be imposed upon people convicted of certain offenses. (523)

mandatory minimum sentencing The imposition of sentences required by statute for those convicted of a particular crime or a particular crime with specific circumstances, such as robbery with a firearm or selling drugs to a minor within 1,000 feet of a school, or for those with a particular type of criminal history. (77)

mandatory release Early release after a time period specified by law. (268)

mandatory sentences Those that are required by law under certain circumstances—such as conviction of a specified crime or of a series of offenses of a specified type. (69)

maximum- or close/high-security prison A prison designed, organized, and staffed to confine the most dangerous offenders for long periods. It has a highly secure perimeter, barred cells, and a high staff-to-inmate ratio. It imposes strict controls on the movement of inmates and visitors, and it offers few programs, amenities, or privileges. (255)

medical model A philosophy of prisoner reform in which criminal behavior is regarded as a disease to be treated with appropriate therapy. (222)

medium-security prison A prison that confines offenders considered less dangerous than those in maximum security, for both short and long periods. It places fewer controls on inmates' and visitors' freedom of movement than does a maximum-security facility. It has barred cells and a fortified perimeter. The staff-to-inmate ratio is generally lower than that in a maximum-security facility, and the level of amenities and privileges is slightly higher. (255)

minimum-security prison A prison that confines the least dangerous offenders for both short and long periods. It allows as much freedom of movement and as many privileges and amenities as are consistent with the goals of the facility. It may have dormitory housing, and the staff-to-inmate ratio is relatively low. (256)

misdemeanor A relatively minor violation of the criminal law, such as petty theft or simple assault, punishable by confinement for one year or less. (7)

mission That which is done to support an organization's purpose.(329)

mitigating circumstances Factors that, although not justifying or excusing an action, may reduce the culpability of the offender. (523)

model of criminal sentencing A strategy or system for imposing criminal sanctions. (69)

mores Cultural restrictions on behavior that forbid serious violations—such as murder, rape, and robbery—of a group's values. (15)

N

net widening Increasing the number of offenders sentenced to a higher level of restriction. It results in sentencing offenders to more restrictive sanctions than their offenses and characteristics warrant. (132)

networking Meeting new people who can give you information about careers, the job market, and specific positions. It is often done through people you know. (A-2)

new offense violation Arrest and prosecution for the commission of a new crime.(123)

no-frills prisons and jails Correctional institutions that take away prisoner amenities and privileges. (452)

nolo contendere A plea of "no contest." A no-contest plea may be used by a defendant who does not wish to contest conviction. Because the plea does not admit guilt,however, it cannot provide the basis for later civil suits. (12)

nominal damages Small amounts of money a court may award when inmates have sustained no actual damages, but there is clear evidence that their rights have been violated. (372)

noninstitutional corrections (also called *community corrections*) That aspect of the correctional enterprise that includes "pardon, probation, and parole activities, correctional administration not directly connectable to institutions, and miscellaneous [activities] not directly related to institutional care." (14)

nonrevocable parole A type of unsupervised parole that cannot be revoked for technical violations; the person does not report to a parole officer. (288)

O

open institution A minimum-security facility that has no fences or walls surrounding it. (257)

operational capacity The number of inmates that a facility's staff, existing programs, and services can accommodate. (250)

P

pains of imprisonment Major problems that inmates face, such as loss of liberty and personal autonomy, lack of material possessions, loss of heterosexual relationships, and reduced personal security. (342)

pardon An executive act that removes both punishment and guilt. (267)

parens patriae A Latin term that refers to the state as guardian of minors and of people who are mentally incompetent. (539)

parole The conditional release of a prisoner, prior to completion of the imposed sentence, under the supervision of a parole officer. (268)

parole eligibility date The earliest date on which an inmate might be paroled. (277)

parolee A person who is conditionally released from prison to community supervision. (280)

paroling authority A person or correctional agency (often called a *parole board* or *parole commission*) that has the authority to grant parole, revoke parole, and discharge from parole. (278)

pay-to-stay jail (also called *self-pay jails*) An alternative to serving time in a county jail. Offenders convicted of minor offenses are offered privileges for a fee from $75 to $127 per day. (196)

penal law See **criminal law.** (16)

penitentiary The earliest form of large-scale incarceration. It punished criminals by isolating them so that they could reflect on their misdeeds, repent, and reform. (216)

Pennsylvania system (also called *separate system*) The first confinement in silence instead of corporal punishment; conceived by the American Quakers in 1790 and implemented at the Walnut Street Jail. (216)

performance-based funding A method of allocating money for programs that present reliable and valid data that they work.

perimeter security officers Those assigned to security (or gun) towers, wall posts, and perimeter patrols. These officers are charged with preventing escapes and detecting and preventing intrusions. (320)

pleasure-pain principle The idea that actions are motivated primarily by a desire to experience pleasure and avoid pain. (61)

precedent A previous judicial decision that judges should consider in deciding future cases. (376)

predisposition report A report that documents (1) a juvenile's background; (2) his or her educational history; (3) information gathered from interviews with the juvenile, family members, and others; (4) available placement options; and (5) recommended dispositions. (550)

presentence report (PSR) A report prepared by the probation department of a court that provides a social and personal history as well as an evaluation of a defendant as an aid to the court in determining a sentence. (69)

principle of least eligibility The requirement that prison conditions—including the delivery of health care—must be a step below those of the working class and people on welfare. (249)

prison A state or federal confinement facility that has custodial authority over adults sentenced to confinement. (4)

prison argot The special language of the inmate subculture. (344)

prison code A set of norms and values among prison inmates. It is generally antagonistic to the official administration and rehabilitation programs of the prison. (343)

prisoner subculture See **inmate subculture**. (342)

prisoners' rights Constitutional guarantees of free speech, religious practice, due process, and other private and personal rights as well as constitutional protections against cruel and unusual punishments made applicable to prison inmates by the federal courts. (370)

prisonization The process by which inmates adapt to prison society; the taking on of the ways, mores, customs, and general culture of the penitentiary. (342)

privatization A contract process that shifts public functions, responsibilities, and capital assets, in whole or in part, from the public sector to the private sector. (199)

probation The conditional release of a convicted offender into the community, under the supervision of a probation officer. It is conditional because it can be revoked if certain conditions are not met. (96)

profession An occupation granted high social status by virtue of the personal integrity of its members. (17)

professional associations Organizations of like-minded individuals who work to enhance the professional status of members of their professional group. (21)

professional development The lifelong or career-long dedication to quality selection, training, and development of employees.

program staff Those staff members concerned with encouraging prisoners to participate in educational, vocational, and treatment programs. (312)

property crime Burglary, larceny-theft, motor vehicle theft, and arson as reported by the FBI's Uniform Crime Reporting Program.

proportionality The sentencing principle that the severity of punishment should match the seriousness of the crime for which the sentence is imposed. (82)

pseudofamilies Family-like structures, common in women's prisons, in which inmates assume roles similar to those of family members in free society. (357)

public accounts system The earliest form of prison industry, in which the warden was responsible for purchasing materials and equipment and overseeing the manufacture, marketing, and sale of prison-made items. (218)

public works system A system of prison industry in which prisoners were employed in the construction of public buildings, roads, and parks. (221)

punitive damages Money a court may award to punish a wrongdoer when a wrongful act was intentional and malicious or was done with reckless disregard for the rights of the victim. (372)

purpose The reason for an organization's existence. (329)

R

rabble management Control of people whose noncriminal behavior is offensive to their communities. (178)

racism Social practices that explicitly or implicitly attribute merits or allocate value to individuals solely because of their race. (25)

rated capacity The maximum number of beds or inmates allocated to each jail facility by a state or local rating official. (195)

recidivism The repetition of criminal behavior; generally defined as *rearrest*. It is the primary outcome measure for probation, as it is for all corrections programs. (107)

reentry The transition offenders make from prison or jail to the community. (201)

reentry court A court that manages the return to the community of individuals released from prison. (298)

reform school A penal institution to which especially young or first-time offenders are committed for training and reformation. (540)

rehabilitation The changing of criminal lifestyles into law-abiding ones by "correcting" the behavior of offenders through treatment, education, and training. (63)

reintegration The process of making the offender a productive member of the community. (63)

release on bail The release of a person upon that person's financial guarantee to appear in court.

release on own recognizance (ROR) Pretrial release on the defendant's promise to appear for trial. It requires no cash guarantee.

relief officers Experienced correctional officers who know and can perform almost any custody role within the institution, used to temporarily replace officers who are sick or on vacation or to meet staffing shortages. (321)

remote-location monitoring Technologies, including global positioning system (GPS) devices and electronic monitoring (EM), that probation and parole officers use to monitor remotely the physical location of an offender. (151)

reprieve An executive act that reduces the severity of punishment (e.g., from death to life imprisonment) but the person remains guilty. (267)

residential community center (RCC) A medium-security correctional setting that resident offenders are permitted to leave regularly—unaccompanied by staff—for work, education or vocational programs, or treatment in the community but require them to return to a locked facility each evening. (154)

residential treatment center A residential facility that provides intensive treatment services to juveniles. (551)

restitution Payments made by a criminal offender to his or her victim (or to the court, which then turns them over to the victim) as compensation for the harm caused by the offense. (68)

restoration The process of returning to their previous condition all those involved in or affected by crime—including victims, offenders, and society. (64)

restorative justice A systemic response to wrongdoing that emphasizes healing the wounds of victims, offenders, and communities caused or revealed by crime. (64)

résumé A list of your job and other related experiences and education. (A-6)

retribution A sentencing goal that involves retaliation against a criminal perpetrator. (60)

revenge Punishment as vengeance; an emotional response to real or imagined injury or insult. (59)

revocation The formal termination of an offender's conditional freedom. (121)

revocation hearing A due process hearing that must be conducted to determine whether the conditions of probation have been violated before probation can be revoked and the offender removed from the community. (121)

right of allocution A statutory provision permitting crime victims to speak at the sentencing of convicted offenders. A federal right of allocution was established for victims of federal violent and sex crimes under the Violent Crime Control and Law Enforcement Act of 1994. (496)

riot Any action by a group of inmates that constitutes a forcible attempt to gain control of a facility or area within a facility. (441)

roles The normal patterns of behavior expected of those holding particular social positions. (311)

S

salient factor score (SFS) A scale, developed from a risk-screening instrument, used to predict parole outcome. (280)

second-generation jail Jail where staff remain in a secure control booth surrounded by inmate housing areas called *pods* and surveillance is remote. (179)

security threat groups (STGs) The current term for prison gangs that describes how they negatively impact the security of prison operations. (435)

self-assessment Learning who you are and what you can and want to do by evaluating your interests, skills, and values. (A-1)

sentence The penalty a court imposes on a person convicted of a crime. (57)

sentencing The imposition of a criminal sanction by a sentencing authority, such as a judge. (57)

sentencing commission A group assigned to create a schedule of sentences that reflect the gravity of the offenses committed and the prior record of the criminal offender. (72)

sentencing enhancements Legislatively approved provisions that mandate longer prison terms for specific criminal offenses committed under certain circumstances (such as a murder committed because of the victim's race or a drug sale near a school) or because of an offender's past criminal record. (74)

serious error Error that substantially undermines the reliability of the guilt finding or death sentence imposed at trial. (526)

sexual victimization All types of sexual activity, for example, oral, anal, or vaginal penetration; handjobs; touching of the inmate's buttocks, thighs, penis, breasts, or vagina in a sexual way; abusive sexual contacts. (193)

social debt The sentencing principle that the severity of punishment should take into account the offender's prior criminal behavior. (83)

social order The smooth functioning of social institutions, the existence of positive and productive relations among individual members of society, and the orderly functioning of society as a whole. (58)

special master A person appointed by the court to act as its representative to oversee remedy of a violation and provide regular progress reports. (451)

special-needs inmates Those prisoners who exhibit unique physical, mental, social, and programmatic needs that distinguish them from other prisoners and to whom jail and prison management and staff have to respond in nontraditional and innovative ways. (398)

specific deterrence The deterrence of the individual being punished from committing additional crimes. (60)

staff roles The normal patterns of behavior expected of correctional staff members in particular jobs. (311)

staff subculture The beliefs, values, and behavior of staff. They differ greatly from those of the inmate subculture. (315)

state use system A system of prison industry that employs prisoners to manufacture products consumed by state governments and their agencies, departments, and institutions. (221)

status offenses Acts that are law violations only for juveniles such as running away, truancy, or ungovernability (sometimes referred to as *incorrigibility* or *being beyond parental control*). (547)

statutory exclusion provisions Provisions under which adult criminal court jurisdiction for certain juvenile cases is established by state law. (556)

street gang An organized group of people on the street often engaged in significant illegitimate or criminal activity. (560)

stress Tension in a person's body or mind, resulting from physical, chemical, or emotional factors. (323)

structured conflict The tensions between prison staff members and inmates that arise out of the correctional setting. (315)

structured sentencing A set of guidelines for determining an offender's sentence. (432)

subculture The beliefs, values, behavior, and material objects shared by a particular group of people within a larger society. (315)

substance-abusing inmate An incarcerated individual suffering from dependency on one or more substances including alcohol and a wide range of drugs. (399)

supermax housing   A free standing facility, or a distinct unit within a facility, that provides for management and secure control of inmates who have been officially designated as exhibiting violent or serious and disruptive behavior while incarcerated. (446)

supervision   The second major role of probation officers, consisting of resource mediation, surveillance, and enforcement. (117)

syphilis   A sexually transmitted disease caused by the bacteria *Treponema pallidum*. If left untreated, syphilis can cause serious heart abnormalities, mental disorders, blindness, other neurological problems, and death. Syphilis is transmitted when infected lesions come in contact with the soft skin of the mucous membrane. (422)

T

tangible losses   Costs such as medical expenses, lost wages, and property losses that accrue to crime victims as a result of their victimization. (478)

technical violation   A failure to comply with the conditions of probation or parole. (123)

teen courts   Courts in which youths adjudicate and impose disposition for a juvenile offense. (556)

therapeutic community (TC)   A residential treatment program in which substance abuse inmates are housed in a separate unit within a prison or jail facility. (404)

third-generation jail   (also called *direct-supervision jail*) A jail where inmates are housed in small groups, or pods, staffed 24 hours a day by specifically trained officers. Officers interact with inmates to help change behavior. Bars and metal doors are absent, reducing noise and dehumanization. (179)

tort   A civil wrong, a wrongful act, or a wrongful breach of duty, other than a breach of contract, whether intentional or accidental, from which injury to another occurs. (372)

total admission   The total number of people admitted to jail each year. (174)

total institution   A place where the same people work, play, eat, sleep, and recreate together on a continuous basis. The term was developed by the sociologist Erving Goffman to describe prisons and other facilities. (340)

totality of conditions   A standard to be used in evaluating whether prison conditions are cruel and unusual. (384)

trap-door/side-door programs   Emergency release options for special docket offenders, generally used to relieve prison crowding. (132)

truth in sentencing   The sentencing principle that requires an offender to serve a substantial portion of the sentence and reduces the discrepancy between the sentence imposed and actual time spent in prison. (83)

tuberculosis (TB)   A highly variable communicable disease that is characterized by toxic symptoms or allergic manifestations that in humans primarily affect the lungs. (417)

U

unconditional diversion   The termination of criminal processing at any point before adjudication with no threat of later prosecution. Treatment, counseling, and other services are offered and use is voluntary. (95)

UNICOR   The trade name of Federal Prison Industries. UNICOR provides such products as U.S. military uniforms, electronic cable assemblies, and modular furniture. (244)

unit management system   A method of controlling prisoners in self-contained living areas and making inmates and staff (unit manager, case manager, correctional counselor, and unit secretary) accessible to each other. (239)

utilitarianism   The principle that the highest objective of public policy is the greatest happiness for the largest number of people. (47)

V

victim   A person who suffers direct or threatened physical, psychological, or financial harm as a result of the commission or attempted commission of a crime or delinquent act. (473)

victim assistance program   An organized program that offers services to victims of crime in the areas of crisis intervention and follow-up counseling and that helps victims secure their rights under the law. (495)

victim compensation   A form of victim assistance in which state-funded payments are made to victims to help them recover financial losses due to crime. (490)

victim-impact statement   A description of the harm and suffering that a crime has caused victims and survivors. (65)

victim notification   Notification to victims of the release or pending release of convicted offenders who have harmed them. (483)

victimless crime   An offense committed against the social values and interests represented in and protected by the criminal law, and in which parties willingly participate. (93)

victims' rights   The fundamental rights of victims to be represented equitably throughout the criminal justice process. (474)

violent crime   Interpersonal crime that involves the use of force by offenders or results in injury or death to victims. In the FBI's Uniform Crime Reports, violent crimes are murder, forcible rape, robbery, and aggravated assault.

vision   The planned future direction of an organization. (329)

W

waiver provisions   Provisions under which the juvenile court orders transfer of the case to adult criminal court. (556)

work detail supervisors   Those who oversee the work of individual inmates and inmate work crews. (320)

working alliance   An effective relationship between a change agent and a client, with negotiated goals and a mutual willingness to compromise when necessary to meet the goals or to maintain a viable relationship. (109)

writ of *habeas corpus*   An order that directs the person detaining a prisoner to bring him or her before a judge, who will determine the lawfulness of the imprisonment. (371)

Y

yard officers   Those who supervise inmates in the prison yard. (320)

youth gang   A gang whose membership generally comprises people between the ages of 12 and 24. (560)

TEXT CREDITS

Chapter 1: p. 15, Exhibit 1-7, American Correctional Association Public Correctional Policy on Role of Corrections Policy. Copyright © American Correctional Association. Reprinted with permission. **p. 18,** Ethics and Professionalism, American Correctional Association Code of Ethics. Copyright © American Correctional Association. Reprinted with permission. **p. 23,** Exhibit 1-8, American Correctional Association Public Correctional Policy on Higher Education. Copyright © American Correctional Association. Reprinted with permission. **p. 26,** Exhibit. 1-9, Corrections Personnel by Gender and Rank. From *Equity Denied: The Status of Women in Policing,* 2001, **p. 9.** Copyright © National Center for Women and Policing. www.womenandpolicing.org. Reprinted with permission. **p. 27,** Commission on Safety and Abuse in America's Prisons: Fighting Prison Abuse. Excerpts from *Confronting Confinement: A Report of the Commission on Safety and Abuse in America's Prisons* by John J. Gibbons and Nicholas de B. Katzenbach, June 2006. Copyright © 2006, Vera Institute of Justice. Reprinted by permission of the Vera Institute of Justice.

Chapter 3: p. 66, Exhibit 3-2, Restorative Justice Principles. Copyright © Restorative Justice Consortium. Used with permission. **p. 67,** Exhibit 3-3, American Correctional Association Public Correctional Policy on Sentencing. Copyright © American Correctional Association. Reprinted with permission. **p. 84,** Exhibit 3-7, Average Prison Time Served Compared with Court Sentence in Florida, 1998–2009. From The Florida Department of Corrections, Bureau of Research and Data Analysis. Reprinted with permission.

Chapter 4: pp. 100–101, Exhibit 4-3, American Probation and Parole Association Position Statement on Probation. Reprinted with permission of American Probation and Parole Association. **p. 103,** Exhibit 4-5, Probation Statistics. Adapted with permission from Camille Graham Camp and George W. Camp, *The Corrections Yearbook 2000,* pp. 170, 172, 176, 177, and 187. Copyright © 2000 Criminal Justice Institute; and Pew Center on the States, "One in 31: The Long Reach of American Corrections." (New York: Pew Charitable Trusts, March

2009). **p. 119,** Exhibit 4-9, Adult and Juvenile Case Load Standards. From *Caseload Standards for Probation and Parole* (Lexington, KY: APPA, September, 2006). Reprinted with permission of Mr. William D. Burrell.

Chapter 5: p. 135, Exhibit 5-2, American Jail Association Resolution. Copyright © American Jail Association. Reprinted with permission. **p. 146,** Exhibit 5-8, American Correctional Association Public Correctional Policy on Community Service and Restorative Justice. Copyright © American Correctional Association. Reprinted with permission. **p. 163,** Exhibit 5-10, American Correctional Association Public Correctional Policy on Community Corrections. Copyright © American Correctional Association. Reprinted with permission. **p. 164,** Exhibit 5-11, States with Community Corrections Legislation. Mary Shilton, "Community Corrections Acts by States, 2007." Center for Community Corrections, centerforcommunitycorrections.org. Reprinted with permission. **p. 165,** Ethics and Professionalism, International Community Corrections Association Code of Ethics. Reprinted by permission of the International Community Corrections Association.

Chapter 6: p. 176, Exhibit 6-1, American Jail Association Mission Statement. Copyright © American Jail Association. Reprinted with permission. **p. 197,** Exhibit 6-9, Comparison of Six Pay-to-Stay Jails. From "For $82 a Day, Booking a Cell in a Five Star Jail," by Jennifer Steinhauer. *The New York Times,* April 29, 2007. Copyright © 2007 The New York Times Co. Reprinted with permission; updates by the authors. **p. 207,** Ethics and Professionalism, Code of Ethics for Jail Officers. Copyright © American Jail Association. Reprinted with permission.

Chapter 7: p. 226, Commission on Safety and Abuse in America's Prisons: Preventing Crime. Excerpts from *Confronting Confinement: A Report of the Commission on Safety and Abuse in America's Prisons* by John J. Gibbons and Nicholas de B. Katzenbach, June 2006. Copyright © 2006, Vera Institute of Justice. Reprinted by permission of the Vera Institute of Justice.

p. 233, Exhibit 7-4, American Correctional Association Public Correctional Policy on Classification. Copyright © American Correctional Association. Reprinted with permission. **p. 252,** Exhibit 7-6, Ratio of Corrections Spending to Higher Education Spending, 2007. From "One in 100: Behind Bars in America 2008," by Jennifer Warren. Published by The Pew Charitable Trusts, 2009. Reprinted with permission of The Pew Charitable Trusts. **p. 253,** Exhibit 7-7, States with the Highest and Lowest Reported Average Annual Operating Costs per Inmate. From *Public Safety, Public Spending: Forecasting America's Prison Population 2007–2011.* Published by The Pew Charitable Trusts, 2007. Reprinted with permission of The Pew Charitable Trusts and The JFA Institute. **p. 262,** Exhibit 7-10, National Crime and Imprisonment Trends, 1931–2007. From *Public Safety, Public Spending: Forecasting America's Prison Population 2007–2011.* Published by The Pew Charitable Trusts, 2007. Reprinted with permission of The Pew Charitable Trusts and The JFA Institute.

Chapter 8: p. 269, Exhibit 8-1, American Probation and Parole Association Policy Statement on Discretionary Parole. Reprinted with permission of American Probation and Parole Association. **p. 273,** Exhibit 8-2, American Probation and Parole Association Position Statement on Parole. Reprinted with permission of American Probation and Parole Association. **p. 275,** Exhibit 8.3, Service Needs of State and Federal Prisoners. From *The Report of the Re-Entry Policy Council: Charting the Safe and Successful Return of Prisoners to the Community.* Copyright © 2005. Reprinted by permission of The Council of State Governments. **p. 278,** Exhibit 8-5, American Correctional Association Public Correctional Policy on Reentry of Offenders. Copyright © American Correctional Association. Reprinted with permission. **pp. 283–284,** Exhibit 8-7, Risk Assessment Instruments Used by Other Jurisdictions Across the United States. From *State of Connecticut Assessment and Validation of Connecticut's Salient Factor Score* by Shamir Ratansi and Stephen M. Cox. New Britain, CT: Connecticut Statistical Analysis Center. Central Connecticut State University, Department of Criminology and Criminal

PHOTO CREDITS

CASE INDEX

SUBJECT INDEX

guideline sentencing, 71–76
guilty pleas, 78–79
Gulf War, 245
gynecological services, 393–394

H

habeas corpus, 13, 368, 371, 527
habitual offender statute, 79. *See also*
   three-strikes laws
Hain, Scott Allen, 531
halfway houses. *See* residential community
   center (RCC)
Hamm, Mark, 333, 335, 439
hands-off doctrine, 367–369
hanging, 37
Hanks, Tom, 319f
Hansen, Robert, 446
Hanway, John, 43
harassment
   of inmates by staff, 188
   of staff by staff, 323
Harris, Mary Belle, 50–51, 51f
Harrison, William, 267
Hate Crime Statistics Act, 480
Hawaii
   education spending *vs.* corrections spend-
      ing in, 252
   parole risk assessment in, 283
   population under community supervision
      in, 125
Hawaii's Opportunity Probation with
   Enhancement (HOPE), 122
Hawes-Cooper Act, 218
Hawkins, Tammy, 558
Hayes, Roxanne, 473
Hayes, Rutherford B., 1
Hayes, Steven, 14f
health care. *See also* HIV/AIDS
   Commission on Safety and Abuse in
      America's Prisons on, 419
   costs of, 421
   deliberate indifference and, 384
   for HIV/AIDS, 407–408
   hospice, 420–421
   prisoners' rights and, 384
   in prisons, 248–250
   sexually transmitted diseases and, 422
   for special-needs inmates, 399
   telemedicine in, 465–466
hearing
   detention, 549–550
   disciplinary, right to council in, 387
   disposition, 550–551
   parole, 280–284
   revocation, 121, 124
Hebrews, 33
hedonist, 346
hedonistic calculus, 48
Heffernan, Esther, 356
Helvetius, Claude-Adrien, 46
Henderson, Thelton, 249
hepatitis C, 274

Herbert, George, 267
herpes, 422
hierarchy, staff, 311–313
high-security prison, 255
Hightower, Melanie, 298f
Hill, Megan, 148
Hispanics
   confusion over census definition
      of, 189
   as correctional officers, 316
   in jail population, 189
HIV/AIDS
   among African American women, 275
   criminal transmission of, 58–59
   deaths from, 406
   definitions of, 406
   education, 410–411
   inmates with, 406–411
   legal issues with, 423–424
   legitimate penological concerns in, 426
   prevalence of, 406, 408
   prevention, 410–411
   testing, 410
   training and, 426
   work assignments and, 423–424
Hobbes, Thomas, 46
Holder, Eric, 277, 434
homicide, in jails, 192–195
homosexual behavior
   among female inmates, 357–358
   among male inmates, 348–351, 365
honor dorms, 239–241
Hoover, Herbert, 271
HOPE. *See* Hawaii's Opportunity
   Probation with Enhancement
   (HOPE)
hospice, 420–421
House of Correction, 41–42
houses of refuge, 539–540
housing assignments, 364
Howard, John, 43, 45–46, 175–176, 539
Howe, S. G., 270
Howe, Trevor, 538
hulks (prison ships), 38
Hume, David, 46
humiliation, public, 40
Hummer, Don, 440
Huskey, Bobbie, 454

I

"iCare" Web site, 195–196
ICCs. *See* intensive confinement centers
   (ICCs)
ICE. *See* Immigration and Customs
   Enforcement (ICE)
Idaho
   death row exonerations in, 503
   education spending *vs.* corrections spend-
      ing in, 252
   population under community supervision
      in, 125
Identity Theft and Deterrence Act, 479

Illinois, 57
   capital punishment in, 519
   day reporting centers in, 150
   death row exonerations in, 503, 530
   education spending *vs.* corrections spend-
      ing in, 252
   intermediate sanctions in, 134, 148–150
   parole population in, 292
   parole risk assessment in, 283
   population under community supervision
      in, 125
Immigration and Customs Enforcement
   (ICE), 249, 434
Impact of Crime on Victims (IOC), 488
importation theory, 343
imprisonment rate, 6f
incapacitation
   definition of, 61
   as goal of sentencing, 59, 61–63
incarceration
   effectiveness of, 260–263
   history of, 41–53
   as punishment, 41–53
   rate
      in jail, 186
      of juveniles, 194
      in prison, 224
      world statistics, 224–225
   shock, 156
*Incarceration of Youth Who Are Waiting
   for Community Mental Health Services
   in the United States,* 191
income
   of correctional officers, corruption
      and, 332
   of jail inmates before incarceration, 184
indeterminate sentencing, 69–71, 430
Indiana
   day reporting centers in, 150–151
   death penalty reversals in, 526
   death row exonerations in, 503
   education spending *vs.* corrections spend-
      ing in, 252
   intermediate sanctions in, 133
   population under community supervision
      in, 125
   reentry program in, 300
Indian country, 189
industrial era, 218, 220–221
industrial schools, 540–541
industrial shop officers, 320
infractions, 7, 8
injection, lethal, 515–517
injunction, 372
inmate management, in jails, 178–182
inmates. *See also* population
   correspondence between, 379–380
   death row, 511–515, 517–519
   elderly (*See* elderly prisoners)
   female (*See* women)
   in jails
      characteristics of, 183–191
      education of, 201–204